D1269198

Heron Conservation

Heron Conservation

James A. Kushlan

Heinz Hafner

Published in collaboration with
the Station Biologique de la Tour du Valat

ACADEMIC PRESS

A Harcourt Science and Technology Company
San Diego   San Francisco   New York   Boston
London   Sydney   Tokyo

This book is printed on acid-free paper.

Copyright © 2000 by ACADEMIC PRESS
© Photographs to named photographers

Academic Press
A Harcourt Science and Technology Company
Harcourt Place, 32 Jamestown Road, London NW1 7BY, UK
http://www.academicpress.com

Academic Press
A Harcourt Science and Technology Company
525 B Street, Suite 1900, San Diego, California 92101-4495, USA
http://www.academicpress.com

ISBN 0-12-430130-4

Library of Congress Catalog Card Number: 99-65070

A catalogue for this book is available from the British Library

Typeset by Phoenix Photosetting, Chatham, Kent
Printed and bound in Great Britain by
Bookcraft (Bath) Ltd, Midsomer Norton, Somerset

00 01 02 03 04 05 BK 9 8 7 6 5 4 3 2 1

Contents

Foreword   vii
James A. Hancock

Preface   ix
Luc Hoffmann

Introduction   xi
James A. Kushlan and Heinz Hafner

Table 0.1   Herons of the world and their distribution   xiii

Contributors   xv

1   **Herons in Europe**   1
    Loïc Marion, Paula Ulenaers and Janine van Vessem

2   **Herons in the Mediterranean**   33
    Heinz Hafner

3   **Herons in South and West Asia**   55
    Christian Perennou, Richard V. Lansdown and James A. Hancock

4   **Herons in East and South-east Asia**   73
    Richard V. Lansdown, Taej Mundkur and Llewellyn Young

5   **Herons in Africa and the Malagasy Region**   99
    Donald Turner

6   **Herons in Australasia and Oceania**   123
    Max Maddock

7   **Herons in North America, Central America and the West Indies**   151
    Robert W. Butler, James A. Kushlan and Ian J. Davidson

8   **Herons in South America**   177
    Gonzalo Morales

9   **Heron Nest Site Conservation**   201
    Heinz Hafner

10 **Heron Feeding Habitat Conservation**   219
    James A. Kushlan

11 **Conservation of Wintering and Migratory Habitats**   237
    Olivier Pineau

12 **Environmental Contaminants**   251
    Thomas W. Custer

13 **Aquaculture**   269
    Loïc Marion

14 Captive Populations   293
Anna Marie Lyles

15 Herons as Indicators   311
R. Michael Erwin and Thomas W. Custer

16 Research and Information Needs for Heron Conservation   331
James A. Kushlan

17 Conservation of Herons   343
*Heinz Hafner, Richard V. Lansdown, James A. Kushlan, Robert W. Butler,
Thomas W. Custer, Ian J. Davidson, R. Michael Erwin, James A. Hancock,
Anna Marie Lyles, Max Maddock, Loïc Marion, Gonzalo Morales, Taej Mundkur,
Christian Perennou, Olivier Pineau, Donald Turner, Paula Ulenaers, Janine van
Vessem and Llewellyn Young*

18 Reflections on Heron Conservation   377
James A. Kushlan and Heinz Hafner

Acknowledgements   381

Bibliography   387

Index   445

Foreword

This book sets the worldwide agenda for conservation of the herons of the world. It gathers together all the details we know about the populations and distribution of the world's herons and, based on this, what we know about their conservation needs.

Nothing quite like this has been attempted before. Each area of the world has been analysed by leading ornithologists who have personal experience carrying out extensive fieldwork in each geographic region. They have evaluated the status of the heron species of their regional fauna and identified the major conservation challenges they face. Specialists in the predominant conservation issues have brought their experiences and a variably complete literature to bear on both identifying challenges and encouraging approaches to conservation of the world's herons.

There has never been a time during the last century when flora and fauna throughout the world have been under such pressure as they are today. Herons are not only charismatic, they are also great survivors . . . and they need to be! Never, throughout the wetlands of the continents of the globe, have threats been so great.

Even in the United States of America and in Europe, where concern for the environment grows steadily stronger, there is constant erosion of heron habitat.

Here is a detailed situation of the spectacular birds as they are today. Here is a benchmark against which to judge the future. Let us hope it succeeds in highlighting one aspect of the serious conservation problems facing the planet as the next millennium begins.

James A. Hancock
Winchester, United Kingdom

Preface

More than fifteen years have elapsed since Hancock and Kushlan (1984) produced the last synthesis of our knowledge of herons. The efforts made since then to deepen our understanding fully justify this new update. The previous work was called *The Herons Handbook*, and the title of the new book, *Heron Conservation*, is highly significant. It reflects the growing threats to heron populations around the world, but also the growing efforts to counter these threats. The studies of the past fifteen years have not only concentrated on fundamental scientific research, but have increasingly focused on forging weapons for the conservation of these fascinating birds. We are now in a position to manage heron populations much more effectively. In addition, analyses of conservation problems have inspired innovative scientific approaches which have led to great strides in our fundamental knowledge.

Herons are of little economic value, although their aesthetic qualities have always inspired artists and thinkers. In the few places where they are still hunted, it is for sport rather than for meat. Diverse and successful heron populations are an expression of healthy wetlands, and their study is an essential part of wetlands research. The position of these birds at the end of food chains makes them particularly vulnerable to environmental contaminants, thus increasing their value as indicators of the state of wetlands.

Heinz Hafner and James Kushlan are particularly well-qualified as authors of this book. They have dedicated a large part of their lives to herons, mainly in the field, but also in the libraries and on the computer. As coordinators of the Heron Specialist Group of Wetlands International, BirdLife and IUCN, they maintain a constant relationship with all those who work on herons throughout the world. A large part of the progress made within the past decades is due to their work and inspiration.

Luc Hoffmann
Tour du Valat
Le Sambuc, France

Introduction

Herons are large, popular, and in many cases spectacular birds found in aquatic habitats worldwide, especially in nearly all temperate and tropical wetlands. In recent years many aspects of their basic biology have become increasingly well understood due to the diligent study by many, worldwide. Understanding their conservation needs has lagged substantially behind an appreciation of their biology. Some populations are very small and localised, others have decreased, some have expanded their ranges, and a few are pests to human activities.

They use a variety of habitats, including many human-altered landscapes. Most species are highly dependent on wetlands, habitats that are under increasing pressure worldwide. Such wetlands are widely acknowledged for the importance of their critical functions in the environmental landscape. Recent understanding of heron basic biology has suggested that herons may reflect the ecological condition of their wetland habitat. The local status of heron populations may reflect the success or failure of conservation action in wetlands. More subtly, aspects of heron biology may also serve as indicators (or biological markers) of the health of wetlands or the success or failure of wetland conservation action. Wetlands generally support several species of herons that coexist by individually using the available mosaic of habitats and resources in different ways. The heron community (or guild) as a whole depends on robust functioning of these wetlands, since each species requires maintenance of its specific range of hydrology, vegetation features, productivity, and the diversity of the fish, amphibian, and invertebrate populations that serve as its prey. Many heron populations are migratory and depend upon conservation of both summer and wintering wetland habitats, not atypically located on different continents. Effective conservation of these wetlands of international importance depends in large part on local and regional socio-economic factors. Herons, to the extent that they require maintenance of wetland functioning, should be an integral part of sustainable wetland conservation.

The international aspect of heron conservation can scarcely be underestimated. Most species are found on more than one continent, and many species migrate across political or continental boundaries annually. Critical feeding or nesting habitats in one country can determine the status of herons in another country at another time of year. Although heron conservation must be undertaken on a local scale, it must be understood and coordinated on the international scale.

Given the increasing understanding of basic biology, an increasing appreciation of the need for local conservation action, and the existence of a worldwide network of heron and wetland specialists, it is an opportune time to synthesise and summarise the state of knowledge of the conservation needs of herons throughout the world. The goal of such a synthesis would be to capture the present understanding of conservation needs of this group, to make suggestions to guide their conservation and management, and to thereby contribute to emerging planning for sustainable conservation.

To accomplish this task we have drawn on the experience and expertise of a multi-national network of over 200 biologists and heron conservationists, many associated with the Heron Specialist Group sponsored by Wetlands International and IUCN. These experts have accumulated significant databases and understanding over the past decades by studying heron biology and conservation in different parts of the world. Many have gained understanding of heron conservation needs on a local scale through their investigations of individual species, specific habitats, single regions, or specific issues such as contaminants or captive breeding. Much of this information has only recently become available, especially from remote areas in less-developed countries. It is critical to synthesise this new information, now available at the local scale, into a worldwide perspective.

More than fifteen years ago, *The Herons Handbook* (Hancock and Kushlan 1984) summarised what was then known on the biology and conservation of the group. Since its publication, there has been a tremendous increase in our knowledge of heron status and conservation needs. So we take *The Herons Handbook* as our base line and attempt to capture new information. It is our purpose to compile presently-available information and understanding of heron populations and conservation needs worldwide, especially changes and increases in knowledge since Hancock and Kushlan (1984), and to synthesise this information in a way that will be of value to conservation action at local, regional and continental scales.

We take two approaches. The status and conservation needs of herons are first summarised on a regional basis, in a series of chapters set at a continental or sub-continental scale. Then we summarise several critical issues of heron conservation in a series of topical chapters. These are followed by an accounting of specific action needs for species and populations we found to be in special need. For consistency and utility we follow the nomenclature for heron species of Hancock and Kushlan (1984). As must be expected, the listing we use is not necessarily the same as other listings of heron species, for example Sibley and Monroe (1990), IUCN (1996), Rose and Scott (1997), and AOU (1998), all of which differ from each other in treatment of some taxa. Our analyses are principally at the species level and continental scale, but where appropriate, especially in Chapter 17, we also treat subspecies or unnamed populations: Table 0.1 lists the species of herons covered and their worldwide occurrence. The species abbreviations of this table are used throughout the book.

This book is a work of many. Our authors are drawn from every continent. They and we have relied on a virtual army of correspondents, colleagues and collaborators who have generously shared their experiences from around the world. Many are specifically noted in the Acknowledgements section at the end of the book. It is our great pleasure to single out two of our colleagues for special acknowledgement. We dedicate this book to Luc Hoffmann and James A. Hancock, whose interests and leadership in heron conservation span decades. Without their innovative and persistent leadership, their mentorship of several generations of heron specialists, and their dedication to wetland conservation, the army of contributors to this book would never have developed. We hope their inspiration will transmit to the next generation of heron conservationists to whom fall the tasks of further supplementing our information base and of implementing the conservation actions suggested in this book.

James A. Kushlan
Annapolis, Maryland, USA

Heinz Hafner
Tour du Valat
Le Sambuc, France

Table 0.1   Herons of the world and their distribution.

Names[1]			Regions[2]						
Abbr.	Scientific	English	EUR	SWA	ESEA	AFR	AUS	NAM	SAM
WH	*Syrigma sibilatrix*	Whistling Heron							×
CpH	*Pilherodius pileatus*	Capped Heron							×
GrH	*Ardea cinerea*	Grey Heron	×	×	×	×	×	×	
GBH	*Ardea herodias*	Great Blue Heron						×	×
CoH	*Ardea cocoi*	Cocoi Heron						×	×
WNH	*Ardea pacifica*	White-necked Heron					×		
BhH	*Ardea melanocephala*	Black-headed Heron				×			
MH	*Ardea humbloti*	Malagasy Heron				×			
IH	*Ardea imperialis*	Imperial Heron			×				
SuH	*Ardea sumatrana*	Sumatran Heron			×		×		
GoH	*Ardea goliath*	Goliath Heron		×	×	×	×		
PuH	*Ardea purpurea*	Purple Heron	×	×	×	×			
GWE	*Egretta alba*	Great White Egret	×	×	×	×	×	×	×
RE	*Egretta rufescens*	Reddish Egret						×	×
PdH	*Egretta picata*	Pied Heron			×		×		
SlE	*Egretta vinaceigula*	Slaty Egret				×			
BH	*Egretta ardesiaca*	Black Heron				×			
TH	*Egretta tricolor*	Tricoloured Heron						×	×
IE	*Egretta intermedia*	Intermediate Egret		×	×	×	×		
WFH	*Egretta novaehollandiae*	White-faced Heron					×		
LBH	*Egretta caerulea*	Little Blue Heron						×	×
SnE	*Egretta thula*	Snowy Egret						×	×
LE	*Egretta garzetta*	Little Egret	×		×	×	×		
SwE	*Egretta eulophotes*	Swinhoe's Egret			×			×	
ERH	*Egretta sacra*	Eastern Reef Heron		×	×	×	×		
CE	*Bubulcus ibis*	Cattle Egret	×	×	×	×	×	×	×
SqH	*Ardeola ralloides*	Squacco Heron	×	×	×	×			
IPH	*Ardeola grayii*	Indian Pond Heron		×	×				
CPH	*Ardeola bacchus*	Chinese Pond Heron			×				
JPH	*Ardeola speciosa*	Javan Pond Heron			×				
MPH	*Ardeola idae*	Malagasy Pond Heron				×			
RBH	*Ardeola rufiventris*	Rufous-bellied Heron				×			

Table 0.1   Herons of the world and their distribution. – *contd*

| Names[1] | | | Regions[2] | | | | | | |
Abbr.	Scientific	English	EUR	SWA	ESEA	AFR	AUS	NAM	SAM
GbH	*Butorides striatus*	Green-backed Heron		×	×	×	×	×	×
AH	*Agamia agami*	Agami Heron						×	×
YCNH	*Nycticorax violaceus*	Yellow-crowned Night Heron						×	×
BCNH	*Nycticorax nycticorax*	Black-crowned Night Heron	×	×	×	×		×	×
NNH	*Nycticorax caledonicus*	Nankeen Night Heron			×		×		
WBNH	*Nycticorax leuconotus*	White-backed Night Heron				×			
WENH	*Gorsachius magnificus*	White-eared Night Heron			×				
JNH	*Gorsachius goisagi*	Japanese Night Heron			×				
MNH	*Gorsachius melanolophus*	Malayan Night Heron		×	×		×		
BBH	*Cochlearius cochlearius*	Boat-billed Heron						×	×
BTTH	*Tigrisoma mexicanum*	Bare-throated Tiger Heron						×	×
FTH	*Tigrisoma fasciatum*	Fasciated Tiger Heron						×	×
RTH	*Tigrisoma lineatum*	Rufescent Tiger Heron						×	×
NGTH	*Zonerodius heliosylus*	New Guinea Tiger Heron			×		×		
WcTH	*Tigrionis leucolophus*	White-crested Tiger Heron				×			
ZH	*Zebrilus undulatus*	Zigzag Heron							×
StB	*Ixobrychus involucris*	Streaked Bittern							×
LsB	*Ixobrychus exilis*	Least Bittern						×	×
LtB	*Ixobrychus minutus*	Little Bittern	×	×		×	×		
YB	*Ixobrychus sinensis*	Yellow Bittern		×	×		×	×	
ShB	*Ixobrychus eurhythmus*	Schrenck's Bittern			×				
CB	*Ixobrychus cinnamomeus*	Cinnamon Bittern		×	×				
DB	*Ixobrychus sturmii*	African Dwarf Bittern				×			
BB	*Ixobrychus flavicollis*	Black Bittern		×	×		×		
SAB	*Botaurus pinnatus*	South American Bittern							×
AmB	*Botaurus lentiginosus*	American Bittern						×	
EB	*Botaurus stellaris*	Eurasian Bittern	×	×	×	×			
AuB	*Botaurus poiciloptilus*	Australian Bittern					×		

[1] Scientific and English names follow Hancock and Kushlan (1984), abbreviations listed here are used throughout the book.
[2] EUR = Europe including the Mediterranean, SWA = south and west Asia, ESEA = east and south-east Asia, AFR = Africa and the Malagasy Region, AUS = Australasia and Oceania, NAM = North America, Central America and the West Indies, SAM = South America.

Contributors

Robert W. Butler
Canadian Wildlife Service
Pacific Wildlife Research Center
5421 Robertson Road, RR1
Delta, British Columbia, V4K3Y3
CANADA

Thomas W. Custer
USGS Upper Midwest Environmental
Sciences Center
2630 Fanta Reed Road
La Crosse, Wisconsin 54603
USA

Ian J. Davidson
Wetlands International
7 Hinton Avenue, N., Suite 200
Ottawa, Ontario K1Y4P1
CANADA

R. Michael Erwin
USGS Patuxent Wildlife Research
Center
Clark Hall
University of Virginia
Charlottesville, Virginia 22903
USA

Heinz Hafner
Station Biologique de la Tour du Valat
Le Sambuc, 13200 Arles
FRANCE

James A. Hancock
Jollers, Sparsholt
Winchester SO21 2NS
UK

James A. Kushlan
PO Box 429
Annapolis, Maryland 21404-0429
USA

Richard V. Lansdown
Ardeola Environmental Services
Floral Cottage
Upper Springfield Road
Uplands, Stroud
Glos., GL5 1TF
UK

Anna Marie Lyles
Wildlife Conservation Society
830 Fifth Avenue
New York, New York 10021-7095
USA

Max Maddock
64 Clarence Town Road
Glen Oak
New South Wales 2320
AUSTRALIA

Loïc Marion
Laboratoire d'Evolution des Systèmes
Naturels et Modifiés UMR Ecobio
Université de Rennes 1
Avenue du Général Leclerc
35042 Rennes Cedex
FRANCE

Gonzalo Morales
Universidad Central de Venezuela
Instituto de Zoología Tropical
Apt. 47058, Caracas 1041-A
VENEZUELA

Taej Mundkur
Wetlands International
3A39, Block A, Kelana Centre Point
Jalan SS 7/19
47301 Petaling Jaya, Selangor
MALAYSIA

Christian Perennou
Station Biologique de la Tour du Valat
Le Sambuc, 13200 Arles
FRANCE

Olivier Pineau
Station Biologique de la Tour du Valat
Le Sambuc, 13200 Arles
FRANCE

Donald Turner
PO Box 48019
Nairobi
KENYA

Paula Ulenaers
Institute of Nature Conservation
Kiewitdreef 5, B-3500 Hasselt
BELGIUM

Janine van Vessem
Wetlands International
PO Box 7002,
6700 CA
Wageningen
THE NETHERLANDS

Llewellyn Young
Peter Scott Field Studies Center
Mai Po Marshes Nature Reserve
Mai Po, Yuen Long, New Territories
Hong Kong SAR
PEOPLES REPUBLIC OF CHINA

1. Herons in Europe

Loïc Marion, Paula Ulenaers and Janine van Vessem

This chapter discusses the heron populations of European countries west to the Ural Mountains and the Great Caucasus of Russia (Fig. 1.1, Table 1.1). The chapter includes all of Turkey. The small countries of Luxembourg, Monaco, San Marino and Andorra are not mentioned because they lack breeding herons. The present chapter covers coastal Mediterranean populations at the country level because these populations are evaluated more fully in Chapter 2. Heron populations of Europe are among the best known in the world, and population status and trends for many species are relatively well understood.

The Heron Fauna

Europe has nine heron species (Table 1.1). A north–south gradient in heron diversity occurs from Scandinavia and the British Isles to the Caspian and Mediterranean Seas. Historically herons have been recolonising Europe from Caspian and Mediterranean areas, which were the last places in Europe favourable to herons during the last glaciation (Harrison 1982). The Grey Heron is the most widespread, found in 34 out of 38 countries, followed by the Eurasian Bittern, Little Bittern, and Black-crowned Night Heron. Ranges are discontinuous for almost all species. Eurasian Bitterns seem more regularly distributed, while most Grey Herons are localised in five countries and nearly all Cattle Egrets in two. A vast majority of Great White Egrets and Purple Herons are in Russia, where information is the poorest. France, Italy, Russia and Turkey are the only countries that support all European species.

No European heron is globally threatened. Some have been recognised as being of conservation concern within Europe, one as declining, two as vulnerable, and two (provisionally) as vulnerable (Tucker and Heath 1994). Overall in Europe, herons number around 462 000 to 722 000 breeding pairs (Table 1.1). The Grey Heron is the most abundant (28% of total), followed by the Cattle Egret (15%), Purple Heron (13%), Little Bittern (12%), Black-crowned Night Heron and Little Egret (10% each), Eurasian Bittern (5%), the Squacco Heron and the Great White Egret (3% each).

Heron Conservation
ISBN 0-12-430130-4

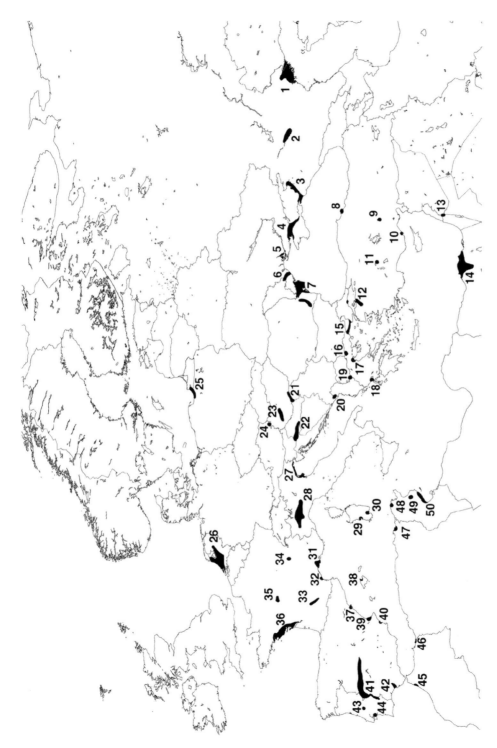

Fig. 1.1   Important heron areas in Europe and the Mediterranean.

Russia supports 29% of European heron populations, followed by Spain (12%), France (8%), Ukraine and Italy (7% each), and Portugal, Turkey and Romania (5% each). The other 30 countries represent less than 2.3% each. Overall heron population size is not well related to size of country as densities are high in some of the smaller countries. There are 34.6 breeding pairs of herons per 100 km^2 in Portugal, 26.5 in the Netherlands, 25.7 in Moldova, 15.8 in Denmark, 15.6 in Spain, 14 in Hungary, 12 in Italy, 11.5 in Romania, 8.6 in France, 8.5 in Croatia, 7.8 in Belgium, 6.3 in Ukraine, 5.9 in Bulgaria, 4.5 in the United Kingdom, and only 1.0 in Russia.

Environmental Conditions

Climate and geography, and the resulting presence of scattered favourable sites, explain much about heron distribution in Europe. Climate, which varies from arctic

Key to Fig. 1.1
1 Russia—Volga Delta
2 Russia—Manik Gudilo
3 Russia—South-east coast of Azov Sea
4 Ukraine—Ozero Sivash and Karkinitsk
5 Ukraine—Mouth of Dnepr and adjacent lagoons
6 Ukraine—Dnestr Delta
7 Romania—Danube, Danube Delta, Dobrogea including Razelm and Sinoie Lakes, Braila
8 Turkey—Kizilirmak wetland complex
9 Turkey—Kurbaga Lake and Sultans marshes
10 Turkey—Goksu Delta
11 Turkey—Eber/Aksehir complex
12 Turkey—Manyas Lake, Lake Izuik, Sarabar Braji
13 Israel—Hula swamp and fishponds
14 Egypt—Nile Delta complex
15 Greece—Lake Vistonis and Porto Lagos lagoons, Evros Delta
16 Greece—Kerkini Reservoir
17 Greece—Axios, Loudias and Aliakmon Delta
18 Greece—Amvrakikos Gulf
19 Greece—Lake Mikri Prespa
20 Montenegro—Skutari Lake
21 Croatia—Kopacki Rit, Ludasko Lake
22 Croatia—Floodplain of the Sava, Lonja and Strug Rivers, Crna Mlaka
23 Hungary—Lake Kis-Balaton
24 Austria—Lake Neusield
25 Poland, Russia—Zalew wislany
26 Netherlands—Dutch Wetlands
27 Italy—North coast of the Adriatic Sea including Laguna di Marano, Venetian Lagoons, Po Delta complex, Comacchio
28 Italy—Rice field area (Pianura Padana) of the Po River floodplain
29 Italy (Sardinia)—Wetlands near Oristano
30 Italy (Sardinia)—Stagno di Cagliari
31 France—Camargue Delta complex
32 France—Mouth of the River Aude and Vendre marshes
33 France—Garonne River floodplain, Moissac and Toulouse floodplains
34 France—Ponds of Dombes
35 France—Ponds of Brenne
36 France—Lake Grand-Lieu, Guerande, Briere, Poitevin, Brouage and Seudre marshes
37 Spain—Ebro Delta
38 Spain (Mallorca)—S' Albufera de Mallorca
39 Spain—Albufera de Valencia
40 Spain—Pantano del Hondo
41 Spain—Guadiana River and floodplains, Volongo, San Betino, Tajo River floodplain
42 Spain—Guadalquivir Delta
43 Portugal—Paul de Boquilobo
44 Portugal—Ria Sado
45 Morocco—Loukos marshes
46 Morocco—Moulouya River mouth
47 Algeria—Wetland complex of El Kala
48 Tunisia—Ichkeul
49 Tunisia—Sebkha Kelbia
50 Tunisia—Kneiss Islands and Sfax-Gabes coastline

Table 1.1   Status of herons in Europe and the Mediterranean. Figures are number of nesting pairs: minimum and maximum given when numbers fluctuate. Brackets: estimated where no figures available.

	Species								
	GrH	PuH	GWE	LE	CE	SqH	BCNH	LtB	EB
Albania	200–500	10–50	(1–5)	500–1500		0–5[1]	50–200	100–300	1–10
Austria	910–950[2]	70–80[3]	554[3]				10[2]–16	(100–150)	(100–150)
Belarus	4500[4]–6500							100–300	950–1200
Belgium	2200[5]–2500						2–3	2–10	2–13
Bulgaria	300–2000	30[6]–100	1–10	500–1000		2000–2500[1]	800[6]–1500[7]	(200–2000)	(10–50)
Croatia	1714[8]	95[8]	21[8]	190[8]–250		50–183[8]	690–1000	1000–2000	(30–50)
Czech. Rep.	1400[9]	1–25[9]		0–1[9]			300–370[9]	40–90[9]	20–30[9]
Denmark	6735[10]							(0–1)	60–100[10]
Estonia	1300[11]								200–300[12]
Finland	50–70[13]								150–220[13]
France	26687[14]	1978[14]	15[15]	9845[14]	4300[16]	68–142[16]	4176[14]	200–300[17]	300–350[18]
Germany	12000[19]	15[19]–40	7–15[20]		0–1[21]		20–30	200[19]	800[19]
Greece	570–600[20]	105–140	500	1055–1230[20]		200–377[20]	490–590[7]	600–700	400–500
Hungary	1200–1600	800–1000		350–400		200–300	4000–4800	3500–6000	20–30
Italy	5156[22]	480–600[22]	2–5[23] (1–5)	16000–22000[22]	65[22]	500–600[24]	14000–24000[22]	(1000–2000)	200–300
Latvia	1100–1500							(10–30)	200–250
Liechtenstein	10								
Lithuania	1500–3000[25]							40–50	
Luxembourg								0–1	
Moldova	1700–2000	100–150	40–60	500–800		50–80	3500–5000	1000–2000	150–200
Netherlands	10000–11000[26]	215–300[26]	5[3]				1–9[6]	5–10[26]	175–275[26]
Norway	5000–10000[27]								
Poland	7000–8500	1–2		3000–5000[28]	25000–28000[28]		80–100[7]	400–700	1100–1400
Portugal	200–300[28]	100–150[29]				1–5[28]	100–200[28]	500–1000	(1–5)
Rep. Ireland	3000[30]								
Romania	1000–3000	800–1250[31]	150–300	1200–2000	2[42]	2150[31]	5000–7000[7]	(10000–20000)	(500–2000)
Russia	20000–25000	(40000–90000)	10000–11500	4500–6000	30–50	5500–9000[32]	10000–15000[7]	(10000–50000)	(10000–30000)
Slovakia	155[33]–200	50[33]–70	1–10	5–15			100–300[7]	300[33]–400	60[33]–150
Slovenia	400–500						(5–10)	20–50	(5–10)
Spain	1430–1600[34]	1200[35]		3486–7600[34]	52000–69000[34]	171–822[34]	1480–2210[34]	1900–2300	25
Sweden	4000[36]–5000								400[36]
Switzerland	880–1050[37]							40–60	
Turkey	(2000–5000)	(2000–5000)	(100–500)	(5000–10000)	(1–50)	(3000–10000)	1000–3000	(1000–10000)	(30–500)
Ukraine	16000–20000[38]	1000–1500[39]	1500–4000[38]	1300–2500[38]		400–600[40]	3700–5000[38]	5000–6000	4000–4300
UK	10300			5[41]				1[43]	16

Data without references are from European Bird Database (1994) for GrH, GWE, LE, CE, and from Tucker and Heath (1994) and Hagemeijer and Blair (1997) for the other species. [1]Hafner and Didner, 1997 [2]Ranner, pers. comm. [3]Munteanu and Ranner, 1997 [4]Samusenko and Wiazovick, pers. comm. [5]Uleaners and Van Vessen, pers. obs. [6]Michev, pers. comm. [7]Fasola and Hafner, 1997a [8]Mikuska, pers. comm. [9]Bjecek, Musil, Petlantova, Statsuy, pers. comm. [10]Frederiksen, 1992 [11]Lillelecht and Leibak, 1993 [12]Kunesoo, Polua, Roja, pers. comm. [13]Lammi, pers. comm. [14]Marion, 1997d [15]Marion, pers. obs. [16]Marion, 1994a [18]Duhautois, 1984 [19]Rutschke, pers. comm. [20]Crivelli et al., 1988 [21]Goutner et al., 1991 [22]Farinha, 1997 [23]Volponi, pers. comm. [24]Fasola, pers. comm.; Hafner, 1997b [25]Svazas, pers. comm. [26]Van Dijk, pers. comm.; [27]Gjershang pers. comm. [28]Dias, 1991 [29]Candeias et al., 1987 [30]Merne, pers. comm. [31]Kiss, Munteanu and Toniuc in Green, 1992 [33]Krivenko, 1991 [33]Darobova, pers. comm. [34]Fernandez Cruz et al., 1992 [35]Hafner, see Chapter 2 [36]Risberg, 1990 [37]Geiger, 1984a [39]Serebryakov and Grischenko, 1989 [40]Mikhalevich et al., 1994 [40]Schogolev, 1992 [41]Lock and Cook, 1998 [42]Munteanu, 1998. [43]Allport and Caroll, 1989.

to warm temperate, is the most fundamental factor. Except for the Grey Heron and Eurasian Bittern, Palearctic herons primarily occur in temperate and tropical areas (Harrison 1982). Northern Scandinavia is arctic and does not support herons. Most of Europe is temperate; the Atlantic and the Gulf Stream influence Western Europe. Although relatively warm, its oceanic climate produces frequent rains in spring, unfavourable for sensitive species (Voisin 1991). Middle and Eastern Europe and Spain have a continental climate, with a favourable hot and dry spring and summer. In winter, the northern part of Europe becomes unfavourable to herons, as temperatures fall frequently to –20°C in the north-eastern countries, where rivers, lakes and even the Baltic Sea freeze. Winter is usually somewhat more temperate on the plains of central Europe and the Iberian Peninsula, while snow is heavy in the Alps.

The resulting diversity of habitats ranges from tundra and boreal forests to temperate and Mediterranean habitats. The long coastline bordering the Atlantic Ocean and the North, Baltic, Barents, Mediterranean, Black, Azov and Caspian Seas supports many estuarine and coastal wetlands.

Europe also has many rivers including several great rivers with marshy deltas or estuaries (Vista, Pechora, Volga, Don, Dnepr, Dnestr, Danube, Po, Ebro, Guadalquivir, Guadiana, Tajo, Rhône, Loire, Rhine). The greater portion of Europe is a plain, covering a large area of Russia, the Baltic states, and half of Scandinavia. This plain narrows toward the west, along the Baltic and the North Seas, before enlarging again in the north-western part of France and the British Isles. This extensive plain, 0–400 m MSL, is bordered in the north by the Norwegian mountains, in the east by the Urals, and in the south by a series of Alpine mountains that circle the Hungarian plain and extend to France, where they are prolonged to the west by the Massif Central and the Pyrenees. In Russia, a large band of this plain, from the Dnestr to the Ural (2000 km by 600 km), is now almost entirely ploughed, while the other part is a mosaic of forests, meadows and crops. European mountain habitats are largely unfavourable to herons, as is the desert steppe covering 450 000 km^2 that borders the northern Caspian Sea, around the Volga Delta.

Changing Status

Data available

This chapter is based on published data, personal investigations of the authors, and the results of a questionnaire sent to local correspondents for recent data, except for some southern countries (Moldova, Slovenia, Greece, Turkey, Spain, and Portugal). When no data were available (half of the figures of Table 1.1), we used the estimates of the European Bird Database (from Tucker and Heath 1994). Some of these may not be very accurate, but at the moment they are the best available. Their estimates give the minimum and the maximum population size for each country, and the recent trend of size and range, with an estimate of the reliability of data. For other sources of data, we have also adopted a minimum and a maximum population size per species and per country. When populations are stable or are regularly decreasing or increasing, we have considered the most recent accurate data (generally post 1985) both for the minimum and the maximum, while when populations are fluctuating we used the minimum and the maximum population size observed in the recent period. This presentation differs from Tucker and Heath (1994) (minimum and maximum 1970–90). For each species and each country, we have added separately the minimum and the maximum figures, and percentages of the European population per country are given in the text by averaging the two values. In the chapter, all trends referring to the 1970–90 period are from Tucker and Heath's estimates (±20–50% of change or ± >50% of change), while precise percentages for other periods have been calculated from the literature. Trends are described from the end of the nineteenth century, but we have given priority to the 1970–1996 period.

Generally, literature cited in the present chapter provides reliable census data. Recent exhaustive censuses (from 1988) are available for tree-nesting, colonial species and for a few countries (Belgium, Denmark, France, Greece, Italy, Portugal, Spain, Sweden and Ukraine). Data reliability differs greatly among countries according to the methods used, including exhaustive censuses of occupied nests by visiting all colonies (e.g. France), partial censuses on a sample of colonies and extrapolation for the country (United Kingdom, Italy), aerial counts for reed-bed colonies of Grey Heron, Purple Heron or Great White Egret (e.g. Lake Neusield in Austria, the Camargue in France, the Volga Delta in Russia), estimates from the number of booming male Eurasian Bitterns, or non-published country estimates from non-heron specialists (e.g. Russia). Reliability of data is given in the text for each species and main countries. Calculating the mean reliability for the whole of Europe by using criteria given by Tucker and Heath (1994) for recent population size and trends (numbers and range) in each country shows that the status of the Cattle Egret may be considered well known, while the status of five species is relatively well known (Grey Heron, Purple Heron, Great White Egret, Little Egret and Squacco Heron).

Species accounts

Grey Heron. The Grey Heron occurs from the Arctic circle throughout Europe and is the region's most abundant species with 150 000 to 180 000 breeding pairs (Table 1.1, Fig. 1.2). The main populations are located in France (16%), Russia (14%), Ukraine (11%), Germany (7%), United Kingdom and Netherlands (6%), and the species is considered to be secure in Europe. It has been well studied, especially in England from 1928, and since the 1970s regular and exhaustive national published censuses have been conducted in France (eight censuses from 1962 to 1994; Brosselin 1974, Duhautois and Marion 1982, Marion 1991b, 1997d). Outside France, the last exhaustive censuses were made in 1981, 1982, 1983, 1986, 1992 in Belgium (van Vessem et al. 1982, van Vessem 1988, van Vessem and Ulenaers, unp. data), in 1978–91 in Denmark (Frederiksen 1992), in 1986 in Sweden (Holst and Persson 1988), 1986 in Ukraine (Serebryakov and Grishchenko 1989), 1985 in the United Kingdom (Marquiss and Reynolds 1986, Marquiss 1989), 1983 in the former East Germany (Rutschke 1985), 1992 for all of Germany (Rutschke, pers. comm.), and 1983 in Switzerland (Geiger 1984a,b). It is difficult to find all colonies because this species may breed in small numbers (see for example Marquiss and Reynolds 1986), can feed as far as 38 km from the nesting site (Marion 1984), and can breed in all kinds of habitats, trees or ground, small marine islands, cliffs, or inland woods, reed beds,

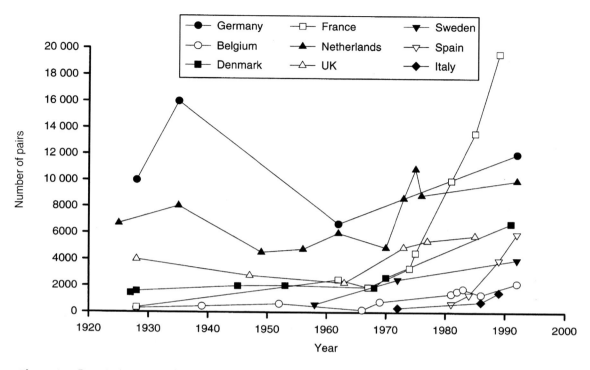

Fig. 1.2 Population size of *Ardea cinerea* in different European countries.

and even in city parks (London, Amsterdam, Nilrijk in Belgium, Oléron in France). Many colonies are mixed with other herons, and sometimes with cormorants or Spoonbills. Grey Herons nest early, especially in France (mainly February–March), frequently attracting other species to their colonies (Marion 1991a, Marion and Marion 1994, Voisin 1991), so the Grey Heron can play an important role for other species.

The history of the Grey Heron in France is one of the best documented. The species was a royal game bird, and under that, protection was widespread until the eighteenth century (Marion 1976). In the nineteenth century, it progressively came to be considered a pest and was systematically destroyed (see Chapter 13). Between 1881 and 1917, for example, 3000 birds were killed in Alsace (del Hoyo et al. 1992). By the twentieth century, the species had almost disappeared. It may be that only one colony remained, in the castle park of Ecury le Grand (Marne), where the site had been protected since 1326 by its owners (Brosselin 1974). During the hiatus in hunting due to the First World War, two important colonies developed at Clairmarais (Nord) and Grand-Lieu (Loire Atlantique). By 1928, about 350 pairs occurred in 5 colonies, which were the source of a population expansion during and just after the Second World War (Berlioz in Lowe 1954). Hunting had decreased except on the coasts, where up until 1950 hunters could shoot herons during the entire year (Voisin 1991). In 1958, one of these colony sites, Grand-Lieu, was probably the most important colony of this species in the world, having 1300 pairs,

Grey Heron, Europe's most widespread and abundant species. Photo: Jacques Delpech.

and was the origin of several new coastal colonies (Marion 1979). North-eastern France was similarly colonised by numerous but small colonies. In 1962, the French population reached 2500–2700 pairs, reduced to 1900 pairs in 1967 after the hard winter of 1963, and 2032 pairs in 1968, in 64 colonies (Brosselin 1974). Just before the species was legally protected in 1975, it reached 4500 pairs in 113 colonies (Brosselin 1974, corrected by Duhautois and Marion 1982), with 33% in the colony of Grand-Lieu (Marion 1981). By 1981, there were about 10 000 pairs in 197 colonies; in 1985, 13 600 pairs in 313 colonies; in 1989, 19 593 pairs in 448 colonies (Marion 1991b), and in 1994, 26 687 pairs in 658 colonies (Marion 1997b). At this time, most of France was colonised. The annual rate of increase was 12% to 16%, driven by a decrease in annual mortality rate of immatures (79% before 1937, 50% after 1975), but curiously not that of adults (39% to 38%, Marion 1981). Since 1984, the two largest colonies have decreased while small, dispersed colonies have become more numerous, and probably are more optimally distributed according to feeding resources (Marion and Marion 1987a, Marion 1988). Overall, the French population, once primarily regulated by a non-density-dependent factor (hunting mortality), is now regulated more by density-dependent factors, feeding resources and territorial feeding behaviour (Marion 1984, 1989b). This suggests that the population will be more sensitive to food resources. Many French herons do not migrate in winter (Marion

1988). Others winter from France to the Mediterranean area, with a few recoveries in Africa in Sierra Leone and Togo.

In England and Wales the population has been regularly censused (the last complete surveys were made in 1964 and 1985) or since 1928 estimated from samples by the British Trust for Ornithology (Nicholson 1929, Marchant 1997). Until 1962, this population was stable, fluctuating around 4000 pairs (5000 pairs to 2800 pairs, as in 1947 after a hard winter). It fell to 2250 pairs following the winter of 1986 after rising to 5600 pairs in 1985 (Stafford 1971, Reynolds 1979, Marquiss and Reynolds 1986). More recently the estimated population increased over four years to reach 6950 pairs in 1995, but decreased by 5.5% in 1996 (6570 pairs, Marchant 1997). The population of Northern Ireland seemed stable until 1985 (396 pairs in 1954, 490 in 1985), while the Scottish population increased: 768 in 1928, 1086 in 1954 (but best coverage), and 3800 pairs in 1985 (Burton 1956, Marquiss 1989). The United Kingdom had 9400 pairs during the last complete census of 1985 (Marquiss and Reynolds 1986).

The Netherlands showed the same trend as in England and Wales, fluctuating around 6000–7000 pairs (1925, 1962), with increases to 8000–8500 in 1935 and decreases to 4500–5000 in 1949 dipping to 3250–3750 in 1964 after cold winters (van der Ven 1964, Rooth and Jonkers 1972). As in England and Wales, the following increase was more dramatic than previously, with more than 10 000 pairs in 1975 (Blok and Ross 1977). The situation was different in Belgium, with 230–480 pairs in 1900, 300 in 1928 and 652 in 1952, before a marked decrease to only 178 in 1966 and 297 in 1969 (Lowe 1954, Lippens and Wille 1972, Verheyen 1966). After legal protection in 1972, the population strongly increased to 1782 pairs in 1983, but fell to 1343 in 1986 after the cold winter of 1984–85 (van Vessem et al. 1982, van Vessem 1988).

The Grey Heron population in Switzerland increased from about 50 to 500–570 between 1900 and 1955 (Géroudet 1978), 350–400 pairs in 1970, 1036 in 1981 and 880 in 1982 (Geiger 1984a). The population in Austria increased from 200 pairs in 1975 (Böck 1975) to 911 pairs in 1990. In Germany, there were already 10 000 pairs in 1928 (Lowe 1954) and 16 000 in 1935 with 200 colonies (Géroudet 1978), but by 1960–61, there were only 4625 in West Germany (Krämer 1962) and 2100 in East Germany (Creutz and Schlegel 1961), just before the hard winter of 1962–63. This decrease was probably in large part due to shooting (Hancock and Kushlan 1984). The protection of species and mild winters increased the eastern population to 4000 pairs in 1978 and 5626 in 1983 (Rutschke 1982, 1985). There have been no federal censuses in Western Germany since 1961, but the trend is probably similar, because in Bavaria the population increased from 527 pairs in 1960 to 1142 in 1981 (Utschick 1983b), and the German population as a whole is considered to be strongly increasing by Tucker and Heath (1994), with 5000(?)–12 000 pairs.

A different pattern was observed in Denmark, with stability from 1880 (1280 pairs) to 1910 (1300, Weibüll 1912), followed by an increase to 1450 pairs in 1927 and 1600 in 1928 (Holstein 1927, Lowe 1954). A second stable period occurred from 1945 to 1968 (around 2000 pairs, Krüger 1946, Dybbro 1970). Then a strong increase occurred, with 2673 pairs in 1978 (Moller and Olesen 1980) and 6735 in 1991 (Frederiksen 1992). In Sweden, the population was estimated at a minimum of 600 pairs in 1943, 1800 in an incomplete census in 1972 and 2500 in 1976 (Svensson 1976), and it was roughly estimated to be 3000–5000 by Tucker and Heath (1994).

The population in Russia was estimated to be 20 000–25 000 without national data, but the Volga Delta (10 000 km²) is annually censused by the Astrakhan Reserve since 1981. There population is stable around 3000–4000 pairs (Gavrilov in Crivelli and Hafner 1991), but this reserve had 18 500 pairs in 1923 and 23 400 in 1935 (Dementiev and Gladkov 1951) before the upper delta was drained. In the eastern part of Russia, del Hoyo et al. (1992) mentioned a tenfold increase in some populations in the period 1969–1982. For all European countries of former USSR, Krivenko (1991) mentioned 50 000–100 000 pairs, but this may be overestimated. For Tucker and Heath (1994), the Russian population seems stable but is poorly documented.

In southern Europe, the Grey Heron has also recently increased. The Spanish population increased from 340 pairs in 1972–73 to 1400–1600 pairs in 1989 (Fernandez Alcazar and Fernandez Cruz 1991, Fernandez Cruz et al. 1992; see Chapter 2). In Italy, the increase was more important, from 680 pairs in 1981 (Fasola et al. 1981) to 5950 pairs in 1992 (Fasola pers. comm.; see Chapter 2). A marked increase also occurred recently in Croatia (1186 pairs in 1990, at least 1739 in 1993; see Chapter 2).

Grey Herons have increased in all other European countries, except Bulgaria, Norway, Estonia, Hungary, Albania, Turkey (however, no quantitative data) and Moldova (Tucker and Heath 1994). Europe-wide increases may have just compensated for the crash at the Volga Delta in Russia. Protection against human disturbance, threats from fish farmers or hunting appear, along with winter freezing, to be the main factors for fluctuations in Europe. The northern expansion is possibly also due to climate improvement (Knief et al. 1997). However, territorial behaviour is the main regulating factor with breeding birds when populations reach their upper limit (Marion 1984). Habitat loss seems less important, except locally (drainage, timber operations—Marion 1991b).

Purple Heron. The Purple Heron is patchily distributed in Europe, with 49 000 to 105 000 pairs (Table 1.1), most of them in non-Mediterranean countries. It is considered to be vulnerable in Europe. Although it is present in 20 countries it is relatively rare, with only 9000–14 000 breeding pairs outside Russia. The Russian population, mainly localised along large rivers and lakes, is poorly known and roughly estimated as 40 000 to 90 000 pairs (Tucker and Heath 1994) or 65 000–98 000 pairs (Bankovics 1997), while Krivenko (1991) only mentioned 28 000 pairs for all the European countries of former USSR. Before the twentieth century, this species was not a regular breeder in many countries but has expanded its range in Central Europe and increased in Germany and the Netherlands from the 1940s (Bauer and Glutz von Blotzheim 1966, del Hoyo et al. 1992), however only temporarily. The Dutch population is today isolated (Bankovics 1997). According to Tucker and Heath (1994), numbers declined between 1970 and 1990 in all countries except the small Slovakian population and in Greece and Portugal. The species is now vulnerable in Europe. The strongest decreases (more than 50%) were in Austria, Bulgaria, Croatia, the Netherlands, Switzerland, Ukraine, Spain and Romania (Tucker and Heath 1994). A recent partial recovery occurred in Spain, with 1200 pairs (Chapter 2). In the Netherlands, breeding population dropped from 900 pairs in the early 1970s to 640 in 1980 and 210 in 1991 (van der Kooij 1992), with a recent increase to 270 in 1993 (Bankovics 1997). In France, after a stable situation between 1974 and 1983, the population decreased from 2761 to 1978 pairs in 1994 (Marion 1997d), with a strong decrease along the Mediterranean coast, before recovering in

1996, 1997 and 1998 (see Chapter 2). The average number of pairs in Germany has decreased in recent years (1989–1993) to only 15 (Rutschke, pers. comm.). In Poland and Switzerland, the population is almost extinct, but in Austria, after the strong decrease noted by Tucker and Heath (1994), numbers slightly increased recently (73 pairs in lake Neusield; Ranner, pers. comm.). In the early 1980s, solitary-breeding Purple Herons were noted in Belgium (Gabriëls, 1985). The breeding range also decreased drastically in the Netherlands and in Bulgaria, Croatia, Spain and Ukraine.

Several factors can explain these changes. This species is extremely sensitive to human disturbance (Moser 1984). It also forages solitarily and defends an exclusive feeding territory, so food availability and quality within foraging range of the breeding site are critical. The size of the older reed beds chosen for nesting (more than 20 ha) influences the number of breeding pairs (Moser 1983, Broyer et al. 1998), as well as water level. Reed bed degradation or drying out may explain decreasing numbers or desertion of colonies in the Camargue (Moser 1984). Changes in feeding habitat (water level, conversion into rice fields, pesticides) are also related to population declines in Spain (see Chapter 2). Fresh water marshes and reed beds have become extremely vulnerable in Europe, and reed beds are locally harvested for thatch (Kayser et al. 1994b). In other areas, Purple Herons do nest in trees and breeding may occur in mixed colonies with other herons such as in the Netherlands (van der Kooij 1991) and on the French western Atlantic coast (Marion unpubl. data). In this case water level in the colony seems less important.

Wintering conditions appear to be a major factor in population dynamics. Most of the Western Palearctic breeders winter south of the Sahara, mainly in the western and central countries, Mauritania, Senegal, Mali, Sierra Leone, Gambia, Nigeria, Liberia, Ghana (Cramp and Simmons 1977). Dutch breeders may migrate via Italy and Greece and winter mainly south of about 10°N (den Held 1981), especially in the Senegal Delta and Central Niger Delta (Moreau 1972, Roux 1973, Curry and Sayer 1979). Following droughts in West Africa, fewer Purple Herons return to their breeding grounds in the Netherlands (den Held 1981), more individuals older than one year being found dead in the winter quarters in such years (Cavé 1983). den Held (1981) showed the same result for Purple Herons breeding in southern France, but Fasola et al. (in press) found only a limited effect of African climate on Mediterranean populations (see Chapter 2).

Great White Egret. Despite its near worldwide distribution and its presence in 16 European countries, the Great White Egret is patchily distributed in Europe, with an estimated population of 12 900–17 500 breeding pairs, most of them in non-Mediterranean countries (11 000–12 500, Table 1.1). It is considered to be secure in Europe. It is found mainly in Russia (71% of the European population) and Ukraine (18%), followed by Austria, Hungary, Turkey, and Romania (Tucker and Heath 1994). Except for Turkey, these populations are reliably known. Small but regular populations occur in East European countries (Crivelli et al. 1988, Chapter 2; Mikuska pers. comm.). It is expanding its range. In Croatia the population increased from 7 to 21 pairs between 1990 and 1994 (see Chapter 2). The species first nested in the Netherlands in 1977 (Poorter 1981, Voslamber 1992), in Latvia in 1977 (Celmins 1992), Italy in 1992 (Volponi pers. comm.) and France in 1994 (Marion and Marion 1994). Breeding may be anticipated within the next few years in the Czech Republic.

Besides population increase, part of this expansion is a recovery from its persecution, for its beautiful plumes, in the nineteenth and early twentieth centuries (del Hoyo et al. 1992). For example, although almost extirpated in Ukraine (Mikhalevich et al. 1994), there and in Russia populations increased at least 20% between 1970 and 1990, although data are incomplete (Tucker and Heath 1994). In Hungary, 162 pairs dispersed in 14 colonies in 1976 (Schmidt 1977) increased to about 500 pairs in 1990 (Tucker and Heath 1994). The sole colony in Austria, at Lake Neusiedl, has continually increased from 100 pairs in 1946 to 260 in 1976 (Voisin 1991), although recently fluctuations have grown more extreme: 152–320 pairs between 1981 and 1987 (Grüll 1988), 429 pairs in 1989, 174 in 1991, 250 in 1992, more than 450 in 1993 and 554 in 1994 (Munteanu and Ranner 1997, Ranner, pers. comm). We do not know if the Hungarian part of the lake is included in these counts or if fluctuating numbers reflect displacement through the border. These changes may be explained by changing water levels of Lake Neusiedl (Dick et al. 1993), a low level resulting in reduced numbers the following year, and conversely. Such fluctuations also occur in the Danube Delta in Romania (0–258%, Paspaleva et al. 1985), with 700 pairs in 1986 (Green 1992) and only 150–300 now (Tucker and Heath 1994, Chapter 2), while Munteanu and Toniuc (1992) mentioned a large decrease from 1977 to 1992. Tucker and Heath (1994) also mentioned a large decrease for the small Bulgarian population and a small decrease in Turkey.

There is a change of wintering habits since the 1960s (Marion and Marion 1994). Before then, the Great White Egret was a short-distance migrant species, moving mainly along the Adriatic, north-east Italy, the former Yugoslavia, Albania, and Greece with only a few birds moving to the Nile Delta or North Africa (Kuhk 1955). Wintering birds in Iran and Iraq were presumably from the former USSR (Cramp and Simmons 1977). In mild winters some birds even stayed late or overwintered in the neighbourhood of the breeding place, except when waters were covered with ice (Bauer and Glutz von Blotzheim 1966). In the 1970s, increasing numbers of birds migrated to north and west, from the Czech Republic to the Netherlands and France, part of them staying for a while during spring. In winter 1991–92, three individuals were recorded in Spain and Portugal (see Chapter 2). Recently, numbers of birds are also overwintering in Austria.

Little Egret. The Little Egret breeds in southern Europe from Spain to Russia (Table 1.1), but its northernmost breeding limit is 50°N in the Dnepr Valley in Russia (Hancock and Kushlan 1984) and recently (1996) in the United Kingdom and Ireland (Anonymous 1998, Lock and Cook 1998). The European population is 47 000–70 000 breeding pairs, distributed in 16 countries, most of them in the Mediterranean area (see Chapter 2). It is considered to be secure in Europe. The highest abundance occurs in large wetlands, lagoons and rice fields (Fasola and Hafner 1997b). The most important population (32% of the European total) is in Italy (see Chapter 2), followed by France (17%), where the population has strongly increased recently (Marion 1997d), and by the poorly known Turkish population, 13% of the total (Tucker and Heath 1994), Spain 9% (Fernandez Cruz et al. 1992) and Russia (9%). Outside the breeding range, the Little Egret frequently "overshoots" during spring migration and is commonly reported in southern Germany, Switzerland, Austria, United Kingdom and Ireland (Voisin 1991). Its range is increasing. Breeding occurred for the first time in the Netherlands in 1979 (Combridge and Parr 1992,

Little Egret. Little Egrets are increasing in number and expanding their range, particularly in western Europe. Photo: Jacques Delpech.

Voslamber 1992), and more recently in the United Kingdom (Lock and Cook 1998) and in Ireland (Anonymous 1998), probably from increasing breeding in western France (Marion 1997b,d).

Population and range increase are following the species' near extirpation in the last century due to the plumage trade (Voisin 1991). In France, where the situation has been well documented particularly since 1974 in national censuses (Brosselin 1974, Duhautois and Marion 1982, Marion 1991b, 1997a,b), the species bred only in the Camargue in the first half of the nineteenth century but had disappeared by the end of the century and only bred again in 1914 (Voisin 1985). This population grew slowly to reach 1150 pairs in 1955–56 (Valverde 1955–1956). Since 1968, numbers in the Camargue annually fluctuated between 1015 (1985) and 5350 pairs (1996; see Chapter 2). The first inland breeding occurred in La Dombes in 1938 (Berthet 1941–45), with about 100 pairs in the 1960s (Lebreton 1977), but only a few pairs remained in 1989 (Marion 1991b). Breeding started also in six other inland areas between 1942 and 1968, but numbers increased slowly or decreased; all inland French colonies only totalled 190 pairs in 1989 (Marion 1991b). In contrast, the Atlantic boom began with the Grand-Lieu Lake from 1949–55 (Marion and Marion 1975). In 1974, there were about 80 pairs in four colonies on the Atlantic coast, 1901 pairs in 1989 (Marion 1991b) and 5955 pairs in 1994 (Marion 1997a). The total for the country was 1549 pairs in 1968 and 2264 pairs in 31 colonies in 1974 (Brosselin 1974), 3161 pairs in 36 colonies in 1984, only 1841 pairs in 35 colonies in 1985, 3861 pairs in 64 colonies in 1989 (Marion 1991b) and 9845 pairs in 105 colonies in 1994 (Marion 1997d). In Spain and Italy, more recent populations are known. A significant increase occurred in Spain since the first national census in the 1970s (Fernandez Alcazar and Fernandez Cruz 1991), but the breeding population has fluctuated more recently (see Chapter 2). In Italy, after the first national census of 1981 (6700 pairs; Fasola et al. 1981), a small decrease occurred after the hard 1985 winter (5760 pairs), but the population increased by 95% the following year and by 38% in 1990 after a four-year stability (see Chapter 2). The species disappeared in Hungary in 1895 and recolonised the country around 1928. In 1951, 83 pairs were counted, and 203 pairs in 1958; then the population fluctuated between 150 and 214 pairs during the 1959–68 period (Cramp and Simmons 1977). It seems the population reached a higher level later, because Tucker and Heath (1994) commented on the actual size of the population (350–400) as a recent decrease of between 20% and 50% in size and range. In Russia, the species was almost entirely exterminated in the Volga Delta in the early twentieth century but was found in larger numbers later in the Astrakhan Reserve (Cramp and Simmons 1977), where about 22 000 birds were observed in autumn 1935 (corresponding to about 5500 breeding pairs). In the lower Volga Delta, there were 575 pairs in 1951, 100 in 1954, 400 in 1955, only 40 in 1956 and 9 in 1957 (Cramp and Simmons 1977). Since the beginning of the 1980s, the population of the whole Volga Delta is stable with some 3000–4000 pairs (Gavrilov in Crivelli and Hafner 1991), and represents the greater part of the total Russian population (see above). A small population breeds in Slovakia regularly since the 1970s, after sporadic nesting occurred in 1953, 1959 and 1963 (Cramp and Simmons 1977).

Fluctuations of European breeding populations can be due to several factors. The winter survival and the movements between populations seem to play a major role, especially the increasingly local wintering along the French coasts since the 1970s, combined with the generally mild winters. Creation of rice fields after the Second World War in the Camargue, Spain, Italy and Africa, provided new feeding habitat used by both breeding and migrating birds, in areas that often dried out seasonally before. Also active protection of Little Egrets is relatively recent in the most concerned European countries (France 1962, Italy 1977, Spain 1981). Protection has suppressed hunting, which was a major cause of mortality in France and to a lesser extent in Africa (Voisin 1985). This results in increased survival rates. Protection has also suppressed destruction of nests, which was a frequent occurrence in France because the Little Egret was strictly dependent on the colonies of the Black-crowned Night Heron before 1981, and its nests were often destroyed with those of this main species which was considered a pest at this time (Brosselin 1974). Finally, the emigration from the Spanish populations during a spring drought (Brosselin 1974) also played a role in the French increase, probably more in the Camargue than on the Atlantic coast (see Chapter 2). The dynamic conditions of the Atlantic population and its recent wintering habit probably explain the increase of vagrant birds in the British Islands and perhaps in the Netherlands. Acclimatisation to a more northern European climate may lead to further range expansion in northern countries, where suitable habitats exist: flooded lowland near the coasts, with lagoons, salt marshes and fresh water marshes.

The wintering movements of the Little Egret are under study and controversial. In the 1970s, few birds were wintering in southern Europe, most moving to Africa (Hancock and Kushlan 1984). Dugan (1983) claimed that more than 95% of the Little Egrets from the most-ringed population in the Camargue spend the midwinter months in tropical West Africa. Voisin (1985, 1991) suggested two autumn migration routes, along the eastern Spanish coast and secondarily through Italy and Tunisia, with wintering in both cases, while some continue to Africa, from Morocco to Egypt or tropical West Africa. More recently it has been proposed that most birds do not migrate far, and there is a local overwintering population in the Camargue (Marion 1987a, Pineau et al. 1992, Hafner et al. 1994). Nevertheless, local wintering in France can be a threat to survival, because hard winters occur periodically. The winter of 1984–85 killed 92% of these non-migrating French birds, and the survival of this population the next year was almost entirely due to the migrating birds (Marion 1987a).

Cattle Egret. With a population of 80 000 to 100 000 breeding pairs, the Cattle Egret is now the second most abundant species in Europe (Table 1.1), and is considered to be secure even if it is only present in seven countries. It is a well-studied species, and recent data modify those published by Tucker and Heath (1994). Nearly the entire population is in Spain and Portugal: about 66% of the European population are localised in Spain, and 29% in Portugal (Dias 1991). France represents 5%

Cattle Egret. The Cattle Egret's expansion in Europe over the past thirty years has been spectacular. Photo: Jacques Delpech.

(exhaustive census of 1163–1171 pairs in 1992, Marion et al. 1993; at least 4300 in 1998 due to increase in southern France from 1078 to more than 4000—see Chapter 2). Curiously the species is almost absent in Turkey and in Greece, whereas a small population has recently established itself in Italy (Chapter 2). In Romania several birds were seen in the Danube Delta in recent years and the first breeding record (two pairs) dates back to 1997 (Munteanu 1998). In Russia it had colonised only the Volga Delta, by 1950, with a small population of 30–50 pairs still being present there (estimated in Tucker and Heath 1994). The northernmost breeding sites are in northern France (Sueur 1993), and in the Netherlands (first breeding record in 1998 of at least one pair which failed in the fledgling stage—Ronald Messemaker, pers. comm.).

   Since the last century, this species has colonised many parts of the world but its expansion in Europe remained slow. Breeding had already occurred in southern Spain and Portugal at the end of the nineteenth century (Voisin 1991). In 1944, Andalucia was the single common European breeding site (Riddell 1944), probably with fewer than 4000 pairs. A first range expansion occurred by the 1960s to the adjacent provinces of Badajoz and Caceres (Bernis 1961, Fernandez Cruz 1975, Voisin 1991), and another by the 1970s with a few colonies on the extreme north-east Mediterranean coast, particularly in the Ebro Delta (Martinez and Martinez 1983). Cramp and Simmons (1977) estimated the Spanish Cattle Egret population to be over 6500 pairs, from details of colonies in Fernandez Cruz (1975). A strong increase occurred more recently, from about 27 000 pairs in 1986 (Fernandez Cruz and Camacho 1987) to at least 51 680 pairs censused in 1989, and probably 69 000 pairs estimated in 1990 by including colonies of 1986 that were not censused in 1989–90 (Fernandez Cruz et al. 1992). A first colony in Portugal seems to have been established in 1930 (Farinha 1997) or between 1935 and 1940 (Voisin 1991). The first national census in 1984 found about 22 000 pairs (Candeias et al. 1987). The census of 1989 found 25 000–28 000 pairs (Dias 1991) but Farinha (1997) mentioned only about 17 000 pairs in 1991, in both cases with a lower rate of increase than Spain. In France, it was first observed in 1953 in the Camargue, followed by several attempts at breeding from 1957 to 1969, and two pairs bred first in 1969 (Hafner 1970a). This population increased rapidly to about 400 pairs in 1980 (see Chapter 2). The French Atlantic coast was colonised in 1981, probably from Spanish birds, first at Lake Grand-Lieu, then the northernmost (47°N) breeding site of the species in the world (Marion and Marion 1982b). It was followed in 1984 by three breeding records further south. The hard 1984–85 winter destroyed these new populations, and even the Camargue population fell to 74 pairs in 1985 (Marion 1987a, Hafner et al. 1992). A rapid recovery occurred there afterward, with three new breeding sites in 1986 and 1989, while the Camargue population reached 580 pairs in 1991 (Hafner et al. 1992). In 1992, a massive influx occurred from Spain; 1078 pairs bred in the Camargue and 85–93 pairs bred at thirteen other sites further north in France, with one site on the coast of the English channel (Marion et al. 1993). During this "invasion" in April, more than 60 observations of vagrant Cattle Egrets occurred in other countries: Switzerland, Austria, Germany, Belgium, the Netherlands, England, and even Poland and Denmark. Previously only a few vagrant birds had been seen in these countries, as well as in Iceland, Sweden, and Hungary (Cramp and Simmons 1977). These previous sightings could have been birds escaped from captivity or from semi-captive colonies in Alsace (France) and Vienna (Bauer and

Cattle Egret dead in snow. The hard winter of 1984–85 destroyed the pioneer population of Cattle Egrets on the Atlantic coast of France. Photo: Jean-François Hellio and Nicolas van Ingen.

Glutz von Blotzheim 1966, Marion and Marion 1982b). A strong increase was recorded in the Camargue from 1993 to 1998 (see Chapter 2). In Italy, the species curiously only bred in Sardinia from 1985 to the beginning of the 1990s with a small population (Farinha 1997). Today up to 50 pairs breed also on the mainland, in the rice field area of northern Italy (Fasola, pers. comm.). The recent expansion and increasing number of Cattle Egrets do not seem to be related to changes in European habitat availability or requirements of this European population, nor to changes in dispersion of colonies of other attractive species. They probably reflect the natural expression of a dynamic species. However, recent mild winters and summer drought probably assisted the recent changes in West Europe. In the main European population, in the south-western part of the Iberian Peninsula, the Cattle Egret was primarily dependent on coastal wetlands, before extending to inland wetlands or dry land. The largest colony reached more than 10 000 pairs along the Guadiana river in 1990 (Farinha 1997). All other European populations use mainly coastal wetlands (north-east Spain, the Mediterranean and French Atlantic coasts, the Volga Delta). There Cattle Egrets feed in wet meadows with cattle and horses (Bredin 1984, Marion et al. 1993), while the dry areas are used only in hard winters. Its diet is more opportunistic than in other regions. If insects and amphibians represent the main prey during breeding, small mammals, amphibians and even reptiles and fish are dominant before breeding and during autumn, while small rodents and earthworms are consumed mainly in winter (Bredin 1984). Consequently this species does not seem limited in its northern expansion by the scarcity of insects, as suggested by Voisin (1991). Its favoured habitats are still frequent in Europe, and its opportunistic behaviour (exploitation of garbage or feeding behind tractors in the Camargue) extends feeding opportunities. So the European scarcity of breeding Cattle Egrets is probably related more to historical factors (particularly in the eastern part of the Mediterranean) and to climate and range limits.

Squacco Heron. The Squacco Heron is Europe's rarest heron, with an estimated population of 14 300–26 800 breeding pairs in 14 countries (Table 1.1). It is considered to be vulnerable in Europe. Its main breeding area is centred in Turkey, Iran and the Caucasus, with an extension to the northern coast of the Black Sea, up to Hungary and the Adriatic Sea by the Danube Valley (del Hoyo et al. 1992). France, northern Italy and Spain are from this main range. The most northern breeding sites are in Russia (Voisin 1991). The main countries are Russia (35% of the European population), Turkey (32%), Bulgaria (11%) and Romania (10%). The populations of Squacco Heron in Russia are probably under-estimated by Tucker and Heath (1994) because they give only 5800 pairs for the European part of former USSR, while Krivenko (1991) reports 9000 pairs there.

Fluctuations seem characteristic of this species and important changes have occurred in its population since the middle of the last century. The Palearctic population was estimated at 16 400 pairs in 165 colonies in 1850–1900 (Joséfik 1969–70); then it fell to about 6800 pairs in 115 colonies between 1900 and 1920, and increased again between 1940 and 1960 to reach some 8200 pairs in 71 colonies (Cramp and Simmons 1977). However, local situations often differed: for instance in Italy the crash (a 90% decrease) occurred in the first half of the twentieth century. In France, the Squacco Heron probably only bred in a single site (Lake Grand-Lieu) at the end of the nineteenth century (Marion and Marion 1982a) before it disappeared, but regular breeding (by 2 pairs) has been observed since 1996 (Marion and Reeber 1997). The species was also known to have bred in the Camargue during the first half of the nineteenth century (Voisin 1975), but breeding was only rediscovered in 1930 (Galet 1931), and numbers fluctuated between 47 and 142 pairs from 1970 to 1998. It was the unique French population until 1950 when a small population of up to five pairs established in the Rhône Valley, in the Dombes (Marion and Marion 1982a). Numbers have recently fluctuated in Italy from 200 pairs in 1978 to 1300 in 1992 and 500–600 in 1995 (Fasola, pers. comm.; Chapter 2). Spain showed the same trend with 171 pairs in 1988 and 822 pairs in 1990 (Fernandez Cruz et al. 1992; Chapter 2). This increasing trend in France, Spain and Italy contrasts remarkably with decreases in the south-eastern European countries, where Tucker and Heath (1994) reported decreasing trends for the 1970–90 period, by 20–50% in Albania, Bulgaria, Hungary, Romania and perhaps Turkey, and by more than 50% in Ukraine. However, they only mentioned 200–290 pairs for the whole of Ukraine in 1986 from Serebryakov and Grishchenko (1989) while Schogolev (1992) found 400–600 pairs in the Dnestr Delta alone from 1979–91. In Greece, Crivelli et al. (1988) reported a decrease in Squacco Herons from 1400 pairs before 1970 to 201–377 pairs in 1985–86 (see Chapter 2). A strong decrease is also reported in a breeding site in Croatia from 478 pairs in 1954 to fewer than 50 pairs recently (see Chapter 2). In Russia, there were 3800–4200 pairs north of the Black Sea, in the second half of the nineteenth century, only 2100–2300 at the beginning of the twentieth, and 4500–4800 in 1950–60 (Cramp and Simmons 1977). The increase continued and the Volga Delta totalled 7000 pairs in 1975, but this population sharply decreased after 1985 and is presently fluctuating between zero and 300 pairs (Gavrilov in Crivelli and Hafner 1991). For the whole of Europe, Tucker and Heath (1994) mentioned that two-thirds of the breeding populations declined by more than 20% between 1970 and 1990, the species now being vulnerable.

Several factors may influence these fluctuations. Remnant effects of the early plume trade may be a factor (Cramp and Simmons 1977). Shooting of breeding pairs by fishermen as well as by ornithologists in the nineteenth century (the latter probably the final cause of disappearance in western France; Marion and Marion 1982a) and more recent protection probably had effects, together with climatic changes, particularly hot and dry summers that favour its breeding (Voisin 1991). Conversely, heavy rains may result in too high water levels in spring or over longer periods. In the Volga Delta the traditional feeding areas of Squacco Herons have been greatly reduced in recent years because of the increase in water level of the Caspian Sea by 170 cm between 1980 and 1991, which may explain the local population crash there (Gavrilov in Crivelli and Hafner 1991). In African wintering areas, drought conditions may increase mortality (Hafner and Didner 1997). Perhaps the most important factor is the increase in rice fields in both breeding and migration areas.

Black-crowned Night Heron. Distributed in low altitudes, this species is present in 22 countries. The European population (50 000–75 000 breeding pairs, Table 1.1) is centred in Italy, representing 31% of the entire population. Russia supports about 20%, Romania 10% and France 7% (Marion 1991b). Russia seems under-estimated by Tucker and Heath (1994) since their figures only totalled 16 000–21 000 pairs for the European part of the former USSR, against 28 000 pairs by Krivenko (1991). We used data from Fasola and Hafner (1997a) for this country.

Formerly more common, the species disappeared completely in some countries in the late nineteenth and early twentieth century, mainly due to persecution (Brosselin 1974) and destruction of habitat in the Netherlands (Fasola and Hudec 1997). After the Second World War, in most areas the population recovered and expanded, such as in France, Poland and the Netherlands (Lebret 1947, Cramp and Simmons 1977). In The Netherlands and Germany it expanded from artificially established colonies (as early as 1908–1909; Lippens and Wille 1969, Brosselin 1974). Since 1970, breeding range has remained stable or has contracted in most countries (Tucker and Heath 1994). Populations tend to fluctuate. In France, numbers dropped from 2159 pairs in 1968 to 1550 in 1974 (Brosselin 1974), before increasing again to 3411 pairs in 1981, 4013 in 1989 and 4176 in 1994 (Marion 1997d), in spite of a strong decrease in the Camargue (Hafner in Marion 1991b). Italy shows fluctuations between 14 000 (1985) and 20 000 pairs (1990), with a mean of 17 380. Numbers have increased in the Czech Republic and a few pairs first nested in Belarus and in Belgium from 1979 (Verhaegen 1981). In Slovakia, where poachers disturb herons throughout the season, numbers seem to fluctuate between 130 and 330 pairs, depending on the flooding of an area in eastern Slovakia (Darlova, pers. comm.). Fluctuations also occur in Ukraine (see Chapter 2). The species appears to be stable in eastern countries (Germany, Poland, Hungary), and decreasing in Spain, Croatia and Romania (Chapter 2), Austria, the Netherlands (where it is almost extinct) and Russia (Tucker and Heath 1994). This species is classified as declining in Europe.

Causes of these various European trends are unclear. The increase in rice fields explains the strong increase of species in Italy after the Second World War, but not elsewhere (Fasola and Hudec 1997). Habitat loss does not seem a major recent factor in Europe, where the species frequently uses man-made habitats such as reservoirs, canals, ponds, and rice fields (Fasola 1983). Local disturbance may affect colonies when visits occur just before and during egg laying, provoking the abandonment of new nests (Tremblay and Ellison 1979, Marion pers. obs.). Abandonment of colonies due to the death of trees is not critical when there are alternative sites. Migrating and wintering conditions probably play a major role in general population dynamic. About 95% of the Black-crowned Night Herons migrate across the Sahara to overwinter in tropical West Africa, especially the Sudano–Sahelian zone (Dugan 1983), where a high proportion of juveniles remain during their first two and maybe three years (Brosselin 1974). The drought prevalent in the Sahel during the 1970s has probably impacted on the European breeding population (Brosselin 1974, del Hoyo et al 1992), but research is needed to correlate survival rates with Sahelian climate and also to determine the origin of an increasing, though still small, number of wintering birds in European Mediterranean countries (see Chapter 2). In the past, feral birds have had an effect, as already noted for Germany and the Netherlands. In Belgium, recent breeding is mainly from birds released from 1978 at Zwin (van Sanden 1989), where the semi-captive colony reached 20 pairs in 1994 (Burggraeve, pers. comm.), with new surrounding small colonies. Feral birds also nest at the Edinburgh Zoo (25–40 pairs) and in Norfolk.

Little Bittern. The Little Bittern is still a widespread species in Europe (28 countries), but it is continuously distributed only in Russia and Poland. Population size is imprecise (37 000 to 107 000 pairs—Table 1.1) and the species is considered to be provisionally vulnerable. However, recent censuses have been conducted in only four countries (Czech Republic, Moldova, the Netherlands and Switzerland), and there are no quantitative data for the larger populations (Tucker and Heath 1994). These authors have roughly estimated the Russian population at 10 000–50 000 pairs but this seems high, because Krivenko (1991) estimated the whole population of the European part of former USSR as 15 000 pairs. del Hoyo et al. (1992) also give lower numbers for the EEC (2700–4500 pairs against 4300–6530). The largest populations outside Russia are in Romania (21%), Ukraine (8%) and perhaps Turkey.

The Little Bittern is poorly known because it is a nocturnal, solitary and dispersed species that breeds late in the season (end of May to August). It was strongly decreasing both in population size and range from 1970 to 1990 in the great majority of countries, mainly in north-west and central Europe, with a reduction of more than 50% in Austria, Belarus, Czech Republic, France, Germany, Latvia, The Netherlands, Slovakia, Slovenia and Spain (Tucker and Heath 1994). For the whole of Europe, Tucker and Heath estimated that 92% of the population declined by 20–50% since 1970. These estimates are probably a minimum decline, because it is even more pronounced in the countries where exhaustive censuses were made. The decrease in France exceeds 85% since 1968 (Duhautois 1984, Marion 1994a). In the Netherlands, it exceeds 90% since 1961–67 (Cramp and Simmons 1977), and the species will probably soon disappear (Bekhuis 1990). There were 100–200 pairs in Belgium before 1960 (Devillers et al. 1988) but it is now disappearing. In 13 other countries, the decrease seems less pronounced (20–50%, Tucker and Heath 1994). The European range decrease (20–50%) confirms the population trend of withdrawing from west to east (Marion 1997c).

Apart from Belgium where the decline in Little Bitterns was primarily attributable to pollution and drainage (Lippens and Wille 1972) or in a few localities in the Netherlands and in France where riverbank development disturbed the nesting habitat (Braaksma 1968, Marion 1983b), the general European decrease is not clearly related to destruction of habitat or to pollution. This species has disappeared from large, apparently favourable wetlands in spite of their protection. Suitable habitats from which Little Bitterns have disappeared are widespread in Europe: reed beds or other thick vegetation mixed with willow along rivers, fringes of lakes and fish ponds and marshes. This human-tolerant heron sometimes breeds in small ponds near habitations. The decline is probably mainly due to an increase in mortality during migration or wintering in Africa, and may relate to droughts in the Sahara and, more recently, in East Africa (Marion 1994a,b). This species could be very sensitive to drought because it migrates east of the Mediterranean Sea via the Arabian Peninsula or across the Sahara to winter primarily in eastern Africa (Hancock and Kushlan 1984). The loss of wetlands normally used as staging areas in the desert during migration (Cramp and Simmons 1977) could have extended the length of flights and thus induced higher mortality. Unfortunately, there are not sufficient ringing data to test this hypothesis. The stable status of Portugal's Little Bittern population could be due to a direct migration route along the western coast of Africa, thus avoiding drought conditions in the Sahara.

Eurasian Bittern. Although the Eurasian Bittern is a widespread species in Europe, its population can be roughly estimated to be only about 20 000–44 000 breeding pairs (Table 1.1). It is considered provisionally vulnerable in Europe. The Russian population, however, representing 63% of this European total, is poorly known with estimates varying from 10 000 to 30 000 pairs (Tucker and Heath 1994). Its abundance clearly declines in Europe from East to West, and in the northern countries. Outside Russia populations are small, the more important being situated in Ukraine (13%), Poland (4%), Romania (4%), and Belarus (3%). Because this species is extremely secretive during the breeding season, pairs are usually estimated using counts of booming males (Bibby et al., 1992, Kayser et al. 1998), so reliable quantitative data are only available for the smallest populations. However, males being polygynous (Percy 1951), it is difficult to consider singing males (one per 8–25 ha, Koskimies and Tyler 1997) as representative of breeding pairs.

The European population has declined steadily in numbers since the nineteenth century, due to drainage, with occasional human persecution and egg collection (Turner 1924, Cramp and Simmons 1977, Day 1981, Diamond and Presst 1987). In some countries, extirpated populations of Eurasian Bitterns recovered at the beginning of the twentieth century, for example the United Kingdom (Diamond and Filion 1987) and Sweden (Cramp and Simmons 1977), but this recovery has been reversed in more recent years. The 1976 census (Day 1981) revealed in most European countries with reliable estimates that the number of pairs and breeding sites decreased from about 1955 onwards. The species disappeared before 1976 in Luxembourg and Ireland. In seven out of 23 countries, numbers decreased during

1970–90, and for the whole of Europe, 79% of the breeding populations declined by 20–50% since 1970 (Tucker and Heath 1994).

The causes of this recent decrease are habitat loss or changes in traditional management (Tyler 1994), including reducing reed cover, effects of boat traffic at the edge of open water resulting in wave-action (Day 1981), human disturbance due to recreation (boat traffic, angling: Hölzinger 1987), and probably pollution (Day and Wilson 1978), either eutrophication that modifies fish populations within reed beds or pesticides that may alter the survival of birds (Newton et al. 1994). As the Eurasian Bittern strongly prefers for nest building tall, dense emergent wetlands with shallow standing water, especially dense one-year-old reed beds and open clear water for fishing, the population is very sensitive to the loss and disturbance of wetlands. Winter conditions seem a major factor.

Populations from areas with hard winters (Denmark, Finland, Germany, Poland, Sweden) migrate south or south-west to winter in the Netherlands (Den Boer 1992), France (Marion 1991b), and in the Mediterranean region. However, some may travel across the Sahara to overwinter in Africa as far south as Zaire (Moreau 1972). In warmer regions, Eurasian Bitterns normally overwinter locally. Eurasian Bitterns may suffer a high mortality, up to 40%, in prolonged hard weather in Britain (Day 1981, Bibby 1981), and in the Netherlands even up to 80 or 90% (Den Boer 1992). In the harsh winter of 1962–63, however, birds found dead in the

Eurasian Bittern in snow. Eurasian Bitterns may suffer a high mortality in severely cold winters. Photo: Jean-François Hellio and Nicolas van Ingen.

United Kingdom came from the Netherlands, Belgium, Germany and Sweden (Day and Wilson 1978), and after that winter many traditional breeding sites in Baden–Würtemberg (Germany) were never occupied again (Hölzinger 1987). In Sweden, population was reduced from 450 to 270–300 pairs after the hard winter of 1979 (Nilsson, pers. comm.). Populations need three to seven years to recover from a severe winter.

Critical Conservation and Regional Management Issues

International policy

Because herons move across national borders, international cooperation is needed for their conservation. Europe has the advantage of an array of international policies and frameworks for bird conservation (European Commission 1992a,b, Paleologou and Salathé 1993, Lyster 1985 and Biber-Klemm 1991). The "Birds Directive" (European Economic Community Directive on the Conservation of Wild Birds =79/409/EEC), came into force in 1981. All heron species breeding in Europe, except the Cattle Egret and the Grey Heron, are listed on Annex I, which constrains Member States to strictly protect them and their more important breeding, wintering or migrating sites. Member States must classify the most suitable territories in number and size as Special Protection Areas (SPAs), where normally protection takes precedence over human activities. Particular attention has to be paid to the protection of wetlands, and especially those of international importance under the Ramsar Convention. Finally, Member States should take appropriate steps to avoid pollution or deterioration of habitats or any disturbance affecting the birds. Protection of the species of Annex I and protection of their major sites are obligatory for the Member States under penalty, in contrast to other international conventions.

The same principle has recently been applied in the "Habitats Directive" (European Economic Community Directive on the Conservation of Natural Habitats of Wild Fauna and Flora =92/43/EEC), which came into force in 1994 and completes the Bird Directive by adding other animals and plants and also protects habitats for their own sake.

The best contribution by the European Union to wetland conservation will be the eventual removal of direct and indirect subsidies for wetland destruction (Hollis and Jones 1991). Agricultural subsidies have frequently led to wetland destruction, by favouring cultivation in traditional wet meadows. In the French Western Atlantic marshes, 35 000 ha of wetlands were drained for this reason between 1973 and 1990, even though they were in the Natural Regional Park of the Marais Poitevin (Servat 1991).

The Bern Convention (Convention on the Conservation of European Wildlife and Natural Habitats) concerns all the Member States of the Council of Europe (24 countries, i.e. those of the European Union and Cyprus, Iceland, Liechtenstein, Malta, Norway, San Marino, Switzerland and Turkey) and invited non-member states in Europe and North and West Africa. The contracting parties recognise the importance of conserving wild flora and fauna and their natural habitats, and the convention provides a framework to take appropriate and necessary legislative and administrative measures to ensure their conservation. All Ardeidae species occurring in Europe, except the Grey Heron, are listed in Annex II (strictly protected fauna). The Grey Heron is listed in Annex III (protected fauna).

Wetland conservation

All European heron species largely depend on wetlands, the most limited and degraded habitat in Europe (Dugan 1993). Ecological requirements of breeding herons differ in part from those of wintering anatids, so only some of the large and important European wetlands (see Finlayson and Moser 1991, Dugan 1993) also support large heron populations. Apart from the Grey Heron and the Eurasian Bittern, main heron populations are localised on coastal wetlands, or along some major rivers (Volga, Dnepr, Danube, Guadalquivir, Ebre, Rhône, Loire). We identify nine critical major wetlands for herons in Europe (more than 4000 breeding pairs; see Fig. 1.1). The delta of the Volga (Russia) covers 1 900 000 ha, but only the lower part has not been drained. About 14 000–17 000 pairs of herons (Gavrilov in Crivelli and Hafner 1991) use its extensive flooded *Salix* forests, reed beds and floating macrophytes (*Lotus*, *Nymphea*). A similar but less extensive area on the Black Sea in Romania is the delta of the Danube (647 000 ha), with about 17 000 breeding pairs of herons (Gogu-Bogdan pers. comm.). In north-western Italy, about 15 000 pairs of herons use 160 000 ha of inland rice fields, mainly along the River Po (Scott 1980, Fasola and Alieri 1992). Another important Italian area is the Western Adriatic coastal wetlands (about 60 000 ha) including the Po Delta and the Venetian lagoon, with about 6000 pairs of herons (Casini and Boldreghini 1994). In Spain, similar but more extensive habitats are represented in the Guadalquivir Delta (360 000 ha), with about 6000 pairs of herons not including thousands of pairs of Cattle Egrets. There are 48 000 pairs of Cattle Egrets within the Tajo and the Guadiana floodplains in Spain and Portugal (Fernandez Cruz et al. 1992). There are also two major French wetlands for herons: the Camargue, a complex of 142 000 ha of fresh water (with rice fields) and brackish water marshes and lagoons, where about 8500 pairs breed each year (Hafner pers. comm.), and the Western Atlantic marshes, a complex of 250 000 ha with Grand-Lieu lake and coastal fresh water and brackish water marshes from the Loire estuary to the Gironde estuary, where up to 11 400 pairs of herons are breeding (Marion 1997d). A similar (8000 pairs) but less varied (essentially Grey Herons) and more diffused population breeds in the Netherlands, almost all the country representing a favourable habitat for them, particularly the coastal dammed-up marshes.

In these wetlands, the suitable habitats are partitioned among the different species. The Eurasian Bittern, Little Bittern and Purple Heron depend upon reed beds and their surroundings for nesting and feeding. Conversely, the Little and Great White egrets feed in open waters or on banks with scarce vegetation, but the former nests in more or less distant tree-colonies, as do other colonial species. The Squacco and the Black-crowned Night Herons feed generally in more vegetated areas. Inland, the Cattle Egret feeds mainly in wet pastures, and in coastal areas such as the Guadalquivir and the Camargue, in a whole variety of fresh water habitats. The Grey Heron is the most opportunistic species and feeds in all the habitats, from terrestrial sites where it catches small rodents, to brooks, torrents, rivers, lakes, marshes with or without abundant vegetation, and man-made habitats such as ponds, gravel-pits, reservoirs or rice fields. It even exploits the seashore all year long in Norway, but only in winter elsewhere, as Little Egrets do in France. The salinity is well tolerated by Grey Herons and Little Egrets, while all other species strictly depend on fresh water.

Herons require a shallow aquatic environment. Even for the most flexible species, the Grey Heron, there is a strong correlation between the size of breeding populations and the water surface area or length of stream banks (Marion 1988). Drying or draining threatens all heron species, and these practices have been common until now. High water levels over a long period also result in unfavourable conditions. This recently occurred in the Volga Delta, involving a severe decline of the important Squacco Heron population as well as breeding European Spoonbills (*Platalea leucorodia*) and Glossy Ibises (*Plegadis falcinellus*) (Gavrilov in Crivelli and Hafner 1991).

Since the beginning of this century, but especially during the second half, the process of transforming wetlands has accelerated, resulting in their destruction across Europe (Hollis and Jones 1991). Many of the wetlands that survive have been seriously degraded due to human activities. Therefore it is of great importance to conserve those few remaining large wetlands in central and eastern Europe, which even now are in danger of degradation by continued human pressure (Hollis and Jones 1991). Many of the valuable wetlands in East and Central Europe are still unprotected, particularly the great river floodplains (Dugan 1993). Major threats are still posed by development programmes, in and around wetlands, for both urban and industrial expansion and tourism. Fisheries activities can also have major impacts and severely change the ecological character of wetlands. Dugan (1993) and Finlayson and Moser (1991) provide overviews of the status and threats to wetlands, including the causes and consequences.

Due to the severe loss and degradation of wetlands in Europe, almost all countries have now developed legislation providing some element of wetland protection, and most countries have joined the Ramsar Convention. Therefore, in their overview of the status of wetlands in Europe, Hollis and Jones (1991) are cautiously optimistic for the future. One reason is the social changes that have brought public pressure for "greener" governmental policies with regard to agriculture and industry. A network of wetland reserves has been created and the public awareness of the wider social and economic importance of wetland functions and values is constantly improving. The strong movement of non-governmental organisations and the more "green" policies adopted by development banks and agencies can only improve the situation of wetlands and their herons in Europe.

Habitat management

Habitat disturbance by man remains critically important, in no small part because the European landscape has been exploited and transformed by man for thousands of years. Fragmented forests and cultivated fields are widespread, whereas wetlands are scarce. Less than 1% of the surface of France is now wetland (Bouche et al. 1991). Remnant wetlands also attract tourism, with its own types of disturbance. Of the main French wetlands 98% are now seriously degraded and their future seems uncertain (Bernard 1994). In Italy a million ha of wetlands were destroyed in a century (Lussana Grasselli 1982), with only about 100 000 ha remaining (Musi et al.

1992). Creating new wetlands in small countries (in the Netherlands or Austria for instance) will partially compensate for these general losses. But many wetlands remain threatened by urbanisation, and an increasingly dense network of roads, railways, and electrical grids—more numerous in Western Europe than in the East. Less adaptable species face reduced possibilities of finding suitable breeding and feeding sites. This problem seems more pronounced in Europe, particularly Western Europe (Tucker and Heath 1994 for all declining bird species) than in many other parts of the world outside the Far East. The mean human density is 99 inhabitants per km^2 in Europe, outside Russia, twice as many in Germany, Italy and the United Kingdom, three times as many in Belgium, 4.5 times as many in the Netherlands. These densities contrast with 28 in the USA and 40 worldwide. Grey Heron excepted, the future of breeding colonies of herons in Europe could increasingly depend on protection of the few main suitable sites.

Some heron populations are also affected by wetland conditions in their wintering areas outside Europe. Four of the five most vulnerable heron species (Little Bittern, Black-crowned Night Heron, Squacco Heron and Purple Heron) are trans-Saharan migrating species. As noted above, drought in wintering areas is a probable factor in the widespread decline of European breeding populations since the 1970s. Migration stopover locales (for instance Mediterranean coastal wetlands in Spain, Italy and North Africa, and oases in the Sahara) and wintering sites (for instance the inland delta of Niger, Lake Tchad, coastal Atlantic wetlands from the Senegal Delta to Dahomey) are relatively few and it would be theoretically possible to manage these wetlands to preserve their water level. However, human activities are often in conflict and of higher government priority and so it will be difficult to obtain sustainable management in these more and more coveted areas.

The Little Bittern, Squacco Heron, Purple Heron, and Eurasian Bittern depend on reed beds for breeding and/or feeding. Reed bed loss due to drainage of marshes, reed harvest, land reclamation for agriculture or industry, disturbance by tourism or pollution all negatively affect these herons. Active local reed bed management, such as in nature reserves, might positively influence their population status. As old reed is needed for nest building by species such as Eurasian Bittern, mechanical harvesting of reed should be avoided, and total or partial cutting/burning (especially early in the season) should be carefully controlled. In Denmark, a general ban on reed cutting exists during March–October (by the Act of Nature Protection in 1992), which prevents destruction of nests of Eurasian Bittern. Furthermore, this species and some others are very sensitive to human disturbance. Therefore there should be reed bed areas without any recreation such as surfing, boat traffic, skating, angling and walking.

Besides active reed bed and wetland management, water quality is critical and needs to be monitored and managed. As herons mostly catch their prey by sight, they need clear water for foraging. Water pollution, particularly turbidity caused by algae and boat traffic, can hinder the search or catching of food. Water pollution can also adversely affect food chains (Koeman et al. 1972, van der Molen et al. 1982) and causes eggshell thinning (Presst 1970a, Marquiss 1983). However, eutrophication impact needs further research because it could in some instances help herons by increasing fish production.

Water level management is crucial in wetlands. One example is the restoration project at Lake Hornborga in Sweden, in which water levels were restored in this lake to create favourable conditions for a large number of water bird species (Hertzman and Larsson 1991, Björk 1994). Dick et al. (1993) and Winkler et al. (1994) demonstrated the dependency of Great White Egret numbers on water levels in Lake Neusiedl, Austria. Low water levels in one year resulted in fewer egrets the following year, while numbers breeding immediately responded to higher water levels. In France, in Dombes and Camargue, water level influences the numbers of breeding Purple Herons (Moser 1984, Broyer et al. 1998), while at Grand-Lieu Lake lower water level due to diversion for agriculture caused a general decrease of aquatic flora and vertebrates, including fish (Marion and Marion 1975, Marion et al. 1989), and restoration of water level had positive effects (Marion and Reeber 1997, Marion 1999). Similar results were observed at the Kerkini Reservoir in Greece (Crivelli et al. 1995).

No specific management plans for the conservation of herons have been developed in Europe except on the local site-specific level—for example in some nature reserves and heron colony sites. Such local area plans are critical at important heron nesting and feeding sites (Musi et al. 1992). Large-scale wetland and waterbird management plans have been developed in some countries, which, indirectly, may benefit herons. Comprehensive management plans for wetlands which reduce the effects of human impact are accepted as essential tools throughout Europe (Hollis and Jones 1991), and the integration of wetlands into regional and national planning has also become established. It is critical that the specific needs of herons be included in these planning efforts.

A very interesting but still rare aspect of wetland management in Europe is wetland restoration. In the Netherlands for instance, nature restoration projects have been initiated to develop "new natural" marshes in the floodplains of large rivers, as in the lower Rhine floodplain. Increases in breeding Black-crowned Night Heron, Eurasian Bittern, Little Bittern and Purple Heron are expected in such new areas. Finlayson and Larsson (1991) and Eiseltová (1994) provide an overview of wetland management and restoration projects, and their benefits for water birds. However, although wetland restoration is an exciting new development in many countries in Europe and has great potential, it is important not to forget that newly created habitats can never replace those which have already been lost.

Such examples emphasise how important a landscape or ecosystem approach is when addressing wetland conservation and management, and the need for monitoring of any ecological change within wetlands used as breeding and feeding habitat by herons. In Denmark, major habitat restoration projects can now (since 1989) be carried out under the Nature Management Act, which provides a modern tool for actively reversing the negative developments affecting nature, and promotes the multiple use of nature areas, so as to increase public awareness about the value of nature (Ministry of the Environment 1992).

Hunting has affected several heron populations in Europe, starting perhaps with the extraordinary persecution during the nineteenth century of herons considered to be pests by fishermen (Chapter 13). In 1947–57, 79% of recovered ringed Grey Herons (from France to Africa) were officially declared as "killed" or "found wounded" (Marion 1981). Today all species are protected in all European countries, except for the Grey Heron in some countries (Marion 1987b, Voisin 1991). The two pioneering countries were Hungary, where the Great White Egret, Little Egret and Squacco Heron were protected in 1912 and other species except Grey Heron in 1954, and Poland where all species except Grey Heron were protected in 1949. In France, the Little Egret was protected in 1962 and all other species in 1974. In Belgium, all species were protected in 1972, while Italy followed in 1977, Spain in 1981 and the Netherlands in 1985 (though there had been with partial protection since 1912). For the most persecuted species, the Grey Heron, a large increase in numbers and range in several countries and changes in habitat use in France (Marion and Marion 1987a, Marion 1997a) followed protection. Illegal shooting occurs in several parts of Europe, and continues in African wintering areas. In the 1970s, killing still remained the major cause of ring recoveries of Grey Herons in "hunting countries" such as France; in 1971–77, 36% of ring recoveries were from birds killed or found wounded (Marion 1981).

The situation with the Grey Heron is a matter of concern. While it is strictly protected (no hunting or control) in Belgium, France, Greece, Italy, Luxembourg, Northern Ireland, Portugal and Spain, it can be hunted in Poland from 16 August to 31 March, in Lower Austria in September, and during the hunting season in parts of the former West Germany and the former East Germany (from 1 July to 31 January for the latter). The species is often seen as conflicting with human interests, such as at fish farms (Chapter 13). In Denmark, Finland, Norway and Poland, it can be shot for this reason all year round inside fish farms although protected outside of them in the first three countries. In Hungary, Grey Herons can only be shot in fish farms between 1 July and 31 January. In Austria they may be shot everywhere under licence. In Hungary, Ireland, the Netherlands, United Kingdom, Sweden and in some German locales, the species is protected but licences can be given to shoot Grey Herons at fish farms if predation is serious. In Romania, all species of herons can be frightened or shot only at fish farms in the Danube Delta, by governmental guards. An optimum number of predatory birds is determined each year in the entire Danube Delta and adhered to by partial destruction of eggs, frightening or shooting the excess birds (Marion 1987b). In Switzerland, official hunters can also frighten or shoot Grey Herons in case of serious damage (Voisin 1991).

Conclusions

Europe is the poorest continent for heron diversity, with only 9 species. Furthermore, much of Europe has even fewer species, as diversity falls from 9 species to 2 or 1 from the south-eastern coastal wetlands to Scandinavia and the British Isles. This is primarily due to climatic conditions, particularly in winter. Nearly half the species (Little Bittern, Black-crowned Night Heron, Squacco Heron and Purple Heron) migrate to Africa, and others partially migrate or shift locally in winter. Part of the paucity of herons is due to historical factors; heron populations may still be expanding from ice age refugia. Despite the few species, overall numbers are relatively high at about half a million breeding pairs. The Grey Heron is the most widespread and abundant species, and, with the Eurasian Bittern, is most tolerant of high latitude conditions. Migratory species are also relatively well distributed, including Little Bittern, Black-crowned Night Heron and Purple Heron, although a localised species, the Cattle Egret, recently became the second most abundant heron.

Information on species ranges is essential for conservation plans that largely depend on political context in each country. With respect to heron numbers, Russia is the principal country of concern, with 29% of the European population. This is followed by Spain, France, Ukraine, Italy, Portugal, Romania and Turkey. National conservation planning is essential in these countries.

Because the European landscape has been so altered and heavily used, there are relatively few sites of exceptional importance for herons. The most important heron areas are: 1) Tajo and Guadiana floodplains; 2) Danube Delta; 3) Volga Delta; 4) North-western Po floodplain; 5) Guadalquivir Delta; 6) French western Atlantic marshes; 7) Dutch marshes; 8) Po Delta and Venetian lagoon; and 9) the Camargue. Seven of these nine areas are coastal wetlands. Even if these sites do not represent the majority of the national populations, they probably act as sources providing emigrants for more unstable and/or diffused populations. When important wetlands represent a great part of countries or when a species is locally very abundant, the density of herons for the whole country is large, and this is frequently the case in small countries like Portugal, Moldova, the Netherlands, and Denmark. Naturally, the role of each country differs for various species. France is essential for the Grey Heron, Spain and Portugal for the Cattle Egret, Italy for the Black-crowned Night Heron and the Little Egret, while Russia is the major location for the Great White Egret, the Purple Heron, the Eurasian Bittern and, with Romania, for the Little Bittern.

Stability in heron populations seems to be the exception. Considerable changes have occurred in range and numbers of breeding herons. In the nineteenth century and the beginning of the twentieth, the general trend was negative, due to habitat loss or human persecution (fish farmers and hunters for Grey Herons and Black-crowned Night Herons considered as pests or game birds, and the plumage trade for Great White Egrets, Little Egrets and Squacco Herons). In the twentieth century, several opposing factors interacted according to species and countries. Direct human persecution generally decreased, due to the ending of the plumage trade, to a positive effect of the two World Wars which mobilised men and prohibited hunting, and finally to a progressive legal protection in all European countries, that was generally achieved in the 1980s. Also, rice field management from the mid century in Spain and Italy had a positive effect on local heron populations, even if destruction of wetlands elsewhere went on. Finally, long-term mild winters in western Europe between 1963 and 1985 involved an improved survival for partially-migrant species (Grey Heron, probably Great White Egret), and for primarily-migrant species like the Little Egret that recently, in some locations in France, changed its behaviour to become partially-migrant or sedentary. A similar behavioural change was observed in the Cattle Egret, in addition to the natural worldwide expansion of this species. A strong increase occurred in numbers and range for such species. The more impressive case is that of the Grey Heron in western countries that multiplied its populations by a factor of 76 since 1928 in France (the largest European population now), by 18 in Switzerland, 7.5 in Belgium and 4.6 in Denmark. It recently expanded toward the south, invading half of France and part of Spain and Italy. This recovery is important for several other species because the Grey Heron is a pioneering species whose colonies frequently attract other herons (Little Egret, Black-crowned Night Heron, Great White Egret, Squacco Heron, Cattle Egret). Eastern European populations of Grey Herons are stable, but in the Volga Delta, this species seems to have lost around 20 000 pairs since 1935, due to drainage. The Great White Egret shows a similar contrasting pattern between western and eastern countries, with local populations increased by three-fold in Hungary since 1976 and in Austria since 1946, and expansion of a few breeders toward the Netherlands, Italy and France, while the population of the Danube Delta has decreased since 1986. For the Little Egret, stability in the Volga Delta contrasts with the increase in Hungary (population increased 4.5-fold since 1951), Italy (by 2.4 since 1981) and France (by 8 since 1955). The more localised Cattle Egret shows a strong increase in Spain (population multiplied by 17 since 1944) and probably in Portugal, while emigrants were firmly established in France from 1970; but curiously the species has not yet really established itself in the south-eastern European countries.

The situation for the migrant species is largely different. The Little Bittern, probably one of the most abundant species in the 1960s, shows the largest and most widespread decrease in range and numbers (92% of the European population declined by 20–50% since 1970), and this heron is now provisionally considered as endangered in Europe. The decrease (about 90%) was particularly dramatic in western, most studied countries (France, Belgium, the Netherlands). In the same period, 99% of the European populations of the Purple Heron declined by 20–50%, and the species is now vulnerable in Europe. In the Netherlands, the population decreased one third of its original size since 1980. The Squacco Heron shows a contrasting pattern, with recent increases in Italy (by a factor of 6.5 since 1978), France (by 3) and Spain (by 4.8 in five years), and a strong decrease in all the south-eastern countries (population divided by 4.8 in Greece, 9.6 in Croatia, 47 in the Volga Delta). For the whole of Europe, 66% of the breeding population declined by 20–50% between 1970 and 1990, the species now being vulnerable. The situation of the Black-crowned Night Heron is less dramatic but 41% of its European populations declined by 20–50% since 1970. The species increased only in France, was stable or fluctuating in central Europe and in Italy, and decreased in southern countries and in Russia. The common characteristic of all these species is their strictly migrating behaviour, with wintering in Africa. The relationship between amount of rain in Senegal, reflecting good feeding conditions in conjunction with the optimal water level in marshes, and the annual survival rates or the number of breeding pairs in Europe the following year, have only been demonstrated for the Purple Heron in the Netherlands (den Held 1981, Cavé 1983). However, a similar effect seems to be general in other migrant heron species, particularly for the Little Bittern, constrained to cross the Sahara or winter in eastern Africa, areas that have been seriously affected by drought since the 1970s. For instance, practically all the large reed beds of one of the more important African wintering wetlands, the inland Niger Delta, have disappeared since the 1970s, and its capacity for waterfowl only represents 50% of that in 1984 (Yeatman-Berthelot and Jarry 1994). European environmental factors, such as habitat losses or disturbance, seem to play a secondary role in this kind of general dynamic at the continental European scale. However, they may be locally important: the dramatic increase of the level of the Caspian Sea by 170 cm from 1980 to 1991 and its cause, bad weather, are certainly the main factor involving the crash of the populations of the Squacco Heron in the Volga Delta (from 7000 pairs to 0–300).

Population patterns of the Eurasian Bittern do not correspond to the African drought hypothesis. For this species, 79% of the European breeding populations declined by 20–50% since 1970, with a contrasting situation between western, southern and eastern countries (decrease observed in 15 countries), and central and northern countries (stability in eight countries, increase in four). Causes of these trends are not clear. The hard winters (1963, 1979, 1985, 1986) seem to play a major role for populations that overwinter or winter in countries that were affected by extreme cold (Germany, the Netherlands, France), while the more migrant populations of the centre and north reveal a less significant effect. However, the decrease in Russia contradicts this hypothesis. Probably local factors (loss or alteration of reed beds) are important for this species.

Herons are generally well protected in Europe, although this protection is rather recent for most of the species. The Grey Heron is the only species for which hunting still occurs in few Austrian and German Länder, while limited shooting licences at fish farms are provided in some countries. Although these often rather small-scale control measures do not necessarily have an impact on the total population, research has often shown that this does not solve the conflict situation at fish farms (e.g. van Vessem et al. 1985, and Chapter 13). In addition, it should be mentioned that although the Grey Heron is doing fine in most parts of Europe, one should not forget that as recently as the 1960s, the population had dropped to an alarmingly low level in most European countries. Therefore, continued efforts to protect all heron species and an integrated approach for the conservation, management and prudent use of their habitats are essential for the conservation of herons in Europe.

Globally, for all the species, the main factor explaining the trends in numbers and range appears to be the relation with Man (hunting, destruction of colonies or habitats), associated for some species with the climate during wintering in Europe or in Africa. Since the protection of all the species in the 1970s, with simultaneously the strong Sahelian and East African droughts, the second factor seems dominant for the strictly migrant species.

Compared to other regions, European heron populations are well studied. Long-term monitoring has been under way in some countries (Belgium, Denmark, France, Greece, Italy, Portugal, Spain, Sweden and Ukraine) since roughly the 1980s, covering especially tree-nesting colonial species. Other species and countries are less well covered. The reliability of data varies among countries depending on the methods used. The Grey Heron has been monitored in England and Wales from 1928, in France since 1968 and in Belgium since the 1980s. Populations of all colonial herons are well monitored in Spain and Italy, since 1981. On the European scale, however, only the status of the Cattle Egret is well known, while the status of five species (Grey Heron, Purple Heron, Great White Egret, Little Egret and Squacco Heron) is relatively well known. Black-crowned Night Heron, Eurasian Bittern and Little Bittern are fairly well known. On the other hand, ecological studies of factors governing the dynamics of populations using modern demographic techniques are very scarce, but include the Purple Heron in the Netherlands (den Held 1981, Cavé 1983), the Grey Heron in France (Marion and Marion 1975, Marion 1981, 1987a, 1988) and in England (North 1979), and the Little Egret in France (Hafner et al., 1998a, Voisin 1985). Demography, survival, and winter habitat/climate effects for both African migrants and more resident populations appear to be the most important study areas for heron conservation.

2. Herons in the Mediterranean

Heinz Hafner

This chapter discusses heron populations in countries bordering the Mediterranean and the Black Seas (Fig. 1.1, Table 1.1). The region corresponds to the Mediterranean bioclimate zone (Le Houérou 1991), extending to the coastal wetlands of the Black Sea. A distinctive Mediterranean climate differentiates the region ecologically from central and northern Europe to the north and from subtropical and tropical Africa to the south. International collaboration among heron biologists around the Mediterranean has created a uniquely thorough information base on numbers and distribution. For these reasons we separate the Mediterranean region from its companion chapters covering Europe, western Asia and Africa.

The Heron Fauna

The heron fauna of the Mediterranean includes the nine European breeding species (see Table 1.1). In addition, the Western Reef Heron (*Egretta garzetta gularis* of Hancock and Kushlan 1984) and the Green-backed Heron (*Butorides striatus*) nest near the region's limits on the coast of the Red Sea, and the race *Butorides striatus atricapillus* probably nests along the Egyptian Nile (Meininger and Atta 1994).

Generally herons are far more abundant in the European Mediterranean than in the near East and North Africa. In Europe, some countries have large and diverse breeding heron populations (Table 1.1). In North Africa, except for the Cattle Egret, herons breed in small numbers following a patchy distribution. Outside the breeding season, North African wetlands become important stopover and wintering areas for all Palearctic heron species.

Overall the Little Egret, Cattle Egret and Black-crowned Night Heron are the most numerous breeding species. However, although a species may be abundant in one or more countries, its distribution over the entire region may be patchy, and one should be cautious in attributing the status of "common" to any of them.

Heron Conservation
ISBN 0-12-430130-4

Environmental Conditions

The fundamental climatic characteristics of the region were defined by Emberger as "a non-tropical climate with seasonal variation in photoperiod, with the rainfall concentrated in the cold or cooler part of the year; the summer, the hottest season, being dry" (translation from Emberger 1954 in Britton and Crivelli 1993). The physiographic diversity of the region results in a wide range of ecoclimates. Mean average temperatures range with latitude and altitude from 5 to 18°C and annual rainfall from less than 100 to 3000 mm (Le Houérou 1990).

Blondel and Aronson (1995) emphasised that there is a rapid increase in evapotranspiration and decrease in precipitation along a north–south gradient. There is also a marked west to east and south to north decrease in winter temperature. The coldest winter temperatures (generally in January) of the coastal regions of the Mediterranean are in northern Greece where wetlands freeze every winter. Similarly seasonally harsh conditions are encountered in the non-coastal areas of the western half of Turkey with its abundance of lakes, while the few wetlands in the east of the country, situated at high altitudes, remain frozen over for two or three months (December to February) of the year. Prolonged cold spells with freezing conditions are encountered each winter along the Black Sea coast.

Further west, winters are generally mild but very large interannual variations occur of both temperatures and rainfall, and extreme cold spells have been recorded along the north-western Mediterranean shore. In January 1985, virtually all the open waters along the Mediterranean coast of France (including saline lagoons) froze over for two weeks, with minimal temperatures reaching –10.6°C. These conditions killed most of the Little Egrets and Cattle Egrets wintering in the region (Hafner et al. 1992, 1994). During the following summer, breeding populations of the Rhône Delta were reduced by 50% and 80%, respectively.

The Mediterranean region is widely acknowledged to be particularly rich in coastal and inland wetlands of importance to herons. Extensive river deltas, lakes and coastal lagoons have provided livelihoods for people since the early Mediterranean civilisations. However, large-scale drainage developed quickly during the nineteenth century to provide agricultural land or to control malaria, which was then endemic in all the Mediterranean countries. The process of wetland destruction accelerated further in the late nineteenth and especially the twentieth century (Hoffmann et al. 1996), mainly for agriculture but also for industrial and residential development. Dugan (1993) estimated the present extent of wetlands in the Mediterranean Basin as follows: 6000–8500 km^2 of coastal lagoons; 8000–10000 km^2 of natural lakes and marshes, mainly lying in river deltas and the region's remaining floodplains; and over 10000 km^2 of artificial wetlands, mostly reservoirs.

The deltas and coastal lagoons along the northern shore of the Mediterranean in Spain, France, Italy, Greece and Turkey are the most extensive and varied wetlands of the region. Most of the inland lakes to the north are fresh and permanent. The wetlands along the southern shore, where freshwater marshes and lakes are infrequent, are more uniform and mostly composed of brackish and saltwater lagoons. Inland lakes are mostly brackish and temporary. Exceptions are the Nile Delta, Lake Ichkeul in Tunisia and the El-Kala region in north-western Algeria. Unfortunately, two of these three internationally important wetlands for water birds (Jones 1993) are today strongly degraded. The Nile is affected by reduced stream velocity and by heavy industrial and agricultural pollution (Meininger and Atta 1994), and Lake Ichkeul, the largest permanent water body in the Maghreb, by a recent damming scheme (Hollis 1986). The once extremely important freshwater areas in the northern part of Ichkeul have gradually become salty, since the dams retain the former freshwater influx. By 1994 the surrounding marshes had been transformed into arid land. The long-term development of this wetland will depend on future management. In contrast, the El-Kala region remains a beautiful 1000 km^2 mosaic of freshwater lakes, freshwater marshes, wet deciduous woods, brackish water bodies and vegetated dunes (Stevenson et al. 1988).

Changing Status of Herons

Data available

The region has probably the most complete data set on heron populations and trends, although the extent of our knowledge differs among heron species and among countries.

Status of the Little Egret is particularly well known, as are the Cattle Egret, Black-crowned Night Heron, Squacco Heron and, over a restricted range, the Purple Heron. Long-term data in several important breeding areas for these species in Italy, Spain and France allow analysis of fluctuations and trends. Although less precise, good information is also available on the remaining two colonially nesting species, the Great White Egret and the Grey Heron. The two non-colonial species, the Eurasian Bittern and the Little Bittern, are least known. Indeed, their secretive behaviour in inaccessible freshwater habitats makes numbers impossible to evaluate.

Reliable quantitative data collected by heron specialists on national censuses of colonial herons are available for Portugal (Dias 1991), Spain (Fernandez Cruz et al. 1992), the Mediterranean coast of France (pers. obs. 1968–1998) and Croatia 1990–94 (Mikuska pers. comm.). Good but less recent information is available for Greece (all known colonies censused in 1985–86—Crivelli et al. 1988) and for Italy (complete national censuses in 1981 and 1986—Fasola et al. 1981 and pers. comm.). In Italy, long-term monitoring of heron populations carried out since 1981 throughout the north-west, where at least 70% of the Italian populations breed (Fasola pers. comm.), provides recent information. Similar long-term data are available for major breeding areas of Spain, southern France and Ukraine (Schogolev pers. comm.). Heron specialists for parts of Turkey, Israel, Egypt, Tunisia, Algeria, and Morocco have also collected recent quantitative information. Major gaps in our knowledge concern Syria, Lebanon and Jordan in the eastern Mediterranean, where the present status of herons remains relatively unknown. For certain countries, for example Romania, Moldova and Turkey, it is difficult to obtain data.

In general, population figures presented in this chapter have been provided by experienced biologists and are considered reliable. BirdLife International provided estimates from the European Bird Database 1994 (called EBD 1994), which has a verification code indicating accuracy and reliability of data, some countries and species being still poorly known. I also refer to Tucker and Heath (1994), who used EBD 1994 to highlight those species with an unfavourable conservation status in

Europe. EBD 1994 is believed to be the best data currently available for a global estimation of population size per country and population size and range trend over the period 1970–1990 (Tucker and Heath 1994). The same data served for the EBCC Atlas of European Breeding Birds (Hagemeijer and Blair 1997).

Italy has the largest breeding populations of colonial herons of any Mediterranean country; the species accounts below often refer to the long-term data collected there. To facilitate interpretation, Table 2.1 shows the results of the 1981 and 1986 national censuses and presents an index of abundance based on the 1981 census (index = 1).

Species status

Grey Heron. Over the past 20 years, the breeding range of this species has expanded considerably along the northern shore of the Mediterranean, especially in France and Italy. There is no doubt that legal protection of the species throughout Europe has been a major cause of expansion.

Time series of data are not available for the eastern part of the region but, according to recent information (EBD 1994) (Table 1.1), the largest numbers of breeding pairs are found in the countries bordering the north of the Black Sea. In the

Table 2.1   Breeding populations in Italy: data from Fasola (pers. comm.)

2.1.1. National census (numbers = breeding pairs)

Year	GrH	PuH	LE	SqH	BCNH
1981	680	480	6650	270	17 350
1986	1516	350	14 227	721	14 227

2.1.2. Population indices for the rice-field area in NW Italy (1981 = 1)

Year	GrH	PuH	LE	SqH	BCNH
1976	0.77	1.29	0.51		0.45
1977		1.50	0.55	0.53	0.66
1978	0.60	1.21	0.92	0.51	0.68
1981	1.00	1.00	1.00	1.00	1.00
1982		0.86			
1984	1.49				0.61
1985	1.67	0.63	0.91	1.26	0.82
1986	1.99	0.84	1.66	2.64	0.90
1987	2.51	1.03	2.47		0.87
1988	3.05	1.20	1.75	1.80	1.31
1989	3.69	0.89	1.89	2.00	1.38
1990	4.22	0.68	3.09	3.85	1.38
1991	4.91	1.14	2.20	2.89	1.13
1992	6.19	1.25	3.05	4.24	1.21
1993	6.75	1.90	3.38	2.03	1.10
1994	6.13	1.45	3.09	2.30	0.94
1995	7.85	1.54	3.68	2.10	0.77
1996	9.31	1.94	4.16	3.63	0.82
1997	11.28	1.63	3.83	0.92	0.69

western Mediterranean significant numbers are known to breed at present in Spain and in Italy, in Mediterranean France (1200 pairs in 1998 (Hafner, Kayser and Lucchesi, unpublished) and in Croatia (1714 in 1993 (Mikuska pers. comm.)). In Italy, a census in Lombardia and Piemonte revealed 4815 nests in 1993 and the extrapolated total for the country was 5156 (Fasola pers. comm.).

Only occasional, incomplete surveys have been carried out in the other Mediterranean countries. In the numerous Turkish wetlands, many of which are difficult to access, there might be several thousand breeding pairs (EBD 1994) (Table 1.1). The relative abundance of the species in the wetlands along the northern shore of the Mediterranean contrasts with the southern shore, where few breeding records exist despite good and recent coverage of major wetlands in Israel (no breeding since 1964, Ashkenazi pers. comm.), Egypt (isolated pairs only, Goodman and Meininger 1989), Tunisia (5–10 pairs at Lake Ichkeul, Smart and Skinner pers. comm.), Algeria (3 pairs at El Kala wetlands complex in 1990, Chalabi and Hafner unpublished) and Morocco (1–3 pairs near Ouarzazat, Thevenot pers. comm.).

In the Black Sea countries the Grey Heron is undoubtedly a common breeding bird (Table 1.1). More than 1000 pairs breed in the Danube Delta complex (Munteanu pers. comm.) and in Ukraine the largest colonies are found along the river Dnepr, around Lake Sivash and the coastal region of the northern Black Sea (Mikhalevich et al. 1994).

Trends show a general increase. In Mediterranean France, the first three pairs were found nesting in 1964 (Blondel 1965). Ten years later 59 nests were located (Walmsley 1975), and since the mid-1980s the population has fluctuated around 1000 pairs (Kayser et al. 1994b, Hafner, Kayser and Lucchesi, unpublished).

A similar and spectacular increase has been observed more recently throughout northern Italy, where the bulk of the national population breeds (Table 2.1). The Spanish population increased significantly during the same period, from 340 pairs in 1972–73 to 786 pairs in 1986, to reach 1400 to 1600 pairs in 1989 (Fernandez Alcazar and Fernandez Cruz 1991, Fernandez Cruz et al. 1992). Finally, although we do not have figures for the Danube Delta, we know that this more easterly population has slightly declined (10%) from 1974–76 to 1987–89 (Munteanu pers. comm.), while in the Dnestr Delta the number of 100–200 pairs has been stable for at least 15 years (Schogolev pers. comm.).

Migratory movements have been reported mainly along the eastern and western shores of the Mediterranean. In winter, the Grey Heron occurs throughout the region, although quantitative information is scanty and figures are probably underestimates because the birds are widely distributed in winter and not necessarily roosting in large congregations like the other colonial species. A minimum of 5000 birds winter at present in Italy (Fasola pers. comm.) and 3486 were recorded in winter 1992–93 during a coordinated census throughout the Iberian Peninsula (Sarasa et al. 1993).

Purple Heron. This species, one of the most vulnerable herons in the region, nests chiefly in mature *Phragmites* stands that must be inundated throughout the breeding season. As a result of the small number of suitable breeding sites remaining in Mediterranean wetlands, the breeding distribution is presently extremely patchy.

Fewer than 10 000 pairs nest in the countries bordering the Mediterranean. Today, the strongholds in this region are (figures in brackets are for 1994): Spain, about 1200 pairs with the major breeding areas Ebro Delta (475 pairs, Gonzalez-Martin 1994) and the Guadalquivir Delta (146–205 pairs, Garcia pers. comm.); Mediterranean France, 1300 pairs in 1998 (Hafner, Kayser and Lucchesi, unpublished.); Italy, (600 pairs, Fasola pers. comm.); Croatia (95 pairs, Mikuska pers. comm.); and Turkey (Table 1.1) where it breeds in many localities (Grimmet and Jones 1989). An important breeding population of 475–500 pairs was discovered in the Kizilirmak Delta on the Black Sea coast as recently as 1992, the first confirmed breeding in this Turkish wetland (Hustings and van Dijk 1993). For the eastern Mediterranean and northern Black Sea I refer to EBD 1994 (Table 1.1). On the Danube Delta, a population estimate in 1986 revealed 1250 pairs (Kiss, Munteanu and Toniuc in Green 1992). In Ukraine the Dnestr Delta sustains a fluctuating population of 100 to 150 pairs (Schogolev 1992).

Purple Herons are rare in the Near East and in North Africa. The only recent breeding records we are aware of are about 20 pairs in the Huleh reserve in Israel in 1991–93 (Ashkenazi pers comm.) and a minimum of 70 pairs (two colonies) found in 1990 in the extensive freshwater marshes of the El Kala region, north-eastern Algeria (Chalabi and Hafner unpublished). In Morocco, Thevenot et al. (1981, 1982) found three nest sites, with a total population of probably not more than 20 pairs. A few pairs probably still bred in 1989 (Brosset 1990). There are no breeding records in Egypt despite good coverage (Meininger et al. 1986, Goodman and Meininger 1989, Meininger and Atta 1994).

The Purple Heron is declining in most of its important Mediterranean breeding areas, and in fact throughout its range in Europe (Tucker and Heath 1994). In southern France (Fig. 2.1) numbers decreased from 794 pairs in 1991 to 550 pairs in 1994, against a mean number of 1230 pairs for the years 1981–1990; similar high numbers (1200–1300 pairs) were again recorded in 1996, 1997 and 1998 (Hafner, Kayser and Lucchesi, unpublished). The population in northern Italy decreased

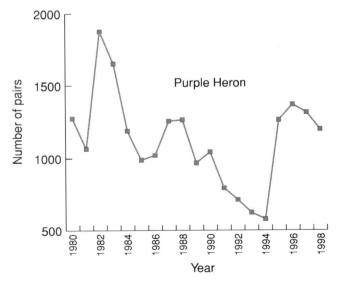

Fig. 2.1 Purple Heron population in Mediterranean France (number of pairs).

Purple Heron. Deterioration of freshwater marshes is an important cause of the decline in Purple Herons in southern Europe. Photo: Jean-François Hellio and Nicolas van Ingen.

from 744 pairs in 1976 to 221 pairs in 1985 (Fasola, pers. comm.), and shows also a clear recovery since (Table 2.1, and Fasola et al. in press). Aerial surveys of the extensive reed beds in the Venetian lagoons and the Po delta revealed 480 pairs in 1993 and 600 pairs in 1994 (Fasola pers. comm.).

In the Guadalquivir Delta in southern Spain the population fluctuates strongly from year to year (minimum 180 pairs, maximum 1500 pairs) (unpubl. data from Estación Biológica de Doñana). The number of pairs is correlated to the amount of rainfall during the previous winter–spring months, probably because the extent of feeding areas in this wetland is highly dependent on rainfall.

In the Ebro Delta, the second important breeding area of Spain, which is dominated by rice fields, dramatic changes have occurred in numbers of breeding Purple Herons. From more than 1000 pairs during the 1960s, the population was down to only 60 pairs in 1973, but has gradually recovered to 475 pairs in 1990 (del Hoyo et al. 1992). A population level of about 500 pairs has been maintained since then (last census in 1994, Gonzalez-Martin, pers. comm., Gonzalez-Martin et al. 1992). Del Hoyo et al. (1992) attribute the decline in the Ebro Delta during the 1960s to pesticides, although reduction of prey availability and habitat modification also played an important role with conversion of some of the most productive freshwater marshes into rice fields (Ruiz pers. comm.).

There are no other long-term data sets. However, for the Danube Delta, Munteanu (pers. comm.) reports a decline of 55% from 1974–76 to 1987–89. The population in the Volga Delta, which is 1500 km east of the Danube, is stable (Gavrilov pers. comm.). In Israel, hundreds of pairs were known to breed in the early 1950s (Paz 1986). By the beginning of the 1970s only about 50 pairs were left and a similar number bred during 1978–81 (Ashkenazi 1983). The decline was probably due to drainage of large areas of freshwater marsh in the Huleh area during the 1950s (Paz 1986).

Only small numbers winter in the Mediterranean Basin (del Hoyo et al. 1992). There are occasional winter observations in south-east Spain and south-west Portugal (Fernandez Cruz and Farinha 1992), in Italy (Fasola pers. comm.) and in southern France (pers. obs.), the Nile Valley and at Lake Nasser (Meininger and Atta 1994), and in Israel (Shy 1990–1996).

The overall decline in Purple Heron numbers and range suggests that the key factor influencing the size of the breeding population may have effect in the species' wintering grounds in tropical West Africa. Survival of adult Purple Herons and population fluctuations in the Netherlands during the 1960s and the 1970s had been shown to be strongly related to hydrological conditions in West Africa (den Held 1981, Cave 1983). However, recent analyses based on long-term series of data on population levels in Italy, Spain, Mediterranean France and Ukraine, and hydrological indicators used by den Held (1981), revealed only limited effects of African climate on population levels (Fasola et al. in press). Although there has been a decline in numbers over the past 20 years throughout the whole range, patterns in the individual areas differ in detail. This suggests that local factors, for example changes in the structure of breeding habitat, affect the breeding populations as well.

Great White Egret. This otherwise cosmopolitan species has presently an extremely patchy nesting distribution in the Mediterranean, and in western Europe as a whole (Hancock and Kushlan 1984). Small relict populations exist in some scattered locales in the eastern Mediterranean, although in other places, such as Italy and the Camargue, the species may be in the process of establishing itself.

The largest populations are found near the Black Sea, in Ukraine in particular (Table 1.1), where populations appear stable (Mikhalevich et al. 1994). The Danube Delta is an important breeding area with an estimated total of 700 pairs in the Romanian part of the delta in 1986 (Kiss et al. in Green 1992). According to Munteanu (pers. comm.), the 1986 figure of 700 pairs represented a decline of 11% since the period 1974–76, and more recently only 150–300 pairs nested throughout Romania (EBD 1994). The Dnestr Delta further to the east supported 250–350 pairs (Schogolev 1992).

Quantitative information for Turkey is sparse (Table 1.1). However, breeding sites are occasionally discovered (Hustings and van Dijk 1994, Guder pers. comm.). There are no breeding records along the southern shore of the Mediterranean.

The species has decreased severely in most of the Balkan countries. In Yugoslavia where 73 nests were counted in 1954 in just one colony, the species was already considered a rare breeding bird by the end of the 1960s (Mikuska 1982). In Greece, only 10–15 pairs were reported for 1970–84 and seven to ten pairs in 1985–86 (Crivelli et al. 1988). Albania had 1–5 nests (EBD 1994).

The population is increasing in Croatia, where seven nests were found in one mixed colony in 1990 (Lukac 1990), seven nests in two colonies in 1993, and 21 nests in 1994 (Mikuska pers. comm.). This recent increase in Croatia is probably related to the healthy, increasing population in Austria which benefits from strict protection measures. Further west it has long been considered an accidental breeder but seems now to be establishing small pioneer populations in Italy and France (Fasola and Volponi pers. comm., Kayser et al. 1994a).

There are no breeding records in Israel and North Africa in spite of good coverage of all the major wetlands.

Birds winter mainly south of the Mediterranean region. However, northern Greece and Turkey have important wintering areas, with up to 1875 birds in January 1987 and 921 birds in January 1990 in Greece (Nazirides et al. 1992) and 1405 birds in Turkey in January 1996 (DHKD (Turkish Wildlife Society) 1996, pers. comm.). 215 birds were recorded in Croatia in January 1993 (Munteanu and Ranner in Hagemeijer and Blair 1997) and a survey of Albanian wetlands in January 1995 (Kayser and Bino pers. comm.) found 170 Great White Egrets.

Numbers of birds overwintering have increased in southern France since the 1960s and in Italy since 1988 to reach several hundred (Assini pers. comm., Hafner 1975, Kayser et al. 1992, 1994a). Since 1991 small numbers also winter regularly on the island of Corsica (Bonaccorsi and Faggio 1997). In winter 1991–92, two birds were also recorded in northern Spain and one in Portugal (Fernandez Cruz and Farinha 1992). These increases could be related to the increasing nesting population at Lake Neusiedl in Austria (Grüll 1988).

For the birds breeding in the Black Sea countries, Israel and Egypt are important during migration and in winter (Ashkenazi pers. comm., Meininger and Atta 1994). In Tunisia the species is a regular winter visitor in small numbers, particularly in the south of the country (Smart pers. comm.).

Little Egret. This is a common species throughout the Mediterranean and is increasing, particularly in the north-western part of the region. About 40% of the Italian population are found in the Po River valley in northern Italy where the egrets exploit about 1600 km^2 of rice fields, the most dense region of rice cultivation in Europe (Fasola 1986, pers. comm.). Populations in Spain and southern France have been increasing, but vary from one year to the next.

The present population in all the countries bordering the Mediterranean Sea is estimated at a minimum of 35 000 pairs, with over 20 000 pairs in Italy (Fasola pers. comm.), 7600 pairs in Spain in 1990 (Fernandez Cruz et al. 1992), 3000 to 5000 pairs in Portugal in 1989 (Dias in Fernandez Cruz et al. 1992), and 6000 pairs in Mediterranean France in 1996 (Hafner and Kayser, unpublished).

In the wetlands of the eastern Mediterranean and the Black Sea, the species is a common breeder though less abundant than in Italy, France, and the Iberian Peninsula. Recent (1993–94) and thorough surveys in Croatia revealed 190 pairs (Mikuska, pers. comm.). A complete survey of Albanian wetlands in 1997 revealed only one small colony of 26 pairs but several hundreds are breeding in the neighbouring Montenegro (Bino, pers. comm.). For the other European countries see Table 1.1. Turkey hosts several thousand pairs each year (Fasola and Hafner in Hagemeijer and Blair 1997) and in the northern Black Sea, the largest Little Egret colonies are in the Danube Delta, along the Dnepr River, and on the Lebyazhyi Islands off the Crimean coast (Mikhalevich et al. 1994).

The most important breeding population in the southern part of the region is in Israel: minimum 1000–2000 pairs distributed in 5–10 colonies (Ashkenazi pers. comm, Shy pers. comm., Shy 1995).

Along the North African coast one finds only a few small, scattered breeding populations. According to Meininger et al. (1986) and Meininger and Atta (1994), the only Little Egret colonies known in Egypt are one in Wadi Rayan (six nests in 1984) and one of several hundred pairs near Aswan, south of our region. In 1992 five nests were found in the Nile Delta and breeding was strongly suspected at another site nearby (Baha El Din 1993). A survey of wetlands along the coast of Libya (Meininger et al. 1994) located only a few birds but no nesting. Tunisia has several small colonies: one on the Kneiss Island off the coast between Gabes and Sfax (Meininger et al. 1994) and three to four small colonies on the mainland, unless drought conditions prevent the birds from nesting, plus one colony at Lake Tunis (Kayser pers. comm.). In north-eastern Algeria, 40 pairs were counted in 1990 near El Kala (Chalabi and Hafner unpubl. data) and the same number was recorded again in 1995 (Belhadj 1996). In Morocco, thorough surveys during the 1980s revealed a fluctuating breeding population of between 200 and 750 pairs in 19 to 31 colony sites (Thevenot, pers. comm.).

An increasing trend is apparent in the western Mediterranean over the past 15 years, especially in Mediterranean France (Fig. 2.2) and Italy (Table 2.1).

In Spain periodic declines occur, sometimes by as much as half, from one year to the next. In southern Spain, with its important breeding areas, this fluctuation is correlated with drought conditions. In contrast, in the Camargue, which is heavily managed for hunting, water levels of many freshwater marshes are maintained throughout the summer, providing a stable aquatic environment that sustains abundant populations of fish and amphibians. The size of the breeding population in the Camargue is affected by winter climate on or near the breeding area (Hafner et al. 1994) and by the amount of winter–spring rainfall in southern Spain (Hafner

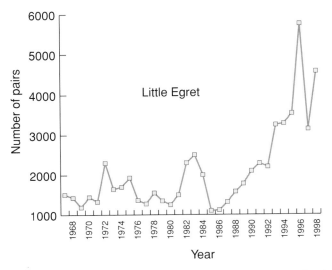

Fig. 2.2   Little Egret population in Mediterranean France (number of pairs).

unpubl. data). Fasola's abundance indices (Table 2.1) suggest that the cold winter of 1984–85 affected the Italian population in a similar way as that of the Camargue.

There is little recent information on trends in the more easterly populations, most of which, in contrast to the western Mediterranean, have decreased between 1970 and 1990 (Fasola and Hafner in Hagemeijer and Blair 1997). In the Danube Delta, a decline of 35% occurred from 1974–76 to 1987–89 (Munteanu pers. comm., from data supplied by the Research Institute of the Danube Delta in Tulcea).

During winter, Little Egrets stay in the south of Europe and Africa. The majority of birds from the Camargue remain in wetland areas along the Mediterranean coast of France and Spain (Pineau 1992), where they have increased since 1985. The first complete census of Little Egrets wintering in the Iberian Peninsula was carried out in 1992 and 1993 (Fernandez Cruz and Farinha 1992, Sarasa et al. 1993), locating about 10 000 birds and confirming the international importance of Spanish wetlands for the West Mediterranean population. During mild winters several thousand birds winter also in Italy (Fasola, pers. comm.). Migrating birds belonging to these populations of the western Mediterranean winter in Tunisia, Algeria, Morocco, Mauritania and tropical West Africa (Voisin 1991 and unpubl. sightings of birds marked in the Camargue).

In the north-eastern Mediterranean and the Black Sea region, conditions are generally harsh in winter and most birds leave for the African continent (Voisin 1991). January counts from 1988–1995 in Israel totalled 1258–2118 birds (Shy 1990–1996). Large flocks are seen wintering in Egypt (2727 counted in winter 1989–90 in the Nile Delta and Nile Valley, Meininger and Atta 1994), and in Tunisia where over 1000 were counted in February 1984 in the Gulf of Gabes (van Dijk pers. comm.).

Cattle Egret. The distribution and numbers of breeding Cattle Egrets in the eastern half of the region and in the North African countries have only slightly changed since Hancock and Kushlan (1984). It expanded its range into Italy, where several hundred breeding pairs are now established on the island of Sardinia (Grussu 1997) as well as a smaller population on the mainland (Fasola pers. comm.). The species was found nesting for the first time in 1991 in Greece, with one pair found in the Axios Delta (Goutner et al. 1991). In Romania breeding (two pairs) was recorded for the first time in 1997 in the Danube Delta (Munteanu 1998). It has expanded in Israel, with new colonies in the semi-desert area, and has regained lost ground in the Nile Delta where several new colonies were located in 1990 in the Faiyum area (Meininger and Atta 1994). It has also expanded in Algeria from coastal wetlands to Kabylie in the centre of the country, where a new colony of 400 pairs was found in 1994 (Moali pers. comm.). The range extension during the 1980s in Morocco occurred as far south as Ouarzazat (Thevenot et al. 1982 and pers. comm.) and discovery of a new colony confirmed a further extension at Tiznit in 1994 (Rousseau pers. comm.).

About 80 000 to 90 000 pairs breed in Spain and Portugal (Fernandez Cruz et al. 1992). In Mediterranean France the population reached more than 4000 pairs in 1998 (Hafner and Kayser unpubl. data; Fig. 2.3). Italy has up to 50 pairs on the mainland (Fasola pers. comm.) and more than 400 pairs were recorded in Sardinia in 1996 (Grussu 1997). A thorough survey of the breeding population in Morocco during the 1980s revealed 15 000 to 20 000 pairs in more than 60 colonies (Thevenot unpubl. data).

Population trends are upwards throughout the area. A significant increase occurred in the Huleh Reserve, Israel, from about 700 pairs in 1980 to 1700 pairs in 1993 (Ashkenazi pers. comm.). In many towns and villages all over the northern and central parts of Israel, large and growing Cattle Egret colonies and roosts represent an increasing nuisance to the inhabitants (Eyal Shy, pers. comm.). The species is increasing in recent years in the Nile Delta, after a severe decline during the 1970s and early 1980s (Baha El Din 1993). The well-known colony at Giza Zoo increased from 1604 pairs in 1987 to 7269 pairs in 1990 (Pineau 1992). The Iberian population increased from about 24 000 pairs in 1986 (Fernandez Cruz and Camacho, in Hafner et al. 1987) to 80–90 000 pairs at present, linked to irrigation of agricultural land in the floodplains of the Tajo and the Guadiana Rivers. Perhaps the most spectacular recent increase has taken place in Mediterranean France (Fig. 2.3), and on the island of Sardinia (Italy), where numbers climbed from 65 pairs in 1992 (Grussu 1994) to more than 400 in 1996 (Grussu 1997).

In winter, Cattle Egrets occur in both Europe and Africa. Portuguese and Spanish Cattle Egrets are partially migrant, wintering mainly in the southern part of the peninsula and, to a lesser extent, in North Africa (del Hoyo et al. 1992). Data are scanty for North Africa. Populations are probably mostly sedentary, making erratic movements when food supplies are depleted (Voisin 1991). Camargue Cattle Egrets winter mainly on or near the breeding area, and winter climate was found to be the main factor regulating the population (Hafner et al. 1992). After the extreme cold spell in January 1985, the subsequent nesting effort fell to only 74 nests (Fig. 2.3), recovering in subsequent years. Movements to the Camargue from the Iberian reservoir of birds and their offspring play an important role in population persistence there (Hafner et al. 1992).

The census of wintering herons throughout the Iberian Peninsula in winters of 1991–92 and 1992–93 found 253 and 242 roosts totalling 150–160 000 individuals (Fernandez Cruz and Farinha 1992, Sarasa et al. 1993).

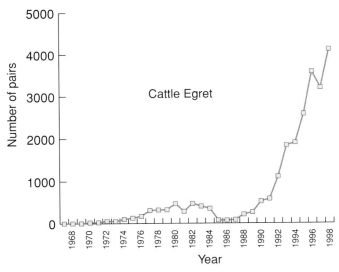

Fig. 2.3   Cattle Egret population in Mediterranean France (number of pairs).

Squacco Heron. This species, highly dependent on freshwater habitats, nests in widely scattered locales in the Mediterranean region where suitable habitat is available, and populations fluctuate from year to year. As a result it is vulnerable in the region.

The largest populations are in eastern Europe. In Romania, Kiss et al. (in Green 1992) estimated that 2150 pairs bred in the Danube Delta in 1986. In western Europe, the largest populations are in Italy, with more than a thousand nests in 1992 (Fasola pers. comm.) and in Spain with 822 nests estimated in 1990 (Fernandez Cruz et al. 1992). In the Camargue, at present the only regular breeding area in France, a record of 142 nests were found in 1992. The species is rare in Portugal (Dias 1991), probably because of the scarcity of freshwater areas in this country (Farinha and Leitão 1996). Elsewhere in the northern Mediterranean recent surveys of all the known heron colonies in Croatia reported 183 pairs in 1993 and 172 pairs in 1994 (Mikuska pers. comm.). It is still relatively abundant in Greece and Bulgaria (Table 1.1). For Albania, EBD 94 give 200–400 pairs. However, a thorough survey of Albanian wetlands during the breeding season 1996 revealed few individuals only and no formal proof of breeding. Estimates of populations in Turkey and the Black Sea countries are given in Table 1.1.

Squacco Heron. The Squacco Heron, the rarest heron in the region, is highly dependent on freshwater habitats. Photo: Jacques Delpech.

The species is rare along the southern shore of the Mediterranean and its clumped distribution follows the few suitable freshwater areas. Meininger et al. (1986) emphasised that there was no proof of breeding in the Nile Delta and that the only area in Egypt where small numbers (maximum 40 nests in 1981) are known to breed regularly is in the southern part of the country near Aswan. However, in July 1992 hundreds of Squacco Herons including recently fledged young were noted at Lake Manzala, and breeding in a nearby reed bed was strongly suspected (Baha El Din 1993). About 100 nests containing chicks were found later near Bilbeis further north, the first confirmed breeding of this species in the Nile Delta (Baha El Din 1993). Israel has probably up to 100 pairs in 6 colonies (Ashkenazi and Eyal Shy, pers. comm.). In Tunisia (Kayser pers. comm.) and Algeria, the species breeds in wet years in small numbers. In 1990, 16 pairs were recorded breeding at Lake Tonga in Algeria and several other pairs were probably breeding at Bou Redim and in the Mekhada marshes (Chalabi and Hafner unpubl. data). In Morocco, according to Thevenot (unpubl. data), surveys carried out during the 1980s revealed a population fluctuating between 15 and 85 pairs.

Trends are variable, and confused by strong interannual fluctuations. Up to two-thirds of the European population occurs in countries which recorded declines over the past 20 years (Tucker and Heath 1994). Nonetheless, the species has recently increased in Italy, southern France, and Spain (Tucker and Heath 1994, Hafner unpubl. data); the situation is reversed in the eastern region (Tucker and Heath 1994). The decline in Greece is well demonstrated by Crivelli et al. (1988) who reported a national total of 1400 pairs before 1970, 1100 pairs during the period 1970–1984, and only 201–377 pairs in 1985–86. Another decline occurred at Kopacki Rit, a breeding site in Croatia. Numbers declined from 478 pairs in 1954 to 190 pairs in 1970 and by the mid-1980s they were down to less than 50 pairs (Mikuska pers. comm.). In Morocco, the population decreased during the 1980s and breeding has not been confirmed since the early 1990s (Thevenot pers. comm.).

The majority of Squacco Herons nesting in the Palearctic are long-distance migrants and most winter south of the Sahara (Voisin 1991). Small numbers have long been known to overwinter in North Africa, from Morocco to Egypt (Cramp and Simmons 1977) but winter occurrence is now regular and has recently increased in Morocco where 56 individuals were reported in January 1992 (El Agbani and Dakki 1992). Similarly, an unusually high number of 632 was reported wintering in 1989–90 in the Nile Delta and Valley (Meininger and Atta 1994). A few were also observed in Israel (Shy 1990–1996), Italy (Fasola, in Hafner et al. 1987), in Spain (Fernandez Cruz and Farinha 1992) and 1–2 individuals spent the winter 1993–94 in the Camargue in southern France (Kayser 1994).

Black-crowned Night Heron. This nearly cosmopolitan species has a patchy distribution in suitable habitat in Europe, especially in the western Mediterranean (Hancock and Kushlan 1984). In the southern part of the region, the breeding distribution is even more discontinuous and limited to a few freshwater areas. This type of distribution can put populations at risk locally, despite overall high population levels.

The total population in the countries bordering the Mediterranean Sea is estimated at 25 000–30 000 pairs. In addition, minimum 20 000 pairs nest in the countries to the north of the Black Sea (Table 1.1). The largest breeding population is

Black-crowned Night Heron. When nesting, Black-crowned Night Herons are markedly arboreal, breeding near extensive freshwater areas. Photo: Karl Weber and Heinz Hafner.

in Italy (Table 2.1). Fewer than 1000 pairs nest in the numerous wetlands along the Mediterranean coast of France, about 2200 pairs in Spain and 100 to 200 in Portugal (Fernandez Cruz et al. 1992).

To the south, Israel is the only country, to our knowledge, with important breeding areas, with an estimated population of 2000 pairs in 1980 (Paz 1987), 50% in the Huleh Reserve (Ashkenazi pers. comm.). In 1993 Ashkenazi (pers. comm.) estimated that 1000 pairs bred at the Huleh Reserve, and in at least four other colonies around the Sea of Galilee each with hundreds of breeding Night Herons (Eyal Shy, pers. comm.). The species is rare in North Africa (Baha El Din 1993, Goodman and Meininger 1989, Thomson and Jacobsen 1979). Algeria has a small breeding population; 30–50 pairs were found near El Kala in 1990 (Chalabi and Hafner unpubl. data). In Morocco, the surveys by Thevenot (unpubl. data) during the 1980s recorded a fluctuating population with minimum 500 and maximum 1500 pairs.

The trend is variable across its Mediterranean range. An eighteen-year inventory in northern Italy (Table 2.1) shows that the most important Palearctic breeding population is relatively stable. Night Herons have declined in the Camargue but show an increasing trend in other French breeding areas. The Spanish population is considered vulnerable, having undergone a major decrease over the past 20 years. The considerable fluctuations that occur from time to time (Fernandez Alcazar and Fernandez Cruz 1991) may well be related to hydrological conditions that, in the important breeding areas in the south, may cause either very dry or wet seasons.

Other declines are reported for Croatia, with only about 500 pairs counted throughout the country in 1993 and 1994 (Mikuska pers. comm.), compared to 800 pairs in just one colony in 1972 (Mikuska 1982). The population of the Danube Delta, which numbered 3100 pairs in 1986 (Kiss, Munteanu and Toniuc in Green 1992), has undergone a substantial decline of 47% between 1974–75 and 1987–89 (Munteanu pers. comm.). Finally, long-term data collected in the Dnestr Delta (Schogolev pers. comm.) indicates a fluctuating population of 1000–2500 pairs.

In winter, most of the Black-crowned Night Herons breeding in the Palearctic cross the Mediterranean and the Sahara, migrating to tropical Africa. A small part of the population remains in the Mediterranean Basin, for instance up to 100 at Porto Lago in Northern Greece (pers. obs.), 100 to 150 in Italy (Fasola pers. comm.), and generally small numbers in several wetlands in southern France (pers. obs.) and Spain (Fernandez Cruz and Farinha 1992). But in January–February 1993, an all time high of 1390 were counted in four roosts in the Guadalquivir catchment area (Sarasa et al. 1993). Large numbers winter also in Israel where mid-winter waterfowl census 1988–1995 recorded 725 (1988) to 1902 (1992) birds (Shy 1990–1996). The species also winters in increasing numbers in Morocco: up to 350 in January 1992 (Thevenot, unpubl. data). In Egypt, Meininger and Atta (1994) noted only small numbers. A winter breeding record was noted in Andalusia by Mackrill (1987) who found several nests containing eggs at the end of January.

Little Bittern. The breeding distribution of Little Bitterns is restricted to freshwater habitat, but these birds use a wide variety of such habitats including marsh, densely vegetated borders of ditches, canals and rice fields, or margins of wet deciduous woods. In the western Mediterranean, the species adapts well to man-made habitats and is therefore locally abundant.

Quantitative data are sparse. In the eastern part of the region, the distribution seems rather patchy. In Turkey, Kasparek (1985) found that, although the species was widely distributed throughout the country, certain wetlands had particularly high densities, such as at least 300 pairs in the Sultan marshes in Anatolia. In 1992, a recent survey throughout the Kizilirmak Delta complex revealed only 15–30 pairs (Hustings and van Dijk 1994). The populations of two Spanish wetlands, the Albufera de Valencia that is largely dominated by rice fields, and a reservoir in the Comunidad Valenciana, were estimated at 200 pairs and 50–100 pairs, respectively (Martinez-Abrain 1991). The floodplain of the Po River in northern Italy, with 1600 km^2 of rice cultivation, is another favourable breeding area. The species is little known in the Rhône Delta in southern France, which offers apparently suitable habitat. In 1994 surveys over a large sample of Camargue marshes located 32 pairs likely to have bred (Kayser pers. comm.). To the south the Nile Delta is an extremely important nesting area, with probably well over 1000 breeding pairs (Meininger et al. 1986). Breeding in Egypt is restricted to the Nile Delta and northern Valley (Goodman and Meininger 1989). The marshes near El Kala in Algeria are another important breeding area with an estimated 100 nests (Belhadj 1996). The species is a rare breeder in Israel (Eyal Shy, pers. comm.) and in Morocco, where breeding by one pair was confirmed in spring 1991 near Rabat (Pouteau et al. 1992).

Trend data are few. In Israel, Little Bitterns were formerly abundant (1960) but their numbers declined and at present five to ten pairs are generally located in the

Rice fields. In the absence of natural feeding habitats, rice fields may offer good alternative feeding areas. Photo: Tour du Valat.

Huleh Reserve and adjacent fish ponds (Ashkenazi pers. comm.). Declines from 1970–90 are thought to have occurred in Spain, France, Italy, Croatia, Albania, Greece, Turkey and especially in Romania (Marion in Tucker and Heath 1994).

Spectacular autumn migration has been observed in Israel, with 2700 Little Bitterns seen in a single day (Paz 1987) and in Egypt along the north coast of Sinai with over 4000 from 15 August to 10 October (Goodman and Meininger 1989). Little Bitterns winter in the Nile Delta, with the local population augmented in autumn by migrants (Goodman and Meininger 1989).

Eurasian Bittern. This Bittern ranges through most of southern Europe (Hancock and Kushlan 1984) where it is confined to freshwater wetlands with extensive *Phragmites* reed beds. Although quantitative data are sparse and difficult to obtain, it is clear that the Bittern is a vulnerable species throughout the region.

Bitterns are locally abundant in the countries bordering the Black Sea. In the Kizilirmak Delta in northern Turkey and neighbouring wetlands, Hustings and van Dijk (1994) estimated the 1992 breeding population at 200–250 pairs. Another population figure is available for the Sivash region in Ukraine where van der Hare et al. (1994) described the Eurasian Bittern as "common" with an estimated 100–250 pairs. Bitterns seem to be rare in the Dnestr Delta (3–6 pairs, Schogolev 1992) but well represented in the Danube Delta (Munteanu pers. comm.) where the most extensive habitat is the large area of freshwater marsh, particularly reed beds.

Known populations in western Europe range from the tens to the few hundreds (Table 1.1, EBD 1994). The species is rare in North Africa, but a few pairs are still breeding in Algeria (Belhadj 1996, Chalabi and Hafner unpublished). The best potential breeding area is undoubtedly the El Kala region, which has minimum five pairs (Belhadj 1996). However, because densely vegetated freshwater areas are rare along the southern rim of the Mediterranean, breeding can only occur in a few small pockets of favourable habitat. In Morocco, one to two booming males were noted in spring in the lower Loukkos marshes in 1976, 1984, 1992 and 1993 (Thevenot unpubl. data). There is no proof of breeding either in the Nile Delta, where the Bittern is a rare winter visitor, or in Israel, where this bird is a common passage migrant (Paz 1987).

The long-term decreasing trend in Europe is well known (Hancock and Kushlan 1984). Data considered by Tyler (in Tucker and Heath 1994) suggest decreasing trends for the period 1970–90 in Spain, France, Italy, Croatia, Albania, Turkey, Bulgaria and Romania, and attribute the recent decline in western Europe to a reduction in availability and quality of large *Phragmites*-dominated marshes.

Overall status

While no Mediterranean heron species is globally threatened, several are declining locally. Long-term decreases in the Eurasian Bittern and Purple Heron require management action to protect their reed bed habitat. Several species are increasing in some areas, such as Great White Egrets, Little Egrets, and Grey Herons. Other species are able to take advantage of human developments, and these are increasing, notably the Cattle Egret and Little Egret. The largest and most diverse breeding populations of herons are along the northern shore of the Mediterranean. Conversely, both population size and species diversity are generally low along the southern shore where, in addition, the distribution of breeding sites is patchy. Populations in the eastern portion of the region remain less well known.

Critical Conservation and Regional Management Issues

North and East Mediterranean and Black Sea

Despite protective laws throughout Europe (Chapter 1 and Voisin 1991) many of the breeding colonies in Portugal, Spain, southern France and eastern Europe are vulnerable to disturbance and habitat destruction. This is even the case in parks, such as the Camargue Regional Nature Park in southern France where all breeding sites are located on private property. They may be exposed to grazing, logging, reed-cutting, burning, or management for hunting purposes such as clearing of marsh vegetation, drainage, or artificial flooding at inappropriate periods. During the 1960s and 1970s, those marshes with large areas of reed beds were the most important breeding sites for the Purple Heron in southern France. Purple Heron population declines in the area are directly attributable to loss and alteration of reed (Moser 1984, Kayser et al. 1994b).

Reed beds and woodlands offering the required structure for successful nesting are vulnerable throughout the region. Even in the Danube Delta, the largest unit of reeds in Europe, there is concern about reed bed degradation (Pons 1992). Huge quantities of reed were harvested there in the past (figures from Pons 1992): 226 000 tons in 1965, the peak year of exploitation, 55 000 tons in 1975 and about 33 000 tons at present. In recent years, a lack of regeneration has become apparent in the extensive polders designed for reed harvest (Pons 1992).

Other negative changes occurred in the Danube Delta. Since 1983, the Romanian part of the delta and adjacent lagoons have lost 23% of natural habitat through land reclamation, pollution affects the remaining natural ecosystems, and declines in fish and bird populations have been observed (Munteanu and Toniuc 1992). In the Dnestr Delta, another important breeding area for herons, the construction in 1983 of a hydroelectric dam 700 km upstream threatens the natural functioning of the delta (Schogolev 1992). Technological developments during the present century have caused severe loss and degradation of coastal wetlands throughout most of the Black Sea region (Wilson and Moser 1994).

Huge areas of wetland habitat have also been reclaimed in Mediterranean countries. Albania has lost about 55 000 ha of coastal wetlands over the past 40 years (Gjiknuri and Peja 1992), Greece about two thirds of the country's wetlands since 1922 (Dugan 1993), Spain more than 60% between 1948 and 1990 (Casado et al. 1992) and Italy 66% between 1938 and 1984 (Istat 1984, in Angle 1992). There is no doubt that the most critical issue over the past decades has been the loss and degradation of wetland habitat for economic reasons.

However, over the past 20 years there has been growing concern for wetlands and increased conservation investment throughout the region. A recent example is the Grado declaration on Mediterranean wetlands and the subsequent creation of a Mediterranean Wetlands Forum (MedWet) (Finlayson et al. 1992). In the western Mediterranean, the Italian heron colonies are a fine example of recent conservation action (Fasola and Alieri 1992). The severe decline in the number of heron colonies during the 1970s and 1980s triggered this long-term conservation programme. At present a total of 22 heron colonies in Italy are located within nature reserves. Destruction of potential breeding habitat, such as woodland and reed beds, for land reclamation was the major cause of decline and today the nesting birds occupy scattered residual patches of wet, deciduous woods in an area of extensive rice cultivation (Fasola and Alieri 1992). Without protective measures, many of these remaining breeding sites would have been lost. The breeding populations of herons (as well as colony size) increased after 1985 (Table 2.1). Unfortunately, creation of reserves for herons is the exception rather than the rule.

Herons have, however, benefited from wetland protection for other species. A comparison of the most important Mediterranean wetlands for grebes, ducks and waders (Charadrii) with those of importance for herons in summer, during migration and in winter, revealed strong agreement between these (Hafner et al. 1987).

Increasing awareness and conservation action is notable in Black Sea countries. Examples are the recent creation of a Biosphere reserve and World Heritage site in the Romanian Danube Delta (Munteanu and Toniuc 1992), IWRB's Black Sea Basin Wetlands Workshop, held in Odessa (Ukraine) in October 1993, and the resulting review and preliminary action plan for the conservation of Black Sea wetlands (Wilson and Moser 1994).

Various anthropogenic factors, not directly involved in habitat loss or modification, may affect heron populations. In Greece, Italy, southern France and Spain mass tourism along the coast causes disturbance in potential nesting areas and may prevent establishment of colonies. It is expected that by the year 2000 about 150 million tourists will be crowding the coastlines of the Mediterranean (Hinrichsen 1994). The situation is aggravated by rapid urbanisation and the northern rim in particular has already suffered much irreversible damage in the last few decades. Persecution by fishermen represents a danger in certain breeding areas in the Black Sea region (Schogolev pers. comm., Munteanu pers. comm.) and in the northern Mediterranean Grey Herons are increasingly accused of causing damage in commercial fish ponds which may finally lead to licences for shooting (see Chapter 13).

In some areas herons are shot during their migration. The island of Malta is particularly well known for slaughter of herons including hundreds of Purple Herons and Squacco Herons each year (Voisin 1991).

Near East and North Africa

In Israel the drainage of large areas of freshwater marsh during the 1950s was probably the major cause of the dramatic decline of breeding Purple Herons and Little Bitterns and the abandonment of breeding by Grey Herons (Paz 1986). According to Ashkenazi (pers. comm.) agricultural development that followed immediately after drainage affected herons in the following way. First, commercial fish ponds replaced the former natural feeding areas. This raised a conflict between man and herons that resulted in shooting activity. Second, crop fields in the Huleh Valley attracted large populations of the social vole *Microtus socialis*, which induced massive use of organochlorine pesticides. This caused direct mortality of Purple Herons, which were known to consume rodents during this period. The Huleh Reserve, a 300 ha wetland and some 1000 ha of freshwater fish ponds nearby sustain the largest mixed heron colony in the country. Like other countries in the southern Mediterranean, Israel faces water shortage problems and this is likely to adversely affect heron populations in the future (Ashkenazi pers. comm.).

Likewise in North Africa, fresh water has become an overstretched resource, primarily through diversion and alteration schemes for irrigation (Hollis 1986, 1992, Meininger and Atta 1994) and increasing demand by people. In these arid countries, fast growing human populations severely increase the pressure on fresh water. In Algeria a 31% population rise is expected to take place from 1990 to 2000 (Hollis 1992). The present expansion of the Egyptian population is estimated at 1 million people every nine months and projected to total 81 million by 2010 and 97 million by 2050 (Anon. 1994b). Compared to standards in the northern Mediterranean, water shortage, expressed as m^3 per person per year (Anon. 1994b) was already dramatic in 1990 in Morocco (1000 m^3), Algeria (690 m^3), and Tunisia (540 m^3).

According to these considerations, the future of North Africa's remaining freshwater wetlands is uncertain and so are the heron populations depending on them. The species diversity could become much reduced in the long term. It would be restricted to the Little Egret and the Cattle Egret, according to the most pessimistic prognosis.

Feeding habitat in the Mediterranean

The fact that the northern Italian rice fields are an extremely favourable foraging area (Fasola and Ghidini 1983) undoubtedly contributed to the increase in herons of northern Italy. At present, these internationally important populations of Black-crowned Night Herons and Little Egrets are concentrated in a 5000 km² region of north-west Italy with few remaining natural feeding habitats, but where some 1600 km² of rice fields offer rich, alternative feeding areas (Fasola 1983, Fasola and Alieri 1992).

The situation is similar in several important breeding areas around the Mediterranean. In Spain, nesting Purple Herons, Little Egrets, Night Herons, Squacco Herons and Little Bitterns are concentrated in areas of intensive rice cultivation (Ebro Delta, Albufera de Valencia and a mixed heron colony near Seville). In the Axios Delta in Greece rice fields support another large mixed heron colony and in southern Turkey (Goksu and Cukurova Deltas), herons also exploit rice fields. In Egypt, rice fields in the Nile Delta were found to be important feeding areas for the recently discovered breeding population of Squacco herons there (Baha El Din 1993). In the Camargue, rice fields were important feeding areas until the mid-1980s (Hafner et al. 1982, 1986) but are exploited to a much lesser extent at present (see below).

In Spain, but not in Italy and France, cultivation methods maintain large areas of rice fields flooded throughout the winter, providing excellent feeding habitat for herons. According to sightings of marked Camargue Little Egrets and count data, two important areas of rice cultivation, the Valencia region and the Ebro Delta, are major wintering sites for Camargue and Spanish Egrets and other heron species. During the winter 1991–92, the Valencia region held 22% (2150 individuals) and the Ebro 24% (2350) of the total number of Little Egrets counted throughout the Iberian Peninsula (Fernandez Cruz and Farinha 1992).

These examples provide clear evidence of the importance of rice fields as a wetland habitat for herons. Any modification in the management of these fields could have detrimental effects on heron populations. However, in regions where most of the natural feeding areas have been reclaimed (northern Italy and the Ebro Delta in Spain) the future condition of the breeding populations will depend on future agricultural policy. This is a major threat. Rice fields are indeed susceptible to changes in agricultural practices. Thus, in the Camargue a considerable decline in the use of rice fields by breeding herons since the mid-1980s may be due to increased pesticide use (Hafner et al. 1986b). In addition, irrigation practices in the Rhône Delta have changed in recent years in order to reduce the cost of irrigation. As a result, with less inflow and outflow of water, oxygenation of the fields is reduced and this no doubt affects prey populations. Similar changes, if they were to take place in Italy and Spain, could have a dramatic impact on heron populations. The importance of rice fields to herons in the Mediterranean region is such that they should be considered an important wetland habitat and consequently deserve environmentally sensitive management.

Requirements for feeding by nesting herons

A special effort has been made by the Heron Specialist Group to learn feeding habitat requirements (size, type) to sustain heron breeding populations of a given size in the Mediterranean (Hafner and Fasola 1992). Perhaps the most important result for conservation and management purposes was that the area (size) and quality of freshwater habitats appeared to be the most important factors limiting the size and diversity of breeding heron populations and that there is a threshold of 800 ha within 5 km of a colony site below which only a very small number of herons breed in this region. Thus very large feeding areas are needed to sustain heron colonies, and certain species (Purple Heron, Black-crowned Night Heron and Squacco Heron) prefer freshwater prey, whether these come from natural marshes or, as in the case of rice fields, from an artificial wetland habitat. Existing heron colonies are the best possible indicators of food availability and both the nest site and the adjacent feeding areas deserve absolute conservation priority.

Conclusions

Since the beginning of this century, but especially during the second half, wetlands have been transformed at an increasing rate, resulting in large-scale destruction of heron habitat in all Mediterranean countries. Many of the wetlands which survive have been seriously degraded by human activities, and major threats are still posed by development programmes in and around wetlands, for both urban and industrial expansion and tourism.

Despite this unfavourable development, large proportions of the herons in the Palearctic continue to breed in the Mediterranean region. Successful breeding by large and diverse heron populations indicates substantial populations of their prey, essentially fish, amphibians and aquatic invertebrates. Outside the breeding season, Mediterranean wetland ecosystems offer important stopover sites for migrating herons and support large numbers of birds in winter. These wetlands are still of outstanding value for the fauna and flora; they all merit conservation action. In certain remote freshwater areas, such as Turkey and north-east Algeria, unexpected, large and diverse breeding assemblages of herons can still be discovered today. There are still important gaps in our knowledge and further investigation through coordinated international collaboration by heron and wetland specialists is still necessary. In areas difficult to access and where local ornithologists are few, for example certain parts of the Middle East, field investigation is urgently required to help identification of conservation priorities. In the western Mediterranean where populations are well known, ornithologists have a high degree of research possibilities, and hence responsibilities. Long-term studies using marking schemes are of particular value for wildlife management because they improve our understanding of the basic population processes. To achieve this goal, we need information on essential demographic parameters: natality, mortality, dispersal and recruitment. At the same time, management can be used to test the appropriateness of the underlying theory.

Thanks to an international collaboration by a network of heron specialists and the resulting synthesis of information, we are today in a much better position to identify the important areas for herons in the Mediterranean region. Many of them were already listed by international conservation organisations as priority sites, on the basis of counts of wintering and migrating waterfowl (grebes, ducks, coots and waders). Other wetlands, however, not recognised as being important for waterfowl, will now complete the list of priority sites. The conservation of the remaining Mediterranean wetlands will be a major challenge for the years to come. If the information in this chapter contributes to this task, then the efforts put in over so many years by enthusiastic ornithologists all around the Mediterranean will have been well worthwhile.

3. Herons in South and West Asia

Christian Perennou, Richard V. Lansdown and James A. Hancock

This chapter discusses the heron populations of the western half of Asia, except the Mediterranean parts covered in Chapter 2 (Fig. 3.1, Table 3.1). It covers more specifically the following areas: south-west Asia including Afghanistan, Azerbaijan, Iraq, Iran; the whole Arabian Peninsula including Saudi Arabia, Yemen, Oman, Qatar, Kuwait, the United Arab Emirates; south Asia including India, Pakistan, Nepal, Bhutan, Sri Lanka, Bangladesh, the Maldives; and central Asia including Kazakhstan, Turkmenistan, Uzbekistan, Tadjikistan, Kirghizia and the central Asian part of Russia from the Urals east to 90°E (Fig. 3.1). The region contains important geographical features, such as the Himalayas, the highest mountain range on earth, and the Arabian Desert. Both act as powerful barriers to heron movements and distributions, isolating heron fauna of tropical Africa from those of south Asia. The region is located between two major zoogeographic regions and between Eastern Asian–Pacific migration routes and European–African migration routes.

The Heron Fauna

The heron fauna of the region comprises 20 species (considering Little Egret and Western Reef Heron as conspecific), about one-third of the world's heron species (Table 3.1). As elsewhere in the Northern Hemisphere, heron species diversity increases from north to south, for example from parts of Russia, where only the Grey Heron, Little Bittern and Eurasian Bittern breed, to Sri Lanka which supports thirteen heron species.

Overall, the Grey Heron is probably the most widely distributed species in this region, but in tropical areas, the Little and Cattle egrets, as well as the Indian Pond Heron in South Asia, are even more widespread and abundant. The Imperial Heron is the most localised and threatened heron in south and west Asia and is one of the most threatened heron species worldwide. The Malayan Night Heron is the next least common species.

A few heron species have ranges that extend into the region only to a limited

Heron Conservation
ISBN 0-12-430130-4

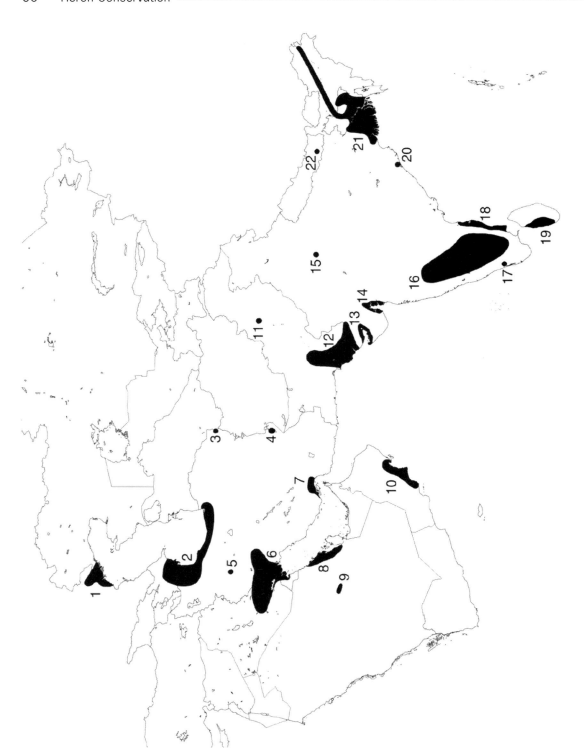

Fig. 3.1   Important heron areas in south and west Asia.

degree. Two (Sumatran and Eastern Reef herons) are primarily south-east Asian species with their western range limits extending into Bangladesh and the Nicobar Islands, and two (Squacco and Goliath herons) are mainly Afro–European, extending east into the Middle East. These species are treated more fully in Chapters 1, 2, and 5. Additional species are vagrants, including the Black-headed Heron, an Afrotropical species, and the Chinese Pond Heron, an east Asian species occurring occasionally in Bangladesh during spring and autumn migrations (Harvey 1990).

Environmental Conditions

The region encompasses virtually all climatic and environmental conditions found on the earth, from polar in Siberia, through desert in the Middle East (to western India), to the tropics in the south. In altitude, the region ranges from the highest mountains on Earth to sea level. High mountain habitats are little used by herons. In the former USSR, from north to south, tundra, taiga, temperate forest, and steppe successively dominate the landscape. The tundra is unsuitable for herons, but the latter habitats are often dotted with extensive wetlands providing adequate habitat for a few heron species. These habitats have been partly transformed by man,

Key to Fig. 3.1   Important heron areas in south and west Asia

1 Russia—Volga Delta (see Chapter 1)
2 Azerbaijan, Iran—South Caspian lowlands, including Aggel (Ah Gol) Lake, Mahmud-Chala and Third Chala Lakes, Kura Delta, Kizil-Agach (Kirov) Bays, Dasht-E Moghan (Aras River), Anzali Marsh, Gomishan Marsh
3 Iran—Sarrakhs Fishpool
4 Iran—Hamoun-I Helmand
5 Iran—Rudbary and Vasej Ab-Bandans
6 Iran, Iraq—Mesopotamian and south-west Iranian wetlands, including Dez Dam and River, Izeh and Shiekhon Lakes, Shadegan Marshes
7 Iran—Coastal marshes of Bandar Abas region, including Hara Protected Region, Khor Tiab and Khor Kohaly
8 Saudi Arabia—Coastal wetlands of Eastern Province including Tarout Bay and Gulf of Salwab
9 Saudi Arabia—Wetlands of Riyadh area including Wadi Hanifah and El Hair Watercourse Reserve
10 Oman—Oman coastline including Masirah Island, Barr al Hikman, Duqm, Dawhat Sawqirah, Dhofar Khawrs
11 Pakistan—Chashma Barrage Reservoir
12 Pakistan, India—Marshes of the lower Indus basin, including Hadero and Drigh Lakes, Great Rann of Kachchh
13 India—Gulf of Kachchh
14 India—Gulf of Khambat
15 India—Keoladeo Ghana National Park, Bharatpur
16 India—Inland tanks of Karnataka and Tamil Nadu including Hidkal Reservoir, Narasambhudhi Tank, Chitrangudi Tank
17 India—Kole Wetlands
18 India—Coromandel Coast with Vedaranyam Great Salt Swamp (including Point Calamere Bird Sanctuary), Pichavaram Mangrove, Puthupalli Alam, Ousteri Tank, Vedanthangal Bird Sanctuary, Simpson Estate, Pulicat and Kaliveli Lakes
19 Sri Lanka—South-west Sri Lanka coastal wetlands including Bopitiya, Course of the Mahaweli Ganga at Kandy, Muthurajawela
20 India—Chilka Lake
21 India, Bangladesh—Lower Ganges and Brahmaputra floodplains including Jhaukhali, Sunderbans, Jonak Char, Hail Hor, Kawadighi Haor, Matian Haor, Pasua Haor
22 Nepal—Koshi Tappu Wildlife Reserve

Table 3.1 Status of herons in south and west Asia

	GrH	IH	SuH	GoH	PuH	GWE	IE	LE	ERH	CE	SqH	IPH	GbH	BCNH	MNH	LtB	YB	CB	BB	EB
Afghanistan	+				+	+/++								++		+				
Azerbaijan	+				++	++		++		++	++			++		++				++
Bahrain	+					+		+		+			+			+/++				+
Iraq	+			?	+	+		+		+				+						+
Iran	++			?	++	++		++		++	++		++	++		+/++				++
Oman	+				+	+		++		+		+	+	+		+				
Saudi Arabia	+			+	+	+		++	?	+/++	+/++		++	+/++		++				+
Yemen	+			++	+	+		+		+			+/++							+
Qatar	+					+		++		+					+	+				
Kuwait	+							+												
United Arab Emirates	+					+		+			+	+	++	+/++		+				
India	++	+/++	++[1]		++	++	++	++	++[1]	++		++	++	++	++	++	++	++	++	+/++
Pakistan	++	+		+	++	++	++	++		++		++	++	++		++	++	++	++	+/++
Nepal	+/++	+			++	++	++	++		++		++	++	++	+		++	++	++	+
Bhutan	+	+				+	+	+		+		+	+							
Sri Lanka	++			+	++	++	++	++		++		++	++	++	+		++	++	++	+
Bangladesh	+	+		+	++	++	++	++	+	++		++	++	++	+		++	++	+	+
Maldives	++				+	+	+	+		+/++		++	++	+		+	+	+	+	+
Kazakhstan	++				++	++		++		++	++			++		++		++		++
Turkmenistan	++				++	++		++		+/++	++			++		++				++
Uzbekistan	+/++				++	++		++			++			++		++				++
Tadjikistan	+/++					++					+/++			++		++				++
Kirghizstan	+/++					++								++		++				++
Russia (Urals E. to 90°E)	++					+/++										++		++	++	++

++ = nesting population, + = present, but not nesting, +/++ = present, but breeding status uncertain.
[1]Andaman and Nicobar Islands only.

especially for cultivation, but the extent of change has not been in general as great as in tropical parts of the continent, although locally or regionally impact has been greater. A striking example of a severely affected wetland system is the Aral Sea, which has shrunk to only a fraction of the former area which it occupied (Aladin et al. 1993). This was caused by the retention of virtually all the water from in-flowing rivers by dams built further upstream, in order to irrigate cotton and other crops in central Asia. On the other hand, the dams have created a string of new, artificial wetlands along all the main rivers in the region.

The Middle East (east to Pakistan/west India) is dominated by deserts and semi-desert habitats, especially in the Arabian peninsula, eastern Iran and south-east Pakistan/north-west India. However, wetlands are well represented and large floodplains exist, for example the Mesopotamian marshes in Iraq, the Khuzestan marshes and the Caspian lowlands in Iran, the Seistan basin marshes on the Iran/Afghanistan border, and the Indus valley in Pakistan. Further south in the Arabian peninsula few inland wetlands exist, and coastal creeks, mud flats and mangrove swamps are the main wetlands, with fine examples in Saudi Arabia and Oman. These habitats are also well represented on the southern coasts of Iran and Pakistan. Inland desert saline lakes are also a characteristic feature of this area. Iran, Afghanistan, Pakistan and north-west India all have fine examples.

Tropical Asia features floodplains of the huge rivers (Ganges, Brahmaputra), which must have been in the past a striking system of floodplains, forested wetlands and marshes. However, the long-established presence of large human populations has virtually extirpated these habitats, except where diking converted natural marshes into freshwater storage reservoirs. For example Bharatpur in north India was converted into a shooting ground by former Maharajahs. A general climatological characteristic of south Asia is the importance of monsoon rains: vagaries of the monsoon regularly prevent breeding at traditional colony sites in very dry years, as for example in Bharatpur (Ali and Vajayan 1986) and south India (Perennou 1990). This natural phenomenon may cause high, although generally biologically insignificant, variation in regional breeding numbers. It is possible that during dry years birds form small colonies wherever suitable feeding habitat can be found, or that birds do not breed every year.

Coastal wetlands have to a certain extent fared better than inland wetlands. Although only tiny remnants of mangrove swamps survive elsewhere in the Indian subcontinent, the Sundarbans in Bangladesh and east India is still the largest single block of mangrove habitat in the world. Large expanses of coastal mud flats still exist, especially in Gujarat in north-west India, south-east India (Great Vedaranyam Swamp, Gulf of Mannar) and in north Sri Lanka. Large lagoons are concentrated on the eastern and south-west coast of India (for example Kerala "backwaters", Pulicat, Kaliveli, Chilka Lake) and in Sri Lanka.

Tropical forests, whether lowland or of medium altitude (up to ca. 2000 m MSL) are an important habitat for some specialised heron species, such as the Malayan Night Heron and the Imperial Heron. They used to be widespread in south Asia, but over-exploitation for fuel and large-scale conversion to agriculture and other uses have reduced their area.

Artificial wetlands occur throughout a large part of the region, especially where the climate is arid (south-west and central Asia) or where heavy tropical rainfall is restricted to a few wet months (south Asia). As a consequence, many dams and reservoirs have been built to support the rapidly increasing human population's need for irrigation, drinking water and hydropower. Reservoirs probably number over 200 000, ranging from less than an acre to hundreds of km.[2] There are over 40 000 in Tamil Nadu, south-east India (Perennou 1990) and over 35 000 in Sri Lanka (T. Hoffmann pers. comm.). In the flat inland or coastal plains, these reservoirs are shallow and have been well colonised by vegetation. The "ab-bandans" in northern Iran, the "tanks" in Tamil Nadu, south-east India and Sri Lanka, and the "jheels" in north India provide an attractive marsh-like habitat for many water birds including herons. In hilly regions, slopes are steeper and reservoirs tend to be large, open water bodies, of more limited interest for water birds.

A number of large canals have also been built recently in the sub-arid regions of Pakistan and north-west India to carry water for irrigation. A striking example is the Indira Gandhi canal in Rajasthan, north-west India. Seepage from these canals has given rise to many new wetlands, providing habitats for herons. Rice fields are other artificial wetlands abundant in tropical Asia, covering millions of hectares in this region. They can change from small mudflats to densely vegetated marshes within a few months, providing habitats for a wide range of water birds.

The Changing Status of Herons

Information available

As is the case with many of the world's regions, before 1984 little detailed information and no long-term studies were available on the status and populations of herons in south Asia and the Middle East, and whatever information did exist was widely dispersed among books and scientific journals. Important summaries include such works as the *Handbook of the Birds of India and Pakistan* (Ali and Ripley 1968) and *The Birds of the Soviet Union* (Dementiev and Gladkov 1951). Knowledge on herons is still very patchy, and trends in populations are usually impossible to assess accurately. An exception may be the former USSR where, however, publication in Russian reduces their availability outside Russia. Very few Russian references have been incorporated in the present review. Further south, main studies have usually been restricted to single sites or small regions. In the past, one of the most thorough studies was probably that of the Western Reef Heron by the team at Rajkot University (Parasharya and Naik 1988). More recently also, *The Herons Handbook* (Hancock and Kushlan 1984), *The Birds of Pakistan* (Roberts 1991), and Asian Waterfowl Census (AWC) summaries (Perennou et al. 1994), brought together historic and recent data allowing a more comprehensive baseline for the herons of the region.

The Asian Waterfowl Census (Perennou et al. 1994) was the first attempt to collect count data and provide baseline winter population estimates against which future trends can be measured. However, cryptic and nongregarious species are not adequately counted, so AWC information is not as useful for the Imperial Heron, Sumatran Heron, Malayan Night Heron, Little Bittern, Yellow Bittern, Cinnamon Bittern, Black Bittern or Eurasian Bittern. Another important source of recent data is the catalogue of known heronries in India, which is still under way (Subramanya 1996) but already yields very valuable data. It has so far received 295 entries from 18 states or union territories. The catalogue covers nine species: Grey and Purple herons; Great White and Cattle egrets; Little Egret and Western Reef Heron (as separate species), Eastern Reef Heron, Indian Pond Heron and Black-crowned Night Heron. We principally used information from the AWC combined with recent publications and personal communication from regional specialists to determine status we report (Table 3.1).

Species status

Grey Heron. This species occurs throughout non-montane areas of the region, and is one of the most abundant and widespread herons in the region. In winter many sites support more than 200 wintering birds. Average winter counts over four years included 2500 at Chilka Lake, Orissa, India and 580 at Gomishan Marsh, Mazandaran, Iran. The AWC has extended the known wintering range of this species to include central Saudi Arabia and Kerala, on the south-west tip of India. It is not possible to establish whether this represents a true range expansion, or simply an increase in our knowledge of the species range. No other changes since 1984 (Hancock and Kushlan 1984) are known, either in breeding or wintering range or numbers.

Imperial Heron. The distribution of this species has always been poorly known. Its original range is considered to have extended from the southern foothills of the Himalayas, southwards at the eastern end through Bhutan and Assam, to north-east and north-west Myanmar. Only two nests have been described, one from the nineteenth century with no locality given (Hume and Davison 1878), another from Arakan in the early part of this century (Baker 1932). In addition eggs have been reported from Sikkim (Walters 1976). However, doubts have been expressed as to the validity of some of these records due to wide discrepancy in the reported size of eggs (Walters 1976). Recent records of the species are sparse, particularly from the western end of its range.

The Imperial Heron is now considered exterminated in Nepal (Inskipp 1989). However, there have been a number of recent records from an area comprising north-eastern Bangladesh, Assam (India), and notably Bhutan (Inskipp and Inskipp 1993a,b). From Bhutan have come repeated sightings of solitary individuals from forested rivers (T. Inskipp pers. comm. 1993). In Bangladesh one solitary individual was seen on a reservoir (Harvey 1990) and a pair flushed from a forested lakeshore in the north-east (Thompson et al. 1993). Finally in India, a solitary individual was seen on a wet thickly-forested river in lowland forest (c. 500 m MSL) in Assam (T. Inskipp pers. comm. 1988), and a solitary bird in Nadampha National Park, in Arunachal Pradesh (Anon. 1994a). An unusual record of a solitary individual at Chilka Lake (Orissa), south-west of the Sundarbans (Jepson 1987) may be linked to a population reported in the Sundarbans (Scott 1989). The species is undoubtedly very rare and is considered to be globally endangered (IUCN 1996, as *Ardea insignis*). It depends on mature trees near wooded water bodies. These habitats are threatened throughout the region, and this species needs to be given high conservation priority.

Sumatran Heron. A good population of the Sumatran Heron appears to exist on the Nicobar Islands (Abdulali 1964, 1967). There have been few records of this species from mainland south or south-east Asia in the last 50 years and it is likely that it has become extinct from much of mainland south Asia this century (Lansdown 1987a, 1992). The Nicobar population may therefore provide an important nucleus for recolonisation of the west coast of peninsular south-east Asia, should habitat protection and management improve.

Goliath Heron. Only a few tens of individuals are known to breed within the region, restricted to the south coast of Iran and Iraq and possibly in the mangroves in Yemen (Brooks et al. 1987), with sporadic records from the Indian subcontinent, including two recent records from Bangladesh (Thompson et al. 1993), where it is also described as occurring in Hail Haor Wildlife Sanctuary in the north-east (Scott 1989).

Purple Heron. The eastern race of the Purple Heron (*A. purpurea manilensis*) occurs throughout much of the region, south of the Himalayas and east of a line from the Hindu Kush in the north to the border between Pakistan and Iran in the south. No new data are available on population trends of the eastern race in the region.

The western, nominate race has a somewhat patchy distribution throughout its range and reaches the eastern extreme of its range within our region. It breeds in suitable sites south and west of a line from Kiev through to the Aral Sea (Dementiev and Gladkov 1951). Aerial surveys during the breeding season in eastern Turkmenistan in 1986 and 1987 recorded a maximum of four birds (A. Poslavski pers. comm.), but this method may not be adequate for such a cryptic species. It has long been known to winter in parts of the Middle East, including the huge reed beds of Mesopotamia (Iran and Iraq) at the northern end of the Persian Gulf (Scott and Carp 1982). Recent drainage and canalisation works in Iraq have very substantially reduced the area of available wintering habitat. However, no data are available on current population trends in this area. Small numbers have recently been recorded wintering along the coastline of the Arabian Peninsula and even inland on artificial waters.

Great White Egret. The species occurs throughout the south of this region, except in areas such as high mountains or desert that lack suitable habitat. The resident race throughout much of the region is *modesta*, while *alba* breeds only in the west in parts of the former USSR and on the Iran/Afghanistan border. Few data indicate the race of birds recorded, and it is therefore impossible to assess whether there have been changes in the population or distribution of either of the two races. Overall, distribution changes include an apparent increase in Pakistan where it used to be rare except in northern Sind in the 1920s (Roberts 1991), and previously unknown wintering populations in the Arabian Peninsula (for example 359 in Oman in 1990), including inland on artificial wetlands (Perennou et al. 1994).

A number of individual sites are considered to be particularly important for wintering populations because they support more than 300 birds, notably: Chilka Lake, Orissa, India (average of 2650 birds over four years); Gomishan Marsh, Iran (average 560 over two years) and Kwadighi Haor (average 600 birds over two years) and Pasua Haor (a single count of 600 birds) in Bangladesh. In the past, Hamun-i-Pusak in south-west Afghanistan held a record 1830 individuals in January 1976 (AWC data). Subramanya (1996) suggests that the Indian population of this species

The Great White Egret. The species occurs in a wide variety of wetlands of south Asia ranging from freshwater to marine habitats. Photo: Jean-François Hellio & Nicolas van Ingen.

(excluding sites in the Sundarbans and at Bhitarkanniaka) is in the order of 2500 pairs, so the AWC estimate of 25 000 for South Asia would include a large influx of migrants in winter. In the United Arab Emirates, Great White Egrets occur mainly on spring and autumn migration, with up to 30 overwintering and one or two remaining through the summer in most years.

Intermediate Egret. Intermediate Egrets occur throughout the Indian sub-continent south of the Himalayas. It is the most common heron species in the large mixed colonies at Bharatpur in India, with up to 700 nests (Ali and Vijayan 1986). It can be quite tolerant of man and at least in India will nest within developed areas, including colony sites in Delhi Zoo and in a popular tourist area at Tilyar Lake, Haryana (Urfi 1993a,b). No apparent trends are known, either in numbers or range. In India the main wintering area is Chilka Lake in Orissa, with an average of nearly 1200 birds over four years.

Little Egret. The nominate white race of the Little Egret occurs throughout the region, except inland in the Arabian Peninsula. It is probably the most widespread heron in south and south-west Asia, occurring in all wetland habitats, including disturbed man-made habitats such as rice fields and areas which are heavily polluted, such as the Bagmati River in Nepal (Tyler and Ormerod 1993). It is the second most common species in the colonies at Bharatpur, with maxima of 300–400 birds (Ali and Vijayan 1986). In Azerbaijan, Patrekeev (1993) mentioned the presence of a large colony at Mahmoud-Chala, with 3000 pairs, and Krivenko (1991) estimated that about 1500 pairs breed in the Asian part of the former USSR, east of the Caspian Sea.

A dimorphic form, the Western Reef Heron, occurs only along the coastline from the Arabian Peninsula to India. Bundy and Warr (1980) reported that it breeds in small colonies around the Arabian Peninsula (formerly also on islands off the Kuwait coast), and Salim and Jensen (1992) counted a total 175–185 breeding pairs in Oman. In 1986, Roberts (1991) re-located a colony in Karachi Zoo in Pakistan that had been previously recorded in 1917. There is no indication of change in numbers or range for either of the races.

In winter, large concentrations of over 600 birds of the nominate race occur in India at Chilka Lake, Orissa (average 900 birds), Narasambudhi tank, Karnataka (800) and Puthupalli Alam, Tamil Nadu (675), and in Sri Lanka at Mahaweli Ganga at Kandy (750) (Perennou et al. 1994). Although concentrations are smaller in south-western Asia, they can reach up to 290 birds (Gomishan Marsh in Mazandaran, Iran). The major winter concentrations of the Western Reef Heron in Asia are located along the Arabian Peninsula, with comparatively smaller numbers occurring further east, into India. Average winter flocks of 770, 600 and 330 were counted respectively at Barr al Hikman, Dawhat Sawqirah and Masirah Island, three coastal sites in Oman (Perennou et al. 1994).

Eastern Reef Heron. In this region, the Eastern Reef occurs as an infrequent vagrant in Bangladesh and breeds only on the Andaman and Nicobar Islands. It occurs in good numbers in south-east Asia (see Chapter 4).

Cattle Egret. The range of the nominate race of the Cattle Egret extends into our region as far east as the Arabian Peninsula and Turkmenistan, whilst the eastern race (*B. i. coromandus*) occurs throughout the Indian subcontinent south of the Himalayas, except areas of Pakistan. The species has been demonstrated to perform regular migrations within India, apparently linked to the availability of water (Santharam 1987, 1988). The species is one of the most numerous herons in our region. Its ability to exploit anthropogenic habitat and exist in close proximity to man, even nesting within cities (Roberts 1991, Urfi 1993a,b, Subramanya 1996), has been recognised as the main reason for its success. It scavenges invertebrates in areas where fish are laid out to dry in India (P. Gole pers. comm. 1994) and extensively exploits rice fields in India and Sri Lanka.

In Azerbaijan, large colonies have been reported by Patrekeev (1993) (for example Aggel Lake 10 000–15 000 pairs and Mahmoud-Chala Lake 1000–1500 pairs), which contradicts Krivenko (1991) who estimated a total population of only 9000 pairs in the former USSR, all west of the Caspian Sea. It is not clear whether this contradiction is a product of changes in knowledge or of species distribution. In India, Subramanya (1996) records it as the most abundant heron species, overall nesting in nearly 57% of colonies reported, and notes that it occurs in particularly high density in cultivated areas in Punjab. In Pakistan, Roberts (1991) reports it as having dramatically increased in the last 50 years.

In winter, the disparate nature of habitat use and its independence from true wetland habitat makes accurate census of feeding birds difficult. Despite this, an expansion of this species' winter range both inland and into new coastal areas is apparent in the Arabian Peninsula and south-west Iran (Perennou et al. 1994), where it appears to be increasing (B. Behrouzi-Rad pers. comm.).

Squacco Heron. The Squacco Heron breeds in parts of the former USSR, but appears to be declining (Krivenko 1991). It is known to winter in small numbers along the eastern shore of the Arabian Peninsula (Oman, United Arab Emirates, Saudi Arabia) (Perennou et al. 1994) and the marshes of Mesopotamia in Iraq (Scott and Carp 1982).

Indian Pond Heron. The Indian Pond Heron occurs throughout the region east of Iran and south of the Himalayas. It is one of the most widespread and abundant heron species in South Asia, occurring on virtually every pond, natural wetlands, rice fields (hence its local name "paddybird") and reservoirs, even in the heart of cities. Its distribution appears to be limited in the north at least in part by altitude. It has been recorded recently for the first time in southern parts of Bhutan (Clements 1992) and up to 400 m MSL in Bangladesh (Katti et al. 1992). Due to its wide dispersal and disparate habitat use, it is inadequately censused by existing monitoring programmes. No recent change in breeding numbers or range is known. As with the Cattle Egret, this species has been found to perform regular migrations within peninsular India, apparently linked to the availability of water (Santharam 1987, 1988). The largest wintering concentrations found were at Mahaweli Ganga, Kandy, Sri Lanka (4200, one count); in India at Chilka Lake, Orissa (660), Kole Wetlands, Kerala (720) and Dharmasagar Reservoir, Andhra Pradesh (510) (Perennou et al. 1994).

Green-backed Heron. This pantropical species is represented in this region by three subspecies, *B. s. chloriceps* in the Indian subcontinent, *B. s. brevipes* along the western shore of Arabia, and *B. s. albolimbatus* in the Maldives. Birds are occasionally reported in the gap between the two continental populations, for instance on the Iran/Pakistan border and south-eastern Arabian Peninsula (Perennou et al. 1994). Breeding was even proved in the United Arab Emirates (Ramadan-Jaradi 1988). Being very secretive and occurring in dense riverine vegetation and mangroves, the species is not adequately monitored by existing schemes. The only important concentration reported was of 150 birds in Sholavandan, Tamil Nadu, India (Perennou et al. 1994).

Black-crowned Night Heron. The Black-crowned Night Heron occurs throughout the region south of the Himalayas where there is suitable habitat. Due to its nocturnal habits, it is difficult to monitor. New data include recently described colonies in the heart of Srinagar City in Kashmir (pers. obs., 1987; P. Gole pers. comm. 1994) and at Koshi Tappu, Nepal in October 1993, estimated at 2000 pairs (Baral 1993). Krivenko (1991) estimates that 2000 pairs currently breed in the Asian part of the former USSR, east of the Caspian Sea. An interesting phenomenon is the occurrence of large, apparently mobile colonies in densely populated cities in Karnataka (Bangalore), Kerala, Tamil Nadu and Rajasthan where some sites are occupied for only a single season, whilst others move within a locality (Subramanya

1996). Movement of Black-crowned Night Heron colonies has been recorded from peninsular Malaysia (Ratnam et al. 1989) and may be a result of damage to supporting trees by nesting birds.

Important wintering concentrations of Black-crowned Night Heron have been found in Drigh Lake, Sind, Pakistan (average of 3300 birds), and in Pichavaram Mangroves (1900) and Simpson Estate, Madras (2400), both in Tamil Nadu, India (Perennou et al. 1994).

As is the case with a number of other heron species, it appears to be increasing its range in the Middle East, including inland in the Arabian Peninsula on artificial wetlands and in Iran (B. Behrouzi-Rad pers. comm.). Previous important wintering populations in the Mesopotamian marshes of Iraq (for example 800 birds at Haur Chubaisah and 1000 at Hammar Marshes) (Scott and Carp 1982) may be threatened by recent wetland drainage.

Malayan Night Heron. As is the case with all the *Gorsachius* night herons, the Malayan Night Heron is little known. The presence of two apparently discrete populations of this species on the subcontinent makes assessment of the current status of the species more difficult. There continue to be regular but infrequent sightings, particularly from the southern and western Ghats (V. Santharam pers. comm. and P. O. Nameer pers. comm.) including a nest in the Silent Valley National Park in May 1990, and also from Guindy National Park (Madras), in October and November, which may involve local movements (V. Santharam pers. comm.). Many of these records are from the winter months, indicating that this species is resident in the area, although resident populations may be supplemented by wintering migrants. Despite suggestions that Sri Lanka is the main wintering ground of populations in the Indian subcontinent, it is considered to be only a rare winter visitor to Sri Lanka (T. W. Hoffman pers. comm. 1994).

It is obvious that Hancock and Kushlan's (1984) statement that "there are still considerable gaps in our knowledge even of its distribution" still applies. There has been virtually no increase in our knowledge of this species in more than fifteen years since this publication. Due to its apparent dependence on mature moist forest, the Malayan Night Heron is not recorded by existing monitoring schemes, nor is it casually encountered by bird watchers. It is also probably threatened by the ongoing deforestation and habitat degradation throughout its range and there is a desperate need for more information on the species' habitat requirements and ecology.

Little Bittern. This species appears to be more widespread in the Arabian Peninsula than previously recognised, with small numbers in Iran (B. Behrouzi-Rad pers. comm.). It is locally common at several sites in the eastern province of Saudi Arabia (Bundy and Warr 1980). It has bred in Bahrain but has not been proven to breed in the United Arab Emirates, Qatar or Oman, where it is considered a passage migrant or uncommon winter visitor (C. Richardson pers. comm. 1994). However, records from the United Arab Emirates show that the species is present from May to June and August to December and it may therefore breed. As with many heron species, it is not possible to assess whether these records indicate a range expansion or simply better coverage of the region. Elsewhere in the region (India, Pakistan), no change in range or numbers is apparent.

Yellow and Cinnamon Bitterns. The Yellow Bittern has been recorded in clumps of tall grasses in rice field complexes in southern India (P. O. Nameer pers. comm. 1994). The largest concentration of Cinnamon Bitterns recently recorded was of 58 birds in Kaziranga National Park, Assam, India (Perennou et al. 1994). Rice fields have been shown to be important for both Yellow and Cinnamon Bitterns in east and south-east Asia (Lansdown 1987b, Lansdown and Rajanathan 1993) and this may be the case too in the Indian subcontinent, although there is little evidence of this.

Black Bittern. The Black Bittern is stated by Roberts (1991) to be common and possibly increasing in Lower Sind, Pakistan, where it was not recorded in the 1920s. On the other hand, it is now regarded as very local and vulnerable in Nepal by Inskipp (1989), due to the loss of habitat.

Eurasian Bittern. The Eurasian Bittern appears to occur in large numbers in Iran (B. Behrouzi-Rad pers. comm.). However, the drainage of marshes on the Tigris and Euphrates Rivers may well affect populations dependent upon the delta. Scott and Carp (1982) mentioned only a few winter records of 1–2 birds in the area in the 1970s. In eastern Turkmenistan, A. Poslavski (pers. comm.) found 22 breeding pairs along water bodies during an aerial survey in 1986.

A male Black Bittern, a species of forest streams and freshwater swamps with thick vegetation. Photo: Jean-François Hellio & Nicolas van Ingen.

Critical Conservation and Regional Management Issues

General wetland conservation issues

Asia overall has over half of the world's human population, which is still growing rapidly. Consequently, natural wetlands are under increasing pressure in a region where water is an increasingly scarce resource, unevenly distributed in space and time. Most threats to wetlands result directly from the need to feed and accommodate this massive population.

For south Asia, the key threats have been identified by Scott and Poole (1989) as fishing and associated disturbances (32% of wetlands from which data were available), hunting (39%), overgrazing (27%), pollution (26%), degradation of the watershed (25%), general human disturbance (23%), and drainage for agriculture (20%). Fifty-one percent of the wetlands were reported to be under an overall moderate to high level of threat, while 21% of their total area was under some form of protection. The habitats most threatened and yet least protected are the interior lakes and marshes of Baluchistan, Pakistan, the wetlands in the Indus Delta and the northern Gangetic Plain, coastal lagoons, marshes and estuarine systems along the west coast of peninsular India, and the wet zone in Sri Lanka. All are important habitats for several heron species, especially the endangered Imperial Heron.

For west Asia, Scott (1993b) reviewed the main threats to wetlands, including hydrological changes (dam building; diversion of water for industry, drinking water supply or agriculture, drainage for agriculture), degradation and pollution (from overgrazing; dredging and landfill for urban developments, industrial, domestic or agricultural pollution, and regional wars), and hunting/egg-collecting. Some case histories are so far-reaching as to deserve specific treatment.

Drainage of Iraqi Marshes. Historically, the Mesopotamian marshes in Iraq covered 15–20 000 km² and harboured significant wintering numbers of herons. Maximum counts in the late 1970s included Purple Herons (35 counted), Grey Herons (564), Great White Egrets (107), Little Egrets (193), Cattle Egrets (50), Night Herons (1820), Squacco Herons (20), and possibly bitterns (Scott and Carp 1982). Since the marshes have never been comprehensively surveyed, the true numbers were probably much higher. A combination of drainage canals and embankments has been developed since the Iran–Iraq war (Prentice 1993), officially to enable the development of agriculture, although strategic reasons have probably also been important. This has resulted in severe loss of wetlands. Non-official sources put the losses at two-thirds by 1993, but reliable figures are difficult to obtain. It is clear that this drainage scheme represents a major threat for herons and other water birds in south-west Asia, although the true impact will never be fully quantified due to the lack of earlier, comprehensive surveys.

Disappearance of the Aral Sea. In the 1950s, 3000 pairs of herons (Grey and Purple herons and Great White Egret) bred in the vicinity of the Aral Sea (Aladin et al. 1993). The gradual drying-up of this sea has severely affected water birds in general, but the impact on herons has not been described in detail. It is likely to have been marked, although the reservoirs upstream that held the water have possibly provided alternative habitats for some species.

Development of artificial wetland habitats. Although many natural wetlands have been lost in Asia, especially in tropical parts, the development of dams and reservoirs can be a viable alternative for many water bird species including herons, provided they have shallow edges that function like marshes. On the other hand, steep slopes preclude their use by wading birds. Therefore, shallow-sided reservoirs located in plains (for example Gangetic, Coromandel, Sri Lanka, South Caspian) can be of high conservation value, while those in hills or mountains, which tend to have steeper banks, will hardly be used by herons. In Sri Lanka old, shallow "tanks" overgrown by vegetation are a much better habitat for water birds than are large, well-maintained ones (T. Hoffmann pers. comm.).

In the Coromandel plains (south India) various species use small irrigation reservoirs (such as Nelapattu and Vedanthangal) for breeding where social forestry programmes have planted trees. Open "tanks" about to dry up may attract up to 1000 feeding herons for several days (Perennou 1990). The thousands of available reservoirs with different drying-up dates ensure a steady food supply, although its distribution constantly changes. Species using reservoirs are also easier to monitor, since this habitat is usually accessible.

In India, rice fields are used by several heron species: Cattle, Little, Intermediate, and Great White egrets; Indian Pond, Little Green and Purple herons, and Yellow and Cinnamon bitterns (Perennou 1990, Subramanya 1996, P.O. Nameer pers. comm.). The first four species are the most widespread in this habitat (pers. obs.). Luckily, both these artificial yet vital habitats are not threatened on the large scale in the immediate future. Water storage is a national priority in several countries, and as a result construction of new reservoirs and restoration of old ones are ongoing.

Rice fields are unlikely to disappear since rice is the staple food in much of Asia, which is unlikely to change. However, local changes are noticeable, which may already affect some herons. In south India, Subramanya (1990) mentions that two heron species (Striated Heron and Cinnamon Bittern) use rice fields planted with tall indigenous varieties, and the extensive cultivation of dwarf hybrids may affect their use of this habitat. Local changes of land-use around breeding colonies are suspected to have affected the breeding population of Little Egrets in Vedanthangal colony (south India), around which dry crops (such as peanut) have partly replaced rice fields (Venkataraman and Muthukrishnan, in Subramanya 1996). Similarly in Kerala (south-west India), conversion of rice fields to cash crops (such as bananas, areca nut and coconut) and to small industries is affecting the extensive Kole wetland (P. O. Nameer pers. comm.), the "rice bowl of central Kerala", where up to 10 000 herons have been counted in winter surveys (Nameer 1993). The uniformity of some large, modern agricultural developments in Sri Lanka (Mahaweli, for example), with no interspersed shrubs or trees, can also reduce their use by herons (T. Hoffman, pers. comm.). Therefore, the shift towards a more modern agriculture (more profitable crops, new varieties of rice, increasing use of agrochemicals and large open landscapes) is a potential long-term threat to many heron populations that had so far been able to adapt to a traditional agriculture.

In Saudi Arabia, development of dams has certainly been profitable to several heron species, whose numbers are locally increasing, such as the Western Reef Heron, Little Egret, Black-crowned Night Heron (C. Richardson pers. comm.). In desert areas, even sewage farms can be of interest for water birds. It appears likely that the recent development of artificial wetlands (reservoirs, sewage treatment lagoons, etc.) has provided suitable habitat where previously none existed, and this may have resulted in expansion of the range of those species capable of exploiting these habitats.

Deforestation in south Asia

The Imperial Heron is mainly restricted to forests and swamps of the Himalayan foothills, and the Malayan Night Heron to the dense forests of north-east and south-west India and neighbouring areas. Most of these forested habitats have already disappeared (Adam et al. 1990), and the rest are being degraded or destroyed at an alarming rate. Due to the naturally low density of these non-gregarious species, a site-specific approach cannot serve their conservation. Their future is linked to tropical forest conservation issues.

Mangroves, which are both coastal wetlands and forests, are under severe pressure, for example on the west coast of India. In the Gulf of Kachchh, their harvesting for green fodder and fuel has resulted in the destruction of breeding habitats for various heron species, notably the Grey and Indian Pond heron, and the Great White and coastal race of the Little egrets (Naik and Parasharya 1987; Mundkur 1991), with damage being highest in recent years of drought (1984–88).

Nest-site protection

In south Asia, deforestation reduces the availability of potential nest sites in many cultivated areas. However, herons are adaptable where there is little disturbance (for example, see Urfi 1993a), which is the rule in our region. They may nest in large cities or towns in Pakistan (Roberts 1991) and in India. There, for instance, Madras (Tamil Nadu) is the home of the large Simpson estate colony site, which harbours 200 pairs of Black-crowned Night Heron (and 2000 birds in winter), plus dozens of pairs of Little, Intermediate and Great White egrets (Anon. 1984b, Gurusami 1988). Srinagar Public Gardens supports a mixed colony (pers. obs.) whilst in the same city, the Jhelum River banks have a large roost and colony of Black-crowned Night Herons (P. Gole pers. comm.). In Bhavnagar new port (Gujarat), a large colony of Western Reef Heron is known (Naik and Parasharya 1987, Subramanya 1996). Out of a survey of 295 colony sites in India, Subramanya (1996) recorded that 46% are located in or around cities, towns or villages.

In India, many traditional breeding colonies are protected officially through sanctuaries or national parks, such as Nellapattu in Andhra Pradesh, Ranganathittu in Karnataka, or the famous Bharatpur in Rajasthan, which may hold up to 1600 pairs of seven species. Other sites have been traditionally protected by local people (Vedanthangal in Tamil Nadu for example; Spillett 1968a) or by sympathetic owners (for instance the Simpson Estate in Madras). Still others are simply ignored and left undisturbed (such as Srinagar Public Gardens, Kashmir).

However in Gujarat, north-west India, there is a difference between small, coastal villages where human predation occurs on nesting herons and larger cities where most people protect the birds (Naik and Parasharya 1987). Subramanya (1996) also records many instances throughout the country of colony sites being disturbed by poaching of adults or young, or development activities (urban growth, factories) or simply destroyed through cutting. Overall, 50 out of 360 recorded sites were considered as threatened by human activities.

Artificial nest/rest sites have in some instances been provided voluntarily, in order to counter a future shortage of nest sites due to the lack of natural tree regeneration (for instance in Bharatpur, India, pers. obs.). Sometimes this end was achieved unintentionally, as in the Social Forestry Programmes in south India where tree planting inside irrigation reservoirs quickly led to trees being used by herons for roosting (pers. obs.) or even breeding, and being abandoned just as quickly as the trees reached harvesting stage (Subramanya 1996).

Contaminants

As Asia develops economically, a heavy increase in pesticide use can be expected. Being at the apex of food chains, herons are likely to become sensitive to this emerging problem (Chapter 12), although we still lack regional evidence. Species widely using rice fields (Cattle, Little and Intermediate egrets, Indian Pond Heron, possibly some bitterns) are the most likely to suffer.

Hunting

Only scattered reports on this threat are available, often in unpublished form. Tribal trappers regularly catch herons in south-east India (such as Indian Pond Heron and egrets, pers. obs.) and offer them for sale as meat, although on a small scale. The same species are regarded as a delicacy in Kerala, and hunted through shooting or poisoning in rice fields (T. Mundkur and P.O. Nameer, pers. comm.). Further north in the Gulf of Kachchh (north-west India), collection of eggs and chicks of several heron species is known to have taken place (Naik and Parasharya 1987, Mundkur 1991). In Bihar and adjacent north-east India, large numbers of herons and egrets are trapped, for food and feathers, while heron meat is available near Chilka Lake and other small towns in Orissa (V. Menon, pers. comm.). In Nepal, human predation on herons in the recently discovered Koshi Tappu large heronry has been recorded (Baral 1993). In south-west Asia, Scott (1993b) describes hunting and egg-collecting as an important threat to waterfowl overall, but whether or not herons are concerned is not explicit. Human predation on herons is therefore widespread in south Asia. Although locally (e.g., in Bihar) it can reach large proportions, its impact on regional populations is probably fairly low.

Conclusions

South and west Asia support one of the most diverse heron faunas in the world, including one-third of the world's species. Until recently knowledge on herons there has been mostly fragmentary and anecdotal. But recent initiatives such as the Asian Waterfowl Census, the Catalogue of Indian Heronries, and increased contacts between former USSR republics and the rest of the world are helping us to better assess the status of the different species, as well as to understand the key conservation issues they face. Overall, out of a regional total of 20, four species are surely declining and/or rare, and would require targeted conservation effort: the Goliath, Sumatran, Imperial and Malayan Night herons, of which the first two are largely extralimital.

For the other species, which are more widespread, the information available enables us mostly to make an initial assessment of distribution and numbers in some countries, but not on a regional scale. In some limited cases, recent trends can be assessed, usually on a local scale (for example the apparent expansion of a few species in the Arabian Peninsula). But there are still important gaps in our knowledge (Iraq, Afghanistan, Azerbaijan for instance) which prevent overall regional assessments, and to which major monitoring efforts should be directed whenever that becomes possible. So, due to this lack of direct information on herons there, the four threatened species listed above are likely to be a mere minimum, and it is not impossible that other species are quietly declining, too, as the fate of some wetlands (such as the Iraq marshes) would strongly suggest.

South and west Asia is a fast developing region, where human expansion is likely to continue to put an extra burden on heron populations and their habitats. So programmes that aim at ensuring a wise use of all the region's wetlands will be a vital complement to the continued protection of the rich, yet necessarily limited, number of protected areas.

4. Herons in East and South-east Asia

Richard V. Lansdown, Taej Mundkur and Llewellyn Young

This chapter discusses heron populations in the countries of east and south-east Asia from the western borders of Mongolia, China and Myanmar, Siberia east of 100°E latitude, south and east to the western tip of Irian Jaya (Fig. 4.1, Table 4.1). This region encompasses a variety of heron habitats ranging from Siberia through the tropics. It is characterised by a large human population with concomitant conservation issues of pollution, land use conflicts, and intense pressures for development.

The Heron Fauna

The heron fauna of the region includes more than a third of the world's herons, including six endemic species (Table 4.1). It is host to 21 endemic taxonomic forms, including races of the Green-backed Heron recognised by Hancock and Kushlan (1984). Populations of a few of the species typical of the region, such as Schrenck's Bittern and Swinhoe's Egret, extend slightly into parts of the former Soviet Union. Conversely, species and races whose main distribution lies outside the region (such as Grey and Purple herons and Little Bittern) extend into the region in China, North Korea or Myanmar.

Environmental Conditions

Because of the geographic scope of the region, temperature differences are extreme, with July temperatures of up to 30°C in south-east China and Vietnam and January temperatures as low as −40°C in northern China and Siberia. Habitats range from the rocky sea cliffs and coniferous woodland in Hokkaido and northern North Korea, through temperate deciduous forests in southern China, to tropical rain forest and coral islands in the Greater and Lesser Sundas and Wallacea. The region contains thousands of islands providing extensive coastal habitat, including mangrove,

Heron Conservation
ISBN 0-12-430130-4

Fig. 4.1   Important heron areas in east and south-east Asia.

sandy, muddy and rocky foreshore, estuaries and coral reefs. High annual rainfall through much of the region produces extensive freshwater marshes, lakes and rivers. These wetlands support most of the heron species occurring in the region.

Taiga extends through eastern Siberia and Ussuriland to Sakhalin Island off the Sikhote-Alin. Vegetation is dominated by open moorland and pine forests with a multitude of small water bodies fringed by willows. The climate is characterised by brief summers and long winters, temperatures being below freezing for six months. The heron fauna of the taiga includes eight species with much in common with western temperate regions. The nominate races of the Grey Heron and the Great White Egret occur here, at the eastern limit of their ranges.

Within east and south-east Asia, the temperate climatic zone is restricted to lowland eastern China. Originally characterised by deciduous forest interspersed with rivers and associated freshwater and coastal wetlands, most land is now under cultivation. Temperature variation is relatively high, with summer highs and winter lows of similar duration. The heron fauna includes many species that occur

Key to Fig. 4.1 Important heron areas in east and South-east Asia.

1 Japan—Kushiro Marsh
2 North Korea—Kwan-Po
3 North Korea—Shijun-Ho
4 North Korea—Ryongol
5 North Korea—Tegam-do, Sogam-do and Sonchonrap-to
6 South Korea—Shin Islet, South Kanghwa, North Yongjong Mudflats
7 South Korea—Upo Marshes
8 South Korea—Nakdong Estuary
9 China—Yellow River Delta
10 China—Zhalong Marshes and Nature Reserve
11 China—Shuangtaizi and Liao Marshes
12 China—Yancheng Marshes
13 China—Shijui
14 China—The Dongting Lakes
15 China—Xi Jiang (Pearl River) Delta, China Kau Kong, Nam Hoi County, Hong Kong Mai Po
16 Taiwan—Chuwei Mangrove Swamp
17 Taiwan—Tatu Estuary, Taiwan Tungshih (Ton-Shou) Mangroves
18 Myanmar—Upper Irrawaddy and Mogawng Chaung
19 Myanmar—Inle Lake
20 Myanmar—Mong Pai Lake Proposed Wildlife Sanctuary
21 Myanmar—Kaladan Estuary, Hunter's Bay and Combermere Bay
22 Myanmar—Mohingyi Lake
23 Myanmar—Gyobyu Reservoir
24 Myanmar—Irrawaddy Delta
25 Thailand—Southern Central Plains of Thailand
26 Thailand—Beung Boraphet
27 Thailand—Tha Ton Marsh
28 Thailand—Sanambin NHA
29 Thailand—Ao Pattani (Pattani Bay)
30 Vietnam—Red River Estuary
31 Vietnam—Cat Tien
32 Vietnam—Mekong Delta including Minh Hai, Bac Lieu, Dam Doi (Ngoc Hien), Nam Can
33 Malaysia—Matang Forest Reserve, Sungei Burung Mangroves
34 Malaysia (Borneo)—Rajang Delta Sarawak
35 Malaysia (Borneo)—Tempasuk Plain Sabah
36 Malaysia—Kinabatangan Floodplain Sabah
37 Philippines—Candaba Swamp Luzon
38 Philippines—Buguey Wetlands Luzon
39 Philippines—Ragay Gulf Luzon
40 Philippines—Lake Lanau Mindanao
41 Indonesia (Sulawesi)—Lake Lindu (Lore Lindu)
42 Indonesia (Sulawesi)—Morowali
43 Indonesia (Borneo)—Danau Bankau and Barito Basin swamps
44 Indonesia—Kangean Archipelago
45 Indonesia (Java)—Pulau Dua, Pulau Rambut, Tanjung Sedari, Muara Cimanuk
46 Indonesia (Sumatra)—Way Kambas
47 Indonesia (Sumatra)—Pulau Betet, Banyuasin Musi River Delta

Table 4.1 Status of herons in east and south-east Asia.

	Species																									
	GrH	IH	SuH	PuH	GWE	PdH	IE	LE	SwE	ERH	CE	IPH	CPH	JPH	GbH	BCNH	NNH	WeNH	JNH	MNH	NGTH	YB	ShB	CB	BB	EB
Russia	++		?		++				++	?			++		++	++						++	++	++	++	++
Mongolia	++				++			?														?	?	++	++	++
North Korea	++				++		++	++	++	++			?		++							++	++	++		++
South Korea	++				++		++	++	+	++	++		?		++							++	++	++		
Japan	++				++		++	++	++	++	++		?		++	++			++			++	++	++		++
China	++		++	++	++		++	++	+	++	++		++		++	++		++				++	++	++	++	++
Hong Kong	++		++	++	++		++	++	+	++	++		++		++	++			+			+	+	++		+
Taiwan	++		++	++	++		++	++	+	++	++	?	++	?	++	++			+			?	+	++	++	+
Cambodia	++		++	?	?		?	++		++	++		+	?	++	++			++	?		++	?	++	++	+
Laos	++		++	?	?		?	++		++	++		+	?	++	++				?		++	?	++	++	+
Vietnam	++		++	++	++		++	++	+	++	++		+	?	?	++				++		++	?	++	++	+
Myanmar	++	++	++	++	++		++	++		++	++	?	+	++	++	?				++		++		++	++	+
Thailand	++		++	++	+		++	++	+	++	++	+	+	++	?					++		++	+	++	++	+
Malaysia	++		?	?	+		+	+	+	+	+		+	+	++		++			?		?	?	++	++	+
Philippines	++		++	++	+		+	+	+	++	+		+		++	++			+	++		++	+	++	++	+
Singapore	++		++	++	+		?	++	++	++	++		+		++	++				+		++	+	++	++	
Brunei Darussalam	++		?	++	?		?	?		?	?		?	?	++	++				?	++	?		++	++	
Indonesia	++		++	++	++	++	++	++	+	++	++		+	++	++	++			?	?		++	++	++	++	

++ = nesting population, + = present, not nesting, ? = status uncertain.

throughout Old World temperate regions supplemented by strictly Asian species such as Swinhoe's Egret, Eastern Reef Heron, Chinese Pond Heron, and four species of *Ixobrychus* bittern.

Dry grassland occurs mainly on the high altitudinal plateau of western China and Mongolia, grading into the southern limits of the Gobi Desert generally over 5000 m MSL. It is characterised by extreme aridity and temperature. By its nature, this habitat supports few heron species, although Eurasian Bittern, Great White Egret and Grey Heron breed, and others such as Little Bittern and Chinese Pond Heron occur on passage (D. Batdelger pers. comm.).

The subtropical zone covers most of the region extending from Myanmar and southern China to Japan and south into the northern Philippines and Indo-China. The climate is generally warm, with high rainfall and clearly defined seasons. Originally it was mainly covered by forest, including mangrove in coastal areas, lowland Dipterocarp, and deciduous and coniferous forests in the mountains. Large numbers of rivers and lakes with associated freshwater and coastal wetlands undoubtedly supported huge populations of water birds. However, much of the forest has been replaced by agriculture and urban development. Mangrove has been converted to fish farms and wetlands drained for rice, with consequent dramatic changes in water bird populations. This zone supports all species of heron occurring in the region, except those restricted to the area south of Wallace's Line. It includes some of the more specialised forest species such as Sumatran Heron, Malayan and Japanese night herons and the two most vulnerable heron species in the region, the Imperial Heron and White-eared Night-Heron.

The tropical zone extends from south-west China and the Philippines, through lowland Indo-China to Australia. It is characterised by high temperatures and high rainfall, with little seasonal variation. This zone was once entirely covered by lush tropical rain forest, mangrove, marshes and riverine swamps, with variation occurring only on a few of the higher mountains. Much of this forest cover has been lost to agricultural and industrial development. This zone contains the main concentration of some of the most vulnerable habitats in the region, such as freshwater swamp forest (concentrated in southern Peninsular Malaysia, south Sumatra and Kalimantan) and mangrove (mainly in east Sumatra, western Peninsular Malaysia and Kalimantan). It supports a diverse heron fauna, including most of the species of the region, either as residents or non-breeding migrants. It also supports breeding populations of the more specialised and vulnerable species.

Changing Status of Herons

Data available

There have been no long-term studies of heron populations in east and south-east Asia. Only in Hong Kong have there been systematic counts, although even these are subject to a high degree of uncertainty in that it is likely that all colonies were not counted each year. Most of the information collected in the region before 1984 was compiled by Hancock and Kushlan (1984), but it was generally anecdotal, providing a poor baseline against which to assess quantitative changes in status. Today, lack of local information still makes it impossible to assess the current status or distribution of the various subspecies. Even with increases in the number of counts of water birds over the last ten years, data are unavailable for a considerable part of the region due to low coverage, often because of political unrest and instability, and difficulties in translation.

Prior to 1984 there were few quantified data on which to base an assessment of the changes in the distribution and status of herons in the region. Consequently, the following account is based mostly on compilation of a variety of anecdotal sources, localised count data and regional surveys over the last ten years. Two important long-term surveys are from Vietnam and Hong Kong (Tables 4.2, 4.3). Rose and Scott (1994, 1997) and Perennou et al. (1994) provide "best guess" estimates of heron populations. Except where information is available for specific colonies, areas or species, the former report is used to provide the population estimates in this chapter. Because these are based on a small sample, they must be treated with caution.

Species status

Grey Heron. This species has a patchy distribution through the region south to Wallace's Line, these herons are generally abundant where they occur. Northern populations (particularly in Siberia where the race *jouyi* overlaps with the nominate race) are summer migrants, but they are abundant residents in China, Korea, Japan and Mongolia and in parts of Indonesia. Small numbers breeding locally in Indo-China and Peninsular Malaysia are augmented by a large winter influx. In Hong Kong, Taiwan, the Philippines and Borneo they occur only as winter visitors. There

Table 4.2 Population trends in Hong Kong heronries (Hong Kong Birdwatching Society records).

Year	GrH	GWE	LE	SwE	CE	CPH	BCNH
1958	–	–	177–200	3+	85	244+	–
1959	–	1	114	9	56	200	–
1960	–	–	72	9	71	170	–
1963	–	–	14	1	32	145	–
1966	–	–	31	2	31	105	–
1967	–	–	50	1	50	?	–
1968	–	–	>50	2	>40	>50	–
1969	–	–	180	3	105	180	–
1970	–	–	25	3	92	15	–
1971	–	–	220–270	2	150	131	–
1972	–	–	30+	1	54+	P	6
1973	–	–	230+	3	600+	P	4
1974	–	–	352	1	44+	67+	8+
1975	–	–	P	2	P	P	4
1976	–	–	P	–	P	50–60	6
1989	–	12	284	–	335	147	196
1990	1	33	252	–	179	250	215
1991	2	10	124	–	129	109	70
1993	5	20	263	–	87	95	171

All figures refer to nesting pairs. P, present but no count available.

Table 4.3 Heron numbers in some southern Vietnamese heronries.[1]

Location/year	GrH	SuH	PuH	GWE	IE	LE	CE	CPH	JPH	GbH	BCNH
Dam Doi											
1978	170		35	40	270	2590	380	380		82	1700
1992	30		10	8	25	1250	140	190		20	650
Cai Nuroc											
1987	80		30	80	4150	2000		600			1600
1992	36		20	20	12	820		280			487
Bac Lieu											
1987	35	12–16	24	105	200	2300	954	720	121	63	1660
1992	10	4–8	8	1300	90	30	349	450	72	20	960
Tan Tien											
1992				74	212	2010		425			372
Tan Thuan											
1992				37	134	480	65			50	

[1] From Duc 1992. Data presented are the lower estimate of number of breeding pairs from the published range.

are few concerns over the status and conservation of most populations, although a number of colonies have been lost recently due to logging and disturbance.

Imperial Heron. This species, listed as globally endangered (as *Ardea insignis*) by IUCN (1996), probably survives in Myanmar, where it was last recorded by Smythies (1986). However, no more recent information is available from that country. The status of the Imperial Heron is covered in more detail in Chapter 3.

Sumatran Heron. Once distributed throughout both coasts of mainland Asia south of 20°N latitude, the Sumatran Heron appears to have suffered a reduction in its range during the last 50–100 years and is listed as near threatened by IUCN (1996). The only records of this species from mainland Asia since the mid 1970s have been from southern Indo-China and coastal islands off Thailand and Malaysia where five nests were found on Pulau Bukom in 1992 but the site was subsequently lost through reclamation. This suggests that most of the population is now restricted to an area bounded by the Nicobar Islands, the Philippines, Singapore and from the Rhio–Lingga Archipelago south through Borneo and Wallacea to Australia. Nowhere throughout the huge range and diverse habitats of this species is it common. Its apparent rarity may be due to population density being limited by ecological constraints, as is the case with the population densities of other large *Ardea* herons, such as Malagasy, Imperial and Goliath herons (Hancock and Kushlan 1984).

The only reliable estimate of population density for Sumatran Herons comes from Australia, where it is estimated at roughly one pair per 600–700 ha of rocky island or one pair per five km of river in coastal mangrove (S. Garnett pers. comm. 1986). This appears to conform to casual observations of birds from other parts of its range (where it continues to survive in reasonable numbers), such as East Malaysia, Indonesia and Papua New Guinea. There is, however, a recent record of ten individuals within a small area south of Singapore.

Most nests located have been solitary and well hidden in dense vegetation over water, but a single nest in the Gulf of Carpentaria was relatively exposed and on the

A Sumatran Heron pictured at the island complex south of Singapore, one of the known strongholds of this species. Photo: Alan OwYong.

outskirts of a colony containing Nankeen Night Herons, egrets and ibises (S. Garnett pers. comm. 1986). Similar nest locations have been described for the Goliath Heron, which is also generally regarded as a solitary nester (Hancock and Kushlan 1984). It is likely that breeding Sumatran Herons depend on dense vegetation with trees strong enough to support nests, and water bodies suitable for feeding, that is, with accessible numbers of large fish.

Within the range of this species, suitable breeding habitats include mature mangrove forest with shallow mudflats or streams, lowland *Dipterocarp* forest with pools and ox-bow lakes, small islands with mature trees and rocky or sandy shores or coral reefs, and large rivers in forested upland areas.

Sites of known importance for Sumatran Herons include the Salu–Sudong–Pawai–Senang group of islands south of Singapore (Lim Kim Seng pers. comm. 1992) and the Rhio–Lingga Archipelago, most coastal mangrove, offshore rocky islands and the Kinabatangan River catchment in Borneo, and throughout Indonesia in coastal mangrove and offshore islands (Lansdown 1987a).

Purple Heron. Purple Herons have a similar status in the region as Grey Heron, although absent from North and South Korea and Japan except as occasional passage migrants. They are generally abundant where they occur and are known to breed through Myanmar to Vietnam, the Philippines, Borneo, Singapore and Indonesia, south to Sulawesi. Purple Herons regularly forage in rice field systems in Malaysia and so are likely to suffer from pesticide contamination, in addition to the loss of natural habitats experienced by all heron species throughout the region.

Great White Egret. Great White Egrets are one of the most widespread and abundant herons of the region. Breeding colonies have been located throughout the region in the past, but there are now no known colonies in Peninsular Malaysia, the Philippines and Singapore. In general, Great White Egrets appear to occur as summer migrants through the northern part of their range in Siberia, northern China, North and South Korea and Japan, residents in Indo-China and Indonesia, and winter visitors to central south-east Asia.

Intermediate Egret. The Intermediate Egret has a more southerly distribution than the Great White Egret, occurring only as far north as southern parts of China, South Korea and Japan. The distribution of the nominate race is then more or less continuous until it joins the race *plumifera* in Indonesia. It appears to be abundant throughout its range, with large winter concentrations in Peninsular and East Malaysia and the Philippines.

Little Egret. The Little Egret is probably the most widespread white egret in the region, the nominate race occurring throughout the south to the Greater Sundas where it overlaps with the race *nigripes*. No significant changes in the perceived status and distribution of this species have occurred since publication of the *Herons Handbook*.

Swinhoe's Egret. Swinhoe's Egret has long been considered one of the rarest and most vulnerable of the world's herons, and it is listed as endangered by IUCN (1996). However, since 1985, a number of small colonies have been discovered on islands off the Korean peninsula and large wintering flocks have been found in the Philippines, suggesting that the world population is probably higher than previously suspected.

Swinhoe's Egret is restricted to the eastern seaboard of continental Asia and

Swinhoe's Egret, a critically endangered species. Photo: Kazuyasu Kisaichi.

south-east Asia. Breeding grounds are in northern temperate or even sub-arctic areas north of 30°N latitude. A large proportion of the population appears to winter in south-east Asia, south of 15°N latitude. In the past, due to a number of historic records of breeding in mainland China and up to nine pairs nesting in colonies in Hong Kong, the eastern seaboard of China and Hong Kong were considered to be the breeding stronghold. Breeding records from Hong Kong were at best irregular, however, and it is unlikely that Swinhoe's Egrets now nest in mainland China (Cheng 1987); similarly records of breeding birds in Taiwan (Swinhoe 1863) are now considered to be erroneous (Mees 1977).

The maximum estimated breeding population of approximately 1000 pairs of Swinhoe's Egrets is distributed over eight colony sites. These are as follows: in China, Second Island off Shanghai, c. 60 pairs (Long et al. 1988); Paifang Island, Nanwan Reservoir, Henan Province, >60 pairs (Wen and Sun 1994a,b); Lushun Kou area, <300 pairs (Pei et al. 1994); in North Korea, Rap-do, 20–250 pairs (Sonobe and Izawa 1987); Sogam-do, 40–50 pairs (Sonobe and Izawa 1987); Yob-do (Austin 1948); Taegam-do, 50–60 pairs (Sonobe and Izawa 1987); in South Korea, Shin Do, c. 400

pairs (Long et al. 1988). Sporadic nesting has occurred in colonies in Japan (K. Sonobe pers. comm. 1987, N. Moores pers. comm. 1992), however there has been limited success to date. Frequent observations of birds on passage north of known breeding grounds have suggested that breeding colonies may occur further north in Ussuriland (Lansdown 1990), a fact proven recently (1998) with the discovery of a colony of 30–40 pairs near Vladivostok, some 600 km north of previously known breeding sites (Litvinenko and Shibaev 1999). It has been suggested that the Swinhoe's Egret may breed in the Philippines (Amadon 1951, Gast and King 1985), but all available records fall within the known migration period of this species and there is as yet no information to substantiate this claim.

Previous data suggested that Swinhoe's Egrets nest exclusively in trees (Hancock and Kushlan 1984) and this has certainly been the case with birds nesting in Hong Kong and Japan. However, all new breeding records are of nests situated on the ground or in low vegetation associated with seabird colonies on offshore islands in China and Korea. All currently known colonies are associated with other colonial birds, including gulls (Laridae) and cormorants (Phalacrocoracidae) on offshore islands and other species of herons in Hong Kong and Japan. It appears likely that, when Swinhoe's Egrets nest in areas where mammalian predators occur, they will nest in trees, and otherwise they will nest on or near the ground.

Birds arrive on the breeding grounds during May, and young fledge in July, initially moving onto nearby coastal wetlands (Sonobe and Izawa 1987). This dispersal then merges into a southward migration with records for July and August from coastal South Korea, Japan and China. Information on non-breeding egrets is shown in Table 4.4. Most migration occurs in September and October and appears to follow two routes. The main population moves through Taiwan (Mees 1977, Severinghaus pers. comm. 1987) and probably the Ryukyu Islands to winter in the Philippines and Borneo (Howes and NPWO 1987, C. Poole pers. comm. 1994) with vagrants reaching Sulawesi (Scott 1989). An observation of a bird wintering in Singapore that had been ringed as a nestling on Shin Do off South Korea (Mundkur 1992) suggests that at least a proportion of Korean birds take the western route. Small numbers move westward through the eastern seaboard of China, where a few overwinter (Waterbird Specialist Group of the Chinese Ornithological Association 1994), then through Indo-China (Scott and Rose 1989, Robson pers. comm. 1993) and Thailand (Robson 1992) to winter in Peninsular Malaysia (Lansdown 1990) with stragglers reaching Singapore (Medway and Wells 1976, Wells 1984, 1990a,b), Sumatra (Voous and van Marle 1988, Robson 1989) and Java (Andrews 1993). However, identification of the wintering grounds has been made difficult by problems of identification of non-breeding birds (Lansdown 1990, Poole et al. 1999). Swinhoe's Egrets depend largely upon rocky offshore islands or coastal heronries for breeding, and coastal wetlands for food. Breeding sites are listed above, and known important stopover and wintering sites are presented in Table 4.4.

In 1990–1992, the Asian Wetland Bureau and Kyung Hee University, Seoul, colour banded 381 fledgling Swinhoe's Egrets on Shin Islet, South Korea. In spite of high observer coverage on wintering grounds, there have been only three sightings of marked birds away from the breeding grounds (in Taiwan, Singapore and the Philippines (Mundkur 1992, Amuerfino Mapalo pers. comm. 1998). Professor Won at Shin Islet saw at least three marked birds in 1993, and a similar number in 1994 (W. Pyong-Oh, pers. comm. 1994).

Table 4.4   Swinhoe's Egret: nesting and non-nesting sites and numbers in east and south-east Asia.

	Breeding site	Number of pairs	Source
P.R.China	Second Island, Off Shanghai	c60	Long et al. 1988
	Paifang Island Nanwan Reservoir, Henan	>60	Wen and Sun, 1994a
	Luchan Kou Area	<300	Pei et al. 1994
North Korea	Rap-do	20–250	Sonobe and Izawa 1987
	Sogam-do	40–50	Sonobe and Izawa 1987
	Yob-do	No recent data	Austin 1948
	Teagam-do	50–60	Sonobe and Izawa 1987
South Korea	Shin-do	c. 400	Long et al. 1988

	Sites used by non-breeding birds	Number of birds	Source
South Korea	Kanghwa Island	92–122 (1988)	
	Yongjong Island	64 (1988)	Long et al. (1988)
	other sites	<35	
Japan	Hakata Bay	Regular in small numbers	N. Moores in litt. (1993)
P.R.China	Jiangsu coast	>100	Waterbird Specialist Group of the Chinese Ornithological Society 1994
	Dongting Hu Nature Rese, Hunan	>100	
	Pangzhai, Henan	>60	
	Quingxu/Huayan Rese, Shanxi	>30	
	Yancheng coast	60	Perennou et al. 1994
Taiwan	Various	<100, apparently stragglers	Severinghaus in litt. (1978)
Hong Kong	Mai Po Marshes	Regular in small numbers	WWF—Hong Kong
Vietnam	Red River Delta	Small numbers 1993	Scott et al. 1989
Thailand	Krabi	<3 (1992)	Robson (1992)
Philippines	Bohol	635 (1991)	AWB (1991)
	Cebu	75 (1990)	
	Palawan	149 (1990), 164 (1991)	
	Others	5–20	
	Ormoc Intertidal Mudflat	1600	Perennou et al. 1994
	Olango Island	36	
West Malaysia	Kuala Gula	<10	Wells (1990a,b)
Singapore	Serangoon Estuary	Regular in small numbers	Wells (1990a,b)
	Kranji Reservoir	Regular in small numbers	
Borneo	Sabah	small numbers	Collar et al. 1994
	Brunei	small numbers	Mann 1987
	Sarawak	small numbers	Howes and NPWO 1986
	Kalimantan	small numbers	Andrew 1992
Indonesia	Sumatra	Straggler	Voous and van Marle 1988
	Java	One record	Andrews 1993

Eastern Reef Heron. Eastern reef herons are restricted to coastal areas. They generally nest on small, rocky offshore islands from Cheju-do (Quelpart Island) off the south coast of South Korea, south to Australia, but some colonies are in mainland coastal mangrove. It is very difficult to estimate populations of this species, as colonies are generally small and widely dispersed through areas which have the lowest observer coverage. However, they appear to be abundant throughout their range and there is no evidence of a decline in numbers.

Cattle Egret. Cattle Egrets are widespread throughout the region except north of central China, and are probably the most abundant heron species. This is partly because they are not entirely dependent upon wetlands and partly because they are very successful in exploiting the agricultural practices which prevail in the region. However, it has been shown in Hong Kong (see below) that there is a decline in the population of this species corresponding with the reduction in use of livestock in agriculture.

Indian Pond Heron. Within the region, Indian Pond Herons appear to be restricted to Myanmar. However, as it is still not yet possible to separate visually the *Ardeola* herons in non-breeding plumage, the large number of pond herons wintering in Thailand may include some of this species. There are no new records from Myanmar since publication of the *Herons Handbook* and so no assessment of trends or current status can be made. This species is discussed further in Chapter 3, which covers the majority of its world range and population.

Chinese Pond Heron. The Chinese Pond Heron is endemic to east and south-east Asia. It breeds from northern China and southern Siberia south to northern Indo-China and winters south to Kalimantan. It appears to be abundant throughout much of its range, with large numbers wintering in rice field systems in Peninsular Malaysia and Borneo. Again, due to the difficulties in separating the *Ardeola* herons in non-breeding plumage, it is difficult to be certain of the exact wintering range of this species, particularly as a number of moulting birds seen in East Malaysia in February 1987 were clearly Javan Pond Herons outside their known range.

Javan Pond Heron. Two races of the Javan Pond Heron occur in and are endemic to the region. *A. s. continentalis* is found from Thailand through southern Indo-China to south-eastern Vietnam, with vagrant birds recorded moulting into breeding plumage in western Peninsular Malaysia. *A. s. speciosa* is found through the Greater Sundas, from Sumatra east to Kalimantan and south to Flores. As is the case with Indian and Chinese Pond herons, the Javan Pond Heron appears to be a common and familiar bird throughout its range, often feeding in rice field systems, where it has been suggested that it may play a role in control of invertebrate pests (Vermeulen and Spaans 1987). Javan Pond Heron (presumably *A. s. speciosa*) has recently colonised the southern part of Mindanao in the Philippines and may be continuing to spread northwards.

Green-backed Heron. Green-backed Herons are widespread and abundant throughout the region and are represented by 9 races: *B. s. actophilus*, *B. s. amurensis*, *B. s. carcinophilus*, *B. s. idenburgi*, *B. s. javanicus*, *B. s. moluccarum*, *B. s. papuensis*, *B. s.*

spodiogaster and *B. s. steini*. Some races, such as *B. s. javanicus*, are sedentary, while others, such as *B. s. amurensis*, are migratory and during the northern winter their ranges overlap. Very few data refer to the different races and there is no easily available guide to their identification. As a result, it is not possible to assess their true status and the abundance of the different races.

Black-crowned Night Heron. Black-crowned Night Herons occur throughout the region south to Borneo and the Lesser Sundas, but are absent from Sumatra except as vagrants (Voous and van Marle 1988). Northern populations are migratory, while southern populations are sedentary. Although the species appears to be abundant throughout its range, it is possible that they suffer from disturbance, as a large colony on the west coast of Peninsular Malaysia is known to have deserted the site following fogging for mosquito control (see below). There has been speculation that hybridisation occurs between this species and Nankeen Night Heron in the Philippines, Java (Hubbard 1976) and Borneo (Sheldon and Marin 1984) where the species' ranges overlap. However, this has yet to be demonstrated genetically.

Nankeen Night Heron. In this region, Nankeen Night Herons are restricted to the Philippines and parts of Indonesia, notably eastern Java, East Nusatenggara, Timor, Sulawesi, the Moluccas and Irian Jaya. Since publication of the *Herons Handbook*, it has become obvious that they breed regularly throughout north Borneo (Mann 1989, Sheldon and Marin 1984) to Luzon at the northern extreme of the Philippines, thus presenting a broader range than was previously thought. However, although the overall distribution of the species is better understood, it is still not possible to assess accurately the status of the populations on different islands, or that of the different races.

White-eared Night Heron. This species is considered critically endangered (IUCN 1996). There were no records of White-eared Night Heron between publication of the *Herons Handbook* (Hancock and Kushlan 1984) and 1990 when a bird was seen in southern Guangxi Province, China (Fang 1993). There have recently been sightings of birds of a similar size and build in the mountains of Hainan (J. MacKinnon pers. comm. 1993) but identification was not possible. In 1990 a White-eared Night Heron was recorded in the Longhu Mountains in Long-an County, Guangxi Province. Subsequently surveys were carried out in Long-an and neighbouring Wuming Counties. No further records were obtained from the Longhu Mountains, but birds were seen on two occasions at two well-separated sites in Wuming County (Fang 1993). A confirmed sighting of a juvenile was made in Guangxi Province in 1998 by ornithologists from Hong Kong.

The White-eared Night Heron is endemic to mainland south-eastern China and the offshore island of Hainan. Early records suggest that it was restricted to a zone between 40°N latitude and 105°E longitude. The species was discovered by John Whitehead in Hainan in 1899 (Ogilvie-Grant 1899) and was subsequently recorded in Hebei, Anhwei, Chekiang, Fujian and Kwangsi provinces (Styan 1902, La Touche 1913, 1917, Gee et al. 1948). It is suspected to occur in Jilin, Liaoning, Shaanxi, Henan, Gansu, Shandong, Sichuan and Xizang Zhizhiqu provinces (Hsu Weishu pers. comm. 1988 and Cheng Tso-hsin 1987). Birds were recorded in southern Guangxi in three different habitat-types in the survey reported by Fang (1993): a small montane river, a reservoir and in rice fields. This indication that White-eared Night Herons can exploit anthropogenic habitats is encouraging, but it is likely that they require extensive montane forest to breed.

Habitats in which the species has been located to date include dense hill-forest (Caldwell and Caldwell 1931) and birds have been recorded roosting in high trees (Styan 1902). This bears strong resemblance to the wintering habitat of the Malayan Night Heron in densely forested sub-montane/montane gorges and river valleys in Sri Lanka (S.W. Kotagama pers. comm. 1987). Therefore, the preferred habitat for this species appears to be well watered and densely forested areas in mountains and foothills.

Nesting has been suspected in pine trees and bamboo, but no nest has ever been described. Although searches may be biased toward these habitats, more success is likely from observing adult birds. La Touche (1917) found or was told of a nest at Fuchou (Fujian Province) in May 1915 and it has been suggested that the bird is a summer migrant to areas north of the Yangtze River, spending the summer in northern China and Tibet (Hancock and Kushlan 1984). However, it is described as resident in Hainan. It is hoped that current surveys will provide more information on the species' status, distribution and habitat requirements (see Chapter 17).

Japanese Night Heron. The Japanese Night Heron breeds in Japan, with a small number of breeding records from Taiwan (Collar et al. 1994). In Japan, it mainly nests on offshore islands, from the Izu Islands south of Yokohama (Hancock and Kushlan 1984), north as far as Niigata Prefecture, Honshu and south to Fukuoka Prefecture, Kyushu (Wild Bird Society of Japan 1978). It is listed as globally threatened by IUCN (1996). Surveys in 1977 recorded six confirmed, fourteen probable and one possible breeding site (Wild Bird Society of Japan 1978). After breeding, birds migrate through the Ryukyu Islands and Taiwan to the Philippines where they are regarded as an uncommon winter visitor (Dickinson et al. 1991), with occasional records in Borneo, Sulawesi and as far south as Halmahera. Rand and Rabor (1960) noted a few summer records from the Philippines, but there has been no suggestion that the species breeds there.

Occasional migrants occur north of the known breeding range in Hokkaido, southern Ussuriland and Sakhalin Island (Collar et al. 1994). Records from Pusan in May and June (Gore and Won 1971) suggest that this species may occasionally breed in Korea, but as yet this has not been confirmed. Similarly migrant birds regularly occur in mainland China and Hong Kong, but there is no proof of breeding. Migration is mainly in late March to April and October, but occasional birds overwinter in the Ryukyu and Kyushu Islands off the south of Japan and there are a few summer records from the Philippines.

Japanese Night Herons appear to favour dense forest, with loose colonies having been located on low trees over freshwater swamp on offshore islands in Japan (Austin and Kuroda 1953). The Japanese Night Heron is undoubtedly very scarce and vulnerable due to its habitat requirements. There are no details available of known stopover or wintering areas. Therefore priorities for conservation of this species must concentrate on areas within the known range offering suitable habitat.

Malayan Night Heron. The Malayan Night Heron has two distinct breeding populations, the western population occurs in south-west India (covered in

Malayan Night Heron. A juvenile of this little known species. Photo: Alan OwYong.

Chapter 3). The eastern population is distributed through the south-western Japanese islands and southern China west to the Nicobars and south to Palawan in the Philippines, with occasional records to Talaud and Halmahera in Indonesia (Coates et al. 1997). Deignan (1963) suggested that the species is resident in Thailand and recent information suggests that the stronghold of eastern populations is in Indo-China, with confirmed breeding throughout northern Thailand (Brockelman 1988, Round 1988), Vietnam (Robson et al. 1989) and Laos (Thewlis et al. 1995, W. Duckworth pers. comm. 1994). The Malayan Night Heron appears to breed throughout the Philippines and a distinct race *G. m. rufolineatus* has been described from Palawan (Hachisuka 1926). This race is said to be resident and if so, would differ enough from the nominate race to merit special consideration for conservation (although see below). As all forest areas in Palawan are under threat from development, logging and slash and burn, *G. m. rufolineatus* must be considered extremely vulnerable.

Records of nocturnal migrants in Peninsula Malaysia and migrating individuals from offshore islands in the Straits of Malacca (Medway and Wells 1976) indicate regular migration, although the sporadic nature of records from Singapore suggest that the majority of these birds winter in the Peninsula or in Sumatra. However, recent records from Taman Negara in the summer suggest the possibility of a Malaysian breeding population. Similarly a recent record of a bird in immature plumage in July from Udjung Kulon National Park (Java) suggests the possibility of a resident population there, as is the case with the population in Palawan. It is possible that these records indicate that the eastern population is largely sedentary, although data are not sufficient to prove this.

Preferred habitat appears to be densely forested wetlands and evergreen forests, largely at moderate altitude and in high rainfall zones. It is possible that this species is widespread and abundant in comparison to its congeners. However, the habitat on which it relies is threatened throughout its range. Rather than concentrating conservation effort upon this species, it may be more appropriate to use it as an indicator of good quality wet forest habitat; however, more detailed information is needed on its habitat requirements before any strong conclusions can be drawn for such assessment.

New Guinea Tiger Heron. There is no new information on the New Guinea Tiger Heron since publication of Hancock and Kushlan (1984), apart from a few casual sightings. There is therefore no possibility to assess the status of current populations and it is listed as near threatened by IUCN (1996). It appears to favour broad, heavily forested lowland rivers (100–300 m altitude) (Hancock and Kushlan 1984). The lack of information alone shows that something needs to be done. The habitat in which it occurs is still relatively widespread through parts of its range; however, much of the lowland forest in Irian Jaya, Papua New Guinea and adjacent islands is under threat from development. Immediate priorities should therefore relate to conservation of lowland forested rivers in these areas and an attempt to assess the status of existing populations.

Little Bittern. The Little Bittern is extralimital within our region, occurring only as a vagrant in Mongolia (D. Batdelger pers. comm.) and parts of western China (Cheng 1987).

Yellow Bittern. The Yellow Bittern is abundant throughout the region and appears to have recently undergone expansion of its breeding range (Lansdown 1987b). The breeding range of the Yellow Bittern was thought to be restricted to Sumatra, Indo-China, the People's Republic of China, Japan, Taiwan and parts of the Indian subcontinent. However, Deignan (1945 and 1963) suggested that it was resident in Thailand. Subsequently, a colony was located on Penang Island off the north-west coast of Peninsular Malaysia (Cairns 1954) and breeding was proven in a number of places in Peninsular Malaysia, Singapore and North Borneo (Lansdown 1987b). Birds were also recorded during the breeding season in Sulawesi (Uttley 1987, Coates et al. 1997). In Malaysia this increase in the known breeding range coincided with increased sightings during the (northern) summer months (D. R. Wells pers. comm. 1987). It is likely that these data indicate an increase in the species' breeding range. This range expansion may be the result of an increase in the area and distribution of rice agriculture in the region.

The birds breed mainly in bushes and reeds adjacent to extensive rice field systems. It is possible that the species has been able to colonise new areas, as forest and lowland wetlands are cleared and converted to wetland agriculture. In parts of its range, Yellow Bitterns have been considered beneficial to rice agriculture as they take large numbers of insects which occur as pests in rice fields (Lansdown and Rajanathan 1993). A similar beneficial role has been attributed to Javan Pond Herons in Sulawesi (Vermeulen and Spaans 1987). However, as the current high populations and success of this species appear to be dependent upon rice fields, it is likely that they will suffer from pesticides used in the region.

Schrenck's Bittern. Schrenck's Bittern appears to have a restricted breeding distribution, being limited to the region bounded by Ussuriland, Japan, Korea and northern China. Very little information is available on populations, although in some areas it has been described as common (Dementiev and Gladkov 1951, Vorobiev 1954, Hancock and Kushlan 1984). However, recent surveys in Japan only located a total of nine sites, of which three referred to proven breeding and the remainder to possible breeding records (Wild Bird Society of Japan 1978). It is listed as near threatened by IUCN (1996). Migrants occur through south-east Asia south to Sulawesi (Coates et al. 1997), but there are few records of wintering birds, and outside the breeding range authors appear to consider this species widely but thinly distributed. The suggestion by Coates et al. (1997) that Schrenck's Bittern breed in Sulawesi is likely to be erroneous. Schrenck's Bitterns are regularly recorded on spring and autumn migration in Hong Kong (Leven and Carey 1993). Records from stop-over sites and the wintering grounds almost exclusively involve isolated individuals, with rarely more than ten sightings per year from any one site. However, these records originate from a huge area. It is therefore very difficult to provide accurate population estimates.

Cinnamon Bittern. Cinnamon Bitterns are widespread and abundant throughout the region from eastern Siberia south to the Greater Sundas, including Sumatra, which is an addition to the known range and where it has been described as a common resident (Voous and van Marle 1988). Northern populations are migratory, while those to the south are sedentary. As is the case with Yellow Bittern, this species exploits rice field systems throughout much of its range and in Peninsular Malaysia will nest within the growing rice, although this may expose it to predation from snakes and rodents (Lansdown 1988). It is likely that resident populations in Peninsular Malaysia and parts of the Greater Sundas are augmented by an influx of wintering birds from the north (Voous and van Marle 1988). In Java (Wetland International data) and Peninsular Malaysia, rice farmers hunt both this species and Yellow Bitterns during the northern winter.

Black Bittern. The Black Bittern is apparently widespread and abundant, from southern China and Myanmar discontinuously south to Australia. Although the ecology of this species is relatively well known from the accounts of the collectors of the nineteenth and early twentieth centuries, we have only a very vague idea of its distribution and abundance. This is probably due to its crepuscular or nocturnal habits and preference for thick scrub. It appears to breed throughout its known range, although birds have been shown to migrate through Peninsular Malaysia through trapping at Fraser's Hill (Wells 1990a,b) and only in very few places has breeding been proven. Indeed we can be almost certain that Black Bitterns breed in

Thailand, as nestlings are occasionally sold at the Bangkok Sunday market (Round 1988), but no nest has been found in Thailand.

Eurasian Bittern. This species is mainly a non-breeding migrant to the region, from populations in Siberia, although it breeds through parts of Mongolia (D. Batdelger pers. comm.) and through northern China to its border with North Korea (Brazil 1992). Birds breeding in northern China, Mongolia and Russia winter south to Myanmar, southern Thailand and Luzon Island in the Philippines. It is nowhere common, but the increasing number of records from its wintering range suggests that populations are still fairly high.

Overall status

Some of the most endangered herons in the world are found in south and south-east Asia, as are some of the very abundant. Historically, most of the colonial herons of the region have been widespread and abundant. This is particularly true for Great White, Intermediate, Little and Cattle egrets, Eastern Reef Heron, Chinese and the *speciosa* race of the Javan Pond Heron, Black-crowned and Nankeen night herons, whilst Grey and Purple herons and the *continentalis* race of the Javan Pond heron are locally abundant.

The species that remain abundant are those that have been able to adapt to land use and other ecological changes. These are generally the least specialised, in particular those white egrets that feed inland and the pond herons and smaller *Ixobrychus* bitterns that now commonly forage in rice fields and fish farms. These areas may now represent the most important habitats for some of these species, reflecting the extent to which they have replaced natural wetlands. The species that have suffered most either have restricted ranges or are generally more specialised and have been unable to adapt to man-made habitats. In particular species that depend on mangroves (such as Sumatran and Green-backed herons) or other types of forest (such as *Gorsachius* night herons and New Guinea Tiger Heron) have suffered in recent years through the dramatic loss of good quality forest habitat. Similarly, coastal species such as Sumatran Heron, Swinhoe's Egret and New Guinea Tiger Heron will have suffered from increased tourism and damage to coastal habitats through development. Recently, conservation organisations have recognised that species such as White-eared Night Heron, New Guinea Tiger Heron and Schrenck's Bittern are now rare or vulnerable (Mountfort 1988), and seven species of heron from the region are internationally listed (IUCN 1996, see Chapter 17).

Critical Conservation and Regional Management Issues

The heron fauna of east and south-east Asia is threatened by a variety of factors resulting from man's activities. These vary from direct effects, such as hunting and exploitation of eggs and nestlings for food, to development and pollution causing loss of suitable foraging sites, to pesticide application leading to reduction in breeding success and adult survival rates. The most effective method of reducing the impact of these activities is through implementation of planning controls and legislation supported by appropriate and effective enforcement.

Colony sites

Colonial species have tended to be the most abundant herons; however, they are highly vulnerable to disturbance and habitat destruction at the breeding sites. Although there are few quantified data to demonstrate population trends, it is highly likely that colonial herons have suffered from man's activities in east and south-east Asia. There has been a dramatic reduction in the area of mangrove and other types of forest, leading to a reduction in the available breeding habitat. Similarly loss of natural wetlands decreased availability of feeding sites, although this has been slightly offset by the gradual increase in land under flooded rice cultivation.

Data from Hong Kong (Table 4.2) show fluctuations which may be real or may also be due to birds moving among sites. Nine heronries were recorded in Hong Kong in 1958, and there were eight in 1993 of which only three were the same as those known in 1958. Overall numbers do not appear to have declined dramatically, but there has been a consistent change in colony site, with a general move away from inland sites dependent upon rice fields, to coastal sites near fish ponds. For most species, overall trends in population size have not changed substantially. The numbers of Black-crowned Night Herons and Great White Egrets have increased in the territory, but Great White Egret only bred for three years. The reasons for the loss of Swinhoe's Egret as a breeding species are not clear, but Hong Kong is on the extreme south-western limit of its breeding range. Short-term colonisation and subsequent abandonment of sites is common for birds in this situation.

Many heronries in Peninsular Malaysia have been abandoned, including a colony of up to 20 000 Black-crowned Night Herons in the Matang mangrove forest, Perak State. This may have been due to pesticide fogging to control mosquitoes. A colony of approximately 20 pairs of Grey Heron in mangrove in Selangor State was abandoned when trees supporting the colony were felled for domestic use. Similarly, all other colonies of large herons which have been located in the Peninsula in the past have subsequently been abandoned.

Data from colonies in Vietnam (Duc 1992) are alarming (Table 4.3), with dramatic declines in all species recorded. The figures presented here suggest that the overall population in those colonies which have been counted has halved in five years. The decline in populations of all species is attributed to a combination of over-exploitation of eggs and young; conversion of colonies to shrimp ponds; felling of mangrove for domestic use and construction; conversion of natural habitats to agriculture; and hunting.

Some of these losses may in part be due to changing attitudes toward wildlife. Where in the past, certain species were considered to bring good luck or good hunting, the respect which this engendered has given over to a more mercenary attitude where land not in use for production is considered wasted. For example, in Taiwan, farmers traditionally considered Little and Cattle egrets to be good omens and that a heronry near the house would bring good fortune. This belief has declined and with development, most people regard heronries as noisy and dirty and regard the birds as pests, accusing them of damaging crops and taking stock from fish farms (L. L. Severinghaus pers. comm. 1993). In Taiwan, there appears to have been a marked trend for a reduction in the overall number of heronries, coupled with general movement of heronries away from inland settlements to the coast (Chung 1992, Yen 1992), which has also happened in Hong Kong (Young and Cha 1995). The known number of colonies in Taiwan dropped from 60 in 1951 (Hachisuka and Udagawa 1951) to 26 in the mid-seventies (Chen and Yen 1977). The replacement of coastal forests with planted Australian pine (*Casuarina equisetifolia*) as windbreaks has provided alternative nesting sites, but suitable feeding sites are less readily available due to pollution and development.

   Disturbance may also be a factor in the loss of breeding colonies. However, it can be seen from two sites in Hong Kong (one adjacent to a busy railway station, the other over a road) and from colonies in Indian cities (see Chapter 3) that colony sites can be established and survive within urban and industrial complexes and other areas with high levels of human activity so long as the herons are not bothered severely. It is likely that if suitable and adequate feeding and nesting sites are retained, herons can tolerate high levels of disturbance.

Habitat loss

The main changes in the region are land-use type and distribution, including: increase in industrialisation and urbanisation; conversion of natural habitats to agriculture and migration of human populations toward urban centres. Generally, freshwater wetlands have been converted to agriculture, while coastal wetlands have been lost to aquaculture and urban or industrial development. The vast majority of these changes in land-use have been detrimental to wildlife populations, generally causing localised extinction and overall decreases in species diversity. However, these impacts have been offset to some extent for species that are able to use created wetland habitats such as rice fields and fish or shrimp farming.

   Many wetland and forest sites in south-east Asia are threatened by development and habitat degradation. This results not only from major regional and local development which can be controlled through planning policy and legislation, but also through casual, uncontrolled and largely unknown changes in land-use such as slash-and-burn agriculture and ribbon development. In addition to the dramatic reduction in breeding heron populations illustrated by trends in breeding numbers in Vietnam and Hong Kong (above), reductions have taken place in the range of other large water birds such as Lesser Adjutant (*Leptoptilis javanicus*) and Milky Storks (*Mycteria cinerea*) in south-east Asia. It is likely that all large water birds are suffering reduction in available breeding sites through felling of trees providing nest sites and loss of foraging areas to urban and industrial development.

   Figures for the historical and recent loss of natural habitats throughout the region are consistently alarming: mangroves in Thailand and Vietnam from 1967 to 1979, 22% (806 km²) and from 1960s to 1970s, 40–50% (124 000 ha); lakes in People's Republic of China from 1950s to 1980s, c. 11% (500 lakes); freshwater swamp in Sumatra and Indonesia to date, 22% (Scott 1989, Whitten et al. 1987). These losses continue, despite the efforts of conservation organisations and national governments. Countries such as Singapore have lost the majority of their natural wetlands, and those which remain are fragmented and generally isolated. Mangrove forest in many areas is being cleared for development (Whitten et al. 1987, 1988), for commercial products such as firewood and charcoal, and for fish farming (Silvius et al. 1986). Similarly, natural freshwater wetlands are being drained and developed, or replaced by commercial fish farms. Where natural wetlands have been replaced by man-made wetlands (for example in much of Java) the need for conservation of the remaining natural wetlands assumes an even greater priority. There is a worrying trend in Hong Kong from artificial wetlands such as rice fields and fish ponds which supported large numbers of water birds, toward increasing industrial and urban development. Across the border in the Shenzen Special Economic Zone of Guangdong Province in China the government incentives to industry are leading to widespread and largely uncoordinated land development on a massive scale. Throughout the region, it is likely that even if large-scale development can be controlled, there will be a period of agricultural intensification leading to reduction in the suitability of artificial wetlands for water birds, as has occurred throughout developed countries.

Many of the natural wetland feeding habitats for herons in Hong Kong were lost in the early part of this century due to their conversion to man-made agricultural wetlands, for instance rice fields, shrimp ponds (called "gei-wai" in Hong Kong and "tembaks" in other parts of Asia) and fish ponds. It appears that the herons were able to adapt to feed in these new habitats, but with decreased profitability of these traditional land uses, large areas have been lost to development (much of which is illegal). At the end of the 1980s, and particularly the start of the 1990s, large areas of fish ponds were illegally filled in for container parks and road-side garages. As a result, the Hong Kong Government enacted planning legislation to prevent such changes in land-use, including establishing zones with fish ponds as Conservation Areas. To support this legislation, the government also commissioned a study into the ecological value of fish ponds. This study concluded that although artificial, they are still a valuable wildlife habitat. In 1995, when the Mai Po and Inner Deep Bay Ramsar Site was designated, the boundary was drawn to include a significant area of fish ponds. This Ramsar site, including the fish ponds has been shown to support numbers of ardeids of regional importance (Carey in preparation). Similarly, in Japan there is a trend for replacement of the traditional open feeder drain systems with culverts, and this has resulted in a 30% reduction in local heron populations (Narasue and Uchida 1993). It is possible that this reduction actually relates to birds moving to other areas to feed and nest, as there has been an increase in fish farming in parts of Honshu and this is apparently linked to a local increase in heron populations (Narusue 1992, M. Narusue pers. comm. 1994).

Water pollution and pesticide use

Water pollution is often an indirect consequence of development, which may take place in a number of ways. Increases in sediment loading and turbidity can arise as a result of erosion through inappropriate land-use, mainly in the upper reaches of the catchment. Gross chemical pollution may derive from discharges from industrial complexes, while residual pesticide and fertiliser run-off from agriculture can cause eutrophication and disruption of aquatic communities. Less significant pollution can be caused by discharge of run-off from highways and other impermeable surfaces, containing heavy metals and hydrocarbons; discharge of inadequately treated domestic wastewater; and release of contaminated leachate from waste disposal sites. All these factors lead to lower water quality, with consequent reduction in species diversity and abundance, and ultimately morbidity or mortality of those organisms higher up the food chain. As top predators, herons are highly susceptible to a build-up of toxins from prey. With the application of huge quantities of pesticides (many of which have long been banned in western countries) to irrigated crops, it is likely that there will be a decline in predators in the region similar to that experienced in the USA and Europe in the 1960s.

Hunting

Within the region, a number of studies have demonstrated that massive numbers of migrant and wintering water birds are taken every year in areas such as Pattani Bay in southern Peninsular Thailand and Javan rice fields (Asian Wetland Bureau data). Ongoing surveys at several colonies around the Great Lake in Cambodia have revealed that the collection of eggs and chicks of colonial water birds, including egrets and herons, for local consumption and sale is a "traditional activity" (Parr et al. 1996, Mundkur et al. 1995). According to local people, the breeding populations of many species have declined. Similarly, the breeding population declines recorded from southern Vietnam (Duc 1992) are in part attributed to over-exploitation of eggs and nestlings. However, a recent study in Java has shown a decline in the numbers caught, thought to be either a result of an education programme, or low profits. There is little quantified information on the effects of exploitation and hunting in the region.

In 1995, a survey of the breeding colonies around the Pearl River Estuary, adjacent to Hong Kong, found that the five colonies located were dominated by Black-crowned Night Herons and supported few white egrets. Neighbouring colonies in Hong Kong support more or less equal numbers of night herons and egrets. This difference may be explained by hunting, as diurnal white egrets are shot or trapped, whereas the nocturnal night herons generally avoid being hunted (Young and Cha 1995). In addition, at two of the colonies in the Pearl River Delta, local villagers have been harvesting chicks annually for 25 years. This harvest is controlled by the village committee and appears to be sustainable (Young and Cha 1995).

Research and monitoring

Further information is needed on a number of species within the region. Unlike the USA and Europe, it is as yet impossible to provide accurate population estimates for any of the herons which occur in the region, except possibly Swinhoe's Egret, although small colonies of this species are still being discovered. With the dramatic loss of wetland and forest habitat, it is likely that many species are declining, and without a quantitative baseline, it will not be possible to recognise significant declines before they have passed recovery. Work being undertaken or supported by organisations such as Wetlands International, the Oriental Bird Club and national branches of the World Wide Fund for Nature will provide some of the necessary data. There is therefore a need for a comprehensive research programme in the region. It is critical to census breeding and roosting populations of the more common species to provide a baseline for future comparison. Although conservation of the wintering grounds and stopover sites is important, it is vital that census work concentrates on breeding populations as these are as yet little known and the vast majority are under threat from habitat degradation, disturbance and development. Imperial Heron, White-eared Night Heron, Japanese Night Heron and New Guinea Tiger Heron are so threatened and little known that we are unable to start to address their conservation needs. It is therefore necessary to establish a baseline from which conservation action can develop, based on distribution, current population size, ecological requirements to assess constraints on populations, and threats.

In Hong Kong the priority for research involves identification of which habitats around colonies are critical for foraging breeding birds. This is carried out by following the flight lines of breeding adults as they leave the colony and has yielded important information such as distances travelled to feed and the relative importance of different habitats (Cornish 1996, Wong 1991, Young 1998). This method is simple and cheap and lends itself well to long-term monitoring.

Surveys and studies of habitat requirements are urgently needed since heron habitats have been lost at an accelerating rate due to the economic boom in many Asian countries, where there is often little consideration of the potential effects of development upon the environment (Lansdown 1991). As a result, many sites have been lost without knowledge of their value.

The value of herons as indicators of wetland habitat quality has long been recognised (Hafner et al. 1987). This application of ecological data could be extended to use of species such as the *Gorsachius* night herons and Sumatran Heron as indicators of good wet forest habitat, as they appear to be dependent upon primary forest with very low human presence. However, more detailed information is needed on their ecological requirements before site protection or management can be based upon their presence.

Planning policy and legislation

There is no specific legislation for the protection of heron species in the region. Many species are listed in national ordinances such as the Wild Animals Preservation and Protection Act (1960, and subsequent amendments) in Thailand, which give protection to a list of species, with exclusions covering those for which a particular method or season for hunting is specified. As such, there is little or no priority protection for rare or vulnerable species. More widespread protection is provided through legislation designating protected areas such as National Parks and Nature Reserves. However, Round (1988) suggests that such protection may have little control over casual, low-intensity exploitation. It is likely that control of exploitation of wildlife within protected areas can only be achieved through improvement in the standard of living and changes in the attitude of local people.

Although there is no specific legislation to protect herons in Hong Kong, the Wildlife Protection Ordinance prohibits all hunting and protects the nesting sites of all birds. Several of the traditional colony sites have been given Site of Special Scientific Interest (SSSI) status and others have been identified as candidate SSSIs. However, the foraging habitats which support these colonies are rarely protected because of the large area involved (Wong 1991; Young 1993), much of which is in private ownership. Therefore, colony sites are being abandoned, not due to problems with the colonies themselves, but through the loss of the surrounding feeding areas. Research is currently under way to identify the foraging areas supporting birds nesting in each colony to improve the overall protection of breeding herons in Hong Kong.

It is vital for the future of endangered and vulnerable species, and for the economies of the countries in the region, that control is exerted over the exploitation

Herons in East and South-east Asia 97

of natural resources. Sound planning policies, taking into consideration environmental values, provide the only method for long-term protection of habitats which support vulnerable species, and for sustainable use of remaining natural resources. However, one of the main difficulties facing countries where such policies have been introduced is effective enforcement.

A combination of strict enforcement of adherence to the Convention on International Trade in Endangered Species (CITES), coupled with enforced habitat and site protection, linked to sound planning policies, is likely to best serve the interests of wildlife conservation in the region. Steps toward such a system have been taken, for example in Malaysia, where the Department of Environment has worked in conjunction with national and international conservation organisations to prepare state plans which incorporate environmental considerations into state planning policy. Similarly in addition to requiring Environmental Impact Assessments (EIA) for development projects of a specified scale or nature, legislation covering EIA in the Philippines states that any development proposed for specified vulnerable habitats must be accompanied by a statement of potential environmental impacts and measures proposed to mitigate these impacts. The main problems with this system arise through difficulty in ensuring that proposed mitigation measures are implemented and monitored to assess their effectiveness (Lansdown 1993).

Conclusions

The main concerns involving conservation of *Ardeidae* in east and south-east Asia are habitat protection and management. This is most urgent for wetlands, particularly freshwater marshes, estuaries and mangrove and primary rain forest, particularly in Japan, southern China and Irian Jaya. There is also a need for rigorous control of exploitation and pollution of coastal and inland water bodies.

These concerns are not specific to the *Ardeidae* and have been a priority for national and international conservation for some time. However, it is clear that unless action is taken in the near future to protect and manage these habitats, particularly in areas known to support White-eared and Japanese night herons, New Guinea Tiger Heron and Swinhoe's Egret, some of these will be lost. Data are needed on the distribution and abundance of these species and Schrenck's Bittern, so as to enable protection of sites and habitats upon which they depend.

The ultimate aim of conservation of herons in east and south-east Asia should be to protect enough sites of sufficient size to enable existing heron populations to exist on a self-sustaining basis. We know that some heron populations are declining and that some are so small that they cannot be considered safe. Therefore if the conservation organisations are serious in their intention to protect and enhance water birds, a major effort must be made to protect herons (at the same time as other water birds and wetlands). The main priorities for conservation of herons in east and south-east Asia are to establish a baseline data set for all species and populations through mapping the breeding distribution, migration routes and stopover and wintering sites, census of breeding populations and continuation of the Asian Waterfowl Census. In addition, there is a need to identify the main threats to each population and carry out studies of the ecological requirements and constraints upon populations of the less known and more threatened species. A catalogue of heronries has been prepared for India by S. Subramanya (see Chapter 3), and a directory of organisations and individuals working on herons for Japan through work by Masae Narasue of the Wild Bird Society of Japan. Such data should be compiled for the region through compilation of existing data (much of which has already been done), followed by the establishment of a network of organisations and individuals involved in heron research and conservation. This will facilitate the production of a comprehensive action plan and should not be too onerous or time-consuming. The data should be compiled into a database which can be updated as new information becomes available. The database can then be used to establish a conservation aim for each species and the means of accomplishing this aim. The consequences (whether or not they are successful) of any action on this basis can be fed back into this database, providing a continuous process of review and assessment through a dynamic action plan. Such a database would be available to all conservation bodies and researchers working on wetlands in the region. This can then guide the conservation funds available so that they can be efficient.

Although data compilation and availability will facilitate appropriate prioritisation of conservation action, this is only a first step toward heron conservation in the region. Conservation of wetlands and the species which they support will only work if it has the support of local people. There are already a number of projects which have successfully involved local people in conservation. An important first step is to make people aware of the relationship between their actions and local ecology, linked to demonstration of the vulnerability of wetland habitats. In many cases local people may not understand that birds which they see regularly are actually rare. Following this, it is possible to involve local people in monitoring populations of rare species to the extent that they begin to take pride in "their" habitats or species.

It is equally vital that public education and awareness projects should not concentrate on single species (although 'flagship' species are a good starting point to raise interest); wetland conservation will only be successful if people have an understanding of ecological relationships and dependencies within local habitats.

5. Herons in Africa and the Malagasy Region

Donald Turner

This chapter discusses the heron populations of continental Africa south of the Sahara (i.e., south of the Western Palearctic as defined by Cramp and Simmons (1977)) together with the islands of the western Indian Ocean known collectively as the Malagasy Region (Campbell and Lack 1985) (Fig. 5.1, Table 5.1). The area covered is generally tropical, including the countries of west, central, east, north-east, and southern Africa. Africa is known as a land of wildlife, and herons are no exception, with many species being very common in suitable habitats throughout the continent. This chapter includes the islands of the Malagasy Region, Seychelles, Aldabra, Comores, Madagascar, Réunion, Mauritius, and Rodrigues, all of which support races of endemic or near-endemic herons.

The Heron Fauna

The heron fauna of the Afrotropical and Malagasy regions comprises 22 species (Table 5.1) including 9 endemic species and 14 endemic races. These account for almost 40% of the world's herons (Table 0.1). African herons include the Black-headed Heron, Slaty Egret, Rufous-bellied Heron, White-backed Night Heron, White-crested Tiger Heron, and Dwarf Bittern. Races endemic to continental Africa include the Intermediate Egret (*Egretta intermedia brachyrhyncha*), Green-backed Heron (*Butorides striatus atricapillus*), Little Bittern (*Ixobrychus minutus payesii*), and Eurasian Bittern (*Botaurus stellaris capensis*).

Due to their isolation, the islands of the Malagasy Region support an array of endemics. The Black Heron is shared between Madagascar, the largest island, and the African continent. Madagascar also has an endemic Grey Heron (*Ardea cinerea firasa*), Purple Heron (*Ardea purpurea madagascariensis*), Green-backed Heron (*Butorides striatus rutenbergi*) and Little Bittern (*Ixobrychus minutus podiceps*). The Malagasy Pond Heron, a Great White Egret (*Egretta alba melanorhynchos*), and a Little

Heron Conservation
ISBN 0-12-430130-4

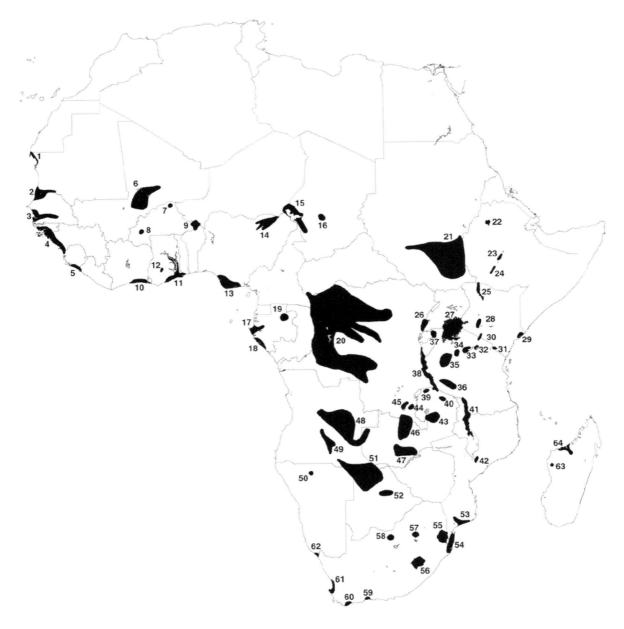

Fig. 5.1   Important heron areas in Africa and the Malagasy region.

Egret (*Egretta garzetta dimorpha*) are shared between the Malagasy Region and continental Africa. The Seychelles have an endemic Cattle Egret (*Bubulcus ibis seychellarum*) and a Green-backed Heron (*Butorides striatus degens*). Other endemic Green-backed Heron races are those of the Comores (*B. s. rhizophorae*) and Aldabra (*B. s. crawfordi*).

Key to Fig. 5.1   Important heron areas in Africa and the Malagasy Region.

1 Mauritania—Banc d'Arguin
2 Senegal—Including Djoudj National Park, Bassin du Ndiael, Senegal Gueumbeul Wildlife Reserve
3 Senegal—Delta du Saloum
4 Guinea, Guinea–Bissau—Including Ile Alcatraz, Iles Tristao, Rio Kapatchez, Rio Pongo, Konkoure, Lagoa de Cufada
5 Sierra Leone, Liberia—Coast
6 Mali—Inner Niger Delta, including Walado Debo, Lac Debo, Seri, Lac Horo
7 Burkina Faso—La Mare d'Oursi
8 Burkina Faso—La Mare aux Hippopotames
9 Burkina Faso, Niger—Parc National du 'W'
10 Ivory Coast—Coast
11 Ghana—Including Muni Lagoon, Densu Delta, Sakumo Lagoon, Songor Lagoon, Anlo-Keta Lagoon complex
12 Ghana—Owabi Wildlife Sanctuary
13 Nigeria—Niger River Delta
14 Nigeria—Hadejia, Komadugu Gana
15 Nigeria, Chad, Niger, Cameroon—Lake Chad
16 Chad—Lac Fitri
17 Gabon—Wingha, Winghe
18 Gabon—Petit Loango, Sette Cama
19 Gabon—Ogoove' River
20 Democratic Republic of Congo (formerly Zaire)—Congo Basin
21 Sudan—The Nile Sudd
22 Ethiopia—Lake Tana
23 Ethiopia—Rift Valley wetlands, including Lakes Ziway, Langano, Abijatta, and Shala
24 Ethiopia—Rift Valley wetlands, including Lakes Awassa and Abaya.
25 Ethiopia, Kenya—Omo Delta and Lake Turkana
26 Uganda, Congo—Queen Elizabeth and Albert National Parks, including Lakes George and Edward
27 Uganda, Kenya, Tanzania—Lake Victoria
28 Kenya—Rift Valley wetlands, including Lakes Nakuru, Naivasha, Elementaita, and Oloiden
29 Kenya—Tana Delta wetlands
30 Kenya, Tanzania—Rift Valley wetlands, including Lakes Magadi and Natron
31 Kenya, Tanzania—Lake Jipe and surrounding wetlands
32 Tanzania—Lake Manyara
33 Tanzania—Lake Eyasi
34 Tanzania—Wembere swamps
35 Tanzania—Malagarasi/ Moyowosi wetlands
36 Tanzania—Rukwa Valley wetlands
37 Tanzania, Rwanda—Kagera wetlands, including Akagera National Park
38 Burundi, Republic of Congo, Tanzania, Zambia—Lake Tanganyika
39 Zambia—Mweru Wantipa wetlands
40 Zambia— Luangwa Valley wetlands
41 Mozambique, Tanzania, Malawi—Lake Malawi
42 Malawi—Lake Chilwa
43 Zambia—Bangweulu Swamps
44 Democratic Republic of Congo (formerly Zaire)—Lake Tshangalele
45 Democratic Republic of Congo (formerly Zaire)—Lake Delcommune
46 Zambia—Kafue River, Lukanga Swamp
47 Zambia—Including Kafue Flats, Lochinvar National Park, Blue Lagoon National Park
48 Angola, Zambia—Camia National Park
49 Angola—Bicavan National Park
50 Namibia—Etosha National Park
51 Botswana, Namibia, Angola—Okavango Delta
52 Botswana—Makgadkgadi Pan
53 Mozambique—Seasonal wetlands
54 Mozambique, South Africa—Including turtle beaches and coral reefs of Tongaland, St. Lucia system, Kosi Bay, Lake Sibaya
55 Swaziland—Seasonal pans
56 Lesotho—Seasonal wetlands
57 South Africa—Blesbokspruit Bird Sanctuary
58 South Africa—Barberspan Nature Reserve
59 South Africa—Wilderness Lakes
60 South Africa—De Mond Nature Reserve Heuningnes Estuary, De Hoop Vlei Nature Reserve
61 South Africa—Verlorenvlei, Langebaan National Park
62 South Africa—Orange River Mouth
63 Malagasy Republic (Madagascar)— Antsalova wetlands including Lake Bemamba
64 Malagasy Republic (Madagascar)— Betsiboka River and Lac Kinkony wetlands

Table 5.1 Status of herons in Africa and the Malagasy Region.

	GrH	BhH	MH	GoH	PuH	GWE	SIE	BH	IE	LE	CE	SqH	MPH	RBH	GbH	BCNH	WBNH	WcTH	LtB	YB	DB	EB
Mauritania	++	++		+	+	++		+	++	++	++	++			++	++			++		++	+
Senegal	++	++		++	++	++		++	++	++	++	++			++	++	++	++	+		++	+
Gambia	+	++		++	+	++		++	++	++	++	++			++	++	++	+	++		+	+
Guinea-Bissau	+	++		++	+	++		++	++	++	++	+			++	++	++		++			
Guinea	+	+		++	+	++		+	+	+	+	+			+	+		++	+	+	++	
Sierra Leone	+	+		+	+	+		+	+	++	+	++			+	+	+	++	++		++	
Liberia	+	+		+	+	+		+	+	++	+	+			++	+	+	++	+		++	
Ivory Coast	++	++		++	+	+		+	+	++	++	+			++	++	++	++	++	+	+	
Mali	++	++		+	++	++		++	++		++	++			++	+	+		++		++	
Burkina Faso	+	++		++	+	+		+	+	+	++	+			++	+			+		+	
Ghana	++	++		+	++	++		++	+	++	++	++			+	+	+	+	++	+	++	+
Togo	+	++		+	+	+		+	+	+	+	+			+	+		+	+		+	
Benin	+	+		++	+	+			+	+	+	+			+	+	+		+		+	
Niger	++	++		+	+	++		+	++	++	++	++			++	++	+		++		+	
Nigeria	++	++		+	+	++		++	++	++	++	++			++	++	++	+	++		+	++
Cameroon	+	++		+	+	+		+	+	++	++	+			+	+	+	++	+		++	++
Chad	+	++		+	+	++		++	++	++	++	++			++	+			+		++	
Central African Republic	+	+	++	++	+	+		+	+	+	++	+			+	++	+	+	++		+	+
Gabon	+	+	+	+	+	+		+	+	++	+	+			++	+	++	++	++		+	+
Equatorial Guinea (Fernando Po = Bioko)										++	+	+			+	+		+	+		+	
Sao Tome and Principe	+				+	+		+		++	++				++				++		+	
Congo (Brazzaville)	+	+		+	+	++			++	+	++	+			+	+	+	+	+	+		

Species

	GrH	BhH	MH	GoH	PuH	GWE	SIE	BH	IE	LE	CE	SqH	MPH	RBH	GbH	BCNH	WBNH	WcTH	LtB	YB	DB	EB
Democratic Republic of Congo	+	++	++	++	++	+		+	++	+	++	++	+	++	++	++	++		++	++	++	+
Sudan	++	++	++	++	++	+		+	++	++	++	++			++	++	++	+	++	++	++	+
Ethiopia	++	++	++	+	+	++		+	++	+	++	++			++	+	++		+	+	+	+
Eritrea	+	+	++	+	+	++			+	++	++	+		++	++	+	+	+	+	++	+	
Djibouti	+		++	+	+				+	++	++	+		++	+	+	+		+			
Somalia	+	++	++	++	+	++		+	+	++	++	+	+	++	++	+	+		+	+	++	
Kenya	++	++	++	++	++	++		++	++	++	++	++	+	++	++	++	+	+	++	++	++	+
Tanzania	++	++	++	++	++	++	++	++	++	++	++	++	++	++	++	++	++		++	++	++	+
Uganda	+	++	++	++	++	++	+	+	++	++	++	++	+	++	++	++	++		++	+	+	
Rwanda	++	++	++	++	++	++	++	+	++	++	++	++	+	++	++	+	+		++	+	+	
Burundi	+	++	+	+	+	++	+	+	++	+	++	++	+	+	+	+		+	+	+	+	
Angola	++	++	++	++	++	++	+	++	++	++	++	++	+	++	++	++	+		++	+	++	+
Namibia	++	++	++	++	+	+		+	+	++	++	++	+	++	++	++	+		++	++	++	
South Africa	++	++	++	++	++			++	++	++	++	++	+	++	++	++	++		++	++	++	++
Botswana	++	++	++	++	++	+		++	++	++	++	++	+	++	++	++	++		+	+	++	++
Zambia	++	++	++	++	++	++	+	++	++	++	+	++	+	++	++	++	++		++	++	++	+
Zimbabwe	++	++	++	++	++	++	+	++	++	++	++	++	+	++	++	++	++		++	++	++	+
Malawi	++	++	++	++	++	++		+	++	+	++	++	+	++	++	++	++		++	+	++	+
Mozambique	+	++	++	++	+	+		+	+	++	++	++	+	+	++	+	++		++	+	+	
Seychelles	+					+				+		+										
Aldabra	++										++	+	++	++	+	+						
Comores	+		+			++				++	++	++	+	++	+							
Madagascar	++		++	++	++	++		++	++	++	++	++	++	++	++	++			++			
Réunion										+	+											
Mauritius	+									+	++			++								
Rodrigues														++								

++ = nesting population, + = present, not nesting.

Environmental Conditions

The African continent is some 100 million years old, having previously been part of the Gondwanaland continental landmass. Today it is a vast and diverse area with varying climatic conditions and a wide variety of wetlands favoured by the heron avifauna (Fig. 5.1). Throughout the continent, Africa's climate is dominated by two broad zones of high pressure that overlie the northern and southern subtropical regions, while a broad area of low pressure (known as the Equatorial Trough) overlies the central equatorial zone. This Equatorial Trough moves north and south during the year, bringing with it the climatic changes so characteristic of the various regions. Recent droughts in many parts of the continent are possibly the result of a reduced northward and southward movement of this rain-bearing trough. North-easterly and south-easterly trade winds blow onshore from the Indian Ocean, each one being respectively north and south of the moving Equatorial Trough, while the westerly air streams that pick up moisture from the Atlantic Ocean are responsible for seasonal monsoon rains over much of West Africa. In the northern and southern tropics there is one main rainy season (June–September in the north; December–February in the south). In the latitudes over which the Equatorial Trough passes there are two rainy seasons each followed by a mainly dry one, hence only two types of seasons: wet and dry. Heavy annual rainfall is largely confined to the equatorial zone, while both the northern and southern subtropical regions contain large areas of desert and are subjected to periods of drought.

While much of the continent comprises savanna, rain forest, dry woodlands, scrub and semi-desert, high mountains are found close to the Rift Valleys in eastern Africa, as well as elsewhere in Cameroon, Rwanda, Uganda, Ethiopia, Kenya, Tanzania and southern Africa. The great rivers, such as the Zaire, Niger, Nile, and Zambezi, and great lakes such as Victoria, Kariba, Malawi, Tanganyika, Turkana, Volta, and Chad provide permanent, although often fluctuating, aquatic systems. Particularly important to herons are the floodplains of the Niger and Zambezi rivers and the Lake Chad Basin, as are several great wetland systems including the Congo freshwater swamp forests, covering some 80 000 km²; the Sudd in the Upper Nile Valley, covering over 50 000 km²; the Lake Victoria Basin wetlands also totalling over 50 000 km², and the Okavango Delta.

African herons, for the most part, depend on these wetlands, which comprise some of the largest expanses of wetland in the world. Among the important heron habitats are mangrove swamps, coastal lagoons, riverine floodplains and woodlands, lakes, seasonal and permanent marshes especially papyrus swamps, reservoirs, and irrigated fields. However, with water resources coming under increasing pressure from urban and industrial users and the demand for agricultural and grazing lands ever-increasing, vast freshwater swamps, floodplains, coastal mangroves and tidal wetlands are being reduced in size, and their productivity is declining. At the same time periods of severe drought have placed increasing pressure upon the rain-fed wetlands of the northern and southern tropics. As a result, many floodplains and marshes once utilised as only dry-season refugia are now being subjected to year-round grazing and permanent cultivation, and so they too are rapidly becoming less productive for the heron fauna.

Changing Status of Herons

Data available

While the geographic range of species is fairly well known, solid population estimates are rather localised. Quantitative trends are seldom possible over large areas due to the lack of prior population assessments. Generally, species whose populations appear to be increasing are Black-headed Heron and Cattle Egret throughout Africa, and the Grey Heron in southern Africa. On the other hand, several species appear to be under some degree of threat, notably the Slaty Egret and Great Bittern in southern Africa; Little Bittern, Grey, Malagasy, Purple, Black and Malagasy Pond herons in Madagascar, and the Green-backed Heron and Yellow Bittern in Seychelles.

Species status

Grey Heron. This species is widely distributed throughout Africa and the Malagasy Region. Sub-Saharan Africa from the Atlantic east to Sudan, Ethiopia and Somalia is the main wintering area for Palearctic breeding birds. Numerous recoveries of ringed birds from Europe have been reported from the Cape Verde Islands, Senegal, Guinea, Sierra Leone, Mali, Burkina Faso, Ghana, Nigeria, Togo, Sudan and Ethiopia. In addition, small sedentary populations breed at the height of

Grey Heron race *monicae*. This pale race nests exclusively on two breeding islands on Banc d'Arguin in Mauritania. Photo: Jean François Hellio and Nicolas van Ingen.

the rains in Senegal, Mali, Niger, Cote d'Ivoire, Ghana, Nigeria, Sudan, Ethiopia, Kenya, Tanzania and Rwanda.

The very pale and sometimes dubiously recognised *A. c. monicae* is a ground-nesting bird on Banc d'Arguin, Mauritania, whose population has ranged from 1100–1600 pairs (de Naurois 1969) to 2400 pairs in 1984–85 (Campredon 1987), while more recently 4188 nests were counted between May and December 1997 (Hafner et al. 1998b). Individuals regularly reach Senegal where at least one bird has shown characteristics intermediate between those of *monicae* and nominate *cinerea* (Dowsett and Dowsett-Lemaire 1993).

In southern Africa, Grey Herons are resident throughout the region with increasing populations in Zimbabwe and South Africa following the establishment of man-made dams, reservoirs and irrigation areas (Vernon 1976, Irwin 1981, Ewbank pers. comm., Tarboton pers. comm.).

In Madagascar a small endemic population (*A. c. firasa*) is constantly threatened by hunting, predation at breeding colonies, and loss of habitat, and although a January 1993 census revealed 565 present on lakes around Antsalova (Rabarisoa 1993), it remains highly vulnerable and largely confined to western areas. While also attributed to the Comores and Aldabra by Langrand (1990), Benson (1960) felt that birds in the Comores were best considered nominate *cinerea*, but Penny (1974) considered Aldabra birds intermediate between *cinerea* and *firasa*. Clearly the true taxonomic position of Grey Herons in the western Indian Ocean (outside of Madagascar) remains in some doubt.

Black-headed Heron. This species is common and widespread throughout the Afrotropical Region with every indication that populations are increasing. The Black-headed Heron is a largely terrestrial species preferring open, grassy and cultivated ground where it is a solitary feeder on frogs, rodents and larger invertebrates. Unlike other *Ardea*, it is often found some distance from permanent water, and can be adequately described as the dry-land counterpart of the slightly larger wading Grey Heron.

It is distinctly migratory over much of West Africa, regularly moving north to breed in the Sudano–Guinean and Sahel vegetation belts as the rains start in May, returning south when they stop in October. A similar movement occurs in the Sudan, while in the Luangwa Valley in Zambia it is present only during the November–May rains (Hancock and Kushlan 1984). Bannerman (1930) found records for only eight out of 22 West African countries, compared to 21 out of 22 now (see Table 5.1). This is further evidence that in recent decades populations appear to be increasing and benefiting greatly from man-made or urbanised habitats. Breeding colonies may be found in several towns and cities (Kampala, Nairobi, Malindi, Arusha, Dar-es-Salaam and Bulawayo) as well as in increasing numbers in mixed colonies with Grey Herons and Cattle Egrets close to man-made dams and reservoirs in Zimbabwe (Vernon 1976, Ewbank pers. comm.). In many year-round occupied urban colonies the number of occupied nests is directly correlated to rainfall, with pronounced peaks in the wettest months and lulls associated with periods of drought (North 1963).

In southern Africa where overall numbers remain fairly constant throughout the year, nestlings tend to disperse widely and rapidly after fledging, the furthermost recovery to date, that of a two-and-a-half year-old bird, was to Zimbabwe, 830 km NE (Tarboton 1977).

Malagasy Heron. This large yet little known Malagasy endemic is reported to have declined alarmingly and to face extinction unless completely protected (Milon et al. 1973). It is considered to be globally threatened (Baillie and Groombridge 1996) and is currently classified as vulnerable (Collar et al 1994, Morris and Hawkins 1998). While currently recorded from four protected areas in Madagascar, its distribution in the north and west of the island is patchy. Although 463 individuals were counted in a January 1993 census in the Antsalova region (Rabarisoa 1993), numbers in most areas remain small and known breeding sites few and widely scattered. Hunting, persecution at breeding sites, and the introduction of rice farming on some lakes are still the major threats to its continued survival, and it remains one of the heron species most in need of protection and constant monitoring.

Goliath Heron. This giant heron is a widespread species of rather patchy distribution throughout Afrotropical Africa, preferring shallow shores of freshwater, rivers and swamps, including mangroves. It is generally sedentary over much of its range, typically in single pairs throughout the year, maintaining exclusive feeding territories. A density of 1 per 4 km^2 along the Kafue River in Zambia (Dowsett and de Vos 1964), and 1 per 11 km of lake shoreline in the Orange Free State, South Africa (Geldenhuys 1984) is indicative of how thinly spread the species is in some seemingly favourable areas. However, it is locally common elsewhere, particularly in many East African swamps (Malagarasi, Moyowosi, Kyoga and the Sudd), and along some lakes and rivers (Lakes Edward, Albert and the Upper Nile valley), where counts of several hundred birds are not uncommon.

Breeding generally coincides with the onset of the rains, and while normally solitary or in small groups, in some areas the Goliath Heron will nest with other herons, cormorants and darters (i.e., Wembere swamps, Tanzania, and the Orange Free State, South Africa).

Purple Heron. A widespread Palearctic passage migrant and winter visitor to much of West and North-eastern Africa, the Purple Heron is also a largely sedentary breeding resident in eastern and southern areas of the continent. Almost the entire Palearctic breeding population (including birds from the Black Sea/Caspian area) winter almost exclusively in sub-Saharan Africa from Senegal, Gambia and Mali east to Sudan, Eritrea and Ethiopia, with ringing recoveries from Mauritania, Senegal, Gambia, Mali, Niger, Sierra Leone, Ghana, Nigeria, Cameroon and Sudan. Small resident populations also breed in Senegal, Mali, Ghana and Congo, while the paler *A. p. bournei* (<200 pairs) is endemic to the Cape Verde Islands (de Naurois 1966).

In East and Southern Africa the Purple Heron is a locally common breeding resident in swamps, reed beds and other dense marshy vegetation, with breeding colonies widely scattered from Uganda and Kenya south to the Okavango Delta and Nyl floodplains in Botswana and South Africa. Most colonies rarely exceed 50 pairs, and the 1000+ recorded breeding in the mixed species heronry in the Tana River Delta, Kenya, in January 1983 was exceptional.

In Madagascar a small endemic population (*A. p. madagascariensis*) is resident on freshwater lakes and rivers, breeding in small monospecific colonies of 3–7 pairs, rarely more (Langrand 1990). However, in view of the continuing degradation of the island's wetlands the entire population must be considered threatened and in need of constant monitoring.

Purple Heron. A large proportion of the Palearctic Purple Heron population spends the European winter in wetlands of sub-Saharan Africa. Photo: Jean François Hellio and Nicolas van Ingen.

Great White Egret. This species is a fairly common and widespread resident with populations largely sedentary throughout both regions. One Russian ringed bird (*E. a. alba*) has been recovered in the Central African Republic. However, despite only limited post-breeding dispersal, there is no evidence of any influx of Palearctic birds to sub-Saharan Africa, or of any major seasonal changes in abundance in the northern tropics of Africa (Moreau 1967, 1972).

The estimated population in the Inner Niger Delta, Mali, 1986–87 was c. 3000 pairs (Skinner et al. 1987), while 1450 pairs were breeding in Parc National du Djoudj, Senegal, November 1988, and a total of 3415 individuals was counted there in January 1991 (Perennou 1991). Elsewhere in Africa a count of 2488 in Tanzania in January 1995 was noteworthy, but in general populations and breeding colonies are smaller. A maximum of 1000 birds were present at the Tana River Delta heronry, Kenya in August 1956, but in all subsequent years numbers there have been greatly reduced. In southern Africa, in January and July 1993 counts in Zambia totalled 3801 and 3376 individuals respectively (Taylor 1993, Taylor and Rose 1994), but were substantially reduced for the period 1994–96 (Dodman and Taylor 1995, 1996, Dodman et al. 1997). In Zimbabwe 200 pairs were recorded breeding in twelve heronries in 1974 (Vernon 1976), and roost counts at Xaxaba in the Okavango Delta, Botswana, October 1986–December 1989 ranged from 186 to 440 individuals

(Randall 1988, 1990). In South Africa the Transvaal population is reported to reach a peak of c. 500 birds in wet years, dropping to <50 in periods of drought (Tarboton pers. comm.).

In the Malagasy Region, it is common throughout much of Madagascar, sometimes occurring in large groups (1000 near Lake Bemamba, November 1985), while counts of 556 (July 1992), 652 (January 1993), 1019 (July 1993), 608 (July 1994), 490 (January 1996) and 296 (July 1996) have been recorded recently (Perennou 1992, Taylor 1993, Taylor and Rose 1994, Dodman and Taylor 1995, 1996, Dodman et al. 1997). It breeds in mixed species heronries and Salvan (1972) estimated 450–600 pairs around Antananarivo alone, but which dwindled to 40–50 pairs (December 1982–March 1983). Breeding colonies, however, are heavily plundered by the local population, resulting in some larger colonies being abandoned in exchange for smaller, less obvious, or inaccessible ones (Langrand 1990). Elsewhere there is a resident population of 50–100 birds on the Comores, breeding in small colonies (maximum 13 nests) on Moheli (Benson 1960).

Slaty Egret. This globally threatened African endemic is largely confined to the swamps and floodplains of the major river systems in Zambia, northern Botswana and the eastern Caprivi, Namibia. While it is subject to some seasonal movement in response to rainfall, shallow floodplains with low grassy or other aquatic vegetation appear to be its required feeding habitat. Breeding in dense reed beds immediately before peak flood levels provides both maximum protection and optimal feeding conditions during the chick rearing stage (Hines 1992, Randall and Herremans 1994). Later, receding water levels make for an abundance of young fish and easy access, yet despite all these factors this egret's population remains low and breeding records are few.

Groups of up to 30 have been recorded in Zambia (Dowsett 1981), and large flocks were reported in the Bangweulu swamps in June 1981. Roost counts in the Okavango Delta (October 1986–December 1989) ranged from 33–159 individuals (Randall 1988, 1990). In March 1985 some 30–35 active nests were observed in the north-eastern Okavango Delta (Fry et al. 1986), and two colonies totalling 26 nests were later reported from temporary wetlands in northern Namibia (Hines 1992). More recently 50–60 pairs were believed to have nested along the Boro River in the central Okavango Delta, Botswana in 1988, 1989 and 1992. It was estimated that no more than 30% of the eggs laid resulted in fledged young in 1988 and 1989, while in 1992 all clutches were lost to predators (Randall and Herremans 1994).

While there is little doubt that temporary wetlands play an important role in the overall biology of the Slaty Egret, the threats to its long-term survival are numerous. Flood regulation has already caused it to disappear from one part of the Kafue Flats in Zambia, and plans to harness the waters of the Okavango Delta and to clear the area of tsetse fly may also seriously affect the ecology of the entire area. Similarly, the proposed development of a rice growing project in the eastern Caprivi may markedly alter the functioning of the Zambezi floodplain. The impact of tourism and livestock industries, together with the constant reduction of potential breeding sites by reed cutting and fires, are all likely to have serious and negative effects on its population. Like the Madagascar Heron, its habitat and population require permanent protection and constant monitoring.

Black Heron. Local and generally uncommon throughout the Afrotropical and Malagasy regions, this heron occurs typically in groups of 5–50, only exceptionally in the thousands. The Black Heron occurs in a variety of fresh and salt water habitats, including swamps, lake margins, flooded grasslands, rice paddies, mangroves and tidal estuaries, and is frequently subject to sporadic local movements (rather than migratory ones), believed governed by the availability of shallow-water feeding areas.

Populations in Africa are generally small: 200–250 pairs in the Inner Niger Delta, Mali 1986–87 (Skinner et al. 1987), while counts of 825 in Cameroon (January 1993) and 245 in Senegal (January 1994) are well above those for other West African countries. Reports of 10 000–20 000 in Guinea Bissau (October–December 1983) are unparalleled and require substantiation before acceptance. Meanwhile, it is in the swamps and floodplains of the Zambezi and Limpopo rivers that the largest concentrations occur, and 1580 in Zambia (January 1994) is the highest count for any African country to date (Taylor and Rose 1994).

Throughout the continent the Black Heron breeds in mixed-species heronries, though rarely exceeding 50 pairs, and again water levels rather than rainfall itself are believed to be an important factor leading to successful breeding.

In Madagascar the Black Heron was formerly common and widespread throughout the island, but its population has declined dramatically over the past 30 years, especially on the High Plateau. A long-established breeding colony near Antananarivo contained 5000 pairs from 1940–50, but due to continued disturbance by man, is now reduced to 20–40 pairs. Elsewhere many large and excessively exposed colonies have disappeared, and it is now rare to find more than 40–50 pairs in a colony (Langrand 1990). However, it remains fairly common in many western wetlands (250 at Lake Bemamba October 1985; 200 at Lake Amboromalandy July 1987). Countrywide counts of 2036 (July 1992) and 1100 (July 1993) offered some hope for its continued survival (Langrand 1990, Taylor 1993, Taylor and Rose 1994). Sadly these have declined to 887 (January 1995), 578 (January 1996) and 252 (January 1997) giving further cause for alarm (Dodman and Taylor 1995, 1996, Dodman et al. 1997).

Intermediate Egret. Locally common throughout Afrotropical Africa, this species favours moist and inundated grassland near water (Blaker 1969b). While there is no evidence of true migrations, like other herons it undertakes local seasonal movements with the rains, and in southern Africa is subject to often considerable post-breeding dispersal. One individual ringed in Cape Province in November 1956 was recovered in Zambia in May 1957, some 2000 km north. Elsewhere vagrants have been recorded from the Cape Verde Islands and Jordan.

Populations appear generally stable, though in West Africa it has increased both its range and abundance since the 1950s (Macdonald 1978). It breeds in mixed-species heronries, often in large numbers: 2000+ nests in the Tana River Delta, Kenya in January 1983, with 400+ at the same site six months later (Coverdale et al. 1983); 1000+ at Lake Tana, Ethiopia in September–October 1969 (Klug and Boswall 1970); 800+ in the Inner Niger Delta, Mali 1986–87 (Skinner et al. 1987). In southern Africa, while up to 1000 pairs have bred at Norton, Zimbabwe (Irwin 1981), there were only 24 breeding pairs on the Witwatersrand, Transvaal during a 1973–74 survey (Tarboton 1977), and roost counts in the Okavango Delta, Botswana (October

1986–December 1989) ranged from 14 to 99 individuals (Randall 1988, 1990). Elsewhere, counts in Zambia (January 1992, 1993) recorded 606 and 1279 respectively (Perennou 1992, Taylor 1993), but which were considerably reduced during the period 1994–97.

Little Egret. The nominate form *E. g. garzetta* is fairly common and widespread throughout Afrotropical Africa on both coastal and inland waters. The Palearctic breeding population is largely migratory, wintering widely across the northern tropics of Africa from Senegal east to Sudan, Eritrea and Somalia, with several ringing recoveries from Senegal, Gambia, Guinea, Sierra Leone, Mali, Ghana, Nigeria, Cameroon and Sudan.

In addition, a resident Afrotropical population breeds over much of Africa, in some areas in large numbers and always in mixed-species heronries including 900–1000 pairs in the Inner Niger Delta, Mali 1986–87 (Skinner et al. 1987), 800+ in Parc du Djoudj, Senegal in November 1988 (Hafner, pers. comm.), and 1500 pairs in the Wembere swamps, Tanzania in February 1962 (Stronach 1968).

In South Africa it is mainly a summer visitor, with winter numbers on the Witwatersrand 90% down on summer numbers (Tarboton 1977). One bird ringed in Cape Province was recovered in Zimbabwe 1840 km north-east, while in Zambia counts of 1504 (January 1992), 2199 (January 1993) and 4031 (July 1993) support the theory that a large percentage of the South African population moves north during the June–August winter months. Elsewhere a countrywide count of 28 120 in

Little Egret. The dark morph of the subspecies *Egretta garzetta gularis* of the Little Egret is common in the coastal wetlands of West Africa. Photo: Jean François Hellio and Nicolas van Ingen.

Tanzania in January 1995 was exceptional and unprecedented, particularly when compared with counts of 963 (Kenya) and 139 (Uganda) over the same period.

Other forms of the Little Egret (as recognised by Hancock and Kushlan (1984)) are more localised: *E. g. gularis* is a common West African coastal heron, where, apart from on Sao Tome in the Gulf of Guinea, dark morph individuals greatly outnumber white ones. Populations are expanding in Senegal (where possibly also migratory), and long-distance vagrants have occurred in the Azores, eastern USA and the Mediterranean.

E. g. gularis breeds commonly throughout the region: on Banc d'Arguin, Mauritania, there were an estimated 900 pairs from 1959–65 (de Naurois 1969); 562 pairs in 1973 (Duhautois et al. 1974); 745 pairs in 1984–85 (Campredon 1987); 750 pairs in 1990–94 (Gowthorpe et al. 1996); and more recently a total of 1897 nests were counted May–December 1997 (Hafner et al. 1988b). Several thousand birds reportedly breed in the Saloum Delta, Senegal (Verschuren and Dupuy 1987), while elsewhere 80–110 pairs bred inland in mixed colonies in the Inner Niger Delta, Mali 1986–87 (Skinner et al 1987). Mangrove roosts of several hundred birds are also known from Senegal, Gambia, Guinea Bissau, Ghana and Nigeria.

E. g. schistacea is common along the Red Sea coasts south to 1°30′N in Somalia, with considerable dispersal south to coastal Kenya, and to Rift Valley lakes in Ethiopia and Kenya. It breeds in all countries bordering the Red Sea and Gulf of Aden, but to date no Afrotropical population figures are available.

E. g. dimorpha is at best an incipient species currently in the process of occupying a niche not occupied by *E. g. garzetta*. It is a common resident along the east African coast between 4 and 10°S, breeding on Kisite, Pemba, Zanzibar and Mafia islands in colonies of 20–100 pairs. Dark morph birds generally outnumber white ones by at least 2:1.

In the Malagasy Region it is a common resident on Madagascar, Aldabra, Cosmoledo and Astove islands. In Madagascar it is common to locally abundant throughout the island, with dark birds more common in coastal areas. It breeds in large numbers in mixed-species heronries, and up to 400 pairs breed regularly at Antananarivo, but like other herons nesting in colonies, suffers disruptions and depredations by villagers (Langrand 1990).

Cattle Egret. This is a common and often abundant species throughout the Afrotropical and Malagasy regions. Unlike most other herons and egrets it specialises in foraging on dry land, often following cattle, large mammals, tractors and ploughs in search of grasshoppers, crickets and other insects, and so has a somewhat distinctive foraging habitat requirement.

During the twentieth century the worldwide distribution of the Cattle Egret has been an ever-expanding process which has resulted in this species achieving a nearly cosmopolitan range (Hancock and Kushlan 1984). In South Africa the period of most significant increase and spread of the bird (1920–1940) was one in which the management of farm livestock, for dairy and meat production, underwent a marked change. During this period, the open rangeland system was replaced by a more intensive one of fenced pastures, planted and planned for rotational grazing. It had its parallel in the USA (Florida) with the close association of Snowy Egrets and cattle (Siegfried 1966).

Current populations of the nominate race in equatorial Africa appear mainly sedentary, but in the northern and southern tropics there is evidence that some are partially migratory, with most northern birds being rains-migrants, while in the south many either winter or disperse northward. On the Witwatersrand in Transvaal, South Africa, numbers fluctuated seasonally in 1973–74 from 13 000–17 000 in summer to 2000 in winter (Tarboton 1977); and several juveniles ringed in South Africa have been recovered in Zambia, Zimbabwe, Tanzania, Congo, Uganda and the Central African Republic. More interestingly, one juvenile ringed near the Caspian Sea in July 1980 was recovered in October of that year in Ethiopia, proof that part at least of the Palearctic population winters in tropical Africa (Nikolaus 1992).

In recent decades there are indications that all populations are increasing, and evidence has emerged of vast breeding colonies in all regions of Africa: 1960 pairs in the Parc du Djoudj, Senegal in November 1988; 63 000–65 000 pairs in the Inner Niger Delta, Mali in 1986–87 (Skinner et al. 1987); 1200 pairs in the Tana River Delta heronry, Kenya in June 1987; 10 000 pairs in the Wembere swamps, Tanzania in February 1962 (Stronach 1968); 2000+ pairs in Zimbabwe in 1973–74 (Vernon 1976); and 1700+ pairs in Barberspan, South Africa in February 1968. Meanwhile a roost of 260 000 birds in late December 1995 at Walado Debo in the Central Niger Delta, Mali is probably the largest ever reported of this rapidly exploding heron species (J.van der Kamp pers. comm.).

In the Malagasy Region the nominate race is a common and widespread resident from Aldabra and the Comores to Madagascar, Réunion and Mauritius. In Madagascar it is very common throughout, in all areas closely linked to the presence of cattle, and breeding in large colonies (c. 1000 pairs at Antananarivo 1971–82, Salvan 1972, Langrand 1990). Elsewhere in the region *Bubulcus i. seychellarum* is considered endemic to the Seychelles, but while some early specimens show evidence of Asiatic rather than African origin, the current population is believed to have been periodically infused with individuals of both *B. i. coromandus* and nominate birds; as such, the true status of *seychellarum* is unclear.

Squacco Heron. This is a common and widespread species throughout the Afrotropical and Malagasy regions. The western Palearctic and south-western Asian breeding populations are migratory with a broad front crossing of the Sahara to wintering areas across the northern tropics of Africa from Mauritania, Senegal and Gambia east to Sudan, Ethiopia and Somalia. Several ringing recoveries have been reported from Mauritania, Guinea, Sierra Leone, Nigeria, Cameroon, Congo and Sudan. Although Bannerman (1930) reported no West African breeding records, there are now colonies in Mauritania, Senegal, Gambia, Sierra Leone, Mali, Ghana, Nigeria, Chad and Congo, all suggesting that it has increased both its range and abundance in recent decades. Skinner et al. (1987) reported 500–600 breeding in the Inner Niger Delta, Mali in 1986–87; and 230 nests were reported in the Parc du Djoudj, Senegal in November 1988, compared to only 12+ in November 1974. Elsewhere, a large resident population breeds in east and southern Africa, in some areas in large numbers: 500 pairs in the Tana River Delta, Kenya (January 1953); 2000+ pairs in the Wembere swamps, Tanzania (February 1962), and up to 550 pairs on the Nyl floodplains, South Africa (Tarboton pers. comm.). A roost of 5120 counted at Walado Debo in the Central Niger Delta (28–29 December 1996) undoubtedly included both resident and wintering populations (J. van der Kamp pers. comm.).

In Madagascar it is a recent and highly successful coloniser of the island, and appears to be better adapted to new man-made environments (i.e. the transformation of wetlands to rice paddies) than the endemic *A. idae*, and around Antananarivo the breeding population has steadily increased from 350+ pairs (1969), 600+ (1970), 500+ (1981) to 1000+ in 1990 (Salvan 1972, Langrand 1990).

Malagasy Pond Heron. This species is a Malagasy breeding endemic (on Madagascar and Aldabra), migrating to mainland Africa each May–October. The population in Madagascar has declined considerably over the past 50 years, with increased competition from *A. ralloides*, and which is more evident on the High Plateau than in other regions (Langrand 1990). It is considered to be globally near-threatened by Baillie and Groombridge (1996).

The breeding population around Antananarivo has been reduced from 700+ pairs in 1945 to 50 pairs in 1981, while elsewhere on the island it breeds only in small numbers in mixed heronries at sites including Maroantsetra, Diego Suarez and Tulear (Milon et al. 1973, Langrand 1990).

During the non-breeding season (May–October) it migrates to tropical Africa, ranging widely from northern Mozambique, north-eastern Zimbabwe, Malawi and eastern Zambia north through Tanzania and southern Kenya to Uganda, Rwanda, Burundi and eastern Congo. Numbers disperse rapidly in Africa, and while few data are available, small groups of 12–15 are regularly observed at Thika oxidation ponds and the Mwea rice scheme north of Nairobi.

Rufous-bellied Heron. A generally local and uncommon species, its strongholds being the grassy floodplains of western and northern Congo, the Kagera swamps in eastern Rwanda, Lake Bangweulu in Zambia, the Okavango Delta in Botswana, and the coastal lowlands of Mozambique. Elsewhere, small numbers are resident north to southern Uganda and south-western Kenya, and south to the Nyl River floodplain, Transvaal, South Africa.

It regularly undertakes local movements associated with the seasonal flooding of riverine floodplains, and breeds irregularly in response to fluctuating water levels with nests no more than 0.5 to 1.5 m above water or ground level. The size of known breeding colonies ranges from 6+ nests in Mara GR, Kenya (April–May 1994), 75+ in Kagera swamps, Rwanda (May 1984), 60–80 in Lake Bangweulu, Zambia (Mwenya 1973), 25 in the Okavango Delta, Botswana (August 1970, yet only 5+ at the same site in September 1981), and 10 pairs on the Nyl River floodplains, South Africa (Tarboton pers. comm.).

Green-backed Heron. While fairly common throughout the Afrotropical and Malagasy regions, on account of its often solitary and crepuscular behaviour, population estimates are difficult to assess. *B. s. brevipes* is restricted to the coastlines and islands of the Red Sea and Gulf of Aden, where it breeds in small colonies in coastal mangroves. Little data and no population estimates are available.

Elsewhere in tropical Africa *B. s. africapillus* is widespread and largely sedentary in all areas. It is particularly numerous in West African coastal mangroves, where in the Sine-Saloum delta, Senegal it breeds in large colonies (100+ nests June–July 1976, and 300+ in 1977, Dupuy and Verschuren 1978). Throughout all inland areas it is generally confined to thick vegetation along lakes, rivers and streams, only rarely venturing into open floodplains. Although no figures are available, all populations appear stable.

In the Malagasy Region, no fewer than five races are considered to occur. *B. s. rutenbergi* is endemic to the island of Madagascar, where present throughout, though rare on the High Plateau. It is generally a solitary breeder in trees overhanging rivers and rice paddies (Benson et al. 1976, Langrand 1990). *B. s. rhizophorae* is endemic to the Comores where it is widespread in all coastal areas. *B. s. degens* is endemic to the Seychelles where now rare and endangered as mangroves continue to be destroyed. *B. s. crawfordi* is endemic to Aldabra, Assumption, Amirantes, Cosmoledo, Astove and Farquhar islands where not uncommon, and there is some evidence of colonial breeding on Aldabra (Penny 1974). *B. s. javanicus* was formerly present on all the Mascarene islands, but is now extinct on Réunion. On Mauritius it inhabits small mangrove islands that grow in the middle of fish ponds, while on Rodrigues it breeds on the rarely visited islets of the lagoon (Staub 1976).

Black-crowned Night Heron. This is a fairly common and widespread species throughout the Afrotropical and Malagasy regions. The majority of Palearctic and south-west Asian breeding birds winter in sub-Saharan Africa from Senegal and Gambia east to Sudan and Ethiopia, with ringing recoveries from Senegal, Gambia, Guinea, Sierra Leone, Mali, Niger, Chad, Nigeria, Cameroon and Sudan. In addition, there are resident breeding populations in Mauritania, Senegal, Gambia, Guinea-Bissau, Cote d'Ivoire, Mali, Ghana, Nigeria, Central African Republic, Congo, Sudan, Ethiopia, Kenya, Uganda, Rwanda, Burundi and Tanzania. In some areas they breed in large mixed species heronries: Parc du Djoudj, Senegal (500+ nests November 1974, and 1375 there in November 1988); 500+ nests in the Central Niger Delta, Mali in March 1995; 300+ nests in the Tana River Delta, Kenya in August 1956, also in June 1974, and 200+ in January 1983; 1000+ nests in the Wembere swamps, Tanzania in February 1962.

In southern Africa it is common throughout the region breeding in all countries with up to 700 pairs on the Nyl River floodplain, South Africa in a wet year (Tarboton pers. comm.). As with other herons, there is some local movement or post breeding dispersal north at least to Mozambique, while a Romanian ringed bird has also been recovered there, confirming that at least some Palearctic birds reach the region (Clancey 1980).

In Madagascar it is fairly common throughout the island, but like other heron species that nest in colonies is subjected to regular nest-raiding by local villagers. In the west, roosts of 300+ have been recorded around lakes near Antsalova in July 1970 and October 1985 (Albignac pers. comm., Langrand 1990).

White-backed Night Heron. Although widespread throughout tropical Africa, it remains little known in all regions. Always solitary or in pairs and strictly nocturnal, it is generally well concealed and inactive in dense vegetation during the day, appearing only at dusk when flying to feeding grounds. Generally local and uncommon almost everywhere, except perhaps along the rivers of the Uelle system in the northern Congo swamp forests (Chapin 1932), and along the Upper Zambezi in Zambia (Winterbottom 1942). It is also resident and breeding in many areas of coastal mangroves in West and East Africa (Pakenham 1979, Verschuren and Dupuy 1987).

White-crested Tiger Heron. This cryptic species is confined to the equatorial swamp forests of tropical Africa from Senegal, Guinea, Sierra Leone and Liberia east to Cameroon, Gabon and Congo. Due to being rarely observed throughout its range, it is difficult to assess its status in terms of numbers, and although remaining little known it does appear to be locally common in parts of Gabon, the lower and northern Congo swamp forests (Hancock and Kushlan 1984, Brosset and Erard 1986).

Little Bittern. Widespread and generally uncommon throughout both regions. Sub-Saharan Africa is the main wintering area for Palearctic and south-west Asian breeding populations of *I. m. minutus*. Despite single ringing recoveries from Senegal, Nigeria and Congo, the bulk of migratory birds is believed to occur east of 10°E, and ranging south to Cape Province, South Africa. Single breeding records of the nominate race are reported from Guinea-Bissau (de Naurois 1969) and Senegal (Morel and Morel 1989).

   I. m. payesii is widespread throughout tropical Africa, though local and generally uncommon in all regions. Populations are largely sedentary, except in the extreme south in Cape Province, South Africa where it is mainly a summer visitor (Langley 1983). A combination of its highly secretive behaviour and confusion with overlapping migrants precludes any accurate population assessments.

   I. m. podiceps is endemic to Madagascar (early reports from Zanzibar now considered erroneous, Pakenham 1979) and known only from very few widely scattered localities (Langrand 1990). In view of the continuing degradation of the island's wetlands, it is clearly in a most vulnerable situation and in need of constant monitoring.

Yellow Bittern. While present in small numbers on Mahe, La Digue, Praslin and Curieuse islands in the Seychelles, it remains scarce and little known. The scarcity of fresh water on the islands has led to considerable speculation as to whether the Yellow Bittern is a naturally occurring species, coupled with the fact that it does not occur in island groups on either side of the Seychelles (Penny 1974). Watson (1980) estimated the population to be less than 100 pairs, with many localities occupied by birds seriously threatened by pressure to drain all marshes, since they are important refuges for mosquitoes. As such he considered the long-term survival of the species in the Seychelles somewhat doubtful.

Dwarf Bittern. A widespread yet obtrusive rains-migrant throughout much of sub-Saharan Africa, and with populations in the northern and southern tropics, it is generally present only during the rainy seasons (July–September and November–March respectively). Elsewhere some populations in moist equatorial regions (i.e. eastern Uganda) may be sedentary (Mann 1976). Throughout its range it appears largely dependent on riverine floodplains and flooded grasslands with scattered trees when breeding, and movements in some areas may be governed by fluctuating water levels. Breeding has been recorded in several west and southern African countries, but in east and north-eastern Africa there are less than five widely scattered records from 1920–90. It has been reported breeding alongside Squacco and Rufous-bellied herons in the Transvaal, South Africa (Tarboton 1967), though the total wet season population in South Africa is probably less than 290 pairs (Brooke 1984). Elsewhere it is reported locally common in the Cunene River floodplain of north-eastern Namibia and southern Angola (Traylor 1963), in the Limpopo River valley, and parts of western Matabeleland, Zimbabwe (Irwin 1981).

Eurasian Bittern. The Palearctic nominate form *B. s. stellaris* has been recorded wintering in several sub-Saharan areas of Africa. Records from Mauritania, Senegal, Mali, Gambia, Ghana, Central African Republic, Nigeria, Cameroon, Gabon, Congo, Sudan, Eritrea and Ethiopia suggest a fairly broad-front movement into the northern tropics, while elsewhere vagrants have been recorded from the Seychelles.

Confined to southern Africa, *B. s. capensis* is in serious decline due to the loss of wetland habitat and its intolerance of human activity. As such it is now exceedingly rare or extinct over much of its former range, and it may be only in the Bangweulu swamps, Zambia and perhaps the eastern Angolan wetlands that it survives in any numbers (Brooke 1984, Leonard pers. comm., Sorensen pers. comm.). In South Africa it breeds only in Natal and Transvaal, with a total population of probably less than 100 individuals (Tarboton pers. comm.). There appears little doubt that the entire population of *B. s. capensis* is in serious decline and endangered. Along with areas of suitable habitat it requires urgent protection and constant monitoring.

Critical Conservation and Regional Management Issues

Wetland management—major African breeding sites

The Inner Niger Delta, Mali. The Inner Niger Delta in Mali is well known for its importance for wintering Palearctic migrants, particularly waterfowl (Roux 1973, Curry and Sayer 1979, Roux and Jarry 1984). Skinner et al. (1987) showed that, with an estimated 87 000 pairs of 15 wetland species, the delta is probably the most important single area on the African continent for breeding colonial water birds, of which herons account for approximately 80%, with the Cattle Egret comprising some 75%, of the total breeding population.

Sadly, during their survey there was evidence that the amount of suitable breeding habitat in the delta was declining, largely on account of the degradation of the acacia woodlands due to extensive dry season grazing by goats and wholesale clearance of some woods to make way for rice cultivation. Since most of the species prefer to nest in flooded woodland, this decline of available habitat may have serious effects on the heron population. As such the protection of the existing woodlands should be a top conservation priority, and which must be done with the cooperation of the local fishermen and goat herders, as it is important that they recognise the heronries as an asset. The potential impact of Cattle Egrets on the grasshopper population (a serious crop pest in the region) and the subsequent enrichment of the water beneath the colonies from droppings, in turn leading to increased fish production, must also be emphasised.

Rounded population estimates (in pairs) for the Delta in 1986–87 were: Cattle Egret 63 000–65 000; Long-tailed Cormorant 17 000–17 500; Great White Egret 2800–3000; Little Egret 900–1000; Intermediate Egret 800–875; Squacco Heron 550–650; Black Heron 200–250; Western Reef Heron (*E. garzetta gularis*) 80–100; Black-crowned Night Heron 1–10; Grey Heron 10–15 (1985); Black-headed Heron (not including monospecific colonies) 10; African Darter 40–45; Sacred Ibis 30–40; African Spoonbill 300–350; Open-billed Stork 30–40.

The Wembere Swamps, Tanzania. The Wembere is an extensive floodplain in western Tanzania, and due to its inaccessibility during the rains has remained little known. It lies south and west of the Eyasi Rift and extends for approximately 85 miles from north to south, and varies in width from 8 to 10 miles. The plain consists of open grassland intersected by drainage lines that dry up in the dry season when the area is grazed by cattle. Bordering the plain are patches of woodland, mainly *Acacia seyal*, and on the slightly higher ground *Acacia drepanolobium*. Ambatch, a swampy shrub, appears in the deeper drainage lines at the beginning of the rains, but dies away in the dry season. Rainfall in the area averages 76–89 cm per annum.

Stronach (1968) gave details of the Chagana heronry situated on the western side of the Wembere, where in February 1962 (following exceptionally heavy rains) an estimated 40 000–50 000 pairs of 17 wetland species were breeding. In addition, numbers of Purple Heron, Little Bittern and Dwarf Bittern were also present, but whose nests were not located. At the time of his survey, heron species accounted for approximately 40% of the total breeding population.

Rounded population estimates in February 1962 were: Cattle Egret 10 000+; Long-tailed Cormorant 10 000+; African Darter 10 000+; Squacco Heron 2000+; Yellow-billed Stork 2000+; Sacred Ibis 2000+; Little Egret 1500+; Black-crowned Night Heron 1000+; Open-billed Stork 1000+; African Spoonbill 250; Glossy Ibis 170; Yellow-billed Egret 150; Great White Egret 100; Black Heron 40; Black-headed Heron 35; Grey Heron 9; Goliath Heron 4.

Elsewhere in Africa major mixed-species heronries are to be found in the Parc du Djoudj, Senegal; the Kagera swamps in eastern Rwanda; the Tana River Delta, Kenya; and on the Nyl River floodplain in South Africa, while many hundreds of smaller monospecific colonies are scattered across the continent. All are highly dependent on rainfall and a minimum of disturbance from man. Very few are in protected areas, and as such their long-term future may be uncertain.

In southern Africa however, it is encouraging to see the numbers of heronries increasing. Smithers et al. (1956) quoted only six breeding records for Zimbabwe, yet by the mid-1970s there were over 500 records of colonial herons breeding, linked almost entirely to the creation of man-made reservoirs and impoundments, now totalling approximately 10 000 (Vernon 1976, Ewbank pers. comm.).

Wetland management—continent-wide

African wetlands provide vital refuges and feeding grounds for herons, as well as supporting the largest numbers and greatest variety of other wildlife in the world. For this reason alone they deserve the highest conservation attention (Denny 1991). In addition to herons and wildlife, African wetlands also support, and are the sole livelihood of, many hundreds of thousands to millions of indigenous people, who are either permanently resident in the wetlands or use them in a nomadic fashion. These people, an integral part of the wetland ecosystems, have for generations lived alongside herons and other forms of wildlife in a generally balanced and sustainable manner. Over the last 50 years, human populations of African countries have increased dramatically, and to such an extent that African wetlands are now among the continent's most threatened ecosystems. Water resources are coming under increasing pressure from urban and industrial users, as is demand for agricultural and grazing lands, and their use to support commercial fishing projects.

In Madagascar the situation is alarming. The slash and burn system of cultivation and the subsequent deforestation has resulted in severe soil erosion, leading to the heavy siltation of rivers and adjacent wetlands. Large areas of once pristine wetland are being transformed into rice fields and fish farms as agricultural development becomes the largest and most important economic activity on the island. As a result, heron populations are in general declining, and some species are the subject of international concern. As with much of Africa, the government must take strong and decisive action, together with the establishment of a firm environmental programme of wetland management for the long-term survival of its wetland fauna.

African wetlands are among the most productive ecosystems in the world, covering 657 000 km² of West Africa, 208 000 km² of East and North-eastern Africa, and 172 000 km² of southern Africa. However, if steps are not taken now these areas will be destroyed at an ever-increasing rate, and heron populations inevitably will become seriously threatened. African governments must be prepared to take strong and firm action on behalf of their future generations. Human population control is the consistently over-riding and often politically sensitive issue.

The character, coverage and threats to wetland resources and similar habitats differ among countries. It is a useful approach to list these characteristics by the many African countries. In Mauritania, West Africa, tidal wetlands, marshes and floodplains cover 7700 km², yet they seem reasonably secure. In Senegal, 15 000 km² of floodplains, estuaries and deltaic systems are threatened by fishing and hydroelectric dams. In other West African coastal countries (Gambia, Guinea–Bissau, Guinea, Sierra Leone, Liberia, Cote d'Ivoire, Ghana, Togo and Benin) wetlands cover from a few hundred to a few thousand km² of mangroves, coastal lagoons, and freshwater swamp forest, all of which are threatened by agriculture, hunting and fishing, and urbanisation. In sub-Saharan Africa, Mali, Chad, Burkina Faso, and Niger have over 160 000 km² of floodplains of rivers as well as the critical Lake Chad system, threatened by population increases, hunting, fishing, agriculture, irrigation, and cattle. Nigeria, Cameroon, Equatorial Guinea, Gabon, and Congo Brazzaville have 180 000 km² of coastal wetlands including mangroves, swamp forests, freshwater swamps, and riverine floodplains affected by population pressures, agriculture, and cattle. The inland Central African Republic has 31 000 km² of river floodplains threatened by shifting agricultural practices and pesticides. The Democratic Republic of Congo has over 200 000 km² of swamp forests, diverse freshwater wetlands, and riverine floodplains.

In the drier north-eastern and eastern Africa, conflicts with water development and use are intensifying. Sudan has over 51 000 km² of permanent swamps and seasonal floodplains, much of which will be affected by the Jonglei Canal project. Ethiopia, Eritrea, Djibouti, and Somalia have tidal wetlands, salt marshes, lakes, and seasonal floodplains, some of which are being affected by the resettlement of refugees. Kenya and Tanzania have over 80 000 km² of tidal wetlands, papyrus swamps, floodplains, and lakes, all of which are affected by increasing population pressures and resultant habitat destruction. Uganda, Rwanda, and Burundi have over 50 000 km² of papyrus swamp, river swamps and floodplains threatened in part by fisheries.

In southern Africa, wetlands are also affected by competition for scarce water supplies. Angola and Namibia have about 35 000 km² of tidal mangroves, salt marsh, riverine swamps and floodplains, while in Namibia are the vast Etosha and Oshakati pans. South Africa (including Lesotho) has only about 6700 km² of wetland, including tidal wetlands, coastal lakes, riverine swamps, and floodplains threatened by increasing urbanisation and industrialisation. In Botswana, Zambia, Malawi and Zimbabwe, over 100 000 km² of seasonal freshwater swamps, including the Okavango and Lake Malawi systems, are threatened by commercial fisheries and other development schemes. Mozambique has over 25 000 km² of freshwater swamps, mangroves, seasonal pans, and coastal lagoons, threatened by clearing of mangroves and hydroelectric development. In Madagascar, 7100 km² of coastal mangroves, riverine floodplains, and lakes are severely threatened by siltation due to the many agricultural projects, forest clearing, and rice production.

The Ramsar Convention (The Convention on Wetlands of International Importance especially as Waterfowl Habitat) is a crucial force in the conservation of African wetlands. It came into force in 1975, and currently some 18 African countries are contracting parties to it. By 1996 African countries accounted for 56 sites and 4 430 363 ha, or just over 8% of the world's Ramsar sites and some 10% of all wetland areas protected. Altogether, 61% of Africa's Ramsar wetlands are coastal, and vary in size from just one hectare (Ile Alcatraz in Guinea) to the huge 1 173 000-hectare Banc d'Arguin in Mauritania. During 1997, Lake Chilwa (Malawi), a 224 800 ha site and the vast Okavango Delta (Botswana) measuring some 6 864 000 ha were expected to join the Convention.

African contracting parties to the Ramsar Convention, number of declared sites and the area of wetlands (ha) are: South Africa, 12: 228 344 ha; Senegal, 4: 99 720 ha; Morocco, 4: 10 580 ha; Tunisia, 1: 12 600 ha; Mauritania, 2: 1 173 000 ha; Algeria, 2: 4900 ha; Gabon, 3: 1 080 000 ha; Niger, 1: 220 000 ha; Mali, 3: 162 000 ha; Ghana, 6: 178 410 ha; Uganda, 1: 15 000 ha; Egypt, 2: 105 700 ha; Guinea–Bissau, 1: 39 098 ha; Kenya, 2: 48 800 ha; Chad, 1: 195 000 ha; Burkina Faso, 3: 299 200 ha; Zambia, 2: 333 000 ha; Guinea, 6: 225 011 ha.

Feeding habitats

Studies have shown that mixed species heronries are limited in size by the area of available feeding habitat surrounding them (Fasola and Barbieri 1978, Gibbs et al. 1987). Under such conditions the loss of any of Africa's major heron breeding sites (Inner Niger Delta, Mali; Tana River Delta, Kenya; the Wembere floodplain, Tanzania; Nyl River floodplain, South Africa) is likely to have very serious consequences for those heron populations, as it is unlikely that other known sites nearby could absorb the displaced birds. Many such wetlands in Africa therefore have high over-riding values which demand the very highest possible protection. The establishment of national parks or reserves, or simply wildlife sanctuaries, may be the appropriate mechanism to provide that protection.

Tourism

It is a well-known fact that profits from regulated wildlife tourism can be sufficient to maintain a conservation area and give much-needed hard currency to the nation. However, for tourism to succeed, local communities must gain from their own efforts. Thus, if tourism is a source of wealth generation, those who underpin it (such as wardens, guides, drivers as well as scientific, technical and managerial staff) must all receive tangible benefits from the conservation area itself. Establishing such conservation areas does not imply that people should be evicted from the area or visitors forbidden from entering them. The rural community is an integral part of all wetland ecosystems; often it has maintained the wetland's current state for generations. The balance of the local community's activities and wetland utilisation is an essential part of the dynamics. Conservation areas are designed to maintain that balance and to ensure that changes in circumstances (i.e. housing, transport, community activities and population structure) do not destabilise the balance irreversibly (Denny 1991).

Therefore, within the framework of sustainable development, the multi-purpose utilisation of African wetlands offers the greatest and in some cases the only hope for the long-term survival of the Afrotropical heron fauna. Most African countries are among the poorest in the world, and as such a concentrated effort is needed to assist them in their environmental tasks. Educational training programmes in environmental studies and wetland management at all levels of society are urgently required for the ultimate protection, conservation and management of the African and Malagasy wetlands and their inhabitants.

Herons play a vital role not only as indicators of the quality of wetlands, but also as an important component of tourism, which has become vital to the economies of several African nations. As ecotourism continues to gain world-wide support, many thousands of tourists flock to wetland areas in Senegal, Kenya, Tanzania, Zimbabwe and Botswana, while many other countries are starting to show increased interest in the value of their wildlife and wetlands. Only by balancing the needs of human demands against the environmental requirements will the future of African wetlands and the long-term survival of heron habitats be safeguarded.

Conclusion

As we see some wetland areas disappearing for ever, we need to look all the more towards providing artificial wetlands that the heron fauna can adapt to, as they appear to be doing successfully in parts of southern Africa. Africa has reached a crossroads; it remains the greatest and most diverse wildlife spectacle on earth, but its rapidly expanding human population threatens not only the survival of all its wildlife, but also the future survival of its own people. Internal civil wars, political and ethnic conflicts, and periods of severe drought have all made their impact on this great continent. The continued survival of Africa's wetlands and their inhabitants (large mammals, resident and migratory birds), as well as the indigenous people, is now of the utmost importance to each and every African nation.

6. Herons in Australasia and Oceania

Max Maddock

This chapter discusses heron populations in Australasia and Oceania, defined here as Australia, Tasmania, and its oceanic island territories, New Zealand and its oceanic islands, the main island of New Guinea (Irian Jaya and Papua New Guinea) and its satellite islands, and the islands of the South Pacific (Fig. 6.1, Table 6.1). The South Pacific Regional Environment Programme defines the South Pacific as extending from Palau east to Pitcairn, consisting of 22 countries or territories including Papua New Guinea. The Pacific Islands are sparsely populated, except Papua New Guinea, which has a population of over one million.

The Heron Fauna

Twenty species have been recorded in the region (Table 6.1) of which 14 are resident in Australia, 15 in Papua New Guinea, 6 in New Zealand and 8 in the Pacific Islands. The others are vagrants or probably incorrectly credited to the region. Some species are widespread, such as the Eastern Reef Heron throughout Australasia and Oceania, and the Great White and Intermediate egrets with extensive populations in both Australia and New Guinea. White-faced, Nankeen Night and Green-backed herons are less widely distributed, the first two being common in their range but little known. The White-necked Heron is distributed widely across Australia and also occurring in New Guinea, while the Pied Heron is found in both tropical north Australia and in New Guinea.

Most populations appear to be stable within limits of the available data. However, over most of the area the species have been little studied. Population numbers and distribution in arid Australia depend heavily on rainfall, drought, and water regulation. The most important breeding sites of the Great, Intermediate and Little egrets outside of the tropical north are in arid inland Australia, vulnerable to threat from water regulation and drought cycles. The Nankeen Night Heron's breeding strongholds also are in inland Australia.

The Cattle Egret is the best-studied species. Its population and range continue to

Heron Conservation
ISBN 0-12-430130-4

Fig. 6.1   Important heron areas in Australasia and Oceania.

expand since it first colonised Australia and New Guinea and established itself as a winter migrant to New Zealand in the middle of the twentieth century. Far less is known about the bitterns and the New Guinea Tiger Heron due to their cryptic lifestyles.

Three species are vagrants in the region. The Black-crowned Night Heron has been recorded on the Cocos–Keeling Islands (Gibson-Hill 1949, Prévost and Mougin 1970) and in the Marianas (Scott 1993a), and the Malayan Night Heron on Christmas Island (Stokes et al. 1987). The Grey Heron is a vagrant in the Marianas (Scott 1993a). One specimen was collected on a ship near New Zealand in 1898 (Parkes 1974). Although rumoured to be a vagrant in Australia, records for Grey Herons (Gould 1865, Broadbent 1910, Dawson 1949, 1951, 1974) are not acceptable (Marchant and Higgins 1990). The record for Swinhoe's Egret on Christmas Island (Hancock and Kushlan, 1984 for example) is incorrect, having been subsequently reidentified as the white morph of the Eastern Reef Egret (Marchant and Higgins 1990).

Environmental Conditions

The region encompasses climates ranging from tropical to temperate zones and habitats ranging from deserts to oceanic islands (Fig. 6.1). Australia extends from the tropics to lower temperate latitudes, with a low mountain range separating a narrow eastern coastal plain from an arid interior. The mountainous island of Tasmania is

Key to Fig. 6.1   Important heron areas in Australasia and Oceania.

1 Indonesia (New Guinea)—North coastal wetlands
2 Indonesia (New Guinea) and Papua New Guinea (New Guinea)—South coastal floodplains including Lorenz proposed park, Pulau Kimaam, Wasur, Rawa Biru, Tonda Wildlife Management Area, Fly River floodplain
3 Papua New Guinea (New Guinea)—Sepik Ramu north coastal floodplains
4 Australia—Western Australia and Northern Territory northern border wetlands including Ord River floodplain, Lakes Argyle and Kununurra, Victoria River floodplain
5 Australia—Darwin area floodplains and tidal wetlands including Cobourg Peninsula, Kakadu National Park Stage 1, Kakadu National Park Stage 2, Mary River floodplain
6 Australia—Gulf of Carpentaria tidal wetlands and floodplains
7 Australia—Cooper system ephemeral wetlands including Coongie Lakes
8 Australia—Paroo system ephemeral wetlands
9 Australia—Murray–Darling basin including Coorong and Lakes Albert and Alexandrina, Riverland, Booligal Wetlands, Kerang Wetlands, Gunbower State Forest, Barmah State Forest, Millewa Forest, Great Cumbung Swamp and Lowbidgee Floodplain (Lachlan–Murrumbidgee), Macquarie Marshes, Lower Gwydir Wetlands, Narran Lakes
10 Australia—Eastern coastal plain including Gippsland Lakes, Queensland and New South Wales coastal breeding colonies
11 Australia—Bool and Hacks Lagoons
12 Australia—Southwestern drainage basin including Lake Toolibin
13 New Zealand—North Island coastal plain: includes Kapuatai Peat Dome and Whangamarino
14 New Zealand—Waitangiroto Nature Reserve (Okarito River)
15 New Zealand—South Island coastal plain
16 New Zealand—Waituna Lagoon

Table 6.1 Status of herons in Australasia and Oceania.

	GrH	WNH	SuH	GWE	PdH	IE	WFH	LE	ERH	CE	GbH	BCNH	NNH	MNH	NGTH	LtB	YB	BB	AuB
Australia																			
Continental	++	++	++	++	++	++	++	++	++	++	++	++	++			++		++	++
Tasmania	+	+		+	++	+	++	+	+	+	++	+	+						+
Barrier Reef Islands							+	+	++	+		++	++						
Torres Strait Islands	+			+	+	+	+	+	++			++	++			?		+	
Macquarie Island										+									+
Lord Howe Island	+						++	+	+	+	+	+							+
Norfolk Island	+					+	+	+	+	+		+	+		+	+			
Christmas Island							+	+	+		+	+	+	+		+	+	+	
Cocos–Keeling Islands							+	+	+		+	+	+						
New Zealand																			
North Island	+			+		+	++	+	++	+		+							++
South Island	+			++		+	++	+	++	+		+				+			++
Chatham Islands				+			+		+	+									
Other islands				+			+		+										+
Indonesia (Irian Jaya) and Papua New Guinea																			
Main Island (Indonesia and Papua new Guinea)	+	+		+	+	+	+	+	++	+	++	+			++	+	+	+	
New Britain (Papua New Guinea)					?	?	?	?	++	++	++	?	?			+	+	?	
Aru Is. (Indonesia)		+	+	++	++		++	?	++						++		+	?	
Bougainville (Papua New Guinea)				+		?	?	?	++			?	?				+	+	

	Species																		
	GrH	WNH	SuH	GWE	PdH	IE	WFH	LE	ERH	CE	GbH	BCNH	NNH	MNH	NGTH	LtB	YB	BB	AuB
Bismarck Islands		+							++		?							?	
Other satellite islands			+	+					++									+	
Oceania																			
American Samoa									+										
Cook Islands									+										
Federated States Micronesia									+										
Fiji									+								+		
French Polynesia									+		++								
Guam										+		+					+		
Kiribati									+	+									
Northern Marshall Islands									+										
New Caledonia							+		+				+						
North Mariana Islands	+						+		+	+	+		+				++		+
Palau						+	+		+	?	+	+	+						
Pitcairn Islands									+										
Solomon Islands				+		+			+	+	+		+						
Tokelau									+									+	
Tonga							+		+	+	+								
Vanuatu							+		+	+	+		+						
Western Samoa									+										

++ = nesting population, + = present but not nesting, ? = status uncertain.

separated from the mainland by the Bass Strait. A number of offshore islands, including Norfolk and Lord Howe Islands, are substantial landmasses in the Pacific Ocean. The Great Barrier Reef and Torres Strait have numerous small coral islands. There are two small oceanic island territories (the Cocos, Keeling and Christmas islands in the Indian Ocean) and an Antarctic island territory (Macquarie Island).

Despite being the world's driest inhabited continent, Australia has a rich array of wetlands (McComb and Lake 1988). Since European settlement, flow patterns of rivers and the distribution of water into wetlands have been significantly altered. Because of the high frequency of severe drought, vigorous competition for water exists among agriculture, mining, domestic and industrial consumption (Giles 1983).

Key wetlands for herons (Fig. 6.1) can be categorised as the tropical north, the eastern coastal plains, the Darling–Murray river system, the inland ephemeral wetlands and the South-western Drainage Division of Western Australia (Lane and McComb 1988), including the Swan Coastal Plain. Numbers and diversity of herons in Australia decrease north to south as productivity declines from tropical to temperate zones (Recher and Recher 1980).

The tropical north includes mangrove and river floodplain areas, which support the richest heron fauna. For example the Morton et al. (1993) aerial surveys of the Alligator Rivers region reported 354 000 herons of several species. Twelve of the 14 resident species have been consistently reported from the region (Blakers et al. 1984, Usbeck and James 1992).

The eastern coastal plain, from Bundaberg (Queensland) south, has a range of estuarine, coastal bay, floodplain lagoons and swamp forests that support herons. Ample moist pasture is favoured by Cattle Egrets and also used by the White-faced Heron. Twenty-one heronries have been identified between Bundaberg and Gosford (Central Coast N.S.W.) (Morris 1979, Pratt 1979, Maddock and Baxter 1991, Geering 1993, Maddock and Geering 1993, 1994, Baxter 1992, McKilligan et al. 1993). Further important breeding and non-breeding heron habitat has been identified in the Gippsland area of Victoria (J. Reside pers. comm., Birkin 1990).

The western slopes of the Great Dividing Range of eastern Australia are drained by the Murray–Darling river system, the tributaries of which flow more or less westward into the arid inland area and join to form the main system that flows south-west to the sea in South Australia. Their vast floodplain supports a complex array of important heron wetlands. Especially important are the Lachlan and Murrumbidgee (Maher 1990). The Macquarie Marshes, including the Ramsar-listed Nature Reserve, are important for breeding Nankeen Night Heron and Intermediate Egret (Brooker 1992). The Murray Valley sector of the Murray–Darling system in Victoria and South Australia has 13 heronries (Pressey 1986) and six Ramsar-listed wetlands, one of the most important of which is Gunbower Island Forest Reserve, a red gum forest seasonally flooded by the Murray, that supports nesting of five species.

Little is known about inland ephemeral wetlands, which occur over vast areas in far north-western New South Wales and south-western Queensland. These are potentially of great importance, even though they may be dry for much of the time (Giles 1983). The Paroo River system (Maher 1991) rises in north Queensland and empties into a basin of freshwater and saline lakes in north-western New South Wales. A major flood event in the Paroo, accompanied by local rainfall downstream, provides abundant productive water bird habitat for 2–3 years, with overlapping events usually ensuring that at least some water remains in the region (Maher 1991).

The Southwestern Drainage Division of Western Australia (Lane and McComb 1988) is a key heron area in West Australia. Some 40% of the state is arid, with erratic low rainfall (Lane and McComb 1988), but the Swan Coastal Plain features a range of permanent and seasonal swamps, winter-wet areas, rivers, drains, estuarine lagoons and artificial wetlands (Storey et al. 1993).

New Zealand extends 1600 km from sub-tropical to lower temperate latitudes (34°E–47°ES), including two major islands (North and South) and small offshore islands, extending into the Antarctic Ocean. The two main islands are divided by a major central alpine mountain range, some areas having active glaciers, reaching altitudes of 3764 metres at Mt. Cook. The Alps are drained by fast flowing rivers, which form extensive deltas or braided channels on coastal plains. Rainfall ranges from orographic rain in excess of 8000 mm on the Alps to 300 mm in semi-arid Western Otago.

New Zealand has an extensive range of wetlands, including coastal and estuarine (fresh, salt and brackish), inland freshwater swamps, riverside swamps and ponds, lakes, alpine tarns and bogs (Buxton 1991). The estuaries, river floodplains and lakes provide supporting habitat for White-faced Herons, Great White Egrets, Little Egrets and Australian Bitterns. Extensive areas of moist pastureland support winter populations of Cattle Egrets. The Okarito River in Westlands on the South Island has the only breeding colony of Great White Egrets in the country. Mangroves are the dominant estuarine plants of the northern third of the North Island, while rushes and succulent herbs dominate further south (Buxton 1991).

New Guinea has a tropical climate (Osborne 1989). Its forested high central cordillera, with three peaks over 4000 m, and forested stream valleys provide the favoured habitat of the New Guinea Tiger Heron. The highlands are flanked by depressions, a northerly one occupied by the Sepik, Ramu and Markham floodplains and a southerly one occupied by the Fly, Strickland, Purari and several smaller floodplains. Fast-flowing rivers plunge down the cordillera slopes and spread to form vast floodplains, deltas, swamps, meanders and oxbow lakes. Spectacular wetlands occur on the coastal floodplains and deltas and extensive nipa palm mangrove systems exist, particularly on Gulf of Papua coast. These, for example the Bensbach River and Tonda Wildlife Management Area in Papua New Guinea, near the West Iryan border (Scott 1989), support a rich heron fauna, including many migrating from Australia. Rainfall varies from about 1000 mm to 10 000 mm annually. Three main rainfall patterns predominate: a wet season in May to August, rain relatively evenly distributed over the year and wet season in December to March (Osborne 1989).

Adjacent islands vary from substantial landmasses (New Britain, New Ireland, Manus and Bougainville) to smaller coral islands (for example the Trobriand Islands). Heron-supporting wetlands have been documented on New Britain, Manus and Bougainville Islands (Scott 1989).

Oceanic islands of the region, widely scattered through the southern Pacific Ocean, include steep volcanic islands with narrow coastal strips which have small lagoons and swamps where rivers have restricted access to the sea, raised coral limestone platforms, and atolls with shallow lagoons enclosed by a fringing coral reef. Coral reefs are important habitat for the Eastern Reef Egret. Freshwater lakes, mangrove forests and melaleuca swamp forests occur on some islands.

Changing Status of Herons

Data available

It is difficult to gain a quantitatively accurate picture of the status of herons in the region because of the fragmentary, intermittent and mostly short-term nature of the information base, much of which has not been published in the scientific literature. There have been no regular censuses. In Australia, the shortage of continuous long-term population, breeding and movement studies, linked with the typical dry–wet cycles of the climate particularly in the inland, make it difficult to assess whether changes are due to climatic fluctuations or represent population trends.

For these reasons, no attempt has been made to quantify populations (Table 6.1) as it could only be based on qualitative evaluation, involving much guesswork, which should not become enshrined in the literature. The conservation status has been derived from the many sources, but it should be noted that trends are not necessarily uniform within or across the regions and depend on the degree of local habitat modification.

Species status

White-necked Heron. This species is widespread in Australia, nesting through most of mainland eastern Australia, the Murray Valley and in the south-west of Western Australia, with scattered breeding records elsewhere in Western Australia (Marchant and Higgins 1990). Range expansion into the south-west of Western Australia is likely to have occurred during the 1950s (Riggert et al. 1965, Serventy and Whittel 1962). It is not found generally in the desert of east Western Australia, western South Australia, and south-eastern Northern Territory (Blakers et al. 1984). It is apparently breeding endemic in Australia, but a visitor to Tasmania and New Guinea and a vagrant to Norfolk Island and New Zealand (Marchant and Higgins 1990).

The White-necked Heron nests in small colonies, but some of more than 100 pairs have been reported (Marchant 1988, Magrath 1992, Corrick and O'Brien pers. comm. 1993). It nested in 29 of 98 wetlands studied by the Victorian Wetlands Survey (Corrick and O'Brien 1993, pers. comm.). Numbers fluctuate where long-term counts exist, for example in the Hunter and Clarence valleys of New South Wales 1973–75 (Gosper 1981). Near Darwin in Northern Australia, it occurs more regularly (Crawford 1972). There have been many reported irruptions, usually between winter and early summer (for example Norton 1922, Carnaby 1933, Serventy 1947, Watson 1955, Sedgwick 1953, Serventy 1953, Boehm 1953, Learmonth 1953, Dell 1985).

Its irruptive habits and lack of detailed studies of movements make it difficult to determine its exact status, and no trend figures are available. However, its population is currently considered to be stable (Marchant and Higgins 1990).

Sumatran Heron. Australia and New Guinea share this species with coastal and island south-east Asia. It is found in the coastal fringe across the north of Australia, but appears to be missing from the shores of the Gulf of Carpentaria (Marchant and Higgins 1990). It has recently been reported as an accidental visitor near Grafton, on the north coast of New South Wales (Gibson 1981), although early historical records indicate its presence there last century (Ramsay 1878, 1888, cited in Marchant and Higgins 1990). There is only one detailed study of breeding in Australia (Seton 1973).

No systematic attempts have been made to determine status or trends. It is reported in densities of less than one bird per kilometre of river (Garnett and Bredl 1985) and up to three per kilometre (Schulz 1989). Beehler et al. (1986) regarded it as a scarce resident of the lowlands and satellite islands of Papua New Guinea. A survey of the Benbach River and the Tonda Wildlife Management Area wetland complex of the Western Province found only 18, compared with counts of 500–1000 individuals of other species (Scott 1989). Its population is probably stable in Australia, although Garnett (1992) lists it under Taxa of Special Concern. Rose and Scott (1997) classify it as declining and the world population is considered to be near threatened (Collar et al. 1994).

Great White Egret. This species is widespread on the Australian continent except for the arid interior. It also occurs in New Guinea and the Solomon Islands (Marchant and Higgins 1990) and as a visitor to the North Mariana Islands (Scott 1993a). In New Zealand, Marchant and Higgins (1990) describe its movements as dispersive, with some regular and seasonal, possibly migratory, and sometimes irruptive. One banded juvenile from a Murray River colony was recovered in Papua New Guinea (Marchant and Higgins 1990), and Geering et al. (1998) recorded long-distance movements of 240 km–750 km from colony sites, with tagged birds having been found returning to their natal colonies to nest. Availability of wintering habitat in inland Australia depends highly on the wet–dry cycle.

The Great White has been regarded as common in suitable habitat in Australia. Hobbs (1961) considered it the most common egret in south-west New South Wales, outnumbering the Little and Intermediate by 25 to 1, being found in flocks up to 150. Gosper (1981) reported it as common in the Hunter Valley and moderately common in the Richmond Valley. It is regarded as common in New Guinea and the Solomons (Scott 1993a) and is accidental on a number of other islands (Table 6.1) (Keith and Hines 1958, Green 1977, McKean and Hindwood 1965, Hermes et al. 1986, Scott 1993a). There have been few surveys of nesting colonies, and because of different methodologies and time frames, they are difficult to link. In evaluating data from 53 colonies found in various surveys of 150 wetlands, I found that colony sizes in Western Australia, Victoria and New South Wales tend to be generally small, with 59% having 50 nests or less and only 6% having more than 200. Inland NSW colonies are generally larger than on the coast.

Trends are not well understood. Jaensch and Vervest (1989) suggested a probable increase in Western Australia. However, a decreasing trend in breeding numbers has been observed in coastal NSW colonies. At Shortland, after initial expansion following colonisation, a decline of 80% was registered from 1988–89 to 1997–98. Decline has also been noted in Victoria, where it has been nominated under the Flora and Fauna Guarantee Act (A. Corrick 1997, pers. comm.). Owing to the importance of the availability of water for nesting, it is difficult to determine whether the recent declines in the number of breeding pairs is a long-term trend or is a response to the climatic cycle. However, the species must be considered vulnerable. Continued long-term monitoring of colony occupation and the numbers of breeding pairs, breeding success and movements will be needed before its status can be confirmed.

The New Zealand race (*maoriana*—Mathews and Iredale 1913) has a small but increasing population (O'Donnell pers. comm.). Expansion has been aided by construction of farm dams and their colonisation by Australian green frog (*Litoria aurea*) (Falla et al. 1975). Millener (1981) considered it rare and Falla et al. (1975) found numbers varying from 50 to 100. It is widespread in coastal areas, but scarce above 500 m and extends to the more remote offshore islands (Falla et al. 1975). The only known breeding colony near Okarito in the South Island, known to the Maoris and reported by Gerhard Mueller in 1865 as consisting of 50 birds, suffered severe decline about 1877 due to vandalism (O'Donnell 1993, pers. comm.). In 1941 only four nests reared chicks, but since 1944, the number of occupied nests and the number of chicks fledged has increased steadily, with about 50 nests and about 35 chicks usually fledged (O'Donnell 1993, pers. comm.). There is no information on migratory movements between wintering habitat on the North and South Islands and the colony.

Pied Heron. This medium-sized heron inhabits coastal and sub-coastal wetland areas up to about 100 km inland across the north of Australia. It also occurs in Sulawesi, the Moluccas, Tanimbar and Aru Islands and New Guinea (Marchant and Higgins 1990). Breeding appears to be nearly confined to Australia, with nesting elsewhere confirmed only in southern Sulawesi (White and Bruce 1986). A Northern Territory Conservation Commission survey of 15 breeding sites in 1993 (R. Chatto pers. comm.) estimated 15 000 adult birds within the heronry area. It is regarded as a partial migrant (Marchant and Higgins 1990). Movement to Papua New Guinea and Indonesia occurs during the dry season following nesting (Halse et al. 1996) but small groups of largely juvenile birds have remained in the Torres Strait Islands (Draffan et al. 1983) and in the Edward River area (Garnett and Bredl 1985).

It is a very common bird in its favoured habitats. In Papua New Guinea, flocks of 20 000–30 000 were recorded by Finch and Howell (1982), and Halse et al. (1996) reported more than 22 000 in their Middle Fly region survey. A 1991 aerial survey of 15 floodplains found a minimum of 10 000 Pied Herons (R. Chatto pers. comm. 1993).

Intermediate Egret. This egret is widespread across northern and eastern Australia, except for the arid west of south-eastern Queensland, north-western New South Wales and most of South Australia (Marchant and Higgins 1990). In New Guinea it is common in the lowlands, and occurs occasionally in the highlands but its breeding status there is unknown and it may be a seasonal migrant from Australia (Beehler et al. 1986, Halse et al. 1996). It has also been reported a vagrant in other parts of the Australasia–Oceania region (Table 6.1) (Marchant and Higgins 1990, Scott 1989, 1993a).

There is little to suggest it is sedentary, but movements are poorly understood and may vary from place to place (Marchant and Higgins 1990). Movements from 133 to more than 2000 km were shown for birds at NSW colonies, including from the Macquarie Marshes to Papua New Guinea and one from Shortland westward across the arid interior to Alice Springs (Geering et al. 1998). A bird banded in New South Wales in January 1975 was recovered in New Guinea (3700 km NNW) about December in the same year—it is unclear whether this is wandering or regular migration (Mees 1982). However, a few birds banded as chicks have returned to their natal colonies to breed (Geering et al. 1998). Movement records show that inland Australian colonies supply birds to the New Guinea population.

The Intermediate Egret ranks in the top numerically of species on the floodplains of the Northern Territory (Finlayson et al. 1988, Morton et al. 1993) and is common in New Guinea (Scott 1989). One thousand birds were recorded in a count in one major wetland in Western Papua in 1988 (Scott 1989), and Halse et al (1996) reported about 130 000 in their Middle Fly region survey. Its status elsewhere is not clear.

Breeding strongholds are in the wetlands of Kakadu National Park in the Northern Territory (where colonies containing 1800–4000 nests have been recorded—Marchant and Higgins 1990) and in the Lachlan–Murrumbidgee and Macquarie Marshes wetlands of western NSW (where up to 6000 breeding pairs have been recorded in the 12 larger colonies—Maher 1990, Magrath 1992). Little is known about the Queensland colonies (Marchant and Higgins 1990). Baxter (1992) recorded it at nine of the 13 egret nesting colonies in coastal New South Wales, with a total of 800 nests. The inland NSW colonies, subject to the vagaries of the flood–drought cycle, in general are much larger than in coastal NSW.

Long-term monitoring data at the Shortland colony in NSW between 1988–89 and 1997–98 demonstrated a breeding population decline of 98% (Maddock unpublished data). In the Macquarie Marshes, a major decline in breeding population of 77% is evident between the peak numbers during the major flood episode of 1990–91 breeding season and 1996–97. No nesting occurred in four of seven seasons between 1991–92 and 1997–98 (from data supplied by W. Johnson pers. comm. and Macquarie

Intermediate Egrets. Nesting success in Australia is highly variable between regions and years in relation to rainfall. Photo: Max Maddock.

Marshes Advisory and Audit Committee 1997). In one of 98 wetlands surveyed in Victoria from the 1970s onwards, one count of 500 pairs was recorded during a flood in 1974, but there are no further significant nesting events for about 20 years (M. O'Brien, pers. comm. 1997). Success and survival of Australian breeding colonies are clearly related to the availability of water (Maddock and Baxter 1991, Baxter 1994, Kingsford and Thomas 1995). Because of decline in Victoria, it has been nominated under the Fauna and Flora Guarantee Act (M. O. Brien pers. comm.). However, it is difficult to determine whether the decline is a temporary reflection of drought or evidence of more serious problems. The weight of evidence is sufficient to regard the species as vulnerable in the region outside of the tropics.

White-faced Heron. The species is widespread throughout Australia, except for inland desert areas, occurs on Pacific islands, and has been reported as a vagrant in a number of locations (Marchant and Higgins 1990, Scott 1993, Bregulla 1992).

Its movements are poorly understood, with no long-term studies of marked birds. Marchant and Higgins (1990) stated that it appears to be locally nomadic, with some regular short-distance movements and some longer distance. Recoveries of three banded birds moving from 229–249 km have been recorded (Marchant and Higgins 1990).

Recher et al. (1983) regarded it as the commonest heron in Australia and evidence in the Hunter Valley of NSW, at least, suggests that its numbers have been sustained (Maddock 1991a), but there have been no recent surveys of its numbers elsewhere in the range. It has shown continued expansion in New Zealand since first reported in 1868. Only 23 confirmed records exist before 1940 but it was verified breeding in 1941 and particularly rapid population growth has occurred since the 1960s (Carrol 1970). It has benefited from clearing, irrigation and construction of farm dams and because of its capacity for solitary nesting in tall trees that are not necessarily in woodland or forest close to water, its breeding has not been adversely affected by clearing.

Little Egret. The Australasian race (*immaculata*) is widespread from northern Western Australia, across the north of the continent and down the eastern periphery to South Australia, and is also found in two small pockets in coastal Western Australia (Marchant and Higgins 1990). However, it only occurs in small numbers, even in the tropical north (Morton et al. 1993). Project Egret Watch observers throughout eastern Australia rarely report it. Hobbs (1961) regarded it as rare (mainly a summer visitor) in south-western NSW. Gosper (1981) regarded it as common on the Hunter River Estuary but less so on the floodplain swamps (mostly fewer than 10) and uncommon in the Richmond River area. It has been a scarce but regular visitor to Tasmania since 1957 (Bolger and Wall 1959, Green 1977, Project Egret Watch records). It was first recorded in New Zealand in 1951 (Falla et al. 1975), and since then mainly in coastal areas, with regular winter appearances in the same locations. Beehler et al. (1986) regarded it as a visitor to the lowlands of New Guinea, where, for example, 150 were reported in a 1988 survey of a western Papuan wetland (Scott 1989), and Halse et al. (1996) estimated 1500 in their 1994 Middle Fly river survey. It is a vagrant on oceanic islands (Marchant and Higgins 1990, Scott 1993a, Table 6.1).

Long-distance movements have been recorded but no distinct migratory pattern has yet been determined. Banded immature birds have been recovered in Papua

New Guinea and New Zealand (Marchant and Higgins 1990), patagially-tagged birds from the Shortland colony in NSW have moved 240–1025 km, and one returned to its natal colony to breed in its second year (Geering et al. 1998).

Few breeding numbers (or localities, for that matter) have been recorded (Marchant and Higgins 1990). Baxter (1992) recorded it in only five of the 13 heronries in coastal NSW. The RAOU Wetland Survey in Victoria found only 40 nests in one of the 148 water bird colonies surveyed (Corrick and O'Brien pers. comm. 1993). Although in general more breeding pairs have been found at inland NSW colonies, numbers are still small.

The Little Egret's range has expanded since the beginning of the century (Blakers et al. 1984), being recorded for the first time in South Australia in 1952 (Parker et al. 1979), Tasmania in 1957 (Bolger and Wall 1959), Western Australia 1965 (Ford 1965) and New Zealand 1951 (Falla et al. 1975). The nesting population at Shortland declined by 86% during the period 1988/89 to 1997/98. It has been nominated under the Flora and Fauna Guarantee Act in Victoria, where the reporting rate has been less than 1.5% in all years since 1970 and the estimated breeding population is less than ten pairs (M. O'Brien pers. comm. 1997). Dependence of breeding success on adequate water (Maddock and Baxter 1991), the deterioration in the conditions of inland breeding colonies, the recent decline in breeding numbers in coastal NSW and its status in Victoria suggest that it can be classified as vulnerable.

Eastern Reef Heron. The Eastern Reef Heron is found around the entire Australian coastline, except for the Great Australian Bight. It is also widespread in the south-western Pacific and New Guinea. Falla et al. (1975) reported it as occurring "sparingly" on the rocky coasts and main islands of New Zealand.

Virtually nothing is known about its movements. The Australian Bird and Bat Banding Scheme has one record of recovery 560 km from the banding site and Recovery Roundup (1985a) recorded one recovery more than 7 years and 6 months after banding at 145 km from the banding site. Some at least are sedentary, with one Queensland recovery at the banding site nearly 10 years after banding as an adult (Recovery Roundup 1991). Some post-breeding dispersal has occurred in South Australia (Parker et al. 1979).

There are very few breeding records in Australia, with only 22 Nest Record Cards from four states up till 1982 (Marchant and Higgins 1990). It breeds in small colonies, the largest of which recorded in Australia consisted of 21 nests (Australian Nest Record Scheme).

Blakers et al. (1984) indicated that it is less common in the Tasmanian region and Victoria than in the past, when both light and dark morphs used to breed in the Bass Strait Islands, but there have been few recent records. The most recent review of its status (Peter 1995) documents its decline in this region from about 1909, gives the most recent confirmed Tasmanian record as 1976 and reports it as currently virtually absent from Victoria. Edgar (1978) indicated a decline in some parts of New Zealand. According to Moon (1967) it is at the south-eastern limit of its mostly tropical range in New Zealand and may be responding to a subtle change in climate and physical changes such as reclamation, pollution, removal of old wooden wharves and increased disturbance on coasts. There is inadequate information on which to base any judgement of trends elsewhere in the Australasia–Oceania region, although it still appears to be relatively common and stable in Oceania.

Green-backed Heron. The Green-backed Heron occupies a thin coastal fringe around Australia in central and northern Western Australia, the Northern Territory, Queensland, New South Wales and eastern Victoria, mainly in mangrove areas. It is resident in Papua New Guinea, occurring sparsely in coastal areas, rivers and on Aru (Beehler et al. 1986) and occurs also in French Polynesia, the Solomons, Vanuatu and Fiji (Scott 1993). It is a vagrant to Tonga, where its visits are becoming more frequent and it may be in the process of colonisation (Scott 1993a).

Its status is unclear, although localised reductions have been noted in Australia (Morris 1975) and habitat loss due to development on the islands of French Polynesia has resulted in a decline. The endemic subspecies (*B. s. patruelis*), confined to Tahiti and highly dependent on the Mita Rapa wetland, has declined significantly over the last 20 years (Monet et al. 1993) and become rare (Scott 1993a). Little is known about its breeding, with only two Australian studies (Morris 1990, Hindwood 1993) and one in Tahiti (Monet and Varney 1998), or about its movements (Marchant and Higgins 1990).

Cattle Egret. The Cattle Egret is widespread in coastal areas of Australia, being very common on floodplains with grazing stock. The two major breeding ranges in Australia are the north of the continent (eastern Northern Territory and the Kimberly region of Western Australia) (Marchant and Higgins 1990, R. Chatto 1993, pers. comm.) and on the eastern coastal plain of Queensland and New South Wales

The Cattle Egret (race *coromandus*). A natural "invader" of the region, the increase and extension of range across Australia and New Zealand since the 1940s has been spectacular. Photo: Max Maddock.

(Woodall 1986, Marchant and Higgins 1990, Baxter 1992, McKilligan et al. 1993, Project Egret Watch records). Minor breeding has been reported in inland New South Wales (Maher 1990, Magrath 1992) and the Murray River system (Parker et al. 1979, Marchant and Higgins 1990). It has also become an annual visitor to Norfolk and Lord Howe, is accidental on other islands (Marchant and Higgins 1990), and a seasonal migrant to Guam and the Marianas (Scott 1993a), (Table 6.1).

The race in Australasia (*coromandus*) is regarded as a natural invader, as part of its world range expansion, perhaps as early as the beginning of the century (Hewitt 1960). Its major expansion dates from about the 1940s (Serventy and Whittel 1962, Lendon 1951), possibly emigrating from the Malay Archipelago via New Guinea. Birds were recorded in western New Guinea in 1941 (Lingren 1971), and Beehler et al. (1986) reported a 15-year history of range expansion, with regular reports from the Fly and Port Moresby areas, although no breeding has been found. Breeding was first recorded near Grafton, New South Wales, in 1954 (Goddard 1955) and since then the range has expanded throughout the eastern coastal plain (Hewitt 1961, Parker et al. 1979, Green 1977, van Gessel and Kendall 1972, Pratt 1979, Gilligan 1979, Maddock 1983). The number of breeding colonies in New South Wales had grown to five (2300 pairs) by 1978–79 (Morris 1979) and to 12 colonies (more than 10 000 pairs) in 1991 (Baxter 1992). Nesting was first recorded in south-eastern Queensland in 1963 (Woodall 1986).

Cattle Egrets breeding in eastern Australia undertake seasonal migration (Maddock 1990, McKilligan et al. 1993, Maddock and Geering 1993, 1994). The Maddock and Geering (1994) study confirmed an out and return major southern and a minor northern migration pattern from colonies in New South Wales and Queensland. Some movements are short distance migrations within the floodplain where the colony is located, and others up to more than 2000 km to the southern states and New Zealand. Faithfulness to wintering locations and to breeding colonies has been demonstrated. Meteorological factors affect timing and staging of movements (Maddock and Bridgman 1992, Bridgman and Maddock 1994, Bridgman et al. 1997, 1998). The major movement from warmer climate to areas with cold winters, such as Tasmania and New Zealand, is an unusual feature of heron migration.

The first confirmed sighting in New Zealand was in 1963 (Turbott et al. 1963), although Brown (1980) considered that it may have been present as early as 1956. Reasonable numbers became regularly reported as winter visitors on both the north and south islands from the 1970s (Heather 1978, 1982, 1986, Jackson and Olsen 1988), with counts from 293 in 1977 to more than 2200 in 1987. Since then, the numbers have declined (Heather pers. comm.).

In 12 years of breeding success records in the Hunter Valley of New South Wales (Maddock and Baxter 1991, Maddock and Geering 1994, Maddock unpublished data) success varied from year to year but was not related to rainfall, high success occurring in years of both high and low precipitation. Very severe drought in 1991–92 obviously influenced the lowest success for the period of the study (1.94 chicks per successful nest). The equally dry 1992–93 season produced the highest success ever (2.86), illustrating the capacity of the species to cope with climatic cycle excesses and for its recovery after setback.

The phenomenal increase in population and extension of range of the Cattle Egret across Australia and New Zealand since the 1940s is a very clear trend (Maddock and Geering 1994) but to date there is no evidence of detriment to the other heron species. Although they breed colonially with the Great, Intermediate and Little Egrets, there does not appear to have been any competition for nesting space and their foraging occupies a niche which is only overlapped to any extent by the White-faced Heron.

Nankeen Night Heron. The Nankeen Night Heron, known in Australia as the Rufous Night Heron, is widespread in coastal and near inland areas of Australia but rare in the arid interior (Marchant and Higgins 1990). Key breeding areas in Australia are the Northern Territory (R. Chatto pers. comm.), and the Darling–Murray system (Maher 1990, Brooker 1992, Magrath 1992, Johnson 1994 pers. comm., Corrick and O'Brien 1993 pers. comm.). Gunbower State Forest in Victoria, with 2000 pairs (Corrick and O'Brien, pers. comm. 1993) and Macquarie Marshes of New South Wales with 1510 nests in 1990–91 (Johnson pers. comm. 1994), are the major sites within the system. The majority of the colonies surveyed (77%) had more than 100 breeding pairs, the inland NSW colonies being subject to drought–flood cycles. A common species within its range, it can be regarded as having a stable population.

Large numbers have been reported in Papua New Guinea, for example a count of 500 at a single wetland in the Western Province in 1988 (Scott 1989). It is also represented in New Caledonia, Palau, the North Marianas and the Solomon Islands. Although regarded as a vagrant in New Zealand, there is a possibility that it may have bred there in 1957–59 (Falla et al. 1975). Its population has expanded in the Cocos–Keeling Islands since it first colonised them in 1941 (Carter 1994).

Its movements are poorly understood. It is generally regarded as nomadic, with some birds sedentary, and there appears to be a northern movement of part of the southern population in winter (Marchant and Higgins 1990). Large numbers have been reported arriving to breed on Raine Island in the Great Barrier Reef, where it is otherwise absent, coinciding with abundance of hatching turtles (Marchant and Higgins 1990). A major drop in the April count in the Halse et al. (1996) survey on the Middle Fly floodplain of Papua New Guinea to 1% of the December count, coinciding with the exodus of Pied Herons and Intermediate Egrets, suggests migration back to Australia. Juveniles and nestlings banded on the Barrier Reef have been recovered in Papua New Guinea, 285–463 km to the north (Recovery Roundup 1985b, 1985c, 1986) and there is one reported Western Australian northern movement of 1323 km (Recovery Roundup 1989).

In Australia, breeding at Macquarie Marshes colonies has been erratic during the survey period due to problems of water supply. There was a peak of 1510 nests in the period of high flood in 1990–91, no nesting in the next two seasons, only 350 in 1993–94 because of inadequate water (Johnson pers. comm. 1994), a resurgence to 4600 in 1996–97 when the first allocation of environmental flow to support water bird breeding was made (Macquarie Marshes Advisory and Audit Committee 1997). Although the species is currently regarded as common, continued overall decline in the water regime in the Murray–Darling River system could have serious long-term consequences for the population. There have been no detailed studies of its breeding habits or success (Marchant and Higgins 1990).

New Guinea Tiger Heron. The current status of this species is uncertain, with little new information since Hancock and Kushlan (1984), although Rose and Scott (1997) classify it as declining. It is a shy, solitary heron inhabiting forest stream edges, breeding in lowland areas of the main island, Aru and Salalwati islands of New Guinea, and occasionally up to 1450 metres altitude in the Central Highlands (Beehler et al. 1986).

Little Bittern. The Little Bittern is only sporadically reported in Australia (Marchant and Higgins 1990). Its strongholds are the Cairns–Townsville areas of Queensland, south-eastern Queensland and New South Wales, Victoria and South Australia inland to the Darling–Murray River systems and in south-west Western Australia (Marchant and Higgins 1990). It has been reported as a vagrant in New Zealand and Lord Howe Island (Marchant and Higgins 1990). There are no trend figures available, although first breeding has been recorded in the north-west of Western Australia, since the completion of the Ord River Dam scheme (Jaensch, R.P. 1988). Garnett (1992) states that surveys in south-western Australia indicate it as common there but lists it under Taxa of Special Concern. There were few reports of the species during the Royal Australasian Ornithologists Union Murray–Darling Water bird Project 1994–97 (M. Hutchison pers. comm.). With reports representing less than 0.7% of bird observations in Victoria in all years since 1970, it has been nominated there under the Flora and Fauna Guarantee Act (Scientific Advisory Committee 1997). Its status in New Guinea, where it is found mostly in the lowlands and is seasonally common near Port Moresby, is uncertain, the dates of reports suggesting that it is a wintering migrant from Australia, although some evidence indicates possible breeding (Beehler et al. 1986). It is assumed to nest throughout its Australian range but most reports have been from the Murray–Darling system (Blakers et al. 1984). Although regarded as migratory (Marchant and Higgins 1990), there is no information on individual movements.

The New Zealand Little Bittern, treated as a subspecies in Hancock and Kushlan (1984) but as a separate species (*I. novaezelandiae*) in Marchant and Higgins (1990), confined to the South Island, is regarded as extinct in New Zealand. It has not been reported for more than a century (Marchant and Higgins 1990).

Yellow Bittern. Rose and Scott (1997) do not list the Yellow Bittern for Oceania, but Beehler et al. (1986) and Scott (1989) record it in New Guinea. It has also been recorded in Micronesia, where it is regarded as a common resident on Yap in a variety of wetland habitats, Guam, Northern Marianas, where it is reported as the commonest resident on Lake Hagoi, and Palau (Scott 1993a). Beehler et al. (1986) reported it as locally and seasonally abundant on the north coast of New Guinea, regarding it as largely a winter migrant. The Yellow Bittern occurred as a cyclone-assisted accidental visitor in West Australia (Ford 1969) and as a vagrant on Christmas Island (Stokes et al. 1987) but other Australian reports are not regarded as acceptable (Marchant and Higgins 1990).

Little information is available on breeding. Beehler et al. (1986) mentioned nesting records from Bougainville and Micronesia and Scott (1989) suggested it was probably breeding on West New Britain. Scott (1993a) referred to it as a "native breeding bird" at the Puerto Rico Mudflats on Saipan in the Northern Marianas. Its status is unclear, but the above information suggests the possibility of an increasing population.

Black Bittern. This species has declined in Western Australia but is widespread elsewhere in its range (Marchant and Higgins 1990). Although it is listed in Schedule 12 in New South Wales (New South Wales National Parks and Wildlife Act 1974) as vulnerable and rare in that state, and Garnett (1992) lists it under Taxa of Special Concern, no reliable trend figures are available. It is a widespread breeding resident of the New Guinea lowlands and Aru Island but is rare at higher altitudes (Beehler et al. 1996). Occurring also on Bismarck Island and in the Solomons, it frequents wetlands fringed by dense vegetation in coastal and near coastal areas around the Australian coastline except for most of Victoria, all of South Australia, south-eastern and central Western Australia (Marchant and Higgins 1990). It was formerly widespread in south-west Western Australia, but has suffered significant decline over the last 50 years (Marchant and Higgins 1990).

The Black Bittern is assumed to breed throughout its Australian range, although there are few recent records (Blakers et al. 1984). There have been no detailed studies of breeding biology (Marchant and Higgins 1990). Very little is known about its movements, with no recorded individual movements. It is regarded as being sedentary but is reported more frequently in eastern Australian coastal areas in summer than in winter (Marchant and Higgins 1990).

Australian Bittern. The Australian Bittern occurs in Queensland, New South Wales, Victoria and south-east South Australia (from the coast inland to the Murray–Darling system), Tasmania and New Zealand. The Murray–Darling system appears to be its stronghold in eastern Australia (Marchant and Higgins 1990). Garnett (1992) lists it as "insufficiently known" (i.e. suspected as being endangered, rare or vulnerable, but more information needed for determining true status). It is listed as rare and vulnerable in Schedule 12 of the New South Wales National Parks and Wildlife Act (1974), as endangered in Collar et al. (1994), and has been nominated under the Flora and Fauna Guarantee Act in Victoria because of its low reporting rate (1.6% of all bird observations since 1970 and only one breeding record in the south-west of the state since 1970—M. O'Brien pers. comm. 1997). Comprehensive surveys in Western Australia indicate fewer than 100 pairs. It is also found in New Caledonia and the Loyalty Islands (Marchant and Higgins 1990).

It is probably sedentary, although some season-related fluctuations of numbers have been noted. No records of movements of individuals are available. Breeding in densely vegetated freshwater wetlands, it is assumed to nest throughout its range, but there are virtually no breeding records and detailed studies of its breeding biology are non-existent (Marchant and Higgins 1990).

Critical Conservation and Management Issues

Wetland management

Loss of wetlands in some areas of Australia has been severe. For example, Riggert (1974, cited in Lane and McComb 1988) estimated that 75% of the wetlands on the Swan Coastal Plain of Western Australia had been filled or drained by 1964. Goodrick (1970) estimated a loss of waterfowl habitat in the wetlands of coastal New South Wales at 60% with further reduction predicted. Pressey and Harris (1988) later reported that 91% of wetland area in the Hunter, Clarence and Macleay floodplains (over 29 000 ha) had been affected by drainage to some extent. Ninety percent of New Zealand wetland habitat has been lost through drainage and development (Bridgewater 1991). Considerable alteration has occurred in catchments, such as Waimea Inlet (Owen and Sell 1985).

Not all habitat alteration has been detrimental to herons. Drainage of swamps and introduction of grazing animals, clearing of swamp forests and water regulation for irrigation on the one hand has reduced available breeding areas for the White-necked Heron, Great, Little and Intermediate Egrets and Nankeen Night Heron. However, creation of a vast number of artificial farm dams, on the other hand, has increased foraging habitat for the same species and the White-faced and Pied Herons. Leach (1994) demonstrated that surface area of farm dams is the most significant factor in attracting water birds, accounting for more than 90% of variation. He recorded White-necked and White-faced Herons, Great, Intermediate and Cattle Egrets using the dams in his sample, White-faced Herons being commonest. Extension of grazing land on floodplains has assisted range expansion of Cattle Egrets.

Although there has been an increasing focus on wetlands and their water birds since the 1960s, only New South Wales, Western Australia and the Federal government have now formally adopted wetland policies or strategies with potential importance for heron conservation. New South Wales introduced its State Environmental Planning Policy covering coastal wetlands (SEPP 14) in 1985, which improved wetland protection in the state by requiring an Environmental Impact Statement before any "designated development" (Pressey and Harris 1988). New Zealand established a Wetland Policy in 1986 and developed a database on Wetlands of Ecological and Representative Importance (Bridgewater 1991).

However, wetland mapping is inadequate (Winning 1991) and not of a quality suitable to support legislation for protective mechanisms (Knights 1991) and there have been few studies analysing environmental characteristics of water bird usage to guide policies. Storey et al. (1993) investigated several factors affecting water bird communities in Western Australia and identified the Swan Plain as an important breeding area, concluding that wetland management for water birds has no routine prescriptions and must be undertaken on a case by case basis. Harper's (1990) monthly water bird counts 1983–87 to investigate relationships between species numbers, season, water depth and rainfall at Bool Lagoon, South Australia found that the White-faced Heron's presence peaked when shallow habitat was available but that no pattern could be identified for the Great Egret. Magrath's (1992) study of habitat factors related to colonial water bird breeding found that almost all egret and night heron colonies occurred in woodlands of more than 50 ha with a high degree of site fidelity by species. A study by Briggs et al. (1995) showed that maintenance of an artificially high water level when an intermittently flooded river wetland was converted to permanent water storage killed nesting trees and prevented any further egret nesting. The consequent management implications require targeting such sites for habitat protection and maintenance of water regimes consistent with breeding requirements.

Allocation of water in regulated river systems in sufficient quantity and with appropriate timing for environmental purposes has emerged as the most critical issue for heron conservation in inland Australia, a focus emphasised by the 1996

Ramsar Conference Recommendation 6.17.4 requesting Australian authorities to consider providing water to inland Ramsar sites in greater quantity and with timing more closely related to natural environment conditions (Ramsar Convention 1996a). Only one successful heron nesting event was reported in the 1994–97 water bird survey of more than 360 Murray–Darling wetlands by the Royal Australasian Ornithologists Union (now called Birds Australia) until after the long drought broke for the 1995–96 season, when active colonies were recorded at eight sites in the region (M. Hutchison pers. comm. 1996). Water quality and competition for limited supply between conflicting interests are still major management issues, especially in the Darling–Murray system, where blue–green algae blooms and problems of lack of water-flow were major difficulties during 1993–94, with flow completely drying up in the Darling at Bourke in 1994.

The case of the Macquarie Marshes is a key example of the problems. Two dams and several diversions cause considerable disturbance to water flow. Variation occurs in the area of available wetland within and between years, but prime-breeding habitat occurs during major floods and suitable feeding habitat most times of the year (Brooker 1992). The management of the water supply upstream is regarded as the most critical issue (Kingsford and Thomas 1995).

The area of wetland vegetation has decreased since 1934. Some areas have been affected by too much water, and only about 14% of the area is reserved for conservation, including only three of the seven Intermediate Egret colonies, with the remaining marshland vulnerable to land use and hydrological changes (Kingsford and Thomas 1995). The future of the marshes is dependent on water entering the system from upstream in the Macquarie River and not on local rainfall (Kingsford and Thomas 1995). Johnson (pers. comm. 1994) identified a lag time of 3–4 months required between the commencement of flooding in the marsh and the onset of nesting. Intermediate Egrets, which require a minimum seven months from beginning nesting until completion of breeding, were the first to be affected by reduction in flood duration.

Developing a management plan, implemented in 1996 (Department of Water Resources and National Parks and Wildlife Service 1996), a major step forward, was fraught with controversy. The primary objective of the plan is to ensure that water regimes in the Macquarie Marshes are capable of maintaining the maximum possible extent, diversity and productivity of wetland habitat and suitable conditions for water bird breeding. It has the unique feature of providing a water quota for wildlife. Views differ widely on the rules for the availability and delivery of the wildlife allocation. Indirect effects and long-term consequences of further development of irrigated agriculture within the marsh system are potentially more serious than the immediate effects of habitat alienation. The first allocation of water for environmental purposes, aimed at approximating the catchment's natural flow and to support water bird breeding, was made in 1996–97. It enabled a successful nesting event (Macquarie Marshes Advisory and Audit Committee 1997) but again no nesting occurred in 1997–98 and the irrigation industry is still applying strong lobbying pressure on the state government.

Similar water management problems exist elsewhere, such as in the Lachlan, Murrumbidgee (Maher 1990, Magrath 1992) and Gwydir sections of the Murray–Darling System. Breeding of egrets ceased after 1983–84 in the Gwydir system, the last natural flood before construction of a major dam, which reduced the watercourse area from about 40 500 ha in the 1970s to about 400 ha in 1992 (J. Southeron pers. comm.). Fullagar and Davey (1983) found that the number of species of herons, ibises and allies known to breed in the downstream Barwon River area was reduced from 11 before 1951 to 4 after 1951, leaving the Macquarie Marshes as the only important breeding area on the Darling system. The Gwydir problem constitutes a serious issue in water management.

An unusually high flood regenerated the wetland in 1995–96, resulting in a major breeding event only supported to a successful conclusion after provision of a special water allocation (K. Yeadon pers. comm. 1996) after strong pressure had been exerted to have it cut off (H. Blackburn pers. comm. 1996). Breeding was again successful in the next two seasons, the last one again dependent on an environmental allocation (H. Blackburn pers. comm. 1997, 1998).

River Management Committees were constituted during 1997, under the NSW water reform process, for six inland river valleys including the Macquarie, Gwydir and Murrumbidgee, three of which reached agreement on environmental flow provisions which were ratified by the Minister for Land and Water Conservation (Desk Diary 1998). The importance of environmental allocations has also been recognised in Victoria, where the Murray Darling Ministerial Council was preparing in 1996 for introduction of a water release strategy for the Barmah Forest Ramsar site, a key heron nesting area, based on requirements for colonial water birds (Leslie 1996).

As a result of regulation, the full amplitude of a natural water regime is still unlikely to occur in any river system in New South Wales, despite these positive steps. However, according to Mitchell and Roberts (1983), although a lack of knowledge about water balance creates difficulties for the formulation of sound principles of water management, diversion of water from a wetland system or maintenance of constantly high water levels should be avoided. Despite the obvious lessons from the Murray–Darling degradation, there are continuing pressures for more water extraction. The rejection in 1997 of a major extraction project to establish a cotton growing industry on the ephemeral Cooper Creek in Queensland, a feeder stream for South Australia's Coongie Lakes Ramsar site, has relieved pressure on that system, at least for the moment. But the Narran Lakes (a heron nesting site) and the Paroo river in the ephemeral internal drainage area, are also likely to come under pressure. A major conference was held in 1998 that brought together proponents of schemes for transporting water to the inland from a number of sources. Under the existing political climate, brought about by prolonged drought and rural recession, such schemes will be very attractive to governments.

The study of egret ecology and conservation issues, with implications for colony management, a pioneer in the Australasian context (Baxter 1992, 1994, Baxter and Fairweather 1994), indicates a need for long-term studies of its kind. The study found that, although the occupation of a colony may be a random event, once a site is occupied it may suppress occupation of other sites within 10–15 km. Relative to non-colony wetlands, there were significantly higher levels of phosphorus and nitrates. It is likely that the imbalance was the likely cause of nest tree death. Thus occupation by a heronry alters the environment to such a degree that vegetation dies and indefinite occupation becomes impossible. Baxter (1992) predicted that only one of the 13 NSW heronries studied had a useful expectancy beyond ten years, and recommended reservation of nesting and feeding habitat based on a more thorough knowledge of the ecology of the birds.

Degradation of the Northern Territory wetlands by *Mimosa pigra*, aquatic weed species such as *Salvinia molesta*, and feral water buffalo threatens favoured habitat of the Pied Heron and Intermediate Egret. Coastal urbanisation has had major impact, with filling of wetlands for garbage disposal, sporting facilities and industrial development and clearing of mangroves for canal estate residential subdivisions. Because of its shy nature, the Sumatran Heron may abandon feeding and breeding areas close to human habitation, such as south of Cairns in Queensland. It is vulnerable to reclamation of mudflat and mangrove habitat (Marchant and Higgins 1990) and localised population decreases of the Green-backed Heron have resulted from reclamation of tidal lands (Morris 1975).

New Guinea

Infestations of the invasive wetland plant species *Salvinia molesta* and the water hyacinth (*Eichornia crassipes*) are causes for concern (Scott 1993a). Concern also exists regarding the possible long-term effects of mine waste disposal on the Fly River system wetlands, which are of importance for herons. The long-term effects of the Ok Tedi and Porgera mines are difficult to predict, but the threats are regarded as real (Scott 1993a). Logging in the forests of the islands may have a long-term effect on the habitat for the New Guinea Tiger Heron.

Oceania

Scott (1993a) reported no systematic study of wetland fauna nor research programme has been set up for Papua New Guinea wetlands or in most of the other island countries, except for the present and former US Territories. In some cases there appear to be no significant wetlands, except for reef systems. Threats to heron habitat vary from island to island (Scott 1993a). The following appear to be the most important: encroachment into and destruction of mangroves for homes and firewood; landfill for industrial, residential and tourist development; degradation of water quality through toxic waste, sewage and garbage disposal, pesticides and fertilisers; soil erosion creating siltation; conversion to agricultural and aquacultural use; and influence of feral animals such as water buffalo and domestic cats.

Conservation in reserves

As at 1997, Australia had 49 sites registered under the Ramsar Convention, some protecting important heron habitat (particularly Kakadu National Park in the Northern Territory, Macquarie Marshes in New South Wales and six Murray River sites in Victoria and South Australia). Only three of 11 Great Egret breeding colony sites in south-west Western Australia (Jaensch and Vervest 1989) and two of 13 New South Wales colonies enjoy protection status. Of the latter, a community-owned reserve, which was established after significant public pressure, protects one (Shortland Wetlands Centre). Of 11 colonies in coastal New South Wales of which the ownership status is known, 8 are on privately owned land, with 2 known sympathetic landholders, one is local government council owned and under threat from potential future road construction (Project Egret Watch Records).

In Victoria, 90% of wetland area is privately owned and only 4% reserved for conservation (Norman and Corrick 1988). In New South Wales, the situation is better, with 45% in private ownership, 32% in reservation, and the rest Crown Land, although coastal floodplain wetlands containing melaleuca swamp forests (identified by Baxter (1992) as preferred breeding habitat for egrets) are poorly represented (Pressey and Harris 1988).

The Northern Territory has 39 wetland parks and reserves, of which the 667 000 ha Kakadu National Park Stage 1 (also on the World Heritage list) and the Cobourg Peninsula Aboriginal Land and Wildlife Sanctuary are Ramsar listed (Finlayson et al. 1988). Administration of wetlands in the Territory is complicated by divisions into freehold and leasehold private land, Northern Territory and Commonwealth administered Crown Land and two park administration services, Conservation Commission of the Northern Territory and the Australian National Parks and Wildlife Service (now called Environment Australia) (Finlayson et al. 1988).

Although Tasmania has 108 wetland reserves, Kirkpatrick and Tyler (1988) claim that no land or water there is safe from development. Queensland has 63 wetland areas in some form of reserve status (Arthington and Hegerl 1988), with two Ramsar sites added in 1993, but even World Heritage Listing did not prevent the destruction of mangroves for a resort development in North Queensland in 1994. South Australia has 52 reserves (Lothian and Williams 1988), but one Ramsar site has been threatened by plans for a bridge development and another by exploration for and likely future extraction of petroleum.

New Zealand had 5 Ramsar sites as at March 1996, of which Waituna lagoon is important for both the Australian Bittern and the White-faced Heron. Whangamarino and Kopuatai Peat Dome support the Australasian Bittern, the former being the country's most important breeding site, providing habitat for about 20% of the population (Jones 1993). There are a number of reserves established by conservation groups (Buxton 1991).

There is no specific environmental legislation aimed at conservation of wetlands areas in Papua New Guinea, although the establishment of conservation areas is possible under a number of different acts (Scott 1989) and the country has one listed Ramsar site (Tonda Wildlife Management Area). Acquisition of sites for reserves is difficult in Oceania because of traditional land ownership systems, and may be inappropriate under local cultural contexts. However, some voluntary conservation areas are being established under the South Pacific Regional Environment Program (R. Jaensch pers. comm. 1998) and some wetland reservation has been achieved in American Samoa, French Polynesia and the Marianas (Scott 1993a).

Wetland assessment

Establishing criteria and presenting local government planners and consent authorities with simple assessment procedures is an important first step in devising strategies for wetland protection and management (Gilligan 1984). Pressey (1981) and Gilligan (1984) combined selected numerically-weighted wetland attributes to produce a value score, a technique which has raised subsequent criticism and debate (Pressey 1985, Beilharz 1989, Winning 1990), the main deficiency being that such techniques can mask the real value of a wetland (Pressey 1985, Beilharz 1989). Use of a single value, such as Beilharz's "breeding site for colonial water birds" is probably the most useful for heron conservation. The major problem under the present political climate is to have such a value accepted as sufficient reason for reserving an area in the face of development or water competition pressures.

Catchment management

Inclusion in a reserve or protection zone does not ensure an appropriate water supply (Pressey and Harris 1988), the Macquarie Marshes being a classic example. McComb and Lake (1988) pointed out that the long-term maintenance of natural wetland values will depend on a greater understanding of processes in the wetlands and their catchments, recommending approaches to total catchment management as a priority area for research. This view was reflected by the 1996 Ramsar Convention with Resolution 6.13 (9) on management planning asking for the Technical Review Panel to investigate most recent advances and best case studies in integrated catchment management (Ramsar Convention 1996b).

The complex effect of dry–wet cycles on wetland catchment management for water birds has been demonstrated at Booligal, New South Wales (Crome 1988). Intermediate Egrets bred best when the swamps had been filled for some time, producing a climax of Ribbonweed and fish, whereas most water bird species, especially ducks, bred best after a flood on a previously dried-out basin. The studies by Kingsford and Thomas (1995) and Johnson (pers. comm. 1994) in the Macquarie Marshes have shown the importance of flooding in the catchment for herons (see Wetland Management).

It has been demonstrated that breeding success of Great, Little and Intermediate egrets is related to the rainfall pattern during the nesting season (Maddock and Baxter 1991). Geering (1993) showed that dry colony sites in northern New South Wales were not used until after flooding. However, little is yet known about the relationship between utilisation of colonies and the climatic cycle. Crome (1988) concluded that for intermittent drying of swamps by drainage to be used on a regional or local scale as a management strategy, it is essential that adequate information be available about water bird concentrations, their breeding activities, and the state of rivers and swamps. This information is frequently lacking when water control authorities make decisions on directing water flows.

A range of catchment management issues affect the health of Australian wetlands and thus heron conservation, including drainage, urban, industrial and agricultural development, water utilisation and regulation, pollution, weed invasion and introduced fauna, too numerous for detailed discussion here. They are well summarised for the separate states and for the continent as a whole in McComb and Lake (1988).

Potentially the most serious of these are in the Northern Territory. The ravages of the feral water buffalo (*Bubalis bubalis*), the impending invasion of the Cane Toad (*Bufo marinus*), introduced weeds such as *Mimosa pigra* and *Salvinia molesta,* and pollution threats from mineral extraction and processing in the catchment of the East Alligator River and the Finniss River, threaten the viability of water bird breeding and foraging habitat.

Colony threats and management

Two Australian colonies have been deliberately destroyed. In New South Wales, an important colony of Great and Intermediate egrets and the Nankeen Night Heron on

Kooragang Island up to the early 1970s was destroyed when the mangrove forest was removed (van Gessel and Kendall 1972). Pollution of the water was one reason given by a private landholder when a Cattle Egret colony was destroyed by removal of the nest trees at Kybong in Queensland (Gympie Times 1987). Another colony was destroyed by artificial change to the water regime (Briggs et al. 1995).

The coastal New South Wales and Queensland colonies are in or close to urban areas, with potential for various forms of human disturbance and predation by domestic animals, which raise special management issues. The Murwillumbah colony is in an industrial and residential area (Pratt 1979), while Boambee, Shortland, Seaham, and Toronto are very close to residences, the latter colony being under threat from proposed road works.

The Bracken Ridge colony in urban Brisbane (Queensland) was threatened with a proposal for the construction of a canal residential estate, which although allowing for the preservation of the nest trees, would have destroyed support habitat (Cameron McNamara 1987). Community lobbying with authorities prevented the development from proceeding and the wetland is now protected as a Wetland Reserve. However, an adjacent housing estate is built on flood-prone land and any serious flood incident may lead to flood mitigation actions, which may affect the colony (R. Sonnenburg 1993, pers. comm.).

The Doboy colony of 11 000 breeding Cattle Egrets has a degree of protection from Doboy Swamp's listing in the "Brisbane Conservation Atlas". It is under pressure from adjacent Noxious, Offensive and Hazardous Industry zones and residential areas (Stock and Venables 1988), with pollution from a nearby skin processing works the likely cause of tree deaths (R. Sonnenburg 1993, pers. comm.). Recommended conservation and management actions (Stock and Venables 1988, 1989) have not yet been implemented.

A strategy for public involvement

An important component of future management for the conservation of herons is public education, which can be facilitated by bringing the community into close proximity to the birds and providing interpretive facilities for education about their ecology and conservation needs. Establishment of such sites brings with it both people and habitat management problems.

Controlled public visitation has been achieved at the Okarito Great Egret breeding colony in New Zealand and at the Shortland Wetlands Centre egret colony of four species in Newcastle, New South Wales. There is easy but uncontrolled public access to the Boambee colony at Coffs Harbour in northern New South Wales and to the Seaham colony north of Newcastle. At Okarito, a concessionaire is licensed to bring visitors to a viewing hide. There has been increasing visitation but so far no detrimental correlation has been found between breeding success and visitor numbers (O'Donnell 1993 pers. comm.). The Shortland Wetlands Centre was set up specifically for wetland education and interpretive facilities are well developed. Access has been managed to minimise disturbance to the colony, but to a degree this has been thwarted by the birds shifting the colony location in 1991, with part of it now directly over one of the walking trails. To date, this does not seem to have had any adverse effect on nesting, as the birds have become accustomed to people moving underneath. It has had educational benefits.

The nesting trees at Boambee and Seaham are right beside public roads in residential areas and attract uncontrolled visitors. A degree of protection has been established by enlisting support of the neighbouring primary schools and local residents, who carry out voluntary policing. There has been no evidence of deleterious effects on occupation or breeding success from continued visitation over at least 10 years at Seaham (Maddock and Baxter 1991, Maddock unpublished data).

A key to mobilising public support for conservation and management of heron populations is community involvement. This has been achieved very effectively through the Shortland Wetlands Centre's Project Egret Watch research and public education programme in eastern Australia and New Zealand (Maddock 1991b, 1992). A core of dedicated volunteers who are closely involved with patagial tagging, colony and winter habitat monitoring, including school children, and a larger, more loosely organised group of observers assist with the research. Feedback to the participants is provided through a quarterly newsletter and personal contact. The general public is given feedback through visitation to the Wetlands Centre and through extensive use of the media.

The key area of community beliefs on water usage needs a focussed educational programme targeted at the rural community, where there is limited understanding of the complex interactive nature of wetland ecology and a pervasive view that water not used for agricultural production is wasted.

Volunteers assist a team of scientists capturing and marking egrets. The Egret Watch research programme in eastern Australia has successfully mobilised public support for conservation of heron populations. Photo: Max Maddock.

Conclusions

There has been insufficient long-term research into the population, breeding and movement of herons in Australasia and Oceania to gauge clearly real current status and population trends. Several surveys have used different methodologies in different time frames, but they are reasonably indicative of the status of colonies in key breeding areas. The issues in Australia are compounded by extremes in the climatic cycle and the complexity of community cultural views. Ensuring an adequate and ecologically-determined water supply to inland wetlands, strongholds of breeding for the vulnerable Great White, Intermediate and Little egrets and the Nankeen Night Heron, is critical for their conservation and also very important for bitterns, about which so little is known.

There is a need for coordinated catchment-based studies of habitat factors on a national basis, integrated with research into heron biology, which can be used as a guide for wetland management policies. At the moment, Australian policy and management decisions are in the hands of several agencies in separate state, federal and territory administrations. Oceania lacks financial resources and skilled people to carry out the necessary work.

Community education is an important component of strategies for both education and conservation management. This can be in part achieved by establishment of special wetland educational reserves where school children and uninitiated adults can have close access to the birds, which in turn requires careful people and habitat management techniques and effective interpretation facilities. Other uncontrolled areas which are visible to the public need appropriate interpretive materials designed and erected and regular use made of the print and electronic media as an educational tool. No matter how extensive the heron biology and habitat research is, it can have little impact without community understanding and cooperation. Because of the migratory nature of many heron species, adequate data on their movements cannot be obtained without recruiting members of the public as field observers.

7. Herons in North America, Central America and the West Indies

Robert W. Butler, James A. Kushlan and Ian J. Davidson

This chapter discusses heron populations in North America, Bermuda, Central America, and the islands of the West Indies including the Bahamas, Greater Antilles, and the island chain including the Virgin Islands and Lesser Antilles (Fig. 7.1). The region includes the large northern countries of Canada and the United States of America (USA) and more southerly countries differing in size and stage of economic development. Ranges, especially migratory ranges, of many species cover the breadth of the region, crossing political borders and making international cooperation an absolute requirement for heron conservation. Seasonal population movements over wide areas are the rule in the region, with few species being endemic or having restricted ranges.

The Heron Fauna

The heron fauna comprises 24 species (Table 7.1). Species diversity is greatest in North America. Twelve species nest north of Mexico; and ten nest only from Mexico south. Several species of recent European/African origin and two species of recent Asian origin occur in the area, some of which may be in the process of establishing themselves in the hemisphere. Most species are abundant and widely distributed. For example, the breeding ranges of the Great Blue and Black-crowned Night herons and Least Bittern extend across the inhabitable portion of the continent from high latitude into the tropics. A few species are more restricted: the Reddish Egret and a dimorphic population of the Great Blue Heron (*Ardea herodius occidentalis*) have limited ranges. The American Bittern is the only regional endemic (as a nesting species), although the Bare-throated Tiger Heron is nearly endemic as it barely ranges beyond our limits into South America. Typical South American species, such as Cocoi, Capped, and Agami herons, range into the region in Central America.

Heron Conservation
ISBN 0-12-430130-4

Fig. 7.1   Important heron areas in North and Central America and the West Indies.

Environmental Conditions

Climatic conditions range from arctic to tropical, arid to humid, and continental to coastal. At high latitudes, landscapes are dominated by short season wetlands (tundra), which give way south to boreal forests (taiga), bogs, prairies, and prairie wetlands, then to temperate forests in humid areas and grasslands and desert in the drier continental interior. Western mountain ranges partition the North American continent, and a single river system (the Mississippi) drains most of the continental interior. Salt marshes occur along the seacoast in the north and are replaced by mangrove swamps further south. Tropical lowlands tend to be dry (especially on islands), and tropical uplands range from scrub to rain forest. Herons use most landscapes having available water, other than those of the far north.

Seasonal distribution of herons is influenced largely by food availability as determined by such factors as seasonal temperatures especially in the north, by seasonal hydrological cycles especially in the subtropics and tropics, by tidal cycles along the seacoasts, and cycles of prey availability in most locations. Temperate zone herons move south of frozen waters in the boreal winter (Hancock and Kushlan

Key to Fig. 7.1 Important heron areas in North and Central America and the West Indies.

1 United States of America—Delaware Bay
2 United States of America—Chesapeake Bay
3 United States of America—Southeastern coastal plain, including the Okefenokee Swamp
4 United States of America—Southern Florida, including Florida Bay and the Everglades
5 United States of America—Mississippi River valley
6 United States of America—Mississippi Delta and Louisiana coastal and inland swamps
7 United States of America, Mexico—Coastal lagoons of Texas and Mexico including the Laguna Madre
8 United States of America, Canada—Puget Sound and Strait of Georgia
9 United States of America—San Francisco Bay and Central Valley
10 United States of America—Imperial Valley and Salton Sea
11 Mexico—Bahia Magdalena
12 Mexico—Sonora and Sinaloa coast
13 Mexico—Nayarit coast including Marismas Nacionales
14 Mexico—Lago Chapala
15 Mexico—Tampico lagoons
16 Mexico—Tabasco lagoons
17 Mexico—Ria Lagartos
18 Mexico, Belize, Guatemala, Honduras—Gulf of Honduras coast and coastal islands
19 Guatemala—Guatemala Pacific coast and Lago Atitlan
20 El Salvador, Honduras, Nicaragua—Golfo de Fonseca
21 Nicaragua—Lago de Managua and Lago de Nicaragua, including Rio San Juan
22 Costa Rica—Gulf of Nicoya including Laguna Palo Verde
23 Costa Rica, Panama—Panama coast including Golfo de Montijo
24 Panama—Golfo de Panama including Bahia de Panama
25 Nicaragua—Mosquito Coast
26 Puerto Rico—Puerto Rico coast
27 Dominican Republic—Hispaniola north coast
28 Dominican Republic—Hispaniola south coast
29 Jamaica—Jamaica north coast
30 Cuba—Cuba south coast including the Zapata Swamp, Golfo de Batabano, Golfo de Ana Maria, Golfo de Guacanayabo
31 Cuba—Cuba north coast including Archipelago de Sabana, Bahia de los Perros, Bahia de Jiguey
32 Bahamas—Andros Island

Table 7.1 Status of herons in North and Central America and the West Indies.

	CpH	GrH	GBH	CoH	GWE	RE	TH	LBH	SnE	LE	SwE
Greenland		+						+		+	
Canada		?	++					++	++		+
USA		?	++		75 000–100 000	2500	75 000–100 000	75 000–100 000	12 000–150 000	+	
Mexico			++		25 000–50 000	500	?	++	25 000–50 000		
Belize						++	?	+	+		
Guatemala			+		++	+	++	+	++		
Honduras			+		++	?	++	+	+		
El Salvador			+		++	+	++	+	+		
Nicaragua			+		++		++	+	+		
Costa Rica			+		++	+	++	++	++		
Panama	++		+		++	+	++	+	+		
Cuba			++	+	++	++	++	+	++		
Jamaica			+		++	++	++	+	++		
Hispaniola			+		++	++	++	+	++		
Puerto Rico			+		++	+	++	+	++	+	
Bahamas			+		++	++	++	++	++		
Bermuda			+	+	+		+		+	+	
Lesser Antilles	+		++	++	+	+	++		++	++	+

++ = nesting population, + = present, not nesting, ? = status uncertain, Number = nesting pairs.

	CE	GbH	AH	YCNH	BCNH	BBH	BTH	FTH	RTH	LsB	YB	SAB	AmB
Greenland		+											+
Canada	++	++			++					++			++
USA	250 000–500 000	++		++	25 000–50 000					++	+	++	++
Mexico	++	++	++	++	++	++	++		++	++		++	++
Belize	++	++	+?		++	++	++		++	++		++	?
Guatemala	++	++	++	++	++	++	++			++		++	+
Honduras	++	++	+	++	++	++	++		++	++		?	?
El Salvador	++	++	?	++	++	++	++		?	++		++	?
Nicaragua	++	++	?	++	++	++	++			++		++	?
Costa Rica	++	++	++	++	++	++	++	++	++	++		++	+
Panama	++	++	++	++	+	++	+	++	++	++			+
Cuba	++	++		++	++					++			+
Jamaica	++	++		++	++					++			
Hispaniola	++	++		++						++			
Puerto Rico	++	++		++	++					++			+
Bahamas	++	++		++	++					+			+
Bermuda	+	+		++	+					+			+
Lesser Antilles	++	++		++	++					+			+

++ = nesting population, + = present, not nesting, ? = status uncertain, Number = nesting pairs.

1984, R. W. Butler 1992). Seasonal and daily fluctuations of temperature and surface water depths control when and where herons forage, and also when and where they nest (Kushlan et al. 1985, Kushlan 1989a, Butler 1993, 1995). Shallow waters created during semiannual or biannual dry periods in subtropical savannas and swamps concentrate prey and attract large numbers of feeding herons. When savannas and wetlands dry completely, herons migrate to lower lying areas or to coastal areas. Lunar tidal fluctuations dictate where and when coastal herons can feed, setting up daily and longer-cycle movements. Seiches and wind-driven tides influence use of shores.

North America has extensive wetlands (Fig. 7.1) (Kushlan 1993a, Livingston 1993), which support its heron fauna. Notable feeding habitats include the following: dense freshwater reed beds (American and Least bitterns, Green-backed and Tiger herons); wooded stream edge (Green-backed, Tricolored, and Agami herons); shallow, relatively open, fresh or brackish water marshes (Little Blue, Tricolored, Great Blue and Black-crowned Night herons, Snowy and Great White egrets); shallow coastal marine waters (Yellow-crowned Night Heron, Reddish Egret, Great Blue Heron); coastal mangrove swamp (Green-backed, Great Blue, Tricolored, and Boat-billed herons); sea beaches (Great Blue and Yellow-crowned Night herons, Great White Egrets); prairie, pasture, and cultivated fields (Cattle Egret, Great Blue and Rufescent Tiger herons), urban grasslands and lawns (Cattle and Great White egrets, Yellow-crowned Night Heron), aquacultural ponds and raceways (Great White Egret, Great Blue and Black-crowned Night herons); and residential and commercial sites where foods such as human hand-outs or fish scraps are available (Great Blue and Black-crowned Night herons).

Extensive wetlands occur in the prairie pothole region of central USA and southern Canada and along the coastal plain of south-eastern USA. In tropical regions, significant wetlands occur along both coasts of Mexico, particularly in Nayarit and Tabasco, and along the Caribbean coast of Central America (Scott and Carbonell 1986, Lopez-Ornato and Ramo 1992, Davidson and Gauthier 1993, Anderson et al. 1996, Wilson and Ryan 1997). Inland, Lakes Managua and Nicaragua support extensive freshwater wetlands. Large wetlands on Caribbean islands include the Zapata Swamp and other coastal wetlands of Cuba, and the coastal wetlands on the Bahamas, Hispaniola, Jamaica, and the French Antilles.

Wetlands were more extensive throughout the region before European settlement. Over half of the pothole wetlands in the Canadian prairies have been converted to other uses, as have two-thirds of the wetlands in southern Ontario, the salt marshes in Atlantic Canada and estuarine marshes on the Pacific Coast (Government of Canada 1991). In the USA, over 4.75 million acres (54%) of palustrine wetlands were lost between mid 1950s and mid 1970s (Tiner 1984). In Mexico 50% of wetlands have been lost since 1970.

Changing Status of Herons

Data available

Although information available on the status of various species of herons is rather extensive, compared to some other parts of the world, only broad conclusions can be drawn regarding status and trends. No national or continental programme yet exists for censusing colonial herons (Parnell et al. 1988, Erwin et al. 1985, 1993). Some smaller regions, particularly some states, have significant information bases from recurring surveys. In some locales information goes back decades and, although of varying reliability (Frohring et al. 1988), is sufficient to identify long-term trends in parts of North America (Ogden 1978, Powell et al. 1989). Comprehensive surveys were undertaken along coasts of eastern North America starting in the 1970s (Portnoy 1977, Kushlan and White 1977, Erwin 1979, Custer et al. 1980) and a national register was operating for several years (McCrimmon 1978). Spendelow and Patton (1988) did a thorough evaluation of these data. Monitoring has been conducted in some USA states, such as Texas, Florida, Louisiana, South and North Carolina (TCWC 1982, Lange 1995, Runde et al. 1991, Bancroft 1989, Keller et al. 1984, Martin and Lester 1991, Dodd and Murphy 1996, Parnell et al. 1997). An annual North American survey of breeding birds, although focusing on land birds, can be used cautiously to infer trends of some of the more visible herons (Robbins et al. 1986, Peterjohn and Sauer 1993, Fleury and Sherry 1995). In boreal winter, bird counts conducted near Christmas each year provide long-term data on herons in count sites (Root 1988, Fleury and Sherry 1995). Fleury and Sherry (1995) found correspondence between these two census methodologies in evaluating wading bird population changes. In the future, breeding bird atlases, which are being developed in various USA states, will provide additional detail of nesting distributions. Each species is being described in the Birds of North America series.

Species status

Capped Heron. The range of this South American species reaches eastern Panama, where it is considered rare or uncommon but probably regular (Ridgely and Gwynne 1989).

Grey Heron. This Old World species has been reported infrequently in Greenland and the West Indies (Barbados, Martinique, Montserrat) (Hancock and Kushlan 1984, Smith and Smith 1990, Raffaele et al. 1998), and outside the region in South America. One bird had been banded in France. These are vagrants, presumably delivered to the New World by favourable winds. The species should be sought also among Great Blue Herons along the east coast of North America.

Great Blue Heron. The breeding range of this widespread species is shown by Butler (1992), updating and clarifying that illustrated by Hancock and Kushlan (1984). Its western range extends as far north as south-east Alaska. To the south it has been recorded breeding in Cuba, in the Virgin Islands, and also in the Galapagos Islands off South America. Its breeding status in Central America requires additional documentation. In the core of its North American distribution, all evidence suggests it remains widespread. Nesting is widespread though localised, and often coincides with areas of human activity, so conflict with changing human land use is its primary conservation challenge.

    Because the Great Blue Heron nests solitarily or in small colonies over a vast area, range-wide population estimates are unavailable. In the late 1970s about 36 000 birds were tallied along the east and south North American coast, almost 40% being counted in the Chesapeake Bay and mid-Gulf of Mexico coast (Spendelow and Patton 1988). Few comparable data are available from large inland areas (for instance Findholt and Berner 1988). Available information, however, suggests populations in various portions of North America are stable or maybe even increasing (McCrimmon 1982, Robbins et al. 1986, Butler 1992). For example, the nesting population in Louisiana doubled from 1976 to 1990, now exceeding 10 000 birds (Portnoy 1977, Martin and Lester 1991) and continuing on an upward trend (Fleury and Sherry 1995).

Individuals do winter as far north as southern Canada in some years, but generally they winter south of the −6° January isotherm (Root 1988), especially along coasts and in the southern USA, Mexico, and Central America south to the Greater Antilles, rarely in the Lesser Antilles, and into northern South America (Byrd 1978, Campbell et al. 1990, Mikuska et al. 1998, Raffaele 1983, Raffaele et al. 1998). In the USA, relatively high winter densities occur on the southern Colorado River, Great Salt Lake, the Gulf of Mexico coast, and Florida (Root 1988). Wintering populations appear high and have increased dramatically in recent years in Louisiana (Fleury and Sherry 1995). Post-breeding dispersal of young individuals extends far north of their nesting range.

Two subspecies deserving special conservation consideration are the southern Florida–Caribbean subspecies (*occidentalis*), characterised by a high proportion of white-plumaged morphs, and the north Pacific subspecies (*fannini*), residing year-round along the coasts of Washington, British Columbia and south-east Alaska (Butler 1997). Powell et al. (1989) provided an excellent understanding of the population changes in extreme southern Florida. The *occidentalis* population doubled each decade between 1930 and 1980 to about 1500 birds. About 1500 birds occur elsewhere in Florida (Kale 1978). The white phase appears to be rare in the West Indies, but additional study is desirable in Cuba. Butler (1997) described population changes in Washington and British Columbia. The *fannini* subspecies appears to be in slow decline, likely as a result of frequent disturbances of nesting birds by humans and eagles.

The Cocoi Heron. The South American analogue of the Great Blue Heron (Chapter 8), this species extends into the region in eastern Panama, but its status there is little known. It is thought to breed, but this is not confirmed (Ridgely and Gwynne 1993).

Great White Egret. Widely dispersed throughout the region, this egret's nesting distribution has not changed much since 1984 (Hancock and Kushlan 1984), but its slow northward range consolidation continues, now including nesting in southern Ontario, Canada.

Coastal USA nesting population in the 1970s was about 114 000 egrets (Spendelow and Patton 1988). The North American nesting population is centred on Louisiana, USA, where over 43 000 were estimated to occur in 11 colony sites in 1990 (Martin and Lester 1991). Florida, USA, supported over 23 000 nesting birds (counted in 1977). A few thousand birds reside in the American states along the mid-Atlantic (Spendelow and Patten 1988), and hundreds live in each of various non-coastal states. Nesting populations are increasing in Louisiana, Texas and California, but may be decreasing in south-western USA (Robbins et al. 1986, Fleury and Sherry

1995). Coastal Mexico is a second population centre, where about 54 000 birds nest in the Tabasco Lagoons (Scott and Carbonell 1986). Its breeding range extends into the West Indies in the Bahamas, Greater Antilles, and northern Lesser Antilles (Raffaele et al. 1998).

In late summer, post-breeding birds disperse into the mid-USA and southern Canada. The wintering range (not depicted clearly in Hancock and Kushlan 1984) includes California, southern Mississippi Valley through Texas, the east and south USA coast, both Mexican coasts, the Caribbean and into northern South America (Mikuska et al. 1998). In the USA, highest wintering abundance is on the Florida Gulf Coast and in Louisiana–Texas; the southern Colorado River and Humboldt Bay in California also support numbers in winter (Root 1988). Wintering Great White Egret populations have been stable from 1960 through 1989 in Florida (McCrimmon pers. comm.) and appear to have increased in Louisiana (Fleury and Sherry 1995). Egrets winter also through the West Indies into the lower Lesser Antilles.

Reddish Egret. This coastal egret nests along the Gulf of Mexico, Caribbean and Pacific coasts. In recent decades, it has expanded its USA breeding range into Gulf coastal Alabama and Louisiana. Further south it nests along the Caribbean and Pacific coasts of Mexico south to Costa Rica (race *dickeyi*), the Bahamas and Cuba (Hancock and Kushlan 1984, Paul 1991, Lopez-Ornato and Ramo 1992). Outside the region covered by this chapter it occurs into northern South America (see Chapter 8).

The species is rather irregular away from its nesting grounds but is found as far as the Lesser Antilles. Wandering birds are increasingly being reported far inland.

The world population of the Reddish Egret is about 6–10 000 adults (Paul 1991). It nests most abundantly in Florida and Texas, USA, and is less common in Central America. In Texas, local breeding populations have fluctuated between about 2000 and 4200 birds since the 1970s (Paul 1991). About 600–800 birds nest in Mexico (Lopez-Ornato and Ramo 1992) and about 600–800 in southern Florida. Highest wintering densities in the USA are around Laguna Largo in Texas and in southern Florida (Root 1988). The Florida population was probably extirpated in the early part of this century but has recovered in Florida Bay, since its rediscovery in the 1930s, to about 200–250 adults in the 1970s (Powell et al. 1989). More recent information is needed. Other populations appear to have decreased somewhat in recent years in Texas and Louisiana (Martin and Lester 1991, Lange 1995).

Tricolored Heron. This species nests from Maine, USA, through the Gulf of Mexico and the Gulf of California to both coasts of Central America, the West Indies (Bahamas, Greater Antilles, Cayman Islands) and outside the region into South America (Hancock and Kushlan 1984, Frederick 1997). Birds occur in Florida and on the Gulf of Mexico Coast year-round. This species expanded its range northward in North America in the present century, and has benefited from coastal habitat modification creating both nesting and feeding sites. Populations have likely increased in Louisiana but may have decreased in southern Florida.

Spendelow and Patton (1988) tallied about 178 000 birds nesting along the USA coasts in 1976–78. Over 133 000 individuals were counted in Louisiana alone. In 1990, Martin and Lester (1991) tallied about 44 000 individuals in Louisiana, but the methods do not allow for comparison to previous surveys. Summer populations may have decreased in Texas (Fleury and Sherry 1995).

Post-breeding birds disperse into the south-central USA. Northernmost populations migrate southward in winter, into the south-eastern USA, the Greater Antilles, Central America, but also into South America (Mikuska et al. 1998). The largest winter populations occur in southern Louisiana wetlands and Texas, but it is also numerous in winter along both Florida seacoasts (Root 1988). Its populations have increased in winter in Louisiana (Fleury and Sherry 1995).

Little Blue Heron. The North American distribution of this species appears to be influenced by proximity to the coast and large lakes and rivers. It nests in the eastern USA south from Maine through Central America, the West Indies, and outside the region through much of South America (Hancock and Kushlan 1984). Recent

Little Blue Heron. Overall nesting populations of the Little Blue Heron are relatively stable in the USA. Photo: Robert Bennetts.

evidence indicates limited nesting in mid-continental sites (AOU 1983), but no important shifts in distribution have occurred in recent years.

The centre of the North American population is on the Gulf Coast of the USA. Coastal populations were estimated to be about 101 000 nesting birds in the 1970s, over 80% in Louisiana (Spendelow and Patton 1988). An additional 34 000 birds were reported from inland colonies in Texas, USA (TCWC 1982). There are indications of decreases in this species in eastern USA (Robbins et al. 1986), but overall nesting populations remain relatively high.

Post-nesting herons disperse into the eastern USA before migrating south. Populations east of the Mississippi River migrate into the Caribbean and South America (Byrd 1978). Birds breeding west of the Mississippi River migrate to the south-eastern USA, Mexico, Cuba, Bahamas, Hispaniola, Puerto Rico, Jamaica, Central America, and northern South America (Mikuska et al. 1998). Important winter sites include the eastern North American coast, lower Mississippi River in Louisiana, southern Florida, and coastal lagoons of western and eastern Mexico and Honduras, Cuba, Hispaniola, Puerto Rico (Root 1988, Fleury and Sherry 1995, Mikuska et al. 1998). Florida wintering populations show evidence of a decrease from 1960 to 1989 (McCrimmon pers. comm.).

Snowy Egret. This species nests from Maine, USA, south along the Atlantic and Gulf coasts, and from California south through coastal Mexico, into the West Indies (Bahamas, Greater Antilles, northern Lesser Antilles to St. Martin) (Hancock and Kushlan 1984, Raffaele et al. 1998). Disjunct populations occur in western American states. Its nesting range expanded between the end of the plume hunting era and the 1970s (Hancock and Kushlan 1984). Populations are increasing in the West Indies (Raffaele et al. 1998). It breeds most abundantly along the coast. Estimates from the 1970s indicated a coastal USA nesting population of about 159 000 birds (Spendelow and Patton 1988). Its population is centred on the Gulf of Mexico coast, where the nesting population in Louisiana may approach 100 000 birds and that of the coastal lagoons of Tabasco may approach 60 000 (Scott and Carbonell 1986). Florida supports the next largest nesting concentration, about 20 000 individuals.

Few data exist on breeding population changes. It is probable that populations decreased into the early 1900s due to the plumage trade, but credible numerical estimates are lacking. In recent decades, summer populations have increased in California (Fleury and Sherry 1995). In southern Florida, USA, between the 1970s and 1980s numbers plummeted from about 5000 pairs in 1976 to about 500 pairs in 1989 (Bancroft 1989). However, for Florida as a whole and range-wide, there is no evidence of significant decrease (Robbins et al. 1986, McCrimmon pers. comm.). Post-breeding dispersal results in a net northward movement through most of the continental USA. North American populations winter in the eastern and south-eastern USA, southern Florida, the Pacific coast from San Francisco through western Mexico, the southern end of the Colorado River, eastern coastal Mexico, the Caribbean, Greater and Lesser Antilles, into South America in coastal Colombia, Venezuela, and French Guiana (Mikuska et al. 1998). Wintering populations have increased significantly in Louisiana (Fleury and Sherry 1995).

Little Egret. Hancock and Kushlan (1984) reported sightings from Newfoundland, Trinidad and Martinique, of which two birds had been banded in Spain. These were evidence of stragglers from the Old World to the New World. Since then the species has become a part of the nesting heron fauna of the Americas (Murphy 1992, Raffaele et al. 1998), an extremely exciting example of recent heron population expansion. Two forms have been reported. The Little Egret (*E. garzetta garzetta)* is now resident on Barbados, with nesting of up to 40 individuals, and St. Lucia and (so far) a nonbreeding resident or vagrant on Puerto Rico, Martinique, and Guadeloupe (Raffaele et al. 1998). The Western Reef Heron (*E. g. gularis, sensu* Hancock and Kushlan 1984) is also reported from the West Indies (Puerto Rico, St. Lucia, Barbados) (Raffaele et al. 1998). Its breeding is to be looked for.

Swinhoe's Egret. No North American records were reported by Hancock and Kushlan (1984), but a single North American record does exist, an adult female from Agattu Island, Alaska, 16 June 1974 and now in the University of Alaska Museum (UAM 2805) (Byrd et al. 1978).

Cattle Egret. This species invaded from Africa to become the most abundant heron in North America within a space of 60 years. Evidence exists that trans-Atlantic colonisation continues (Telfair 1994). Its range now covers much of the landscape of North America from southern Canada, Central America and the Caribbean. Telfair (1994) provides an excellent evaluation of its changing status (also Telfair 1983, Arendt 1988, Campbell et al. 1990).

Spendelow and Patton (1988) found coastal nesting populations in the 1970s numbered about 439 000 individuals, with over 248 000 birds along the Florida coast. These totals do not include extensive inland populations. Populations have continued to grow over recent decades; expansion continues along the range periphery, such as in California (Fleury and Sherry 1995). However, in most places the rate of population increase has slowed, suggesting that population growth is levelling off continent-wide (Telfair 1994).

Northern populations migrate south in the winter. Densest wintering populations occur in Florida, the Salton Sea in California, the coastal plain in Texas, and Mississippi River swamps in Louisiana (Root 1988). Wintering areas include Mexico and the Greater Antilles, and Central America, into northern South America (Mikuska et al. 1998).

Green-backed Heron. This species is widely distributed in North and Central America and the West Indies (Davis and Kushlan 1994). Hancock and Kushlan (1984) showed the northernmost range as Washington State, USA, but small numbers now reside year-round in British Columbia, Canada, and it is extending slowly northward along the Pacific coast of Canada.

Population size data are few because of its widely dispersed nesting habits. Breeding bird surveys (Robbins et al. 1986, Fleury and Sherry 1995) suggest that populations are largest in Florida and Louisiana and that continent-wide increases are occurring. It is an abundant resident in Central America, particularly Nicaragua and Costa Rica where it is the most abundant heron species.

In winter, northern populations move southward into Florida and Mexico, and perhaps into South America (Chapter 8). Highest wintering densities in the USA were in southern Florida and in southern California (Root 1988).

The Green-backed Heron. This species normally nests solitarily or in small colonies. Consequently population sizes are poorly known. Photo: Robert Bennetts.

Agami Heron. This tropical bird of pools and streams in dense forests nests in Mexico and Costa Rica, and outside the region in South America (Marin 1989). Little is known about its requirements, and deforestation might threaten its survival. As a result it is considered to be near threatened (IUCN 1996).

Yellow-crowned Night Heron. This species nests through most of eastern North America, Central America, and the Caribbean, and outside the region in South America and the Galapagos (Chapter 8). Its North America nesting distribution, unclearly presented in Hancock and Kushlan (1984), is from Kansas, Nebraska, Iowa, Wisconsin, Michigan, Ontario, Ohio and Pennsylvania to Massachusetts, southward along the Atlantic Coast and into the mid continent in Texas, Colorado, and Oklahoma. It also nests along both coasts of Mexico and Guatemala, through the Bahamas, Greater Antilles, Virgin Islands, and northern Greater Antilles. Also outside this region, it occurs on the Galapagos and coastal South America, the southern birds being recognised as the race *bancrofti*. The species was reintroduced to Bermuda in the late 1970s (Wingate 1982).

Northern populations migrate south to western and southern Florida, with smaller numbers along the Gulf and Atlantic coasts (Root 1988), and some into the West Indies.

The population size of this dispersed species is poorly known. Spendelow and

The Yellow-crowned Night Heron. This species is widespread in North America. Some West Indian populations seem to be threatened by increasing pressure from human activities. Photo: James A. Kushlan.

Patton (1988) tallied about 1800 birds in coastal USA in the 1970s but this is an underestimate because the censuses they analysed clearly overlooked many birds. Breeding Bird Survey data indicate increases in summer in Louisiana (Robbins et al. 1986). There is no evidence of breeding population decreases in North America.

Some West Indian populations may be a matter of concern. For example the nesting population on Tobago is reported from only three wetlands there. Boccoo Reef is a state-owned reserve, while Kilgwyn and Bon Accord Swamps are private. All face pressures from livestock grazing, fishing, crab-collection, and garbage dumping, and there is the probable construction of large tourist resorts, which would eliminate habitat (see also Chapter 8). More information is needed on the status of this species in the West Indies.

Black-crowned Night Heron. This bird nests throughout much of North America, in the west from southern British Columbia and east of the mountains from southern Saskatchewan, Manitoba, Ontario and Quebec, and outside the region through much of the world (Hancock and Kushlan 1984). The northern edge of the North American breeding range has not changed from the 1960s (Palmer 1962) to the 1980s

(Godfrey 1986), and there is no evidence of other changes in overall nesting distribution.

Nesting population estimates are tenuous because of difficulty in counting these cryptic, nocturnal birds in their many small colony sites. Along the North American Atlantic coast, over 48 000 individuals were tallied in the 1970s with the greatest concentrations being on the mid-Atlantic and Louisiana coasts (Spendelow and Patton 1988). These numbers are undoubtedly underestimates, and do not include inland colonies. Local changes in numbers have been suggested, including possible decreases in the central North America plains and mid-Atlantic but also increases in the north-eastern states (Robbins et al. 1986, Williams et al. 1990, Erwin and Spendelow 1991, Davis 1993).

Birds breeding in Oregon and Idaho colonies migrate to the central coast of Mexico. Night-herons breeding in Nevada winter in southern California, southern Arizona and southern Texas (Henny and Blus 1986). Largest numbers occur in the USA along the Oregon–California border, in California, on the California–Arizona border, the Texas coast, and the west coast of Florida (Root 1988). Other birds migrate into the southern West Indies.

Contaminant levels in some Pacific North-west colonies had been sufficiently high to threaten productivity (Henny et al. 1984) but have generally declined in recent years (Custer et al. 1983a, Henny et al. 1985, Chapter 12).

Boat-billed Heron. The range of this species includes South America, Central America and Mexico, where four subspecies are recognised, and outside this chapter's region in South America (Chapter 8). Few data exist on nesting populations anywhere within its range. It appears common where it is found and its populations stable, but habitat loss may affect it in the future.

Bare-throated Tiger Heron. Although known as a bird of mangrove swamps and coastal lagoons, it does occur inland along rivers. It is nearly restricted to Central America, breeding from southern Mexico into Colombia (Hancock and Kushlan 1984, Lopez-Ornato and Ramo 1992). Nothing is known about population sizes or trends.

Fasciated Tiger Heron. This primarily South American species (Chapter 8) occurs in the south of the region in Panama and Costa Rica. Nothing is known of its population size or trend there. Because of its limited distribution it is considered near threatened (IUCN 1996).

Rufescent Tiger Heron. This primarily South American species (Chapter 8) occurs south of Chiapas, Mexico. Little is known of its population size or change, but it is widely distributed in Central America and is a common species found along rivers, lakes and even grasslands.

Least Bittern. The nesting range of this species includes eastern USA, eastern Mexico and the West Indies (Greater Antilles, northern Lesser Antilles), and localised areas in western North America, Mexico, and Central America (Hancock and Kushlan 1984, Gibbs et al. 1992a), and outside our region into South America (Chapter 8). There is no known recent change in breeding range.

The secretive Least Bittern. Photo: Robert Bennetts.

It is secretive and often overlooked on surveys, so estimates of population trends are scant. Birders reported the species as being reduced over much of its range (Tate 1986), but there is some evidence of increases in the north-eastern part of its range (Robbins et al. 1986).

Northern populations migrate to the south-eastern USA and Mexico. There is weak indication of decreases in wintering populations in Louisiana (Fleury and Sherry 1995). In North America, preservation of wetlands >10 ha appears to be its most urgent conservation need (Gibbs et al. 1992a).

South American Bittern. This bittern breeds in freshwater swamps and rice and sugarcane fields of southern Mexico, Costa Rica, Nicaragua and Guatemala, as well as outside the region in South America (Chapter 8). Nothing is known about its population sizes or trends in the region.

American Bittern. This secretive species is widespread in North and Central America (Gibbs et al. 1992b). Breeding populations have been recorded from Texas, the Great Basin, California, and Florida, USA (unclearly labeled in Hancock and Kushlan 1984).

Population data are few. An analysis of breeding bird surveys for the north central states suggested decreases in numbers (Hands et al. 1989). Loss of wetland and wet grassland habitats is the most likely cause for any declines (Hands et al. 1989).

This bittern winters from the southern USA through Mexico and the West Indies to Panama. Centres of winter abundance in the USA are southern Florida and the San Joaquin River in California, with smaller numbers reported from marshes along the North Carolina coast, the Okefenokee Swamp between Georgia and Florida, and the swamps along the Louisiana coast (Root 1988). Winter populations in Louisiana may be declining (Fleury and Sherry 1995).

Hands et al. (1989) recommended that conservation should focus on wetlands >10 ha and adjacent grasslands. They suggested that under natural conditions, the species could move among sites as plant succession proceeded, but today it might be necessary to maintain a complex of protected wetlands in different stages of succession for populations to grow in the long term.

Overall status

No heron species in the region is globally threatened (Groombridge 1993, IUCN 1996). No species has suffered a critical range decrease; most have expanded their range: at least two have newly established breeding populations in the New World in this century. The several quantitative data sets that are available (comparative censuses, Christmas Counts, and Breeding Bird Surveys) suggest that no continent-wide population decreases can be documented. It is likely that continent-wide Great Blue Herons, Cattle Egrets, and Green-backed Herons have increased in abundance in recent years. Some data suggest localised decreases, but for such highly mobile species, localised decreases may be offset by increases elsewhere. The most apparent example of compensatory change in abundance is the decrease of some species in south Florida, stability elsewhere in Florida, and increases in Louisiana (Bancroft 1989, Fleury and Sherry 1995).

However, population data for even the best-known species can only provide some sense of large-scale trends, and data for rare or highly dispersed species are scant to non-existent. Even the best available data cannot detect small changes in numbers of any species. Thus, much needs to be done to develop appropriate monitoring programmes for these species. It is essential that a continent-wide programme of population monitoring of both breeding and wintering populations be developed (Erwin et al. 1993, Kushlan J. and Steinkamp M., pers. comm.).

A few populations that have small ranges in the region or specific habitat requirements deserve conservation attention for those reasons. The white morph and North Pacific Coast populations of Great Blue Herons, Reddish Egrets, and newly established Little Egrets have restricted ranges. Bare-throated Tiger Herons, Fasciated Tiger Herons, and Agami Herons may be likely candidates to become at risk if their limited habitats are altered; the Fasciated Tiger Heron and Agami Heron are considered to be near threatened (IUCN 1996).

Critical Conservation and Regional Management Issues

Conservation of herons and other water birds in the northern New World requires multifaceted approaches (Parnell et al. 1988, Bildstein et al. 1991, Custer et al. 1991, Erwin et al. 1993 and Kushlan 1992, 1993b). Overriding concerns throughout the region include habitat (especially wetland) loss and alteration, human competition, and contaminants. Conservation of herons in North America requires habitat protection, legislation, and management action at local to international levels, and wise use of their wetland habitats (Bildstein et al. 1991). Conservation needs to be undertaken at the local scale as guided by continental scale goals set out through regionwide conservation planning.

Bermuda

We have included Bermuda in our region for biogeographic reasons, as it derives its heron fauna from North America. Several North American herons occur there in migration (Wingate 1973). Bermuda is the site of one of the great success stories in heron conservation—the establishment of Yellow-crowned Night Herons by David Wingate (Wingate 1982). But the small size of this population requires continued vigilance.

Mexico and Central America

Mexico and Central America support many nesting and wintering herons, including species not found elsewhere in the region. The major conservation issues for herons in Mexico and Central America are habitat loss and degradation, especially along the coast. Davidson and Guthier (1993) summarised the direct and indirect causes of wetland loss in Central America, finding the following to be critical: deforestation, removal of mangrove bark, clearing for shrimp and salt production, agricultural clearing, uncontrolled forest fires, uncontrolled tourism development, hunting and poaching, agro-chemical contamination, raw sewage and industrial waste dumping, dams and irrigation channels, and other wetland development.

Large numbers of wading birds reside and migrate to coastal wetlands and mudflats in Mexico and Panama (Wilson and Ryan 1997, Morrison et al. 1998). Conversion of mangroves to salt ponds and aquaculture is a particularly major concern, given their importance for resident and wintering herons (Butler et al. 1992). However, some aquaculture ponds also provide additional feeding sites. Oil exploration along the coast may also become a factor in the quality of local habitats for herons.

Conversion of inland forests affects not only downstream wetlands, because of increased sedimentation, but also more directly the habitat of forest and stream-edge heron species. Further loss of remnant inland forests in El Salvador (now 2% of original) and Costa Rica (5% of original) and rapid acceleration of the agricultural frontier along Caribbean coasts undoubtedly threaten forest-dependent species. Information on these species is urgently needed.

Atlantic flyway

The migration flyway along the eastern coast of North America encompasses nesting, migration, and wintering habitats of herons breeding from eastern Canada and north-eastern USA southward into Florida, the Bahamas and the Caribbean (Custer et al. 1980, Spendelow and Patton 1988).

The Atlantic coast supports substantial nesting populations, with Florida being one of the three most important areas in North America (Bancroft 1989). Although nesting and wintering populations remain high in most areas of this state, nesting numbers have decreased in extreme southern Florida, despite the persistence of huge areas of wetland, owing to changes in water management practices affecting food availability (Kushlan and White 1977, Bancroft 1989, Ogden 1994). On the other hand, appropriate habitat conditions have increased for some species along the Atlantic coast. In New York and Ontario, reforestation of abandoned agricultural lands has positively affected Great Blue Heron populations (McCrimmon 1982).

Herons nesting in north-eastern North America migrate along the Atlantic coast, coastal plain, and Appalachian Mountains. Herons nesting in the south shift further southward in winter. Wintering areas include Florida, the Gulf of Mexico coast east of the Mississippi Delta, Cuba, Jamaica, Dominican Republic, the Lesser Antilles to Trinidad and coastal northern South America (Byrd 1978, Hancock and Kushlan 1984, Mikuska et al. 1998).

The Atlantic Flyway has the greatest human population densities in the USA (Southworth 1989). Conservation threats to herons involve competition with humans for the herons' nesting and feeding sites and various threats from contaminants. Herons do continue to nest as part of developed landscapes in parks and along watercourses near even the largest cities. It is expected, although not assured, that future wetland habitat losses in the USA and Canada will be ameliorated by continued enforcement of strict wetland protection legislation. In the Caribbean, losses of scarce wetland habitat continue through drainage and conversion (K. Shephard, pers. comm.).

Several Ramsar sites are located in this flyway (Jones 1993). Delaware Bay, Chesapeake Bay, and the Okefenokee Swamp support nesting, migratory and/or wintering populations of herons. Trinidad's Nariva Swamp supports many nesting and wintering herons.

Coastal wetlands and lagoons along the Atlantic Flyway are of special concern because of their importance to all species of herons, but especially white morph Great Blue Herons and Reddish Egrets. The drainage of coastal wetlands for agriculture and development, other alterations of hydrology, and pollution are especially disconcerting given the narrow habitat requirements and ranges of these species. Powell and Powell (1986) showed that the white morph Great Blue Heron population of extreme southern Florida was under food stress, probably owing to changes in food availability. Disturbance also becomes a factor in such restricted populations. Kale (1978) recommended prevention of unauthorised landings by boaters at nesting sites to protect coastal Great Blue Herons. Increased access to heron feeding areas, by increases in various watercraft including jet-propelled personal watercraft, should be examined for effects on feeding birds.

Mississippi flyway

The Mississippi River, its tributaries, and associated wetlands are major features affecting North American herons, serving as nesting grounds, a migration corridor, and winter destinations. The river and its tributaries serve as conduits for migrant herons breeding as far as central Canada, the Midwest and southern USA states east of the Rocky Mountains. Herons originating in Canada, Wisconsin, Illinois, and Minnesota follow the Mississippi drainage to the Gulf Coast, eastern Mexico and Central America (Byrd 1978). Inland and coastal wetlands of Louisiana are the most important heron habitats in North America (Portnoy 1977, Spendelow and Patton 1988, Root 1988, Martin and Lester 1991). The coastal lagoons of Texas and Mexico support the largest North American nesting populations of the Reddish Egret. The wetlands of Tabasco and Campeche, Mexico, are one of the three most important nesting areas for herons in the region.

The Louisiana wetlands are the most important destination for migrating and wintering herons in North America (Fleury and Sherry 1995). Further south, the coastal lagoons of Texas and Mexico form a chain of stopover and wintering sites (Anderson et al. 1996, Mikuska et al. 1998). This beadwork of coastal lagoons includes the Laguna Madre, Laguna Tamiahua, Usumacinta Delta, Laguna de Terminos, and the Rio Lagartos (a Ramsar site). Less known areas include the extensive coastal wetlands of Central America, where herons appear to be widespread. The Bay of Panama supports large numbers of herons (Butler et al. 1992). In the West Indies, it is likely that the Zapata Swamp and other parts of coastal Cuba, the western Bahamas especially Andros and the Caicos (including a Ramsar site) may be important wintering grounds (Mikuska et al. 1998). Ramsar sites in the Netherlands Antilles and Aruba (Het Lac, Het Pekelmeer, De Slagbaai) support several heron species.

Habitat protection is the most critical issue in this region. In North America, this means wetland conservation. Conservation and management of Louisiana wetlands, Laguna Madre of Texas–Mexico, the many shallow, isolated wetlands of the Mississippi watershed, and Mexican wetlands are of prime importance (Paul 1991, Gibbs et al. 1992a, Wilson and Ryan 1997). In the Louisiana wetlands, there is strong evidence that heron populations have grown in response to seasonal food supplies from aquaculture (Fleury and Sherry 1995).

Further south, harvest of mangroves, development of shrimp farming, and increasing drainage for agriculture, especially banana plantations, threaten wetlands used by herons. Butler et al. (1997, 1998) showed that the highest densities of wading birds in Panama were associated with mangrove ecosystems near regions with ocean upwelling.

Pacific flyway

In western North America, some herons disperse in winter to nearby habitats along the coast and mountain valleys (Gill and Mewaldt 1979, Butler 1992) while others migrate south to Arizona, Texas and western Mexico (Byrd 1978, Henny and Blus 1986). Therefore the relatively coastal wetlands of the Pacific coast assume critical importance. These include the lagoons of Huizache–Caimanero, Nayarit, and Jalisco, in Mexico, and other coastal lagoons south to Palo Verde, Costa Rica, a Ramsar site that supports nesting and seasonal heron populations. Conservation issues in the region involve disturbance, habitat loss, and contaminants.

Increasing human populations in the area have intensified competition with herons for nesting sites, although the long-term effects are not yet clear (Vos et al. 1985, Werschkul et al. 1977, Butler 1997). In recent years, growing numbers of Bald

Eagles (*Haliaeetus leucocephalus*) along the coast of Washington, USA, and British Columbia, Canada, have become important predators of chicks, immature and adult herons (Norman et al. 1989, Butler 1995, 1997).

Habitat protection is critical, as over two-thirds of the coastal wetlands between southern British Columbia and California have been lost in the last 100 years (Speth 1979, Butler and Campbell 1987). Protection of wetlands along the Central American coast is similarly essential to heron conservation (Morrison et al. 1998).

Through much of this flyway, contaminants have been found in heron eggs and tissues (for example Blus et al. 1980, 1985, Henny et al. 1984, 1985, Ohlendorf et al. 1988, Elliott et al. 1989, Ohlendorf and Marois 1990, Chapter 12). Some herons may be accumulating pesticides on their wintering grounds in the USA and Mexico. Sudden declines of Great Blue Heron and Great White Egret populations and disappearance of breeding populations of Cattle Egrets and Snowy Egrets in the Salton Sea area (W. Radke, pers. comm.) are cause for alarm.

Habitat conservation

The loss of wetland habitat in North and Central America is one of the principal conservation concerns for herons in the region. Wetland conversion, mostly for agriculture or residential development, was national policy in both the USA and Canada for many years. Incentives were provided for reclaiming the "waste land" (Alderman 1965). Even lacking definitive information of effects on herons, it can be expected that wetland conversions over the past centuries have had effects on heron populations, at least locally.

Today, however, legislation and executive policy in both the USA and Canada mandate some level of wetland protection. In Mexico, Central America, and the West Indies wetland loss to drainage, conversion to aquaculture, and tree harvest continues. Adoption of the Ramsar Convention by every nation in North and Central America as well as several nations of the West Indies including the Netherlands (for Netherlands Antilles and Aruba), United Kingdom (for Turks and Caicos) has raised attention to the value of wetlands for herons and other birds. Important heron sites need to be protected and managed to conserve their sustained viability as heron habitat (Mikuska et al. 1998).

Wetland conservation has become national policy for governments in Canada and the USA (Government of Canada 1991). Policies of "no net loss" recognise wetlands as important components of national and global landscapes and economies. However, only about 29% of Canada's wetlands are on federally-owned lands and many are north of the range of herons. Most wetlands within the range of herons in southern Canada are within the jurisdiction of provincial governments, and policies differ among provinces. In the USA, federal initiatives in wetland protection are enforced at the federal level through requirements over issue of permits, and are being adopted by many states and some local governments. The federal government protects many wetlands in parks and wildlife refuges that support many herons. It is likely that, overall, the loss of wetland area has been halted in Canada and the United States.

However, the downward trend in wetland viability continues in many parts of North America. Despite protection of wetland area, functional alterations continue and the role as suitable heron habitat of restored and created wetlands (built as replacement for lost wetland area) is not yet understood. Protection of heron habitat needs to be extended throughout the range of herons including Mexico (Wilson and Ryan 1997), Central America, and the Caribbean. However, as wetland conservation increasingly conflicts with development and agricultural interests, the resolve of government to protect these habitats may be weakening and the outcome remains in doubt.

Barriers to accomplishing wetland conservation involve economic and social factors because wetland protection carries significant costs in loss of immediate economic opportunity. Issues of the appropriate balance between governmental regulation and private ownership rights remain to be resolved in the United States, as do the relative roles of federal, state/provincial, and local governments. In developing countries, human population increases have exacerbated stress on wetlands. In both developed and less-developed economic zones of the region, the need for integrating policies that promote wise use of wetlands is paramount.

Heron habitats need also to be viewed at larger spatial and temporal scales. Changes in habitat may be due to long-term changes such as climate change, sea level rise, and landscape fragmentation. Heron habitat needs to be conserved and managed within the context of these larger-scale processes, particularly those operating at the landscape or watershed scale.

Habitat quality

As noted above, habitat quality is as important as habitat area in conserving herons. Important approaches to maintaining habitat quality are those that seek to retain habitat diversity, natural functioning, food supplies, and sustainable human use of wetland ecosystems (Boyd and Pirot 1989). Preserving habitat quality specifically for herons includes maintenance of vegetation at colony sites, prey base and suitable hydrology. Despite their flexibility, herons require the presence of species-appropriate nesting sites. In that herons can damage sites, making them unsuitable, a succession of sites needs to be available in most areas. Most studies in the region show that maintenance and accessibility of a suitable prey base is essential to maintaining heron populations. Given the importance of water depths to wading birds, hydrological management is often a crucial consideration. The example of wading bird declines in the southern Florida Everglades owing to hydrological alteration and changes in prey availability are testament to the result of declining habitat quality (Bancroft 1989). In this regard, on wetland preserves, management for game species (waterfowl) may not coincide with optimal management for herons, and such potentially conflicting conservation concerns need to be optimised at each locality.

International conservation

The importance of international cooperation in protecting heron populations in the region becomes clear when their breeding and winter distributions are examined. For example, six species that nest in Canada (American and Least bitterns, Cattle Egret, Green, Great Blue, and Black-crowned Night herons) (Godfrey 1986) spend the winter from southern USA and southward. Some individuals of most of the 12 species that breed in the United States winter in the West Indies, Mexico, or Central and even South America, so important areas for wintering North American herons extend well south of the USA border (Mikuska et al. 1998). Two restricted populations that might especially benefit from an international approach to conservation are the white morph Great Blue Herons in Florida, Bahamas and Cuba and Reddish Egrets in Mexico and USA. Throughout the region, laws, treaties, policies, and conservation programmes to arrest wetland losses hold promise of protecting heron habitat.

In North America, bilateral and trilateral migratory bird treaties have played important roles in the conservation of habitats of value to herons. The most critical treaties are between the United States, Canada, and Mexico, along with Russia and Japan. The North American Waterfowl Management Plan by Canada, the USA, and Mexico is designed to protect wetlands for waterfowl especially. This has more recently been supplemented by environmental sub-agreements associated with the North American Free Trade Agreement. International cooperation occurs at operational levels, with over half the funds derived from the USA Wetland Conservation Act being directed to wetland conservation in Canada and Mexico. Habitat planning and restoration activities under the North American Waterfowl Management Plan will help conserve wetland-dependent herons, especially the American Bittern, Least Bittern, Great Blue Heron and Black-crowned Night Heron. Trilateral planning for bird conservation recently began under the auspices of the trilateral council for the North America Bird Conservation Initiative (NABCI). A component of NABCI is a recent initiative for planning the conservation of colonial water birds in North America (Kushlan and Steinkamp in prep.).

In Central America, there are a number of pertinent international conservation initiatives under way (Davidson and Guthier 1993). Costa Rica and Nicaragua have created a bilateral programme to protect areas, including wetlands, along their border. The Central American biological Corridor Project proposes to link protected areas from Guatemala to Panama, many of which will conserve heron habitat.

All North and Central American nations have become signatories to the Ramsar Convention, which requires them to make "wise use" of wetlands of international importance (Boyd and Pirot 1989, RCB 1998). Nearly all Ramsar sites sport herons. Thirty-five sites have been designated as Ramsar sites in Canada, 15 in the USA, seven in Costa Rica, six in Mexico, and three in Guatamala, Honduras, and Panama.

Conservation of herons in the region requires increasing hemispheric planning and international cooperation and coordination. This involves developing a multinational conservation planning effort and the establishment of reserve networks similar to those developed to protect sites used by shore birds (Myers et al. 1987, Boyd and Pirot 1989, Erwin et al. 1993). In North America, heron conservation will be a part of the North American Colonial Waterbird Conservation Plan and similar efforts for non-colonial marsh birds. This plan will coordinate with continental planning efforts for other groups of birds to be enacted on a coordinated regional basis. We also envision a network of sites from Canada to South America that are identified as important to heron populations (Mikuska et al. 1998), able to attract and maintain conservation activities.

Contaminants

Contamination of eggs and tissues of herons by pollutants is widespread in North America and probably Mexico and Central America, but currently effects on regional heron populations appear to be minimal (Custer et al. 1991, Rattner et al. 1993). Local conditions do appear to be deleterious in places such as the Salton Sea in California, parts of Mexico, and parts of the Gulf Coast (Mora 1991 and Chapter 12). Herons have been used as sentinels and indicators of contamination (Kushlan 1993b and Chapter 15).

Hunting

Throughout the region, herons are killed by people for various reasons, but mostly for food or in response to their apparent or real depredations on aquacultural crops. Dramatic decreases in some heron populations occurred around the turn of the 1900s when adults were hunted for their plumage at colony sites (reviewed by Butler 1994). Herons are now protected as migratory species by treaties between Canada, the USA, and Mexico. They are, however, considered pests to aquaculture. In the United States permits are issued for aquaculturalists to kill thousands of herons annually (Fleury and Sherry 1995). Available studies suggest that herons, unlike some other bird species, have little adverse impact on aquaculture (Chapter 13), and killing is seldom justified. Almost nothing is known about the potential population impact of depredation reduction programmes, especially given the constraints of relatively crude population monitoring techniques in use, which can detect only large population changes.

Colony site protection

There is no evidence that heron populations are limited at present by shortage of nesting sites in North America (Butler 1994), and in some areas nesting habitat is increasing due to forest development, wetland conservation and construction, and dredge spoil island construction (see for example Parnell et al. 1988). However, nesting sites are frequently affected and destroyed by urban, agricultural or recreational developments or other human disturbance (David 1994, Butler 1997). Many suitable colony sites exist in the vast swamps of the south-eastern USA, but they are more restricted near populated areas. Many colonies are located on artificial lakes and artificial dredge spoil islands, created by channel dredging. In such areas, policies for spoil disposal and competing uses of colony sites pose challenges. Protecting of existing and potential nesting sites will be essential for the future well being of heron populations in an increasingly developed North American landscape.

  To date, herons have proven resilient in using urban and suburban environments for nesting and feeding (Erwin et al. 1991, for example). Extensive use is made of zoos, parks and suburban green spaces for colonies and winter roosts. Some colony sites have been around for decades, but others are considered nuisances. Additional study is needed of how heron colonies can be compatible in developed areas.

  Colony abandonment rates in most areas are relatively low, indicating long-term site stability (McCrimmon and Parnell 1983). Turnover is greater where many alternative sites occur (Bancroft et al. 1988). Perhaps the greatest threat of colony site destruction is to Great Blue Herons, which nest in many scattered sites, often in forests, often near people. Developments frequently encroach on heron colony sites, either destroying them, disturbing them with construction activities, changing nearby foraging sites, or encouraging other forms of disturbance. Some of these activities require permits, a restriction through which the needs of herons can be provided for. Given how widespread such conflicts are, much additional study is needed to determine appropriate approaches for sustainable development near sites containing heron colonies.

It is not clear what long-term effect disturbance of colonies has on breeding populations, although in the short term it can cause abandonment and reduced fecundity of individuals (Werschkul et al. 1977, Vos et al. 1985). Large colony sites should be provided with the strongest protection, such as by purchase, posting, easements and perhaps guarding. In developed areas, fencing may be needed. State and province-wide programmes of identifying and securing heron colony sites are required.

Aquaculture

Aquaculture appears to have important effects, both positive and negative, on North American herons. The most important wintering area for most species of North American herons in southern USA coincides with large-scale pond aquaculture. Increases of aquaculture in Louisiana, especially the areal extent of crayfish ponds, correlate strongly with an increase in heron numbers in the region (Fleury and Sherry 1995). Thus it is possible that aquaculture may be responsible for the present stability and increase in some heron populations in North America.

However, the aquaculture industry regards herons as pests, even though the birds may take only a small proportion of the available stock (Fleury and Sherry 1995 and Chapter 13). Great Blue Herons were found to consume two catfish per hour and Great White Egrets 1.3 per hour, which extrapolates to as many as 24 catfish per day for Great Blue Herons (P.G. Ross and J. Armstrong pers. comm.). Although small compared with the standing stock of fish in a location, such consumption inevitably will lead to damage control and continued conflicts between herons and aquaculture in North America.

Less is known about the effects of conversions of mangroves to aquaculture in the tropics. Natural habitat is lost, but artificially enhanced feeding sites are provided. Controls on killing offending herons are minimal, so much needs to be learned about these sites.

Species of concern

The Reddish Egret is adapted to hypersaline coastal shallows, mostly around the Gulf of Mexico, which are threatened by housing and industrial developments. In addition, the reproductive rate of these egrets appears to be low (Paul 1991).

The white morph of the Great Blue Heron is confined to mostly estuarine habitats of southern Florida and the Caribbean. The special needs of these species are summarised by Kale (1978).

The Pacific coast subspecies of Great Blue Heron is restricted to the coastal strip along the north-east Pacific coast of North America (Butler 1997).

Bitterns are adapted to marshes and nearby grassland habitats, which have been greatly diminished in the USA and Canada. Protection of even small wetland patches would benefit these species in the middle USA, and artificial wetlands may benefit Least Bitterns (Hands et al. 1989, Gibbs et al. 1992b).

The Tiger Herons and Agami Heron of Mexico are little studied, to some extent because they are less social than other species. Nonetheless, information is needed on their status especially in light of their dependence on tropical rain forests.

Conclusions

Our review has suggested that most species and populations of herons in North and Central America and the Caribbean are widespread and, to the extent of available data, seem mostly to have maintained or increased breeding ranges and continental population sizes over recent decades. Species are being added to the fauna through colonisation from the Old World. International agreement on migratory bird hunting and killing, the extent of protected wetlands, land use management, increases in artificial heron habitat due to aquaculture, international conservation planning efforts, the activities of numerous organisations dedicated to the protection of wetlands and water birds, all contribute to this very positive situation.

However, such current optimism must be tempered by the lack of information on some species and on important habitats and locales in Mexico, Central America, and the Caribbean. Loss of wetlands continues apace south of the USA and alteration of wetland functions continues throughout the region. A critical problem is the inability to detect numerically even large changes in heron populations. The inadequate quality of long-term monitoring is a critical issue in most areas, even where such programmes have existed for some time. Only the most massive of population changes can be detected with any statistical confidence. The development of a statistically sound continent-wide monitoring programme seems essential.

Populations of special concern, for various reasons, include the mid-continental American Bittern, mid-continental Least Bittern, Reddish Egret, white morph and north-east Pacific coast subspecies of the Great Blue Heron, Agami Heron, Bare-throated Tiger Heron and Fasciated Tiger Heron. Of these, breeding habitats for the bitterns can be secured by current wetland conservation programmes but their special needs must be considered in actual habitat management schemes. The Reddish Egret and Great White Heron require protection of coastal lagoons, and the Agami Heron and Tiger Herons require protection of tropical rain forests.

Only international conservation planning and action will suffice in North and Central America and the West Indies. We recommend the institution of North American, Central American and West Indian conservation plans that include herons. We also recommend the formation of a wading bird reserve network similar to the Western Hemisphere Shorebird Reserve Network to conserve and manage sites and areas of importance to herons (Mikuska et al. 1998 for example). Technical experts need to be mobilised through increased coordination of existing organisations including Wetlands International and its specialist groups, the Waterbird Society, the National Audubon Society, Federal and State governments, and other share holders in heron conservation.

8. Herons in South America

Gonzalo Morales

This chapter discusses the heron populations of South America, a continent particularly rich in bird life, having about 2930 species (Blake 1977) and 33 major areas of endemism (Cracraft 1985). The region includes the Galápagos, Falkland Islands, Trinidad and Tobago, and the Netherlands Antilles and covers almost 18 million square kilometres (Fig. 8.1). Due to the latitudinal and altitudinal gradients in environmental conditions, a wide range of natural and man-made wetlands are available to wading birds. Although herons are among the most common aquatic birds, there are few studies of their distribution and status, or of their ecology, conservation, or impact of wetland use and management.

The Heron Fauna

The heron fauna comprises 22 species (Table 8.1), most of which are exclusive to the Americas. Nearly all have their population centres in South America, and six currently recognised genera (*Syrigma*, *Agamia*, *Pilherodius*, *Cochlearius*, *Tigrisoma*, *Zebrilus*) are endemic or nearly endemic to the region (some range slightly into Central America—Chapter 7). Eleven species are truly neotropical, seven also occur elsewhere in the Americas, and only four occur outside the Americas. Two species (Reddish Egret and Great Blue Heron) are primarily North American, but winter along the northern coast of South America. Two species (Little Egret and Grey Heron) are accidental, although they may be establishing themselves in the hemisphere (Chapter 7).

Most herons are widely distributed in inland freshwater wetlands. Only three species (Great Blue Heron, Reddish Egret, and Tricolored Heron) and five subspecies from offshore islands can be considered primarily marine. The endemic species are less abundant, relatively sedentary, and nest and forage solitarily or in small groups.

Heron Conservation
ISBN 0-12-430130-4

Fig. 8.1   Important heron areas in South America.

Key to Fig. 8.1   Important heron areas in South America.

1 The Netherlands (Aruba)—Spaans Lagoon
2 The Netherlands (Bonaire)—Lagoons of Lac and Pekelmeer
3 Venezuela—Morrocoy National Park and Jatira–Tacarigua Dams
4 Venezuela—Tacarigua Lagoon
5 Venezuela—Gulf of Unare
6 Venezuela—Orinoco Delta
7 Venezuela—Central–western Llanos, wetlands of the Arauca Fauna and Flora Sanctuary
8 Venezuela—Swamps of Juan Manuel de Aguas Blancas and Aguas Negras
9 Trinidad—Nariva Swamp
10 Colombia—Saline Lagoon of San Juan and Swamp of San Agustin
11 Colombia—Zapatosa Swamp
12 Colombia—The Great Swamp of Santa Marta, Isla de Salamanca National Park, the Swamps of Totumo, Guajaro, and de la Virgen, and the Bay of Cartagena
13 Colombia—Gulf of Urabá, the lower Atrato River and Los Katios National Park
14 Suriname, French Guiana, Brazil—Guianas coast including coastal wetlands of Bigi Pan and Wageningen Swamps, of Braamspunt, Matapica and Motkreek areas, wetlands of Coppenamebank, Coppename River Mouth, area of Wag naar Zee, coastal wetlands of Wia-wia and Galibi, coastal marshes of Sinnamary and Iracoubo, Kaw Marshes, coastal wetlands and savannas of Pointe Behague and the lower Oyapock River, Cabo Orange and Cassipore Marshes
15 Colombia—Bay of Buenaventura
16 Colombia—Lake Tota, Lagoons of Fuquene, Lagoon of La Herrera and marshes of La Florida and Funza
17 Ecuador—Lagoons of Cuyabeno
18 Ecuador—Upper Napo River and its tributaries
19 Ecuador—Upper Blanco River
20 Ecuador, Peru—Peninsula of Santa Elena, mangroves of Churute in the Gulf of Guayaquil, mangroves of Los Tumbes
21 Ecuador—Saline lagoons of the Galapagos Islands (not mapped)
22 Peru—Lagoons of Playa Chica and El Paraíso
23 Peru—Villa Marshes
24 Peru—Agua Santa Marshes and wetlands in the Paracas National Reserve
25 Peru—Wetlands in Manu National Park
26 Peru—Wetlands in Tambopata Wildlife Reserve
27 Peru—Lagoons of Mejia and Ite
28 Peru—Lagoons of Launillas and Umayo
29 Peru—Wetlands of Pacaya-Samiria National Reserve
30 Peru, Bolivia—Lake Titicaca
31 Bolivia—Wetlands in the Ulla-Ulla National and Biological Reserve
32 Bolivia—Lake Uru-Uru
33 Bolivia—Baures and Zapecos Rivers
34 Bolivia—Mamoré River
35 Bolivia—Wetlands of the Beni Biological Station
36 Bolivia—Lakes of Beni Department
37 Brazil—Lakes on lower Japura River
38 Brazil—Middle and lower Purus River and lower Solimoes River
39 Brazil—Central Amazon and lower Madeira River
40 Brazil—Lower Tapajos River and adjacent Amazon
41 Brazil—Lower Xingu River
42 Brazil—Lower Tocantins River
43 Brazil—Floodplain of Araguaia River and the Bananal Island
44 Brazil—Bay of San Marcos and estuary of Mearim River
45 Brazil—Ninhal do Barreiro
46 Brazil—Estuary of Doce River, Juparana Lakes, and Linhares Marshes
47 Brazil—Mangroves near the cities of Santos and Cubatao
48 Brazil—Lagoons of Tramandai
49 Brazil—Lagoon of dos Patos and adjacent marshes
50 Brazil, Paraguay—The Pantanal, including the Pantanal do Mato Grosso, wetlands and flooded savannas of Pantanal Matogrosense, Pantanal of the eastern Chaco, Paraguay River, Ypoa Lake, Pantanal of Neembucú
51 Argentina—Iguazú River and tributaries
52 Argentina—Pilcomayo River and Blanca Lagoon
53 Argentina—Wetlands in Chaco National Park
54 Argentina—Submeridional lowlands of Chaco Province
55 Argentina—Esteros del Iberá
56 Argentina—Figueroa Marshes
57 Argentina—Marshes of Dulce River, Delta of the Mar Chiquita Lake, Marshes of Cañada de Los Tres Arboles and Los Morteros
58 Argentina—Etruria Lagoon
59 Argentina—Marshes of the Saladillo River
60 Argentina—Marshes of the lower Paraná River
61 Paraguay—Salto Grande Dam
62 Uruguay—Arazati Marshes and Santa Lucia River
63 Uruguay—Lagoons of José Ignacio and Garzón
64 Uruguay—Marshes of Santa Teresa and Laguna Negra
65 Uruguay, Brazil—Lagoon of Merin, San Miguel Marshes, Lagoons of Mirim and Mangueira, Taim Marshes
66 Chile—Lagoon of El Peral
67 Chile—Cruces River and Carlos Anwandter Sanctuary
68 United Kingdom (Falkland Islands)—Carcass Island
69 United Kingdom (Falkland Islands)—Hawk's Nest Ponds

Table 8.1 Status of herons in South America

	Species										
	WH	CpH	GBH	CoH	GWE	RE	TH	LBH	SnE	CE	GrBH
Venezuela	5000–25000	++	250–500	5000–50000	50000–250000	+	++	5000–50000	5000–50000	5000–50000	5000–25000
Trinidad			+	+	++	+	++	++	++	++	++
Colombia	++	++	+	++	++	250–500	++	++	++	++	++
Guyana		++	+	++	500–2500		++	++	++	++	++
Suriname		++	+	6000	6000		35000	40000	10000	1000–5000	++
Fr.Guiana		++	+	++	500–2500		2500	5000	5000	++	++
Ecuador		++	++	++	++		++	++	++	++	++
Peru	++	++	+	++	++		+	++	++	++	++
Brazil	++	++	+	++	++		++	++	++	++	++
Bolivia	++	++		++	++			++	++	++	++
Paraguay	++	++		++	++			++	++	++	++
Chile	+			++	++			++	++	++	?
Uruguay	++			++	++			++		++	++
Argentina	250–500			500–2500	25000–50000			++	150000–225000	5000–25000	++
Falkland Is.				+	++				++	++	++

	Species										
	AH	YCNH	BCNH	BBH	BTTH	FTH	RTH	ZH	StB	LaB	SAB
Venezuela	++	++	50000–250000	++		++	5000–50000	++	++	++	++
Trinidad	+	++	++	++		?	++		++	++	++
Colombia	++	2500–5000[1]	++	++		++	++	++	++	50–250[3]	++
Guyana	++	++	++	++	++		++	++	++	++	++
Suriname	++	11000	2500	3250			++	++	++	++	++
Fr.Guiana	++	++	++	++			++	++	++	++	++
Ecuador	++	++	++	++		++	++	++	?	++	++
Peru	++	++	++	++		++	++	++	+	++	+
Brazil	++	++	++	++		500–2500[1,2]	++	++	++	++	++
Bolivia	++	?	++	++			++	++	++	++	?
Paraguay	?		++	++			++		++	+	++
Chile			++						++		
Uruguay			++			?	?		++	?	+
Argentina			++	++		500–2500[1,2]	++		++	+	++
Falkland Is.			5000–6000[1]								

++ = nesting population, + = present, but not nesting, ? = status uncertain, Numbers = nesting pairs.
[1] Rose and Scott (1997); [2] Race *fasciatum* only: Argentinian and Brazilian populations total less than 10000 individuals; [3] Race *bogotensis* only.

Environmental Conditions

Continental South America ranges between 13°N and 55°S and 35–80°W, with a northerly displacement of the climatic zones (Strahler 1973). The Andes, the dominant mountain range, extends along the Pacific coast. The Guyana and the Brazilian Shields, remnants of Gondwanaland, lie to the north-east, mostly below 800 m altitude. Most of the continent lies below 500 m, and the two major rivers flow easterly. The three largest river basins are below 300 m and drain to the principal rivers, the Orinoco (2–10°N), the Amazon (2°N–18°S), and the Paraná–Paraguay (15–35°S).

The climate and vegetation of South America vary with latitude, elevation, and distance from the coast (Mather 1974, Walter 1985). Along the Pacific coast Andes, there is a latitudinal succession of climates and life zones. From north to south, the warm and rainy coastal climate in western Colombia becomes drier in Ecuador. Between 10°S and 32°S along coastal Peru and Central Chile is one of the driest deserts on Earth. Below this latitude, the climate is temperate, becoming increasingly seasonally cold and rainy southward.

East of the Andes, the warm and humid climate in the northern Amazon valley allows the development of tropical rain forest. The Amazon forest extends well south along the Atlantic coast of Brazil, although in a very narrow belt. To the north of the Amazon are the lowlands (Llanos) of the Orinoco basin, mostly savannas with a warm climate and strongly seasonal (summer) rains. South of the Amazon are the Brazilian tablelands and campos cerrados, and Chaco in Paraguay and Argentina, which also have a highly seasonal climate, with seasonally heavy rains. The grasslands and open forests are similar to those of the Orinoco Llanos.

Eastward the climate is humid, subtropical to warm-temperate (lower Paraná basin in Argentina and Uruguay), but much drier, even desert, in the centre and south of the continent (Argentina). The original vegetation of lower Paraná was evergreen subtropical forest. The southernmost central part of the continent is covered by extensive temperate grass steppes (Pampas) in Argentina.

Besides the latitudinal effect, climate and vegetation in the tropical Andes change rapidly with the altitude. Semi-desert areas prevail near sea level, with a rapid succession of deciduous (1000 m), semi-evergreen (1500 m), and cloud forests (2000 m). This sequence may continue through the upper forest limit (3000 m) to the alpine belt (paramo), dominated by sparse, dwarf and hairy bushes.

Due to the prevailing tropical to subtropical climates, use of natural wetlands by herons largely depends on local and regional habitat conditions. Low temperatures in austral winter have significant influence only in the southernmost parts of the continent. Although herons use a wide range of natural wetlands, some of them are especially critical, namely mangrove swamps, coastal lagoons, tidal mudflats, flooded savannas, inland forested wetlands, high altitude marshes and lagoons, and a number of man-made water bodies. Scott and Carbonell (1986) and Morrison and Ross (1989) give details on many of these habitats.

Mangrove swamps, coastal lagoons and tidal mudflats are a prime habitat for the three marine herons, for the endemic island races of the Galápagos and for cosmopolitan species like the two night herons, *Egretta* species, the Green-backed Heron, and the Boat-billed Heron. All over the tropical coasts, mangroves are frequently associated to tidal mudflats, where herons find year-round food and shelter.

Flooded savannas of the Orinoco Basin harbour about 15 heron species, mostly resident (Kushlan et al. 1985). The gallery forests are very important for a number of rather solitary, non-flocking species like Agami Heron, Rufescent Tiger Heron, Green-backed Heron, Capped Heron, Boat-billed Heron and the night herons. Drier or little-flooded savannas and forest edges are typical habitat for the Whistling Heron (Kushlan et al. 1982). The Pantanal flooded savannas and the floodplains of major Amazon tributaries are among the most critical areas for resident and wintering (from the south) herons. Wetlands along the coast of Uruguay and southern Brazil, the Paraná–Paraguay basin, and several wetlands in northern (inland) Argentina are also critical for these species.

The huge forested wetlands within the Amazon and Orinoco basins seem to be the primary habitat for Zigzag Heron, as well as important areas for 17 other heron species. Only missing or rare are the Whistling Heron, Yellow-crowned Night Heron, Fasciated Tiger Heron, and Streaked Bittern. Except for the southern Andes, fast-flowing streams in mountainous forests seem critical for the Fasciated Tiger Heron.

High altitude freshwater lagoons, marshes, and reservoirs, at 2500 to 5000 m above sea level, are important habitat types for bitterns and Black-crowned Night Herons. Many of these critical wetlands, often isolated by mountain barriers over 6000 m high, are scattered along the Andes from Colombia through Bolivia, and seem to be linked to heron endemism.

Increasing agriculture and cattle ranching are opening new habitats for Cattle Egrets and perhaps Whistling Herons. In equatorial lowlands, the rice fields may harbour large populations of the common, more aquatic herons like Great White Egret, Little Blue Heron, Snowy Egret and the two night herons. However, other herons from marshes with grassy or reed-covered shores, like the bitterns, can also be attracted to these sites.

Changing Status of Herons

Data available

The geographical range of most species is not well documented in detail (see Hancock and Kushlan 1984 for best estimates). Data on distribution in Table 8.1 are derived from Armonía (1995), del Hoyo et al. (1992), Hancock and Kushlan (1984), Haverschmidt and Mees (1994), Lowen et al. (1997), Narosky and Yzurieta (1987), Parker et al. (1982), Sibley and Monroe (1990), Sick (1984), Stotz et al. (1996), and Tostain et al. (1992), and other sources noted in the species accounts. Sound numerical estimations are very few (Table 8.1). A principal source of information on distribution is the inventory of over 700 neotropical wetlands compiled by Scott and Carbonell (1986), including some site-specific population estimates of herons. A second source is a bird census conducted in the austral winter in 270 wetlands from Argentina, Uruguay, southern Paraguay, Chile, and Brazil (Blanco and Canevari 1992). These data have an error of 10–20% (assumed throughout chapter). A third, less reliable, source is the worldwide waterfowl population estimates compiled by Rose and Scott (1994), who also include judgments on trends and status. These figures are wide estimates based on best judgment. A fourth data source is the census programme for Scarlet Ibises (*Eudocimus ruber*) in northern Brazil and the Guianas, which also provides data on the Cocoi Heron and Great White Egret (Spaans 1990). In addition, McNeil et al. (1990) and Morales et al. (1981) estimated population densities of some heron species from the eastern coast and the Llanos of Venezuela, respectively. Most of the information available refers to species that are widespread, visible, diurnal, large, brightly coloured, or active, but many South American herons do not fit this description. In this chapter, I use the concepts of short, medium, and long terms to refer to 5, 10, and 20 or more years, respectively.

Species status

Whistling Heron (Garciolo Real, Pacopaco, Garza Silbadora, Chiflón, María-faceira). This species is endemic to South America, its two populations being separated by the Amazon basin. Its semi-aquatic habits and use of open places make this species less dependent upon pristine habitats than other herons. In Venezuela and Colombia, the northern race *fostersmithi* is common in pastures and other anthropogenic habitats. Although there are no records of breeding in Colombia (Hilty and Brown 1986), this is very likely. The southern race *sibilatrix* similarly exploits managed savannas in Brazil (D.M. Teixeira, pers. comm.) and Argentina (di Giacomo 1988). Antas et al. (1986) recorded the species in southern Brazil, and Blanco and Canevari (1992) in Chile. *S. s. sibilatrix* is expanding its range southwards in Argentina (T. Narosky pers. comm.). Recently, Olmos (pers. comm.) recorded the species (*S. s. sibilatrix*?) well outside its accepted range, in a semi-arid region of Serra de Capivara, in north-eastern Brazil.

In the middle term, their populations seem stable or increasing due to the current expansion of pasturelands. Nevertheless, the Whistling Heron depends partially upon aquatic prey and isolated nesting trees, so in the long term, clearing of lowland forests for agriculture or ranching may pose limits.

Capped Heron (Garza Real, Garciolo Real, Garça-real). The Capped Heron occurs mostly in the Orinoco and Amazon basins and north-western Colombia (Hancock and Kushlan 1984). Available data add nothing to this range, so its colonising abilities may be very limited. It occurs rarely outside the region on both Pacific and Caribbean slopes of Panama, according to Ridgely and Gwynne (1993). Despite occurring commonly in the Guianas, the species is apparently absent from Trinidad and Tobago (ffrench 1980). It uses forested swamps or open areas close to gallery forests and is usually considered to be typical of undisturbed-forested wetlands. In Colombia, it is thinly spread along riverbanks and less frequently in open wetlands (Hilty and Brown 1986). Its current geographical distribution in the Amazonian and Orinoco lowlands is probably shrinking as cattle ranching, gold mining and forest clearing progress.

There is no information on population levels. However, since the regional population is being restricted steadily to smaller habitat patches, a declining population trend is expected in the long term.

Grey Heron. This Old World species is accidental in Brazil, Trinidad and the Guianas (ffrench 1980, Sick 1984).

Capped Heron. Its distribution is restricted to the Orinoco and Amazon basins. Photo: Bruno Pambour.

Great Blue Heron (Garzón Cenizo, Garza Azul Mayor, Garzón Azul). Primarily a North American species, this species is now a rare visitor in Panama (Ridgely and Gwynne 1993) but winters regularly in coastal Ecuador and Colombia (Hancock and Kushlan 1984, Mikuska et al. 1998), Trinidad and Tobago (ffrench 1980, James et al. 1986). Its winter range has recently been extended to Amazonas, Brazil (Parkes 1998). It probably breeds in Venezuela (de Schauensee and Phelps 1979), which may be a significant range extension since the species was previously described as a regular visitor there. Coastal wetlands in Aruba and Bonaire are also important. It occurs in the Galápagos Islands as an endemic race (*cognata*).

In South America the Great Blue Heron uses mostly marine habitats, often-brackish lagoons and tidal flats associated to mangrove forests where its most common prey are fish and intertidal invertebrates. However, it also occurs in a few high-altitude freshwater marshes in Colombia (Hilty and Brown 1986).

Because no censuses covering its huge wintering areas are available and the scattered published data on *A. h. herodias* are few, it is impossible to estimate the population wintering in South America. *A. h. cognata* remains common along the shores of the Galápagos (Kushlan pers. comm.).

Cocoi Heron (Garza Morena, Garza Gris, Garza Mora, Garza Cenicienta, Garza Cuca, Baguari). The Cocoi Heron is a common and widespread South American species. The main populations are centred in the middle and northern part of the continent. Northwards, it reaches outside the region into Panama (rarely), where its breeding is probable but not confirmed (Ridgely and Gwynne 1993). It has occasionally been recorded in the Falkland Islands (Hilty and Brown 1986, De la Peña, pers. comm.).

It is found both in still freshwater and in coastal habitats, either open or forested. Likewise, it frequently uses tall trees for nesting, but uses reeds on non-forested islands. However, it has been recorded over 2600 m high in northern Argentina (Peris and Alabarce 1991) and also in the desertic western Peruvian coast (Plenge et al. 1989).

It is sometimes abundant in tropical lowlands. Rose and Scott (1994) report the total in the Neotropics is 100 000 to 1 000 000 birds, a numerical range that reflects the lack of real data. It is patchily distributed in some areas and some seasons. Nores (1986) found the species in only three out of 60 surveyed wetlands in Argentina, and Schlatter and Espinoza (1986) did not record the species in 50 Chilean wetlands. Blanco and Canevari (1992) report only 780 birds of this species all over the southern part of the continent in austral winter, which may support the suspected post-breeding dispersal northwards. According to the few available data, the population trend is stable or probably increasing.

Great White Egret (Garzón Blanco, Garceta or Garza Real, Garza Blanca, Garça branca-grande). Being one of the most versatile and least shy species, it is found all over the Americas. In South America, breeding populations occur as far as 44°S (Nores 1986). Wintering birds from North America occur into Colombia (Hilty and Brown 1986, Mikuska et al. 1998). It may forage and nest solitarily or in groups on trees, bushes, or reeds as reported by De la Peña (pers. comm.) in northern Argentina. This is a highly opportunistic species that has established urban populations in several cities.

During austral winter, 4853 birds were observed in southern South America (Blanco and Canevari 1992). Population trends are most probably stable or increasing.

Reddish Egret (Garceta Rojiza). The Reddish Egret is a typically marine fish-eating heron that occurs along open shorelines and tidal flats of the northern South American tropics. The subspecies *rufescens* is reported from the eastern Venezuelan coast westward through the Colombian side of the Goajiran Peninsula, but it is absent from this location north to the Panama Isthmus. It also seems to be absent along the Pacific Colombian coast, despite having been recorded along the Pacific coast of Central America through Panama (Ridgely and Gwynne 1993). It seems to breed in the Goajira (Naranjo 1986) and Bonaire (Spaans 1974a). Although common along the Venezuelan coast, the Reddish Egret is not reported for nearby Trinidad (ffrench 1980, James et al. 1986).

Only a small proportion of the total population size of about 10 000 (Chapter 7) occurs in South America. Important areas are the coastal wetlands of Aruba, Bonaire, north-western Venezuela, and the Caribbean coast of Colombia. It seems the Reddish Egret breeds in the San Juan Lagoon and the Swamp of San Agustín,

Colombia (Fig. 8.1). Numbers seem stable or even increasing in the short term, but habitat loss and degradation in the Caribbean may affect local populations in the long term.

Tricolored Heron (Garza Flaca, Garza Pechiblanca, Garça Tricolor). The Tricolored Heron is primarily coastal in South America, using marine and freshwater coastal wetlands, feeding on fish in shallow waters, most frequently as solitary individuals. In northern South America, it occurs primarily near mangrove forests along the coasts, but it was recorded in very dry habitats in Ceará, north-eastern Brazil (Teixeira et al. 1993). The overall range is from Peru and Ecuador, through Colombia, Venezuela, Trinidad and Brazil (Hancock and Kushlan 1984). North American birds winter into Colombia and Ecuador (Mikuska et al. 1998).

The taxonomic status and distribution at the subspecific level deserve further study. Currently the race *tricolor* has two populations recognized, one on each side of the continent, and *ruficollis* ranges in between (Hancock and Kushlan 1984). Blake (1977) restricted *tricolor* to Brazil and the Guianas, and *ruficollis* for the rest of the range except Trinidad, where a third race is identified. These subspecific definitions may have conservation implications.

The distribution of this species appears stable, but the information is variable. Antas et al. (1986) did not report the species all over its expected Brazilian range, although Teixeira (pers. comm.) more recently confirmed the expected range and also observed the species regularly in Amapá Province (neighbouring French Guiana). On the Pacific coast, Scott and Carbonell (1986) reported 30 birds near the Arequipa coast (southern Peru), and Castro et al. (1990) observed the species near Lima.

Available information suggests that local populations may fluctuate widely over time, but the overall population trend seems stable in the short term. In the long term the species might be affected by losses of coastal habitats.

Little Blue Heron (Garcita Azul, Garça-Azul). These are among the most common herons in the Americas, exploiting a wide variety of shallow wetlands, including human habitats such as rice fields, populated areas, and aquaculture ponds. Primarily fish-eating, it feeds on an extremely high variety of other prey. In South America it is widely distributed all over the Caribbean shore, Amazon basin, and southwards along the Pacific coast through Peru to near the Chilean border. It is accidental to the Andes of Peru and Colombia at 3500 m altitude or more (Fjeldsa and Krabbe 1990). North American birds can migrate as far south as coastal Venezuela, Colombia, and Ecuador (Mikuska et al. 1998). It has not been reported for Paraguay, Bolivia or Chile. None was seen by Blanco and Canevari (1992) in southern South America in winter 1991, but the species was found in coastal Brazil (78 individuals), at the same latitude. Contreras (1993) made the first report for Argentina, near the Paraguayan border. These data suggest that substantial migrations may occur. Information suggests its population trend is stable due to its colonising abilities, and may be increasing in the short term.

Snowy Egret (Garceta Nívea, Chusmita, Garcita Blanca, Garza Chica, Garça branca-pequena). The Snowy Egret is one of the most common and widely distributed herons in South America, where it uses a variety of habitats but also exploits man-made wetlands such as rice fields, fish ponds and shrimp ponds, and even channels within large cities. North American birds winter as far south as coastal Venezuela and French Guiana (Mikuska et al. 1998). Its geographical range seems stable, and its numbers are increasing in Argentina (Narosky and De la Peña pers. comm.), where plume hunting was particularly intense in earlier decades. In the austral winter, 2611 birds were recorded by Blanco and Canevari (1992) over the south of the continent, but mainly in Argentina. Overall, the population trend is stable.

Little Egret. This Old World species has occurred on Trinidad and Suriname (ffrench 1980, Haverschmidt and Mees 1994). A recent sighting in Trinidad was of a Western Reef Heron (*Egretta garzetta gularis* of Hancock and Kushlan 1984) (Murphy and Nanan 1987, Murphy 1992). Nesting has recently been reported in the Lesser Antilles, showing that an invasion of the New World has taken place recently (Chapter 7).

Cattle Egret (Garza del Ganado, Garceta Bueyera, Garça vaqueira). The African race *ibis* of the Cattle Egret arrived in Suriname in 1877–1882 and from there spread to most of the New World (Telfair 1994). Its feeding habits take advantage of cattle grazing and agriculture, and it can nest in urban sites in warm-climate cities. Formerly expected to range south to 35–40°S (Hancock and Kushlan 1984), it has more recently exceeded expectations, extending south to the Falkland Islands and Tierra del Fuego at 55°S (De la Peña pers. comm.) and, outside the region, to the South Shetland Islands, probably deriving from Argentina and Chile (Moenke and Bick 1990). In Peru it breeds at 4000 m above sea level (Fjeldsa and Krabbe 1990). North American birds winter as far south as Colombia (Mikuska et al. 1998).

Although population estimates are slim, it is likely that the trend in South America may be still increasing due to the expansion of agriculture at the expense of wetlands and forests.

Green-backed Heron (Garza verde, Garza Rayada, Chicuaco, Garcita Azulada, Socozinho). This small heron is a solitary feeder that uses almost any forested wetland of any depth. Nesting can be solitary or in small, often mixed colonies. Although not shy, the Green-backed Heron is easy to overlook in its preferred habitats. It is found throughout the continent, including the Andes up to 4000 m altitude (Fjeldsa and Krabbe 1990).

Its taxonomic situation at the species/subspecies level remains unresolved. The black race *sundevalli* is endemic to the Galápagos Islands, where it is common along shores (Kushlan pers. comm.). The typical South American form (*striatus*) is found over most of the continent from Panama south through Rio Negro in Argentina, and is extending its range slightly southwards (De la Peña, pers. comm.). Distribution of the North American form (*virescens*) is unclear. Although Hancock and Kushlan (1984) limit the southern distribution of *virescens* to Panama, two races of the former *Butorides virescens* have been reported in Colombia, Venezuela and the Guianas (Blake 1977). Northern birds of the *virescens* types are generally considered restricted to coastal wetlands, while *striatus*-type birds are found both in freshwater and marine shores. However, Naranjo (1986) recorded "*B. virescens*" as a nearctic migrant in continental southern Colombia, at about 1000 m above sea level, which extends its range southward and inland. Fjeldsa and Krabbe (1990) report this race as accidental to the central Colombian Andes at 2600 m altitude.

Population data are slim and population sizes may have been underestimated. There is no evidence of population decreases, although the species may be facing drastic habitat loss due to clearing of mangroves and large-scale damming.

Agami Heron (Garza Pechicastaña, Garça-da-mata, Garça-beija-flor). This large and little-known heron inhabits forested freshwater wetlands. Feeding mostly on fish, this shy species nests solitarily (do Nascimiento 1990, first record for Brazil) or in small, mixed-species nest groups (Ramo and Busto 1982 for the Venezuelan Llanos, and Blanco pers. comm. for Peru). In South America it ranges south to include the equatorial Amazon basin, and along the Pacific coast, Panama through northern Ecuador and, most recently, to Amazonia Peru (Blanco pers. comm., 1998). It is accidental to the high Colombian Andes up to 2600 m altitude (Fjeldsa and Krabbe 1990). Important sites for this species include the wetlands of Manu, Tambopata, Cabo Orange, and Cassiporé marshes (Fig. 8.1).

Available data do not clarify its range, nor is there any information on population sizes or trends. Collar et al. (1994) and Armonía (1995) consider it as near-threatened. Deforestation, chemical pollution, and/or large-scale damming in the Amazon and Orinoco basins may produce a declining trend in the long term.

Agami Heron. This shy and little known heron inhabits South America's gallery forests. Photo: Bruno Pambour.

Yellow-crowned Night Heron (Pedrete Enmascarado, Chicuaco Enmascarado, Martirão). This New World night heron is not shy and is less nocturnal than the Black-crowned Night Heron. In South America it uses mangrove forests both for nesting and foraging. It also breeds in inland wetlands of the Llanos and upper Orinoco basin and Amazon basin. It is becoming common in the city of Rio de Janeiro (D.M. Teixeira pers. comm.).

Four sub-species are described for South America: *pauper*, endemic to Galápagos Islands; *bancrofti*, from Tobago but also along the Caribbean coast and small islands offshore from Venezuela (de Schauensee and Phelps 1979); *caliginis*, found from Panama and along the Pacific coast through Ecuador; and *cayennensis*, widespread along the South American coast from Colombia to Brazil and inland in the Venezuelan and Colombian Llanos (Figueroa and Seijas 1986; Naranjo 1986), middle Amazon Basin (Araguaia river, Antas et al. 1986), and upper Orinoco Basin (Willard et al. 1991). However, it was not recorded in Pantanal (south-western Brazil) near the Bolivian border (Yamashita and Valle 1990b, Willis and Oniki 1990). In the north it overlaps with *bancrofti*.

Population data are scant. In austral winter, Blanco and Canevari (1992) observed only four birds. McNeil et al. (1990) recorded 38 birds (no subspecies given) in seven eastern coastal wetlands in Venezuela. *Pauper* is common on the Galápagos (Kushlan pers. comm.). Despite occurring in low numbers, all indications are that the Yellow-crowned Night Heron populations are stable, especially in the interior. Some range expansion seems to be occurring for *cayennensis*. Loss of mangrove forests and other coastal South American wetlands may have long-term effects.

Black-crowned Night Heron (Perro de Agua, Guaco, Garza Bruja, Huairavo, Boca-d'água, Coá). One of the most abundant and widely distributed herons, this species is a habitat and food generalist, nesting on many substrate types. It is very aggressive while breeding and tolerates human intervention well. It is usually associated with habitats with some plant cover, mostly inland forests and man-groves.

In South America there are three subspecies: *falklandicus*, a small-sized race endemic to Falkland Islands; *obscurus*, ranging from southern Chile and Argentina through Tierra del Fuego, and *hoactli*, on most of the rest of the continent and the Galápagos. Fjeldsa and Krabbe (1990) report a breeding population of this race at 4800 m above sea level along the Andes of Peru through Chile. Recent data confirms its expected presence in the Amazon basin (Yamashita and Valle 1990b, Willis and Oniki 1990, Cintra and Yamashita 1990). As far as is known, the distribution of *obscurus* remains unchanged from Hancock and Kushlan (1984). Sparse populations breed in high-altitude wetlands along the Andes, like the lagoons of Lagunillas and Umayo, the lakes of Titicaca and Uru-Uru, and the wetlands of Ulla-Ulla (Fig. 8.1).

Blanco and Canevari (1992) recorded 2835 individuals during the 1991 austral winter. Scott and Carbonell (1986) estimated 90 breeding pairs of *falklandicus* (called *cyanocephalus*) in two colonies. The South American population trend seems stable or increasing. There is no apparent risk for *falklandicus*: this opportunistic heron seems able to profit from the accelerated changes occurring in South American wetlands.

Boat-billed Heron (Garza Cucharón, Pato Pico de Barco, Pato Cuchara, Garza Cucharona, Arapapá). This neotropical night heron inhabits forested fresh waters and mangrove swamps, breeding solitarily or in small colonies. It is widespread in South America, with the predominant subspecies, *cochlearius*, absent only on the Pacific coast south of Panama, in Chile, Uruguay, and north-eastern Brazil. However, north-eastern Brazil may be within its range since there are large populations in Suriname (de Jong et al. 1986, Haverschmidt and Mees 1994) on the north; it also occurs southerly in Brazil. It was reported for the uppermost Orinoco river (Willard et al. 1991) and as accidental to the Andes of Colombia and Venezuela, at 2600 m altitude (Fjeldsa and Krabbe 1990). The southern limits of distribution (north-eastern Argentina) remain unchanged (Hancock and Kushlan 1984). Another race, *panamensis*, is found in the northern lowlands of Pacific Colombia (Blake 1977).

Although widespread, it is rarely abundant. The population trend is uncertain, due to scarcity of data. It seems stable in the short term, but habitat losses may reverse the trend in the long term.

Bare-throated Tiger Heron (Garza-tigre Cuellinuda). In South America, this Central American tiger heron is restricted to north-western Colombia (Gulf of Urabá, Hilty and Brown 1986), and there is almost no information about this local population.

Fasciated Tiger Heron (Garza-tigre Barreteada, Pájaro Vaco Oscuro, Hocó Oscuro, Socó). This largely unknown heron usually inhabits fast-flowing rivers of variable size along foothills. Schulenberg et al. (1984) recorded the species at 2000–2350 m above sea level, and Fjeldsa and Krabbe (1990) up to 3300 m in the Peruvian Andes. Food and feeding behaviour remain almost unknown. Hancock and Kushlan (1984) suggested it is nocturnal, but Ridgely and Gwynne (1993) report rather diurnal habits.

In South America three subspecies are recognised: race *pallescens*, from north-western Argentina (bordering Bolivia); *fasciatum*, from north-eastern Argentina through south-eastern Brazil and Mato Grosso; and *salmoni*, in Bolivia through Panama and Costa Rica, including Venezuela (northern Orinoco basin). Yamashita and Valle (1990a), who observed two adult birds in Goias, central Brazil, significantly expanded the known range of *fasciatum*. The birds were seen in open woodland, a different habitat from those previously reported.

Its naturally low abundance and the lack of population data preclude assessing the population or human impacts on its isolated populations. However, a decreasing trend seems likely because its geographic range overlaps extensively with areas under heavy deforestation and urbanisation. Yamashita and Valle (1990a) believed that this species exploits oligotrophic stream habitats, and so requires large areas to meet its food needs. Collar et al. (1994) and Armonía (1995) consider this species as near-threatened or declining.

Rufescent Tiger Heron (Garza-tigre Castaña, Garza Serpiente, Pájaro Vaco, Hocó Colorado, Socó-boi). The Rufescent Tiger Heron is a largely South American species. It inhabits mainly lowland freshwater swamps and the forested shores of slow-flowing rivers. It is shy, forages solitarily while standing, and usually preys on crabs, shrimp, and often large fish and eels.

There are two subspecies recognised but their status is uncertain. The northern, *lineatum*, is reported from southern Honduras through north-eastern Bolivia and

The Rufescent Tiger Heron. This is a bird of forested borders, of freshwater swamps and slow-moving rivers. Photo: Bruno Pambour.

central Mato Grosso (Brazil), whereas the southern race, *marmoratum*, is reported from south-eastern Mato Grosso through northern Argentina. A wide overlap of races is said to occur in the Amazon basin and Argentina (Blake 1977) and the diagnostic black crown of *marmoratum* also occurs in one of the preadult plumages of *lineatum* (Hancock and Kushlan 1984). No recent data suggest modifying the species range (cf. Hancock and Kushlan 1984).

The total population of this widespread species is large, although Blanco and Canevari (1992) observed only 85 birds in the southern continent in winter. Major threats are deforestation and damming of lowland forests, but given the shy character of the species, hunting and motorboating in pristine areas may affect nesting activities. Its status seems stable in the short to middle term, but habitat loss may reverse this in the long term.

Zigzag Heron (Garza Cebra). This is one of the least known herons. Almost nothing is known about status or distribution, or about its behaviour, nesting, habitat or food habits. The few published observations are from forested wetlands, but Hilty and Brown (1986 and references therein) provide data on semi-terrestrial foraging.

Recent reliable distribution records include those from Flores (1986) in Tumi Chucua Lake, north-eastern Bolivia, Ortiz (1986) in two localities of the Amazon slope of Ecuador, and Robbins et al. (1991) on the southern bank of the Amazon in north-eastern Peru. The latter two records are range extensions to Hancock and Kushlan (1984) and Blake (1977). Recently it has been recorded near forested streams in managed pasture lands in the Venezuelan Llanos (C. Sharpe, pers. comm.). Critical areas to the species include the remaining undisturbed wetlands of Cabo Orange, Manu, Tambopata, the Mamoré and Cassiporé rivers, the lower Amazon wetlands, and the Orinoco River delta (Fig. 8.1).

No data are available on population sizes or trends of this rare heron. The loss of its primary habitat and disturbances due to hunting are probably the main threats to the species. Armonía (1995), Collar et al. (1994) and IUCN (1996) regard the Zigzag Heron as near threatened by extinction. Although we follow this categorization, available data are not sufficient to support a firm understanding of its conservation status. Clearly, much more information is needed.

Streaked Bittern (Garza Enana Amarilla, Mirasol Común). This small South American endemic is described as a rather solitary bird of secretive habits. Hancock and Kushlan (1984) reported tropical grassy marshes as typical habitat, but some new findings seem noteworthy. Nores (1986) reported a breeding population in the northern Argentinean Andes at 3500 m above sea level, and Flores (1986), in a fast-flowing river in southern Bolivia. In both cases the habitat was also used for livestock grazing and/or agriculture. Antas et al. (1986) observed the same near the city of Rio de Janeiro.

Available data suggest a wide geographical distribution. In northern South America, it was recorded patchily in Venezuela, Colombia, Trinidad and the Guianas. In Suriname it was reported as migrant (Haverschmidt and Mees 1994). The southern range includes southern Brazil to central Argentina and, separated by the Andes, southern Chile. Recent records seem to be filling the Amazon gap between the two known ranges. Terborgh et al. (1984) reported this species in south-eastern Peru; Olmos (1988) collected a bird for the first time in north-eastern Brazil; and the record of Flores (1986) also seems to extend the range northwards, along the Andean foothills. The possibility that the southern population migrates northwards in winter seems still unresolved.

Although this species is common within its range in Argentina (De la Peña, pers. comm.), Blanco and Canevari (1992) recorded only 23 birds in over 270 wetlands in southern South America in winter. Neither Willis and Oniki (1990) nor Cintra and Yamashita (1990) recorded the species in 10 sites in Mato Grosso, Brazil at any time between 1982 and 1988. These results may mean that migration, if it occurs, may reach equatorial latitudes. In fact, Hilty and Brown (1986) reported the species as being fairly common in the western Meta River (Colombia, nearly 4°N) in boreal summer. This suggests that the Streaked Bittern is more widespread and common than expected, but its seasonal movements remain largely unknown. Also, it seems able to use some man-made habitats involving drastic environmental changes. No population data are available, but the trend may be stable or even increasing.

Least Bittern (Garcilla, Mirasol Menudo, Gallito, Alcaravancito, Garza Enana, Socoí-vermelho). The Least Bittern is widely distributed in the Americas (see

Chapter 7), with three out of the five described subspecies breeding in South America. These are: *peruvianus*, endemic to the central coast of Peru; *bogotensis*, endemic to Sabana de Bogotá (2500–3000 m above sea level in the Colombian Andes); and *erythromelas*, the most widespread, occurring from central Panama through Venezuela, northern Colombia, Trinidad, the Guianas, eastern Brazil, Paraguay, to northern Argentina. Some new data expand the species' range. Cintra and Yamashita (1990) recorded it in Mato Grosso (south-western Brazil), so confirming its expected presence (Blake 1977). Scott and Carbonell (1986) report birds (most probably *peruvianus*) near Lima, in coastal, intensely disturbed areas.

Population data are slim. The race *bogotensis* is still common in its typical range, but according to Naranjo (1986), its wetlands are threatened by a number of factors, and Procam-Inderena (1986) considers this race as threatened by extinction. The Peruvian race also seems threatened, but is little studied. The widespread race *erythromelas* seems relatively less troubled, and its populations may be stable in the short term.

South American Bittern (Garza Tamboruda, Mirasol, Mirasol Grande, Socó-boi-marron). The South American Bittern exploits freshwater swamps with dense herbaceous cover, including rice fields (Hilty and Brown 1986). The range of the South American race (*pinnatus*) extends into Central America (Chapter 7) and, in the region, includes north-western Venezuela, Trinidad, the Guianas, eastern and central Brazil, Paraguay, northern Argentina (where it is rare—De la Peña pers. comm.), and Uruguay (Blanco and Canevari 1992). Although reported for Mato Grosso (south-western Brazil), it was not observed there by Willis and Oniki (1990) or by Cintra and Yamashita (1990). Remsen (1986) did not observe the species in north-eastern Bolivia either. Recently, di Giacomo (1997) made the first report of nesting of this species for Argentina. These data show very little progress beyond Hancock and Kushlan (1984) in understanding the details of its range. The Zapatosa Swamp, Kaw Marshes, and Lagoons of Tramandai (Fig. 8.1) are reported as important habitats for this species.

As for most large bitterns, little information is available on population sizes. In Colombia, it is regarded as locally threatened by extinction (Procam-Inderena 1986).

Overall status

No species or subspecies of South American heron is globally threatened (IUCN 1996). Three species are considered to be near threatened, namely Agami Heron, Fasciated Tiger Heron, and Zigzag Heron. All three seem to occupy stream-edge forests and are little known. Populations of several species are considered threatened by local authorities, including the South American Bittern in inland Colombia and the Least Bittern in Colombia and Peru. The known distribution of several species is highly patchy, which may put them under threat, but it is not clear whether this is a true biogeographic feature or is due to incomplete survey coverage. The Zigzag Heron is a good example; concerns for its welfare derive as much from a lack of knowledge about its distribution as from real knowledge about the threats it faces.

Currently, there are no estimates of trends in South American heron populations due to a lack of long-term data, so the population trends proposed here are tentative.

Herons have been monitored in the northern savannas and during a winter survey in the south. However, the huge Amazon basin and the tropical Andean foothills remain the most challenging areas to cover. Oren and de Albuquerque (1991) estimate that well over 50% of the Brazilian Amazon basin is ornithologically underexplored or totally unexplored. Overall, however, available information suggests that heron populations appear to be doing well, although it is clear that there are important threats in the long term.

Critical Conservation and Regional Management Issues

At a continental scale, the most important issue in heron conservation is the loss of habitat, especially wetlands, and this phenomenon is tightly linked to regional economic conditions. The need for increased food production and the deficit of hard currencies are the basis of the worst environmental problems. World Resources Institute (1994) estimates over 746 000 km^2 of marshes and wetlands in South America, but there are no data on current loss rates. Heron habitat conservation requires a clear demonstration that: 1) wetlands are extremely valuable habitats as sources of goods and services; 2) loss of wetlands can be very costly to local people; and 3) herons are key biotic elements of wetland dynamics. Because South American

A mixed foraging aggregation of Great White Egrets, Scarlet Ibises and Wood Storks in a mangrove swamp of Venezuela. Photo: Bruno Pambour.

heron species may not always be able to fulfil requirements as flag species, a habitat approach may work better for their conservation. Here, I discuss the conservation of heron habitats and some promising efforts being made at the population level.

Degradation of heron habitats

Eutrophication and silting of watersheds and coastal habitats is a general problem, since there is little or no treatment of sewage in the region (World Resources Institute 1992). Andean watersheds are among the most severely damaged, and several of the largest basins, such as those of Paraguay, Plata, Orinoco, Magdalena, and Amazon rivers, are among the most polluted and carrying the heaviest sediment loads worldwide (Lean and Hinrichsen 1994, Hayes 1996). There are four major difficulties underlying water pollution in South America. First, not all countries have adequate regulations on water pollution, land use, or habitat management. Second, there is a generalised weakness in law enforcement, which is most dramatically manifest away from the main urban centres. Third, there is little monitoring of water quality. Fourth, there is a very heavy use of and an increasing demand for natural areas by local people.

Croplands are subject to the poorly controlled use of insecticides, including organochlorines long ago banned in their countries of origins. In rice fields, roosts of (presumed) bird pests have been sprayed with pesticides (Spaans 1974b, Basili and Temple 1995). Gold mining is affecting the Amazon and Orinoco basins in several ways, mostly through a heavy silting of water and releasing of mercury (Padovani et al. 1995). Chlor-alkali plants have also been reported as sources of mercurial pollution in northern South America (Ishizaki and Urich 1985). Coastal lagoons and tidal flats, often associated to mangrove forests, are very important for the marine herons and for cosmopolitan species like Great White Egret and Snowy Egret. Usually, these habitats are at river mouths, so receive heavy loads of domestic sewage and contaminants.

There are a number of reserves and protected sites, but law enforcement is often lax and environmental education is still incipient or non-existent. Nearly all South American countries (including Trinidad–Tobago and Netherlands Antilles) have ratified the Ramsar convention. By 1997, they had declared 40 wetlands of international importance (Jones 1993, Frazier 1996, J. Beltrán, pers. comm.). Herons use most of them, although many other sites are also of importance. Figure 8.1 shows 69 wetland areas of key importance to South American herons. These sites need to be censused, monitored, and managed to protect their value to continent-wide heron populations.

Managed wetlands

Damming is a type of alteration potentially causing important transformations in whole basins. For instance, the plan of Eletronorte (the Brazilian agency for hydroelectric power development in the Amazon region) is to flood near $100\,000$ km² by the year 2010. Currently, in the lower Amazon basin dams in advanced design stage or already in operation have created a flooded surface of nearly $30\,000$ km². Besides the loss of floodplain forests, damming in tropical South America has been especially adverse to wildlife because of the drastic ecosystem change to a lake environment. This shift includes the blockage of fish migrations, the desiccation of large tracts downstream from the dams, and fundamental changes in the chemistry of the impounded waters. For instance, Santos (1995) reports significant changes in fish communities after the damming of Jamari River in Rondonia, Brazil. Likewise, J.P. Myers (1993) and Hayes (1996) warned of the huge environmental impact to be caused by the Hidrovia project on the Paraná–Paraguay basin, potentially involving the Pantanal, one of the largest continuous wetlands in the world.

Some managed areas like pastures, rice fields, and shrimp ponds may become suitable habitats for herons, although it is important to realise that they are often developed at the expense of pre-existing floodplains, seasonally flooded savannas, mangrove forests or natural marshes. The net result usually is that common, generalist heron species may increase local populations, but those shyer species and habitat-specialists may be forced to abandon the area.

Mangrove forests in the Caribbean and equatorial Pacific shores are heavily harvested for wood, which may be managed in sustainable ways. However, these wetlands are also being converted to recreation facilities and for shrimp and fish aquaculture. No data are available on mangrove swamp losses, but in South America, this habitat type covered nearly 40 000 km^2 early in the 1980s. If the trend is similar to Africa and Asia, 50% or more may already be lost (Lean and Hinrichsen 1994, N. Myers 1993). This may be a significant habitat loss for the three marine herons and the Yellow-crowned Night Heron.

Recreational disturbance

Coastal recreation and widespread duck hunting are frequently reported as common sources of disturbance for herons, both in natural and in managed habitats. In both cases, nesting herons are the most sensitive, but wintering species along the northern continental coast can also be impaired. Unlike other birds such as flamingoes, scarlet ibises, and migrant shorebirds, herons have not been included as species of concern in preparing hunting regulations and tourism management. Likewise, almost nowhere but in some protected areas like national parks or wildlife sanctuaries are herons considered when planning routes for boats or other vehicles. When this does occur, only the most common, colonial species are considered. It is critical that herons be considered with other water birds in managing other natural resources.

Conservation at the population level

It is a fortunate circumstance that the plume trade caused no mass extinction of herons in South America at the turn of the century. This and the extent of remaining wetlands mean that herons remain an abundant and visible component of wetlands and other areas. Common herons are important scenic elements in the ecosystems where they occur. Others are less obvious. For instance, the distribution of all bitterns remains poorly known (Stotz et al. 1996). A challenge is how to conserve herons and the habitats that still remain over much of South America.

Large flocks of white-coloured herons, usually associated with Scarlet Ibises (*Eudocimus ruber*) or storks, have inspired official protection of several wetlands and also encouraged habitat conservation by private landowners. This has happened particularly in northern South America, where in boreal winter the progressive dry season promotes huge concentrations of wading birds. Although ecotourism based on some bird species can be sustainable and profitable, such as in Trinidad (Hilty 1992), the low visibility of several herons makes it difficult to convince governments or landowners to save large areas. This remains a serious obstacle for using herons as emblematic species for on-site conservation or education programmes (see P. J. Butler 1992 on parrots). Further, the strategy of appealing to local pride for heron conservation would work with the species or races endemic to one country, state or province, which in South America only includes two inland, three Galápagos, and one Falkland subspecies. Thus to be successful, the conservation of local heron populations must be highly imaginative and integrated into other conservation programmes.

Species and races of concern

Its high level of endemism best expresses the particular richness of the South American heron fauna. Here I discuss specific sources of concern for heron populations.

The Colombian range of the Bare-throated Tiger Heron is reported to be Golfo de Urabá and Rio Atrato. The gulf is unprotected, faces urban expansion, occupation of river margins, and discharge of domestic sewage. The river is poorly known and partially protected, but there are traditional fishing, livestock grazing, deforestation, and agriculture practices. The status of this subpopulation should be assessed, especially along the shoreline of the gulf.

The status of the endemic race *bogotensis* of the Least Bittern is uncertain at present since its typical habitat, the wetlands of Savanna de Bogotá, Colombia, has been heavily used. Several lagoons and marshes occur in this extensive area, mainly over 2000 m above sea level. Many of them receive water discharges from the Bogotá River, now heavily polluted by domestic sewage and pesticides. Although there are scattered patches of protected, forested land, a project for controlling the river flow and eventually for draining the entire area is under way. Nearly all wetlands face hunting pressure, draining for pasture, burning of marsh vegetation, silting, and reed-cutting. Among the most important areas to preserve are Lake Tota, La Florida and Funza Marshes, and the lagoons of El Sonso, Fuquene, Cucunuba, Suesca, and La Herrera.

The race *peruvianus* of the Least Bittern occurs in several lagoons and marshes along a narrow, desertic coastal belt of Central Peru, mostly north of Lima (perhaps the most densely populated areas of the country). Over this little-explored range, there are traditional activities of fishing, duck hunting, reed collecting for the local basket industry, pesticides from nearby croplands, public recreation, livestock grazing, and drainage. The presence of this subspecies needs confirmation since available reports are at the species level. The most important sites are the Lagoons of Playa Chica and El Paraíso, the marshes of Villa and Agua Santa, and the Lagoons Medio Mundo and San Felipe. The coastal wetlands from the Provinces of Ancash, Lambayeque, Piura, and Tumbes are also worthwhile to survey.

There is almost no information on the Chilean population of the Streaked Bittern, which is reported for the provinces of Aconcagua, Region Metropolitana de Santiago, Libertador General Bernardo O'Higgins, Maule, Bio-Bio, La Araucana, and Los Lagos. The presence and the status of bitterns in this large area remain virtually undetermined. Likewise, there is the possibility of finding breeding populations in Province Rio Cruces and in the Sanctuary Carlos Anwandter. The species is also reported for Guyana, but the information available is minimal. So far, Guyana has no protected wetlands, very few natural wetlands remain undisturbed, and the unchecked collection of birds and eggs for subsistence and trade may be very intense (Ramsamujh 1990). The remaining and much disturbed coastal plains are the most probable habitats for the bitterns, but towards the interior, the swamp forests may harbour some viable populations. In this situation, urgent conservation action is needed.

The subspecies endemic to the Galápagos Islands (Ecuador) and Falkland Islands deserve special consideration. There are three heron races endemic to Galápagos: *Ardea herodias cognata, Butorides striatus sundevalli*, and *Nycticorax violaceus pauper*. While secure in recent years, bird populations of the Galápagos in general are under pressure from human migration, increased land conversion, tourism, and introduction of alien species. In the Falklands there is an endemic race of the Black-crowned Night Heron (*falklandicus*). The situation there seems benign to herons and their habitats.

The Caribbean population of the Yellow-crowned Night Heron (race *bancrofti*) reaches northern South America. There is need to census and evaluate the viability of Caribbean populations, especially on nearby Tobago (see Chapter 7), as well as the possible interbreeding with the race *cayennensis* in South America.

The range of the *pallescens* race of the Fasciated Tiger Heron is very local in north-western Argentina. The validity of this subspecies should be confirmed since there is an apparent overlap with the race *salmoni* in Bolivia. Immediate actions are censuses of the population in the typical localities, as well as in El Pilon Creek, Salta Province, Argentina.

Conclusions

Since the continent is an ecological, cultural and idiosyncratic mosaic, there are sharp differences in local knowledge, use, and attitude towards wildlife. Consequently, few conservation actions may be operative in more than one country or region. However, I suggest here some initiatives for South American herons.

Considering the limited base of real data, basic inventory and monitoring programmes are needed. Besides the points dealing with subspecies (see above), other studies seem critical. These include evaluation of rates of wetland loss, assessment of water pollution in natural and managed wetlands, and, for some races, population censuses, migration patterns, and viability analyses.

Given that most of the species are reported for more than two countries, a network of heron-concerned individuals and agencies that cross national boundaries needs to be established to keep each other updated on research progress or immediate threats to herons or their habitats. This kind of organisation has also proven to be influential on decision makers.

In some places, it is possible to appeal to native pride, ancestral knowledge, or traditional use of nature to adopt herons as local symbols or foci of conservation. For endemic races, there is a good chance of success if entire communities are involved. Landowners should also be advised on alternative, profitable uses of wetlands used by herons.

Involvement of governments is essential. Governments must be key actors in any conservation process since the management of species and habitats is usually under their authority. Few, if any, heron species are specifically protected as flamingoes, ibises or macaws are. Governmental authorities should be informed of the multiple value of herons as scenic resources or indicators of environmental quality.

International treaties for protection of herons and their habitats are essential. Governments should be lobbied to ratify international agreements likely to protect herons and their habitats. The Convention on Biological Diversity can be a general framework for more specific agreements. The Ramsar Convention is useful in protecting heron habitats, and declaration of Ramsar sites needs to be encouraged. Key sites for heron conservation (Fig. 8.1) must be monitored and managed to protect their value for South American heron populations.

9. Heron Nest Site Conservation

Heinz Hafner

A safe nest site is a fundamental requirement for successful breeding in birds. Reproductive success, defined as the contribution of an individual to the next generation, requires production, survival, and recruitment into the breeding population of young birds. Since safe nest sites are a key requirement of breeding birds and their young, heron conservation must incorporate protection of areas where colonial and solitary breeders are known to nest, especially those sites containing important portions of critical populations. In that breeding success depends not only on a safe nest site but also on the quality of the surrounding feeding areas, conservation attempts need to focus not only on breeding site protection but also on large scale habitat preservation near nesting colonies (Kushlan 1997; Chapter 10).

The heron family contains a complex mix of species with differing breeding patterns, including those that nest colonially, facultatively colonially, and solitarily. Coloniality, or group nesting, characterises only a few bird families, about 10% of the total number of bird species in the world (Siegel-Causey and Kharitonov 1990). However, most species of day herons, Ardeinae, the largest heron subfamily, are colonial. Several other species are facultative colonial nesters, including the Great Blue Heron, Grey Heron and Purple Heron. The Least Bittern, Cinnamon Bittern, African Dwarf Bittern and Black Bittern also have been described as both solitary and colonial breeders (Krebs 1978).

Only three species of day herons are solitary nesters exclusively, the Goliath Heron, Imperial Heron and Sumatran Heron (Krebs 1978, Hancock and Kushlan 1984). In contrast, three out of seven species of night herons are solitary breeders. The other two distinctive groups of herons, the tiger herons and the bitterns, typically nest solitarily. Several of the most vulnerable species of herons are solitary site breeders and the conservation of their breeding areas should be a priority.

Heron Conservation
ISBN 0-12-430130-4

Conservation Issues

Conservation implications of coloniality

Colonial nesting is a dynamic phenomenon (Siegel-Causey and Kharitonov 1990) and has undoubtedly evolved as a result of a variety of selection pressures. Although the survival value of colonial nesting can be studied among heron populations, factors influencing the evolution of colonial breeding are still not well understood. The value of coloniality may differ among heron species and may vary with changing ecological conditions. The evolution of coloniality in herons remains controversial.

There is a strong association between colonial nesting and social feeding (Kushlan 1977, 1978a, Krebs 1974, 1978. Siegfried 1971, Burger 1981a, Bredin 1983, Gregory 1990, Voisin 1991). There is much evidence to support the correlation of colonial nesting and roosting in herons as an adaptation to their feeding conditions. Colonial nesters frequently have conspicuous plumage and nest visibly in trees whereas solitary nesters which frequently nest on or near the ground generally have cryptic plumage (Hancock and Kushlan 1984) and tend to feed under dense cover where the possibility of flock feeding is reduced (Krebs 1978). Observations of Little Egrets in the Camargue (Dugan et al. 1986, Kersten et al., 1991, Hafner et al., 1993) strongly support the idea that coloniality aids the birds in detecting the most profitable food patches. Social feeding among egrets in the Camargue resulted in an increase in chick weights and brood size (Hafner et al. 1993).

Predation avoidance is another frequently-cited benefit of colonial breeding (Patterson 1965, Buckley and Buckley 1980, Burger 1981a, Wittenberger and Hunt 1985, Siegel-Causey and Kharitonov 1990). Moser (1984) proposed predation to be a main factor contributing to the development of coloniality in the Purple Heron. In contrast, Krebs (1978) in his analysis of heron coloniality, concluded that although predation is clearly important in other groups of colonial birds, there is no evidence to support the notion that social breeding has developed as a result of predation. Observations of mixed species colonies in the Camargue provide further descriptive evidence against the predation hypothesis in colonial herons.

A possible predation-related benefit of coloniality, however, has been recognised regarding chicks. Many chicks regurgitate their last meal upon the approach of a predator. The predator eats the regurgitated fish and leaves the chicks unharmed. A Marsh Harrier (*Circus aeruginosus*) may provoke hundreds of Little Egret, Cattle Egret and Black-crowned Night Heron chicks to regurgitate their food (Hafner unpubl. data). It has been observed, however, that parent birds simply emitted alarm calls and rarely exhibited other defensive behaviour in response to the presence of the predator. Instead of mobbing the Marsh Harrier, the adult birds left the top of the trees to hide below the canopy. Parents tended not to defend the contents of their nests from the predator. Four cases of this type of predation have been observed in the Camargue over the years: in two Little Egret nests, one Cattle Egret nest and one Black-crowned Night Heron nest, each containing eggs and small chicks. The parent on guard remained near the nest during the encounters with the predator (Hafner unpubl. data).

Colonially breeding herons form spectacular nesting assemblages. Hundreds of nests have been observed within a single tree and certain colonies may contain tens of thousands of pairs. The largest colonies are found in tropical and subtropical regions. Some large colonies become locally or nationally famous, such as Avery Island in Louisiana, with 22 204 nests recorded in 1912 (Peterson and Fisher 1955). In the temperate zones of the Palearctic, the largest colonies with up to 9000 pairs of Cattle Egrets are found in central Spain (Fernandez Alcazar and Fernandez Cruz 1991).

A very large colony is more vulnerable than several medium-sized colonies distributed over a wider area. For the Mediterranean region, data are available on colony sites and surrounding feeding areas in Spain, Portugal, France, Italy, Greece, Turkey, Israel, Tunisia and Algeria (files Tour du Valat). On a regional level, the data suggest that the several exceptionally large nesting assemblages of a few thousand tree-nesting heron pairs and several hundred Purple Heron pairs are the result of a shortage of woodland and reed bed nesting sites rather than of particularly rich and extensive feeding areas. On a site-level, however, colony size declines in the Mediterranean region, as local resources become less available (Hafner and Fasola, 1992). Similar relationships between feeding area and herons have been shown in other parts of the world (McCrimmon 1978, Beaver et al. 1980, Gibbs et al. 1987, Marion 1988, Gibbs 1991). On a regional level in Florida, dramatic heron population declines have been attributed to wetland degradation (Kushlan 1979a, 1991).

Nesting habitat requirements

Although different heron species vary in their habitat preferences, diet and behaviour, they have certain fundamental common requirements. Research shows that nesting occurs on a variety of site types having several characteristics in common. A site generally provides protection against predators including humans, offers adequate stability and materials to support and construct the nest, and is accessible to adequate feeding areas within foraging range (Valverde 1955, Hafner 1977, 1982, Thompson 1977, Beaver et al.1980, Moser 1984, Gibbs et al. 1987, Hafner et al.1987, Marion 1988, Hafner and Fasola 1992, Fasola and Alieri 1992, Hafner 1997a).

Colonial day and night herons generally prefer to nest in trees and bushes, but in the absence of their preferred habitat, pairs will nest in shrub, reed or other marsh vegetation. More solitary nesters, especially the bitterns, use reed beds more often than shrub or low tree habitats. One of the more intriguing habitat specialists is the Purple Heron, which depends on reed beds (*Phragmites australis*) in many of its breeding areas.

Ground nesting may occur in some colonial heron species. Examples include the Little Egret in parts of Kenya (Turner pers. comm.), Turkey (Siki pers. comm.), Tunisia, southern France, southern Russia (Hafner pers. obs.), and the Grey Heron race *monicae* in Mauritania (Erard et al. 1986). Successful ground nesting occurs if the nests are generally protected against predators by extensive areas of surrounding water or other protective buffer.

The size, structure, shape, and the orientation of the nest site are important in providing shelter against adverse weather, particularly high winds. To construct an adequate nest, large quantities of suitable nest material must be available within or near the colony. The most frequent nest materials are small branches and sticks used by tree-nesting herons, and reeds used by the Purple Heron and Great White Egret. Little Egret nests in the Camargue contain an average of 180 sticks (Hafner 1977)

In Mauritania where nest supports are virtually non-existent and materials to construct nests rare, the Grey Heron builds its nest on the ground using bones of White Pelican. Photo: Pierre Campredon.

while in South Africa, Siegfried (1971) estimated that 1 500 000 sticks, weighing 2000 kg, are needed to support a Cattle Egret colony of 5000 nests. When nest density is particularly high and suitable nesting materials are exhausted, individual nest volume declines (Arendt and Arendt 1988). Consequently, nest contents may become more vulnerable to predation and adverse weather as colony density increases.

Nests in a colony must have a surrounding security zone (Valverde 1955, Hafner 1977, Thompson 1977). In most situations, a security zone is provided by water surrounding the nest site. In the case of ground nests, nesting islands are often located several kilometres from shore. In other colonies, protection can also be provided by dense undergrowth (Valverde 1955, Hafner 1977, Thompson 1977). Many colonies appear to be protected by a combination of water, undergrowth and height above the ground. In the complete absence of surrounding water or undergrowth, nests may be placed 25 metres or more above the ground. The Grey Heron colonies in villages and towns in Europe are an example of this phenomenon. Nesting birds in large urban and traditionally protected colonies in certain parts of Asia, India (Perennou 1990, Subramanya 1994, Chapter 3) and Hong Kong (Chapter 4) are quite tolerant of disturbances.

Solitary nesting herons

Data on the population status of species that form only small and dispersed colonies or which are solitary nesters are virtually impossible to obtain. This is particularly

One of the two islands in Mauritania where Grey Herons of the race *monicae* breed. Their nests are well protected against predators by the surrounding sea. Photo: Pierre Campredon.

true for certain small, cryptic and secretive species of high conservation priority in tropical regions: the tiger herons in Central and South America, New Guinea, and tropical Africa, and the Zigzag Heron and Streaked Bittern in South America. More information on the ecology of these species is needed in order to develop effective nesting season conservation measures. Although these heron species are difficult to study, a monitoring programme encompassing a wide variety of areas is an important step in understanding their ecology. In the interim, preliminary habitat conservation programmes should be established to protect large areas where these species have been recorded.

Purple Heron nesting habitat requirements

The Purple Heron's dependence on reed beds makes it one of the most specialised species. It does nest in other habitats, such as on dead stems of reed mace (*Typha* spp.), in extensive stands of bullrush (*Scirpus lacustris*) and in some places in bushes (Subramanya 1994, Hafner pers. obs.). In western France the species breeds frequently in deciduous trees, at three to ten metres (Voisin 1991). Nests at an exceptional height of 20 metres have been observed in poplar trees in Switzerland, presumably because the local reed bed normally used had been thinned as a result of commercial exploitation (Hofstetter et al. 1949). Tree-nests at considerable height were also found in Singapore (Lansdown pers. comm.), and in Australia, isolated nests have been observed in Eucalyptus trees (*Eucalyptus* spp.) at a height of 15 metres (Maddock pers. comm.).

In response to the steep decline in numbers of breeding pairs of Purple Herons in the Camargue and in other parts of Europe (Chapters 1 and 2), colonies of this vulnerable species have received increasing attention over the past ten years. Due to recent efforts, we now have a greater understanding of the ecological requirements for successful nesting. In this part of its range, Purple Herons require good quality reed beds for nesting and productive freshwater marshes for feeding.

Moser (1984), in a comprehensive ecological study of a population in the Camargue, found a relationship between the number of pairs in each colony and the surface area of suitable reed beds available for nesting. Reed beds smaller than 20–30 hectares physically limited the size of the colony, whereas colony size in larger reed beds was limited by other factors. Moser found that suitable reed bed sites remain inundated throughout the breeding season, and nest desertion occurs in sites that become dry. The presence of open water seems to be a prerequisite for successful nesting. Secondly, only mature stands of reed were occupied by nesting birds. Purple herons construct their nests in spring from the dead reeds of the previous season, before significant reed growth can occur. Reed cutting or burning eliminates this material, which hinders nest building unless undamaged areas remain. Moser found that reed beds which had been heavily grazed, or degraded by repeated cutting, were not occupied. Finally, the study showed that Purple Herons are particularly sensitive to disturbances while establishing their colonies. They are less tolerant of human activity than most other species, and repeated disturbances may prevent nesting in otherwise suitable reed bed sites.

Data collected in the Camargue suggest that habitat modification has caused a significantly steep decline in the local population (Kayser et al. 1994b). Reed bed structure has been increasingly altered as a result of cutting and management practices for hunting purposes. Because the conservation of Purple Herons in Europe has become an urgent priority, the framework for a long-term monitoring programme of reed bed distribution and quality has been established. Studies in the major breeding areas of Spain, France and Italy are presently being conducted. Ideally this work will provide the information needed to develop effective conservation strategies for significant reed bed areas. In order to implement conservation measures, cooperation among specialised groups and institutions will be essential in addressing the economic and political concerns that may arise.

The feeding area

Feeding requirements of herons are considered in Chapter 10. The aim here is to emphasise the considerable demand placed on food resources, even by a small heron colony. A breeding population can only be maintained if the surface area of the various feeding site types and the prey population numbers are large enough to meet the requirements of the birds. Population size of herons is correlated with the amount of habitat available (Kushlan 1978a, Hafner and Fasola 1992).

In his study on the Grey Heron in Brittany, France, Marion (1988) provided evidence that flight distances to foraging grounds increase with colony size, from between 5 to 10 km, to a mean foraging range of 25 km for Europe's largest known Grey Heron colony (1300 pairs). In a study conducted in Maine, USA, it was found that the Great Blue Heron, another large species, flew 15 km, about the farthest distance these birds regularly travel between the nest and the foraging sites (Gibbs 1991).

Smaller heron species generally do not fly as far as the Great Blue or Grey herons. During the incubation and chick-raising period, the Squacco Herons in the Camargue, for example, are rarely found farther than five km from their colony (Hafner unpubl. data). Chinese Pond Herons near Hong Kong foraged on average about 1.5 km from their nests (Young 1993).

In other breeding areas around the world, radio telemetry and observational studies of the Grey Heron (van Vessem et al. 1984, Gregory 1990), Purple Heron (Moser 1984), Little Egret (Dugan et al. 1986, Wong 1991, Hafner et al. 1986b, 1993), Great White Egret, Snowy Egret and Louisiana Heron (Custer and Osborn 1978), have shown that during the incubation and nesting period, adult birds generally feed within ten kilometres of the colony. Consequently, the quality of the nearby feeding habitat likely influences the size and species composition of the heron colonies.

Artificial colony sites

In response to the alarming decline in numbers of certain species of colonial herons, there is an increasing need to apply practical conservation measures to maintain breeding populations at current levels. Practical yet drastic measures are particularly needed at colony sites. Unfortunately, wet and dense woodlands, the most popular nesting sites for many species of colonial herons, are becoming increasingly vulnerable. Since small woodlands can host thousands of breeding pairs, regional colony site management and restoration programmes in heavily-frequented wetland areas are needed to maintain and increase the availability of suitable nesting sites.

Habitat degradation (often a natural result of colony occupancy), disturbance, or other factors frequently cause colonies to relocate. Thus multiple suitable sites need to be available in a region. Colony sites may have to be relocated deliberately because they are in unsuitable areas such as airports (Finkenstaedt and Heckenroth 1974), urban areas (Dusi 1979), near residences, or because of their increased vulnerability for various other reasons. If a colony is to be relocated, birds may be attracted to a new site by various techniques. In this way, birds in vulnerable colonies can be encouraged to relocate to sites that will offer long-term protection. Each instance of intervention needs to be carefully planned and executed, often with participation by local interests, and only after other management options have been considered. The new sites should receive perpetual follow-up protection and management.

The use of captive egrets is undoubtedly the best technique to attract wild birds to an artificial site, particularly if the captive birds are nesting (McIlhenny 1934, Hafner 1982). It is generally worthwhile to apply carefully timed disturbance at their former nesting site. In certain areas, artificial nest sites may be constructed, provided that the surrounding feeding area is suitable to sustain a colony. Through appropriate management and protection measures, it may be possible to increase the existing breeding populations or to return them to their former status. The example detailed in the next section provides a case history of the successful movement of a colony to an artificial site.

The water bird colony at the Bharatpur Bird Sanctuary in India is located on an artificial nesting site. Local woodland areas had been heavily grazed by cattle, preventing tree regeneration. Consequently, the national forestry department planted stands of acacia trees (*Acacia nilotica*), which were readily accepted as nesting sites by herons, storks and cormorants. In Tamil Nadu in South India, several breeding sites have been created inadvertently as a result of new social forestry programmes. Trees planted near irrigation reservoirs now support some of the largest tree-nesting colonies in the region (Subramanya 1994). The results are encouraging, and suggest that similar success may be obtained in other regions that contain few nest sites but rich feeding grounds.

In northern Italy, large areas of rice fields, rich in amphibians, provide suitable foraging grounds for herons (Fasola and Barbieri 1978). However, few suitable nest sites are available and the density of breeding bird colonies is limited. A regional management plan proposal suggests the establishment of mixed plantations of alder (*Alnus* sp.), poplar (*Populus alba*, *Populus nigra*), ash (*Fraxinus* sp.) and willow (*Salix* sp.) trees, which represent traditional local nesting sites. The trees will be planted at various densities depending on the availability of the surrounding foraging habitat (Fasola et al. 1992, Fasola and Alieri 1992).

In contrast to woodland habitats, only relatively large reed beds, covering several tens of hectares, offer a safe nesting site for large numbers of herons. In areas dominated by freshwater marshes, it may be possible to re-create suitable breeding sites. Marsh habitats, required by vulnerable reed-nesting species such as the Purple Heron and the Eurasian Bittern, are far easier to create than woodlands required by tree-nesting birds.

The suitability of an artificial nesting habitat follows certain principles and must be planned with great care. Site conditions must be optimal, protection must be provided against predators and human disturbance, and adequate feeding areas must be available within foraging range.

Creating an artificial colony for tree-nesting herons: a case study

Between 1948 and 1970, data collected on breeding colony distribution in the Camargue suggested there was a lack of suitable breeding sites for tree-nesting herons. As a result, after careful study, it was decided to create an artificial colony on previously farmed land (Hafner 1982). The island was created with the intention of ensuring the permanent availability of an adequate nesting site in the event that local natural sites became unsuitable.

The future colony site was prepared based on data gathered from other colonies in the Camargue. Protection from human intrusion and wind were important criteria in the selection of the site. The area was transformed into an artificial island 80 × 40 m in size, oriented with the longer side facing the prevailing winds. An artificial marsh was created around the island and a water pumping system was used in order to flood the site periodically.

In 1970, approximately 5000 saplings, ash and alder, some white poplar and a few willows, were removed from local woodlands and raised in a nursery for one year.

The following autumn the same saplings were planted on the island and on the banks of the artificial moat. It took about 10 years for the trees to reach a structure similar to that of the egret colonies in the Camargue. Subsequently, egrets from a local zoo, decoys, artificial nests and tape recordings of nesting egrets were used to attract the tree-nesting herons to the island. In 1981, more than 300 pairs of Little Egrets, Cattle Egrets and Black-crowned Night Herons nested successfully at the

Decoy Little Egrets nesting in captivity serve to attract wild birds to the artificial colony site in the Camarge. Photo: Heinz Hafner.

artificial site (Hafner 1982). After several years, however, the colony relocated to a traditional nesting site four km from the island. Since heron population numbers have increased and breeding success is high at the current site, there was not a conservation need to make further attempts to attract the herons and egrets back to the artificial island.

To increase the possibility of providing herons with suitable breeding habitats in the Camargue, a second wood lot containing approximately 6000 two-year-old trees was established on abandoned farmland in 1978. Since the two artificial colony sites were created eight years apart, there is a significant difference in vegetation structure between the islands. As a result of forest succession and growth, as vegetation becomes less suitable for herons in one site, breeding pairs may select the other site for nesting purposes. The artificial sites will eventually be altered by colony site managers on a rotating basis and will be returned to the stage most suitable for heron nesting.

The artificial colony in the Camargue, however, was created to determine if the site would provide the ecological requirements in an area where several successful colonies already existed. The birds were attracted to and successfully bred on the artificial site, confirming that the site provided breeding pairs with adequate resources (Hafner 1982). The ultimate goal of this conservation project was to ensure the availability of a suitable nesting site in the event of the degradation of existing colonies.

Disturbance

Among the most serious threats to nesting herons is human disturbance. Herons are spectacular birds and their large and noisy colonies have attracted humans for thousands of years. Although it is not unusual to find heron colonies in towns and villages, human intrusion and indirect colony disturbance linked to human activities have been major factors negatively affecting breeding over the centuries. The use of heron feathers for decoration and trout flies, and the collection of eggs and chicks for food, were frequent activities in many parts of the world. Any long-lasting and intense disturbance may cause the birds to desert a nesting site permanently. In some circumstances, some are able to re-locate and restart the nesting process. Favourable alternative colony sites, however, are not an inexhaustible resource, and substitute sites are often in less favourable areas and contain smaller numbers of birds. Fragmentation of the breeding population can occur.

Intrusion by humans into heron colonies is especially disastrous early in the breeding season (see for example Allen 1938, Dusi and Dusi 1968, 1987, Blaker 1969a, Hafner, 1970b, 1977, Majic and Mikuska 1970, Tremblay and Ellison 1979, Quinney 1983, Drapeau et al. 1984, Utschick 1983b, Franchimont 1986, Parnell et al. 1988, Frederick and Collopy 1989c). If the disturbance occurs in the presence of avian predators such as crows or ravens (Valverde 1955, Jenni 1969, Milstein et al. 1970, Taylor and Edwin 1971, Burger and Hahn 1977, Marion 1988) or during unfavourable weather (Galet 1931, Yeates 1950, Valverde 1955, Hoffmann 1958, Penot 1963, Hafner 1977, 1978, 1982) the effects on the colony may be quite severe.

Several cases of complete and permanent colony desertion have been caused by heavy and prolonged disturbance during egg laying and incubation (Voisin 1975). One large mixed colony of more than 1000 pairs located on a private estate within the Camargue Nature Park was destroyed by the owner because he was disturbed by the noise and smell of the colony (Hafner 1982). This is a common occurrence worldwide. In the Camargue, characterised by frequent and high winds, Valverde (1955) found hundreds of eggs and small chicks which had fallen from the nest trees in a colony that had been disturbed by tourists during a gale. The estimated losses of eggs and chicks were about 50% of the total production of the colony. Undisturbed, an incubating heron secures its brood with its body and in most protected sites only a few losses occur when the trees are shaken by winds (Hafner 1977).

In developed countries, the causes of disturbances have changed over the years, and colony sites are protected in many parts of the world. However, habitat is still being lost to development projects, for recreational facilities in particular. Many golf courses, marinas and cottages have been rapidly encroaching on prime heron nesting habitat. Heron colonies are a spectacular sight for well-meaning tourists, and as a result, are frequently disturbed in certain areas. Scientific research, if not planned carefully, may also cause heavy disturbances which reduce the reproductive success of breeding herons. Urban and industrial development continues to expand, and conflict for resources frequently arises between fishermen and herons.

Few studies have attempted to quantify the effects of colony disturbance, including that of researchers or conservationists, on bird behaviour, colony occupancy, or breeding success. The limited results are rather controversial. Great Blue Herons in Oregon tended to raise fewer nestlings in a colony disturbed by logging activity than in undisturbed colonies (Werschkul et al. 1976). Tremblay and Ellison (1979) noted that field visits to Black-crowned Night Heron colonies early in the season provoked the birds to abandon their newly-constructed nests, resulting in a loss of eggs to predators. Research activity also induced some mortality in chicks. Kushlan (1979b) found few effects of airplanes during aerial censuses. At least three other studies indicate that disturbance caused by researchers is not detrimental to breeding success in herons. In a Cattle Egret colony, the frequency of disturbances did not influence reproductive parameters (Goering and Cherry 1971). Black-crowned Night Heron chicks became accustomed to frequent handling and remained in their nests during the field visits, while chicks unaccustomed to human intruders moved some distance away (Parsons and Burger 1982). Frederick and Collopy (1989c) found no difference in reproductive success between two Tricoloured Heron colonies, one frequently disturbed and one investigated on occasion. Similarly, Davis and Parsons (1991) found no difference in pre-fledgling survival rates between Snowy Egret chicks which had been handled every second day from hatching, and a control group which had not been handled before banding. Finally, unpublished data on Little Egret colonies in the Camargue (Hafner unpubl. data) indicate that weekly examinations of nests which included egg and chick handling did not affect fledging success. A comparison between colonies that were studied and undisturbed colonies revealed no difference.

It has become clear that the extent of the reaction of breeding herons to disturbances depends on the habitat structure of the colony. In densely vegetated colonies in the Camargue, a slowly-moving observer can approach the incubating herons without causing them to flush. In contrast, Little Egrets, Cattle Egrets and Black-crowned Night Herons found nesting in a more open habitat, such as a pine (*Pinus* spp) stand, tend to react earlier and more intensely to a disturbance. Vos et al. (1985) found a similar difference based on the vegetation structure in the Great Blue Heron, and the same pattern was described for wading birds in general by Erwin (1989b) and for several species of heron by Rodgers and Smith (1995).

Purple Heron colonies in the Camargue and the Ebro Delta in Spain vary substantially. Certain Camargue colonies are spread out, with distances between nests reaching 20 to 30 metres. In the Ebro Delta, nests are close together and a researcher can sample them in a short period of time. More importantly, the crow, which predates on heron nest contents, is common in the Camargue and absent in the Ebro Delta. Nest sampling by researchers in the Camargue will inevitably cause the destruction of clutches by crows, and the danger increases in highly dispersed colonies. In the Ebro, however, it is possible to sample a large number of nests in a short time without causing nest predation (Gonzalez-Martin 1994).

Buffer zones are critical factors in colony site management. Buffer zone size can be determined by recording the distance at which nesting birds flush as a human intruder approaches. In Florida, one study showed that flush distances for the Great Blue Heron, the Tricolored Heron, the Black-crowned Night Heron and the Great White Egret averaged between 30 and 32 m when a human intruder slowly approached the nest site (Rodgers and Smith 1995). Rodgers and Smith recommended buffer distances for wildlife observers to be between 88 m

(Tricoloured Heron) and 100 m (Great Blue Heron). The calculated distance includes an additional buffer zone of 40 m (also recommended by Vos et al. 1985) because it was observed that the birds became agitated before the observer reached the flush distance. Even in habituated colonies, although the flush distances of these birds are small (around 15 m for certain colonies in India for example—Perennou pers. comm.), they nevertheless exist.

In some parts of the world, herons and other colonially nesting water birds have been respected and protected since ancient times. In India, this has led to the establishment of numerous heron colonies in villages and cities such as Srwagar and Madras (Perennou 1990, Subramanya 1994; Chapter 3). A colony in the town of Vedanthangal, South India, has been actively protected since at least 1790. The guano of cormorant and stork colonies provides farmers with an effective natural fertiliser and accounts for much of the impetus to conserve the birds' nesting sites (Spillett 1968).

Although many of the reasons for colony disturbance have changed over time, both human intrusion in, and activity near, breeding sites remain serious threats to birds throughout much of the world. Increasing disturbances caused by urbanisation, industry and tourism continue to reduce the availability of suitable colony sites and affect solitary nesters. Even in remote areas, ecotourism, if not managed carefully, may affect nesting birds.

Harvest

Under conditions of poverty and famine, heron and egret colonies are particularly prone to human disturbance, as the chicks and eggs are taken for food. During the 1940s in Spain, professional egg-collectors, who gathered tens of thousands of Cattle Egret eggs, were considered a serious threat to the conservation of the birds (Riddell 1944). During the same period, towards the end of the Second World War, the systematic slaughter of Little Egret and Black-crowned Night Heron chicks in the Camargue provided much needed protein for the villagers and townspeople living in the vicinity of the breeding area (Yeates 1950). Inhabitants of the small town of Port St. Louis near the mouth of the Rhône maintained the tradition, and continued to harvest the egret chicks year after year (Lomont in Voisin 1975). Since few quantitative data are available on the status of herons in Spain and the Camargue during this period, it is difficult to estimate the extent of the destruction which humans inflicted on the heron and egret populations. Although in some areas human activities probably had a significant negative effect, much of the region contained no human settlements and many colonies are likely to have survived unaffected.

In many parts of the world, herons, eggs and chicks are still harvested for human consumption. In Cambodia for example, bitterns and egrets have been sold for food as recently as 1994, and the eggs and chicks of colonial herons were collected in all known colonies for domestic consumption and trade (T. Mundkur, pers. comm.). In the inner Delta of the Niger River in Mali, West Africa, the breeding season of herons and egrets coincides with annual September–November floods. During this period, the fish, an important food source for the natives, disperse widely and become difficult to catch. The nest contents of the large heron and egret colonies provide an alternative food supply that the local tribes exploit to avoid famine (J. Skinner, pers. comm.).

Young (pers. comm.) reports a case of the sustainable harvesting of heron chicks in a village near Hong Kong. Black-crowned Night Herons, Little Egrets and Chinese Pond Herons have been breeding near this village for over a century. For many years the colony was left undisturbed because the birds were thought to have brought good luck. Towards the end of the 1950s, however, the villagers began to collect the chicks. Before the practice of chick harvesting began to deplete the colony, the head of the village forbade the community from exploiting the chicks. The village now sells the harvesting rights to an outside party for an annual fee of US $25,000. This practice has stabilised harvesting pressure to a sustainable level and has provided the villagers with a regular income and a stronger incentive to protect the colony. The harvest is sold to nearby restaurants and on the markets.

Solitary nesting herons have also been traditionally exploited by humans for food. For the Ebro Delta, Ruiz (pers. comm.) reports that during the first half of the twentieth century it was common practice to use the chicks of the Eurasian Bittern to obtain fish. A collar was put around the chick's neck to prevent it from swallowing the fish fed to it by its parents. Fishermen then collected these fish. In addition, the fledglings as well as the adults were much appreciated table birds.

In Europe, conflict arose between fishermen and herons, initiating the heavy persecution of the Grey Heron during the nineteenth century (see Chapter 1). Due to recent protection measures, this species has increased considerably throughout Europe over the past few years. As a result, the conflict between humans and herons

Chicks of Black-crowned Night Heron, Little Egret and Chinese Pond Heron for sale at a market in China. Photo: Llewellyn Young.

has become serious once again. Other species throughout the world have also been affected as they compete with humans for resources (Chapter 13).

The most significant predation on herons by humans undoubtedly occurred during the commercial plume trade at the end of the nineteenth and beginning of the twentieth century. During this period in various parts of the world, millions of adult herons and egrets were slaughtered for their feathers, which were used to decorate women's hats. According to the detailed description in del Hoyo et al. (1992), massive killings took place on almost every continent. Because the birds, in full breeding plumage, were killed at the height of the breeding season, the adults, eggs and chicks were lost. The extremely lucrative plume industry caused the reduction of the populations of many heron species to alarming levels. The Great White Egret, the Snowy Egret and the Little Egret were particularly affected.

London, Paris, New York, Berlin and Vienna were the principal plume trade centres. In Paris and the surrounding area alone, more than 10 000 people were employed by the plume industry (del Hoyo et al. 1992). Ironically, the plume trade played a major role in the establishment of important conservation movements in the United States and Great Britain, such as the Audubon Society and the Royal Society for the Protection of Birds. Due to the efforts of these organisations and other conservation movements, the plume trade was banned around 1920.

Monitoring

Monitoring heron numbers, nesting success, and ecosystem conditions are essential to support conservation action. This must be undertaken at every scale. Locally wherever possible, every colony and important breeding area for non-colonial species should be surveyed at least annually. These activities are often best done by local resource managers, park managers, or volunteers. At the regional and national scale, coordinated monitoring schemes and data management programmes are needed to assure that the most critical sites and larger portions of populations are monitored and that the data are available for regional analysis. Internationally, data management networks are required to assess breeding population size and trends across national boundaries. Colony census techniques should be recorded and where possible standardised. In addition to numbers, important sites should be monitored for nesting success. Given inherent variability in nesting effort from year to year, censuses should be conducted as frequently as possible in order to be able to assess trends statistically.

Numbers, and in some cases production, in certain breeding areas in Europe and North America have been well documented for several decades. As a result, changes in ecosystem conditions from year to year can be detected. This type of biomonitoring is used to identify the variables of a wetland system, which have influenced the reproductive performance of herons over time. Information on breeding parameters, hydrological conditions and prey populations may help researchers to distinguish between poor and favourable breeding seasons. Cause and effect relationships may then be determined and used as a basis for the development of a management plan. Ideally, the most effective management plan can be developed through the interdisciplinary cooperation of biologists, land-use planners, managers and engineers.

Accurate quantitative data exist only for a few heron colonies in Asia, Africa and

South America, and data for even fewer sites have been collected for longer than a one-year period. There are dramatic differences in the research needs among the continents and there is a fundamental requirement for tropical countries to establish a directory of heron colonies. Following the development of a directory, the preparation of detailed regional conservation action plans for heron colonies is needed. This can only be done through interdisciplinary research and collaboration with local and regional administrators, decision-makers and the general public.

The recent work by Subramanya (1994), on cataloguing heron colonies in India, will be invaluable for the conservation of herons in several regions. Similar cataloguing efforts in other countries will facilitate colony site protection and help to identify priorities for action. Large or more vulnerable colonies containing rare or threatened species should be targeted for immediate action.

Ecotourism

An active heron colony is a spectacular natural sight and the educational opportunities alone may justify conservation and protection measures. Many species of herons show a high tolerance for people, so long as the visitation is unobtrusive and there is ample opportunity for the herons to acclimatise to their presence. The increasing restriction of heron colonies to parks and other protected areas provides both opportunities and responsibility for using them for educational purposes. There are many examples of colony sites and heron conservation becoming a central theme for an environmental education or ecotourism centre. One of the outstanding examples is the Shortland Wetlands Centre and Project Egret Watch in Australia (Maddock 1991b, 1992). Boardwalks through and around colony sites, towers that allow distant viewing, interpretive stations, and public involvement through monitoring and interpretive activities lead to herons becoming a focus of local conservation action.

Colony sites, their nesting birds, and feeding areas need to be protected and actively managed if visitors are to be allowed or encouraged. As also noted above, unrestricted ecotourism can disturb colonies and damage colony sites. Training is essential for guides and researchers visiting colonies. That colony sites shift over time, a fundamental characteristic of nesting herons, needs to be factored into reserve planning, ranging from actively influencing site selection (see above), maintenance of alternative sites, or, if many alternative sites are available, making visitor-use investments non-permanent.

Research

Effective colony and nest site conservation can only be achieved through integrated multidisciplinary field research studies. Such research provides the background required to develop effective management practices for nesting heron colonies. As the fundamental requirements of herons are uncovered through new research efforts, land managers and researchers will be better able to design effective proposals for heron colony conservation. Changes in ecosystem conditions should be quantified and the subsequent responses by heron populations should be assessed. Long-term monitoring of nesting bird numbers and breeding parameters may provide particularly useful information. Site-specific data on clutch and brood size, for example, are indicative of the suitability of an ecosystem for heron breeding.

In addition to monitoring breeding parameters, causal research on abiotic factors, such as hydrological effects known to affect food supplies, is needed (Hafner et al. 1994). This kind of integrated research is essential for the conservation and management of feeding areas vital to existing heron colonies.

Additionally, conservationists also frequently require information on the feeding ecology of a vulnerable species. In the Mai Po nature reserve near Hong Kong (Young, pers. comm.), for example, data on the foraging range and feeding habitat of several species of nesting herons was used to justify the prevention of the development of golf courses and other projects on a vital heron feeding ground. Similarly, in the Mediterranean region, it was found that in order to sustain a large and diverse breeding community of herons, an extensive freshwater area is needed (Hafner and Fasola 1992). These findings provide quantitative data, essential in the development of conservation programmes (Fasola and Alieri 1992). Around the world, research results have been used to justify the conservation of nest sites and surrounding feeding areas.

The results of the comprehensive studies should be made easily accessible to park managers, administrators and decision-makers, who can then incorporate the information into new conservation initiatives. The development of a management plan must be a collaborative effort between policy makers, researchers and local residents.

Conclusions

Since safe nesting sites are required for successful nesting and population stability, colony sites must be protected and managed. Every opportunity needs to be taken to secure, protect, and manage the habitat patches used by colonies and the marshes used by non-colonial herons. Such action is especially critical for the larger colonies and other important heron sites that are responsible for the security of a significant portion of a species, a national population, or a regional population. A standard criterion for determining an important heron site is that it supports 10% or more of a population of concern. Related conservation action needs to focus on preservation and management of feeding grounds used by the nesting herons. To improve conservation of existing nest sites, site managers need to make use of the results of studies on the basic ecological requirements for successful nesting.

Heron conservation not only ensures the protection of valuable wetland areas, it also provides the general public with an opportunity to become involved in and learn about the preservation of unique local species. If possible, observation facilities should be constructed on suitable sites to allow visitors to enjoy the spectacular sight of a thriving heron colony. By becoming emotionally involved in heron conservation, local residents become active participants in the protection of a species. Large heron colonies are a spectacular sight and should be open to the public to enjoy. However, colony viewing must only occur in controlled situations. Colonies should be protected by observation blinds and conservation personnel must be available to enforce access restrictions. Since heron colonies are susceptible to human disturbance, land managers require quantitative information in order to determine the size of the buffer zone needed to protect the nest site from observers. Only a few studies have focused on this important aspect, and further work is required.

Well-trained personnel should be available at heron sites, accessible to the public, in order to inform visitors, both local residents and visiting tourists, about the natural history of the different species in a colony. It is important that any misconceptions about heron behaviour and ecology are dispelled. Local fishermen, for example, should be reminded that, although many herons feed on fish, only a few species are strictly piscivorous birds. Furthermore, herons feed commonly on non-commercial fish and on insect larvae known to predate on fish eggs and fry. Damage to fish farms caused by herons is not universally demonstrated (see Chapter 13).

Comprehensive research and educational programmes are ambitious but necessary projects. Since herons are high-profile study subjects, and there is an existing global network of protected areas, heron conservation efforts are feasible undertakings. Because all heron species are dependent on wetlands, the most threatened habitats in the world, the birds are important indicators of wetland functioning and play an integral role in wetland conservation. The development and expansion of a network of protected sites, based on heron ecology, will be an important contribution to wetland conservation worldwide.

10. Heron Feeding Habitat Conservation

James A. Kushlan

Without food and suitable feeding locations, there is little to be done to conserve herons. On occasion heron habitat alteration is massive and obvious, such as the complete drainage and conversion of a highly productive marsh. Much of heron habitat alteration is more subtle, insidious, and prolonged. Although heron feeding habitat requirements can be generalised to a degree, the suitability of a site is very much a local matter owing to an array of factors including such variables as the species of heron, intraspecific and interspecific competitors, energy needs, seasonal nesting and migration schedule, prey type, abundance and availability, present and past hydrological conditions, vegetation cover and interspersion, distance to suitable nesting or roost sites, distance to other feeding patches, predators, and disturbance regime, all of which may vary within an annual cycle or from one year to the next. Habitat issues are complex for colonial herons in that they require a juxtaposition of nesting and roosting locations and feeding sites (Chapters 9, 11). This chapter seeks generalised patterns useful to local conservation action. The most critical finding is that, given increasing competition for land and resources, heron habitat availability and suitability cannot be taken for granted, but must be evaluated, monitored, and often explicitly managed if herons are to be conserved over the long term.

Habitats Used by Herons

Herons and wetlands

Wetlands are the typical habitat of herons, which are fundamentally adapted to feed by wading around in shallow water. Dry land habitats are used by a few species usually, and by many species facultatively. Even typically dry-land herons depend on damp conditions at least seasonally. The dependence of herons on wetlands places the larger issues of wetland conservation at the core of heron conservation. Wetlands are themselves diverse and changeable (Finlayson and Moser 1991, Kushlan 1993a, Livingston 1993). The international wetland conservation movement

Heron Conservation
ISBN 0-12-430130-4

Little Egrets. These birds prefer open wetland habitat where they forage in the most profitable patches, often in large feeding aggregations. Photo: Jean François Hellio and Nicolas van Ingen.

is well developed, led by such organisations as Wetlands International, IUCN Wetlands Programme, and the Ramsar Bureau. Conservation of herons is tied to the success of these and other local, regional, national and international programmes of wetland conservation.

Most herons are surprisingly flexible in their ability to use various sorts of shallow-water aquatic environments, as well as other situations. Given some limits and notable exceptions, they may be considered generalist, at least as contrasted with storks and ibises. Herons of one sort or another at one time or another may be expected in almost any shallowly flooded place within their range. This flexibility is central to the continuing success of the group, which has seen few forms become extinct in historic times and has few species now endangered worldwide.

Herons and uplands

Uplands also are important to some species, and to other species periodically. One group of upland herons, epitomised by the Cattle Egret, depends on grasslands, both natural and managed rangeland. Maintenance of grassland habitat through grazing, fire and other forces, variability of the invertebrate prey base, and management of grazing commensal herds are also critical to its usefulness for herons. Another group of herons, epitomised by the Agami Heron, uses forests,

The Cattle Egret. This species is less dependent upon wetlands than other herons. It is often associated with grazing animals. Photo: Jacques Delpech.

especially streamside forest habitat. For these, forest conservation practices are critical, and also to heron populations depending on the forest stream itself.

Specific habitats used

In freshwater marshes and swamps, presence of surface water and a supply of suitable prey organisms are the principal features of importance to herons. Thus the range of wetland types used is great, and it is in some ways easier to characterise the wetlands in which herons are seldom found. Those include wetlands that have insufficient prey base for herons to access economically because they are too ephemeral, too far from other wetlands, too isolated from prey recruitment sources, too salty, too acidic, or too deep. This leaves a wide variety of freshwater wetlands that are used by herons, including various sorts of grassy marshes, wooded swamps, reed swamps, fens, wet meadows, shallow streams and stream edges, ponds, and lake margins. Wetlands which herons use more heavily can be characterised as being larger, better watered, well interconnected, having prey refugia, often naturally fluctuating, relatively productive, and having suitable feeding sites.

Some species are more particular in their wetland habitat preferences. Bitterns, Purple and Squacco herons prefer thick reed beds. The endangered Imperial Heron's natural habitat includes impenetrable, often marshy, elephant grasslands. Less thick herbaceous vegetation is attractive to most species of day herons, night herons, and tiger herons. Stream-edge forest is the preferred feeding site for Agami Herons,

Zigzag Herons, pond herons, and Green-backed Herons. White-necked Herons and Whistling Herons appear to prefer more sparsely vegetated feeding sites where their views are unobstructed. Night herons and Boat-billed Herons frequent shallow pools, usually during their night-time feeding activities. Black Egrets and Goliath Herons use lake-edge marshes or shallow but open lake-edge zones. The Fasciated Tiger Heron prefers fast-flowing streams.

Estuarine wetlands support herons along both temperate and tropical coasts. Salt marshes, mangrove swamps, coastal lagoons, tidal flats, and shallow coastal streams are heavily used by many species of *Ardea* and *Egretta* herons and night herons that are very typically found along coasts. Swinhoe's Egret winters along tidal flats. Black, Yellow, and Cinnamon bitterns, Great White Egrets, medium-sized *Egretta* such as the Little, Snowy, Tricolored, and Intermediate egrets, the *Ardea* herons, and Green-backed Herons are typical mangrove species throughout the tropics wherever this habitat occurs.

Herons less use open marine habitats, but some species are found there characteristically. Eastern Reef Herons, Reddish Egrets, and Caribbean Great Blue Herons are specialists in using coastal marine lagoons. The Eastern Reef Heron uses shallowly exposed reefs. Seashores themselves are more difficult habitats for herons to use, as they must contend with tide and wave action. Rocky shores are used by coastal and island populations of the Green-backed Heron, Eastern Reef Heron, and Yellow-crowned Night Heron. Sandy beaches will on occasion be used by various species of medium to large day herons, notably Little and Great White egrets.

Green-backed Heron. Forested water margins and mangrove-bordered shores and estuaries are favoured habitat types for this species. Photo: Robert Bennetts.

Drier habitats are also important. It is likely that individuals of most species can be found feeding on dry land if sufficient quantities of catchable food are present. Yellow-crowned Night Herons, Great White, Snowy and Little egrets, and the *Ardea* herons are particularly adept at feeding on land occasionally. Snowy Egrets appear to have increased their use of dry land, as improved short grass pasturage increased in North America. Stream edges in forests are the typical habitat of several species, including the Agami and Zigzag herons and Fasciated Tiger Heron. The Cattle Egret is well known as a dryland heron, especially its association with grazing animals. Other savanna species, such as the Black-headed, Capped and Whistling herons, actually use a gradient of conditions from dry to wet habitats, depending on food availability. They generally occur in damp to moist conditions, and often take advantage of recently flooded pastures or short stature grasslands in addition to drier grasslands.

In fact, terrestrial herons generally require or benefit from association with damp or shallowly flooded habitats. The Cattle Egret is more appropriately thought of as a bird of the short-grass margins of damp sites, particularly floodplains subject to seasonal flooding and slow drying (Siegfried 1988). It uses aquatic sites for nesting. Cattle Egrets nesting near freshwater foraging areas raise more chicks than those depending entirely on terrestrial habitats for food (Siegfried 1972). So even this, the most terrestrial of heron species, depends on wet conditions.

Artificial habitats cannot be overestimated in their importance to herons, an importance increasing annually. Throughout their range, most heron species take advantage of feeding opportunities presented by human-made wet places having sufficient prey base. These locales are often shallow and productive, and may offer more prey than nearby natural habitats. Nearly any regional consideration of heron conservation needs to take into account the use and preservation of artificial feeding sites: some populations depend on them.

Ditches are perhaps the most commonly used artificial habitat, and their importance is usually overlooked. *Ardea* and *Egretta* herons, pond herons, and Green-backed Herons often use ditches, particularly seasonally when shallower wetlands dry or when prey become plentiful in the ditches for other reasons. In addition to fish, ditches house small mammals, amphibians, and invertebrates also eaten by herons. Territorially-feeding herons, such as *Ardea*, seem to stake out ditches as part of their foraging area. Heron use of ditches has been little studied.

Herons often use dumps and sewage ponds. Production is high in such locales, and feeding conditions often ideal. Pied Heron, Great White, Cattle and Snowy egrets are frequent users. At times such sites are important to nesting birds (Frederick and McGehee 1994).

The role of reservoirs and smaller water management sites must not be overlooked in regional planning for heron conservation. Reservoirs in dry areas have allowed the expansion of heron populations. For example, reservoirs in mid-continent North America have led to range expansion of the Green-backed Heron into this otherwise arid portion of the continent (Ryder 1979). Irrigation reservoirs have become important heron feeding habitats in South Asia (Chapter 3). Farm ponds in Australia have become important feeding sites for White-faced and Pied herons and Great White, Little and Intermediate egrets (Chapter 6).

Herons frequently use agricultural land. It is usual around the world to find herons, particularly Cattle Egrets, following tractors to take advantage of the prey

The Eurasian Bittern. This species is confined to densely vegetated freshwater wetlands. Phragmites stands are preferred nesting and foraging sites. Photo: Jean-François Hellio and Nicolas van Ingen.

stirred up by ploughing or cutting. Pastureland is often marshy, leading to seasonal use. The ability of Cattle Egrets to use hoofstock as beaters is well documented. Agricultural practices that flood land or supply concentrated prey can benefit herons.

The most important artificial heron habitat, worldwide, is the rice field. Rice cultivation covers 1.5 million km^2 with 40% of the world's human population depending on rice production (Forés and Comín 1992). Herons use (and even have come to depend on) rice fields in parts of North America, South America, the Mediterranean, and Asia. Grey Heron, Little, Intermediate, Great White, and Cattle egrets, Squacco Herons and other pond herons, Black crowned Night Herons, and *Ixobrychus* bitterns are usual rice field herons. Asian herons in some areas have become highly dependent on this habitat (Chapter 3; Subramanya 1990, Lansdown and Rajanathan 1993, Young 1993). Rice fields have replaced natural wetlands in many locales; for example in the critically important Ebro Delta of Spain, 74% of total submerged land is now rice fields (González-Solis et al. 1996). It has been shown that rice fields have substituted for the loss of natural wetlands in the Mediterranean and that the stability of heron populations now depends on them (Fasola and Ruiz 1996, Fasola et al. 1996). In Japan the rise and fall of egret populations was directly related to the expansion of rice cultivation, followed by its conversion to dry farming practices (Narusue 1992). Such impacts are undoubtedly the case in other regions where rice fields have come to dominate the wetland. Rice field management must be an active concern for heron conservation, wherever rice is cultivated in wetlands. Rice fields are often critical habitats for heron populations.

Fish farms are also a locally important agricultural habitat for herons (Chapter 13). These sites are the ultimate expression of the high production wetland patch that many herons are adapted to find and to exploit. *Ardea* and *Egretta* herons, night herons, and pond herons appear among the most common users of aquacultural facilities, particularly the Great Blue Heron, Grey Heron, and Black-crowned Night Heron. In some areas such as southern North America, aquaculture has positively affected wintering and breeding heron population levels (Fleury 1996). In Hong Kong, fish ponds have become critical habitats for feeding herons, particularly in winter (Young 1993). As aquaculture is rapidly developing worldwide, particularly in the tropics, similar effects can be expected elsewhere in the world. Fish farms often displace natural wetlands used by herons. The other severe adverse effect is the conflict of heron use with the fish farmer, which has led to killing, in the name of predator control, of substantial numbers of herons (in fact substantial portions of heron populations—see Chapter 13). It would be ideal to develop situations where herons are allowed to access excess aquacultural stock (perhaps in compensation for the loss of natural habitat) without severe economic consequences to the farmer. This in fact turns out to be the case in the instances that have been properly studied. In Hong Kong, and also elsewhere in Asia, there is little persecution of the many wintering herons that feed in ponds when they are being dried down, as the birds are understood not to seriously interfere with the fish harvesting (Young 1993).

In Spain, rice fields are flooded in winter in order to create habitat for hunting. They are favourable feeding habitats for Little Egrets. Photo: Emmanuel Vialet.

While it should not cause conservation complacency, the versatility of heron species should not be discounted as this provides flexibility for successful conservation action. Great White, Little and Cattle egrets, night herons, and Green-backed Herons are among those that appear particularly eclectic in their habitat use.

Conservation of Wetlands

Wetland loss and alteration

Wetlands and other shallow aquatic ecosystems have been under human pressure for thousands of years, a pressure accelerating in the present century. In the United States of America, for example, it has been estimated that 53% of wetlands have been lost since the late eighteenth century (Shaw and Ferdine 1956). In the Mediterranean, 80–90% have been lost (Fasola and Ruiz 1996—more details in Chapter 2). In various areas of Australia, the loss is 70–90% (Chapter 6). Wetland conversion continues throughout the world, although recently at a reduced rate in some developed areas, such as North America, where regulatory constraints are high (Dahl and Johnson 1991). Habitat losses in the past undoubtedly affected heron populations, in mostly undocumented ways. The extent to which wetlands continue to be lost can be expected to impact populations further.

Most loss of wetland habitat has been caused by its conversion to agriculture. Some of this is wetland agriculture, such as rice farming, aquaculture, or wet meadow grazing, that may continue to provide or enhance habitat for herons. However, much of the conversion has been by drainage, which eliminates heron habitat except for drainage ditches and other water control features. Once drained, wetlands almost inevitably come to provide additional living space for humans, which increases pressures for further flood control and competition with herons for the benefits of the water supply. A good example of this typical pattern is Hong Kong (Young 1993). Beginning 100 years ago, coastal mangrove wetlands were reclaimed, first for brackish water rice fields, then for intertidal shrimp ponds, then for intensive fish culture. All the while the herons were able to acclimatise to the changes. The last stage in this typical example is draining the fish ponds for urban development, which is the stage that must be resisted if herons are to persist—a conservation action being lead by WWF in Hong Kong.

Many of the remaining wetlands, while not drained completely, have been altered functionally by human intervention. This is the subtle, insidious, and prolonged part of wetland alteration. A bird that wades requires water depths within certain slim limits set by their own height. Plants, on which feeding herons have to perch and which provide cover for prey, require specific hydroperiods and water depths for germination, growth, and persistence. Heron prey, especially fish, amphibians, and aquatic invertebrates, also require certain water depths and certain patterns of seasonal water level fluctuations. It is probable that functional changes can adversely affect the usefulness of a site to herons nearly as much as its complete drainage.

Although heron extinctions are not explicitly attributable to loss or functional alteration of aquatic habitats, population changes and range changes certainly are. Population changes in Florida and Louisiana, both in the southern USA, are among the best-documented example (Frohring et al. 1988, Kushlan and Frohring 1986, Ogden 1994, Fleury 1996). South Florida heron populations decreased in recent decades despite the persistence of a million hectares of superficially suitable wetland habitat, the decrease being due to anthropogenic changes in the hydrologic cycle. Heron populations coincidentally increased in Louisiana due to habitat enhancements from aquaculture.

Influencing the pressures for wetland loss and functional transformation must be on top of every agenda for heron conservation. Preventing the further conversion of natural wetlands needs to be a central tenet of heron conservation worldwide. Heron conservation also requires the preservation of natural ecological processes or the beneficial manipulation of hydrological and vegetation variables by wetland managers.

Habitat availability

To be useful to herons, suitable wetlands must be available to them in appropriate size, dispersion, and temporal sequencing. The most fundamental finding from many studies is that feeding habitat area determines to a large extent how many herons can be supported in a region. This has been demonstrated at both landscape and local scales (Kushlan 1978a). For example: at the landscape scale, the number of herons in states along the Atlantic coast of North America is correlated with the area of coastal wetlands in each state (Osborn and Custer 1978); at the patch scale, habitat area available during nesting may be correlated to nesting numbers where habitat is limiting (Craufurd 1966, Fasola and Barbieri 1978, Gibbs et al. 1987, Gibbs 1991, Hafner and Fasola 1992, Gibbs and Kinkel 1997, Farinha and Leitão 1996), although not necessarily where habitat is more extensive (Erwin et al. 1987). Habitat quantity and its dispersion over the landscape must be taken into account in local and regional heron conservation planning.

For many species feeding habitat limitations become particularly acute during the nesting season, when herons become more place-bound. They are then limited in the distance they can feed from their nest by constraints of time and energetic cost/benefits. Generally 5 km is the usual flight distance for large to intermediate sized herons, shorter distances for the smaller, more localised species, and somewhat larger distances for larger herons (Chapter 9; Custer and Osborn 1978, van Vessem et al. 1984, Hafner and Britton 1983, Erwin and Spendelow 1991, Smith 1995). Competitive forces also come into play (Gibbs et al. 1987). Marion (1988) found that the distance travelled from the colony site to feed increases with the size of colony, suggesting an effect of local competition. Knowing flight ranges from nesting and roosting sites to feeding sites is critical for local area conservation, in order to determine an inventory of feeding sites that must be secured through conservation planning and also to understand habitat-mediated population size limitation for a local population. These data can be inferred from the literature or, better yet, determined for each area.

Evidence of the importance of habitat availability can be drawn from the recent history of several species, but none more dramatic than the Cattle Egret, expanding from southern Africa to much of four continents (Blaker 1971, Siegfried 1988, Telfair 1983, 1994, Maddock and Geering 1994). Its initial expansion in Africa is correlated with advances in irrigated farming, increasing its favoured moist ground habitat, followed by explosive range expansion into expanding areas of moist short-grass pasture nearly worldwide.

Patch dynamics

Understanding interactions of heron foraging ecology with selection and use of foraging patches is a critical aspect of determining heron habitat quality. Fortunately these issues have been well studied (e.g., Kushlan 1978a, 1981, 1989a,b, 1997, Erwin 1983, 1985a, 1989a, Hafner and Britton 1983, Kersten et al. 1991, Hafner et al. 1993, Hafner 1997a). Variables influencing patch use vary given the species of concern, interacting species, time, location, habitat variables, and prey availability. Also it appears that classical foraging theory has not often been shown to have predictive value for herons (e.g., Kushlan 1978a, Erwin 1985a). Yet it is clear that herons do not use available habitat or prey randomly.

The overriding conclusions to be drawn from the literature are that each species needs to be treated separately and that, based on knowledge of species biology, each foraging habitat or colony site needs to be evaluated. Armed with information on heron biology and habitat characteristics, local conservation and management plans can be drawn. Below (based on numerous studies) are discussions of some of the important habitat variables that need to be understood for heron habitat management.

Prey Fluctuations. Being highly mobile birds, herons choose to feed where prey is sufficiently available to meet their energetic and nutritional needs. So they select among locally-available foraging patches. Prey must be abundant enough that the heron can be sufficiently successful in its feeding. Prey must also be physically accessible. In many cases that means in sufficiently shallow water depths or at a place where perches or banks can support the feeding heron. If prey are not sufficiently available, herons go elsewhere.

Prey availability varies over time. Prey may become more available as their populations increase seasonally, as wetlands flood, as water depths fall and they are concentrated in remaining pools, as perches become available for herons to use, or as water conditions cause prey to surface or to move to other locations where they can be eaten more easily. Prey become less available when populations are low or well dispersed, when fish kills or episodes of intensive predation reduce stocks, when water is too deep for herons to feed, when perches or other means of access are unavailable, or when water temperatures decline or ice cover develops. Among water quality conditions affecting prey availability to feeding herons are diurnal oxygen and turbidity (Kersten et al. 1991, Cezilly 1992). Prey availability often varies with some periodicity, such as winter–summer cycles, dry season–wet season cycles, or daily cycles. Episodic events also occur.

Winter–summer cycles can limit seasonal habitat use by temperate species, which find that their predominantly poikilothermic prey become less available during the winter or that their feeding habitats become inaccessible due to ice cover (North 1979). Most herons respond to such seasonal changes in foraging habitat availability by short-distance shifts or long-distance migration. For those not migrating the severity of winter can have an impact on survival and subsequent population sizes (Hafner et al. 1994). Temperate species wintering in the tropics may encounter very different habitats. Many North American species, which nest in interior freshwater wetlands, winter along the mangrove swamps and other coastal wetlands of Central America. European birds of coastal and inland wetlands repair to the river swamps of sub-Saharan Africa. Similarly, dry–wet season cycles may limit distribution of subtropical and tropical species. Such populations may undertake intraregional movements seasonally that alter their habitat use patterns. In many areas, both temperate and tropical individuals participate in post-breeding dispersal, often related to seasonal water conditions, which brings them into habitats other than those they used during nesting.

Daily fluctuations affect herons inhabiting tidal environments. They must respond to changes in water depths and to prey movements by changing feeding locations with the tidal cycles. Prey also fluctuates over a period of days, as patches dry or are fed-out by herons, at which time the birds have to move to different sites (Hafner and Britton 1983).

Floods or droughts can drastically alter available feeding habitat by rendering large areas of usually suitable feeding habitat inhospitable to either prey or predator. Such events often cause widespread dispersion of heron populations.

In addition to temporal variation, prey availability varies over space. Differences and variation in the many factors affecting prey availability directly impact the spatial dispersion of feeding patches. As seasonal or daily fluctuations in water conditions make patches available or unavailable, herons must respond to these changes by moving. In large wetlands, herons may follow receding or rising water levels, as patches become available. In smaller wetland matrices, herons may have to change feeding patches. Along the coast, herons change feeding sites as tidal conditions fluctuate.

The Little Egret in the south of France (Pineau 1992, Hafner and Fasola 1992) can illustrate the flexibility of spatial and temporal habitat use exhibited by a single population. During nesting, egrets feed near the colony site in permanent freshwater marshes, temporary freshwater marshes, and coastal lagoons. Of these the permanent freshwater marshes appear to be more productive in supporting egrets, primarily because they have higher fish densities (Crivelli 1981). After nesting, herons disperse up to 100 km to drying wetlands which have easily accessible prey. When these wetlands dry, they move to staging areas, which are flooding at the time, prior to migrating southward. In winter in Morocco, egrets feed in permanently flooded coastal wetlands early in winter, moving to seasonally flooded freshwater habitats toward the end of winter. Little Egrets from France wintering in Spain use permanently flooded rice fields.

A different pattern of changing habitat use can be illustrated by the Great Blue Heron in western, coastal Canada (Butler 1991). Herons shift sites seasonally as dictated by food supplies and tides. During nesting, female herons respond to inshore movement of fish into tidal lagoons, by feeding along beaches. As food supplies decrease in winter, herons move to feed in marshes and interior grasslands, although some males feed along riverbanks.

Herons may require or benefit from a choice of alternative feeding habitats (Custer and Osborn 1978, Dimalexis et al. 1997). Choice of feeding sites within the matrix of those accessible depends on availability and also species-specific preferences. Custer and Osborn (1978), for example, showed how several species chose distinctive feeding sites, correlated primarily with their size. In New York,

USA, Snowy Egrets use different feeding sites depending on water levels that are affected by tide and rainfall, whereas Great White Egrets are more consistent in their feeding site choice, being less dependent on very shallow sites (Maccarone and Parsons 1994). Having accessible a diversity of feeding habitats is probably beneficial to overall feeding success of herons. The proximity of colonies to different feeding habitats may affect productivity. For the Little Egret for example, egrets nesting near permanent freshwater marshes in the Camargue had higher rates of food return than those nesting near temporary marshes or saline lagoons (Hafner et al. 1986b).

Hydrology. The most universal determinant of prey availability is a wetland`s hydrology. Nearly all wetlands that herons use vary in water depth and areal extent of water cover, at least seasonally. This variation is fundamentally due to seasonality of rainfall patterns and resulting discharge variation. In the temperate zones, these may be modest. In the subtropics and tropics annual or biannual dry and wet seasons significantly constrain heron use of feeding habitats. In many cases, the seasonal cycle of heron nesting and migrations, and sometimes nesting success, are tightly correlated with hydrologic conditions in their foraging habitat (Kushlan 1989b, Maddock and Baxter 1991, Frederick et al. 1992, Hafner et al. 1994, Baxter 1994, McKilligan 1997). The specific correlations may differ among species and among areas. Some species in some areas nest when water levels rise, others when they fall. Some migrate into an area when rains begin, others migrate out. The communality is that an important portion of the heron's annual cycle in any location may be driven by local hydrology. The hydrologic cycle and the heron's responses to it must be understood in developing management plans for local heron habitat.

Vegetation. The structure of the vegetation is crucial for its use by certain herons. As noted above, different herons require perches, dense emergent plants, open fields, or water edge to feed. These must be provided in the habitat. To the extent that drought, burning, flooding, logging or other human activity affects habitat structure, heron use can be affected. These forces are also tools that can be used to create and maintain suitable vegetation structure within managed wetlands.

Wetland management strategies

Heron conservation, having a large part of its focus on wetland conservation and management, benefits greatly from the widespread and increasingly successful wetland conservation movement worldwide. Wetland management and conservation enjoys a substantial core of scientific information on wetland structure, ecological function, societal values, hydraulic engineering, modelling, water management and vegetation management (see for example Mitsch 1994). Programmes of wetland restoration and wetland creation provide new or improved wetland habitats, often for a specific function such as water quality improvement (Hammer 1989, Marble 1992, Moshiri 1993). These programmes can enhance a region's heron habitat inventory, especially if the needs of herons are taken into account in the design, construction and operations of the enhanced wetland. It is becoming clear that created wetlands seldom completely mimic their natural wetland models. Their value for herons deserve additional study, and it may be that the versatility of herons gives them the necessary scope to make good use of such artificial habitats.

Wetland conservation around the world is developing a common set of principles (Kushlan 1995) and common management goals and practices. Among these are: the importance of regional inventory and monitoring (Costa et al. 1996); the role of wetlands in preserving biodiversity (Giesen 1997); assessing wetland function and values (Kusler and Riexinger 1985); adopting wetland sustainability and sustainable use as overriding management goals (Frazier 1996); achieving multiple, sustainable use through local community involvement (Claridge and O'Callaghan 1997); mitigating for impacts and losses of wetlands and their ecological functions (Kusler et al. 1988); managing from a watershed or catchment perspective (Kusler et al. 1995); and the identification of wetlands of particular importance for preservation and sustained management (e.g., Frazier 1996).

Each of these conservation emphases can be of value to heron conservation. Wetland inventories provide a geographically explicit identification of potential heron habitat. Herons can be used in a symbolic role in conservation of wetland biodiversity. Planning for the sustainable use of wetlands places heron use in a broad ecological and economic context, which is especially valuable if wetland managers (Chapter 15) adopt their role as bioindicators of wetland health and function. Community involvement in wetland conservation is of particular value to species that are well regarded by participants, as herons often are. Mitigation requires the re-establishment of wetlands or their functions that can provide additional or enhanced heron habitat. Identification of wetlands of regional, national, and international importance provides the framework and international network of habitats of value to heron populations worldwide. Heron conservation planning must adopt, partner with, and encourage wetland-planning initiatives.

Conservation of Upland Habitat

Much of the basic understanding of heron biology and conservation in wetlands is undoubtedly applicable to terrestrial habitats. Patch dynamics, the role of prey abundance and availability, seasonal and other variability in habitat availability appear to be fundamental to heron biology and should provide a basis for conservation planning. As noted previously, little is known about the specific biology of herons in terrestrial habitats. As a result there is little to guide specific conservation planning for herons in these habitats. Clearly more information is needed if heron conservation is to be eventually integrated into the conservation of their terrestrial habitat.

Management of Artificial Habitats

Rice fields

Water management and related cultivation practices in rice fields totally determine their utility to herons (Fasola and Ruiz 1996). In traditional rice cultivation, fields are periodically flooded for the growing season, for renovation after harvest, or for waterfowl use in winter, and are also periodically drawn down for harvest and for cultivation. This variation creates a changing patchwork of habitat availability. Unless a rice field is double cropped with fish or crayfish, heron feeding is seldom detrimental to rice culture. Removal of crayfish can even reduce their undermining of the dikes. Water is manipulated by canals, ditches, floodgates, dams, and pumps, depending on the situation. These features too become part of the rice culture complex used by herons. Conservation planning should take into account the seasonal pattern of use of the aquacultural habitat mosaic and how the various practices benefit or are detrimental to herons.

A long-standing issue in the use of rice fields as feeding habitat is the effect of pesticides (Chapter 12). Increasing use of short-term, low-toxicity pesticides should reduce exposure and eliminate bioaccumulation. Heron conservation planning should encourage the use of non-persistent, highly targeted pesticides in rice culture.

Rice cultivation is changing in many parts of the world. In India the substitution of dwarf varieties for the tall indigenous varieties reduces field use by the Cinnamon Bittern and Green Backed Heron (Subramanya 1990). Small paddies are giving way to larger fields more suitable for mechanical farming, thereby reducing variation within the aquacultural mosaic that provides sequences of feeding opportunities (Chapter 3). Old varieties of rice needed prolonged flooding, but recently farming has been carried out in shallower water, which reduces water costs but also productivity of potential heron prey. More recently, dry-ground rice farming is expanding. Although it is less productive, costs of water management are significantly reduced. Transition to dry land farming will put at risk heron populations now depending on flooded fields. In northern Italy, where the heron populations have come to require rice wetlands, one-third of the fields have already been converted and further losses could affect up to half of the breeding population (Fasola and Ruiz 1996). Other changes in farming practice can also affect herons. For example, in Japan changing water delivery from canals to pipes decreased food availability for herons because of reduced recruitment of fish to the rice fields (Narusue and Uchida 1993). Changes in winter flooding regimes would affect migrant and wintering birds. Also of concern is the loss of rice fields through changing to other crops that have higher market value or lower costs of production, thereby eliminating flooding. The fundamental threat to many rice fields, immediately or eventually, is the loss of flooded fields to human development.

The regional importance of rice fields to herons can scarcely be overestimated. Heron conservation planning must take into account local human practices and through planning and research influence the institution or continuation of practices beneficial to herons.

Aquaculture

Aquaculture can have important benefits to herons (Chapter 13). Fish farms make ample foraging opportunities available, with optimal prey in near-optimal feeding conditions (angry farmers notwithstanding). Positive population responses have been documented, and the expansion of aquaculture can be expected to increase foraging opportunities for both resident and wintering herons. It is crucial that the true impact of herons on fish farms be understood and that, in the ideal case, heron predation be allowed (although perhaps constrained). A good example is the study of Ashkenazi and Yom-Tov (1996) which argues that heron predation causes little detriment and even some benefit to the farm. Heron use of fish ponds does not necessarily have an economic impact and need not be controversial, as indeed is the case in Hong Kong (Young 1993). But an objective, locally-relevant information base is required to influence aquacultural practice and the opinions available to farmers.

Reservoirs

The control of surface water by reservoirs is common worldwide. Some reservoirs create fringing wetlands in the desert, whereas others feed rice fields. Herons can quickly come to depend on these water sources. Lakes, ponds, rivers, and even large wetlands are similarly under specific water management regulations. The well-known example of the Florida Everglades is essentially the effect of water management in large shallow reservoirs. Where water is managed and herons are present, heron conservation planning needs to understand the positive and negative effects of water management practices and attempt to influence them for the benefit of the herons.

Regional Management

We need to understand the feeding habitat conservation needs of local heron populations, continental populations and entire species. We also need to understand how management practices are affecting these groups at the local, regional, and national levels. While high-scale (regional, national, or continental) planning is essential to set overarching goals, real conservation action of value to herons happens locally. The most appropriate way to integrate goals on different scales is through regional and local planning, preferably on a watershed basis in concert with national or continental goals.

Flyway management

The success of managing hunted waterfowl on a flyway basis has been well established. Migratory herons must fulfil their habitat requirements not only while nesting, but also while on migration and while wintering (Chapter 11). Flyway management for non-hunted species involves the identification of large habitat areas and of key sites for nesting, migratory, and wintering herons along the flyway, and the coordinated protection and management of these sites. Key sites (or Important Bird Areas) are the important locales used by a significant portion of a population for at least part of the year (see for example Pineau 1992, Mikuska et al. 1998). By linking important areas, the conservation and management of local habitat is placed in the appropriate higher scale context. Heron conservation can establish its own reserve networks, or more realistically partner with flyway-based management schemes for various wetland birds. Examples of flyway programmes that can serve as a template for heron conservation include the North American Waterfowl Management Plan (Streeter et al. 1997), Western Hemisphere Shorebird Reserve Network (Davidson 1997), African–Eurasian Waterfowl Agreement (Boere and

Lenten 1997), and the Asia–Pacific Migratory Waterfowl Conservation Strategy (Mundkur and Matsui 1997).

Watershed management

It is clear that preservation of aquatic habitats suitable for herons is essential for heron conservation worldwide. Parks, refuges, reserves, easements, zoning, wetland protection laws, and private preservation activities are a workable array of methods used for conservation of wetlands. Such actions preserve aquatic habitats from being drained and developed in ways adverse to herons.

However critical as a foundation, habitat preservation alone will be inadequate for conservation of most heron habitats in the long run. Vegetation, water depths and their fluctuations, patch sizes and dispersion are all subject to manipulative action. In the Mediterranean, for example, available freshwater feeding sites are manipulated to increase fish production by controlling water levels (Britton 1982). In larger systems where water discharges are controlled by dikes, water depth fluctuations can be manipulated to create conditions suitable for heron feeding. Wetlands will inevitably be increasingly managed and manipulated.

Heron use of artificial sites poses both opportunities and difficulties for heron conservation. Sites such as rice fields provide feeding habitat that otherwise might not be available, or as productive. In some cases these fields have replaced natural freshwater marshes preferred by herons, but without them the natural habitats might well have been drained. Changes in management practices, such as the extent of flooding and resulting ability to support fish and amphibians, could affect these habitats' usefulness to herons. More drastically, economic pressures may change the value of rice farming in certain areas, leading to abandonment of rice cultivation.

It is the regional mosaic of potential habitat that is used by herons. So it is the regional mosaic that needs to be the geographic basis for conservation planning. This mosaic may encompass combinations of natural wetlands and artificial sites, of colony and feeding sites, or of breeding, post-breeding and wintering sites.

Herons are not the only users of their feeding habitats, and their needs will have to be reconciled with the multiple use of these habitats by other wildlife and humans. The sustainable use of wetlands is a core principle of modern wetland conservation. This principle serves herons well in that they have a degree of flexibility in adapting to sustainable use strategies. It is likely that heron conservation will require some active management or the continuation or enhancement of various activities. Thus it is essential that herons' needs be made part of the wider sustainable use planning at a watershed scale.

Conclusions

Management and conservation of heron feeding habitat should be a conservation priority in areas having large concentrations of herons or supporting rare species. In such areas, the geographic pattern of heron habitat use and the temporal pattern of use within the geographic pattern need to be understood. Conservation and management of heron feeding habitat should be undertaken on a regional basis, and as part of more encompassing strategies of sustainable, multiple use. Habitat conservation requires maintenance of such characteristics as water depths, water fluctuations, vegetation, prey base, and dispersion of patches. Feeding habitat is often not continuous, so its patchiness, including patch size and dispersion, affect heron use. Small patches may not contain sufficient food or shelter to support herons. It is likely that the larger the individual patches within the matrix of available feeding sites, the more herons can be supported. The temporal dispersion of patches is also important in that herons can feed sequentially in patches if they become suitable in an orderly sequence, allowing herons to change patches efficiently. The size and physical and temporal dispersion of patches can determine the length of time a heron can feed in an area.

Certain species require specific vegetative structural characteristics, especially those that feed in dense herbaceous plants and those that feed from bushes and trees overhanging the water. For these species, maintenance of vegetation structure is required for their use of a habitat. If a heron is physically able to access a patch through the feeding repertoire available to it, its presence will be determined primarily by prey availability. Irrespective of other characteristics, insufficient prey availability will cause a heron to avoid a potential feeding patch.

The pattern, timing, and extent of water level changes, as determined by rainfall or overland flows, often determine prey availability, and therefore feeding patch suitability. In dry seasons, falling water conditions concentrate prey, make it available in shallower locations, and present a succession of feeding patches. In wet seasons, flooding allows prey populations to expand, both spatially and numerically. Timing of each is crucial, as the herons' reproductive and migration phenology must be in synchrony with local and regional patterns of food availability. To the extent that the timing of hydrological fluctuations determines patterns of prey abundance and dispersal, maintenance of such fluctuations is critical to heron habitat use.

Heron feeding habitat conservation can be built on an already solid foundation of heron biology and wetland ecology. To be successful it needs to be locally based, regionally compatible, and placed in the appropriate national and flyway perspective. Heron feeding habitat conservation, especially, should be based on herons' being an integral part of sustainable land use, and flyway, national and international water bird management plans.

11. Conservation of Wintering and Migratory Habitats

Olivier Pineau

In the temperate zones of the world, many species of heron move away after the breeding season. Some populations are resident, such as Grey Herons in Ireland, Scotland, northern and central England (Voisin 1991). Other herons, such as the Little Egret in southern France, are partial migrants with many individuals spending the winter on or relatively near the breeding area. A smaller proportion of egrets winter thousands of kilometres to the south in Africa (Pineau 1992), where they mix with other typical long-distance migrants from the Palearctic, such as the Purple Heron and the Squacco Heron, and with Afro-tropical species.

In contrast to the breeding sites and surrounding feeding areas, the protection of herons on migration and on the wintering grounds has so far received little consideration (Mikuska et al. 1998). Yet this is the period when the birds are at risk, during the least favourable time of the year (Hafner 1997a). Colony site and feeding habitat requirements during nesting are today to some extent understood (Chapter 9) and this knowledge has led to successful conservation projects for nesting herons (Hafner 1982, Fasola and Alieri 1992, Hafner and Fasola 1997). Clearly, nest site and feeding habitat protection and management for breeding birds when they are restricted to a limited home range (Chapter 9), is far more feasible than trying to identify, protect and manage wetlands on an intercontinental scale. However, during the critical period outside the breeding season, herons can be severely affected by any changes to their environment resulting from anthropogenic and meteorological factors such as urbanisation, management for agriculture and hunting, drought or freezing. Under unfavourable circumstances their only option is to abandon stopover sites or wintering areas and to migrate further towards more hospitable regions. These migrants must face the dangers of hunting, predation, electric powerlines, habitat modification, and climatic unpredictability on their passage and final resting areas. They must also share their passage and wintering habitats with other individuals of the same or different species. This competition presents a further risk to be faced during this period.

Heron Conservation
ISBN 0-12-430130-4

Finally, over a large proportion of the earth herons inhabit warm tropical regions where the climate is more constant and where species can find wetlands that provide favourable conditions for them throughout the year. But seasonal movements of herons occur here as well. These movements are often related to the rainy season. In Senegal, for instance, Squacco Herons breed at the end of the rainy season (August–September), but they will abandon if water levels fall too rapidly (Voisin 1991).

The ecology of herons outside the breeding season is still rather poorly understood and represents an immense field of investigation for the future (Hafner 1997a). We need urgently more studies on feeding ecology, interactions with other species on stopover sites and in wintering areas, and on bottleneck areas and periods. Banding studies and marking schemes are important tools indicating locations of important stopover and wintering sites (Pineau 1992, Mikuska et al. 1998) and providing estimates of mortality and survival rates of yearlings and of adults (Hafner et al. 1998a). For Camargue Little Egrets, a recent sensitivity analysis using a Leslie Matrix model with existing parameter estimates has indicated that population change for this species is far more sensitive to adult and juvenile survival than to reproduction (Bennetts and Hafner, unpubl. data, Hafner et al. 1999). It is generally acknowledged that population change in birds with long generation times

A marking scheme for individual recognition of Camargue Little Egrets has provided new information on movements and dispersal of this local population. Photo: Emmanuel Vialet.

is more sensitive to adult survival than to fecundity. This kind of information based on recent advances in capture–mark–recapture methodology (Lebreton et al. 1993) is particularly useful for the design of research aiming at conservation, since the logical follow-up will be the identification of factors influencing the sensitive parameters. Unfortunately the solitary species, many of which are of conservation concern (Chapters 9 and 17), are too difficult to study using banding and marking schemes. Therefore movements and sites used outside the breeding period by these birds are virtually unknown.

Observation pressure varies greatly between regions. In large areas of South America, Africa and Asia, it is insufficient to reveal the movements that herons undertake, movements that become all the more complex the nearer one approaches the equator. Many questions on their biology in general and their movements in particular will remain unanswered as long as intensive studies on these species or in these localities are not undertaken.

Migratory Status

Different statuses can be defined, depending on the amount of time spent each year in the breeding and wintering grounds and the extent of the movements that the birds undertake between two breeding seasons.

Sedentary species

In equatorial or tropical regions, where wetlands are subjected to no seasonal climatic changes, herons can find the resources they need to survive throughout the year. However, totally sedentary species are rare. They include the tiger herons which live along water courses in heavily forested areas and mangroves (Rufescent Tiger Heron) which are stable and predictable biotopes all year round, and the Little Bittern of tropical Africa (*Ixobrychus minutus payesii*) (Hancock and Kushlan 1984, del Hoyo et al. 1992). These species nest singly, and egg laying in these tropical species takes place throughout the year. The clutch size is low and few chicks are raised. For little-known species such as the New Guinea Tiger Heron, the Rufescent Tiger Heron and the White-crested Tiger Heron, the few nests that have been found only contained a single chick (Brosset 1971, Hancock and Kushlan 1984, del Hoyo et al. 1992). Other species considered essentially sedentary live in the tropics as well: the Capped Heron, the South American Bittern, the Indian and the Javan Pond Heron (Hancock and Kushlan 1984).

Others are sedentary in parts of their range only, such as the Eurasian Bittern in west and south Europe (Koskimies and Tyler 1997), Grey Herons in Ireland and parts of Great Britain (Voisin 1991), and the American Bittern, which is sedentary in central America but migratory in the northern part of its range (del Hoyo et al. 1992). Whether or not sporadic or regular movements occur is still virtually unknown at present for at least one species, the Zigzag Heron (Hancock and Kushlan 1984, del Hoyo et al. 1992).

Migratory species

Herons breeding in areas that are subject to great seasonal climatic variation are the most inclined to migrate. When ecological conditions become difficult for the prey that comprise their food and some prey organisms enter dormancy and are no longer available, predators must either switch to other prey or migrate. Prey availability may decline either because of low temperatures in high latitude regions, from which birds move towards more temperate countries (for example Purple Heron, Squacco Heron, Black-crowned Night Heron nesting in the Palearctic region) or by drought (in Africa, southern Asia and Australia) where movements are related to rainy seasons and species such as Black-headed Heron, Intermediate Egret, White-faced Heron, and Rufous-bellied Heron will shift locally with water conditions.

Strict migrants

According to present knowledge only two species out of the 60 are strict migrants (i.e. when all the individuals of a given species migrate between two breeding seasons), Swinhoe's Egret and Schrenk's Bittern.

Partial migrants

The great majority of heron species fall into this category. Their breeding distribution occupies a major part of the world, and with the exception of equatorial regions where meteorological conditions are more stable, they are elsewhere subjected to seasonal climatic variations which affect their habitats and make them less hospitable for part of the year. Under these conditions, some populations or a certain number of individuals must move.

Movements

To escape from unfavourable conditions, migrants undertake movements of variable distances. In the tropical regions, the timing of the rainy season dictates to a large extent the movements of herons, which in some cases can undertake true trans-equatorial migrations (Curry-Lindhal 1981). At high latitudes some populations are able to be sedentary, such as the Grey Heron in Ireland and the United Kingdom (Rydzewski 1956, Voisin 1991) or the Great Blue Heron spp. *fannini* along the Pacific seaboard of North America (Palmer 1962), because of oceanic currents that lead to mild winters. But birds further inland must move south or towards seacoasts to escape from the continental climate (Rydzewski 1956, Byrd 1978, Bartolomé et al. 1996). Individuals that attempt to winter in these areas without moving face the risk of heavy losses during severe cold spells (North 1979, North and Morgan 1979, Day and Wilson 1978, Day 1981, Hafner et al. 1992, 1994). In the Little Egret (spp. *garzetta*), the majority of the western Palearctic population travels south to south-west (Moreau 1972). Those in tropical Africa are sedentary (Brown et al. 1982). Those of the Mediterranean region winter either in their breeding range or as far south as equatorial Africa (Dugan 1983, Voisin 1985, Pineau 1992). Its counterpart in the New World, the Snowy Egret, behaves in a very similar way (Ryder 1978, Mikuska et al. 1998).

Colour marking of Little Egrets in the Camargue has shown that birds were faithful to an area throughout the winter (in the Camargue, Spain, Morocco and Senegal) and that there were several instances of birds recorded at exactly the same

Great White Egret. Freezing conditions in Europe can severely affect herons. The only option to survive is to move further south. Photo: Jean François Hellio and Nicolas van Ingen.

site, such as specific marshes and lagoons, during successive winters in the Camargue, in the Ebro Delta in Spain and in Senegal (Hafner, unpubl. data). The same phenomenon of site fidelity has been recorded in Australia with the Intermediate Egret (Maddock, pers. comm.).

Movements generally take place at night (Suchantke 1960, del Hoyo et al. 1992) and in small flocks (Paran and Shulter 1981, Moore 1984, Turrian and Schmid 1984, Voisin 1996). Migrating birds may well use weather systems in their migration (Maddock and Bridgman 1992). For migrants coming from the Palearctic the network of oases scattered over parts of the Sahara desert seems to play an important role, judging from records of Purple Herons (Voisin 1991) and of Little Egrets and Squacco Herons (del Hoyo et al. 1992). Little Bitterns are able to cross the Sahara desert in a single flight but are known to stop at oases as well (Voisin 1991). In the central Sahel (southern part of Niger) the importance of numerous small, scattered wetlands for both Palearctic and Afrotropical species in January–February has been discovered only recently (Mullié et al. 1998). Eleven species of heron were recorded in a small sample of these lakes, with hundreds of Grey Herons, Little Egrets, Squacco Herons and Black-crowned Night Herons. These extensive African wintering areas, often difficult to access, are still subject to important discoveries. Another example is the unusual observation of a concentration of more than 5000 Squacco Herons in the inner delta of the Niger (Mali) in December 1996 (Jan van der Kamp, unpubl. data).

Status of Migrating Herons

Differential movements may occur between sex and age classes. In herons this aspect is still very poorly researched since there are so few banding and marking programmes. Opportunity to collect information arises occasionally, when extreme climatic conditions cause high mortality (Wallace 1990, Hafner et al. 1992, 1994).

If overwinter survival on the breeding grounds depends on limited food resources, only part of the population can gain access to these whereas other individuals must migrate. In birds, males are generally larger than females and are dominant, while older birds dominate younger individuals (Wilson 1975, Myers 1981, Gauthreaux 1982).

Analysis of 260 dead *Egretta garzetta* found at roosting sites during severe winter weather in the Camargue showed that young birds were affected first, then adults, with males succumbing last, if the cold spell persisted. It seems likely that the latter had better territories and/or larger fat reserves (Wallace 1990). There were strongly biased sex and age ratios amongst the dead bodies, suggesting that adult males are the class of individuals least likely to migrate whilst juveniles are the most likely. Male Little Egrets are larger, on average, than females and may well therefore be at an advantage in cold weather (Wallace 1990).

In herons siblings differ considerably in size as a result of the asynchronous hatching of the clutch. This reproductive strategy favours first-hatched chicks, which grow faster. A high proportion of the last-hatched in a brood die of starvation (e.g., Fujioka 1985, Inoué 1985, Mock 1986, Mock and Parker 1986). Furthermore, it would seem that the effect of asynchrony is felt later, at the time of migration, as suggested by sightings and recoveries of Little Egrets ringed as chicks in the Camargue colonies. The first-hatched birds of a given brood tend to be more sedentary, whereas the last-hatched tend to migrate (Pineau 1992). One advantage of such a compromise would allow part of the population to replace the other in the event of either wintering groups being wiped out on their wintering grounds due to disastrous climatic conditions, such as drought in the Sahel or winter severity in the Camargue.

Dispersal

The most frequently proposed explanation for dispersal in birds is competition for resources such as breeding sites, food, or mates (Bowen et al. 1989, Aebischer 1995, Delestrade et al. 1996, Miller and Smallwood 1997). In this rapidly changing world, the capacity of a species to explore and adapt to changes in the environment is a key element to its survival. The mechanism of dispersal is frequent in herons and both sedentary and migratory species disperse after the breeding season, particularly young birds soon after they become independent. This dispersion takes place in all directions, even in directions opposite to the normal migratory route taken by most herons (May 1929, Rydzewski 1956, Siegfried 1970, Byrd 1978, Ryder 1978, Voisin 1991, Erwin et al. 1996b). By moving to favourable habitats that were previously unused, this dispersal can decrease competition close to breeding sites where feeding areas are overcrowded at the end of the breeding season. In the northern hemisphere, at the end of the breeding season birds are more likely to find wetlands that still contain water by dispersing north than by resting further south where drought may affect wetlands at the end of the summer.

Erratic dispersal can also be a mechanism for range expansion. The colonisation of new continents by the Cattle Egret could at least partly be explained by this post-fledging dispersal (Hancock and Kushlan 1984, Voisin 1991) and the same could be true for the Little Egret in North America (Murphy 1992).

In contrast to post-fledging dispersal, herons observed far to the north of their normal distribution range in the spring are due to "overshooting" by migrants (Elkins 1983, Voisin 1991).

Habitat and Diet Changes

For the conservation of herons it is critical to identify habitat and food resources along migration routes and in the major wintering areas. This aspect is still rather poorly known. Most species of herons may be considered generalists and they adapt remarkably to fluctuating food resources and changing environment (Fasola 1994). Only for the few strictly sedentary species is it doubtful that they change their diet with the seasons, given the stability of the habitats in which they live. Migratory herons with precise habitat requirements such as the Purple Heron and the Squacco Heron seem to seek similar freshwater environments to those they used on the breeding grounds, when on the staging or wintering areas in Africa (Hafner, unpubl. data). Records of a Little Bittern and a Squacco Heron in hypersaline habitat are exceptions and presumably the result of stress situations (Hafner unpubl.).

Many migrants from temperate zones and wintering in the tropics may have to accommodate to very different habitats. Great Blue Herons that remain in high latitude regions inland shift to maritime provinces and hence to more saline habitats less prone to freezing (Butler 1992). Migrant bird species are opportunistic feeders that readily adapt to new conditions imposed by the climate. In particular their diet varies considerably with season (Lack 1986). Except a few strictly sedentary species in certain tropical areas, food will necessarily change between seasons for both long-distance migrants and partial migrants. In the Camargue, southern France, when earthworms, a common winter food, are no longer accessible because of frost, Cattle Egrets switch to small mammals (Bredin 1983, 1984). The same phenomenon has also been reported in the Ebro Delta in Spain with a peak in mouse consumption in November (Ruiz 1985). Grey Herons in France are essentially piscivorous during most of the year but earthworms and small rodents become major food items during certain winters (Marion 1991a). Change in diet of Grey Herons related to a switch in biotope in the winter was also recorded in Belgium (Draulans and van Vessem 1987) and other cases of diet switching coinciding with a habitat change have been reported in Little Egrets (Balança 1987) and Great Blue Herons (Butler 1992).

In North Africa, prey items of local and transient Little Egrets must be different in

The Squacco Heron. This species is a typical long-distance migrant. These two individuals (1 adult and 1 young) use a stop-over site which does not offer their favoured vegetated freshwater habitat. Photo: Jean François Hellio and Nicolas van Ingen.

autumn when the preferred habitats are permanently-flooded wetlands with marine influences (salinas, lagoons, tidal saltmarshes) and in early spring when the freshwater habitats (mostly seasonally-flooded) become important after flooding by winter rains (Pineau 1992).

Competition

Most heron species share their staging and wintering areas with individuals of the same species or with closely related species.

Size is a factor segregating birds in terms of their choice of wintering sites. In winter, in Greece, Great White Herons and Grey Herons occur in the north of the country with a colder climate, whereas Little Egrets winter further west in regions with milder climate (Nazirides et al. 1992). Large individuals should be at an advantage in cold weather as they are more able to resist harsh conditions and fasting. Even within a species, larger individuals seem to be favoured during cold weather, as suggested by analyses of egret carcasses in the Camargue (Wallace 1990, see Movements section above). Palearctic migrants arrive in tropical Africa with, or soon after, the end of the rainy season (August–October). Tropical rains considerably increase the available area of wetlands (such as Sudd and Inner Niger Delta in Africa, the Llanos and Pantanal in South America, the Ganges Basin in Asia). This is also the time of year when local species start their breeding season and huge concentrations of wading birds aggregate to breed (Skinner et al. 1987). Moreau (1972) expressed the opinion that Palearctic migrants had a dramatic impact on local birds in certain wetland areas of Africa, but no quantitative studies are available. In South American wintering grounds, where studies have been conducted, no competition has been demonstrated to occur between different species of wintering wading birds (Duffy et al. 1981), nor between local wading birds and winterers from further north (Swennen and Spaans 1985).

If populations are regulated outside the breeding season, and even if climatic conditions seem to be the proximal factor, density may be the more significant factor and must play an important role especially when extreme climatic conditions are involved. Besides, in their stopover sites and wintering grounds, migrant herons encounter prey species and predators they are not used to in their breeding areas.

Changes in Migratory Status

Recent changes have become apparent in the migratory behaviour of some species in the western Palearctic. There is no clear explanation for this phenomenon but it may be related to improved protection and, in the case of the Grey Heron, the Little Egret and the Cattle Egret, to increase in population size and range expansion. However, the two migrants Black-crowned Night Heron and Squacco Heron neither increased nor expanded; and the effect of climatic changes (Burton 1995) cannot be discounted.

The presence of small groups of Black-crowned Night Herons overwintering in Mediterranean countries has been known for 20 years, but their numbers have increased in southern Spain to up to 1390 (Sarasa et al. 1993) and winter breeding has been reported in the same area (Mackrill 1987).

Generally most Squacco Herons from the western Palearctic migrate to the northern tropics of Africa although small numbers are known to winter in western Morocco, the southern Mediterranean, Iraq, Iran and the Persian Gulf. However, in recent years individuals were recorded wintering in the Camargue (Kayser 1994), Spain and Italy and unusually high numbers were seen in Morocco (56 in January 1992; El Agbani and Dakki 1992), and in Egypt (632 wintering in 1989–90; Meininger and Atta 1994).

Pressures on Wetlands

Investigations into the main adversities that migratory birds face tend to show that natural habitat destruction and degradation are the most important threats (Collar and Andrew 1988). For wetland birds this process of destruction has been particularly accelerated over the past two centuries. Each of the status chapters in this book, which cover the world, leads to the conclusion that the most important heron conservation issue is the loss of wetland habitat and that this phenomenon is tightly linked to regional economic conditions. These differ among countries and continents and include increasing population pressures inducing competition for scarce water supplies, habitat loss and fragmentation due to urbanisation, industry and agriculture, and loss of wetland quality through alteration of natural functioning. Since historical times, wetlands have been modified for agricultural and industrial development. Increasing human population has led to ever-greater use of wetlands, and everywhere in the world the level of utilisation of wetlands is today extremely high (Chapters 1–8). The wintering and staging areas used during migration are located in wetlands that are liable to sudden transformation. The threats faced by these wetlands are either directly related to human activities (such as hydrological changes, agricultural and industrial development, leisure activities, etc.) or indirectly so (for instance global climate change).

Hydrological Changes

Damming of all the major river systems is widespread in the world, for hydropower and irrigation purposes, for industrial and domestic uses or to reduce seasonal flooding. Together with other hydrological schemes this has radically altered the downstream wetlands, which depend on this water. The same is true of pumping from aquifers, and river diversion schemes.

One of the most striking examples is the Aral Sea (Ellis 1990, Aladin et al. 1993) but other projects have also had major implications, although at a smaller scale. Examples include: damming and dike construction on the Senegal river (Braakhekke and Marchand 1987), groundwater extraction in Spain (Llamas 1988; Hollis et al. 1989), and draining of the floodplain of the Euphrates and Tigris. Other side-effects of these modifications are the reduction in the amount of silt reaching deltas after the construction of dams upstream and the erosion of the delta coastline (for example the Aswan High Dam and the Nile Delta; Stanley 1988), changes in water levels and nutrient inputs in silt reflected in lowered agricultural and fishery yields (Adams 1985, Awachie 1976).

The effect of hydrological changes on heron populations is not readily perceptible, except locally (for example in the Volga Delta, Gavrilov, pers. comm.; see Chapter 1, and the Dniestr Delta; Schogolev 1992), since they have been accompanied by the creation of artificial water bodies which have provided substitute habitats for many species. So far, the only species to be directly threatened by a hydrological scheme could be the Slaty Egret because of the modification of the Okavango Delta (Collar and Stuart 1985; see Chapters 5 and 17).

Man-made wetlands such as reservoirs, ponds and gravel pits are becoming increasingly frequent, not only in developed but also in developing countries. In some countries they have even become the most important waterfowl habitats, either because they have replaced natural habitats as in Europe, or because there were no alternative natural sites in the regions where they were created (Chapters 5 and 6).

The existence of these artificial wetlands, which have some of the characteristics of natural wetlands, has led developers to argue against unnecessary protection of natural wetlands where they can be replaced or recreated. However, the complexity of natural wetland functioning and especially their critical hydrology, is difficult to engineer and to replace.

Degradation and Pollution

Agriculture

In developing countries, the conversion of natural habitat to agricultural land is commonplace. When transformed into rice fields, for example, wetlands can still play an important role for Ardeidae, but not if they are highly mechanised and heavily sprayed with pesticides (Mullié et al. 1991).

In developed countries, the transformation of wetlands into agricultural land is an ancient practice that developed greatly with the coming of steam and diesel-powered pumps, and is still taking place despite conservation measures. For example, the agricultural intervention of the Common Agricultural Policy of the European Union has adversely affected Mediterranean wetlands. Price stability has encouraged land reclamation through drainage. Price guarantees have encouraged increased production levels which have often been achieved through heavy applications of agrochemicals that find their way into watercourses and hence into wetlands (Hollis 1992).

Urban and industrial development

The effect of industrial development is even more dramatic on wetlands than agricultural transformation. In addition to landfill and dredging for urban and industrial developments, wetlands have been polluted with domestic sewage, industrial effluents and other waste products. However, from the 1970s onward, the rate of major industrial development has declined, partly because of economic crises and also because of the emergence of the environmental movement. In contrast, housing development has continued and has been responsible for the destruction of many wetlands both in developed and developing countries. In countries where economic pressure is high and especially in the recent economic crisis era, wetlands have become increasingly difficult to protect in the face of arguments for socio-economic benefit.

Aquaculture

The transformation of wetlands into fish farms is also a type of degradation affecting both developed and developing countries. In developed countries, management of fish farms renders them unavailable for herons because of excessive water depth, netting and scaring techniques (Chapter 13). Because herons are considered as a pest at these places, they are either directly killed or scared away. Thus, wetlands transformed into unavailable fish ponds are a net loss to herons even if the damage they cause here is often regarded as negligible (Chapter 13).

In developing countries fish and shrimp farms are very attractive for herons because of their location and structure (Huner 1993a,b). But in the future, profitability motives may make competition intolerable and they are likely to become subject to the same persecution as in more northerly countries, with results that will be all the more disastrous since these farms are established in places which host numerous sedentary as well as migratory and wintering herons and other piscivorous birds. In these countries, fish farming has developed mostly at the expense of mangroves, and the ecological and environmental costs of these transformations caused by the loss of valuable nursery habitat for seed fish and natural fisheries (Trent et al. 1976) detract from any gains due to aquacultural production (see also below).

Specific wetland loss

Mangroves in southern USA, Africa and south-east Asia have been heavily deforested and converted to rice fields and for aquaculture, and also for fuelwood, timber and urban development. Puerto Rico has lost 75% of its original mangrove areas, Thailand up to 20% in recent decades and the Philippines as much as 50% between 1968 and 1981 (Gosselink and Maltby 1990). As mangrove is an important biotope for little-known and shy species of herons such as the Sumatran Heron, Bare-throated Tiger Heron and White-crested Tiger Heron (Hancock and Kushlan 1984), any encroachment in the mangrove would have a double impact through clearance and disturbance.

Disturbance

Disturbance through human activities degrades the habitat function of wetlands to a large and probably increasing extent. Disturbance has been identified as a threat in 35% of Mediterranean wetlands (Hollis 1992), and in 32% of wetlands in South Asia (Scott and Poole 1989). Hunting seems to be the most important cause of disturbance in wetlands, but tourism can also have disturbing consequences if its development is poorly managed.

In northern countries, herons are no longer of interest to hunters as they are well protected by laws. Nevertheless, they are still considered competitors by fish farmers and special permission can be readily available to limit them. Further south, their importance as quarries for hunters increases. In the Mediterranean islands, where local game has been decimated so that hunters rely entirely on passing birds, herons are killed in hundreds. On the Maltese Islands, the number of migrating herons shot annually is estimated at 3000–5000 (Sultana 1991). Elsewhere in the eastern Mediterranean islands (Chios, Crete) precise numbers are unavailable, but hunters take a heavy toll on herons (Magnin 1991, Choremi and Spinthakis 1992).

In developing countries, herons are still caught for their meat. Professional trappers provide markets with every kind of bird including many herons. In Egypt, hundreds of herons are still offered for sale in the Nile Delta (Goodman and Meininger 1989) and the Purple Heron is still the second most sought-after quarry by hunters in North Sinai (Baha el Din and Salama 1991). In Africa, herons, together with ducks, flamingoes and storks, are still a common prey for trappers in the Inner Niger Delta in Mali (J. Skinner, pers. comm.).

In south-east Asia, massive numbers of migrant and wintering water birds are trapped every year. Mass capture of herons is carried out in coastal Thailand (Nabhitabhata and Somrang 1986). In Indonesia, an estimated 38 000 herons are caught annually (Parish and Howes 1990). In the Philippines, ten different species of herons are trapped in the Dalton Pass (Alonzo-Pasicolan 1992). Herons are caught massively elsewhere in south-east Asia, for instance in Cambodia (T. Mundkur, pers.

comm.), China (L. Young, pers. comm.) and Laos where nestlings are considered a delicacy.

In South America, subsistence hunting is widespread, but except in Venezuela, where the Zigzag Heron is said to be vulnerable due to uncontrolled hunting by natives (Collar and Andrew 1988) no notable destruction is reported. Mist netting seems to be the commonest method of capture, but shooting, snares, dazzling and poisoning are also widely used.

In western South America, where these activities are carried out for sport, only better enforcement of the existing laws will stop them. Elsewhere, the socio-economic situation needs to be considered before undertaking rigorous conservation measures. These captures are made by a few village inhabitants who derive a major proportion of their income or food from this source, and they only involve the commoner species of heron, and with the exception of the Zigzag Heron, do not appear to endanger any species. The capture of abundant bird species is not incompatible with the concept of the rational use of the resources provided by wetlands. Moreover, it is probable that these activities will tend to decline in the future as the standard of living of the inhabitants of these countries improves.

Nevertheless, activities aimed at regulation, education and protection should be conducted in certain sensitive areas when species are endangered.

When tourism plays an important role in the economy, the protection of wetlands for multiple wetland-oriented recreational activities can be positive for herons. But its impact in the disturbance of water birds is far from negligible: mass tourism can alter the more sensitive areas such as the staging areas along the coast during the southward migration (Burger 1981b).

Conclusions

With the exception of a few species that are sedentary in tropical regions, most herons undertake movements of variable extent, particularly as a result of climatic conditions which alter the habitats on which they depend for breeding. These herons which migrate must however find favourable conditions at staging posts and areas where they spend the adverse season, which will allow them to accumulate sufficient reserves to survive, undertake the return journey and arrive in good physical condition on their breeding grounds. Yet the wetlands on which they depend are undergoing profound changes, particularly as a result of human activities, which is making them increasingly less hospitable.

The size and distribution of heron populations depend on the occurrence of favourable wetlands, but human activities have had, and continue to have, a phenomenal adverse impact on the world's wetland resources. Species with precise requirements but whose habitat is profitable to man in one way or another are particularly vulnerable, such as the White-eared Night Heron, Imperial Heron and Malayan Night Heron, confined to forested areas. Many species, however, show a remarkable plasticity in their use of habitats that have been radically changed by man, both during the breeding season and during wintering and migration.

The value of wetlands is officially recognised and recommendations relating to their protection have become customary in the last 30 years at the end of each of the many conferences that are devoted to them. In view of ever-increasing economic pressures, the principles are difficult to implement. The only way is to reconcile the need for human development and natural resources and the needs of water birds, starting at the regional scale and gradually extending the strategy to meet the conservation requirements of intercontinental migrants. Planning and implementing conservation actions for whole flyways must take into account development policies (Prentice and Jaensch, 1997). Local community input to planning sustainable wetland management by local people and increasing community awareness of wetland values must be part of the planning. International conservation organisations are working very hard toward this goal and multilateral approaches such as the Ramsar Convention, the Agreement on the Conservation of African–Eurasian Migratory Waterbirds (AEWA), the North American Waterfowl Management Plan (NAWMP) and the Asia–Pacific Migratory Water Bird Conservation Strategy play an essential role in achieving sustainable use of wetlands across national and continental boundaries.

12. Environmental Contaminants

Thomas W. Custer

Throughout the world, individuals and populations of herons are affected by
environmental contaminants, leading to direct mortality, decreased reproductive
success, or degradation of feeding habitat. Contaminants suspected or known to
affect herons include organochlorine compounds, organophosphorus insecticides,
trace elements, and petroleum (Parnell et al. 1988). General reviews on the effects of
pesticides on birds (Risebrough 1986, 1991) and colonial water birds (Nisbet 1980)
are presented elsewhere. The objective of this chapter is to review toxic effects of
contaminants on herons. Unless otherwise noted, contaminant concentrations are
presented as parts per million (ppm) on a wet weight (ww) basis.

Conservation Issues

Organochlorine insecticides

The insecticide DDT (o,p'-dichlorodiphenyltrichloroethane) came into wide
agricultural use in the late 1940s. Catastrophic population declines in certain species,
notably raptors, and related eggshell thinning were well documented after 1946, the
period associated with the widespread use of DDT and other organochlorine
insecticides (Ratcliffe 1967, Hickey and Anderson 1968, Anderson and Hickey 1972,
Risebrough 1986). DDT was banned in the United States in 1972. In Britain, DDT use
declined during the 1960s, but continued substantially until restricted in the early
1980s (Newton et al. 1993). Dieldrin, one of the more toxic organochlorine
insecticides (Stickel et al. 1969), came into wide use in the mid-1950s. Dieldrin was
banned from use in the United States in 1975 and in Britain during 1986.
Organochlorine pesticides were banned for agricultural practices in Italy in 1978
(Fasola et al. 1987). Peakall (1976) reported that organochlorine pesticides used for
agriculture would be banned in South Africa in 1976. Ramesh et al. (1992) reported a
recent ban on DDT for use in agricultural practices in India, but they also noted
increasing demand for organochlorines in developing countries.

Heron Conservation
ISBN 0-12-430130-4

Unsafe waters. A sign on Grand Calumet River, Indiana, USA, indicates that fish are unsafe to eat. Colonial waterbirds, including Black-crowned Night Herons, regularly feed on this river and are exposed to industrial chemicals and petroleum. Photo: Thomas W. Custer.

Organochlorine-caused mortality of adult herons and egrets has been attributed primarily to dieldrin exposure. Four adult Great Egrets found dead or moribund in a California, USA heronry had toxic levels of dieldrin in their brains (Faber et al. 1972). One Great Blue Heron found dead in South Dakota, USA in 1975 was diagnosed as having died from DDE (o,p'-dichlorodiphenyldichloroethylene) (Call et al. 1976), the main metabolite of the insecticide DDT. Ohlendorf et al. (1981) analysed brains of 51 herons found dead or moribund in the USA from 1966 to 1977. Eight herons probably died of dieldrin poisoning; four others had elevated levels of dieldrin. One heron probably died of endrin poisoning and another had a potentially lethal concentration in the brain. One heron died of DDT poisoning and another had elevated concentrations of DDE.

The accelerated declines in several species after 1945 in North America probably resulted mainly from lowered reproductive success and not acute mortality to adults or juveniles. This conclusion is based upon an analysis of banding returns of 16 avian species in North America, including Great Blue Herons and Black-crowned Night Herons, in which post-fledging mortality rates did not increase significantly after the widespread use of DDT (Henny 1972).

Members of the order Ciconiiformes were classified by Peakall (1975) as highly sensitive to DDE-induced eggshell thinning. This classification was based on 1970 data demonstrating up to 16% eggshell thinning (25% decrease in thickness index) in several heron species after the use of DDT (Faber and Hickey 1973). In the following, I summarise research on the effects of organochlorine insecticides on heron reproduction, identify organochlorine concentration trends in heron eggs and tissues through time, and note for selected species and locations whether reported concentrations were elevated or at background levels.

Grey Herons. Eggshell thinning in herons was first documented in Grey Herons. In 1967, incubating Grey Herons in a colony in Britain were observed breaking their eggs, a behaviour suspected to be linked with pesticide residues (Milstein et al. 1970). Elevated concentrations of DDE and dieldrin were reported in adults and eggs collected from 1966 to 1968 (Prestt 1970a). The mean shell thickness index of eggs collected in 1968, 1970, and 1973 was 12, 16, and 9% thinner than those collected before 1947, the pre-DDT era (Cooke et al. 1976). Shell thickness index was inversely

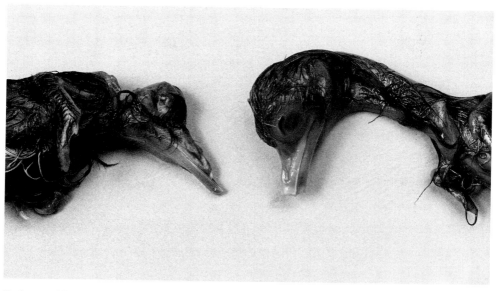

Deformed Black-crowned Night Heron embryo (left) from San Francisco bay, California, USA, an area contaminated with a variety of environmental contaminants. The embryo on the left lacks eyes, has an exposed brain, and a shortened upper bill; the embryo on the right is normal. Photo: US Fish and Wildlife Service.

related to egg concentrations of DDE, but not dieldrin or polychlorinated biphenyls (PCBs). In addition, a linear relationship existed between the proportion of pairs breaking eggs and mean residues of DDE and dieldrin in surviving eggs (Fig. 12.1). Even though more than half of the pairs broke eggshells in some years, Grey Heron populations did not decline, perhaps because of their ability to repeat clutches (Cooke et al. 1976).

Recently, organochlorine concentrations in Grey Herons have decreased. Concentrations of DDE and HEOD, the active ingredient in the insecticide dieldrin and a metabolite of the active ingredient in the insecticide aldrin, declined in livers of Grey Herons between 1963 and 1990 (Fig. 12.2, Newton et al. 1993). DDE concentrations (mean = 6.6 ppm dry weight [dw] or about 1.3 ppm ww assuming 80% moisture) in Grey Heron eggs from the Delta of the Danube in Europe were relatively low (Fossi et al. 1984). Low concentrations of DDE were found in eggs of Grey Herons from Doñana National Park, Spain, in 1983–1984 (Hernandez et al. 1987). One Grey Heron collected in the Transvaal, South Africa, had relatively low DDE concentrations (Peakall 1976).

Black-crowned Night Herons. Black-crowned Night Herons have been well studied in North America and are one of the few species where a relationship has been demonstrated between concentrations of DDE in eggs and reproductive effects. Anecdotal evidence suggested that populations of Black-crowned Night Herons decreased in the 1960s and early 1970s in New England and Michigan, USA (Ohlendorf et al. 1978a). This decrease coincided with the use of the pesticide DDT. Eggshells collected after the introduction of DDT were thinner at some locations when compared to those collected pre-1947 (e.g., Anderson and Hickey 1972, Faber and Hickey 1973, Ohlendorf et al. 1978a).

Black-crowned Night Herons studied in 1972–1976 along eastern Lake Ontario, Canada had high DDE concentrations in eggs (means 4.5–12.4 ppm), 14–17% shell thinning, low hatching success (36–54%), and low fledging success (less than 1 per

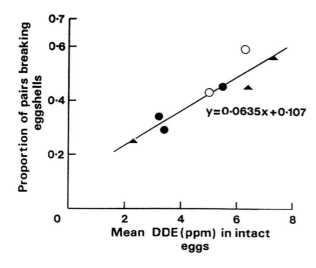

Fig. 12.1 Relationship between proportion of Grey Heron pairs breaking their eggs and mean DDE residues (ppm ww) in surviving eggs. Symbols refer to different colonies. Figure from Cooke et al. 1976.

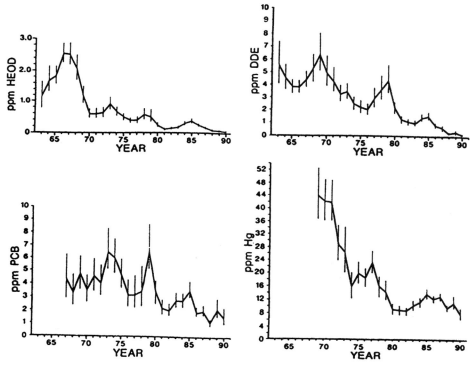

Fig. 12.2   Concentrations (ppm ww) of contaminants in livers of Grey Herons, 1963–89. Lines show 3-year moving geometric means of residue levels, and bars show geometric standard errors. Figure from Newton et al. 1993.

pair) (Price 1977). Because PCB concentrations were also high (means 10–63 ppm), the low reproductive success could have been related to residues of DDE, PCBs or a combination of both. In contrast, night herons studied in the St. Lawrence Estuary, Canada in 1975 and 1976 had relatively low DDE concentrations (mean = 2.2 ppm) in eggs, no evidence of eggshell thinning, and reproduction seemed normal (Tremblay and Ellison 1980).

An extensive survey of Black-crowned Night Heron eggs in the eastern United States in 1972 and 1973 (Ohlendorf et al. 1978a) reported that organochlorine concentrations were higher in the northern than southern Atlantic coast colonies and there were significant decreases in eggshell thickness compared to pre-1947 eggs. Changes in eggshell thickness could not be related to specific organochlorines because of the intercorrelations among the various compounds; DDE, however, had the highest correlation with shell thinning.

By the late 1970s to early 1980s, there were still many locations where DDE contamination was adversely affecting night heron reproduction; however, residues of DDE in eggs generally were decreasing with time. A threshold of 3.8 ppm was identified below which DDE had no apparent effect on hatching success; 10 ppm was projected to cause a 50% decrease in hatching success (Custer et al. 1983a).

Dented eggs, such as the one on the far left in the Black-crowned Night Heron clutch pictured here, have been associated with high concentrations of DDE. Photo: Harry Ohlendorf.

Although the data suggested an effect of DDE on hatching success in two New England, USA colonies, the impact on overall reproductive success seemed minimal.

Of eight Black-crowned Night Heron colonies investigated in Washington, Oregon, and Nevada, USA in 1978–1980, one colony on Ruby Lake, Nevada had high levels of DDE in eggs (means = 8.2 and 4.1 ppm) and low productivity (0.4 young fledged per pair, Henny et al. 1984). Eggshell thickness was significantly correlated with DDE (Fig. 12.3) and PCBs (weaker than DDE). When DDE levels in sample eggs exceeded 8 ppm, clutch size and the frequency of cracked eggs increased and productivity decreased (Table 12.1). Radio telemetry and banding indicated that the less-contaminated Oregon and Idaho, USA night herons wintered primarily in coastal Mexico, whereas the more contaminated Ruby Lake, Nevada, night herons wintered primarily in the south-western United States (Henny and Blus 1986). High concentrations of DDE in night heron eggs, eggshell thinning, and effects on productivity were also reported in 1979 in Colorado, Wyoming (McEwen et al. 1984) and Idaho, USA (Findholt and Trost 1985).

High concentrations of DDE (geometric mean = 8.6 ppm) were found in night heron eggs from the Salton Sea, California, USA in 1985 (Ohlendorf and Marois 1990). In the same study, night heron shell thickness in four other California colonies was 4–12% thinner than the pre-1947 norm. Of night heron eggs from two colonies along the Pecos River, New Mexico, in 1983, 40% had concentrations of DDE greater than 8 ppm (White and Krynitsky 1986), a concentration associated with decreased productivity in night herons (Custer et al. 1983a, Henny et al. 1984).

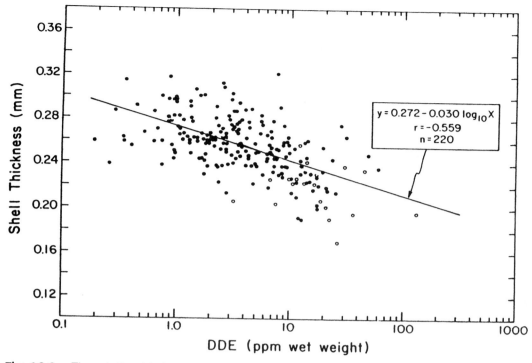

Fig. 12.3 The relationship between Black-crowned Night Heron eggshell thickness and the log-transformed residues of DDE. Figure from Henny et al. 1984.

DDE concentration in night heron eggs from two New England, USA colonies decreased between 1973 (Ohlendorf et al. 1978a) and 1979 (Custer et al. 1983b) and in a northern Italian colony between 1978 and 1994 (Fasola et al. 1998). DDE concentrations in night heron eggs also decreased from 1979 to 1983 in Idaho, Nevada, and southern Oregon, USA (Henny et al. 1985), from 1978–1980 to 1991 in colonies in Washington and northern Oregon, USA (Blus et al. 1997), and from

Table 12.1 Residues of DDE (ppm wet weight) in Black-crowned Night Heron eggs in relation to productivity, shell thickness, and egg breakage. Table modified with permission from Henny et al. 1984.

DDE (ppm)	No. of nests	Percent nests successful	Mean no. young/ successful nest	Shell thickness (mm)	Clutches with cracked eggs
≤1	19	79	2.53	0.272	0
>1–4	72	79	2.18	0.264	1 (1%)
>4–8	33	73	2.08	0.253	2 (6%)
>8–12	19	58	1.90	0.239	3 (16%)
>12–16	11	55	1.80	0.235	3 (27%)
>16–25	11	45	1.80	0.220	4 (36%)
>25–50	7	29	1.50	0.232	4 (57%)
>50	2	0	–	0.217	1 (50%)

1978–1980 (Heinz et al. 1985) to 1991 (Custer and Custer 1995) in Green Bay, Wisconsin, USA. DDE concentrations were generally low in night heron eggs collected from Israel (range 0.1–5.0 ppm, mean = 1.6 ppm; Perry et al. 1990), the Delta of the Danube (mean = 5.3 ppm dw or about 1.1 ppm ww assuming 80% moisture) (Fossi et al. 1984), Italy (range 0.23–0.74 ppm, Fasola et al. 1987), and San Francisco Bay, California, USA (Hothem et al. 1995). One adult and one immature night heron collected in the Transvaal, South Africa (Peakall 1976) and nine night heron nestlings collected in wetlands of Thermaikos Gulf, Macedonia, Greece (Albanis et al. 1996) had relatively low DDE concentrations.

Great Blue Herons. Even though Great Blue Herons generally had higher organochlorine residues in eggs than other heron species from similar locations (Ohlendorf et al. 1979a), there have been no studies documenting effects of organochlorines on nest productivity. Great Blue Herons experienced significant eggshell thinning following the introduction of DDT (see for example Anderson and Hickey 1972, Faber and Hickey 1973, Ohlendorf et al. 1979a) and a negative relationship was documented between DDE concentrations and eggshell thickness (Vermeer and Reynolds 1970, Vermeer and Risebrough 1972, Custer et al. 1997 for instance). Egg-eating behaviour was reported in Great Blue Herons at a colony in Iowa, USA, where extremely high concentrations of dieldrin (>13 ppm) and DDE (>115 ppm) were reported in three newly hatched chicks from one nest (Konermann et al. 1978). In addition, Great Blue Heron broken eggshells from a colony in California, USA were 17.2% thinner than pre-1947 specimens; hatched eggshells were only 7.8% thinner (Faber et al. 1972). However, eggshell thinning rarely exceeded 15% and there was no documented effect of organochlorine contaminants on Great Blue Heron productivity (King et al. 1978, Blus et al. 1980, Mitchell et al. 1981, Laporte 1982, Fleming et al. 1984, Nosek and Faber 1984, Fitzner et al. 1988, Speich et al. 1992).

Great Egrets. Great Egret eggs collected from the eastern United States in 1972 and 1973 did not show significant eggshell thinning (Ohlendorf et al. 1979a). DDE concentrations in eggs collected along the Mississippi River, USA were low (mean = 1.8 ppm) and eggshells were not significantly thinner than eggshells collected pre-1947 (Nosek and Faber 1984). In contrast, the percentage of successful Great Egret nesting attempts decreased from 52% to 28% between 1967 and 1970 in a California, USA colony (Faber et al. 1972). Eggshells in this colony were 15% thinner than eggs collected before 1947. No eggs were analysed for organochlorines, but high concentrations of dieldrin in brains of four adults found dead suggested dieldrin poisoning. Extremely high concentrations of DDE (geometric mean = 24 ppm) were reported in Great Egret eggs collected from the Salton Sea, California in 1985 (Ohlendorf and Marois 1990).

Green-backed Herons. A relationship was demonstrated between concentrations of DDE in eggs and reproductive effects in Green-backed Herons. Green-backed Heron eggs collected in 1981 near a former DDT manufacturing site in the Tennessee Valley, USA had elevated DDE concentrations (mean = 3.9 ppm, Fleming et al. 1984) and there was a significant relationship between DDE in eggs and eggshell thickness; eggshells were 7.6% thinner than eggshells collected prior to 1947. A study in Mississippi, USA in 1984 demonstrated a relationship between DDE concentrations in sample eggs and hatching success of eggs remaining in the nest (White et al. 1988). DDE concentrations between 5.1 and 10 ppm reduced hatching success of eggs. Mean concentrations (mean = 7.4 ppm) of DDE in eggs were higher than the Tennessee study and shell thinning was 11% when compared to pre-DDT era eggs. In contrast, low DDE concentrations and lack of eggshell thinning was documented in a survey of 16 eastern United States Green-backed Heron colonies (Ohlendorf et al. 1979a).

Snowy Egrets. Concentrations of DDE in Snowy Egret eggs were related to reproductive success in the north-western United States. Relatively high concentrations of DDE (mean 4.2 and 4.8 ppm) were detected in two Snowy Egret colonies in Idaho in 1979 (Findholt 1984). Eggshell thickness was inversely correlated with DDE. When nests were divided into high DDE (>5 ppm) and low DDE (<5 ppm) groups, eggs were thinner and hatching success was lower in the high DDE group. In contrast, an extensive survey of eastern United States Snowy Egret eggs (Ohlendorf et al. 1979a) reported no significant change in eggshell thickness and generally low organochlorine concentrations. DDE concentrations in Snowy Egret eggs were also low in San Francisco Bay in 1982 (Ohlendorf et al. 1988) and 1989–1991 (Hothem et al. 1995); eggshell thickness was not correlated with DDE concentrations (Ohlendorf et al. 1988).

Cattle Egrets. Circumstantial evidence suggested that Cattle Egrets decreased in the Nile Delta and the Suez Canal area as a result of DDT use on cotton (summary in Mullié et al. 1992). The population started to recover in the 1980s, corresponding to a shift away from the use of DDT.

Cattle Egret eggs collected from the United States (Ohlendorf et al. 1979a, Heinz et al. 1985), Mexico (Mora 1991), Spain (Ruiz et al. 1982), Israel (Perry et al. 1990), and Egypt (Mullié et al. 1992) generally had low concentrations of DDE. Eggs from one of 16 Atlantic coast colonies had somewhat elevated concentrations of DDE (Yazoo National Wildlife Refuge; range 0.4–18 ppm; mean = 4.3 ppm; Ohlendorf et al. 1979a). Eggshells of Cattle Egrets from Baja California, Mexico, in 1987–1988 were 9.3% thinner than pre-1953 museum clutches, and eggshell thickness was correlated with DDE and PCB concentrations (Mora 1991). Although the DDE concentrations from the Ebro Delta in Spain (Ruiz et al. 1982) were relatively low, eggshell thickness was negatively correlated with DDE concentrations and egg breakage was reported.

Breast muscle samples of Pond Herons and Cattle Egrets from south India had means of about 0.5 ppm DDT + metabolites (Ramesh et al. 1992). HCH (hexachloro-cyclohexane) isomers in these same birds were more than two times higher than DDT + metabolites. HCH residues were expected to increase further because of continuing use in agriculture and anti-malaria campaigns. DDT levels were expected to fall because of a recent ban for agricultural purposes in India. HCH residues in birds have been documented throughout the world, with some of the highest residues from Suriname, Costa Rica, and India (Ramesh et al. 1992). The consequences of increasing levels of HCH residues to herons are unknown.

Purple Herons. Low concentrations of DDE were found in eggs of two Purple Herons collected in south-west Spain in 1972 (2.0–2.1 ppm; Baluja et al. 1977) and

Purple Herons from Doñana National Park, Spain, in 1983–1984 (Hernandez et al. 1987).

Little Egrets. Low concentrations of DDE were found in eggs of Little Egrets from Doñana National Park, Spain, in 1983–1984 (Hernandez et al. 1987), from Israel (mean = 1.6 ppm; Perry et al. 1990), and from northern Italy (Fasola et al. 1998). Little Egret nestlings collected in wetlands of Thermaikos Gulf, Macedonia, Greece (Albanis et al. 1996) also had relatively low DDE concentrations.

Squacco Herons. Eggs and nestlings of Squacco Herons collected in wetlands of Thermaikos Gulf, Macedonia, Greece (Albanis et al. 1996) had relatively low DDE concentrations.

Polychlorinated biphenyls (PCBs)

PCBs are synthetic halogenated aromatic hydrocarbons that have many uses including insulating or cooling agents in transformers and capacitors. Environmental contamination has resulted from several sources including industrial discharge, leaks from closed systems, disposal to sewage treatment plants, and incomplete incineration of PCBs. They have been prohibited in the United States since 1979 (Eisler 1986).

With the exception of locations within the Great Lakes and the Upper Mississippi River, USA, PCB concentrations were generally low and not associated with impaired survival or reproduction of herons. As stated earlier, Black-crowned Night Heron eggs on eastern Lake Ontario had high PCB concentrations (means 10–63 ppm) and low reproductive success (Price 1977). The low reproductive success was possibly related to residues of DDE that averaged 4.5–12.4 ppm, PCBs, or a combination of both. Night heron eggs collected from Green Bay, Wisconsin, and Saginaw Bay, Michigan, USA in 1984 had a higher frequency of abnormal embryos, enlarged livers, smaller femurs, elevated microsomal AHH, and lower hepatic DNA concentrations than a reference colony (Table 12.2, Hoffman et al. 1993). Total PCB concentrations in night heron embryos (Rattner et al. 1993, 1994) but not nestlings

Table 12.2 Morphological development and liver biochemistry in pipping Black-crowned Night-Heron embryos from Great Lakes colonies and a captive reference colony. Data summarised from Hoffman et al. 1993.

	Controls	Green Bay	Saginaw Bay
N:	14	5	10
Liver weight : body weight ratio × 100	2.5A[1]	3.2B	2.9AB
Femur length : body weight ratio × 100	55.5B	50.6AB	49.1A
Microsomal AHH (pmol/min/mg protein)	15A	45B	47B
Microsomal protein (mg/g liver)	13.1A	12.8A	15.7B
Abnormal embryos[2] (%)	0	60[3]	40[3]

[1]Rows not sharing the same letter are significantly different by the SNK multiple-range test (P <0.05).
[2]Mainly edematous.
[3]Significantly different from controls (P <0.01).

(Rattner et al. 1996) collected from Green Bay were correlated with liver enzyme activity. PCB concentrations in Black-crowned Night Heron eggs collected from Green Bay declined from 1978 and 1980 (means 15 and 24 ppm PCBs, Heinz et al. 1985) to 1991 (mean 11.0 ppm PCBs, Custer and Custer 1995).

PCB concentrations increased with weight of Great Blue Heron chicks on the Upper Mississippi River in 1976 and suggested elevated PCB concentrations in local food sources (Ohlendorf et al. 1979b). Great Blue Heron and Great Egret eggs collected from the Upper Mississippi River in 1978 (Nosek and Faber 1984) had relatively high PCB concentrations (14.1 ppm Great Blue Heron, 13.3 ppm Great Egret). However, a collection of Great Blue Heron eggs in 1993 on the Upper Mississippi River suggested that PCB concentrations had declined significantly since the late 1970s (3.0 ppm, Custer et al. 1997).

PCB concentrations in night heron eggs were negatively correlated with embryonic weight in night herons from San Francisco Bay, California, USA in 1983 (Hoffman et al. 1986); PCB concentrations, however, were relatively low (mean 4.1 ppm) and microsomal AHH activity was not significantly induced above reference values. PCB concentrations in Black-crowned Night Heron and Snowy Egret eggs were generally low from several colonies in San Francisco Bay during 1989–1991 (Hothem et al. 1995).

Total PCBs were higher in the heron eggs from northern than southern Atlantic, USA colonies (Ohlendorf et al. 1978a, 1979b) and higher in Great Blue Herons than smaller-billed species (Ohlendorf et al. 1979a). Between 1973 and 1979 concentration of PCBs in eggs from two New England, USA, colonies decreased significantly in one colony (10.2 to 6.1 ppm) but not the other (7.2 to 6.2 ppm) (Custer et al. 1983b). PCBs declined significantly (63 to 28 ppm) in night heron eggs between 1972 and 1976 at a colony in eastern Lake Ontario, Canada (Price 1977). PCBs also declined steadily in the Grey Heron in Britain between 1967 and 1989 (Fig. 12.2; Newton et al. 1993). PCB concentrations were low in Little Egret and Black-crowned Night Heron eggs from northern Italy (Fasola et al. 1998), in Great Blue Heron, Tricoloured Heron, and Snowy Egret eggs from the Lower Laguna Madre, Texas, USA (Mora 1996), and in Great Egret, Snowy Egret, and Little Blue Heron eggs from south Florida (Rodgers 1997).

There are 209 possible congeners of PCBs (Safe 1987). Some of these PCB congeners induce cytochrome P450-dependent mixed function oxygenases and may act as a catalyst for many mutagens and carcinogens. Because of the distribution of PCB congeners within samples, total PCBs may not adequately reflect toxicity (Boumphrey et al. 1993). For example, total PCBs in Black crowned Night Heron eggs were 2.7 times greater from Green Bay, Wisconsin, USA (9.3 ppm, Rattner et al. 1994) than from Baltimore Harbor, Maryland, USA (3.4 ppm, Rattner et al. 1997); however, the toxicity of the PCB congener mixture, based on dioxin equivalents assigned to each of the congeners (Safe 1987), was only 1.8 times greater from Green Bay (2977 pg/g) than from Baltimore Harbor (1691 pg/g).

Dioxins and related compounds

Dioxins are highly toxic and teratogenic contaminants associated with the manufacture of chlorophenols, and are suspected to have had an adverse effect on Great Blue Heron embryonic development at some locations. Hepatic microsomal ethoxyresorufin-O-deethylase (EROD) activity in Great Blue Heron hatchling livers was correlated with TCDD, the most toxic of the dibenzodioxins (Bellward et al. 1990). When TCDD equivalents of the PCB congeners were added to TCDD, the significance of the correlation with EROD did not increase, indicating that PCBs were not a major factor in enzyme induction. In contrast, TCDD concentrations were at background levels in Black-crowned Night Heron eggs collected from colonies in Washington and northern Oregon, USA (Blus et al. 1997) and in Great Blue Heron eggs collected from colonies on the Upper Mississippi River, USA (Custer et al. 1997).

Pairs of Great Blue Heron eggs were collected from three British Columbia colonies with low, intermediate, and high dioxin contamination. One egg was incubated to hatching while the other was analysed for contaminants. Dioxin concentrations in eggs, although not related to mortality, were correlated with depressed embryonic growth and increased frequency of edema (Hart et al. 1991). Subcutaneous edema was observed in 33% of hatchlings from the most TCDD-contaminated colony, 15% from the intermediate TCDD-contaminated colony, and none from the lowest TCDD-contaminated colony. Additionally, the brains of Great Blue Heron hatchlings from contaminated colonies displayed gross morphometric intercerebral asymmetry that was associated with TCDD contamination (Henshel et al. 1992). Chlorophenols, used in wood preservation, are the most likely sources of polychlorinated dibenzodioxin (PCDD) contamination in Great Blue Heron eggs in the Strait of Georgia, British Columbia (Elliot et al. 1989).

Polychlorinated dibenzo-p-dioxins and dibenzofurans were quantified in the livers of Grey Herons in the Netherlands (van den Berg et al. 1987). The suspected sources of these contaminants included PCBs, chlorophenols, and fly-ash combustion. No attempt was made to evaluate the effects of these contaminants on the Grey Herons. TCDD injected into embryo (Sanderson et al. 1997) and adult (Janz and Bellward 1997, Sanderson et al. 1997) Great Blue Herons at environmentally relevant concentrations induced EROD activity but did not result in overt toxicity.

Organophosphorus and carbamate insecticides

Organophosphorus (OP) and carbamate insecticides are the most widely-used group of pesticides in North America. These anticholinesterase (antiCHE) compounds act by inhibiting the enzyme cholinesterase, causing the accumulation of acetylcholine at nerve synapses and the consequent disruption of nerve function (O'Brien 1967).

Herons, probably because of their aquatic feeding habits, are generally not as exposed to antiCHE compounds compared to some other avian species. Only one of 31 incidents of wildlife mortality associated with antiCHE compounds included herons (Grue et al. 1983). Zinkl et al. (1981) documented poisoning of herons (Great Blue Heron, Great Egret, Snowy Egret) by fenthion (an OP) in an area sprayed for mosquito control. A laboratory study was conducted on Black-crowned Night Herons in an exposure chamber where the birds were allowed to wade and drink, or wade only, in fenthion-treated water (Smith et al. 1986). When the water was treated with 1 and 10 times the field application rate of fenthion, cholinesterase activity was significantly inhibited in plasma but not the brain. The conclusion of this study was that field application rates of fenthion were probably not life-threatening to this species.

Trace elements

Trace elements of concern to herons include mercury, lead, cadmium, and selenium (Scheuhammer 1987, Ohlendorf 1989).

Mercury (Hg). Mercury has been used by man for at least 2300 years, most recently as a fungicide in agriculture, in the manufacture of chlorine and sodium hydroxide, as a slime control agent in the pulp and paper industry, in the production of plastics and electrical apparatus, and in mining and smelting operations (Eisler 1987). One major consequence of increased Hg use, coupled with careless waste disposal practices, has been a sharp increase in the number of epidemics of fatal Hg poisoning in humans, wildlife, and aquatic organisms.

Background liver concentrations of Hg were generally below 10 ppm (about 33 ppm dry weight [dw], assuming 70% moisture) in wild birds in north-western Ontario, Canada (Fimreite 1974). Great Blue Herons collected in 1970–1971 downstream from a chlorine alkali factory in north-western Ontario had much higher mercury concentrations in their livers (3–128 ppm, mean = 50 ppm) than herons collected elsewhere (Fimreite 1974). Concentrations of Hg in livers of adult Great Blue Heron (medians 8–17 ppm, range 0.8–144 ppm) collected in western Lake Erie in 1972–1973 were elevated, and some individuals had extreme values (Hoffman and Curnow 1979). In contrast, concentrations of Hg in livers of adult, juvenile and nestling Black-crowned Night Herons and Great Egrets, and juvenile and nestling Great Blue Herons, were generally within the background range.

Exceptionally high Hg concentrations were also discovered in the livers of four Great Blue Herons (15, 66, 136, and 175 ppm) from Lake St. Clair, USA, in 1970 (Dustman et al. 1972). Elevated levels of Hg in Lake St. Clair were attributed to discharge along the St. Clair and Detroit rivers. Mercury discharge was curtailed in this region in 1970. Concentrations of Hg in Black-crowned Night Heron eggs collected from the Lake St. Clair area declined between 1970 (mean = 0.77 ppm) and 1973 (mean = 0.44 ppm; Stendell et al. 1976).

A combination of high Hg levels and stress from cold and starvation may have contributed to a die-off of Grey Herons in the Netherlands during the winter of 1975–76 (van der Molen et al. 1982). The die-off resulted in an estimated 19% decrease in the breeding population. About 20% of the 41 necropsied herons had extremely high Hg concentrations (>160 ppm dw) in the liver; 2 individuals had lethal levels (>500 ppm dw). The local use of Hg as an agricultural fungicide was the probable source of the contamination.

Mercury concentrations were high (range 0.05–74.5 ppm ww in liver) in herons in Florida, USA, and were related to location, size of fish eaten, age of the heron and to decreased body fat (Sundlof et al. 1994). Great White Herons with >6 ppm Hg in the liver more frequently died from chronic, often multiple, diseases than birds with <6 ppm Hg in the liver (Spalding et al. 1994a). Based on Hg concentrations in feathers, Great White Herons and Great Egrets in southern Florida may be at risk from Hg poisoning (Beyer et al. 1997).

Great Blue Herons in Washington and Idaho, USA (Blus et al. 1985), Lake Erie, USA (Nims 1987), Little Egrets from the Camargue, France (Cosson et al. 1988), Eastern Great White Egrets from central Korea (Honda et al. 1985), and Cattle Egrets in Puerto Rico (Burger et al. 1992) were all within background concentrations of Hg.

Mercury contamination in Grey Herons in England has steadily decreased since the early 1960s (Fig. 12.2; Newton et al. 1993).

Mercury concentrations have been reported in heron eggs (for example by Blus et al. 1985, Custer et al. 1997, Custer et al. 1998, Elliot et al. 1989, Faber and Hickey 1973, Fleming et al. 1984, Fossi et al. 1984, Heinz et al. 1985, Hothem et al. 1995, Mullié et al. 1992, Nims 1987, Ohlendorf et al. 1978a, 1988, Rodgers 1997, Stendell et al. 1976), but are difficult to interpret. The concentration of Hg associated with reproductive failure varies by species (Ohlendorf et al. 1978b) and a critical Hg level in eggs has not been measured for any heron species. Mean concentrations of Hg in Black-crowned Night Heron eggs from Lake St. Clair (Stendell et al. 1976) and San Francisco Bay (Ohlendorf et al. 1988) were above the 0.5 ppm level reported to affect Ring-necked Pheasant (*Phasianus colchicus*) reproduction (Fimreite 1971), but below that reported to affect reproduction in Mallard (*Anas platyrhynchos*) (0.85 ppm; Heinz 1979), Common Tern (*Sterna hirundo*) (1.0 ppm; Connors et al. 1975), or Herring Gull (*Larus argentatus*) (>16 ppm; Vermeer et al. 1973).

Lead (Pb). Aquatic birds at risk from Pb include water birds that frequent hunted areas and ingest Pb shot, avian predators that eat game wounded by hunters, and aquatic birds feeding near smelters, refineries, and Pb battery recycling plants (Eisler 1988). Herons and egrets are generally not at risk from Pb, because they do not normally ingest Pb shot and forms of Pb other than shot do not generally cause clinical signs of Pb poisoning in birds.

Lead concentrations in livers of herons were within the range of background concentrations (<6.7 ppm dw) in livers of other wild birds (Friend 1985), including Grey Herons in the Netherlands (Hontelez et al. 1992), Great Blue Herons in Washington and Idaho, USA (Blus et al. 1985), Black-crowned Night Herons along the Atlantic coast, USA (Custer and Mulhern 1983), Little Egrets from the Camargue, France (Cosson et al. 1988), Tricoloured Herons and Cattle Egrets from Texas, USA (Hulse et al. 1980; Cheney et al. 1981), Cattle Egrets from India (Husain and Kaphalia 1990), Eastern Great White Egrets from central Korea (Honda et al. 1985), and Great Blue Herons, Snowy Egrets, and Cattle Egrets from south Florida (Rodgers 1997).

Cadmium (Cd). Cadmium contamination of the environment can be severe in the vicinity of smelters and urban industrialised areas (Eisler 1985a). There is no evidence that Cd, a relatively rare heavy metal, is biologically essential or beneficial; on the contrary, Cd is a known teratogen and carcinogen, and is a probable mutagen. Cadmium concentrations may be greatly elevated in the tissues of some estuarine and marine birds, such as shearwaters, fulmars, puffins, murres, and scoters (Ohlendorf 1993). Lesions have been observed in the kidneys of some pelagic seabirds having high concentrations of Cd in their tissues.

Herons generally do not accumulate Cd. Grey Herons in the Netherlands (Hontelez et al. 1992), Great Blue Herons in Washington and Idaho, USA (Blus et al. 1985) and Lake Erie, USA (Nims 1987), Black-crowned Night Herons along the Atlantic coast, USA (Custer and Mulhern 1983), Little Egrets from the Camargue, France (Cosson et al. 1988), Tricoloured Herons and Cattle Egrets from Texas, USA (Hulse et al. 1980, Cheney et al. 1981), Cattle Egrets from India (Husain and Kaphalia 1990), Eastern Great White Egrets from central Korea (Honda et al. 1985), and Cattle Egrets from Baja California, Mexico (Mora and Anderson 1995) were all within background Cd concentrations of <3 ppm dw in the liver and <8 ppm dw in the kidney (Scheuhammer 1987).

Selenium (Se). Selenium is a naturally-occurring trace element that is essential for animal nutrition, but the range between dietary requirements and toxic levels is relatively narrow (Eisler 1985b, Ohlendorf 1989). Disposal of Se-containing fly ash from coal-fired power plants and drainage water from agricultural fields can increase the potential for adverse effects of Se on wildlife. Selenium from agricultural drainage water accumulated to high enough levels in plants and animals to cause mortality and impair reproduction of aquatic birds at several areas throughout the western USA (Ohlendorf 1989).

High Se concentrations have not been documented in herons. Background Se concentrations in livers of several species of birds from freshwater averaged 1–3 ppm (4–10 ppm dw) and normal egg concentrations were 0.4–0.8 ppm (1–3 ppm dw; Ohlendorf 1989). Selenium concentrations within this background level were reported in livers of Little Egrets from the Camargue, France (Cosson et al. 1988), in livers of Cattle Egrets from Mexicali Valley, Baja California, Mexico (Mora and Anderson 1995), in eggs and livers of Great Blue Herons from Lake Erie, USA (Nims 1987), and in eggs of Black-crowned Night Herons (five colonies) and Great Egrets (one colony) from California, USA (Ohlendorf and Marois 1990). Somewhat elevated Se concentrations were found in Great Blue Heron eggs from the Upper Mississippi River, USA (mean = 3.1 ppm dw, Custer et al. 1997) and Indiana, USA (mean = 4.0 ppm dw, Custer et al. 1998), Grey Heron (mean = 3.5 ppm dw) and Black-crowned Night Heron eggs (mean = 5.9 ppm dw) from the Delta of the Danube (Fossi et al. 1984), Black-crowned Night Heron eggs (mean = 1.1 ppm) from the Salton Sea, California, USA (Ohlendorf and Marois 1990), and Black-crowned Night Heron (colony means = 2.9–5.7 ppm dw) and Snowy Egret (colony means = 3.0–5.3 ppm dry weight) eggs from San Francisco Bay, California (Hothem et al. 1995). Captive Black-crowned Night Herons were not as sensitive to dietary Se as were mallards, which in turn were less sensitive than chickens (Smith et al. 1988).

Petroleum

Birds are affected by petroleum through external oiling, ingestion, egg oiling, and habitat changes (Ohlendorf et al. 1978b, Albers 1991). External oiling causes matting of feathers and eye irritation; mortality often results from hypothermia and drowning. Petroleum can be ingested through feather preening, consumption of contaminated food and water, and inhalation of fumes from evaporating oil. Ingestion of oil is seldom fatal, but it can cause many debilitating sub-lethal effects that produce mortality from other causes, including starvation, disease, and predators. Avian embryos are highly sensitive to petroleum (Hoffman 1990); small quantities of some types of oil are sufficient to cause death, particularly during early stages of incubation. Petroleum spilled in avian habitats can have immediate and long-term direct and indirect effects on birds. Fumes from evaporating oil, shortage of food, and clean-up activities can reduce use of an affected area, but long-term effects are more difficult to document.

Genetic damage in Black-crowned Night Heron embryos in Louisiana and chicks in Texas was suspected to be caused by petroleum-related contamination (Custer et

Great Blue Heron found dead after being exposed to oil. Photo: James Runningen.

al. 1994). The coefficient of variation of DNA content (CV) of blood collected from embryos suggested cytogenetic damage at a site in Louisiana known to be contaminated with petroleum. Blood CV from chicks suggested genetic damage at a site in Texas also known to be contaminated with petroleum.

Operational Issues

While considerable research has been conducted on some contaminants in some species, there are significant gaps in knowledge. In order to establish levels of contamination, baseline contaminant information should be gathered from countries not yet well sampled, especially developing countries. Beyond baselines, long-term studies on trends in residues should be encouraged. The long-term study on organochlorine and Hg residues in Grey Herons (Newton et al. 1993) is a good example of the value of such studies. Investigation should especially be conducted on species and locations where the effects of specific contaminants measured are not well understood: for example, Pond Herons and Cattle Egrets nesting in India in relation to increasing use of HCH (Ramesh et al. 1992). Studies on species and locations reported or suspected to have population declines or reproductive problems should be continued. Additional biomarkers need to be developed that can rapidly screen heron populations for potential contaminant problems (Chapter 15).

Even though most of the approaches presented in this chapter are often technical and expensive, there are steps that can be taken by local managers to evaluate the potential threat of environmental contaminants to local and regional heron populations. Long-term population surveys of breeding herons either by amateur or professional ornithologists should be encouraged. If population declines are suspected, this information can be used to lever more intensive investigations. Field research on breeding herons should also be encouraged. Intensive investigations, even if not focused on contaminants, can give important clues to the health of particular colonies. For example, observations of chick deformities or reduced reproduction may lead to further study. Finally, these research efforts should be intensified in habitats suspected to be contaminated, such as areas associated with intensive agricultural or industrial activity.

Conclusions

Except for anecdotal evidence concerning Black-crowned Night Herons from New England and Michigan and Cattle Egrets from the Nile Delta, Egypt, no heron population declines worldwide were noted following the use of organochlorine insecticides in the mid-1940s. This is in sharp contrast to raptor population declines in Europe and North America. Following the use of organochlorine insecticides in the mid-1940s, acute mortality associated mainly with dieldrin, a highly toxic organochlorine, was documented in herons. Eggshell thinning was documented in several heron species after the mid-1940s and DDE concentrations in eggs were correlated with eggshell thinning and reduced reproductive success. After the ban on DDT and dieldrin, organochlorine concentrations decreased significantly in herons both in Britain and North America. Hot spots of organochlorine insecticide contamination still remain, however, that may affect local populations of herons. PCBs and dioxins may be responsible for decreased reproductive success in herons, but the effects seem localised. Organophosphorous and carbamate pesticides, trace elements (mercury, lead, cadmium, and selenium), and petroleum do not seem to have had a significant impact on heron populations. Hot spots of mercury were reported and may have been partially responsible for a 19% decline in the breeding population of Grey Herons in the Netherlands in 1976. Mercury concentrations in herons, however, have steadily decreased since that time.

13. Aquaculture

Loïc Marion

Aquaculture is the captive rearing of aquatic animals, including fish, molluscs, crustaceans, reptiles or amphibians. Aquaculture has been around for thousands of years and has probably always come into conflict with natural competitors such as fish-eating birds. The idea that species are to be deemed useful or harmful to human activities developed in Europe in the nineteenth century, and in the early twentieth century in the USA (Draulans 1988). Any species that could potentially feed on crops, domesticated livestock or even wild animals used by man was considered a pest and doomed to various forms of persecution (d'Hamonville 1898, Pycraft 1934, Hewitt 1936, Ikeda 1952). Fish-eating Ardeidae were immediately grouped into this category (Creutz 1981), although the true impact of these birds was little understood. There were major consequences to some European heron populations, particularly the Grey Heron (Chapter 1), which, once hunted, became a part of hunting culture, especially in Latin countries (France, Spain, Portugal). Many aquacultural management practices produce a concentrated, easily available food source for herons, which are well adapted to find these concentrations of prey. Conflict between herons and aquaculture remains a worldwide concern for heron conservation and is increasing as aquaculture further develops. On the other hand, food resources provided by aquaculture appear to have had a positive influence on some heron populations (Huner 1995).

The Aquacultural Industry

At least 152 species are raised in aquaculture in North America alone (Price and Nickum 1993). Worldwide, aquaculture is dominated by the carp, 40% of production by weight as of 1993 (ICLARM 1995); in contrast salmonids accounted for 3.8% and shrimp 5.6%. In each country, one or two species dominate, based largely on the cultural preferences of the market. Catfish account for a third of production in the USA in 1800 fish farms but are considered a trash species in Europe. Cyprinids dominate in eastern Europe and Asia; trout are reared preferentially in France and salmon in Norway, Scotland, the Faeroes, and Chile (Folsom and Sanborn 1992). Specialised production sometimes dominates in certain regions, such as ornamental aquarium fish in Florida (Price and Nickum 1993) and Italy (Tinarelli et al. 1993) and crawfish in Louisiana (Huner 1993a, 1995).

China leads world aquacultural production with 6.7 million tons of carp, molluscs and shrimp in 1988, followed by Japan (Price and Nickum 1993). Asia accounts for 81.5% of the estimated world production of about 16 million tons, compared to 11.4% for Europe, 5% for North America, 2% for South America and only 0.1% for Africa (Anonymous 1994b). Eleven countries produce more than 80% of the world's aquacultural products, six of them being developing countries of China, India, Indonesia, Philippines, Thailand and Bangladesh. Other important producers are Japan, the USA, South Korea, France and Taiwan (ICLARM 1995). Aquaculture is widespread in the tropics because of the more optimal growing conditions there, and that segment of the industry is expanding rapidly. Production increased in these countries by 78% between 1984 and 1993 (82% of world production), compared to a 26% rise in developed countries. Aquacultural expansion in tropical countries is often to the detriment of coastal wetlands (ICLARM 1995), posing considerable threat to those populations of herons that depend on these natural habitats. Fish farming conflicts and reduction of natural habitats in tropical countries can affect both resident and wintering birds.

Aquaculture is now a worldwide phenomenon, accounting for 16 million tons in 1993, i.e. 22% of wild catch (ICLARM 1995), compared to 8.7 million tons produced in 1980 (Price and Nickum 1993). The latter authors predicted that world aquacultural production would probably reach 20 to 22 million tons in about the year 2000, accounting for 25% of world fish production (40% in terms of value), and according to ICLARM (1995) will be 33 million tons in 2010.

Character of the Conflict

Conflict between fish farmers and fish-eating birds goes back to the earliest days of aquaculture but has intensified in extent and impact in the current century. In one of the regions of Europe most noted for its herons, the Danube Delta, thousands of nests and entire colonies of any bird suspected of eating fish were destroyed between 1949 and 1953 (Catuneanu 1958), and 106 340 fish-eating birds were killed as late as 1956 (Paspaleva et al. 1985). In Denmark, between 4000 and 7000 herons were killed each year until 1979, 29% of them at fish farms, equivalent to 25% of the autumn population in the country (Moller and Olesen 1983). The problem was somewhat less intense in other continents, because of lower farming intensity and human population density and because of differing cultural impediments to killing birds. Protection was especially encouraged by cultural practices in parts of Africa and India. On the other hand, in China after Mao it was considered a civic duty to kill pest birds. Conservation movements began sufficiently early in the twentieth century in the USA and some other western countries (Fortbush 1921) so as to avoid, or at least postpone, the situation that occurred in Europe at that time. In Europe, protective measures appeared in the 1940s but only became effective in the 1970s in many countries. Protection has resulted in an astonishing recovery in the populations of some species of herons in Europe (Marion 1997a, Chapter 1).

Paradoxically, however, this recovery brought about new conflicts with fish farmers in regions where for decades they had become accustomed to living without herons (Bungenberg de Jong et al. 1989). From the 1980s onwards, protests from fish farmers and fishermen became more vociferous (Marion 1983a, Utschick 1983a, Draulans 1988, van Vessem et al. 1985, Marion 1997a). Legalised killing to reduce depredation is increasingly leading to fears of reduced protection. Illegal shooting is common and poisoning of Grey Herons on fish farms may be widespread in Belgium and France (van Vessem et al. 1985, Marion pers. obs.). Even in the United Kingdom, illegal shooting at fish farms accounted for 4600 Grey Herons killed each year (Cadbury and Fitzherberg-Brockholes 1983).

In the United States where protective laws are strong, conflicts have become increasingly numerous since the late 1980s (Scanlon et al. 1978, Parkhurst et al. 1987, Hoy et al. 1989, Stickley and Andrews 1989, Williams 1992). The number of permits to kill increased 55-fold between 1986 and 1991 in the most important fish farming region in the south-eastern USA (Huner 1993a). For a long time, shooting and trapping were the methods most frequently used against birds by fish farmers in the USA (Lagler 1939, Randall 1975). The latter reported that fish farmers in nine eastern states in the USA destroyed 10 000 birds in one year, including Great Blue Herons and Black-crowned Night Herons. This slaughter was roundly condemned by the conservation community (Morrisson 1975, Randall 1975), which demanded non-lethal methods be used (Mott 1978). Nevertheless illegal killing is becoming ever more frequent, with up to 20 000 birds known to have been killed on a single fish farm, including 200 night herons poisoned with cyanide in a single night (Williams 1992). In California, one fish farm killed 15 000 cormorants and herons over five years (Conniff 1991). These conflicts derive primarily from a considerable development in aquaculture in wetlands, whose national production increased 5-fold between 1980 and 1990 (Price and Nickum 1993). In Louisiana, it is likely that the increase in the area of crawfish farms can explain the growth in the wintering populations of herons and ibises since 1949 (Fleury 1993).

As in the past, accusations now made by fish farmers against fish-eating birds are seldom substantiated as having serious economic consequences (Mills 1967, Creutz 1981, Marion 1983a, 1989b, 1990a, 1997a,e, Draulans 1988, Huner 1993a, Marquiss and Carss 1994). There are many studies of the diet of herons and other fish-eating birds, but very few of them deal with their impact on prey populations (Bungenberg de Jong et al. 1989). Such a study would require simultaneous studies of both the fish and bird populations (Mills 1967, Draulans 1988, Marion 1990a, Marquiss and Carss 1994). The presence of fish-eating birds at an aquaculture facility is highly visible and seems to compel the farmer to take action. The condemnation of fish-eating birds often seems to be a gut-level reaction separated from proven economic consequences (see Alexander 1977). The diversity of situations and the small number of studies make it difficult to assess real impacts of heron predation. There is little in common between an extensive lake or marsh fish farm, where the fish population dynamics follow natural rules, and an intensive fish farm where attempts are made to control all variables. Professional fishermen and sports anglers also have different attitudes towards predators depending on whether they are on natural habitats (sea, rivers) or recreational water bodies. Growing heron populations tend to bring on adverse attention (Draulans and van Vessem 1985a).

The Species of Herons Incriminated

Of the 60 species of heron (Hancock and Kushlan 1984), 90% are piscivorous from the semi-quantitative data provided by these authors, and at least half of the species have a diet consisting mainly of fish (Table 13.1). Among these, very few have actually been accused of causing damage at fish farms. Those causing damage are the largest, most abundant and frequently gregarious species, which are likely to capture the largest number or size of prey. For these reasons, the Grey Heron is the most frequently incriminated species in Europe. This is expected in those countries

Table 13.1   Percentage of fish in heron diet, generally from Hancock and Kushlan 1984.

0% fish

Whistling Heron	Black-headed Heron	Cattle Egret
White-eared Night Heron	Javan Pond Heron	Malayan Night Heron

0 to 20% fish

White-backed Night Heron	White-faced Heron	Squacco Heron
Yellow-crowned Night Heron	Nankeen Night Heron	White-necked Heron
Japanese Night Heron	Boat-billed Heron	Yellow Bittern
African Dwarf Bittern	Australian Bittern	

20 to 50% fish

Pied Heron	Black Heron	Little Egret
Swinhoe's Egret	Eastern Reef Heron	Chinese Pond Heron
Black-crowned Night Heron	Rufous-bellied Heron	Malagasy Pond Heron
New Guinea Tiger Heron	Streaked Bittern	Little Bittern
South American Bittern	Cinnamon Bittern	American Bittern

50 to 80% fish

Capped Heron	Grey Heron	Great Blue Heron
Cocoi Heron	Imperial Heron	Sumatran Heron
Goliath Heron	Purple Heron	Great White Egret
Slaty Heron	Tricoloured Heron	Intermediate Egret
Little Blue Heron	Snowy Egret	Western Reef Heron
Bare-throated Tiger Heron	Green-backed Heron	Indian Pond Heron
White-crested Tiger Heron	Rufescent Tiger Heron	Fasciated Tiger Heron
Zigzag Heron	Least Bittern	Schrenk's Bittern
Black Bittern	Eurasian Bittern	

80 to 100% fish

Malagasy Heron	Reddish Egret	Agami Heron

Because the Grey Heron is among the most piscivorous herons, fish farmers in many parts of the world consider this bird a pest. Photo: Jacques Delpech.

where it is the only colonial species (the United Kingdom, Belgium, Scandinavia, Switzerland and Cyprus), but also in many other countries such as France, the Netherlands, Italy, Germany, the Czech Republic, Slovakia and Austria (Creutz 1961, Meyer 1981, van Vessem 1982, Marion 1983a, 1990a, 1997a, Anonymous 1984a, Utschick 1984a, Bungenberg de Jong et al. 1989, Carss 1993). This is also the case in Israel, but the Black-crowned Night Heron also poses problems there (Ashkenazi and Yom-Tov 1993), as it does locally in Italy (Tinarelli et al. 1993) and in France (Marion 1983a). In North America, the Great Blue Heron is considered to be the main heron predator (Mills 1980, Hanebrink and Byrd 1989, Price and Nickum 1993, Ross 1995), but the Black-crowned Night Heron and Great White Egret are also implicated. In addition to the herons, ibises are of concern on crawfish farms in Louisiana (Huner 1993a). No Asiatic, African or South American species is mentioned in the literature as causing an overwhelming problem.

The inquiry conducted by the EIFAC Working Party (Bungenberg de Jong et al.

1989) on the impact of fish-eating birds in all European countries plus Israel clearly indicates the general opinion of fish farmers towards herons. These birds are accused not only of predation but also of wounding fish, transmitting diseases to them and disturbing them. However, herons were on the whole judged to cause less damage than cormorants, pelicans, gulls and grebes in those countries where these birds are abundant (Israel, Hungary, the Netherlands, Romania, and since 1990, France) or where their attacks are concentrated on particular types of fish farm (by gulls in Ireland, for example). Fish-eating birds only account for a part of the predation. In Canada for instance, the Great Blue Heron is only responsible for 4% of the predation on salmon rearing facilities, the great majority of the losses being due to seals (Price and Nickum 1993). It must not be overlooked that the fish themselves can be predators both in natural environments (Nillson and Nillson 1976) and in fish farms (Marion and Marion 1987b).

The Diversity of Production Systems

There are as many situations as there are types of fish farms. Three main categories of inland fishery activity can be distinguished, intensive aquaculture, extensive aquaculture, and harvest in open waters. The areas and annual yield for each category in 1989 are given in Fig. 13.1. Since then, trout rearing has greatly increased

Success in catching fish by the Grey Heron requires elaborate behaviour, experience, and favourable prey availability. Photo: Jean François Hellio and Nicolas van Ingen.

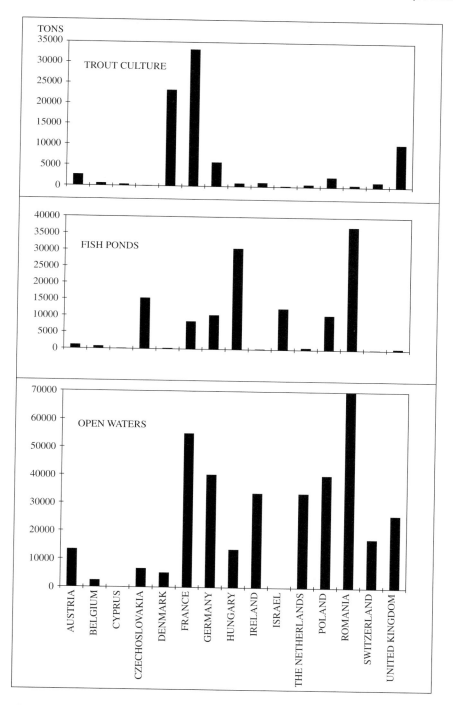

Fig. 13.1   Annual production of fish in Europe and Israel in 1989.

(for example, 50 000 tons in France in 1993), whereas the yield from extensive fish pond aquaculture seems to have remained stable (Anonymous 1994b).

Intensive aquaculture specialises in the rearing of Salmonidae. It has developed relatively recently (end of the nineteenth century in Europe) and has increased greatly since 1960. The ponds are small with steep banks, and are either close to trout rivers or cold springs or on the coast in floating cages, in fresh or saline (Scotland, Norway) waters. They are semi-industrial operations. They occur especially in Europe (Norway, France, the United Kingdom, Germany, Austria, Belgium, Denmark), in Asia (Japan, China), and in the United States and Canada.

Extensive pond culture is the more traditional form of aquaculture, dating from 2400 years ago in China, 1900 years ago in Japan and from the Middle Ages in Europe, when flat areas with poor soils were converted into fish ponds. In Europe they are mostly restricted to the countries of the former Soviet Union, Romania, Hungary, Poland, Germany, the Czech Republic, Slovakia and France. This type of habitat is rare in mountainous countries (Scandinavia and Switzerland) and for historical reasons in the United Kingdom and other continents, except for Israel where they were introduced by eastern European immigrants. Rice fields are used as supplementary fish- or shrimp-producing systems in China, Japan, India, the USA and Africa (Billard 1980). In Japan and Thailand, salines are being reconverted into fish ponds.

Fish harvest also occurs by amateur or professional fishing in the natural environment (lakes, rivers) or in artificial ponds not created as fish ponds. This type of activity is found in countries with vast marshes or a dense network of water bodies, such as South-east Asia, the great lakes of Africa, to some extent in North America and more locally in Europe (Romania, Ukraine, France, Germany, Norway, Sweden, Poland, the Netherlands and Ireland). The world freshwater fish catch has only slightly increased in the last 20 years and currently stands at six million tons, of which Asia accounts for two-thirds, followed by Africa, the main species being carp and tilapias (ICLARM 1995). In addition to this professional catch is that of amateur anglers, especially in the United States, Europe (4.5 million in France, 3 million in the United Kingdom, and 1 million in the Netherlands and in Norway, Marion 1989a).

The attractiveness of aquatic sites to birds varies greatly depending on how the sites are built and the number, size, and quality of potential prey. Water depth, steepness of banks, occurrence of perches, and tranquillity affect the suitability of a site, which often is the result of centuries-old traditions of fish pond creation (Draulans 1987a, 1988). In trout farming, the annual yield per hectare varies from 0.8 tons/ha in Belgium to 57 tons in Denmark and even 187 tons in Ireland (From 1989). Large extensive fish ponds are much less attractive. They have yields of 40 to 500 kg/ha/year in Europe, except in Hungary where yields reach 1400 kg and in Israel where 4000 kg is reported, and where artificial feeding makes these fish ponds more similar to intensive ponds (Bungenberg de Jong et al. 1989). This is also the case in China (Tapiador et al. 1977). In rice fields, yields vary between 70 and 1100 kg/ha/year (Borgstrom 1978, Billard 1980). The yield from natural environments, where amateur and professional fishing takes place, is largely unknown; the number of fishermen is estimated to be 15 million in Europe, who take about 100 000 tons (ca. 6.4 kg/ha/year, Bungenberg de Jong et al. 1989). In China, the yield from lakes and reservoirs averages 373 kg/ha/year (Tapiador et al. 1977).

Predation Rates by Herons

Quantitative studies of heron predation

There are few quantitative studies of the true impact of the predation exerted by herons, covering some of the many types of production systems. Predation in natural habitats appears to be variable according to the situation (Table 13.2) so the evaluation is divided into natural and artificial habitats (Fortbush 1921, Bowmaker 1963, Utschick 1984a,b). In two studies, Grey Herons took only about 6% of available prey from a permanently flooded wetland in France and trout rivers in Switzerland (Feunteun and Marion 1989, 1994, Geiger 1983, 1984a,b, Fischbacher 1984, Kramer 1984, Müller 1984, Swiss studies summarised in Anonymous 1984a). Utschick (1984a) supported these conclusions, showing that Grey Herons had no effect on trout density and represented compensatory mortality. Based on the Swiss results, especially that heron predation contributed partly toward decreasing major causes of mortality, the Swiss working group (including fishery and environmental authorities, fishery interests and conservationists) concluded that priority should be given to protecting the Grey Heron.

Predation in natural areas can be much higher when high densities of fish are

Table 13.2 Review of studies measuring heron predation rate on fresh water fish stocks.

Authors	Species	Predation[1]		Habitat and Country
NATURAL HABITAT				
Kushlan 1976	wading birds	76%	B-N	seasonal pond, USA
Pinowski et al. 1980	wading birds	32%	B	seasonally-flooded savanna, Venezuela
Geiger 1984b, Anon. 1984	Grey Heron	6.3%	B	trout rivers, Switzerland
Feunteun & Marion 1994	Grey Heron	6.5%	B	natural marshes, France
ARTIFICIAL HABITAT				
Marion 1990a	Grey Heron	0.3%	B	extensive fish ponds, France
Perennou 1986	Grey Heron	1.4%	N	intensive fish pond, France
Ashkenazi & Yom-Tov 1993	BCNH and Little Egret	12.8%[2]	N	intensive fish pond, Israel
Meyer 1981	Grey Heron	0.4%	N	intensive fish farm, England
Marion & Marion 1987b	Grey Heron	1%	B	intensive fish farm, France
Ransom & Beveridge 1983	Grey Heron	0%	N	intensive cage farm, Scotland
Carss 1993	Grey Heron	4%[3]	N	intensive cage farm, Scotland
Génard et al. 1988	Grey Heron	3%[4]	N	experimental pond, France
Le Louarn 1988	Grey Heron	36%[4]	N	experimental ponds, France

[1] B= on biomass, N= on number
[2] not measured and probably overestimated due to data from captivity
[3] recalculated from the 7% mentioned by the author in order to obtain the predation for the whole fish farm
[4] overestimated because the number of fish was non-representative of commercial fish farms

In northern countries Grey Herons resist well to winter cold and are therefore the cause of concern throughout the year. Photo: Jean François Hellio and Nicolas van Ingen.

concentrated by falling water levels. In the Everglades, falling water level concentrates fish in water holes, where herons (Great Blue Heron, Great White Heron, Snowy Egret, Little Blue Heron, Tricoloured Egret, Black-crowned Night Heron) and also ibis and storks feed on them. Bird predation led to a 76% decrease in biomass, whereas without predation the reduction due to oxygen depletion (higher density of fish) was 93% (Kushlan 1976). The finding that the birds' predation was compensatory for other mortality bears study in other systems. In one such study, in rather similar seasonally-flooded wetlands in Venezuela, Pinowski et al. (1980) recorded a lower predation rate by wading birds (32%), this predation also having a beneficial effect.

In artificial habitats, studies have generally found predation impact to be relatively low (Table 13.2). In most quantitative, comparative studies (for example Marion 1990a, Perennou 1986, Génard et al. 1988), predation was low compared to other losses of fish. Perennou (1986) found predation by a territorial Grey Heron accounted for 2% loss in a fry-rearing pond compared to 73% lost for other reasons including heat stress, feeding problems, lack of oxygen, stranding on the mud or grid during emptying and predation by dytiscus beetles. Comparing protected and unprotected parts of ponds, Génard et al. (1988) found predation rates 3% of the fish in the unprotected portion, despite its being of a very favourable feeding depth; natural mortality in the protected part amounted to 33%. On the other hand, predation by cormorants was much higher (64%). Higher rates were found in small ponds by Le Louarn (1988): the Grey Herons' take was of 36% compared to 22% loss in protected ponds. In Israel, predation on carp was estimated to be 12.8% of initial stock (Ashkenazi 1985, Ashkenazi and Yom-Tov 1993), based on energetic calculations. The economic impact was on the whole low, especially as herons preferentially capture parasitised fish, and they fed especially when dying fish became available as the ponds were dried. A study by Draulans (1988) attributing a loss of 8% in fish ponds is not cited in Table 13.2 because of imprecisions in the calculations.

Studies have generally shown predation rates to be relatively low in intensive pisciculture, in most cases contrary to the impressions of the farmers. One of the largest trout farms in England, thought to be subject to heavy predation (leading to the killing of 88 Grey Herons), in fact suffered a predation rate of 0.4% of the annual yield (Meyer 1980, 1981, Cadbury and Fitzherberg-Brockholes 1983). Accidents accounted for 2.5 times the annual predation. In an identical situation in France, predation accounted for only 1% of losses (Marion and Marion 1987b). On the basis of monitoring fish numbers alone, the study pond subject to predation had higher losses than the control, but it turned out that these were due to an epidemic and to male trout responding to migratory instinct and crowding (Utschick 1984a), leaping from the ponds onto the banks, where the fish farmer found them in the morning and accused the resident heron of having taken them from the water without eating them. This study demonstrates the importance of monitoring all the variables, since if the study had restricted itself to just comparing the total losses between the two ponds it would have arrived at a predation level that was 14 times higher than reality.

When an intensive fish pond is highly attractive relative to natural feeding sites, for example when the density of accessible fish is much higher than in the natural environment, heron predation can occur even if it is protected by nets. A floating-cage trout farm in Scotland suffered 6.6% loss and 0.5% injury of fish from heron predation through the nets, whereas mortality not due to predation was 10% (Carss 1993). At another farm with netted cages, herons injured 2.5% of the fish present through the net (Ransom and Beveridge 1983).

Other predation reports

Other reports on bird predation, usually observational rather than experimental, give higher rates. The 1990 statistics of the U.S. Department of Agriculture indicated

A fish pond in France protected against avian predators with wire and ropes. Photo: Pierrick Marion.

that predation by fish-eating birds on catfish farms only accounted for 9% of the total mortality (Price and Nickum 1993). More locally, bird predation is reported to be 32% of total catfish mortality in North Carolina, 24% in Missouri and 22% in Oklahoma, 15% in Florida (Anonymous 1991, in Price and Nickum 1993). These figures do not however seem derived from detailed, experimental studies but from the declarations of the fish farmers, which is why they cannot be included in the review of scientific data (Table 13.2).

These reports refer to impacts of all fish-eating birds, not just herons. The body of work on predation by fish-eating birds and aquaculture suggests that herons cause far less loss than most other species of concern to the industry. Cormorants, for example, can take 20–50% of the fish stock (Suter 1991). Pelicans, due to their large body size and efficient feeding methods, may have even more impact. The relatively small role that herons play in predation can be explained partly by their anatomy (which restricts them to shallow water) and secondly because of their feeding behaviour which is less efficient than in other fish-eaters (cormorants, pelicans, mammals). Nillson and Nillson (1976) have already estimated, by an indirect energetic approach, that the Grey Heron only takes 10% of the fish consumed by fish-eating birds in Swedish lakes, and that predatory fish consume as many prey as the birds, which reduces heron predation to 5% of the total. In France, an important country for Grey Heron, Marion (1997a) estimated that the species only takes a very small percentage of the whole national fish stock.

Other sources of stock loss

In rivers, 75–90% of trout disappeared each year for many reasons (Utschick 1984a). In fish farms the non-predation losses were estimated to be 73% by Perennou (1986), 33% by Génard et al. (1988) and by Ashkenazi and Yom-Tov (1993), 22% by Le Louarn (1988), 17% by Marion and Marion (1987b), and 10% by Carss (1993). Meyer (1981) also cited cases of very high mortality which over short periods could exceed annual predation losses by 2.5 times. The 1990 statistics of the U.S. Department of Agriculture indicated that disease (46%), floods and oxygenation stress were the most important mortality factors, but curiously, predation was emotionally ranked first by fish farmers (Price and Nickum 1993). For catfish, 70% of losses nationally were due to disease and another 10% to oxygen depletion, while birds accounted for only 7% (Conniff 1991). In Florida poor water quality was the main cause of losses (56%), with predation and disease each accounting for 15% (Anonymous 1991, in Price and Nickum 1993). Also in Florida, disease accounted for 27–32% of losses from ornamental tropical fish farms, compared to 24% for predation (not just birds), whereas poor water quality was responsible for 11–12% and other and unknown causes 32–35% (Anonymous 1992 in Price and Nickum 1993). According to a recent worldwide report by ICLARM (1995), traditional non-integrated fish farmers, on a world scale, face suffering total production losses at least once and possibly twice every ten years from a variety of causes including: disease, equipment breakdown, adverse weather conditions, eutrophication and theft.

Conclusions on predation

The objective studies on heron predation reviewed in this chapter found that documented predation losses were low. For eleven studies (minus those of naturally falling water levels) the mean is 6.52% ± 3.16. Excluding also one study in which predation was estimated indirectly (Ashkenazi and Yom-Tov 1993) and the two conducted on low numbers of fish, mean predation rate was 2.49% ± 1.2 (N= 8 studies). Injuries inflicted on non-ingested fish also were found to be at relatively low levels in aquacultural cases where they have been quantified (Meyer 1981: 0.016%; Carss 1993: 0.5%; Ransom and Beveridge 1983: 2.5%; Carss 1988: 3.6%), although it is higher for trout in rivers (Utschick 1980: 3–17%). Losses to predation by herons are low relative to other sources of mortality, especially disease, accidents, and water quality, and the impact of herons is also much lower than other predation losses.

The true importance to fish population dynamics of losses attributed either directly or indirectly to predation is always difficult to assess. In the absence of detailed studies, it is still debatable whether these losses are additional to natural mortality, or whether they partly or entirely substitute for it, in which case they would have no effect on the final fish yield. It is probable that predation is additive in intensive fish farms and canalised rivers (Suter 1991) but is more or less compensatory in more natural habitats.

Other Damage Attributed to Herons

In addition to direct predation and causing injuries, fish farmers also blame herons for such damage as transmitting diseases, reducing production because of stress, and for preventing fish from feeding. These charges are difficult to prove or disprove, or to estimate the extent of effect.

It is particularly difficult to assess what role herons and other fish-eating birds may have in transmitting fish diseases (Beveridge 1989). Fish diseases are most often transported by water or between fish, and according to Michel (1983), fish viruses do not survive for long in birds, as their body temperature is unsuitable. Studies finding fish pathogens in birds' faeces suggest that birds can theoretically transport some fish pathogens (Eskildsen and Vestergaard Jorgensen 1973, Taylor and Lott 1978, Flick 1983, Olesen and Vestergaard Jorgensen 1982, Peters and Neukirch 1986, Willumsen 1989). There are no studies of epidemiology, on actual transmission, or even the viability and infectiousness of pathogens in or on herons.

Birds have been shown to play a role in transmitting two viruses that occur in both North American and European fish farms: IPN (Infectious Pancreatic Necrosis) by gulls and VHS (Viral Haemorrhagic Septicaemia) by herons (de Kinkelin et al. 1985). Paradoxically, the tests conducted by Sonstegard and McDermott (1972), intended to show that IPN, the most resistant virus known, could survive in the alimentary tract of herons, were very inconclusive according to Michel (1983). VHS can survive a few hours on a heron's beak but transmission by this route is not demonstrated. According to Michel (1983) and Stickley (1990), birds could only play an insignificant role compared to other means of transmission. According to de Kinkelin et al. (1985) the main vectors for viruses and bacteria are the boots and hands of man, plus vehicles and the transport of fish and equipment.

A recent study on IPN virus in birds is full of errors of interpretation (McAllister and Owens 1992). This study collected faeces (duck, heron, and mixtures of various species) directly from the earth, pontoons and dykes of fish farms and in a few cases from drowned birds, and compared the virus content with those of the kidneys and spleens of farmed salmon. The authors concluded that the occurrence of viruses in the faeces proved that birds could be contaminated and could transmit viruses. Difficulties in the study included non-aseptic methods of faeces collection, no study of virus viability or epidemiology, and failure to explain absence of pathogens in dead birds. The results of this study could equally well be interpreted completely differently: (i) that the fish were just as heavily contaminated when birds were present as when they were absent, (ii) that other more abundant species of birds at the fish farms were more contaminated than herons (71% compared to 28%), and (iii) that a wide range of environmental factors could contribute to infestation. The figures could demonstrate that potentially the role of herons is very slight to zero, a conclusion not shared by the authors.

Although the role of herons in the transmission of viral and bacterial diseases remains unproven, birds are certainly involved in the transmission of some parasites (cestodes and trematodes), for which they are obligate third and final hosts, following a mollusc or crustacean and then a fish. In Europe the life cycle of the cestode *Ligula intestinalis* includes any bird species, copepods and then fish. The worm occupies most of the fish's abdominal cavity and renders it more liable to predation. The trematode *Posthodiphostomum cuticola,* which causes melanosis, is transmitted by gulls, cormorants and herons to planorbid snails and then from these to fish, which acquire black spots, rendering them unsuitable for sale, but there is little mortality except for fry. *Diplostomum spathaceum,* which causes cataract and can make fish blind, is transmitted by gulls and cormorants (but not herons) to *Lymnaea* snails which contaminate the fish. Taraschewski and Paperna (1982) showed that the infestation of a fish by a trematode (Heteropyidae) in two sites in a mangrove lagoon in Egypt was higher close to a colony of *Ardea gularis,* the presumed definitive host. This study has the advantage of being comparative, but the disadvantage of being correlative. Comparative, experimental, causal studies are needed.

Injuries inflicted by herons favour secondary bacterial or fungal infections (Michel 1983, Bungenberg de Jong et al. 1989, Carss and Marquiss 1992, Price and Nickum 1993). The extent of such secondary infections is also influenced by water quality, crowding, handling and other elements of culturing (Utschick 1984a, Michel 1983). Stress caused by birds has been suggested as a cause of reduced growth, an impact especially proposed for the cormorant (Osieck 1982, Im and Hafner 1984, Moerbeek 1984, Moerbeek et al. 1987), whose underwater and flock fishing behaviour is likely more stressful than the ambush tactics of herons. Information on this suggestion is scarce. Le Louarn (1988) showed that the fish growth in ponds with heron predation was comparable to that in protected ponds.

Fish farmers tend not to accept the concept that herons can be beneficial in reducing numbers of unhealthy fish through their preferential feeding, even though this has been clearly shown by many studies. Ashkenazi and Yom-Tov (1993) found herons preferentially took parasitised fish. Carss (1993) found that fish captured by Grey Herons in a fish farm had more cataracts compared to non-captured fish; the herons also took the smallest fish and those in poorest health. Van Dobben (1952) found that cormorants select parasitised fish. Marion and Marion (1987b) found fish deaths from an epidemic exceeded the feeding capacities of the heron. Ashkenazi and Yom-Tov (1993) reported the beneficial effect that herons reduced invertebrate fish predators such as *Notonecta* and *Corixa* (14.9% of egret and 1.3% of night heron prey), which are responsible for 80–90% of fry losses in Israeli nursery ponds (Hepher and Pruginin 1981). Fish-eating birds consume part of rearing fish or the progeny of uncontrolled spawning in fish farms (Ashkenazi and Yom-Tov 1993), reducing density and benefitting growth of the other fish (Gulland 1971, Backiel and Le Cren 1967, Hepher 1967, Hepher and Pruginin 1981, Huner 1990). This is not always the case, however (Le Louarn 1988). In natural habitats, birds also often decrease competition between commercial species and non-commercial species (usually the more abundant and more heavily consumed) (Suter 1991).

State of Scientific Understanding

With a few exceptions, quantitative studies reviewed in Table 13.2 reported on a single species, the Grey Heron. Broad scientific understanding of heron predation is hampered by lack of information on most species and most locations. Aquaculturists tend to blame the Grey Heron, Great Blue Heron, Great White Egret, and Black-crowned Night Heron for most depredation; these are species (or superspecies in the case of the *Ardea* herons) that are found nearly worldwide. This suggests firstly that most heron species are not an issue with respect to impacts on aquaculture. This also suggests that comparative studies focusing on understanding the nuances of feeding biology of a few species at a range of aquacultural sites would provide scientific understanding helpful in explaining, alleviating, or discounting predation conflicts with aquaculture.

Studies available to date (Table 13.2) are narrowly focused and are generalisable only with great care. Available studies describe predation over a limited period, rarely a full year and usually the fish production cycle of a few weeks (Perennou 1986 for example) to several months, whereas understanding predation impacts in light of all other mortality factors over an entire annual cycle is required. Another defect of most current studies is that predation is expressed either with respect to the initial number of fish or weight but not both, thus inhibiting cross-study comparison.

It is essential that controlled studies be conducted, investigating all pertinent variables (Fig. 13.2) simultaneously. Some experimental studies are also based on too few fish subjected to predation, under conditions not representative of normal commercial exploitations (see for example Le Louarn 1988, Génard et al. 1988), whereas in real fish farms predation by one or two herons would be "diluted" among tens of thousands of fish. The usually territorial behaviour of the *Ardea* herons restricts the number of birds frequenting fish farms unless available fish densities achieve high levels (Marion and Marion 1987b, Draulans 1988, Marion 1990a). This problem of differing fish density is a primary obstacle to making comparisons: the 9000 fish consumed in Meyer's (1981) study only represented a 0.4% loss, whereas the approximately 360 fish taken in Le Louarn's (1988) study accounted for a 36% loss. Account can only be taken of studies conducted at full commercial scale, i.e. of stocks of fish weighing several tons.

Only those few studies measuring both heron consumption and the size of the fish stocks have been included in Table 13.2, as this evaluation is essential to assess predation impact. Most studies have evaluated these variables inadequately. Objective counts of the birds present are largely lacking, critically since herons may frequent fish farms throughout the year, seasonally, or for only part of the day

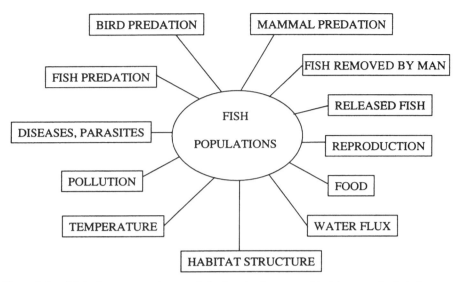

Fig. 13.2   Main factors acting on fish density in natural habitats or in fish farms.

(Marion and Marion 1987, Meyer 1981, Utschick 1983a, Draulans and van Vessem 1987, Carss 1993). Food consumption is seldom directly measured and indirect measure or calculation is inadequate. For instance Ross (1995) calculated an erroneous daily consumption of 1.7 kg for the Great Blue Heron in catfish farms by only taking into account number of "anonymous" birds, rhythm of captures and mean size of fish in stocks. Birds at a site may or may not be feeding for their entire stay (much of their day being occupied by resting or preening) and calculations of impact based on metabolic energy requirements assume not only standard energy intake, but also that all energy is obtained from fish ponds, which is seldom true. Further, daily energy requirements of fish-eating birds are often overestimated: this hardly exceeds 16% of body weight. The Grey Heron's requirement is closer to 270 g than the 500 or 800 g cited in the literature (Creutz 1964, 1981) on the basis of data obtained in captivity—which are overestimates since captivity leads to displacement over-consumption (Marion 1990a).

Impact cannot be determined by analysis of stomach contents of birds killed at fish farms, since they reflect instantaneous consumption and not a mean, whereas the daily consumption of herons can fluctuate widely (Marion 1988). Similarly the food requirements of nestlings have been greatly overestimated in some studies (Meyer 1981, Draulans 1988), since there is a great difference between the optimum theoretical requirements and the quantity of food actually brought by the parents (Marion 1979, 1988).

Nor do studies take into account the huge individual variation in behaviour and activity seen in herons (Draulans and van Vessem 1985b, Draulans et al. 1986, Marion 1984, 1988). The feeding effectiveness of herons also varies among age classes (Recher and Recher 1969, Cook 1978, Quinney and Smith 1980, DesGranges 1981, Cadbury and Fitzherberg-Brockholes 1983, Draulans and van Vessem 1987, Draulans et al. 1986, Draulans 1987a, Carss 1993). Fish farms are especially frequented by immature birds (Draulans and van Vessem 1987). Marquiss and Carss (1994) were of the opinion that simple approaches based on the diet and number of birds could only provide rough estimates of the probability of a problem. They suggested that it was necessary to confirm by experimentation if the impact was heavy, which has only been done in a few limited cases.

Any study is fundamentally flawed that pretends, without adequate experimental controls, to measure predation on a fish farm simply by comparing the number of fish initially stocked with the number harvested and assume that the difference is due to bird predation. Other potential losses (such as death through poor environmental conditions, competitive or handling stress, disease and parasites, predation by other fish, invertebrates and/or cannibalism—Fig. 13.2) are unquantified but may be very heavy. Yet many fish farmers form and act upon their impressions of bird predation by limited and incomplete observation: scientific studies are absolutely required.

Overall, gaps in knowledge are more ichthyological than ornithological (Marion 1990a, 1997a, Price and Nickum 1993). Our knowledge of the ecology, behaviour, dynamics and management of fish populations, especially under captive conditions, is very poor and often empirical compared to what we understand of birds. But both aspects of the problem must be understood to calculate the impact of one on the other. For example, it is practically impossible to evaluate the true losses due to predation when there is uncontrolled recruitment in the fish pond. This was the case in the study by Ashkenazi and Yom-Tov (1993) and is also the reason why it is impossible to quantify predation on crawfish in the USA (Huner 1990) or in any pond where there are great annual variations in production that are independent of predation. In a review of experimental studies of the impact of all piscivores on fish communities in temperate lakes and rivers, Marquiss and Carss (1994) showed that fish populations depend on the synergy between feeding, predation and environmental factors, that the action of the birds must be expressly demonstrated, and that it is not sufficient to assume that an increase in predators necessarily leads to a decrease in fish numbers.

Calculating the true impact of fish-eating birds requires intensive scientific study based on controlled, experimental, quantitative variables encompassing comparisons (Marion 1983a, 1990a) and comparing areas subjected to predation with areas protected with nets on the same farm, with identical initial fish populations and with prolonged observations of bird behaviour. Marquiss and Carss (1994) rightly considered that such experimentation was easy in small closed systems, but is very difficult on large or open systems, with a continuous throughput of fish. In such cases protocols with sequential crossover between control and experimental sites must be used.

With respect to heron conservation, it is critically important that the effects and impact of heron predation be divorced from those of other fish-eating birds. All evidence suggests that herons are of minor significance compared to other fish-eating species. Thus it is essential to document the effects of the several heron species in each situation so as to determine those situations (probably the majority) in which herons are insignificant and therefore should not be subject to control.

Given the requirements for scientifically valid inference on one hand and the ease to rush to judgement based on casual observations, it is not surprising to find a gulf in viewpoint between the fish-farming profession and the scientific community.

Each views the claims of the other with scepticism (Creutz 1981, Marion 1983a, 1990a, 1997a, Draulans 1988, Suter 1991, Huner 1993a, Price and Nickum 1993, Marquiss and Carss 1994, 1997). There is an enormous divergence between the questionnaires supplied by fish farmers and objective economic studies taking into account all the operating variables. It must be admitted that it is extremely difficult to produce such objective demonstrations, such as the exemplary study by Carss (1988), where all variables were monitored (see Fig. 13.3).

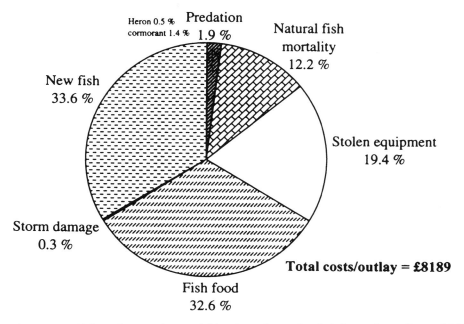

Fig. 13.3   Value of operating variables in an intensive fish farm, from Carss 1988.

Protecting Fish Farms

If damage is confirmed and is sufficiently severe to make protective methods economically viable, the most appropriate control method suitable to local ecological and operating conditions must be found. It should be irrational for a farmer to spend money on protection if it were to cost more than the losses from predation (Salmon and Conte 1981, Marion 1990a, Price and Nickum 1993). Several reviews of methods of protecting fish farms have appeared (Lagler 1939, Creutz 1981, Salmon and Conte 1981, Ueckermann et al. 1981, van Vessem 1982, Parkhurst et al. 1987, Draulans 1987a,b, Littauer 1990a, Marion 1990a,b), and these are simply summarised here with some indication of their effectiveness.

Site design measures

The location of fish farms plays an important role (Littauer 1990b). When creating a fish farm, it is essential not to choose a site that is inherently at risk such as an area favoured as feeding grounds by fish-eating birds, such as marshes, lakes or large rivers, or on the flight line coming from colonies or roosts. It should be more than 25 km from the nearest heron colony, since those close to colonies suffer the heaviest damage (Hanebrink and Byrd 1989, Marion 1989b). Unfortunately, the extension of world aquaculture is taking place increasingly on the site of natural wetlands, most extensively in coastal tropical wetlands in Asia and the Americas (Huner 1993a, 1995, ICLARM 1995, Kushlan pers. comm.), in the Mediterranean (Hafner and Moser 1980) and along the European Atlantic coast (Marion 1990a). This increases conflicts, decreases the area available for heron populations, and can increase heron mortality if they are shot or poisoned on fish farms. The most flagrant example is the fish ponds in the Huleh region of Israel, where there are hardly any natural freshwater habitats left, as they have all been converted to aquaculture.

Unlike for some other species, discouraging herons by proper pond design is relatively straightforward (Lagler 1939, Ranftl and Zur Mühlen 1976, Meyer 1981, van Vessem 1982, Utschick 1983a, Marion 1990a,b). Herons cannot normally feed in water deeper than 40 cm without expending a considerable amount of energy. The best protection for fish stock is to constantly maintain water deeper than this, to eliminate perches and other ambush sites and to design banks that are steep and raised more than 40 cm above the water level. Herons that cannot wade generally feed from the banks, so large ponds reduce the access of herons (Hanebrink and Byrd 1989, Marion 1990a). Herons can catch fish while flying or swimming, but their efficiency is low and this is effective only at high levels of fish availability such as when fish densities are high or oxygen levels low, which should be avoided by good husbandry practices. Means must also be provided in the form of shelter to allow fish to protect themselves. To reduce costs, all these features must be planned when designing the fish ponds.

Operational measures

The fish-farming calendar may be adjusted to reduce risks, since predators are often only present at certain times of year (Meyer 1981, Utschick 1983a, Draulans and van Vessem 1987, Carss 1993, van Vessem et al. 1985, Marion and Marion 1987b). The fish farmer may be able to take account of these dates in selecting the period of stocking and harvesting, the availability of fish of a size preferred by herons, and so forth (Meyer 1981, Salmon and Conte 1981, Marion 1990a). Often fish-farming activities take place at traditional dates guided by historical or legal reasons (dates of rental agreements) and thus independent of biological considerations. Hanebrink and Byrd (1989) reported that monoculture practice in the USA favours predation. Diversifying production should therefore logically decrease losses. An alternative approach to reduce losses would be to decrease effective predator density by using more ponds (Marion 1990a), although this is not always economically possible.

For territorial herons (Grey Heron, Great Blue Heron) (Marion 1984, 1989b, 1990a, van Vessem et al. 1984, Draulans 1988, Marion and Marion 1987b) it is in the fish farmer's interest not to kill or disturb the "owner" of the site, as this bird keeps out others of its species, and if it disappears it is likely to be replaced by flocks of non-territorial herons (Marion 1984, 1990a).

A solution involving diverting herons from fish farms by attracting them to other ponds regularly stocked by non-commercial fish species has been proposed by Ranftl and Zur Mühlen (1976), Creutz (1981) and Utschick and Weber (1980). This method, which is costly and time-consuming, can give good results (Tinarelli et al. 1993) provided that these ponds are more attractive than the fish ponds (with respect to type and size of prey, ease of capture) and that they are sufficiently distant from the fish ponds not to increase the attractiveness of the latter (Draulans 1987b, Marion 1990a). In the long term, however, this method could increase the survival rate of the fish-eating birds and favour further growth in their population (Marion 1990a). So its true effectiveness still needs to be assessed (Draulans 1987b).

When scaring programmes are used, it is best to begin when first migrating birds arrive, before they establish feeding habits, because conditioning the early birds to avoid production ponds may prevent later arrivals from being as much of a problem (Littauer 1990b).

Scaring and killing

Scaring involves frightening the birds using visual and/or acoustic methods, suggesting the presence of humans (scarecrows, streamers, flags, fireworks, detonations, alarm calls or blank shots). The classic scarecrow placed on the pond margins quickly loses its effectiveness. On the other hand, one or more scarecrows faithfully representing a human silhouette, and dressed as a hunter or in the fish farmer's usual clothing, with for example a lifelike mask, and infrequently displayed can give especially satisfactory results. Movement is crucial (Littauer 1990b). It is placed in a boat moored to a buoy in the centre of the water body and free to move around with the wind (Marion 1990a), or an inflatable model can emerge periodically (Conniff 1991). A gibbet of dead herons (a method often prohibited), silhouettes of predators, or the use of a dog are completely ineffective (Schiemenz 1936, Creutz 1981, Utschick 1983a, Marion 1990a). Aluminium streamers suspended from strings are not effective in the long term (Lagler 1939), nor is floodlighting (Draulans and van Vessem 1987, Marion and Marion 1987b, Marion 1990a).

Acoustic scaring has been attempted with variable success (Littauer 1990b). The most successful method is playing recordings of heron alarm calls at variable intervals while regularly changing the position and direction of the loudspeakers (Behlert 1977, Ueckermann et al. 1981, Im and Hafner 1984 and Utschick 1983a against the Grey Heron, Spanier 1980 against the Black-crowned Night heron and Tinarelli et al. 1993 against both species). From time to time it is useful to combine the alarm calls with real human disturbance to prevent birds becoming accustomed. These alarm calls are specific and do not therefore disturb game species on water bodies that are used both for fish farming and hunting. This method is, however, costly and its true effectiveness on the scale of the fish farm and over a sufficiently long period has only been tested recently for Black-crowned Night Heron and Great Blue Heron. It was ineffective for the latter while the first one quickly habituated after a 48% decrease in numbers during the 11-day treatment period (Andelt and Hopper 1996). Classical acoustic bird scarers (gas cannons) can be effective against herons if used under the same conditions as alarm calls (Mott 1978, Meyer 1981, Salmon and Conte 1981, Marion 1990a, Littauer 1990b). However, most birds become accustomed to them after a few days to weeks, except for those on passage

(Creutz 1964, Ranftl and Zur Mühlen 1976, Ueckermann et al. 1981, Utschick 1983a, Draulans 1987b). This method is usually sufficient to protect the ponds during emptying, especially if it is combined with a visual scarer in the form of an object that is hurled vertically for several metres along a ramp (Marion 1990a). In contrast, devices such as suspended tin cans, which emit a regular noise, are completely ineffective (Lagler 1939). All scaring methods become more effective if humans are present; human presence alone will scare off herons if it is associated with danger (which is not everywhere the case). For this reason the Grey Heron visits fish farms especially at night and weekends (Draulans and van Vessem 1985b,c, 1987, Marion and Marion 1987b, Marion 1990a, Carss 1993). Whenever possible, fish farms should be designed so that the farmhouse is at the centre of the ponds to increase the dissuasive effect of human presence.

Shooting is seldom economic or effective, requiring much effort for few results (Draulans 1987b, Marion 1990a). In the United Kingdom, 240 fish farmers killed 4600 herons in one year, 30% of the national recruitment of young in one year and 17% of the adult population. No change was recorded in the numbers of herons visiting fish farms (Meyer 1981), in that herons killed were immediately replaced by others that had been waiting for an empty territory. The same phenomenon was recorded in Belgium (van Vessem et al. 1985). No difference in heron numbers was recorded on a fish farm where 100 herons were killed, compared to a neighbouring farm where the herons were tolerated, nor was there any change at a third fish farm after 200 herons were killed. The ineffectiveness of shooting in scaring herons has been shown by Mott (1978), van Vessem (1982), Reichholf (1982), Utschick (1983a) and Ransom and Beveridge (1983). In contrast, Lagler (1939) considered that shooting and trapping were effective, but this study was at a time when herons were less abundant, which probably prevented those shot from being replaced immediately. The effectiveness of killing by shooting, trapping or poisoning probably depends on the intensity of killing and/or the size of the floating population existing in the region, and can only be effective when the population is held down to a very low level, which is incompatible with species protection. For Marquiss and Carss (1997), casual shooting is ineffective in reducing bird numbers but where it is sufficiently intensive to be effective, it will have impacts on the bird population over a much wider area than the fishery concerned, involving a cull of the wider population. Unfortunately, killing is a method that is still used by fish farmers, who often confuse wariness by herons towards man (nocturnal feeding, desertion on distant approach) with true desertion (Draulans 1987b). In practice, killing birds does nothing to change the attractiveness of a fish farm (Meyer 1981, Utschick 1983a, van Vessem et al. 1985, Draulans 1987b).

Protective measures

The most effective method of heron deterrence is to completely cover the water body with a well-stretched net of suitable mesh size, taking care to prevent birds from entering from the sides (Lagler 1939, Pough 1941, Salmon and Conte 1981, Pinkington 1981, van Vessem 1982, Utschick 1983a, Marion 1990a,b, Littauer 1990a,b). The methods used depend on the size of pond, the duration of protection needed, the type of piscivorous bird and the compatibility with fish-farming procedures. Small ponds can be covered with removable panels, fitted on rails or hinges, or free. For larger ponds a permanent installation may be justified with the net held on cables stretched between the banks, 40 cm above the water, or on posts that allow a tractor or boat to pass underneath (McAtee and Piper 1937). All types of salmonid-rearing facility can be effectively protected at an acceptable cost. Cases of predation through the net, reported especially from Scotland (Carss 1993, Marquiss and Carss 1994), were a reflection of poorly designed protection. In the case of improperly stretched nets, herons can reach the fish by perching on the nets (Carss 1993, Price and Nickum 1993). Large ponds are impossible to protect this way due to the operational situation and economics (Littauer 1990b).

For water bodies of less than 10 ha, parallel nylon ropes can be spread at intervals of one meter suspended 40 cm or up to several metres above the water surface and attached to posts (Lagler 1939, Salmon and Conte 1981, Ueckermann et al. 1981, Utschick 1983a). Another design is in the form of a "circus tent", with a central pillar about 5 to 10 m high from where ropes radiate towards the banks at intervals of about 1.5 to 5 m (van Vessem 1982, Marion 1990a). Stretched ropes do seem to be more effective against cormorants and gulls than herons, according to Naggiar (1974). It is likely that this finding referred to arrangements without a surrounding fence, because this device on the banks is generally effective on its own (Creutz 1964, Ranftl and Zur Mühlen 1976, Ueckermann et al. 1981, van Vessem 1982, Utschick 1983a, Marion 1990a). Such fences can either be vertical or horizontal, in the latter case being at least 40 cm above the water surface. Two stretched wires, 30 cm apart, or a single electrified wire can also be used (Staude 1966). A coloured plastic ribbon, similar to that used on roadworks or by the police, fixed at 50 cm above the ground, has also given good results (Ueckermann et al. 1981). The fence can also be placed in the water, or replaced by a single wire under water, or on the surface held up by floats: the heron usually lands on the bank and then wades into shallow water where it will trip against such a device with its legs. This device is usually sufficient to dissuade a heron (Meyer 1981, Draulans 1987b).

Methods of using protection

Each fish farm is an individual case because of its configuration, pond size, surrounding conditions, water quality, presence of predators, aquacultural practices and schedule, and the type, size, quantity, and quality of the fish being reared. Therefore the most appropriate means of management vary between fish farms (Marion 1990a). Need and potential effectiveness of a protection measure must be assessed in relation to inevitable fluctuations by measuring the real losses and not just by counting the birds (Mills 1967, Draulans 1987b). A fall in the number of herons does not necessarily mean a decrease in fish losses (Draulans and van Vessem 1985b).

In practice, each fish farmer must make a double cost–benefit analysis, one for the business and one for the bird. Each bird makes decisions based on the attraction of the fish farm versus the disadvantages of visiting it (Draulans 1987b, Marion 1990a). The former depends on ease of capture of profitable prey in terms of quality and size that can be ingested in a given time, compared to what is available outside the fish farm in natural or artificial habitats. The disadvantages include human disturbance, aggression from conspecifics and physical difficulties in capturing fish (water depth, steep banks, protective measures). The fish farmer can adjust both sides of this equation by decreasing the attractiveness of the fish farm (lower fish density, which also has advantages in terms of diseases, food competition and behavioural problems among fish) or by increasing the difficulties for the predator.

In most cases there is an effective solution against heron predation, although other species pose greater challenges. Nevertheless, the larger the fish pond, the more difficult the problems are to resolve. The same is true of fish ponds that are used both for rearing fish and for waterfowl hunting, since the protective measures can also repel game species (Marion 1990a). The most frequently encountered problem with protective measures is habituation, which means that the fish farmer must show imagination and use many and varied systems (Salmon and Conte 1981, Risley and Blokpoel 1984, Littauer 1990b). When the fish density is too attractive, herons may prefer to use fish farms rather than natural habitats (Ross and Armstrong 1993). Or they may adopt atypical feeding behaviours such as swimming or capture in flight, or overcome electric fences, or go trampolining on the nets to catch fish (Williams 1992, Ashkenazi and Yom-Tov 1993, Ross and Armstrong 1993, Marion pers. obs.). The aquaculturist has to be smarter than the bird.

Conclusions

Thirty years ago, Mills (1967) stated that our knowledge of the true damage caused by fish-eating birds was almost non-existent, and ten years ago Draulans (1987b) concluded that very little progress had been made since. In recent years a little progress has been made in that several serious, quantitative, experimental studies have found only a slight impact caused by heron predation, and much less than losses from other causes. Each of these studies was conducted in situations in which predation was thought, a priori, to be very heavy, at least to the extent that it attracted the attention of the fish farming profession, researchers and the necessary funding for the studies. To some extent, the study situations bias our ability to generalise in that no study has been conducted on fish farms that have not encountered bird problems. On a country-wide scale (Marion 1997a) or even more so a world scale, fish farms where serious damage from herons is likely are the exception.

Although notable progress has been made, much research remains to be done, more so in terms of the biology and responses of the fish. We know far less about the fish than the herons. The main current handicap of fish farming is that most aquacultural species are only marginally domesticated and are therefore ill-adapted to captivity and to the high densities imposed on them for economic reasons. Even the most intensive of fish farms is still subject to the vagaries of adverse environmental conditions, especially to poor water quality. Heron predation seems to be a minor (albeit highly visible) problem for most of them. Given that herons are among the least detrimental of the fish-eating birds, it is instructive that bird predation is not even mentioned as a factor for world aquacultural production (ICLARM 1995).

Development and maintenance of fish-farming activities can have beneficial effects by creating or maintaining attractive habitats for aquatic birds (Nassar et al. 1991, Fleury 1993, Huner 1993b). To the extent that aquaculture and herons can coexist, this food source will support heron populations, even leading to increases.

However, it also seems that the forecast strong growth in world aquaculture in the forthcoming decades, particularly in developing countries, probably threatens the integrity of coastal wetlands, and especially mangroves. To that extent it will be detrimental to herons. Thousands of fish farms will be installed in these habitats, since aquaculture seems to be the only means of overcoming the inevitable stagnation or decline in marine and inland fisheries (ICLARM 1995). It is to be feared that the protection of herons will carry little weight in countries where there is little or no conservation movement. Even in countries where such a lobby exists, there is little reason to be optimistic. Controversies are even taking place in Europe and in the United States, where government authorities have played an ambiguous role by managing conflicts for political purposes while authorising destruction in the absence of convincing proof of damage, as required by law. The situation described by Williams (1992) in the USA, despite recent attempts at conciliation between fish farmers and bird conservationists (Huner 1993a), is entirely representative of the situation existing in some European countries and particularly France.

14. Captive Populations

Anna Marie Lyles

Herons frequently occur in zoological parks and aquariums, or zoos, where they may be highly visible to the public and are a potentially useful tool in heron conservation. Zoos not only maintain captive heron stocks but also provide nesting and foraging places for wild populations that become semi-feral on the zoo grounds and nearby. Maintenance of captive heron stocks has several functions, but the primary purpose is not, as it is popularly misperceived, for future reintroduction efforts. Zoos may indeed rescue individual birds and sequester them in the safety of captivity. Using intensive care methods of captive propagation, endangered captives can often be bred so that progeny may potentially restock wild populations. However, rescue from extinction is generally not the primary justification for captive breeding because it is expensive and risky (Beck 1995). Resources are highly limited for maintaining viable captive populations of even the most charismatic animals (Conway 1986), let alone herons. Zoos are developing new, diverse conservation strategies to better utilise finite captive resources (IUDZG/CBSG 1993, Wiese et al. 1994). Application of these diverse strategies to heron conservation is the focus of this chapter.

This chapter begins with a review of the changing status of herons in captivity and segues into conservation issues. Captive heron conservation strategies are feasible from a husbandry perspective; herons are relatively easy birds to keep and breed in captivity (Table 14.1; Young 1985). The impact of captive animals on wild populations, positive or negative, depends upon husbandry, quality of management, and the appropriateness of the programme. For a few highly endangered species of herons, captive breeding may well be one way to bring them "from the brink of oblivion". Other appropriate captive approaches to heron conservation are also discussed.

Status of Captive Populations

Captive herons mostly reside in public zoos. Herons are seldom found in the wildlife collections of private citizens, and they are rarely kept as pets. Relatively insignificant numbers can be found in a few other settings, such as research facilities and wildlife rehabilitation centres.

Heron Conservation
ISBN 0-12-430130-4

Table 14.1 Status of captive heron populations[1]

Species	Species	Main Zoo[2] Regions	Global ISIS data Census	# Zoos	Europe Census	# Zoos	N. America Census	# Zoos	Breeding[3] History
Whistling Heron	WH	NA	2	1	3	1	2	1	+ m
Capped Heron	CpH	SA	1	1					+
Grey Heron	GrH	various	45	24	408	73			++ m
Great Blue Heron	GBH	NA	19	15			27	15	
Cocoi Heron	CoH	SA	1	1					
White-necked Heron	WNH	Aus.	1	1					
Black-headed Heron	BHH	various	13	7			8	4	+[4]
Goliath Heron	MH	various	24	10	17	5	16	6	+
Purple Heron	PuH	Europe	5	4	17	9			++ m
Great White Egret	GWE	various	38	19	54	10	9	7	++ m
Reddish Heron	RE	NA	1	1			2	1	++ m
Pied Heron	PdH	Aus.	33	6	6	1			+ m
Black Heron	BH	—							+
Tricoloured Heron	TH	NA	8	4			1	1	+
Intermediate Egret	IE	Asia	5	3					+ m
White-faced Heron	WFH	Aus.	25	7	2	2			+ m
Little Blue Heron	LBH	NA	52	16	3	1	52	17	+ m
Snowy Egret	SnE	NA	80	18			56	17	++ m
Little Egret	LE	Europe	217	25	355	40			++ m
Swinhoe's Egret	SwE	Japan	1	1	1	1			
Eastern Reef Heron	ERH	Europe	6	1	6	1			+
Cattle Egret	CE	various	616	93	638	58	294	50	++ m
Squacco Heron	SqH	Europe	12	2	29	3			+ m
Indian Pond Heron	IPH	Asia	8	3	17	2	3	1	+ m
Chinese Pond Heron	CPH	Europe	11	2	6	1			+
Javan Pond Heron	JPH	Europe			5	2			+
Green-backed Heron	GBH	various	90	28	3	1	49	19	++ m
Yellow-crowned Night Heron	YCNH	NA	34	16			28	14	+ m
Black-crowned Night Heron	BCNH	various	249	45	449	51	42	17	++ m
Nankeen Night Heron	NNH	Aus.	35	4	1	1			+ m
Boat-billed Heron	BBH	NA	185	30	44	9	146	29	++ m
Bare-throated Tiger Heron	BTTH	—							+
Fasciated Tiger Heron	FTH	—							+
Rufescent Tiger Heron	RTH	—							++ m
Least Bittern	LsB	NA	1	1					+
Little Bittern	LtB	Europe	3	2	1	1			+
Yellow Bittern	YB	Japan	1	1					
Schrenck's Bittern	ShB	Japan	1	1					
Cinnamon Bittern	CB	—							+
Black Bittern	BB	Aus.	1	1					+
American Bittern	AmB	NA	4	2			2	1	+
Eurasian Bittern	EB	Europe	5	4	14	7			+
Australian Bittern	AuB	Aus.	1	1					+

[1] Inventory data as described in text. ISIS current to September 1998, Europe data from 1994, N. America from end 1997.
[2] Regions keeping most of captive population; abbreviations: NA=N. America, SA=S. America, Aus.=Australia, various indicates multiple.
[3] Breeding history from IZY-BBC as described in text. Data through 1994: + = has bred, ++ = reliably bred, m = multiple generations.
[4] Black-headed Heron was bred at San Diego Zoological Park during 1998.

Data sources

Data on captive herons were gleaned from the sources described below. For additional information on rare species, the author also contacted all Regional

Conservation Coordinators of the IUCN-SSC Conservation Breeding Specialist Group.

Estimates of global numbers of herons and numbers of zoos keeping them were obtained from ISIS, the International Species Information System. ISIS is a non-profit computer registry for zoo animals. The ISIS network serves nearly 500 member zoos and aquariums in 54 countries; it has records for around 250 000 living specimens. The ISIS database is most complete in North America and Australia. Data used in this paper are current through September 1998, and can be accessed at the Internet site www.worldzoo.org.

Censuses of captive herons were obtained for Europe and North America. These are the most complete inventories available for captive herons. The North American census was done by the author and is current as of 31 December 1997. The author supplemented ISIS data with a telephone survey to zoos that were suspected to have under-reported herons to ISIS (although calls were not placed to Mexican zoos). The European Census was conducted in June of 1994, with surveys returned by 214 (78%) of member zoos in the European Association of Zoo and Aquarium, and by another 14 (70%) of non-member zoos (Brouwer et al. 1995).

Data on breeding success of herons in captivity was gathered from the International Zoo Yearbook's Breeding Bird Census (IZY-BBC). This census has been published for years 1959 through 1994. The editors attempt to include all of the world's major zoos and aquariums in the annual survey. Reporting is voluntary and not all zoos respond every year. Since successful breeding is a point of pride among zoos, reporting rates are reasonably high.

Little has been published on herons in captivity, and there are no prior reviews on the family's captive status (but see Young 1985 on *Nycticorax*). There exists, however, a rich literature on the history of zoos and zoo animals. This literature documents rapid zoo evolution—from menageries and living museums, to conservation centres and bio-parks (Cherfas 1984, IUDZG/CBSG 1993, Tudge 1992). Captive heron populations and exhibits are also in transition; a transition can be seen in zoo databases and is confirmed from conversation with zoo "old-timers".

Past

Herons have been kept in captive collections for at least a century. Earlier in this century, herons were collected for their beauty, for their rarity, or to add diversity to a collection. Collections mainly consisted of wild-caught herons because captive breeding was uncommon. Wild birds were mainly captured and sold by professional dealers and collectors; zoos either bought commercially-available birds, or they mounted a costly expedition to capture exotics themselves. During this century, zoos reported keeping almost every heron species somewhere in the world (data from review of back issues of the International Zoo Yearbook census of rare animals in captivity, and Avicultural Magazine). One such case, the Capped Heron, is now virtually unknown in captivity, but in the past it was kept and bred at a few zoos (Hubbell 1962).

The bird collecting era, at least in the USA, ended in the early 1970s, when quarantine laws were enacted to guard against Newcastle's disease (Bridges 1974). Modern zoo motives for keeping herons have expanded to include educational exhibition, to give homes to injured and non-releasable native wildlife, for studies of heron biology, and to develop propagation techniques. Local, abundant heron species can usually satisfy these goals, and international trade in herons has been negligible for the last few decades. Herons are rarely advertised for sale by professional dealers and they are seldom seen in international bird markets; herons are not on the list of "coveted ones" (Nilsson 1981).

Present

Modern zoos tend to keep the more common species of herons such as Grey Heron, Little Egret, Cattle Egret or Black-crowned Night Heron. As can be seen in Table 14.1, they also tend to display species that occur locally. ISIS member zoos hold 36 of the 60 heron species, or 60%. Non-ISIS reporting zoos mostly keep the most common, readily available herons. However, a few rare specimens are kept in non-ISIS zoos, and thus do not appear in Table 14.1. For example, the Rufescent Tiger Heron is kept and occasionally bred in some South American Zoos, which do not report to ISIS; two zoos with Javan Pond Herons were found in the European Census but did not report these birds to ISIS. Table 14.1 also presents European and North American captive heron census data, as well as a summary of breeding success, which will be discussed later.

The ISIS global database registers 1833 living ardeids. ISIS membership includes only about a third of federated zoos (IUDZG/CBSG 1993). Assuming there are approximately the same number of herons in ISIS member and non-member zoos, one can estimate a real global captive heron population of roughly 5500. A different way to estimate global numbers is to scale up from a relatively complete census. North American zoos represent 14.6% of the world's federated zoos, and approximately a quarter of the world's federated zoos are in Europe (IUDZG/CBSG 1993). North American zoos hold 737 herons of 16 species, which scales up to a world estimate of approximately 5050 herons. The European survey probably included most of the large bird collections, and found 2079 herons of 22 species; scaling this up gives a global estimate of over 8300 captive herons. Overall, the three estimates are within the same magnitude, and one may reasonably assume that something like 6260 ($\pm$ 1460) individual herons live in zoos worldwide.

The global estimates from these three data sets are broken down in Figure 14.1 by tribe. Day herons constitute 60–70% of captive specimens; another 20–30% are night herons. Negligible numbers of tiger herons occur in captivity, and less than 10% of captive herons are bitterns. The most numerous species of day herons and night herons in captivity are those that can be housed in breeding colonies, as can be deduced from a comparison of the Table 14.1 columns for Census and # Zoos. One can also see that zoos tend to keep only one or a few specimens each of the non-colonial species. Colonial herons may be less expensive to keep, and thus favoured over more solitary herons (Conway 1986). ISIS registered zoos hold 71% of all day heron species, and half of the species in the night heron tribe. By contrast, none of the tiger herons and 62% of the bittern species (although none in viable populations) are kept in ISIS member zoos.

Limited space on the Ark

Organised conservation programmes involving captive ciconiiforms are beginning to develop around the world through regional zoo professional association "taxon

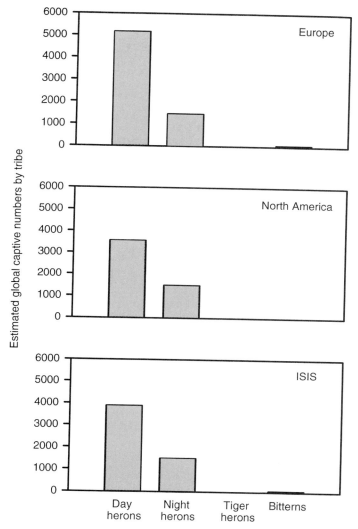

Fig. 14.1 Estimated global numbers of captive herons, by tribe.

advisory groups". But successful captive conservation also depends upon space and other resources, interest, and feasibility. Feasibility, or the ability to successfully manage captive populations, is the focus of the next sections.

Interest in heron conservation among zoo professionals is mixed. Few can deny the beauty of herons in a well-designed exhibit. Herons are also appealing to zoos because they are hardy, and they are appropriate denizens for wetland exhibits. However, herons currently seem to have a bad reputation with aviculturists. Aviculturists stereotype herons as aggressive birds that poke at their keepers' eyes and rob chicks from the nests of cage-mates (Young 1985, and my informal survey of zoo bird curators in USA, Europe and Asia). Like most stereotypes, this one is only partially correct. Not all heron species have aggressive personalities, and aggressive heron personalities can usually be managed through appropriate husbandry practices (Young 1985; see also discussion on husbandry below). A second prejudice against herons is that most of them are thought to have less appeal to visitors than some other colonial waterbirds, like flamingos, ibises and storks, that use similar zoo space; herons also compete for zoo space with species like vultures and cranes. A third strike against captive herons is that many will sit still for long periods of time, while active animals tend to better engage visitor attention.

Given current attitudes towards captive herons, one can expect little change in the zoo space and other resources that will be available for herons. Substantial space is needed to maintain a viable captive population in the long term. For instance, an ideal population of 50 animals could maintain 90% of genetic diversity for 20 generations (Willis and Wiese 1993). This ideal population of 50 probably corresponds to a real heron population of at least 150–350 well-managed individuals, depending upon life history variables and how tightly genetics and demographics can be controlled. Assuming there is space in the world's zoos for 6260 herons, and making a further optimistic assumption that about two-thirds of these herons would be managed in cooperative breeding programmes, then there is potentially space to manage only 14 species with 300 individuals each. This is a fraction of the 36 species currently found in captivity.

Zoos only maintain a few species in large numbers (see Table 14.1); nearly half (47%) of the species in the ISIS database number eight or fewer individuals. Almost no rare herons are kept in zoos. There were 4–5 Swinhoe's Egret in total at: Ueno Zoological Gardens, Tokyo (A. Komori pers. comm.); Tierpark Berlin, Germany (Brouwer et al. 1995); and possibly one at Kuala Lumpur Bird Park in Malaysia (as of 1991, N. Yaacob pers. comm.). A few Japanese Night Herons were kept in Japan before 1991, but none are kept at this time (A. Komori pers. comm.); Rangunan Zoo, Jakarta kept one Malayan Night Heron as of January 1991 (N. Yaacob pers. comm.). Schrenck's Bittern was represented by two individuals at Ueno Zoological Gardens, Tokyo (A. Komori pers. comm.), and one Malagasy Heron was kept at Parc Tsimbazaza, Antanarivo, Madagascar (seen by author in 1989).

Feasibility of Heron Conservation Breeding

Zoos do not currently keep the heron species that might be candidates for conservation breeding. If conservation breeding, or *ex-situ* (off-site) programmes for herons are to be developed, founders of these species will need to be collected from the wild. Many zoo professionals feel that collecting rare founders is only justified after careful consideration of various factors such as whether the probability of captive success is high, and whether the impact of collection is positive in terms of overall biological diversity (Koontz 1995).

"Successful" captive management means more than merely getting animals to breed in captivity—it usually means managing populations better than random. Because *ex situ* space is expensive and limited, there is good reason to keep captive populations as small as possible (Conway 1986). Small populations need intensive management to maintain their genetic and demographic health. Hence, it is very important that managers can reliably breed most individuals in the population when needed, and that survival rates are high. Successful maintenance and breeding both depend upon husbandry knowledge. This section will suggest that the odds for successful captive management of herons are good, but that much preliminary work needs to be done.

Breeding success and survival

Herons, once established, can survive longer in captivity than in nature, some living for 20 or 30 years. Even before the advent of modern veterinary medicine and technology, there are good longevity records. For example, the archives of Bronx Zoo/Wildlife Conservation Park, New York, USA, record a Cocoi Heron from 1913–1947 and a Goliath Heron from 1912–1935. Ages of wild-caught birds were usually unknown at acquisition, so these individuals lived for more than 34 and 23 years respectively.

Theoretically, survival rates for captive adult herons should be at least 85–90% per annum for long-term population management. Actual crude survival estimates were obtained from ISIS as means of 5 annual rates from 1988–1992. Species with less than 10 individuals at the end of 1992 were not included, leaving 19 survival estimates. About half of these crude survival rates were over 85%. The data concur with the general opinion of zoo bird curators that herons are hardy and relatively disease-free birds, with the exception of wild-caught herons that have not yet acclimatised to captive conditions.

Reliable propagation of most herons is probably possible. A few descriptions of heron propagation events are published (Hubbell 1962, Grummt 1964, Yealand 1964, Falzone 1989), The IZY-BBC documents zoo breedings of 33 heron species in the last three decades, and a further species, the Black-headed Heron, was bred during 1998 (see Table 14.1). The 27 species not yet propagated (most of these do not appear in Table 14.1) include tropical night herons (*Gorsachius* sp. and White-backed Night Heron), tiger herons except those of genus *Tigrisoma*, and the Agami Heron.

Some of the reported breedings were undoubtedly fortuitous "accidents", that is, species that only bred one or a few times at one or a few zoos for unknown reasons. Multiple generation breeding is usually considered a good sign of "reliable breeding", and when many zoos have bred a species it is an even stronger indication. For this review, a species that has bred at more than ten zoos is considered reliably bred, and ten heron species meet this criteria (see Table 14.1, species with ++). These reliably bred species are represented in good numbers in captivity, and they are generally widespread and common in nature.

Basic husbandry techniques

Much is understood about husbandry for herons, both from the general experience of keepers and the literature. The following information largely represents conventional wisdom in North America (Lyles 1994a,b).

Banding and Identification. Metal leg bands are commonly used for permanent identification, with males banded on the right leg and females on the left if sexes are known. Many institutions also use a second form of identification for back-up when bands fall off, for example implanted microchip transponders. For visual identification, coloured bands, laminated plastic bands and coloured electric cable ties are the most common choices. If coloured leg bands with etched numbers are used, it may be desirable to use bands with two sets of numbers, so if the band rotates on the bird's leg, then it will still be possible to read the bands from a distance. Wing tags may be preferable in some exhibits or studies because they are more visible.

Sex Determination. Laparoscopy is widely used for determining the sex of herons. It is most accurate in reproductively mature birds, but it has been reported to work in 3-month-old Boat-billed Herons. However, laparoscopy entails capture, separation from the flock, restraint, and often anaesthesia; other sexing methods are less stressful. Least invasive is sexing based upon behavioural differences, variation in calls, or sexual dimorphism; unfortunately these techniques are not well established for herons. Sexing based upon karyotyping is not commonly used for herons. Recently, sex-specific DNA probes have been developed and several commercial genetics laboratories offer diagnostics using a feather, blood or other tissue sample.

Handling. Most zoos tend to use hands-off management. Herons can be dangerous to handle, as they will stab at the handler's eyes with their sharp beaks. Herons are trapped or netted from exhibits when necessary for exhibit work, shipments, veterinary care, or for management reasons such as sexing or banding. Individuals of some colonial species do poorly when isolated for quarantine or treatment; a typical problem is not eating. Providing a companion, or housing birds within visual and auditory contact of companions, seems to help.

Health problems. Bumblefoot and dry, cracked toes are a recurring problem. Water and soft substrates are important to prevent these problems. Trauma is another commonly reported problem. Traumatic injuries are most likely when birds are first introduced to an exhibit or when they are captured. Head trauma is a common cause of mortality. In general, long-legged birds are also prone to broken legs, and long-billed species are prone to broken mandibles.

Diets and dietary supplements. Zoos commonly feed herons fish, meat, soaked dog-chow, fish meal, shrimp meal, trout chow, or commercial flamingo food. Supplementation of some vitamins and nutrients may be required to balance diet, especially vitamin E and thiamin, as health problems have been correlated with deficiencies (Carpenter and Spann 1979). Live insect foods can be used as "treats". Hidden treats may be beneficial for behavioural enrichment. The amount provisioned should vary with a flock's consumption level. Seasonal caloric adjustments are recommended for birds that are housed outdoors, as they may need extra calories to keep warm during winter. It is not known whether herons should be fed a seasonally varied diet to stimulate reproduction. An artificial fish substitute may be needed in the future because fish are becoming increasingly expensive and difficult for zoos to obtain.

Housing. Captive herons seem to feel more secure when they can perch high to escape disturbance, or to roost or nest. Some herons, particularly disabled, non-releasable ones and also larger herons, are kept in open-top yards or islands; if not disabled, these must be wing-clipped or surgically pinioned to prevent flight.

Pinioning may reduce egg fertility in some herons, particularly long-legged ones, because it may affect their ability to balance well during copulation. Herons kept with hoof-stock and other large mammals seem to have increased risk of traumatic injury. If herons are kept outside in open yards, care must be taken to protect them from predators. Flightless individuals may be more comfortable and safer in an exhibit with ramps that allow them to reach high perches.

Most herons are kept in covered aviaries where they can fly. Ideally, the exhibit layout should provide several different kinds of areas for the birds, keepers and public. For captive nesting, some species may need to feel particularly secure and isolated from disturbance. In choosing a nest site, these birds seem to take a combination of factors into account, including site height, cover, isolation, and whether the location is over water. So, for instance, if an aviary has no high nest sites, placing nest platforms over water, in an area with cover, might encourage birds to build nests. Most wild colonial water birds feed away from the nest area; hence separating the nest area from the feeding area may decrease aggressive interactions near nests. Some institutions have designed feeding areas that also serve as a trap.

When kept in numbers, herons are messy and sometimes smelly. Cleaning is generally easier when nests and perches are kept over water. Some species dip their food in water before ingesting, thus food pans are often placed over or near water.

Most species can be housed with other species of ciconiiformes, cranes, waterfowl, shorebirds, small perching birds and parrots. Predation by herons on the young of other birds can be minimised by keeping heron numbers low, removing vulnerable species from the enclosure or moving the predatory individuals into another enclosure during nesting season, and by providing ample food (Young 1985). Because hybridisation occurs in captivity (see Table 14.2), similar species should not be housed together; nor should solitary, similarly sized individuals of opposite sexes.

Propagation. There are a number of unproven theories about how to stimulate nesting in herons. In single-species and mixed-species colonies it may be important to have at least one pair of proven breeders per colony. Another idea is to mimic natural migration by moving captive herons seasonally (for example to and from the

Table 14.2 Hybrid offspring for herons[1]

	>1 zoo	>1 year
With genus		
GrH × PuH[2]	yes	yes
SnH × LE	no	no
SqH × CPH	no	no
YCNH × BCNH	no	no
Between genus		
CE × LE	yes	yes
CE × BCNH	no	no
LE × BCNH	no	yes
SnH × NNH	no	no

[1] As reported in IZY-BBC, summarised by relationship between parents.
[2] Hybrid offspring of GrH × PuH successfully backcrossed.

winter quarters). Many herons will build their own nest if provided with a secure nest platform and nesting materials (i.e. sticks, twigs, hay, grasses), and it is not known if old nests should be removed after the nest season.

Chicks. Most institutions encourage herons to rear their own offspring, rather than having a keeper incubate eggs and hand-rear chicks. Parents with chicks may be given an increased number of feeds to ensure availability of fresh food. Parents generally regurgitate to their chicks, and provided they have a balanced diet, no major diet changes are needed for the chicks. However, chicks may be intolerant of salty food (Bennett et al. 1992). Diets may be supplemented with small fish or pieces of meat, which parents may prefer. Depending upon the substrate, it may be advisable to place food pans over water; this prevents adults from accidentally coating food with sand, which can cause gut impaction in chicks.

Hand-rearing herons is not difficult. A variety of species have been hand-raised successfully in zoos, including Goliath Herons, Cattle Egrets, Boat-billed Herons, and Black-crowned Night Herons. A general hand-rearing strategy is to start small chicks on small chunks of neonatal mice or fish, or on a blended milkshake that gets increasingly solid as chicks mature. For fish-eaters, a balanced frappe formula is: 1000 g homogenised whole fish + 100 mg thiamine + 100 IU vitamin E (E. Dierenfeld pers. comm.). The natural diet of herons is primarily fat and protein (for example crustaceans, insects, fish, frogs) with little carbohydrate; they may lack enzymes to break down milk sugar, so milk should be avoided (E. Dierenfeld pers. comm.).

Recently hatched chicks are usually started in a brooder box, at 90–95°F. Chicks are placed inside a stick nest (important for preventing foot problems). Feedings are initially 5–6 times daily. If a liquid formula is fed, it may be delivered through a feeding tube apparatus, or poured in the mouth with a narrow spoon. As chicks age and become more mobile, the temperature is reduced, and they are moved into a larger enclosure with perching so that they can clamber about. Feedings can be gradually reduced to 2–3 daily, and water should be provided when chicks become mobile.

Imprinting can be a problem for hand-reared wading birds, but putting fledglings back in with the colony quickly may help reverse imprinting. Rearing several together may reduce imprinting problems. Group-reared chicks usually make the transition to self feeding better than solitary ones do. However, there may be competition within a group of chicks. Groups should be monitored to make sure all the chicks are getting food, and that none are pecked excessively by other chicks.

Husbandry research needed

One way to improve the odds of successfully keeping and breeding a particular heron species is to develop robust husbandry methods, possibly starting with a related surrogate species that already occurs in zoos, or is common enough in nature that collection would not damage wild populations. For example, captive Goliath Herons are already kept by a dozen ISIS member zoos, and frequently bred. This majestic heron might serve as a husbandry surrogate for other great herons like the Malagasy Heron or Imperial Heron. Even when husbandry methods are successful with a surrogate, a minimum of 5 years should be allowed to adapt husbandry techniques for the target species.

Keeping and breeding herons in captivity is currently more of an art than a science. Many aspects of heron husbandry are poorly known, and some of the unanswered questions are relevant to both *ex-situ* and *in-situ* management of herons. Cues necessary to trigger breeding are not well understood, for example some species may need seasonal adjustments of diet or lighting. One critical factor for breeding is probably getting the correct social grouping, especially for colonially nesting species. For species that nest with other species in the wild, assembly of a mixed-species heronry may be beneficial in captivity. The spatial and micro-habitat requirements of herons are important but poorly understood. Curators tend to use educated guesswork and aesthetic considerations to design the configuration of perches, feed areas, water, nest sites and other habitat variables. Sometimes natural history can help guide enclosure designs, but not always. For instance, the natural temperature range that a species encounters is often not identical to its apparent temperature comfort range. Many tropical birds can tolerate cold weather if they are provided with plenty of food, open water, and shelter.

Feasibility of Heron Reintroduction

An organised attempt to reintroduce captive-born herons into nature has not yet occurred. Records from translocations, releases and hacking of herons gives reason to be optimistic that captive-born herons can be successfully repatriated. In addition, the use of captive birds and decoys to attract wild birds to a nest site may be one of the most effective ways to establish a new colony (see Chapter 9 for a case study and examples).

Mature herons have been captured and translocated from one wild population to found another. This has been done on numerous occasions with the Cattle Egret, often successfully (Lever 1987). Following their decline due to plume hunting in the early part of the century, a population of Snowy Egrets was re-established on Avery Island, Louisiana, USA, when the pepper sauce founding entrepreneur E.A. McIlhenny captured seven birds and moved them to the island (Kenyon 1993). Now 20 000 herons and egrets nest in the Avery Island refuge, and 30 truckloads of twigs are dumped for their nest building annually (Kenyon 1993). Twelve Grey Herons were translocated to the Blankaart, Belgium, in 1967 where they probably attracted three additional pairs of wild herons; in 1968 there was breeding of 11 pairs including some of the introduced birds (Houwen 1968).

Zoo herons have been released or have escaped on numerous occasions. Most releases were not monitored or documented, and it is usually not clear whether the released birds were wild born or captive born. In the 1920s and 1930s, Cattle Egrets were released in England at Whipsnade, Surrey and Dublin Zoo. Apparently, these birds wandered widely but did not breed (Lever 1987). As part of an effort to establish Cattle Egret in the Hawaiian Islands (for pest control), the Honolulu Zoo released 48 herons on Oahu (Lever 1987). Yellow-crowned Night Heron escaped from decaying flight cages in Juraspore, India and Avery Island, USA and apparently naturalised (cited in Wingate 1982). Tel Aviv University Zoo released Black-crowned Night Herons onto its grounds; a colony established and is increasing (Lever 1987; see also Chapter 1).

Hacking is a technique that has been perfected by raptor conservationists. It involves hand rearing of nestlings and release after fledging. Wingate (1982) used hacking to successfully reintroduce Yellow-crowned Night Herons to Bermuda. Nestlings were taken, in sibling groups, from a colony site in Tampa Bay, Florida, over three consecutive breeding seasons (1976–1978), to Nonesuch Island, Bermuda, and held in a derelict house. They were primarily fed land crabs and allowed to fledge and to disperse. The fledglings began hunting local land crabs without any assistance. No nestlings were lost during transition to independence during the first two years, but two were lost during the third year. Breeding commenced after a few years in a secluded reserve area. Hacking techniques have also been used to restore Great White Egrets in the Tennessee Valley, USA (Pullin 1987). Groups of wild-hatched, pre-fledge egrets (3–5 weeks old) were moved to a release site cage, and released after fledging. To lure the egrets from the hacking cages, an egret decoy was used. As a result of this release programme, Great White Egrets are again nesting on Guntersville Reservoir in northern Alabama (B. Pullin pers. comm.).

The above cases involved establishment of non-migratory populations, or establishment of colonies within the range of an existing population. It is not clear how zoo birds could be taught migratory routes when no experienced birds remain to teach them. Nor is it known how to induce naive, reintroduced herons to found a brand new nesting colony, although decoy techniques are promising (see Chapter 9). When the original population of a highly colonial or migratory heron is gone, repatriation may be difficult. Reintroduction of ecological specialists may also present a significant challenge.

Costs and Benefits of Captive Heron Populations for Conservation

Research and expertise in intensive techniques

Zoo heron collections have long served as living scientific resources, and little basic research with captive herons has occurred outside of zoos (see for example Rhoades and Duke 1975, Mock et al. 1987, Ashkenazi 1983). A number of taxonomic studies have used zoo herons. Dickerman et al. (1982) studied plumage development and sub-species variation in a captive colony of Boat-billed Herons. Mendelssohn (pers. comm.) undertook long-term breeding studies of herons at the Research Zoo of Tel Aviv University, Israel. One aspect of this programme was studies of the effect of pollutants on egg fertility and breakage, and egg residues (Mendelssohn 1975). For research on the inheritance of behaviour patterns in herons, Mendelssohn hybridised Purple Herons and Grey Herons and back-crossed the fertile male hybrids (IZY-BBC, and pers. comm.). The IZY-BBC reports hybrid offspring. A compilation, in Table 14.2, demonstrates intra- and inter-genera crosses. Hybrid offspring are produced more infrequently under modern zoo management.

Captive herons can be observed more closely than herons in the field. Hence, there are a number of ecological and behavioural questions that are well suited to zoo study. Zoos provide a convenient "laboratory" for studying the basic biology and microhabitat preferences of some poorly-known, or taxonomically unusual, species like Boat-billed Herons. Birds in *ex-situ* collections can be handled for individual identification and sex-determination. Life history and behaviour can be quantified for individuals of known age and sex. And in large heron collections, cross-species comparative studies are possible. However, zoo resources for research are highly limited, and priority is generally given to applied problems of most relevance to current conservation programmes.

Zoo personnel use intensive techniques and are developing hands-on expertise that can be employed in *in-situ* conservation programmes. Most zoo herons receive basic veterinary health care, including regular screening for parasites, blood-work, surgical care, and pathology. Some institutions employ nutritionists, who study dietary requirements. Endocrinologists have done little work with zoo herons, and high-tech reproduction techniques, such as artificial insemination or frozen embryos, have not yet been developed for herons. Zoo personnel regularly assist reproduction in captivity through providing artificial nests or nest platforms, and through artificial incubation of eggs and hand rearing of chicks. One can easily imagine a need for some of the above intensive techniques when, for example, a heronry must be moved because the colony site is listed for development. Captive herons can also be used to test and refine equipment and techniques before trying them in the field.

Education programmes

Exciting, educational heron exhibits are potentially zoos' preeminent contribution to conserving herons and wetland habitats. Worldwide, zoos are estimated to attract over 600 million visitors annually (IUDZG/CBSG 1993). The majority of these visitors live in urban areas and otherwise have little contact with wildlife. Zoos are beginning to study and develop approaches to mobilising visitors for conservation through innovative exhibit and educational programmes.

A number of zoos display herons in walk-through wetlands exhibits. These exhibits should deliver clear conservation messages about wetlands and herons. Computer technology might be a good way to link exhibits with wetlands conservation messages; the Wetlands Center, Australia, while not a zoo, has pursued this approach with its Window on Wetlands computer programme (Chapters 6, 9). Zoo-based heron education programmes need not end at the exit gates. Zoo educators and graphic artists can also develop heron and wetland conservation curricula that can be used within the target species' native range; this kind of *in-situ* education has been proposed for Madagascar's herons.

Supporting *in-situ* conservation

Engaging exhibits can do more than educate; they can also kindle support for wild populations by raising conservation funds. Exhibits might link zoo colonies with wild colonies or wetlands through an "adopt a colony" or "adopt a wetland" programme. Yet another way zoos can support *in-situ* conservation and ecotourism is through zoo members' tours to areas with heron populations.

Collection of founders

Good captive management reduces the number of founders, or wild-born breeding stock, needed for long-term population viability. Theoretically, the required number of founders is 25 picked at random from a wild population (Ralls and Ballou 1986), but many captive populations start with only a fraction of this number. Even with good management, however, new founders may need to be added, since not all founders will produce the ideal number of offspring. Founders should be collected with minimal impact on the wild population. The way that this is done depends upon the natural history of the species and specifics of the programme.

Collection of one egg or nestling per nest is a good approach for herons, since typically only part of the clutch usually survives in nature. An advantage of collecting eggs or nestlings is that human rearing may facilitate adaptation to captivity, provided the human-reared herons are not imprinted. Care must be taken when entering wild breeding colonies to collect. Human disturbance may result in egg or chick loss, or even colony desertion. When collection from breeding colonies causes excessive disturbance, it may be better to collect adults.

A low-impact approach to collecting founders is to salvage injured, non-releasable wild birds and orphaned nestlings. But this opportunistic approach has several serious disadvantages: acquisition of sufficient founders can be slow, and disabled wildlife can constitute poor stock for breeding.

Zoos as refuges

Zoos often provide homes for displaced, injured or confiscated wildlife. Thus, zoos help wildlife authorities enforce regulations by providing homes for seized wildlife. However, as there is little trade in herons, few herons have found their way into zoos through confiscation. More commonly, zoos provide wildlife rehabilitators with homes for injured and non-releasable native herons.

Artificial and natural wetlands within zoo grounds provide habitat for an unknown, but probably significant, number of free-ranging, wild herons. Examples of free-flying herons harboured in zoos include: Grey Herons at Barcelona, Spain and Eekholt, Germany (Brouwer et al. 1995); a large breeding colony of Yellow-crowned Night Herons at San Antonio Zoo, USA; Nankeen Night Herons at Melbourne Zoo, Australia; Cattle Egret and Black-crowned Night Herons at Jurong Birdpark, Singapore (K. Nazimuddeen pers. comm.); and a variety of wading birds at Delhi Zoo, India (Young 1985). Because these colonies may be concentrated, they may damage vegetation; however, it may be possible to manage the colony in ways that mitigate damage (Baxter 1996).

Contact between captive and wild herons

Where free-ranging herons use zoo grounds, they may come into contact with captive stocks. Captive colonies can attract wild individuals and disrupt natural range patterns. Black-crowned Night Herons, for example, were probably attracted outside their former range by aviary conspecifics at Bird Sanctuary "Zwin", on the Dutch border with Belgium (Wille and Wille 1969).

Mixing between captive and wild stocks could foster the transmission of disease-causing pathogens. I know of no example of pathogens being transmitted from zoo ciconiiformes to wild ones. There are examples of transmission from wild to zoo stocks (Locke et al. 1974 for example).

Another concern is that escaped herons could introduce genes exotic to the local population. ISIS records show that releases, or escapes, are not uncommon. For example, they accounted for one ninth of registered Yellow-crowned Night Heron losses from zoos between 1987 and 1991. However, the vast majority of these releases are of native, usually rehabilitated wildlife (and these numbers are probably trivial compared to what wildlife rehabilitators release). Native wildlife releases have led to establishment of free-flying colonies on or near zoo grounds, for example ones at Tel Aviv, Israel and Perth, Australia (Young 1985).

Infrequently, non-native species do escape. In 1950–51 some Black-crowned Night Herons (North American subspecies *hoactli*) escaped through a roof hole in Edinburgh Zoo aviary (Young 1985). A small population of 25–40 persists, and nests in the zoo gardens. There is no evidence of nesting outside the zoo grounds. Supplemental feeding may be keeping birds on grounds. The main food seems to be diets of other zoo animals, put out during the day. The herons also forage in intertidal areas and wetlands. British ornithologists are concerned that these zoo herons may hybridise with the European subspecies *nycticorax* (Lever 1987).

Zoos should not be castigated for past releases, as these were not seen as irresponsible at the time (Baker 1986). Modern zoos should follow guidelines for responsible releases. Guidelines are under development by a number of authorities, such as IUCN's Reintroduction Specialist Group (Stanley-Price 1994).

Suggested Captive Conservation Priorities

Conservation breeding will rarely be needed to "rescue" a heron species. More commonly, conservation of a viable population outside of the original habitat (*ex-situ*) can complement field conservation efforts (IUDZG/CBSG, 1993). As there are currently no viable *ex-situ* populations of rare herons, an opportunity exists for field biologists and zoo biologists to cooperatively design new initiatives.

Species that are recognised to be critically endangered, endangered, and vulnerable (i.e. 1996 IUCN Red List of Threatened Animals) are the most obvious candidates for conservation breeding. The annotated list below suggests potential captive actions for each of these species.

Imperial Heron. None occur in captivity and sightings in nature are extremely rare. Before contemplating conservation breeding, field research is needed to locate animals and gather basic information on their ecology. Zoos have been fairly successful with other large herons, so prospects seem favourable for keeping and propagating this heron species in captivity. If nests could be located in nature, it should be possible to collect captive stocks as eggs, with little impact on the wild population.

Malagasy Heron. This species would probably benefit from a captive population, because wild populations are small, declining, persecuted and unlikely to recover in nature at present. Zoos currently support other conservation breeding programmes in Madagascar, so a political infrastructure exists to support a zoo project with this species. However, zoos would probably proceed cautiously with developing a conservation breeding programme, since the biology of this species is little known, it has not been maintained in captivity in any numbers, and space for large herons is limited.

Swinhoe's Egret. Locales of wild breeding colonies are known, so it should be relatively easy to collect founders for a captive population of this species, should it be deemed desirable. Captive stocks for reintroduction efforts are probably not needed, given the current size of wild populations. However, captive birds could be useful for developing artificial nests, egg management techniques or other techniques that could be used to support the wild colonies. More importantly, captive egrets in educational exhibits, particularly within the range area zoos, could serve as ambassadors for conservation of their habitat. These egrets have been kept in captivity but not bred. Egrets generally breed well in zoos, so the prospects of success are relatively good.

Slaty Egret. Wild populations are small, and declining for reasons not fully understood. Thus, establishing a small captive population might be good insurance against extinction. No egrets of this species occur in captivity. Some zoos with African-themed exhibits might be willing to undertake a project with this species, perhaps including support of field research. Otherwise, recommendations for this species are similar to those for Swinhoe's Egret.

White-eared Night Heron and/or Japanese Night Heron. Much needs to be learned about the *Gorsachius* herons. None are currently kept in captivity and none have been captive bred. Although attractive, their secretive nature may make them poor candidates for zoological display. A pilot captive programme with a small number of these birds would probably yield much valuable information for *in-situ* or *ex-situ* conservation planning. A programme with the Malayan Night Heron would be similarly valuable.

Australian Bittern. Conservation breeding is not indicated for recovery of this species at present. However, a small captive group might provide some useful information on the biology of the species. Australian zoos would need to lead any potential programme. If captive birds prove suitable for display in educational exhibits, they might serve as conservation ambassadors.

Captive programmes for less-threatened herons have already been developed for a few species, and are recommended for some others. These are described in the next annotated list.

Boat-billed Heron. This heron is popular in North American zoos, and also occurs in some European zoos. A North American studbook (i.e. registry and genealogy) exists for this heron; its purpose is to manage a self-sustaining captive population and to improve husbandry techniques. Currently the population receives minimal genetic or demographic management, because population management techniques for colonially breeding birds are poorly developed. This is currently the only managed captive-breeding programme for a species of heron.

One of the priorities of the Ciconiiformes Advisory Group of North American zoos is to develop a wetlands conservation education initiative, possibly with an internet website component. This project commenced with the Wood Stork, *Mycteria americana*, but the curricula should be expanded to include herons, because they are more available for zoo exhibition than are the Wood Storks. Perhaps this programme could eventually also be adapted for other regions of the world.

Madagascar Pond Heron. The St. Louis Zoo, USA and the American Zoo Association's Madagascar Fauna Group have recently sponsored 3 years of breeding-season surveys in the vicinity of Antananarivo. Numbers are much lower than were found breeding in previous surveys. The next step will be to expand the survey to the entire range. Findings suggest that more aggressive intervention may be indicated. Steps might include establishing a captive population in cooperation with the local zoo, as well as an in-country education campaign for heron habitat.

Tiger Herons. Some populations of tiger herons are doing poorly in nature. Tiger herons are currently kept in negligible numbers by zoos. However, tiger herons are, reputedly, good exhibit animals. South American zoos could take the lead in establishing a captive population, which would allow zoos to gain more experience with these birds, in case conservation breeding is required. Tiger Herons could be featured in educational exhibits.

Feral populations. Zoos can contribute to heron conservation by providing protected habitats and nesting sites, and perhaps safe food sources, for some feral herons. This contribution may be especially important where rare herons occur within a zoo's range. Feral colonies may have some undesirable aspects, such as causing damage to vegetation, or producing odours and faeces. Zoos might cooperate to develop techniques to counter these negative aspects. The educational advantages of having a wild heron colony on zoo grounds should not be overlooked. By proper management, a wild colony can be an exceptional asset to a zoo's education and conservation programme.

Conclusions

There are a number of heron conservation actions upon which captive specialists can commence immediately. Zoos should improve conservation education programmes for existing heron exhibits. They can provide protected habitat for feral herons. Zoos should minimise negative impacts on wild herons. They should limit propagation of common species unless there are good zoo homes for the offspring. Zoos should document husbandry techniques. Zoos can start working with surrogate species for endangered herons, especially if a need for intensive management is anticipated. Those working with *ex-situ* surrogates can develop linkages with *in-situ* heron specialists, and try to provide technical assistance or other support for the target species. In appropriate cases, the surrogate may eventually be replaced with a captive population of the target species.

Zoos wish to play a responsible role in conservation and they can offer heron field specialists complementary resources. Zoo professionals tend to be generalists, and specialised knowledge of herons is largely absent in the profession. Heron specialists should collaborate with zoo professionals to develop effective heron and wetlands conservation initiatives.

Heron field biologists also have a responsibility to help develop effective captive conservation programmes. They can work with local zoos, advising them on ways to improve heron exhibits and habitats. They should help zoo advisory groups develop projects and priorities for *ex-situ* conservation. Heron specialists who anticipate a need for conservation breeding should start collaborating with zoos as early as possible; they should not wait for the final decline of a species when these approaches are extremely costly, if not too late.

15. Herons as Indicators

R. Michael Erwin and Thomas W. Custer

An indicator is "an organism or ecological community so strictly associated with particular environmental conditions that its presence is indicative of the existence of these conditions" (Merriam–Webster 1961). In environmental biology, this definition has been modified and extended to other levels of biological organisation, indicators of environmental change being called "bioindicators". A number of authors agree that using suborganismal (*sensu* Kushlan 1993b) or organismal bioindicators in birds, including herons, represents an effective means of monitoring both for effect and for exposure to some "insult" such as a contaminant or other environmental challenge (Gray 1980, Hill and Hoffman 1984, Morrison 1986, Fox and Weseloh 1987, Custer et al. 1991, Kushlan 1993b). At levels of organisation above the organism, use of birds as bioindicators has been challenged (Morrison 1986, Temple and Wiens 1989) largely on the claim of birds' lack of sensitivity to change. Another criticism is that the term bioindicator may have been used too broadly, which may cloud its meaning in some contexts.

Kushlan (1993b) suggested that certain biological cues at hierarchical levels above the organismal, from populations to the ecosystem, could be useful as bioindicators. He called these the PCE indicators (i.e., Population, Community, and/or Ecosystem). Kushlan (1993b) and Temple and Wiens (1989) realised, however, that the higher the organisational level, the less direct (i.e., lower correlation coefficients) will be the connection between the bioindicator measurement and the environmental elements of concern. Time lags may also be associated with changes in population sizes, community changes, or habitat shifts (Newton et al. 1993). Resource managers concerned with making rapid assessments and evaluations of environmental conditions or concerned with enforcing a regulatory mandate may not have access to more reliable lower-level indicators, but instead have to rely on long-term (PCE) indicators as a primary signal. Biomonitoring programmes are also suggested to be most effective when a combination of biological indicators (at different levels of organisation) and chemical/physical indicators are used (Gray 1980, Zonneveld 1983, Spellerberg 1991, Burger 1993).

Biologists involved in biomonitoring programmes need to be clear about what a

Heron Conservation
ISBN 0-12-430130-4

Cattle Egrets. Growth and condition of small chicks such as these may serve as bioindicators of prey availability. Photo: Heinz Hafner.

particular biomarker or variable is "indicating" (Kushlan 1993b). The attributes of interest at the higher levels of organisation (ecosystems) may or may not be closely correlated in function, time, or space with the biological parameters being measured (Table 15.1). The challenge in any biomonitoring programme is to find one or a few parameters (measurable in a cost-effective way) that are closely coupled with the environmental conditions of interest, at least in a statistical if not causal way. Whether bird monitoring fits this description is a matter of controversy (see Morrison 1986). Some recent advances have helped mitigate some early confusion by modelling and trying to integrate the individual components of chemical exposure, effects, individual responses, and population responses (Hallam et al. 1996).

Individuals and agencies responsible for conservation of birds have reason to know the size and trend of the populations under their care. As a result birds, including herons, have been monitored in various places around the world. Reasons for this vary, but the intrinsic value of birds to the public and their recreational importance (for example hunting of certain species) argue for maintaining programmes and databases of breeding, migrating, and/or wintering population estimates (Diamond and Filion 1987, Nichols 1991). Population-level changes of

Table 15.1 The potential use of herons for monitoring changes in ecosystem state or condition.

Ecosystem processes (p) or variables (v)	Responses by Herons[1]			
	D/I	S/O	Population	Community
Production (p)	I		Reproduction (clutch size, success, growth)	Diversity, composition
Trophic web ratio (v)	D			Herons as a top carnivore component
Succession (p)	D			Changes in species over time
Habitat quality (v)				
Nesting habitat area	D		Local colony size	Total (all species) colony size
Feeding habitat area	I		Size of feeding assemblages (single species); reproduction	Reproduction
Habitat quality (v)				
Contaminants	D	several s/o biomarkers	reproduction (hatching success, deformity rate)	
Parasites	D		Mortality of young	
Disturbance level	D		Reproduction (success)	Presence/absence of certain species

[1] Response is direct or indirect (D/I) and can be detected at 3 levels of organisation: S/O = Suborganismal/organismal; population, or community.

birds certainly do not, under most circumstances, closely track environmental changes in space or time (Temple and Wiens 1989); however, when coupled with other types of environmental data, they may corroborate impressions of major ecosystem changes (Terborgh 1989) or changes in human activities such as agricultural pesticide applications (Newton et al. 1993). The decline in many populations of birds of prey due to the widespread use of DDT in agriculture is one of the clearest, and probably the most celebrated, example of using birds as indicators of environmental degradation (Carson 1962). For wetland species, changes in numbers of herons, egrets, ibises, and Wood Storks (*Mycteria americana*) in the Everglades were some of the first signals that major system deterioration had begun (Kushlan 1993b, Ogden 1994). Because of the heightened interest in wetland conservation throughout the world, herons and egrets have become a valuable and popular monitoring guide because of their conservation value, their vulnerability and their conspicuousness (Kushlan 1993b, Ogden 1994).

Reviews of colonial water birds as bioindicators are available elsewhere (Fox and Weseloh 1987, Kushlan 1993b). The objective of this chapter is to provide a more detailed focus on those indicators that have been evaluated with respect to herons. In the following we discuss both the benefits and liabilities of various biomonitoring methods.

Suborganism and Organism Level Indicators

General reviews of biochemical, physiological, and histological biomarkers (Huggett et al. 1992) and embryotoxic and teratogenic effects (Hoffman 1990) have been published. In the following, we concentrate on those suborganism indicators that have been evaluated for herons.

Contaminant concentrations

Concentrations of environmental contaminants in tissues (or even in excrement; see Fitzner et al. 1995, Spahn 1997) can be used to evaluate the chronic or acute exposure in herons. They can also be used to make comparisons among species, locations, or time periods. Several examples of the above are presented in Chapter 12. Contaminant accumulation rates and the use of feathers as indicators of trace elements are discussed below.

Contaminant accumulation in chicks. Residues in heron eggs have been used to indicate local or regional contamination (see for example Ohlendorf et al. 1974). However, because herons may be migratory, contaminants present in the female at laying could have been accumulated elsewhere (Henny et al. 1984, 1985, Henny and Blus 1986 for example). In order to overcome that limitation, heron chicks have been collected, and their tissues analysed (Ohlendorf et al. 1978b, Custer et al. 1991). Because food fed to heron chicks comes from within a few km of the nesting colony (Custer and Osborn 1978, Erwin et al. 1991, and Chapter 9), their tissue composition should reflect local contamination.

The mass (total µg) of PCBs in carcasses of sibling night-heron chicks collected in Narragansett Bay, Rhode Island, USA, increased between 5–10 and 10–15 days of age (Fig. 15.1; Custer et al. 1991). The rate of increase (µg/day) could be used to compare species, locations, or time periods. An assumption of this method, that residues among eggs within clutches are similar, has been documented for Black-crowned Night Herons (Custer et al. 1990). It has also been demonstrated that no noticeable loss of contaminant mass occurs from night-heron eggs to chicks (Custer and Custer 1995). Accumulation based on contaminant mass has also been demonstrated for trace elements in chicks of the Eastern Great White Egret in Korea (Honda et al. 1986).

Trace elements in feathers. Trace element concentrations in feathers can be useful indicators of contaminant exposure because feather concentrations reflect tissue concentrations at the time of feather formation and comparison among species, location, and chronological trends can be evaluated (Burger et al. 1992b, Burger and Gochfeld 1993). Additionally, feathers can be collected without killing the individual and can be archived for many years without degradation (Burger 1993). Exceptionally high values of trace elements in feathers can be used as justification for further biomarker or chemical analysis. For example, concentrations of lead in feathers from herons from Hong Kong and Szechuan, China were among the highest in the world, and this was attributed to the use of leaded gasoline (Burger and Gochfeld 1993).

Burger (1993) reviewed the state of knowledge of metals in avian feathers and provides an exhaustive list of the relative concentrations of various metals in feathers vs. body tissues and organs in a number of bird species. Earlier, Honda et al. (1986) found that between 10% (iron) and 50% (mercury) of the total body burdens of 8 trace elements in Great White Egret (from eastern USA) adults and chicks were

Purple Heron. Being dependent on freshwater prey, chicks are particularly sensitive to variation in environmental conditions and high nestling mortality may occur in certain years. Photo: Heinz Hafner.

in the feathers. A recent study involving Little Blue Herons suggested that high levels of cadmium in feathers of growing young may reduce growth rates (Spahn 1997).

One limitation of using trace element concentrations in feathers is that, because the relative body burden that is sequestered into body feathers differs among metals, there is no general conversion factor between residues in feathers and residues in other tissues (Burger 1993). Additionally, only a few studies are available to interpret the significance of trace element concentrations in feathers to the health of the organism. For example, mortality from chronic diseases in Great White Herons was associated with mercury concentrations in livers that exceeded 6 ppm (wet weight) (Spalding et al. 1994a), which is comparable to 9.7 ppm (dry weight) in wading bird

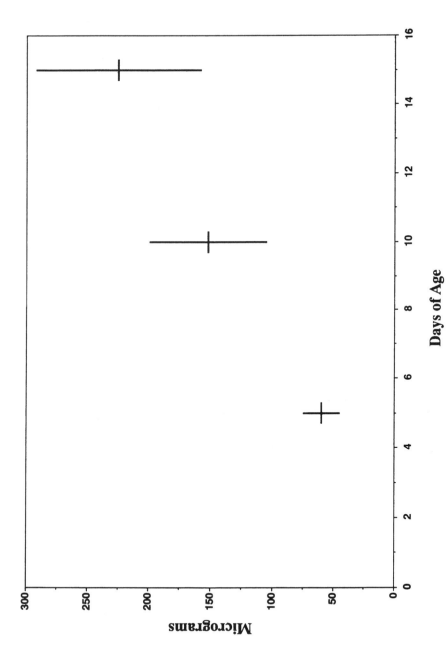

Fig. 15.1 Total PCBs (µg) of 5-, 10-, and 15-day-old skinned carcasses from seven broods of Black-crowned Night Herons collected from Gould Island, Narragansett Bay, Rhode Island in 1987. Horizontal lines are the arithmetic mean; vertical lines represent one standard error. Data redrawn from Custer et al. 1991.

feathers (Beyer et al. 1997). In another study, feather concentrations of lead above 5 ppm (dry weight) were associated with behavioural deficits and impaired growth and survival in Herring Gull (*Larus argentatus*) chicks injected with lead in the laboratory (Burger and Gochfeld 1995). Another issue regarding trace element concentrations in feathers is that the relative contribution of trace elements from body burdens compared to external contamination may be uncertain, because some trace elements (for example cadmium and lead) adhere externally to feathers and cannot be entirely removed by washing prior to chemical analyses (Fasola et al. 1998).

Eggshell thickness/quality

As documented repeatedly in Chapter 12, eggshell thickness is a good indicator of DDE contamination. One concern in measuring eggshell thickness is that it might change with stage of incubation, regardless of contamination. Field evidence suggested this not to be the case for herons (Ohlendorf et al. 1979a) and this was further verified using eggs at various stages of incubation from a captive colony of Black-crowned Night Herons (Bunck et al. 1985).

In addition to structural changes in the eggshell following DDE contamination (Cooke et al. 1976), data on Common Tern (*Sterna hirundo*) eggs suggested reduced pore area in the shell, regardless of thinning (Fox 1976). Shells of eggs in which embryos died had 44% fewer pores, and evaporative water loss was 39% less than from eggs that hatched. Similar information is not available for herons.

Cholinesterase

Measurement of cholinesterase (ChE) activity is frequently used as an indicator of exposure to organophosphorus or carbamate insecticides. Brain cholinesterase activity >20% below reference values or two standard deviations below the average of reference values indicates probable exposure to a ChE inhibitor, and mortality is usually associated with brain ChE activity >50% below controls (Ludke et al. 1975). Because brain ChE activity of Black-crowned Night Heron, Great Egret, and Snowy Egret chicks (and other species with altricial young) increases with age, age must be considered when evaluating exposure of chicks to cholinesterase-inhibiting chemicals (Custer and Ohlendorf 1989). As mentioned in Chapter 12, herons are generally not exposed to cholinesterase-inhibiting chemicals. An exception may be the Cattle Egret, because it tends to feed in uplands.

Cytochrome P450, H4IIE Rat Hepatoma Cell Bioassay and TCDD-equivalents

Planar halogenated hydrocarbons (PHHs) include a possible 209 different polychlorinated biphenyls (PCBs), 75 polychlorinated dibenzo-*p*-dioxins (PCDDs) and 135 polychlorinated dibenzofurans (PCDFs) congeners (Safe 1987). Some of these PHH congeners induce cytochrome P450-dependent mixed function oxygenases and may act as catalysts for many mutagens and carcinogens. Because of the distribution of PHH congeners within samples, estimates of contaminants based on total PCBs, PCDDs or PDFs may not adequately reflect toxicity (Boumphrey et al. 1993). One method to evaluate PHH toxicity is to measure P450-associated monoogenase activities and P450 proteins. Hepatic microsomal EROD activity was 2.6 times greater in Great Blue Heron hatchlings exposed to high, contrasted with low, levels of PCDD and PCDF contamination (Bellward et al. 1990); hepatic microsomal EROD activity was correlated with concentrations of 2,3,7,8-TCDD. Black-crowned Night Heron embryos collected from PCB-contaminated Green Bay, WI, and Saginaw Bay, MI, USA in 1984 had elevated microsomal AHH activity when compared to embryos from a captive colony (Hoffman et al. 1993). Cytochrome P450 activity in livers of Black-crowned Night Heron embryos collected from Green Bay, WI were up to 85-fold higher than reference values (Rattner et al. 1993) and P450 activity was correlated with total PCB concentrations (Fig. 15.2) and the sum of PCB congeners when expressed as dioxin equivalents (Rattner et al. 1994, 1997). In contrast, total PCBs and dioxin equivalents were apparently not sufficiently elevated to induce cytochrome P450 activity in Great Blue Heron embryos from the upper

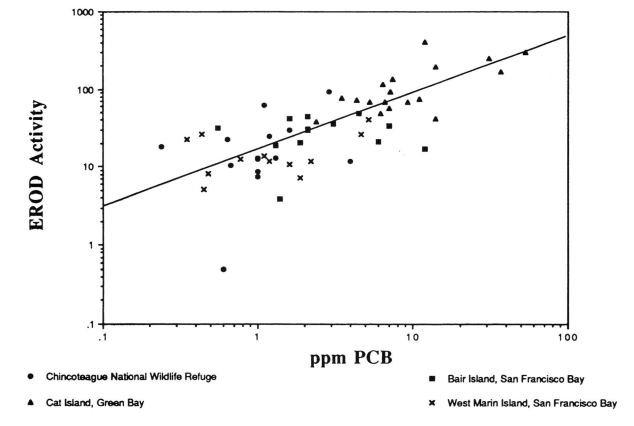

Fig. 15.2 The relation between log-transformed total PCB burdens and hepatic microsomal EROD activity of pipping Black-crowned Night Herons, with detectable values collected from reference and contaminated sites (r = 0.72, p <0.05) (Rattner et al., 1993).

Mississippi River, USA (Custer et al. 1997) and from northern Indiana, USA (Custer et al. 1998). Background levels of cytochrome P450 activity for embryos and 13-day-old Black-crowned Night Herons and embryos of Great Blue Herons are presented by Melancon (1996).

One limitation of using P450s as indicators is that the relationship between exposure and induction in adults is much less predictable than that for embryos (Rattner et al. 1989). Also, samples must be quick frozen when collected, controls must be analysed concurrently with each new collection, and samples should be analysed within a year.

A second method to evaluate overall PHH toxicity is the H4IIE rat hepatoma cell bioassay (Tillitt et al. 1990, Rattner et al. 1994). In this method cultured rat liver cells are challenged with the environmental sample, and cytochrome P450 catalytic activity of the rat liver cells is measured. The advantage of this method over direct measurement of P450 activity of field organisms is that controls do not have to be analysed concurrently, there is no time limit for storage, and the samples do not have to be quick frozen. An underlying assumption of this method is that P450 activity of rat liver cells is similar to that of the organism being sampled.

A third method to estimate PHH toxicity is to calculate 2,3,7,8-TCDD equivalents (TEQs) of the PHH congeners using various potency estimates or toxic equivalency factors (Safe 1987, Kubiak et al. 1989, Custer et al. 1997, 1998, Rattner et al. 1994, 1997). One limitation of this method is that the interactions (e.g. synergism, antagonism, additivity) among the individual PHH congeners are not well understood. An equally important consideration is the high cost of the chemical analysis necessary to measure the various PHH congener concentrations.

Genetic damage

Genetic damage can result from exposure to radiation, petroleum, and some heavy metals. Methods to measure genetic damage include strand breakage, flow cytometry, relative concentration of DNA and RNA/DNA ratios in various tissues, DNA adduct formation, methylation of DNA, and exchange of DNA by sister chromatids (Kushlan 1993b). Hepatic concentrations of DNA in Common Tern embryos were lower in Saginaw Bay than a reference site. However, DNA concentrations in Black-crowned Night Heron embryos did not differ among Saginaw Bay, Green Bay, and a control colony (Hoffman et al. 1993).

The flow cytometry method is a rapid and simple means of quantifying cellular characteristics from suspended cells (Bickham 1990). If blood is used, the technique can be non-lethal to the bird. The coefficient of variation of DNA (CV), measured by flow cytometry, was positively correlated to chromosome breaks in white-footed mice (*Peromyscus leucopus*; McBee and Bickham 1988).

Flow cytometry and DNA concentrations have been investigated in herons. The CV of blood collected from Black-crowned Night Heron embryos suggested cytogenetic damage at a site in Louisiana known to be contaminated with petroleum (Table 15.2; Custer et al. 1994). Blood CV from night heron chicks suggested genetic damage at a site in Texas also known to be contaminated with petroleum. Although the flow cytometry method holds promise, further laboratory and field studies are needed before this technique can be used as a reliable indicator of chromosomal damage.

Table 15.2 Geometric mean coefficient of variation (CV) of DNA content in blood of Black-crowned Night Heron embryos and chicks collected at five locations in the United States. Data from Custer et al. (1994).

Location	Geometric mean CV of DNA content	
	Embryo	Chick
Reference (Virginia)	3.57 BC[1]	3.44 B
Baltimore, Maryland	3.45 C	3.45 B
Green Bay, Wisconsin	3.87 B	3.59 AB
Houston, Texas	3.83 B	3.86 A
Sabine NWR, Louisiana	4.37 A	3.54 B

[1] Among site means not sharing the same letter are significantly different (1 way ANOVA, P <0.05, Bonferroni multiple separation test).

Delta-Aminolevulinic Acid Dehydratase (ALAD)

The measure of ALAD in blood is a useful indicator of lead exposure in birds (Dieter et al. 1976, Blus et al. 1991). As stated in Chapter 12, herons are generally not exposed to lethal or sublethal concentrations of lead. One exception may be the high concentrations of lead in feathers from herons from Hong Kong and Szechuan, China (Burger and Gochfeld 1993). Analysis of blood for ALAD would allow an evaluation of lead exposure in these birds. An advantage of this method is that it is not lethal to the organism.

Deformities

The Canadian Wildlife Service has established a registry of congenital anomalies in fish-eating colonial water birds of the Great Lakes (Fox and Weseloh 1987).

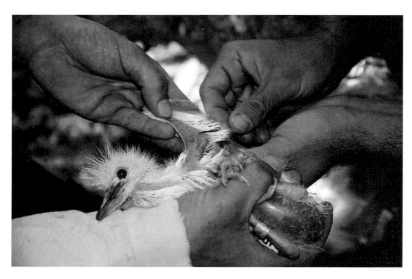

Blood sampling of a Little Egret nestling in the Camargue. Samples are collected to provide molecular and physiological bioindicators. Photo: Emmanuel Vialet.

Deformities observed in the Great Lakes are thought to be related to specific PCBs congeners, dioxins and dibenzofurans. One of 72 Black-crowned Night Heron chicks in 1971–73 (Gilbertson et al. 1976) and none of 574 chicks in 1975–80 (Gilbertson et al. 1991) from Lake Ontario were deformed. Dioxin concentrations in Great Blue Heron eggs from three British Columbia colonies were correlated with depressed embryonic growth and the increased frequency of oedema (Hart et al. 1991). Subcutaneous oedema was observed in 33% of hatchlings from the most TCDD-contaminated colony, 15% from the intermediate TCDD-contaminated colony, and none from the least TCDD-contaminated colony. Additionally, the brains of Great Blue Heron hatchlings from contaminated colonies displayed gross morphometric intercerebral asymmetry, and the asymmetry was associated with TCDD contamination (Henshel et al. 1992).

A high incidence of abnormal embryos occurred in Black-crowned Night Heron embryos from Green Bay and Saginaw Bay (Chapter 12; Hoffman et al. 1993). Most of the abnormalities were characterised by subcutaneous oedema; one embryo from Saginaw Bay had a shortened lower mandible. Recently, bill deformities were reported in two Reddish Egret chicks in a south Texas colony. Field studies have been initiated to evaluate these findings (M. Mora pers. comm.).

Metallothionein induction

The induction of metallothioneins, metal-binding peptides and proteins, may be indicative of metal contamination. However, interpretation is difficult because induction is not related to specific metals, including non-toxic metals (Kushlan 1993b). Concentrations of metallothionein-like proteins were only correlated to zinc in liver samples of Little Egrets collected from the Camargue, France (Cosson 1989).

Population Level Indicators

In the following sections, we review some of the PCE bioindicators that have been used in herons and others that may have potential. Some of these suggest a direct response to a specific environmental change, while others are quite indirect.

Mortality

Collecting dead birds, either isolated individuals or a number from one location, can provide useful indicator information. Finding even a few dead birds in an area where pesticides are used is usually indicative. As mentioned in Chapter 12, archived collections of herons identified mortality of adult herons and egrets caused by organochlorine. Ohlendorf et al. (1981) analysed brains of 51 herons found dead or moribund in the USA from 1966 to 1977. Eight herons probably died of dieldrin poisoning; four others had hazardous levels of dieldrin. Finding a number of dead heron adults at one location is unusual. Such cases might occur from unusually severe weather conditions (for instance lightning strike or hail), disease, or aerial spraying of an organophosphate or carbamate pesticide on agricultural fields. As mentioned in Chapter 12, only one instance of organophosphate or carbamate pesticide poisoning has been reported in herons, probably because of their general lack of association with agricultural habitat.

Using mortality as an indicator is, by its nature, a *post hoc* rather than a prescriptive protocol for assessing environmental change. Its primary weaknesses are its serendipitous nature, dependence on rapid discovery, and lack of sampling rigour. Costs are generally very low because of the erratic frequency of sampling and because few specimens are needed to determine cause of death in large, episodic events. When a cause can be determined, mortality may be a primary response to an environmental "insult" (agricultural pesticides for example) or a secondary response (such as parasitism from local fish at a sewage treatment lagoon).

Distributional changes

Changes in either the breeding or wintering distributions of herons can be used as a potential bioindicator of landscape-level changes in wetland quality or quantity. However, simply assessing presence/absence patterns as reported in state breeding bird atlases is probably not sensitive enough to be a bioindicator (e.g., Andrle and Carroll 1988). Broad-scale distributional changes by the Cattle Egret, for example, have little to do with changes in habitat quality or quantity; the change has more to do with this species expanding into a "vacant niche" (Telfair 1993).

However, recovery of former ranges may strongly indicate general improvement in habitat quality. The reappearance of the Cattle Egret in the Nile River Delta after its extirpation was presumed to result from declines in DDT application (Mullié et al. 1992). Other examples are found for other groups of water birds (United States Fish and Wildlife Service 1985, Weseloh et al. 1995), attributed in part to a reduction in levels of organochlorine compounds, hence improved water quality.

Breeding Populations. Changes in the relative abundance of breeding herons over larger spatial scales may indicate large-scale changes in habitat quality or quantity. For instance, the changing hydrology in the Everglades–Florida Bay region, USA, has had substantial impact on the distribution of breeding herons, egrets, and other wading birds in Florida over the past 25–50 years (Powell 1983, Ogden et al. 1987, Frohring et al. 1988, Kushlan 1989b). This method is expensive and requires substantial manpower and aircraft time, especially for species that cannot be estimated or photographed from aircraft.

The problems associated with census accuracy and standardisation have been raised on many occasions (cf. Kushlan 1993b), but these do not seem to be any more intractable than are census data from other wildlife species. Another problem is that distributional changes are usually slow to occur and may reflect changes that have been occurring for a number of years (Frohring et al. 1988). In spite of these shortcomings, however, this method does yield valuable direct information about responses to changing habitat conditions over a landscape scale and should continue as the "backbone" of regional and state monitoring programmes.

Monitoring of breeding colonies has occurred in a number of countries outside of North America. In Australia, a Project Egret Watch has developed over recent years (Chapter 6). In the Mediterranean Basin, a number of regions such as Portugal, coastal Spain, southern France, northern Italy, and Greece, have included heron censusing as part of a regular wetland monitoring programme (Chapter 2) and a new initiative is under way to conduct basinwide inventories (N. Hecker, Station Biologique de la Tour du Valat, pers. comm.). In the United Kingdom, a Grey Heron survey has been conducted for decades (Reynolds 1979). These monitoring efforts have documented population increases (for example Grey Herons and Cattle Egrets) in parts of Europe and Australia. In Europe, water bird population monitoring seems to couple fairly well with changing agricultural practices; in northern Italy, for instance, rice field areas seem to explain the abundance and distribution of Black-crowned Night Herons (Fasola and Alieri 1992).

Wintering populations. In the western Palearctic, Wetlands International has been coordinating winter (January) censuses of important wetlands in Europe for migratory water birds (van Vessem and Rose 1993). Although the thrust of the effort and analysis has been directed at the Anatidae (Rüger et al. 1986), census data are also collected on herons and other waders. No analyses have been done of these data.

In the USA, little effort has been made to assess changes in wintering numbers of herons and other waders, except by the National Audubon Society's Christmas Bird Counts (CBC) (Root 1988). For most bird species, maps based on average numbers for certain areas over a 10-year period are shown (Root 1988). Only recently has there been any attempt to examine CBC trends as a monitoring tool (McCrimmon et al. 1997, J. Sauer pers. comm.). Preliminary results of these CBC analyses suggest some significant winter population increases for Great, Snowy, and Cattle egrets, Green and Black-crowned Night herons (Table 15.3). Little Blue Herons show a negative (but not significant) trend. Some general qualitative changes in some heron species in certain regions have become apparent. For example, the expansion of aquaculture in western Mississippi and Louisiana has attracted increasing numbers of Great Blue Herons and other aquatic birds to the point where economic impacts are being felt (Nettleship and Duffy 1995). In Florida, where wetland losses have been most pronounced, populations of Snowy Egrets and Tricolored Herons appear to have declined over the past three decades of the CBC; however, Great Egret and Little Blue Heron numbers appear to be relatively stable (McCrimmon et al. 1997).

Table 15.3 Summary of Christmas Bird Count (USA) trend analysis for selected heron species, 1966–1989.

Species	Trend[1]	No. circles[2]	Probability[3]
Great Blue Heron	2.20	1643	0.001
Great Egret	2.45	490	0.003
Snowy Egret	2.02	317	0.028
Little Blue Heron	−0.24	224	0.749
Tricolored Heron	0.55	185	0.614
Cattle Egret	2.81	350	0.016
Black-crowned Night Heron	2.85	545	0.002

[1]Trends listed as percent change per year, using weighted regression methods developed by J. Sauer (USGS Patuxent Wildlife Research Center).
[2]Circle is a 15-mile (24.3 km) diameter search area.
[3]Probability that the trend estimate = 0.

Interpreting data from winter bird censuses, whether in Europe or North America, must be done with caution. Water (or ice) conditions during the very short period of the CBC in December or the International Waterfowl Census period in January probably explain much of the distributions of wading birds and therefore are unlikely to reveal much about changing environmental quality in general. Nonetheless, data for many other bird species may be valuable and therefore collecting additional data on herons and their allies can be used as another (albeit minor) source of population trend information.

Reproductive performance

Reproductive parameters may be the most sensitive of the PCE bioindicators because they reveal primary responses to environmental changes (Temple and Wiens 1989). Below are listed several potential bioindicators that focus on the breeding season.

Timing of nesting. At least in some areas, the dates of nesting and clutch initiation by herons may be used as a proximal indicator of the local conditions (for example hydrology) of wetlands (Kushlan 1986, Frederick and Collopy 1988). In general, when wading birds defer nesting, wetland conditions are suboptimal for feeding success; hence success may be lower than in years when nesting begins early (Frederick and Collopy 1988, J. Ogden pers. comm.). Monitoring timing of egg laying is inexpensive, but reflects relatively little about the wetlands except that feeding conditions are not particularly good at that time. If however there is a chronic shift in the timing of nesting such as that experienced by Wood Storks in the Everglades (Ogden 1994), then this monitoring information could prove useful at a gross scale when coupled with other information.

Clutch size. Some evidence has shown that, in years with low average clutch sizes in herons, survival and fledging success (per hatched egg) may also be reduced (Frederick and Collopy 1988, Parsons 1994, Erwin et al. 1996a, T. Custer unpubl. data). This suggests that local prey abundance within the foraging range of the colony influences reproductive activities early and throughout the season. Thus, an early, simple-to-measure method (estimating average clutch size in a colony) may be used as a surrogate for nest success in heron colonies, at least where predation and weather do not exact major egg losses. Such an assessment can be made with two visits to a colony. On the first visit, during early- to mid-incubation, a sample of nests and eggs are marked. On the second visit, several days later, completed clutches are recorded. The method is cost-effective but the response (i.e., clutch size) may not be sensitive for some species to a particular environmental insult (Parsons 1994).

Hatching and fledging success. Hatching success of eggs and fledging success of chicks can be influenced by a number of variables including predation, climatic factors, food availability (hence, habitat quality of the wetlands in which they feed), disease, and contaminants (e.g., Henny et al. 1984, Kushlan 1989a, Frederick and Collopy 1989a, 1989b). Hatching success has been repeatedly used to evaluate effects of contaminants on herons (see Chapter 12). For example, when DDE concentrations in sample Black-crowned Night Heron eggs exceeded 8 ppm, clutch size decreased, the frequency of cracked eggs increased and productivity decreased (Henny et al. 1984).

The utility of using nesting success as a bioindicator however depends on the relative importance of food as a limiting factor during breeding and the individual species involved. Some species such as Great Blue Herons or Black-crowned Night Herons are extremely generalised in feeding (Erwin and Spendelow 1991, Butler, P. J. 1992); declines in fish in a tidal wetland may simply result in a habitat switch to non-tidal wetlands or even uplands (see Diet of young, below). For species such as Snowy Egrets or Tricoloured Herons, however, their dependence on intertidal wetlands for feeding makes them better potential indicators of environmental change in estuarine wetlands (see for example Ramo and Busto 1993, Parsons 1994). Snowy Egret fledging success did not recover to pre-oil spill levels at a New York estuary even two years after the spill (Parsons 1994); in contrast, she found that the success of Black-crowned Night Herons showed little change as a result of the spill. For certain metals such as cadmium and lead, survival of young Little Blue Herons may provide a sensitive bioindicator (Spahn 1997).

The use of nesting success as a method is costly in time because it requires regular visits to colonies, at least once per week. Visiting the colony results in disturbance, which can either have negligible or significant consequences to the estimate of success of the species being studied (Chapter 9). Also, because of the mobility of young, "nest success" for most wading birds generally is estimated only to about two weeks of age. Most wading bird young require at least 6 weeks to fledge (Palmer 1962). Data from radiotelemetry studies on several heron and egret species have shown that nestling mortality can be significant after the first two weeks (H. Hafner unpubl. data, Erwin et al. 1996a). Thus, "success" as reported in most studies necessarily overestimates fledging success. In spite of these problems, we recommend monitoring of this sensitive parameter for certain species that are relatively specialised in their prey and/or feeding habitats. For the heron group, this includes Snowy Egrets, Tricoloured Herons, Little Blue Herons and Yellow-crowned Night Herons in North America. In Europe, the Purple and Squacco herons may be good candidates.

Growth rates of young. Growth rates of young are often correlates of nestling survival (Custer and Peterson 1991, Parsons 1994, Spahn 1997). The magnitude of difference in masses among chicks in asynchronous broods may hypothetically parallel survival differences and reveal the degree to which colonies are food-stressed over space and time (Lack 1966). In field studies in Virginia, we found a significant relationship between the magnitude of mass differences between first- and third-hatched chicks and the number of young surviving to 14 days for Snowy Egrets, but not Black-crowned Night Herons (Table 15.4, Erwin et al. 1996a). For certain contaminants such as cadmium, reduced growth rate of young may be related to high levels found in the feathers in Little Blue Herons (Spahn 1997).

Investigators have usually measured several growth parameters in herons: body mass, culmen length, and/or tarsus length (Custer and Peterson 1991, Parsons 1994). Culmen and tarsal growth have been used to age heron and egret chicks (Custer and Peterson 1991); however, we found at a Virginia colony that the culmen growth rates of Black-crowned Night Herons may vary significantly between years (Table 15.5). We also found that culmen length is much less variable than is mass

Table 15.4 Relationship between mass difference between A vs. C chicks[1] and number of young surviving (14 days) for Snowy Egret and Black-crowned Night Heron broods at a Virginia, USA, colony, 1992–93.

Species	N	T value[2]	P	Model
Snowy Egret	50	2.93	0.005	Percent mass = 35.53 + 10.72 (no. chicks)
Black-crowned Night Heron	43	0.12	0.91	Percent mass = 65.99 + 0.40 (no. chicks)

[1] A = first-hatched, C = third-hatched chicks in a brood.
[2] Randomisation test (1000 permutations) for the regression.

Table 15.5 Relative variation in culmen and body mass growth rates for Black-crowned Night Herons at a Chincoteague, Virginia, USA, colony, 1992–1993.

Chick	N	Culmen[1] (mm/d)	C.V.[2]	Mass (g/d)	C.V.
1992					
A	8	1.87[3]	17	31.28	34
B	7	1.90	13	35.94	27
C	4	1.59[4]	36	7.41	137
1993					
A	10	2.23[3]	8	39.33	14
B	9	2.21	10	34.88	21
C	9	2.17[4]	17	33.85	35

[1] Means for culmen and mass growth.
[2] C.V. = coefficient of variation.
[3] Significant year difference; ANOVA "A" chick, F=7.03, P<0.03.
[4] Significant year difference; ANOVA "C" chick, F=3.92, P<0.05.

growth, hence is not as statistically sensitive to between-colony or between-year variation as is body mass. Linear measurements of morphological features with important survival function are probably of limited utility as bioindicators; they are undoubtedly under strong genetic constraints (i.e., are canalised *sensu* Waddington 1957). At the other extreme, mass changes are highly variable. Measurements of mass of heron chicks are highly subject to the vagaries of feeding schedules. We have found that regurgitated boluses of Black-crowned Night Herons may constitute from 1% to more than 20% of the gross mass of a chick during the first two weeks of age (Erwin et al. unpubl. data). Thus, true body mass may be difficult to estimate in the field.

Given the problems associated with growth parameters, we feel that using growth rates as a biomonitoring tool requires further research before it is widely used. At present, it does not seem to be a cost-effective biomonitoring method for herons and their allies.

Parasite loads

Wetlands may differ in quality as well as quantity. In a number of wetlands created for municipal sewage treatment in Florida, the fish eaten by herons are highly infected with nematodes capable of killing young (Spalding 1990, Spalding et al.

1994b). Similar parasitic infections in herons have also been reported at a large colony in Delaware (Weise et al. 1977), and the Houston Ship Channel, Texas (Franson and Custer 1994), although the source of the fish was not known in these studies. Monitoring for parasites is a simple method but, in itself, parasitism rates of young are unlikely to reveal a chronic condition of the wetlands. Little information exists relating parasitism in fish and other aspects of wetland function.

Diet of young

Monitoring the diet of young herons is facilitated by their propensity to regurgitate. Thus, direct measures of fresh prey (including contaminant assessments) can be made to compare with parallel measures in the young. Dietary composition can be used to determine whether the source of prey is freshwater, marine, or terrestrial. During periods of drought in the Everglades of Florida, herons and other waders nest and feed mostly in brackish water areas (Frederick and Collopy 1989a, Bancroft et al. 1990). As a result, few amphibians or freshwater fish were found in the diet. On the other hand, the diets of Black-crowned Night Herons at one colony in coastal Virginia included fish, shrimp, frogs, small mammals, and even small Laughing Gull (*Larus atricilla*) chicks (Erwin et al. unpubl. data). Monitoring diets of opportunistic species may be more difficult to interpret; however, after an oil spill in New York Harbor, Parsons (1994) found that the night herons switched from feeding in estuarine wetlands to refuse facilities.

   Another caveat concerns seasonality in diet. Examination of diet in the incubation period of a heron species may not be indicative of diets fed to the young; similarly, diets of very small young may differ from those near fledging. Bildstein (1993) documents the shift in the diets of young White Ibis (*Eudocimus albus*) as a result of changing salt tolerances in their prey.

Community Level Indicators

Using changes in community (i.e., multi-species) attributes of herons usually includes other associated wading birds such as ibises, storks, spoonbills, etc. Monitoring the relative changes in numbers of species that depend on more specialised habitats should provide an indication of long-term changes in wetland conditions. For example, an increase in Tricolored Herons or Snowy Egrets may indicate saltwater intrusion into wetlands, while an increase in Little Blue Herons may suggest a shift to more freshwater conditions (Frederick et al. 1992). This bioindicator would result from an evaluation of censusing data and therefore is a secondary assessment that would be used only as ancillary information.

   Another type of community bioindicator is one of habitat use. In areas with intense human disturbance along the coast, herons and their allies have shifted from nesting on barrier islands to man-made dredged deposition material islands in a number of states in the USA (Erwin 1980). Such a dramatic change in habitats over time may not be common. More subtle shifts may occur as food conditions change gradually (Frohring et al. 1988, Frederick et al. 1992). For instance, in northern Italy, most wading birds are associated with rice fields, not natural wetland sites (Fasola and Alieri 1992). Monitoring colony site use and general habitat association in this region has suggested that natural wetland habitat has been lost; although the overall population size of some species (for instance Black-crowned Night Heron) has increased, the number of heronries has actually decreased (Fasola and Alieri 1992). Thus, simply monitoring the colony and roost site use of herons over time and its habitat association may provide valuable "indicator" information.

Ecosystem Level Indicators

Kushlan (1993b) mentions several ecosystem-level functions of relevance to herons, such as bioenergetics, community respiration, and decomposition rates. However, because herons are only a small part of most ecosystems and because of their mobility and seasonality in most systems, using system parameters such as those mentioned by Kushlan (1993b) is probably not feasible. Monitoring at the ecosystem level is plagued with problems when trying to assess cause–effect relationships (Spellerberg 1991). Even if major ecosystem functions being monitored were found to change, it is unlikely that some change in the heron community would have been implicated.

Operational Issues

The selection of the appropriate suborganismal/organismal bioindicator depends on the perceived need for each situation. For example, in an area comtaminated with PCBs, such as the Great Lakes, contaminant accumulation in chicks coupled with measurements of liver enzyme induction would allow an evaluation of potential effects. On the other hand, if herons are found dead near an agricultural field following an organophosphorus pesticide application, the measurement of brain cholinesterase would seem appropriate. The following suborganism/ organism biomonitoring tools are the major ones that have been successfully used for herons:

1) Contaminant accumulation in chicks can indicate local contamination of a wide variety of contaminants.
2) Trace elements in feathers can be used to compare species, locations, or time periods. However, the toxicity of the individual trace elements cannot be evaluated.
3) Eggshells collected where organochlorine pesticides were or are used, can serve as an indicator of DDE pesticide contamination.
4) The measurement of liver enzyme induction can be used to evaluate contamination by planar halogenated hydrocarbons (PCBs, dioxins, dibenzofurans), but suffers from not being specific.
5) The flow cytometry method shows promise as a non-destructive tool for evaluating genetic damage caused by exposure to radiation, petroleum, and possibly some metals.
6) Measurements of cholinesterase and delta-aminolevulinic acid dehydratase are useful tools for measuring exposure to organophosphorus or carbamate pesticides and lead, respectively.

There are also many potential indicators available at levels above the organism. Depending on the logistical constraints and the primary objectives of the programme, we recommend the following approaches to heron monitoring. The following examples apply again to the perceived information need and the manpower and funds available to conduct the studies:

1)   Adult herons found dead can be frozen and archived for necropsy and possible contaminant analysis. This is especially useful in developing countries that continue to use organochlorine pesticides.
2)   Monitoring of breeding colony locations and estimates of population size can reflect population sizes and the environmental conditions constraining them. Censuses should be conducted (with the same observers using replicate counts if possible) at least for large colonies on a periodic basis (annually or at 3–4 year intervals). When possible, roost locations should also be mapped on a year-round basis.
3)   Estimates of the timing of nesting and clutch sizes of selected species can be used to determine primary population responses to stress. In mixed-species colonies where eggs cannot be discriminated, initial brood sizes of a sample of nests can be measured within a week post-hatching.
4)   At a more intensive level of monitoring, an index of reproductive success (e.g., number of young surviving to about 2 weeks) can be attempted at a sample of colony sites on a periodic basis. Supplemental data on relative chick size (mass of C- vs. A-chicks) can easily be added. Growth rates of young require further evaluation.

Conclusions

The use of population or higher level measures for biomonitoring of birds as indicators of environmental change has been challenged by earlier authors. The chief criticism is that there is little coupling in either time or space between population phenomena in birds and specific environmental changes. Another criticism is that many of the biological responses that are measured are not specific to individual contaminants. However, most authors agree that using suborganismal/organismal bioindicators in herons and other species, while not always "chemical-specific", represents an effective means of monitoring both for effect and exposure to contaminants. Biomonitoring programmes seem to be most effective when a combination of biological indicators (at different levels of organisation) and chemical/physical indicators are used.

Concentrations of environmental contaminants in tissues (or excrement) of herons can be used to evaluate the chronic or acute effects on herons. They can also be used to make comparisons among species, locations, or time periods. Other suborganism indicators and their application are mentioned in Recommendations. Adult and juvenile herons found dead should be archived for necropsy and possible contaminant analysis. Maintaining an inventory of breeding colony (and roost) sites for herons and their allies and estimates of population sizes is a minimal requirement at broad spatial scales (regions within countries). Measurements of "primary population parameters" (e.g., timing of nesting, clutch size, hatching success and/or fledging success) are all valuable additions to a biomonitoring programme, as resources allow.

Although they are not a comprehensive "bioassay" of environmental change by themselves, herons and other wading birds have been selected as a key biological indicator group in a number of regions, including the Florida Everglades in the United States, the Fraser River Delta region of British Columbia, Canada, and in Mediterranean basin wetland areas of Europe and North Africa. Recognising the importance of wading bird (and other water bird) populations, new international efforts have been launched in North America, Europe, and North Africa to monitor populations and their wetland habitats. These efforts involve partnerships among national, regional, provincial, and non-governmental organisations.

16. Research and Information Needs for Heron Conservation

James A. Kushlan

The edifice of heron conservation must be constructed on a firm foundation of scientific information. Fortunately, as shown in previous chapters, there exists for many herons and in many areas a considerable body of pertinent information. This information base is derived from surveys, studies, and conservation action undertaken around the world, much of it within the last two decades (Chapter 17). As much as feasible, this information base has been summarised in previous chapters of this book.

Nonetheless, there also remain significant information needs that must be filled through inventory, research, and long-term monitoring if heron conservation is to proceed. For a few species the information base is limited to a few observations of their presence and behaviour. For many species, we know little more than places they occur and their basic biology. Even for the best-known species and continents, significant information gaps exist. For example, only in Europe is the understanding of population sizes and dispersion sufficient to understand population status in any quantitative way.

Information needs include population data, ecological information, and basic biology. It would be remiss however to confine discussion to biology alone. The fundamental threat to herons is not their biology but the economic and political forces affecting the landscape.

In this chapter, various information needs are noted to focus attention on the studies most needed. The results of the previous chapters underlie much of this discussion, and it also draws on previous syntheses (Hancock and Kushlan 1984, Kushlan 1992, 1997, Sheldon and Slikas 1997, Hafner 1997a, Cezilly 1997, Bildstein 1997).

The Literature

It should be recognised that much of the information of value to heron conservation remains unpublished or poorly published. A scan of the chapters will reveal how

Heron Conservation
ISBN 0-12-430130-4

much of the information of this book is derived (thankfully) from personal communications. Information resides in unpublished reports, the "grey" literature, in people's memories or notebooks, theses and so forth. An important slice of the published literature is unavailable to most western authors because it is published in a language not traditionally used by international science; see for example the chapters on Asia. A critical need is to continue to discover and access this information, to produce translations of various works, to develop international data banks to which data can be easily contributed, and to continue to develop expert networks such as professional societies and the Heron Specialist Group. The first information need for heron conservation is to continue to access and synthesise what is already known.

Socio-economics

The connectivity of herons with human dominance of the landscape is central to understanding heron conservation issues. Human cultures that value or protect wildlife or animals or all of nature provide protection for herons as well. The status of herons on the Indian subcontinent is specifically enhanced in Hindu areas. Human cultures that have achieved a high level of prosperity can afford to appreciate environmental protection of their wildlife and natural landscape. There is a critical need for study and evaluation of the relationship of human cultural attitudes to heron conservation. In developing species – or regional – conservation plans these cultural understandings need to be explicitly considered in planning.

The economics of heron conservation have been little studied. The gravest threats to heron conservation worldwide are wetland loss and alteration and human depredation, especially in aquacultural situations. These threats are entirely economically driven. In the developed portion of the world, formal environmental assessment and impact analysis require an understanding of the impact of economic forces on heron populations, and conversely the economic impact of herons (both positive and negative). The economics of heron conservation require intense study.

Population status

From the information summarised in the geographic chapters, it is clear that data on the numbers of herons composing regional and national populations are severely limited. For most continents, the chapter authors can do no more than indicate the presence or absence of a species from a country in their status tables. Western Europe enjoys the best population estimates due to having few species, a restricted number of nesting sites, an admirably long-standing tradition of counting birds, and the core presence of the Heron Specialist Group. Overall, the best population knowledge is found especially in the United Kingdom, France, Netherlands, and northern Italy. On other continents, breeding population estimates could be in error by ten or even a hundred fold. This is true even in North America, where population estimates can be inferred from the hit-or-miss record of surveys, but the reliability of the estimates within a power of one or two remains suspect.

For many herons, counting is made easier by their periodic concentration in colony and roost sites. However, colonies need to be found and the birds then counted, with some acceptable degree of accuracy. Herons also gather in wintering sites. Estimates there also are few and less exhaustive because most wintering areas

The gravest threats to heron conservation are economically and politically driven. This aquaculture development destroyed large mangrove areas in Cambodia. The impact of economics on herons and conversely the economic impact of herons represent an immense potential for future research. Photo: Taej Mundkur.

are relatively inaccessible. Many species instead of concentrating are highly dispersed, and wintering birds may be indistinguishable from year-round residents. So it is not clear what populations are being counted.

The state of knowledge of the status of non-colonial species is even worse than for those that congregate at times during their annual cycle. These species are often cryptic, shy of people, highly dispersed, and in inaccessible habitat. These species require the development of inventory techniques uniquely suitable to their unique situation.

It is well appreciated that accurate population estimates provide the most useful metric for conservation. Population numbers are the surest way of monitoring population changes. Knowing the size of the overall population and the proportion of a population using specific sites allow the identification of important heron areas and assessment of risks faced by population segments of concern. Knowledge of global or regional population sizes is particularly critical for determining and asserting the importance of specific sites as key to the population. Since we recommend using the Ramsar criteria, whereby 1% of a population using a site renders that site key to the species, the ability to estimate the total population size is paramount.

However, determining and evaluating heron population numbers require advances in both methodology and conservation infrastructure. Regarding methodology, a fundamental need is for detailed studies of the efficacy of available techniques in individual applications. Dodd and Murphy's (1995) study of Great Blue Herons is an excellent model for such research. Although aerial surveys have long been used both to locate and count colonies, it has become increasingly apparent that errors (generally underestimates) are too high for conservation purposes (see for example Rodgers et al. 1995, Frederick, Towles et al. 1996, Dodd and Murphy 1995). While random or systematic aerial surveys can be used to locate colony sites, only small colonies of large, top-nesting birds can be counted with sufficient accuracy from the air. Aerial censuses, if used, must be corrected by ground counts in ways that are appropriate for each application (Pollock and Kendall 1987). Accuracy and precision problems are also found in ground-based census techniques (Erwin 1980b, Dodd and Murphy 1995). One of the most significant research needs for herons is to study and account for bias in counting techniques, to develop monitoring programmes that measure the bias, and to develop models to estimate population size incorporating the biases of the data.

The difficulty of compiling an inventory of heron populations in lesser developed countries, the bulk of their range, cannot be overstated. Some of the areas thought to be most critical for herons are inaccessible due to remoteness, cost of access, lack of infrastructural support, or—very importantly—civil unrest.

Regarding infrastructure, within each appropriate political or environmental entity, government agencies, NGOs, and citizens need to work together to develop inventory and monitoring programmes to provide more accurate estimates of heron populations, in both summer and winter. It should not be overlooked, however, that there are considerable political impediments for governments and NGOs to work together in most parts of the world. It is even more difficult to connect governments and NGOs to the local human populations that control the outcome of heron conservation in most locations. Since scarce resources must be combined to accomplish conservation objectives, research and models are needed to discover and demonstrate mechanisms by which collaborative conservation can be undertaken.

The resources and organisational structure must be developed to provide for repeated censuses. How this is to be accomplished will differ among applications, and various models need to be tried, evaluated and reported. Development of monitoring infrastructure may, in itself, be considered a research need. The special challenges of accomplishing this in lesser-developed countries, noted above, should be carefully considered. Creating interacting networks of important locations of shared heron populations, developing continental monitoring schemes, north–south and east–west dialogue and assistance, and developing cost- and manpower-effective techniques are needed. Models that work are critically needed.

The importance of population estimates notwithstanding, for many applications the trend of population change rather than absolute numbers may be what is required for conservation monitoring. This too needs to be quantitative within regions and within populations, and must account for bias. Techniques used in any application should aim to allow detection of at least a 20% change in numbers between years of the populations being monitored (Parnell et al. 1988).

Of course an important consideration is that population indices must be sensitive enough to reveal such trends, and this requires considerable additional research.

Evaluation of trend data can suggest when population trajectories are such as to require management intervention. Monitoring programmes need to be developed at several scales, local, national, and continental. To make monitoring data useful, monitoring data collected at different scales need to be collected in a standardised way (Erwin 1985b). Furthermore, new ways of sampling wild populations, particularly using capture–recapture models, hold great promise for development of effective population and trend estimation (North and Morgan 1979, Kushlan 1992, Nichols 1992). The data need to be shared through communal data management systems, which in the best situation should allow data to be made available electronically to any interested person who may wish to conduct analyses. The development of compatible, accessible monitoring programmes requires considerable research and development in the many different kinds of settings in

Little Egret. An individually recognisable bird in the Camargue. Capture–recapture models are increasingly used to estimate demographic trends and also for bias estimation. Photo: Olivier Pineau.

which monitoring has to occur. Sharing ideas and models through publication of case histories is essential.

The success of trend analysis is generally dependent on the messiness of the data. Designing monitoring programmes with sufficient statistical rigour to conduct predetermined analyses is essential, and an exceptionally high priority in heron conservation. In the past, uncertainties inherent in combining data sets taken over different times, areas, and methods have reduced interpretive reliability. Studies leading to standardised monitoring protocols are highly desirable; and, if history is a guide, developing techniques to evaluate unstandardised or "messy" data sets will remain equally important.

Population numbers or trends are necessary but not sufficient to appreciate population status. For most species, basic demographic parameters are little known. This need is especially acute in relatively long-lived birds such as herons, in which current population sizes in themselves are seldom indicative of the long-term health of the population. Without knowing and monitoring age-specific survival, gender-specific survival, age at first breeding, short- and long-term reproductive success, and the factors influencing success and adult survivorship, it is difficult to understand the causes of trends being observed and therefore to begin appropriate conservation measures. It is particularly critical that additional studies be conducted of heron survivorship. Cezilly (1997) pointed out that the efforts put into assuring nesting success may be futile if the fate of the population depends more on variation in adult survival.

Distribution

The geographic distribution of herons can change over surprisingly short periods of years. Expansion of the Cattle Egret throughout much of the world in this century is the most notable example, but other species on all continents have expanded or contracted ranges in recent decades. Range changes need to be monitored. Some range changes are geographic shifts without population change. When distribution changes are detected, studies into causes are needed in order to determine if conservation action is required.

The vagility of some heron species suggests that conservation is usually required at a scale above that of the local colony site or feeding area. Populations need to be understood in terms of their regional demographics. It is likely that the source–sink concept of metapopulation analysis would be a valuable approach to heron population biology. To accomplish this, studies need to be undertaken of dispersal (Cezilly 1997). Ringing, colour marking, and perhaps genetic studies are needed.

Most herons are migratory, and for most of these species, little is known about their movements, particularly the range of decisions available to individual birds. Studies in the Mediterranean suggest that annual differences occur in the numbers of birds migrating and the extent of their movement. For some species, conditions on the wintering grounds are believed to significantly affect survivorship (Chapter 11). It is therefore critical that important stopover locales and wintering areas be identified and sufficiently understood to support conservation action if needed. Even in North America, wintering locations are only superficially known (Mikuska et al. 1998). Locations where a significant proportion of a population winters need to be identified and put under conservation protection, as important heron areas. Research on heron dispersal, migration patterns, stopover locations, and wintering sites is needed. Fortunately techniques are available, involving ringing, visible marking, radio telemetry, and satellite telemetry, if the resources to conduct the studies can be secured. The recommendation for increased ringing and telemetry study is critical to heron conservation. In winter, roost site dynamics and foraging habitat may play roles in bird survival and need to be better understood.

As noted above, there are probably specific locales for most species that support a significant portion of a population. While the criteria for such areas may differ among species, the Heron Specialist Group in this book adopts the Ramsar criterion that a site is important to herons if it supports 1% or more of a species or a species segment for some part of the year. These locales, which can be called Important Heron Conservation Areas, need to be identified and described for all heron species worldwide, as a significant research task. The maps in this book are a starting point for further research.

Conservation populations

One of the more fundamental information needs, in heron conservation is determining what constitutes a population of conservation interest (Kushlan 1997). Although a principal goal of heron conservation should be to preserve the genetic diversity of the family worldwide, the genetic structures of heron populations are totally unknown. The study of the biochemical genetics of widespread species is essential to understand the scope of variation to be conserved and how this variation is packaged within population segments suitable for conservation planning. Herons such as the Great White Egret, Little Egret, Green-backed Heron, and Black-crowned Night Heron need to be characterised genetically over their nearly cosmopolitan ranges. For the first three of these, there even remain doubts as to the most appropriate species limits, thereby requiring higher-level biochemical taxonomic study (Hancock and Kushlan 1984). A number of species are currently subdivided into subspecies, which must be re-examined using biochemical techniques if they are to become useful conservation units. In this book, we identify some populations that have not been taxonomically discriminated as being of conservation importance (Chapter 17). It is crucial that genetic studies be brought to bear on the question of what is a population of conservation interest.

Population biology

Much is known about the population biology of many herons. However, there continues to be a critical need for demographic studies of herons, particularly reproductive success and survival. This requires long-term studies, utilising ringing, telemetry, state of the art analytical tools and modelling. Recent reports of such long-term studies, such as Hafner et al. (1998a) and Thomas et al. (1999), show the value of understanding the roles of competition, differential survival, nesting success, and survival on population stability. Analytical techniques and the sophistication of the scientific questions that can be asked of a data set are developing quickly. The availability of long-term demographic data sets is critically limited. There is a crucial need for long-term population biology studies to produce the data sets that can be mined by the quickly developing field of population biology.

A Squacco Heron chick. A capture–recapture study on the local Camargue population was initiated in 1999. Photo: Carol Durand.

Habitat conservation

Habitat quality is as essential to herons as it is for other species (see Chapters 9, 10, 11). However, defining habitat quality is not easy and, despite overlapping requirements, differs somewhat among species and among geographic areas. A fundamental research need for each species is to identify the critical habitat elements that are required for its life cycle. While these differ among species, nesting and feeding habitat requirements are often similar for sympatric colonial nesting species.

For most of the heron world, understanding of heron biology requires understanding of the functioning of wetlands. Research on the ecology and function of wetlands is an essential prerequisite to heron conservation. What should be especially encouraged is the study of wetland function as it directly affects herons.

The strong connection of herons with wetlands should not divert attention from other heron habitats. Some of the most endangered herons use forests rather than wetlands. Our knowledge of what constitutes quality for herons in forest habitats is non-existent. Research is needed on the effects of felling trees, clear cutting, stream alteration, runoff changes, burning, and other human-caused changes on herons in forests (Chapter 4).

Nesting habitat

Much is known about the basic nesting habitat of a majority of species (Chapter 9). For several species, requirements are known in sufficient detail to guide creation of artificial nesting sites and feeding habitats. For little-known species, requirements often can be inferred from what is known of similar species. As a result conservation action in protecting nesting habitat can in many cases proceed without additional research. The effectiveness of such action does however need to be monitored, scientifically evaluated, and reported on.

Interspecies interactions are less known. The effect of nesting site competition among species in mixed colonies is unclear in most cases. To the extent that competition has conservation implications, these interactions should be better understood. Known or suspected examples include colony site effects of expanding heron populations, especially Cattle Egrets, as well as the effects of other species, such as cormorants.

Human interactions with nesting herons and their habitat need to be further studied. It is well known that humans and their domestic animals can adversely affect heron habitat; conversely humans can also protect and manage heron habitat. Herons can be disturbed by intrusive human activities, and herons also have the ability to acclimatise to non-intrusive human activities. Additional study on the many and diverse relationships of heron nesting and heron habitat to human activities is crucial, in all areas and for many species.

Herons are well known to affect the plants on which they nest. In some situations, long-term occupancy of colony sites leads to changes in plant community structure and not uncommonly to the death of trees and shrubs they are using. Provided that sufficient alternative colony sites are available, herons can readily shift from a damaged site to another to begin the habitat cycle anew. If sufficient alternative sites are not available, it may prove necessary to actively manage the limited supply of potentially suitable sites. In these situations, it is necessary to study more precisely the direct causes of impact so as to develop habitat management strategies.

In many areas there seem to be shifts of nesting herons from inland sites to the coasts. Presumably this is due to a reduction of quality in inland sites, and perhaps even an increase in quality of coastal sites. In that this seems to be a common response of herons to development pressures, it needs to be studied in both the local context and as a generality.

Feeding habitat

The conservation of heron feeding habitat is profoundly more complex than that of nesting habitat. Physical features of the habitats typically used by herons differ among species, ranging from deep water (large *Ardea*), coral reefs (reef herons), densely vegetated marshes (bitterns), river banks (Agami Heron), and damp pastureland (Cattle Egret), to dry grassland (Black-headed Heron). Even species that feed communally use their habitat in subtly different ways. Furthermore, herons are for the most part flexible species with wide habitat potentiality. Thus habitat conservation needs to take into consideration the individual needs of each species, in the various kinds of conditions in which each species occurs. As a result research is needed on the individualised habitat requirements of various species in various locations at various times of year. Because habitat conservation is inherently accomplished at the local scale, studies similarly need to be local, even if guided by the generalised knowledge of the species. Such studies need to be a priority in locales deemed to be Important Heron Conservation Areas.

Most herons, most of the time, depend on wetlands for their nesting and feeding habitat. As a result heron conservation is intimately tied to wetland conservation (Kushlan 1997). Protection, management, loss, alteration, enhancement, restoration, and creation of wetlands can profoundly affect the status and trends of local heron populations. Many studies have documented how many species of herons use wetlands, one lesson being that subtle changes in the functioning of a wetland can adversely affect heron population stability. Local studies are still required to test generalisations and determine best management practices for local situations. Especially it is essential that heron conservation be linked tightly to wetland conservation activities; how this is to be done in specific situations needs to be studied. Regional management of heron habitat, in concert with other ecosystem and bird conservation goals, appears to be the most hopeful approach to local heron conservation (Kushlan 1992). However, how such management plans can be devised and implemented requires considerable study. Successful and unsuccessful case histories need to be published for wider evaluation and adoption.

Because of the extent of alteration of wetlands, the principal heron habitat worldwide, conservation often involves wetland restoration or even wetland creation. Herons, with their ecological flexibility, are often among the most obvious species to use a restored or created wetland, and may be suitable indicators of restoration success. It is essential to understand how wetlands may be restored in ways that are conducive to supporting heron populations. With such knowledge the role of herons as indicators of wetland restoration success can be enhanced and appropriate strategies developed for use in other applications.

Past studies uniformly indicate that the most crucial feature of a heron's habitat is food availability. Availability has at least three components: suitability (including species, size, capture susceptibility), abundance, and accessibility. As a result, prey availability depends in complex and changing ways on such habitat variables as water depths, speed and direction of water depth change, temperature, dissolved oxygen levels, rainfall, and timing of availability (tidal, seasonal, day–night). There is also a geographic component in that prey must be available sufficiently close to colony or roost sites and must vary temporally in ways that the herons can adjust to.

With respect to habitat selection, it is likely that variability may be as important as availability. So for each combination of species and locale, the relative importance of these and other variables need to be determined relative to their impact on herons. From a conservation perspective, these need to be understood within the context of available conservation strategies and active management options. Again, such studies are of highest relative priority in areas deemed to be Important Heron Conservation Areas.

Wintering habitat

Habitat used in the non-breeding seasons is as crucial as that used in nesting seasons (Chapter 11). The role of wintering habitat on the population stability of European herons has been well appreciated (Chapter 1). It is likely to be similar for other populations. So little is known about heron ecology on their wintering areas that few

Squacco Heron. The wintering sites of birds that nest in Europe are not well known. Photo: Jacques Delpech.

conservation recommendations are available at present. The additional study of herons on their wintering habitat is a crucial link in heron conservation.

Artificial habitats

While it is essential to understand how herons survive in natural conditions, increasingly habitats available to herons have been altered by human activities. It is in most situations not a matter of whether heron habitat has or will be altered, but to what extent it is being altered. What needs to be understood is how specific alterations alone and as cumulative impacts affect heron habitat use, and therefore population stability. Like other habitat questions, these need to be determined in each application, following guidance provided by general species knowledge.

Aquaculture will be an increasing threat and benefit to herons, worldwide (Chapter 13). Current information suggests that herons are of economic consequence in aquaculture under only restricted conditions. Herons, nonetheless, are often blamed for economically significant losses. It is essential that the true economic impact of herons in various aquacultural situations be definitively determined. In that in many situations other water birds seem to have far greater impact than herons, it is crucial that the relative roles of all potential predators be understood.

Studies to determine alternative, heron-friendly aquacultural practices remain necessary as a high priority.

Contaminants

Contaminants are fundamentally habitat issues, in that herons gain exposure through habitat use, especially via feeding. Tissue concentrations of contaminants in heron tissue are known from many areas around the world, and there is little evidence of population-scale effects of contaminants on herons (Kushlan 1997). However, sub-lethal effects of contaminants on herons in nature are poorly known.

Contamination continues to be a significant issue in heron conservation worldwide (Chapter 12). Baseline contaminant information needs to be gathered from countries and areas not yet sampled. The value of long-term monitoring of contaminant burdens in herons is clear (Chapter 12). Such studies should be continued and expanded. Contaminants especially need to be studied in populations that appear to be declining or otherwise show signs of stress.

To the extent that herons accumulate or show sub-lethal responses to contaminant exposure, they may serve a bioindicator function (Kushlan 1993b; Chapter 15). Further research is required on the long-term, population-level effect of sub-lethal contaminant exposure on herons and on the degree to which such effect can be used in bioindication.

Conservation scale

To the extent all conservation is local, management action must be local as well. Examples, models, and case histories of successful and unsuccessful heron management need to be published.

Heron conservation undoubtedly must also be managed at a higher scale, given herons' large home ranges and seasonally variable use of the landscape. So local management needs to be placed within a regional context. Determining the best approaches to accomplish integrated management across geographic scales requires new approaches. Landscape level analysis, geographically explicit models, geographical information systems, decision support systems, adaptive management, and other weapons in the developing arsenal of landscape ecology need to be applied to questions of heron conservation. Research and adaptive approaches need to be used to determine the most effective conservation delivery systems in various settings. Case histories need to be published so as to increase transference of experiences to similar situations.

17. Conservation of Herons

Heinz Hafner, Richard V. Lansdown, James A. Kushlan, Robert W. Butler, Thomas W. Custer, Ian J. Davidson, R. Michael Erwin, James A. Hancock, Anna Marie Lyles, Max Maddock, Loïc Marion, Gonzalo Morales, Taej Mundkur, Christian Perennou, Olivier Pineau, Donald Turner, Paula Ulenaers, Janine van Vessem and Llewellyn Young

It has been over 15 years since the publication of the Herons Handbook (Hancock and Kushlan 1984) and over 17 years since the establishment of the Heron Specialist Group, in cooperation with IUCN, BirdLife International (then the International Council for Bird Preservation) and Wetlands International (then the International Waterfowl Research Bureau) (Hafner et al. 1986a). Since these events, our knowledge of the world's herons and of their habitats and conservation needs has increased exponentially thanks to the enthusiastic commitment of a multinational group of professional biologists and heron conservationists. The many results of their investigations on all continents and over many specific regions, presented in the previous chapters, may now serve conservation purposes.

In this chapter representatives of the Group synthesise this knowledge in a condensed version of a global-scale conservation action plan. This plan outlines general and specific action required to maintain or enhance heron populations of concern throughout their present ranges. It represents the first complete assessment of existing knowledge of the global and regional conservation status of herons at species, subspecies and population levels. Not surprisingly there are taxa and regions for which data remain poor or non-existent. Gaps in our knowledge are emphasised in this chapter in order to challenge field biologists to fill major gaps in geographical coverage and to further understanding of heron biology and conservation needs in remote areas. The world's remaining wetlands, perhaps the most vulnerable and fragile of all habitats, are under ever-increasing threat from many sides. High consideration is therefore given to habitat and site conservation requirements without which species-conservation action would be futile.

Although this is the first compendium, it is anticipated that future research and conservation action will lead to periodic updating. Because conservation action must be built on ever-developing foundations of knowledge, the synthesis presented

Heron Conservation
ISBN 0-12-430130-4

below may be viewed as one milestone along the road to successful conservation and management of heron populations and the habitats that sustain them.

Assessing and Presenting Conservation Status

For consistency and utility we use the IUCN's most recent threat categories (IUCN 1996), which are based on criteria developed by Mace and Lande (1991), Mace et al. (1992), Mace and Stuart (1994) and Collar et al. (1994). The categories are listed in Table 17.1 and the criteria for each category are listed in Appendix 17.1. These criteria were intended for assessment at a species level. Additionally, we found that lower taxa and non-taxon populations also require evaluation and categorisation. So we used these criteria to assess conservation status for each heron species and subspecies (Table 17.2) and for some non-taxon populations. In the section Taxon Conservation, these are presented according to their conservation status, from Critically Endangered (CR) to Lower Risk (LR), and not in taxonomic order (for the latter see Table 17.2).

In most cases, we found the IUCN categorisation to be accurate. However we have also categorised threats to species based on new knowledge and also categorised threats to subspecies and certain populations. These are listed as Heron Specialist Group (HSG) status in Table 17.2. HSG status follows the criteria of IUCN status except that populations at threat in an area not encompassing the range of a taxon (species or subspecies) is considered Regionally Endangered (REN) or Regionally Vulnerable (RVU). We also make use of the category Data Deficient (DD) (Table 17.2). Although none of the herons of the world has been listed by IUCN in this category, the HSG found it suitable in a number of cases for which information on the current population is lacking and for which immediate action required is data collection. Finally, to indicate data lapses, the HSG uses the following subcategory to complete categories such as Endangered (EN) or Vulnerable (VU): dd, hl, where dd indicates data deficiency and hl that habitat loss is clearly a major problem (Appendix 17.1.).

Taxonomic classification of the herons is by no means settled (see introduction). We intend Table 17.2 to be as useful as possible, so we have attempted to be comparable to other listings. Of course, total consistency among listings is not possible. For consistency with the rest of this book, we followed the species categorisation and taxonomy of Table 0.1 (from Hancock and Kushlan 1984). This differs somewhat from IUCN (1996).

For conservation purposes, it is useful to pay attention to various populations even if considered taxonomically dubious by some. For utility we followed sub-specific categorisation of Rose and Scott (1997). The difference between the taxonomy of Hancock and Kushlan (1984) and other listings falls outside the scope of this work and is not discussed. Hancock (1990) emphasises the need for DNA to be carried out on a number of species to finally resolve the situation.

Notable differences among treatments are:

Ardea imperialis = Ardea insignis (IUCN 1996);
Egretta garzetta gularis = Egretta gularis (Rose and Scott 1997);
Egretta garzetta dimorpha = Egretta dimorpha (Rose and Scott 1997);
Butorides striatus virescens = Butorides virescens (Rose and Scott 1997);
Butorides striatus sundevalli = Butorides sundevalli (Rose and Scott 1997);

Table 17.1   Threat Categories used by IUCN and the Heron Specialist Group (from IUCN 1996).

Category	Definition
Extinct (EX)	A taxon is Extinct when there is no reasonable doubt that the last individual has died.
Extinct in the Wild (EW)	A taxon is Extinct in the Wild when it is known only to survive in cultivation, in captivity or as a naturalised population (or populations) well outside the past range. A taxon is presumed extinct in the wild when exhaustive surveys in known and/or expected habitat, at appropriate times (diurnal, seasonal, annual), throughout its historic range have failed to record an individual. Surveys should be over a time-frame appropriate to the taxon's life cycle and life form.
Critically Endangered (CR)	A taxon is Critically Endangered when it is facing an extremely high risk of extinction in the wild in the immediate future, as defined by any of the criteria (A to E) listed in Appendix 17.1.
Endangered (EN)	A taxon is Endangered when it is not Critically Endangered but is facing a very high risk of extinction in the wild in the near future, as defined by any of the criteria (A to E) in Appendix 17.1.
Vulnerable (VU)	A taxon is Vulnerable when it is not Critically Endangered or Endangered but is facing a high risk of extinction in the wild in the medium-term future, as defined by any of the criteria (A to D) in Appendix 17.1.
Lower Risk (LR)	A taxon is Lower Risk when it has been evaluated, does not satisfy the criteria for any of the categories Critically Endangered, Endangered or Vulnerable. Taxa included in the Lower Risk category can be separated into three subcategories:
1. Conservation dependent (cd)	Taxa which are the focus of a continuing taxon-specific conservation programme targeted towards the taxon in question, the cessation of which would result in the taxon qualifying for one of the threatened categories above within a period of five years.
2. Near threatened (nt)	Taxa which do not qualify for conservation dependent, but which are close to qualifying for Vulnerable.
3. Least concern (lc)	Taxa which do not qualify for conservation dependent or near threatened.
Data Deficient (DD)	A taxon is Data Deficient when there is inadequate information to make a direct, or indirect, assessment of its risk of extinction based on its distribution and/or population status. A taxon in this category may be well studied, and its biology well known, but appropriate data on abundance and/or distribution is lacking. Data Deficient is therefore not a category of threat or Lower Risk. Listing of taxa in this category indicates that more information is required and acknowledges the possibility that future research will show that threatened classification is appropriate. It is important to make positive use of whatever data are available. In many cases great care should be exercised in choosing between DD and threatened status. If the range of a taxon is suspected to be relatively circumscribed, if a considerable period of time has elapsed since the last record of the taxon, threatened status may well be justified.
Not Evaluated (NE)	A taxon is Not Evaluated when it is has not yet been assessed against the criteria.

Where there was uncertainty as to the correct classification for a population, the precautionary principle was adopted, recommending investigation to clarify the existing status towards a potential revision of the classification. This is particularly important for those taxa for which there are little or no data. As for all such categorisations, ours is data-dependent and we anticipate future revisions with the availability of new information.

Table 17.2   Conservation Status of Herons of the World. (Extinct taxa excluded)

Species	Subspecies	Distribution	IUCN 1996 Status[1,2]	HSG Status[1,2]
Syrigma sibilatrix	S.s.sibilatrix	South America		LR, lc
	S.s.fostersmithi	South America		LR, lc
Pilherodius pileatus		South America		DD
Ardea cinerea	A.c.cinerea	Europe, Africa, Asia		LR, lc
	A.c.rectirostris	Asia		LR, lc
	A.c.altirostris	Sumatra		VU
	A.c.monicae	Banc d'Arguin (Mauritania)		VU
	A.c.firasa	Madagascar		EN
Ardea herodias	A.h.herodias	North America		LR, lc
	A.h.fannini	North America		VU
	A.h.hyperonca	North America		LR, lc
	A.h.treganzai	North America		LR, lc
	A.h.wardi	North America		LR, lc
	A.h.santilucae	North America		LR, lc
	A.h.occidentalis	Caribbean		VU
	A.h.cognata	Galapagos		LR, lc
Ardea cocoi		South America		LR, lc
Ardea pacifica		Oceania		LR, lc
Ardea melanocephala		Africa		LR, lc
Ardea humbloti		Malagasy Subregion	VU	VU
Ardea imperialis		India, Bangladesh	EN	CR
Ardea sumatrana		Asia, Australia, New Guinea	LR, nt	LR, nt
Ardea goliath		Africa		LR, lc
		Asia		RVU
Ardea purpurea	A.p.purpurea	Europe and North Africa		RVU
		Africa		LR, lc
		Asia		LR, lc
	A.p.madagascariensis	Madagascar		VU
	A.p.bournei	Cape Verde Is.		CR
	A.p.manilensis	Asia		LR, lc
Egretta alba	E.a.alba	Europe and North Africa		RVU
		Africa		LR, lc
		Asia		LR, lc
	E.a.melanorhynchos	Tropical Africa		LR, lc
	E.a.modesta	Asia, Australia, Oceania		LR, lc
	E.a.maorianus	New Zealand		CR
	E.a.egretta	N. America, Neotropics		LR, lc
Egretta rufescens	E.r.rufescens	North America		VU
	E.r.colorata	Mexico		VU
	E.r.dickeyi	San Luis Is.		VU
Egretta picata		Asia, Oceania		LR, lc
Egretta vinaceigula		Africa	VU	EN
Egretta ardesiaca		Africa		LR, nt
Egretta tricolor	E.t.tricolor	NE Neotropics		LR, lc
	E.t.ruficollis	N. America, Neotropics		LR, lc
	E.t.trufimentum	Trinidad		DD
Egretta intermedia	E.i.intermedia	Asia		LR, lc
	E.i.brachyrhyncha	Africa		LR, lc

Table 17.2 *continued*

Species	Subspecies	Distribution Status[1,2]	IUCN 1996 Status[1,2]	HSG
Egretta intermedia	E.i.plumifera	SE Asia, Australia, New Guinea		LR, lc
Egretta novaehollandiae		Oceania		LR, lc
Egretta caerulea		N. & S. America		LR, lc
Egretta thula	E.t.thula	Neotropics		LR, lc
	E.t.brewsteri	North America		LR, lc
Egretta garzetta	E.g.garzetta	Africa, Europe, Asia		LR, lc
	E.g.nigripes	Java—New Guinea		LR, lc
	E.g.immaculata	Australasia		LR, lc
	E.g.gularis	W. Africa		LR, lc
	E.g.schistacea	NE Africa, SW Asia		DD
	E.g. dimorpha	Africa		DD
Egretta eulophotes		East Asia	EN	EN
Egretta sacra		Asia, Oceania		LR, lc
Bubulcus ibis	B.i. ibis	Africa, Europe, Asia, the Americas		LR, lc
	B.i.seychellarum	Seychelles		DD
	B.i.coromandus	Asia, Australasia, Oceania		LR, lc
Ardeola ralloides	A.r.ralloides	Europe and North Africa		RVU
		Africa		LR, lc
	A.r.palludivaga	Tropical Africa		LR, lc
Ardeola grayii	A.g.grayii	Southern Asia		LR, lc
	A.g.phillipsi	SE Asia		VU
Ardeola bacchus		Asia		LR, lc
Ardeola speciosa	A.s.speciosa	Greater Sundas		LR, lc
	A.s.continentalis	Mainland SE Asia		LR, lc
Ardeola idae		Malagasy Subregion	LR, nt	LR, nt
Ardeola rufiventris		Africa		LR, nt
Butorides striatus	B.s.striatus	N. Neotropics		DD
	B.s.anthonyi	N. America, Mexico		DD
	B.s.frazari	Baja—Mexico		DD
	B.s.bahamensis	Bahamas		DD
	B.s.maculatus	Caribbean		DD
	B.s.margaritophilus	Pearl Island		DD
	B.s.curacensis	Curacao Island		DD
	B.s. patens	Panama		DD
	B.s.robinsoni	Margarita Island		DD
	B.s.cyanurus	Central S. America		DD
	B.s.fuscicollis	Bolivia		DD
	B.s.brevipes	E. Africa, SW Asia		DD
	B.s.atricapillus	Africa		LR, lc
	B.s.rutenbergi	Madagascar		LR, lc
	B.s.rhizophorae	Comoro Islands		DD
	B.s.degens	Seychelles		EN
	B.s.crawfordi	Aldabra		LR, lc
	B.s.albolimbatus	Chagos Islands		VU
	B.s.didi	N. Maldive Islands		VU
	B.s.albidulus	S. Maldive Islands		VU
	B.s.chloriceps	Southern Asia		DD

Table 17.2 *continued*

Species	Subspecies	Distribution Status[1,2]	IUCN 1996 Status[1,2]	HSG
Butorides striatus	*B.s.spodiogaster*	Andaman Islands		DD
	B.s.amurensis	South-east Asia		DD
	B.s.abbotti	Malaysia		DD
	B.s.connectens	China		DD
	B.s.actophilus	South-east Asia		DD
	B.s.javanicus	Indonesia		DD
	B.s.moluccarum	Moluccas		DD
	B.s.solomonensis	Solomon Islands		DD
	B.s.papuensis	Northern New Guinea		DD
	B.s.macrorhynchus	Southern New Guinea		DD
	B.s.stagnatilis	North Australia		DD
	B.s.patruelis	Tahiti		VU
	B.s.rogersi	Southern Australia		DD
	B.s.virescens	The Americas		DD
	B.s.sundevalli	Neotropics		DD
Agami agami		South America	LR, nt	LR, nt
Nycticorax violaceus	*N.v.violaceus*	Central & N. America		LR, lc
	N.v.gravirostris	Socorro Islands		LR, lc
	N.v.caliginis	Colombia		LR, nt
	N.v.cayennensis	Neotropics		DD
	N.v.bancrofti	Baja—Mexico		DD
	N.v.pauper	Galapagos		DD
Nycticorax nycticorax	*N.n.nycticorax*	Europe and North Africa		RVU
		Africa		LR, lc
		Asia		LR, lc
	N.n.hoactli	Neotropics, N. America		LR, lc
	N.n.obscurus	S. Neotropics		LR, lc
	N.n.falklandicus	Falklands, Malvinas Is		LR, lc
Nycticorax caledonicus	*N.c.caledonicus*	New Caledonia		LR, lc
	N.c.manillensis	Philippines		LR, lc
	N.c.minahassae	Sulawesi		LR, lc
	N.c.pelewensis	Palau Island		DD
	N.c.mandibularis	Solomon Islands		DD
	N.c.hilli	Australia, New Guinea		DD
	N.c.cancrivorus	Bismarck Archipelago		DD
Nycticorax leuconotus		Africa		DD
Gorsachius magnificus		China	CR	CR
Gorsachius goisagi		Eastern Asia	VU	VU
Gorsachius melanolophus	*G.m.melanolophus*	Asia		LR, nt, dd, hl
	G.m.kutteri	Philippines		LR, nt, dd, hl
	G.m.rufolineatus	Palawan (Philippines)		VU, dd, hl
	G.m.minor	Nicobar Islands		LR, nt, dd, hl
Cochlearius cochlearius	*C.c.cochlearius*	N. Neotropics		DD
	C.c.zeledoni	W. Mexico		DD
	C.c.phillipsi	S. Mexico		DD
	C.c.ridgwayi	N. Central America		DD
	C.c.panamensis	S. Central America		DD
Tigrisoma mexicanum	*T.m.mexicanum*	N. Neotropics		LR, nt

Table 17.2   *continued*

Species	Subspecies	Distribution Status[1,2]	IUCN 1996 Status[1,2]	HSG
Tigrisoma mexicanum	*T.m.fremitus*	Sonora		DD
Tigrisoma fasciatum	*T.f.fasciatum*	S. Brazil, N. Argentina	LR, nt	LR, nt
	T.f.salmoni	W. Neotropics	LR, nt	LR, nt
	T.f. bolivianum	Argentina, Bolivia	LR, nt	LR, nt
	T.f.pallescens	NW Argentina	LR, nt	LR, nt
Tigrisoma lineatum	*T.l.lineatum*	N. Neotropics		DD
	T.l.marmoratum	S Neotropics		DD
Zonerodius heliosylus		PNG, New Britain	LR, nt	LR, nt
Tigriornis leucolophus		Africa		LR, lc
Zebrilus undulatus		South America	LR, nt	LR, nt
Ixobrychus involucris		South America		DD
Ixobrychus exilis	*I.e.exilis*	The Americas		LR, lc
	I.e.bogotensis	Colombia		DD
	I.e.pullus	Sonora		DD
	I.e.limoncochae	Ecuador		DD
	I.e.peruvianus	Peru		DD
Ixobrychus minutus	*I.m.minutus*	Europe and North Africa		RVU
		Asia		DD
	I.m.payesii	Tropical Africa		LR, lc
	I.m.podiceps	Madagascar		VU
	I.m. dubius	Australasia		VU
Ixobrychus sinensis		Asia, Seychelles, Oceania		LR, lc
Ixobrychus eurhythmus		Eastern Asia	LR, nt	DD
Ixobrychus cinnamomeus		Asia		LR, lc
Ixobrychus sturmii		Africa		LR, lc
Ixobrychus flavicollis	*I.f.flavicollis*	Asia		LR, lc
	I.f.gouldi	Australasia		LR, lc
	I.f.australis	Timor		DD
	I.f.woodfordi	Solomon Islands		DD
	I.f.pallidor	Rennell Islands		DD
	I.f.nesophilus	New Britain/New Ireland		DD
Botaurus pinnatus	*B.p.pinnatus*	Neotropics		DD
	B.p.caribaeus	Central America		DD
Botaurus lentiginosus		North America, Caribbean		LR, nt
Botaurus stellaris	*B.s.stellaris*	Europe and North Africa		RVU
		Asia		DD
	B.s.capensis	Southern Africa		CR
	B.s.orientalis	East Asia		LR, lc
Botaurus poiciloptilus		Oceania	EN	CR

[1] IUCN = Categorisation from IUCN 1996; HSG = Categorisation from the Heron Specialist Group.

[2] For abbreviations and explanation see Table and Appendix 17.1.

The knowledge base and conservation needs differ considerably among continents and regions. After a brief summary of the situation characterising each region, the status of herons and the conservation issues discussed in the previous chapters are reconsidered at a species by species and at subspecies and population levels to derive recommendations for conservation priority.

Regional Perspectives

Europe and North Africa

Reliable data on heron populations exist for most European countries and for the most important breeding areas of north Africa (Chapters 1 and 2). Major gaps in our knowledge concern Syria, Lebanon and Jordan in the east Mediterranean since the present status of herons in these countries is virtually unknown.

No European heron species is listed of important conservation concern by IUCN (Baillie and Groombridge 1996). This is entirely justified on a global scale. On a regional scale, BirdLife International considered five species (Purple Heron, Squacco Heron, Black-crowned Night Heron, Little Bittern and Eurasian Bittern) to belong to their SPEC Category 3 based on their being "not concentrated in Europe but with an unfavorable conservation status in Europe" (Tucker and Heath 1994). This statement is in agreement with the assessments made in Chapters 1 and 2, which underline the urgent need for regional and local action plans for these European populations of species that globally are not threatened.

Asia

Asia (Chapters 3 and 4) supports the largest number of species, subspecies and populations of herons of the regions used in this book (see Figs 3.1 and 4.1). In spite of this, for the majority of Asian heron populations, there are no historical and few contemporary quantitative data and it has therefore not been possible to analyse population trends. As a result it is difficult for most of the species to assign them confidently to the relevant IUCN categories. It is clear that this continent hosts the two presently most critically endangered herons of the world, the Imperial Heron and the White-eared Night Heron, and several other vulnerable species.

Africa

For the majority of African heron populations, there are no historical or contemporary quantitative data, and it is therefore not possible to quantify population changes. The conservation of several species and subspecies on the African continent is in particular need of updated information on numbers, distribution and habitat use (Chapter 5 and Fig. 5.1). The Slaty Egret for instance is considered so vulnerable that one hesitates to initiate research activity, which could cause disturbance during breeding. Similarly, the Eurasian Bittern subspecies *capensis* is today considered endangered, with very low numbers, and almost certainly still declining due to shrinking and deteriorating habitats, and its intolerance of man. The Malagasy subregion, which includes the island complexes Seychelles, Aldabra, the Comores, Madagascar, Réunion, Mauritius and Rodrigues, supports fifteen species of heron, with five subspecies of *Butorides striatus* and two of *Bubulcus ibis*. Of these, two species and eight subspecies are endemic to the subregion.

Australasia and Oceania

The continent of Australia, the large islands of New Zealand and Papua New Guinea, and thousands of small islands scattered across the Pacific Ocean (Chapter 6) are important heron habitats. On the Australian continent the climate fluctuates from a period of extreme drought conditions to periods of extreme flooding and because of the short-term nature of surveys which have been conducted, it is difficult to determine whether population fluctuations are merely a reflection of the climatic changes or of more serious ecological problems. Regulation of inland rivers for water supply and irrigation has significantly altered seasonal hydrological characteristics of wetlands, with detrimental affects on heron breeding; recent moves to provide environmental flows to mimic natural processes have important potential for a resurgence of breeding in the inland and needs to be pursued and monitored. Only the Cattle Egret has been extensively studied in Australia and New Zealand and research data on other heron species is fragmentary. Very little research has been carried out in the island countries. Herons are known to move between the island of Tasmania and the Australian mainland, between Australia and New Zealand, and between Australia and Papua New Guinea. In many areas of this extensive region data are too sparse to provide detailed accounts of populations and trends. Consequently several species in this region are categorised as Data Deficient.

North America

In contrast to the Neotropics, heron populations have been rather extensively studied in North America (Chapter 7). The situation is similar to Europe where intensive research programmes initiated decades ago in certain areas continue to form a basis of knowledge on which conservation action can be built. However, as is also the case in Europe, detailed information exists for important regions and sites whereas continental-scale or even national initiatives for coordinating long-term censuses of colonial herons usually fail. There is a continuous need for monitoring programmes in order to improve insight in status and trends.

South America

South America, with its numerous and diverse wetlands and extensive floodplain forests (see Fig. 8.1), supports a particularly rich heron fauna, with a high level of endemism (Chapter 8). This immense field of research remains largely underexploited. Data on the population status of species which form only small and dispersed colonies or which are solitary nesters are virtually impossible to obtain. This is particularly true for certain small, cryptic and secretive species of high conservation priority such as the Zigzag Heron. The scarcity of quantitative data on the heron fauna in general does not allow trends to be estimated, and even distribution ranges cannot be attributed confidently to most of the species. IUCN (1996) lists only three species under the category "Lower risk: near threatened". South America hosts some of the least known herons of the world. To acquire more knowledge is at present a major concern, and also a challenge in view of inaccessible areas to cover such as the huge Amazon and ParanaBasins.

Taxon Conservation

In this section we synthesise the conservation status and needs of various heron taxa, following the IUCN categorisation for species and that of the Heron Specialist Group. Table 17.2 provides the categorisation for all taxa. Below we discuss certain taxa and populations.

Extinct taxa

According to IUCN (1996), the following taxa are considered extinct (Category EX): Mauritius Night Heron (*Nycticorax mauritianus*) on Mauritius by 1700; Rodrigues Night Heron (*Nycticorax megacephalus*) on Rodrigues Island in 1761; unidentified Night Heron (*Nycticorax* sp.) on Réunion Island by 1700 and Black-backed Bittern (*Ixobrychus novaezelandiae*) in New Zealand by 1900.

Species of conservation concern (listed in order of conservation status)

White-eared Night Heron (*Gorsachius magnificus*) *IUCN and HSG Category Critically Endangered (CR)*. The White-eared Night Heron is the most threatened Heron species in the world; it is currently only known to occur in south-western China. There have been only a handful of sightings since 1980. Three sightings in the wild in Guangxi, on a survey with funds from the Oriental Bird Club, included one in degraded habitat (Zhou 1996). In May 1998, during a survey by Kadoorie Farm & Botanic Garden (KFBG), a conservation charity based in Hong Kong, a juvenile caged bird was recorded in a market in the town of Nanning, Guangxi (Lee 1999). This bird was reared to adulthood by Prof. Zhou Fang of Guangxi University, and

White-eared Night Heron. The most threatened heron in the world. The juvenile bird pictured here was found in May 1998 on a market in south-western China. Photo: Lee Kwok-Shing, Kadoorie Farm and Botanic Garden.

subsequently, following quarantine, released in the Da Ming Shan Nature Reserve. The finding prompted KFBG to fund a twelve-month survey of both markets and potential habitats in Guangxi by Professor Zhou in collaboration with the Guangxi Forestry Department. As of July 1999, one breeding site had been confirmed in Fusui County; several old nests were found high in the forest canopy, one of which contained a dead sub-adult bird which had apparently died there of injuries sustained elsewhere. Another live sub-adult was found in a market in Shajing Town, a suburb of Nanning. KFBG plans further study and conservation action following completion of the present survey, having established a good working relationship with the Guangxi Forestry Department. In neighbouring Guangdong province, two specimens have been recently reported by Professor Gao Yu-ren, one from Shixing County, northern Guangdong, killed by a hunter and the second a specimen being sold in Chee Hing County.

There are no recent records from Hainan, Anhui, Zhejiang or Fujian Provinces, where it was formerly recorded (La Touche 1934, Cheng 1987). In view of the precariousness of the species, it should be the highest global priority for heron conservation. The species was classified as Critically Endangered by Collar et al. (1994).

Conservation action: immediate conservation action for the White-eared Night Heron is critical. The current KFBG surveys will provide a basis for this, but current efforts are restricted by the limited expertise available in southern China.

Besides locating the breeding and roosting sites of the species, conservation activity must include: nest site protection, creation of awareness among local human communities, creation of incentives to protect the species, data gathering during breeding including that on reproductive success and causes of failure, on dispersal and on wintering. Radio-tracking of known birds might be considered. However, in view of the vulnerability of the species and the possibility of research activity reducing breeding success if not carefully planned (Chapter 9), access to breeding sites by experienced heron biologists must only be decided if preliminary surveys reveal a situation judged relatively safe for this kind of work.

Other urgent actions are assessment of habitat requirements and habitat inventories, and important area inventories during breeding, migration and wintering. Finally, if sexually mature individuals exist in captivity, captive breeding should be considered immediately.

Understanding of the ecology of this species is presently insufficient to provide guidance for its efficient conservation. Surveys must be combined with collection of data on the ecology of the species to provide an account of its ecological requirements as a basis for conservation action. There, the primary objective must be to establish its habitat preferences and requirements. This sort of information can only be collected through detailed studies throughout the year. It will be necessary to monitor the species' seasonal presence to assess to what extent it migrates, as the results will influence identification of priority sites and habitats for protection. It will be important to clarify the annual movements of birds with regard to protection of suitable sites throughout their range.

The data may serve to create and enhance understanding and awareness of conservation in areas that support this species. It is of concern that the most recent records of this species include birds captured for human consumption. Although the degree to which this sort of activity may affect populations is unknown, an effort should be made to discourage capture of White-eared Night Herons. Awareness is therefore an important conservation issue. Because the area from which recent records derive supports a low standard of living, it is unlikely that there exists any significant degree of consideration of the environment per se. Therefore promotion of conservation awareness should be included as a fundamental component of any conservation project for this species. As a cautionary note, it should be remembered that rarity of species is sometimes viewed as an attractive feature among Chinese consumers. The market birds recorded so far have been on sale for quite low prices (US$6 or less), no higher than those of commoner species. If recognised as rare, the price and demand for the bird might increase. Thus there may be a risk attached to publicising the rarity of the species without engendering a conservation ethic towards it.

Little information is currently available on the status of natural and semi-natural habitats in the area where this species has been recorded in recent years. The forest in the region is threatened by clearance for agriculture (as can be said for most forest throughout east and south-east Asia). Hunting is rife throughout its range. Consequently, site protection combined with enforcement of protection of the species must be considered.

Conservation action for the White-eared Night Heron is designed initially to compile data to enable the design and implementation of suitable conservation action plans. It is particularly important that project design be an ongoing process and that the relationship between design and action be iterative. Eventually, captive breeding may become necessary to prevent extinction.

Imperial Heron (*Ardea imperialis*) *IUCN Category Endangered (EN); HSG Category Critically Endangered (CR).* Although it is apparently widespread in suitable habitat over a fairly large area in Asia, its solitary habit and large size mean that population densities are never likely to be high. The species seems to have disappeared from Nepal, and this combined with the paucity of records since 1980 suggest that the species is uncommon where it occurs. Classified as Endangered by Collar et al. (1994), there is today no justification for a population estimate of over 250 mature individuals. This scarcity when combined with the known degree of habitat destruction and degradation over this species' range justifies classification as Critically Endangered (CR). Therefore, until further information becomes available, any site that supports more than two individuals should be considered to support more than 1% of the world population.

Imperial Herons appear dependent upon mature trees associated with wetlands (rivers, marshes and lakes) and large forest rivers (see Inskipp and Inskipp 1991), a habitat complex which is threatened throughout the region. To date, nothing is known of the ecology of this species.

Conservation action: the species is little known and the primary conservation objectives should be to identify its habitat preferences and to assess whether or not migration or seasonal movements occur. Information on movements and distribution throughout the year may help designation of priority sites for protection over a wide range.

The most urgent recommendations are: to approach the governments of India and Bangladesh to address the potential for legal protection of the species and sites upon which it depends; to provide an accurate assessment of the current distribution and numbers of Imperial Herons; to study the habitat requirements for different aspects of the species life cycle; to establish a baseline for population monitoring in the long term. This kind of work should lead to recommendation of a preliminary list of sites for protection and to identification of areas of potential suitable habitat.

Australian Bittern (*Botaurus poiciloptilus*) *IUCN Category Endangered (EN); HSG Category Critically Endangered (CR).* This species is very poorly known. The current population is estimated to be not more than 10 000 individuals. Following the Ramsar criteria, any site supporting more than 100 individuals therefore qualifies for designation as a Ramsar site. In Australia, it occurs in Queensland, New South Wales, Victoria and Tasmania. It also occurs in New Zealand, New Caledonia and the Loyalty Islands. The species has been nominated in Victoria under the Flora and Fauna Guarantee Act because it is in a demonstrable state of decline and prone to future threats which are likely to result in extinction; only one record of breeding has been reported in Victoria since 1970 (O'Brien, pers. comm.). Precise information on the populations occurring at individual sites is virtually non-existent. The Heron Specialist Group raises conservation status of the species into the category Critically Endangered (CR, Table 17.2.).

Conservation action: in view of these considerations it is most urgent to: clarify the distribution and population of the species; identify the most important sites for its conservation; create awareness and provide information to local people; implement strict protection of the species and sites on which it depends; and establish a baseline for a comprehensive monitoring programme.

Swinhoe's Egret (*Egretta eulophotes*) *IUCN and HSG Category Endangered (EN).* The total known population is estimated at 1800–2500 birds, therefore any site which supports more than 20 birds is eligible for Ramsar status. The breeding population is concentrated on a small number of islands in the Yellow Sea. None of the colonies numbers more than 1000 mature individuals. In addition, known stopover sites are limited and threatened. Consequently, the species is likely to be vulnerable to a variety of anthropogenic influences. It is classified as Endangered (Criteria C1; C2a) by Collar et al. (1994), who consider that the main threats to the survival of this species are wetland reclamation and coastal development at breeding and wintering sites, particularly an airport being built on Yongjong Island which will destroy the most important feeding area for the South Korean breeding population.

  Although this species has been considered to be one of the most severely threatened in the world, as a consequence of the discovery of a number of breeding colonies on islands in the Yellow Sea in the 1980s (Chapter 4) the population appears to be today fairly robust and stable. The Swinhoe's Egret is now one of the better known Asian heron species. In spite of this, it is clear that this stability needs direct conservation action, supported by pertinent legislation. Chapter 4 gives the most recent figures available for non-breeding individuals. This information is presented to provide a clear account of the differing importance of sites as indicated by the numbers of birds that have been recorded. It must be recognised that many of the sites are stopover sites on migration and may at any one time only support a very small number of birds. However, such sites may have a high turnover during migration and consequently data from a single count may give an inaccurate picture of the true importance of the site.

Birds disperse widely from the breeding grounds, travelling southwards along the coasts of the People's Republic of China, South Korea and Japan; then the majority of the population travels south to the Philippines, sometimes stopping over in Taiwan. A smaller proportion of the population passes through coastal Indo-China to Peninsular Malaysia and Singapore, possibly continuing to Sumatra.

Conservation action: based on the information available we recommend: to encourage the relevant governments to protect the known breeding, stopover and wintering sites; to support surveys designed to clarify the distribution and relative value of breeding and non-breeding sites; and to promote and support studies into the ecology of the species on the breeding grounds and staging and wintering sites.

Increased access and observer coverage in coastal areas of mainland China, North Korea, and South Korea, combined with increasing ease of exchange of data, have greatly improved our knowledge of the location and size of breeding colonies. However, there remain a number of potentially suitable sites in the Yellow Sea and along the coast of Russia north from Vladivostok. A colony discovered in 1998 is located near Vladivostok 600 km north of the previously known breeding range (Chapter 4).

Finally, a sufficient number of active breeding colonies have been located since the mid-1980s to enable establishment of a comprehensive monitoring programme which would accurately indicate population trends, and a long-term monitoring programme should be initiated.

Slaty Egret *(Egretta vinaceigula) IUCN Category Vulnerable (VU); HSG Category Endangered (EN).* The small, localised population is poorly known, largely confined to the swamps and floodplains of the major river systems in Zambia, northern Botswana and the eastern Caprivi, Namibia. Flood regulation has already caused it to disappear from one part of the Kafue Flats in Zambia and the population is threatened by a variety of proposed actions, such as plans to harness the waters of the Okavango Delta. Plans to clear the area of tsetse fly may also seriously affect the ecology of the entire area. The proposed development of a rice-growing project in the eastern Caprivi may markedly alter the functioning of the Zambezi floodplain; and the impact of tourism and livestock industries, together with the constant reduction of potential breeding sites by reed-cutting and fires, are all likely to have serious and negative effects on the remaining Slaty Egret population (Chapter 5). In view of this situation of serious concern the Heron Specialist Group raises the species into the category Endangered (Table 17.2).

Conservation action: it is most important to carry out quantitative surveys to achieve legal protection of all sites supporting 1% of the world population (i.e., 50–100 birds, Rose and Scott 1997) at any time, and to continue to identify and monitor risks to the long-term survival of the species.

The first action needed is a comprehensive survey, to enable a suitable response to be given to the importance of different sites, in response to the various development proposals. Secondly, an assessment is needed of the current level of legal protection of sites which support this species, and of the existing capacity for implementation of legal protection.

There is little information on the factors limiting population size, apart from general assumptions relating to habitat availability. It is therefore recommended in terms of site protection to study the ecological requirements of the species through all aspects of its life cycle, including monitoring of nesting success. However, in view of the vulnerability of the species and the possibility of research activity causing disturbance at the nest site (Chapter 9), the possibilities of studying breeding parameters must be carefully evaluated.

Reddish Egret (*Egretta rufescens*) *HSG Category Globally Vulnerable (VU)*. This species has a restricted geographical range in southern North America, West Indies and northern coast of Venezuela and Columbia. It exploits exclusively coastal wetland areas, a vulnerable habitat which is increasingly subject to disturbance and degradation by human activity (Chapter 7). Many of these areas are threatened by housing and industrial development. Changing the hydrology through building dikes and thus altering the natural functioning of a coastal wetland reduces the food supply for these birds. Estuaries are also much exposed to environmental contamination.

Conservation action: with only 6000–10 000 adults, this population is in need of a continuous monitoring programme. The results of surveys must be used to re-evaluate the list of priority areas and sites during the breeding season, during migration and in winter. Protection and policies promoting wise use of these coastal wetlands are critical.

Japanese Night Heron (*Gorsachius goisagi*) *IUCN and HSG Category Vulnerable (VU)*. The Atlas of breeding birds in Japan shows only six confirmed, fourteen probable and one possible breeding site (Wild Bird Society of Japan, 1978) combined with anecdotal accounts of a recent decline. The only records of this species outside the breeding season refer to isolated observations. Even if the species is relatively widespread, data are insufficient to properly address its conservation requirements.

Conservation action: the most urgent conservation action at present is: to clarify the current distribution of this species during and outside the breeding season and to provide a population estimate as a basis for monitoring. Such basic data must lead to ecological studies into habitat requirements and assessment of the viability of existing forest to sustain the populations. This information must be fed into the conservation strategy to ensure protection and address potential for habitat protection and management. Habitat protection is most important. The WBSJ Atlas provides a sound basis for establishment of a network of forest reserves for this species in Japan. The six confirmed and fourteen probable breeding sites should be surveyed to re-confirm presence and provide them with legal protection. The species should be accorded full protection in Japanese legislation.

Migration occurs through the Ryukyu Islands and there appears to be a regular wintering population in Taiwan (Chapter 4). Protection of remaining forested areas in these two areas would contribute significantly to the viability of the existing populations of this species.

Malagasy Heron (*Ardea humbloti*) *IUCN and HSG Category Vulnerable (VU)*. This species is still present in relatively strong numbers in parts of north-west Madagascar, where it has a patchy distribution. Possibly it breeds also on the Comoro islands (Collar et al. 1994). According to Rose and Scott (1997) the total population is now below 5000 individuals, a situation already suspected by Collar et al. (1994). The species is threatened by hunting and nest predation by locals and by conversion of natural wetlands to rice agriculture (Chapter 5).

Conservation action: there are a clear suite of problems, mainly related to habitat destruction and degradation, which affect the survival of a number of waterbird species and endemic subspecies in the Malagasy subregion, particularly on Madagascar. We are aware that much has been done in Madagascar by International and National Conservation Institutions such as the World Wide Fund For Nature, the Jersey Wildlife Preservation Trust, and others. It is therefore possible that actions which we propose here will already be being undertaken. A first stage in the conservation strategy for herons in this region must involve liaison with conservation organisations active in the Malagasy subregion, to establish an accurate overview of the current state of conservation. Rigorous protection of the known nest sites is essential. The success of this may depend on efficient wardening combined with awareness campaigns. Surveys to update information on distribution and numbers must form part of the strategy. However, surveys are likely to be constrained by logistical problems and must not take precedence over site protection and wardening.

Sumatran Heron. This species is in need of surveys to clarify its status and distribution. Photo: Alan OwYong.

Sumatran Heron (*Ardea sumatrana*) *IUCN and HSG Category Lower Risk (LR), Subcategory near threatened (nt).* This species seems to have disappeared from mainland south-east Asia (except parts of Indo-China) in the last 50 years. Due to an apparent significant range reduction, the existing population of the Sumatran Heron has been split into two discrete geographic areas. One involves scattered records in coastal Indo-China and islands off the south-west coast of Thailand, with a probably isolated sub-population in the Andaman islands. The other occurs through much of Indonesia, south to the northern coasts of Australia. There is little current information on the size of these sub-populations, mainly due to a combination of low observer coverage and difficulty of access. The species appears to be dependent upon mature woodland and fairly extensive coastline or wetlands, which are threatened throughout the regions.

Conservation action: the primary conservation aim must be to clarify the population size and status and its distribution. The most appropriate approach involves provision of financial and technical support to wetland surveys for a better coverage of suitable areas. In Asia, the project could be linked to conservation action for the Malayan Night Heron (see below).

Black Heron (*Egretta ardesiaca*) *African and Madagascar populations HSG Category Lower Risk (LR), Subcategory near threatened (nt).* Although the world population may appear secure, the species cannot be considered common anywhere in Africa and there is suspicion that it is declining. The population in Madagascar, where it was formerly common and widespread has severely declined over the past 30 years (Chapter 5).

Conservation action: in Africa we recommend a survey programme to establish the current situation and compare this with historic data where available. The survey method and data must be used to establish a basis for long-term monitoring, so that if there is a real decline in the overall population, this can be recognised and appropriate action developed. In Madagascar where colony sites disappeared or declined dramatically due to excessive disturbance by man (Chapter 5), the remaining wetlands in the west of the country are the last stronghold of the island. They deserve priority for protection since they are also the strongholds for the globally threatened Malagasy Heron.

Malagasy Pond Heron (*Ardeola idae*) *IUCN and HSG Category Lower Risk (LR), Subcategory near threatened (nt).* The population size of this endemic species to Madagascar is presently estimated at less than 10 000 individuals (Rose and Scott 1997). There has been a sharp decline over the last 50 years, possibly related to competition with the more recently established Squacco Heron which seems to exploit rice fields as feeding grounds more successfully (Hancock and Kushlan 1984). The Malagasy Pond Heron is threatened by conversion of natural feeding areas for rice-growing.

Conservation action: there are several very active conservation organisations in Madagascar and inventories of important sites to this species certainly exist. These organisations collaborate with the governmental departments in order to create awareness and achieve site protection. This seems indeed the most urgent and efficient conservation action to recommend.

Rufous-bellied Heron *(Ardeola rufiventris) Africa HSG Category Lower Risk (LR), Subcategory near threatened (nt).* Local and uncommon. Breeding is apparently sporadic, in response to fluctuating water levels (Chapter 5). To date, we have very poor data on populations.

Conservation action: the species may well be of higher conservation concern than stated here. However, in order to attribute a new status confidently, it is urgent to update a baseline population estimate and distribution map from all available information and carry out surveys to improve knowledge on the current population and identify priority sites for conservation. After this initial phase the data should be used as a baseline for long-term population monitoring and a tool enabling a quick response to concerns identified through future assessment of trends. Further, in collaboration with universities and other institutions, ecological studies should be envisaged to test the hypothesis that the species depends for breeding upon the availability of feeding habitat, as a product of varying water levels. There is a need to achieve a better understanding of this relationship, to help understand population trends and, in certain protected areas, to take appropriate management action.

Agami Heron *(Agamia agami) IUCN and HSG Category Lower Risk (LR), Subcategory near threatened (nt).* This little-known and shy South American heron is confined to forested freshwater wetlands where it nests solitarily or in very small mixed species nest groups (Chapter 8). Few scattered records do not allow clarification of the range and virtually nothing is known on population sizes or trends. Deforestation and damming of rivers may well be a major threat.

Conservation action: habitat conservation programmes should be established to protect areas where the species has been recorded. Research could be initiated in these areas as a second step towards conservation. Data on ecological requirements and factors influencing breeding success would be helpful, although the study of this solitary species in this type of habitat will be difficult. In addition the work will no doubt be constrained by considerable logistical problems. As with any other vulnerable species, research activity must avoid disturbance and priority must be given to protection.

Fasciated Tiger Heron *(Tigrisoma fasciatum) IUCN and HSG Category Lower Risk (LR), Subcategory near threatened (nt).* This species which occurs in South and Central America is very little known and seems to occupy stream-edge forests, a vulnerable habitat (Chapter 8).

Conservation action: improved knowledge on the distribution and habitat use by the species is most urgent before developing proposals for their conservation. A higher threat status may well be justified.

New Guinea Tiger Heron *(Zonerodius heliosylus) IUCN and HSG Category Lower Risk (LR), Subcategory near threatened (nt).* There are no population data for this species, which is confined to parts of Indonesia and Papua New Guinea (Chapters 4 and 6). The sum total of recent information amounts to less than 30 confirmed sightings in the last 15 years. Only one nest has ever been described and the species is only known to be relatively easy to see at one site. Throughout its range, its apparently preferred habitat is under extreme pressure from logging, clear-fell and pollution, as well as increased turbidity as a consequence of mining activities in the catchment. This Heron is suspected to favour broad, heavily forested lowland rivers.

Conservation action: the most urgent action recommended is to clarify the current distribution and provide a population estimate as a basis for monitoring; and to carry out ecological studies into the habitat requirements of the species.

Proposals should be put forward to protect remaining forested lowland rivers, with concern for this species included as part justification. New information may well justify raising the species into a higher threat category.

Zigzag Heron (*Zebrilus undulatus*) *IUCN and HSG Category Lower Risk (LR), Subcategory near threatened (nt).* The situation of this species which occurs in northern South America is identical to that of the Fasciated Tiger Heron.

Schrenk's Bittern (*Ixobrychus eurhythmus*) *IUCN Category Lower Risk (LR), Subcategory near threatened (nt); HSG Category Data Deficient (DD).* The species may have a high population within a restricted breeding distribution. Records from the wintering grounds almost exclusively involve isolated individuals, with rarely more than ten sightings per year from any one site. This species, which is probably declining, has never really been considered rare or particularly vulnerable. This is probably because the bird occurs (as do most of the Asiatic *Ixobrychus* species), frequently in open wet grassland and rice fields and is easy to see; consequently, the overall impression is that it is not uncommon. However, records in recent years show that although widespread, it appears never to occur in high densities and is actually considered an occasional visitor through most of its range.

Conservation action: it is most urgent to clarify the range and location of sites of importance for this species outside the breeding season, and to establish a more precise estimate of breeding populations. Although existing data suggest that the main non-breeding distribution is in the Philippines, there are annual records from various sites and habitats throughout south-east Asia. Surveys of sites are necessary where the species is known to occur to identify the main non-breeding distribution more accurately. The current breeding distribution is fairly well known (Chapter 4), but more information must be collected, particularly in far eastern Russia, which may hold the main breeding population. The results of investigations will provide useful arguments for site protection including hunting control.

American Bittern (*Botaurus lentiginosus*) *North America, Caribbean populations HSG Category Lower Risk (LR), Subcategory near threatened (nt).* Although still widespread in North and Central America, the species has specific habitat requirements similar to those which characterise the Eurasian Bittern (Chapter 7). Because these shallow marshland habitats with vegetation cover and grasslands are generally threatened by reclamation for agriculture, urbanisation and other development projects, the species deserves conservation attention. It is thought to decline in the North–Central states (Chapter 7), and del Hoyo et al. (1992) consider it endangered in the states of Illinois, Indiana and Ohio, and of special conservation concern in others.

Conservation action: the overriding issue for this species is the lack of information on population status, given the difficulty of censusing its numbers over large areas. Data are needed to strengthen arguments for conservation. It would be useful to identify and designate in selected states the most important areas for bitterns, and undertake yearly sample counts during the breeding season to investigate trends in numbers. The only way to obtain information is to count the singing (booming) males (Koskimies and Tyler 1997, Kayser et al. 1998). The list of priority sites resulting from this monitoring may serve to promote statutory protection. Surveys of breeding habitat and management practices (see under Purple Heron and Eurasian Bittern) are equally important.

Subspecies and populations of conservation concern (listed according to their conservation status)

Purple Heron *(Ardea purpurea bournei) HSG Category Critically Globally Endangered (CR).* This subspecies is endemic to the island of Santiago, Cape Verde Islands and there is evidence that the population has declined significantly since its discovery in 1951, from an estimated 75 pairs to a recent population estimate of 20 pairs (Hazavoet 1992).

Unlike the majority of heron taxa and other Purple Heron populations, this subspecies appears independent of wetlands; it nests in trees and forages on arid hillsides during the breeding season. There is no information on foraging habitat outside the breeding season, but it is suspected to use isolated, dry river valleys (Hazavoet 1992).

However, it is possible to implement conservation action that will ensure that it has the best possible chance of survival.

Conservation action: the proposed conservation action is to develop management and protection strategies for this subspecies on the Cape Verde Islands, through characterisation of current habitat use, assessment of the area of suitable habitat available and establishment of protected sites.

The main habitat survey priority must involve survey of all suitable trees on the island (these are very limited in number and therefore this is not as impractical as it sounds) and identification of foraging habitat and site use. Population monitoring is essential. The two known colonies are located near villages (Hazavoet 1992) and it appears that they can be counted without risk of disturbance (although this must be confirmed). It is clear that the current population must be protected from hunting, disturbance and habitat destruction.

Great White Egret *(Egretta alba maorianus) HSG Category Critically Globally Endangered (CR).* Endemic to New Zealand, population currently estimated at 100–200 birds (Chapter 6). The viability of such a low population is uncertain and will be critically dependent upon environmental and anthropogenic influences.

Conservation action: the colony and surrounding feeding areas are looked after by the Department of Conservation Te Papa Atawhai. Research efforts need to be extended for the current emphasis on breeding success to include seasonal migration habits.

Eurasian Bittern *(Botaurus stellaris capensis) HSG Category Critically Globally Endangered (CR).* This subspecies is confined to southern Africa; it is in serious decline due to loss of wetland habitat and its intolerance of human activity. As such it is now exceedingly rare or extinct over much of its former range, and it may be only in Zambia and perhaps in the poorly known eastern Angola wetlands that it survives in any numbers. In South Africa it breeds only in Natal and Transvaal, with a total population of probably less than 100 individuals. There appears to be little doubt that the entire population is in serious decline and endangered (Chapter 5). Last minute information (October 1998) suggests that the Bangweulu swamps in Zambia do still hold a sizeable population.

Conservation action: there is limited information on habitat preference, but Brook (1984) proposes protection of "large reed and bullrush beds in big swamps". Surveys of "booming" Bitterns are recommended in order to obtain information on the current distribution. This will help define the important areas and sites. Further action should then focus on habitat protection.

Grey Heron (*Ardea cinerea firasa*) HSG Category Globally Endangered (EN). The taxonomic status of Grey Herons in the Comores and Aldabra is uncertain and this subspecies is presently considered endemic to Madagascar, where it is threatened by human activity and habitat modification (Chapter 5).

Conservation action: as the threats are clearly recognised, site protection combined with awareness campaigns must be a priority. Wardening of breeding colonies should be envisaged and conservation priority directed to all sites which support 1% or more of the population i.e., 50–60 individuals.

Green-backed Heron (*Butorides striatus degens*) HSG Category Globally Endangered (EN). This subspecies is endemic to the Seychelles, where it is becoming rare and endangered as mangrove, the only habitat used for nesting, is increasingly destroyed (Chapter 5).

Conservation action: the mangrove of the Seychelles represents an extremely vulnerable habitat and conservation must focus on protection of the remaining areas.

Grey Heron (*Ardea cinerea altirostris*) HSG Category Globally Vulnerable (VU). This population was not recognised as a subspecies by Hancock and Kushlan (1984) and its taxonomic status needs confirmation. It is restricted to the island of Sumatra, in the Greater Sundas (Voous and van Marle 1988) where it occurs over a restricted range in habitats which are under threat. Information on water bird populations on the island is sparse and it is not currently possible to provide a population estimate greater than 700 mature individuals.

Conservation action: surveys covering the known or suspected distribution of the Grey Heron in Sumatra are needed to improve knowledge on the taxonomic status, the distribution and the abundance of these birds on the island. If the results suggest that there is a real cause for concern, then a more intensive conservation strategy should be prepared.

Grey Heron (*Ardea cinerea monicae*) HSG Category Globally Vulnerable (VU). This small population (up to 8000 individuals) is confined to the Banc d'Arguin in

Mauritania and subject to considerable fluctuations of numbers of breeding birds. Recent aerial surveys revealed 4188 incubating birds in 1997 (Hafner et al. 1998b), and only 1067 in 1998 (Pineau and Hafner, unpubl. data). There is no evidence of a decline since the censuses in 1984–85 by Campredon (1987) who counted 2400 occupied nests.

Conservation action: the breeding islands are extremely difficult to access and they are part of the Banc d'Arguin National Park, which has strict regulations. Similarly, the feeding areas are very extensive and human population is so low that there is practically no disturbance to these birds. The Station Biologique de la Tour du Valat in France collaborates with the National Park and the aerial surveys will be continued in the long term.

Great Blue Heron *(Ardea herodias occidentalis) HSG Category Globally Vulnerable (VU)*. This population is found in southern Florida and the Caribbean. It is a typically dimorphic population with a limited range, largely confined to estuarine habitats of southern Florida and nearby islands of the West Indies (Chapter 7).

Conservation action: the status of the species is little known outside of southern Florida, and surveys need to be conducted to determine its range and population sizes. Within southern Florida, there are indications that habitat conditions are deteriorating in large parts of its habitat, despite much of it being in national parks and refuges. The breeding success of the population may largely depend on artificial food sources. The population requires close monitoring of size, distribution, and productivity. Restoration of the estuary, especially the birds' natural food base, is required.

Great Blue Heron *(Ardea herodias fannini) HSG Category Globally Vulnerable (VU)*. This population is confined to the northeast Pacific coast of North America.

Conservation action: The population has been surveyed around the Strait of Georgia since 1989 and the largest colonies have been protected from destruction and disturbance by humans. Studies into the sudden increase in Bald Eagles and subsequent predation on herons are required. Close monitoring of the heron population is also required.

Purple Heron *(Ardea purpurea madagascariensis) HSG Category Globally Vulnerable (VU)*. This small population is endemic to Madagascar and depends on freshwater lakes and rivers.

Conservation action: in view of the continuing pressure on these habitats in Madagascar, there is a need for constant monitoring of the population and the state of wetlands. Conservation organisations, which are active in Madagascar, need continuous support.

Indian Pond Heron *(Ardeola grayii phillipsi) HSG Category Globally Vulnerable (VU)*. The apparent area of occupancy, the Maldives (Rose and Scott 1997) is restricted and exposed to pressure from tourism. This subspecies is therefore vulnerable to habitat degradation.

Conservation action: in the short term, the most important action must be to establish the current size of the population, together with an assessment of habitat availability and the degree of threat to breeding and foraging habitats. There appears to be some degree of capture and sale of wildlife in towns in the Maldives (anecdotal information) and capture of herons should be discouraged. Promotion of conservation awareness should be included as a fundamental component of a conservation project.

The following four subspecies of the Green-backed Heron are considered HSG Category Globally Vulnerable because of their restricted range on offshore islands which exposes them to natural and/or anthropogenic habitat degradation.

Green-backed Heron *(Butorides striatus albolimbatus) HSG Category Globally Vulnerable (VU)*. According to Rose and Scott (1997) this bird is now restricted to the Chagos Islands (unless the distribution on the Chagos and Maldives given by Hancock and Kushlan 1984 is more accurate).

Green-backed Heron *(Butorides striatus didi) HSG Category Globally Vulnerable (VU)*. Apparently restricted to the northern Maldive Islands (Rose and Scott 1997).

Green-backed Heron *(Butorides striatus patruelis) HSG Category Globally Vulnerable (VU)*. It is restricted to Tahiti and has declined over the last twenty years and is now considered rare.

Green-backed Heron *(Butorides striatus albidulus) HSG Category Globally Vulnerable (VU)*. Apparently restricted to the southern Maldive Islands (Rose and Scott 1997).

Conservation action: in view of the increasing pressure on these islands by mass tourism, action must be based on a recent assessment of the current distribution to help define the important areas and sites. Habitat requirements must be assessed during breeding as well as outside the breeding season. This is particularly important in terms of site protection. The four subspecies of the Green-backed Heron exploit coastal wetlands; parts of these are seasonal and sometimes ephemeral but nevertheless important in the bird's life cycle. This may render difficult the definition of the boundaries of protected areas but it is necessary to take even temporary wetlands into account. The data collected should form the basis for a priority list of areas and sites for full protection.

Malayan Night Heron *(Gorsachius melanolophus rufolineatus) HSG Category Globally Vulnerable (VU)*. The Malayan Night Heron is little-known throughout its range, in spite of its wide distribution and apparent local abundance. This is mainly due to its nocturnal habits and preference for dense humid forest. All recognised populations of this species are insufficiently known to propose detailed conservation action (Chapter 4). Recent records from Sumatra and Peninsular Malaysia suggest that these areas may also support resident populations, while it is not known whether the apparently healthy populations recently located in Cambodia, Laos, Thailand and Vietnam are sedentary or migratory.

Conservation action: the first aim must be to clarify the distribution and status of the species as a whole, particularly in areas where there appear to be small, isolated, resident populations threatened by logging. This is definitely the case of the race *G. m. rufolineatus* of Palawan in the Philippines (Chapter 4), where it appears essential to protect all the remaining forested areas. However, *G. m. melanolophus*, *G. m. kutteri,* and *G.m. minor* also qualify for subcategory dd, hl: data deficient but clearly suffering from habitat loss (Table 17.2).

Little Bittern *(Ixobrychus minutus podiceps) HSG Category Globally Vulnerable (VU).* This subspecies is endemic to Madagascar, consequently subject to all the threats and pressures affecting wetlands on the island (Chapter 5).

Conservation action: the subspecies seems to occur only in few scattered localities (Chapter 5). These need absolute conservation priority and continued monitoring of the population must be envisaged.

Little Bittern *(Ixobrychus minutus dubius) HSG Category Globally Vulnerable (VU).* This subspecies has been declared rare and vulnerable in Australia.

Conservation action: Recent information on known or suspected distribution may be used to establish a priority list of areas and sites for protection.

Yellow-crowned Night Heron *(Nycticorax violaceus caliginis) Colombia population HSG Category Globally Lower Risk (LR), Subcategory near threatened (nt).* Very little known, this subpopulation comprises apparently less than 10 000 individuals but reliability of data is low (Rose and Scott 1997). In such a case it is difficult to choose between category DD and others. However, *N. v. caliginis* is largely confined to coastal habitat which is generally more threatened by human activity than inland wetlands. Because only small numbers have been reported, the HSG attributes presently the status Lower Risk, near threatened (Table 17.2).

Conservation action: as a first step, a regional population and distribution estimate is essential as a basis for developing a conservation strategy.

Bare-throated Tiger Heron *(Tigrisoma mexicanum mexicanum) Northern Neotropic population HSG Category Globally Lower Risk (LR), Subcategory near threatened (nt).* The race is reported for the Gulf of Urabá and for Rio Atrato in north western Colombia. To date, the gulf is to our knowledge unprotected, faces urban expansion, settlement of river margins and discharge of domestic sewage. The river is poorly known and partially protected only. Livestock grazing, deforestation and developing agriculture threaten the habitat.

Conservation action: the most urgent action is to assess the status of this subpopulation, especially along the shorelines of the gulf.

Goliath Heron *(Ardea goliath) South Asian and South-west Asian populations HSG Category Regionally Vulnerable (RVU).* The south Asian and south-west Asian populations of the Goliath Heron may be a coastal extension of the main African population. There is no evidence to suggest that these populations were ever large. Due to their small size (Chapter 3) they are vulnerable to degradation of coastal habitats. However, the main African population is considered to be of least concern (subcategory lc, Table 17.2).

Conservation action: despite the healthy status of the species as a whole, these regional populations are of conservation concern. They should be assessed continuously in collaboration with other ongoing wetland surveys.

Purple Heron *(Ardea purpurea purpurea) European and North African populations HSG Category Regionally Vulnerable (RVU).* Numbers have declined between 1970 and 1990 throughout Europe and the species is a rare breeding bird in North Africa (Chapters 1 and 2).

Conservation action: in several countries breeding populations have been monitored during many years. Without these surveys the decline would have gone unnoticed and they should be continued. In southern France nest sites have become a limiting factor due to various management practices including commercial exploitation of reed (Chapter 9). Assessments of seasonal and annual variation of the physical characteristics of wetlands are essential to understand the impact of management practices on the local population size and colony distribution. Certain indicators of wetland quality for this species, such as the extent of flooded habitat and emergent vegetation (nest sites), may be obtained from aerial surveys. The possibilities of using GIS and satellite imagery to monitor physical characteristics of reed beds (size, inundated versus dry, commercial exploitation of reed, etc.) is presently being investigated and if successful this method may be used for large scale monitoring programmes.

Breeding populations in Europe are presumably regulated by winter survival but there is a lack of information on numbers and distribution in the main African wintering areas. Such information is badly needed since there are such heavy pressures to exploit wetlands through damming of river systems for hydropower and irrigation purposes (Chapter 5). The possibility of collecting information on the availability of aquatic habitats using large-scale satellite techniques is presently being investigated. A network of collaborators in the African wintering (European winter) areas must be established in order to clarify the present range and location of the most important wintering sites. As a second step data collection on habitat use and factors limiting survival may be envisaged.

Great White Egret *(Egretta alba alba) European populations HSG Category Regionally Vulnerable (RVU).* Tucker and Heath (1994) consider the Great White Egret, Grey Heron, Little Egret, and Cattle Egret secure at the European scale. Regarding the three latter species, Chapters 1 and 2 confirm this statement. In contrast, the Great White Egret should be considered of conservation concern. It is indeed difficult to accept the status "secure" for this species if one compares it with the status of the Black-crowned Night Heron, considered vulnerable by Tucker and Heath (1994).

Rose and Scott (1997) give for the Mediterranean/Black Sea wintering population 7000-17 000 individuals (no estimates of numbers of breeding birds). According to the most up-to-date information (Chapters 1 and 2), this species is localised in Europe (no breeding records in North Africa), although it has been expanding in a westerly direction in recent years.

Conservation action: despite this apparently favourable development the Great White Egret deserves continued monitoring effort, particularly in the Eastern Mediterranean, the Black Sea regions and Russia where the strongholds of the population are and where the status "apparently secure" needs to be reconfirmed.

Squacco Heron *(Ardeola ralloides ralloides) European and North African populations HSG Category Regionally Vulnerable (RVU).* It is patchily distributed and particularly in south-west Europe and in North Africa, the small local populations (Chapter 2) are quite susceptible to local extirpation from catastrophic events. The greatest threat is loss and deterioration of freshwater habitat for feeding and wet woodland for nesting (Hafner and Didner 1997). The largest Squacco Heron populations of western Europe today use rice fields. Changes in agricultural practice could have a negative impact on prey populations.

Conservation action: monitor the breeding populations in the major breeding areas of western Europe (Italy, southern France and Spain), in particular the availability and quality of nest sites, and promote conservation and management of wet woodlands, the preferred breeding habitat; synthesise existing data on habitat use and feeding ecology across the major rice production areas in the Mediterranean region to prepare management proposals for environmentally sensitive agricultural practices. Continue to assess the importance of rice fields versus natural/seminatural habitats through field observations.

Like the Purple Heron, the Squacco Heron is a long-distance migrant, although in recent years it is seen in increasing numbers in winter in Morocco and in Egypt (Hafner and Didner 1997). Most however will migrate to the northern tropics of Africa and project links must be made for Squacco Heron/Purple Heron in order to assess the present major wintering areas.

Black-crowned Night Heron *(Nycticorax nycticorax nycticorax) Europe HSG Category Regionally Vulnerable (RVU).* Although it is present in 22 European countries, locally in rather impressive numbers, the distribution is patchy, especially in the western Mediterranean (Chapters 1 and 2). The largest, apparently stable breeding population is in northern Italy (31% of the European population). This species has similar habitat requirements (freshwater dependency) as the Purple Heron and the Squacco Heron. The major European and North African nesting areas of Squacco Herons are also the most important ones for Black-crowned Night Herons, where the two species nest in mixed colonies.

Conservation action: a very large proportion of the European breeding population of Black-crowned Night Herons is sustained by rice fields. Changes in agricultural practices could therefore affect the European population very seriously. Consequently the conservation strategy outlined for the Squacco Heron is also recommended on behalf of the Black-crowned Night Heron, and project links must be established through international collaboration.

Little Bittern *(Ixobrychus minutus minutus) European and North African populations HSG Category Regionally Vulnerable (RVU).* The species has strongly decreased both in population size and range between 1970 and 1990 in most European countries and the overall decrease in Europe in range was between 20 and 50%, withdrawing from

Little Bittern. This species has strongly decreased in most European countries. Its wintering areas are virtually unknown. Photo: Jean François Hellio and Nicolas van Ingen.

west to east (Marion 1997c). The southern rim of the Mediterranean has two important known breeding areas, the Nile Delta and the wetlands of the El Kala National Park in north-east Algeria (Chapter 2).

This species, which is highly dependent on freshwater areas, is extremely difficult to study. Furthermore it is most likely that the decline in European numbers is largely due to high mortality of birds during migration or when wintering in Africa. The decline seems largely to have occurred since the 1970s, over a period which covers severe drought conditions in African staging and wintering areas; through desertification the drought caused the loss of formerly important staging areas which increased the length of the Sahara crossing (Marion 1997c).

Conservation action: efforts in Europe and North Africa should concentrate on maintaining favourable breeding habitat over large areas to ensure that sufficient habitat exists, should conditions in Africa again improve. The aims of the strategy are: to assure availability of suitable breeding habitat in as many areas as possible by protecting wet scrubland and reedbelts, both in the known strongholds of the species and in areas where it has disappeared. In addition, efforts should be made to identify the most important wintering areas. The distribution in winter of this species remains a major gap in our knowledge.

Eurasian Bittern *(Botaurus stellaris stellaris) European and North African populations HSG Category Regionally Vulnerable (RVU).* As for the previous species, a notable decrease has been reported from 1970–1990 across Europe (Chapter 1). In North Africa the species is extremely rare and confined to the few pockets of favourable freshwater areas (Chapter 2). Russia holds 10 000 to 30 000 pairs, about 75% of the

Eurasian Bittern. This species has declined over much of its range. Habitat loss and alteration are major threats. Photo: Jean François Hellio and Nicolas van Ingen.

European population (Koskimies and Tyler 1997). The Eurasian Bittern is less common in western and northern European countries, where high densities of this bird are restricted to the rare extensive reed beds.

Conservation action: In general the Eurasian Bittern is confined to large wetlands dominated by Phragmites reedbeds. Therefore a project link is recommended with the strategy developed for the conservation of nesting habitat of the Purple Heron. The large scale monitoring of Phragmites beds aimed to inform local, national and international conservation organizations, development agencies and decision makers will be a valuable contribution to the conservation of the two species.

Conclusions

The HSG has made use of the meticulous work organised by the IUCN (Mace and Lande 1991, Mace et al. 1992, Mace and Stuart 1994, Baillie and Groombridge 1996), BirdLife International (Collar et al. 1992, 1994, Tucker and Heath 1994) and Wetlands International (Rose and Scott 1994, 1997) evaluations. Of the 60 heron species recognised by Hancock and Kushlan (1984), IUCN 1996 attributes a global threat status to 14 of them (Table 17.2). The HSG proposes few additions or amendments to the list at present. It should be noted that in spite of the large amount of information accumulated, there is still a significant lack of data. This prevents us in a number of cases from attributing confidently a global threat status to a species. The Malayan Night Heron is a good example. It has a wide distribution, is locally abundant and therefore considered safe. However, one subpopulation in particular (island of Palawan in the Philippines) is clearly threatened because mature forest, to which it is apparently restricted, is disappearing at an alarming rate as a result of logging. Although the IUCN 1996 criteria are intended for assessment at a species level, we recognised throughout this chapter that there are threatened subspecies and populations within species considered safe, and added therefore 20 taxa which, according to our database, qualify for global threat categories: Critically Endangered (CR), Endangered (EN) or Vulnerable (VU) (Table 17.2). In addition, we consider 7 other taxa threatened at regional level.

The amount of information obtained over the past 30 years and synthesised here leads to concrete proposals for conservation action for a relatively small proportion of the taxa. Gaps in our knowledge must challenge field biologists, and during the years to come the HSG will certainly not decrease its activity. The collaboration by the international conservation organisations, as well as by national and local institutions, will be essential, as will the continued collaboration by members and correspondents of the HSG. The complete Heron Conservation Action Plan will necessarily be a separate document. This plan is being prepared with a five-year horizon in mind, 2001–2005. Priority for application of recommendations during these five years will be given to the globally-threatened taxa. An action plan must be a life document, subject to constant updating when new information comes in. During the period 2001–2005 the HSG will also be working, together with its partners, toward the next five-year plan 2006–2010. Today too many taxa suspected as threatened are listed under DD, Data Deficient. To declare a species, subspecies, race or population globally or regionally threatened is a responsibility which must rely on solid data.

Appendix 17.1   Criteria for Critically Endangered, Endangered and Vulnerable Species (IUCN 1996).

Critically Endangered (CR)
A taxon is Critically Endangered when it is facing an extremely high risk of extinction in the wild in the immediate future, as defined by any of the following criteria (A to E):

A. Population reduction in the form of either of the following:
1. An observed, estimated, inferred or suspected reduction of at least 80% over the last 10 years or three generations, whichever is the longer, based on (and specifying) any of the following:
    a. Direct observation
    b. An index of abundance appropriate for the taxon
    c. A decline in area of occupancy, extent of occurrence and/or quality of habitat
    d. Actual or potential levels of exploitation
    e. The effects of introduced taxa, hybridisation, pathogens, pollutants, competitors or parasites.
2. A reduction of at least 80%, projected or suspected to be met within the next ten years or three generations, whichever is the longer, based on (and specifying) any of b, c or e above.

B. Extent of occurrence estimated to be less than 100 km² or area of occupancy estimated to be less than 10 km², and estimates indicating any two of the following :
1. Severely fragmented or known to exist at only a single location.
2. Continuing decline, observed, inferred or projected, in any of the following:
    a. Extent of occurrence
    b. Area of occupancy
    c. Area, extent and/or quality of habitat
    d. Number of locations or subpopulations
    e. Number of mature individuals.
3. Extreme fluctuations in any of the following:
    a. Extent of occurrence
    b. Area of occupancy
    c. Number of locations or subpopulations
    d. Number of mature individuals.

C. Population estimated to number less than 250 mature individuals and either:
1. An estimated continuing decline of at least 25% within 3 years or one generation, whichever is longer, or
2. A continuing decline, observed, projected, or inferred, in numbers of mature individuals and population structure in the form of either:
    a. Severely fragmented (i.e. no subpopulation estimated to contain more than 50 mature individuals)
    b. All individuals are in a single subpopulation.

D. Population estimated to number less than 50 mature individuals.

E. Quantitative analysis showing the probability of extinction in the wild is at least 50% within 10 years or 3 generations, whichever is the longer.

Endangered (EN)

A taxon is Endangered when it is not Critically Endangered but is facing a very high risk of extinction in the wild in the near future, as defined by any of the following criteria (A to E):

A. Population reduction in the form of either of the following:
    1.   An observed, estimated, inferred or suspected reduction of at least 50% over the last 10 years or three generations, whichever is the longer, based on (and specifying) any of the following:
        a.   Direct observation
        b.   An index of abundance appropriate for the taxon
        c.   A decline in area of occupancy, extent of occurrence and/or quality of habitat
        d.   Actual or potential levels of exploitation
        e.   The effects of introduced taxa, hybridisation, pathogens, pollutants, competitors or parasites.
    2.   A reduction of at least 50%, projected or suspected to be met within the next ten years or three generations, whichever is the longer, based on (and specifying) any of b, c or e above.

B. Extent of occurrence estimated to be less than 5000 km² or area of occupancy estimated to be less than 500 km², and estimates indicating any two of the following:
    1.   Severely fragmented or known to exist at no more than five locations.
    2.   Continuing decline, inferred, observed or projected, in any of the following:
        a.   Extent of occurrence
        b.   Area of occupancy
        c.   Area, extent and/or quality of habitat
        d.   Number of locations or subpopulations
        e.   Number of mature individuals.
    3.   Extreme fluctuations in any of the following:
        a.   Extent of occurrence
        b.   Area of occupancy
        c.   Number of locations or subpopulations
        d.   Number of mature individuals.

C. Population estimated to number less than 2500 mature individuals and either:
    1.   An estimated continuing decline of at least 20% within 5 years or 2 generations, whichever is longer, or
    2.   A continuing decline, observed, projected or inferred, in numbers of mature individuals and population structure in the form of either:
        a.   Severely fragmented (i.e. no subpopulation estimated to contain more than 250 mature individuals)
        b.   All individuals are in a single subpopulation.

D. Population estimated to number less than 250 mature individuals.

E. Quantitative analysis showing the probability of extinction in the wild is at least 20% within 20 years or 5 generations, whichever is the longer.

Vulnerable (VU)

A taxon is Vulnerable when it is not Critically Endangered or Endangered but is facing a high risk of extinction in the wild in the medium-term future, as defined by any of the following criteria (A to E):

A. Population reduction in the form of either of the following:
1. An observed, estimated, inferred or suspected reduction of at least 20% over the last 10 years or three generations, whichever is the longer, based on (and specifying) any of the following:
   a. Direct observation
   b. An index of abundance appropriate for the taxon
   c. A decline in area of occupancy, extent of occurrence and/or quality of habitat
   d. Actual or potential levels of exploitation
   e. The effects of introduced taxa, hybridisation, pathogens, pollutants, competitors or parasites.
2. A reduction of at least 20%, projected or suspected to be met within the next ten years or three generations, whichever is the longer, based on (and specifying) any of b, c or e above.

B. Extent of occurrence estimated to be less than 20 000 km^2 or area of occupancy estimated to be less than 2000 km^2, and estimates indicating any two of the following:
1. Severely fragmented or known to exist at no more than ten locations.
2. Continuing decline, inferred, observed or projected, in any of the following:
   a. Extent of occurrence
   b. Area of occupancy
   c. Area, extent and/or quality of habitat
   d. Number of locations or subpopulations
   e. Number or mature individuals.
3. Extreme fluctuations in any of the following:
   a. Extent of occurrence
   b. Area of occupancy
   c. Number of locations or subpopulations
   d. Number or mature individuals.

C. Population estimated to number less than 10 000 mature individuals and either:
1. An estimated continuing decline of at least 10% within 10 years or 3 generations, whichever is longer, or
2. A continuing decline, observed, projected or inferred, in numbers of mature individuals and population structure in the form of either:

a.   Severely fragmented (i.e. no subpopulation estimated to contain more than 1000 mature individuals)
b.   All individuals are in a single subpopulation.

D. Population very small or restricted in the form of either of the following:
1.   Population estimated to number less than 1000 mature individuals.
2.   Population is characterised by an acute restriction in its area of occupancy (typically less than 100 km^2) or in the number of locations (typically less than 5). Such a taxon would thus be prone to the effects of human activities (or stochastic events whose impact is increased by human activities) within a very short period of time in an unforeseeable future, and is thus capable of becoming Critically Endangered or even Extinct in a very short period.

E. Quantitative analysis showing the probability of extinction in the wild is at least 10% within 100 years.

Additional Subcategory (HSG)

dd, hl: when there is a lack of information on the distribution and the number of individuals belonging to a species, subspecies or a population but when there is nevertheless evidence that the taxa are threatened by habitat loss. This category applies to species which depend upon habitat which is particularly threatened, e.g. tropical forest, mangroves.

18. Reflections on Heron Conservation

James A. Kushlan and Heinz Hafner

Herons are intriguing animals. Most are highly noticeable elements within their environment. Worldwide their well-appreciated images are often painted and sculpted; they grace signage of businesses, homes and government; they serve as symbols of conservation and scientific organisations, and otherwise have come to represent what is beautiful, natural, and serene within their landscape. A stately heron gazing in a sunlit pool, perhaps framed by swamp trees, is an experience commonly shared by observers of nature.

They are intriguing too because they are for the most part survivors. They belong to one of the oldest bird orders still surviving, the Ciconiiformes, which dates back some 55 million years. After having admired the grace of flying and foraging herons, an observer who is able to penetrate into a colony will be amazed by the sight of thousands of noisy chicks struggling for life, the smell of guano and decay, and the sight of regurgitated prey below the nests. It is a strange world that contrasts remarkably with the one humans are used to now. One feels propelled thousands of years back into a world in which man is nothing but an intruder from another time. Heron colonies today probably look very much the same as they used to for time immemorial.

Today, some species are in the process of expanding or consolidating their ranges, and probably have been for thousands of years. Just within the last 15-year period that this book particularly covers, species have invaded new continents and have shifted their population centres within continents. The adaptability of many of these species in the face of human alteration of the landscape is a marvel.

Yet there are clearly limits to the inherent adaptability of herons. Several species are reduced to a few individuals and others have become extremely restricted geographically, and such species, subspecies and populations are certainly worthy of being considered as endangered or threatened or of special concern, as we have done.

Defining the limits of these generally adaptable species is the crucial step in designing conservation action. We need to understand their biology sufficiently to understand their limiting factors. And we need to understand their habitat requirements sufficiently to understand how to manage habitat for their benefit.

Heron Conservation
ISBN 0-12-430130-4

Herons offer an immense field of research to answer important biological questions of general interest both for science and for conservation. This is because many important wetland areas host a guild of sympatric species coexisting there. Their biometrics, morphology and behaviour differ considerably among species, making them an ideal subject to study adaptive behaviour, interspecific competition and resource partitioning. Marking schemes allowing recognition of individuals in nature, developed during the 1980s showed that at least certain species of colonial herons are suitable for studying fundamental demographic parameters, such as survival, mortality and dispersal. The results of these studies offer new possibilities to conservationists who require good knowledge of the functioning of both wetland ecosystems and bird populations they want to protect.

In this book, we have attempted to bring together what is known about the distribution and conservation needs of these species. Much of this information is new and is derived from the on-the-ground experience of many correspondents from whom the authors drew much of the data for their analyses. The present population numbers of many species, the depth and breadth of understanding of basic heron biology, and developing approaches to establishing inventory and monitoring systems suggest that these herons are species for which conservation action could be rewarding.

Conservation action must take place at all scales. Most especially heron conservation is a local matter. The fate of an individual or a population is fundamentally in the hands of those who protect, manage, conserve, use, develop, drain or alter their nesting or feeding habitat and who protect, secure, harass, or kill individuals. Without local involvement in heron protection, larger-scale conservation action has little chance of succeeding. We encourage wildlife officers, wardens, local refuge, sanctuary and park managers, local and regional planners, developers, local public officials, conservationists and conservation societies to consider herons in their planning and enforcement efforts. Preserving and protecting a local colony site, managing a local feeding site, protecting local birds from depredation, bringing herons into local environmental education programmes all are essential efforts that should be undertaken by those concerned about their local environment. To the extent that aspects of heron biology can serve as indicators of ecosystem health and as symbols of their natural areas, herons hold the potential of being used to address more general environmental concerns. The ideal local heron conservation plan is one that places herons within the context of wise and sustainable use of the landscape. In this way herons should be a part of the larger scheme of local conservation action.

Conservation also needs to be coordinated at regional, national, flyway, and continental scales. The multitude of local activities need to sum into a population-wide strategy that assures the survival of the population of concern. Monitoring and multi-colony and multi-site conservation action must be coordinated. Again, it is best if herons are considered not just by themselves, but as integral parts of larger conservation initiatives. This is particularly the case for species dependent on wetlands, which must be managed on a watershed basis.

The dependence of many species and populations of herons on wetlands is both a challenge and a benefit. It is a challenge because wetlands are under threat worldwide—not only from drainage, but also from very subtle hydrological and biological alterations and from over-exploitation. It is a benefit because wetlands have a high priority for conservation and management in many parts of the world. In this situation, heron conservation can be placed in the more encompassing context of regional wetland conservation and management.

It is important not to equate herons entirely with wetlands, as some species of herons do not depend on traditional wetland habitats. They use stream edges, forests, grasslands, coral reefs, and seashores. It turns out that these heron species are among the most threatened, and we know little about their requirements. These habitats too are under increasing threat from human activities. It is crucial that our lack of understanding of herons in these environments be rapidly remedied.

Herons are one group of birds that have the potential to remain a part of the human dominated landscape. But this will not be assured without intervention. Herons need their champions, so that management of the landscape by humans will not proceed without the needs of herons being considered. Herons need conservation plans, at local, national and continental scales, that define these needs. Herons can be used by conservationists to develop broader plans that benefit the herons by achieving more encompassing conservation goals leading to sustainable human use of the landscape.

We honour the founders of heron conservation, such as those to whom this book is dedicated. We cherish the many colleagues who have worked so hard for the past decade and more for heron conservation. We anticipate eagerly the work of the next generation of heron conservationists, new ideas, new information, new understanding and exciting new successes in conservation of herons and their habitats. We hope that this book will prove of some value along the way.

Acknowledgements

We thank the many people and institutions who made this book possible. Most especially we thank the over two hundred correspondents of the Heron Specialist Group and the many other ornithologists, conservationists, and wetland scientists whose information, understanding, and insights, all graciously provided to the authors, form the core of this book. The authors thank their home institutions whose support was crucial to the project's completion, The University of Mississippi (USA), USGS Patuxent Wildlife Research Center (USA), Smithsonian Environmental Research Center (USA), Station Biologique Tour du Valat (France), University of Rennes 1 (France), Institute of Nature Conservation (Belgium), Wetlands International (Netherlands, Canada, Malaysia), Peter Scott Field Studies Center (Hong Kong), Shortland Wetlands Centre (Australia), Canadian Wildlife Service (Canada), Universidad Central de Venezuela (Venezuela), USGS Upper Mississippi Science Center (USA), and the Wildlife Conservation Society (USA). We thank the Station Biologique de la Tour du Valat, the University of Mississippi, the organisers of the XXI and XXII International Ornithological Congresses, Wetlands International (formerly IWRB), BirdLife International (formerly ICBP) and the International Conservation Union (IUCN) for their institutional support for the Heron Specialist Group and its activities on this project. We especially thank L. Hoffmann and J.P. Taris for their support and encouragement of this project.

We thank S. Golden, D. Wilker, and A. Johnson for French to English editing. We thank M. Arnoux, F. Daubigney, Ch. Heurteaux, B. Knight, J. Ratliff and M. Whitehead, for secretarial assistance. We thank K. Boone and R. Lansdown for preparing the maps.

Photographic credits are as follows (authors and page numbers): Robert Bennetts: 159, 162, 165, 222; Pierre Campredon: 204, 205; Thomas W. Custer: 252; Jacques Delpech: 8, 13, 15, 45, 221, 273, 341; Carol Durand: 338; Heinz Hafner: 209, 312, 315; Jean-François Hellio and Nicolas van Ingen: 17, 22, 39, 63, 67, 105, 108, 111, 220, 224, 241, 244, 274, 278, 369, 370; Kazuyasu Kisaichi: 82; James A. Kushlan: 163; Lee Kwok-Shing, Kadoorie Farm and Botanic Garden: 352; Max Maddock: 133, 136, 148; Pierrick Marion: 279; Taej Mundkur: 333; Harry Ohlendorf: 256; Alan

OwYong: 80, 88, 358; Bruno Pambour: 184, 188, 191, 194; Olivier Pineau: 335; James Runningen: 266; Tour du Valat: 49; US Fish and Wildlife Service: 253; Emmanuel Vialet: 225, 238, 320; Karl Weber and Heinz Hafner: 47; Llewellyn Young: 213. Front cover: Emmanuel Vialet. Back cover: Jacques Delpech.

Funds supporting preparation of this book were provided by the Basler Stiftung für Biologische Forschung, IUCN and Wetlands International, and the Port Authorities of Marseille, France.

We especially wish to thank and acknowledge our editor, A. Richford, and Academic Press for their support throughout the course of the project.

Chapter 1. We thank the following colleagues for the information they provided on their countries: A. Anselin and K. Devos (Belgium), G. Aubrecht and A. Ranner (Austria), V. Bjecek, P. Musil, J. Pellantova and K. Stastny (Czech Republic), A. Darolova (Slovakia), V. Keller (Switzerland), A. Kuresoo, G. Polma and R. Raja (Estonia), E. Lammi (Finland), O. J. Merne (Rep. of Ireland), T. Michev (Bulgaria), H. Skotte Møller and S. Pihl (Denmark), D. Munteanu (Romania), L. Nilsson, S. Svensson and T. Larsson (Sweden), T. Nygard (Norway), E. Rutschke (Germany), I. Samusenko and Y. Viazovich (Belarus), V. Serebryakov (Ukraine), S. Svazas (Lithuania), A. J. van Dijk (The Netherlands), J. Viksne (Latvia), and M. Wieloch (Poland). We also acknowledge W. Hagemeijer (SOVON, Netherlands) for his help in our securing data from the European Bird Atlas, G. Tucker and M. Heath (BirdLife International) for the updated information of the BirdLife Database, S. Bouche (EC Brussels) for legislation documents, E. Kuijken, Director of the Institute of Nature Conservation (Belgium), for the opportunity for Paula Ulenaers to work on this project, E. Boaerts and M. Rombouts (Institute of Nature Conservation) for updating the heron literature, H. Hafner for providing data on Mediterranean wetlands, and, with J. Kushlan, for comments on various drafts and for their continuous enthusiastic support throughout the project. We are grateful for permission to use the data of the European Bird Census Council EBCC BirdLife European Database.

Chapter 2. We thank the dedicated ornithologists around the Mediterranean region whose commitments and contributions made the species accounts possible. Special thanks are due to A. Araujo, S. Costa Marques, J. C. Farinha, R. Rufino (Portugal), G. Atta (Egypt), S. Ashkenazi, Y. Kaplan, E. Shy (Israel), T. Bino, G. Jorgo (Albania), B. Chalabi, G. Belhadj, A. Si-Bachir (Algeria), A. Crivelli, V. Goutner, S. Katzanzidis, G. Papakostas (Greece), M. Fasola (Italy), M. Fernandez-Cruz, M. Gonzalez-Martin, J. Prosper, C. Ramo, X. Ruiz (Spain), J. Franchimont, M. Thevenot (Morocco), G. Magnin (Turkey), T. Mikuska (Croatia), T. Michev (Bulgaria), D. Munteanu (Romania), I.V. Schogolev (Ukraine), M. Smart (Tunisia), who have all taken a leading role in collecting and compiling information on heron populations in their respective countries. In Mediterranean France, Y. Kayser, J. L. Lucchesi, M. Moser, O. Pineau and J. Walmsley provided important contributions to the database. A marking scheme allowing capture–mark–recapture methodology applied to Little Egrets in southern France has considerably improved our knowledge of heron biology over the past ten years and we thank the French National Ringing Centre (C.R.B.P.O.) and the French Ministry of Environment for their permission to capture and mark egrets. The author is particularly grateful to L. Hoffmann, the founder and president of the Station Biologique de la Tour du Valat, for his enthusiasm and constant encouragement over the past 35 years, and for allowing the author to carry out so many surveys throughout the Mediterranean.

Chapter 3. We thank the following, who have provided extensive help in the form of literature searches, unpublished data, and comments on earlier chapter drafts: B. Behrouzi-Rad (Iran), T. Hoffmann (Sri Lanka), A. M. Lyles (USA), R. Manandhar, C. and T. Inskipp (Nepal), R. Nation (Qatar), A. N. Poslavski (Turkmenistan), C. Richardson (United Arab Emirates), V. Santharam, T. Mundkur, S. Subramanya, V. Gurusami, P. O. Nameer, V. Menon, and P. Gole (India), E. H. Sultanov (Azerbaijan) and C. Tailhardat (France).

Chapter 4. We thank W. Duckworth, S. Garnett, M. Heath, Hsu Weishu, S. W. Kotagama, J. MacKinnon, K. Matsunaga, N. Moores, M. Narusue, C. Poole, N. Redman, Kim Lim Seng, K. Sonobe, C. Robson, Y. Sawara, L. Liu Severinghaus, M. J. Ueta, D. Wells and Won Pyong-oh for providing unpublished information and advice and E. C. Dickinson and T. Pankhurst for comprehensively reviewing drafts. We also thank the following people for contributing time and information for a desk study by the chapter's senior author, which provided much of the information included in the chapter, including supplying lists of references and their own published and unpublished data: M. Brazil, N. Collar, E. C. Dickinson, T. Fehringer, S. Garnett, C. Hails, D. Holmes, P. Holmes, J. Howes, N. Ichida, R. Jaensch, R. E. Johnstone, K. Kamolphalin, B. King, S. Kotagama, J. Kushlan, T. Lamb, the late K. Curry Lindahl, C. Mann, G. Mees, D. Melville, T. Mundkur, the late R. M. Naik, R. Ollington, D. M. Parasharya, F. Parish, J-Y. Pirot, C. Prentice, M. Rands, H. F. Recher, D. Scott, F. Sheldon, M. Silvius, K. Sonobe, S. Stuart, Cheng Tso-hsin, C. Viney, L. Wei-ping, Hsu Weishu, D. R. Wells, M. Xianlin, D. Yong, L. Young, and Cheng Zhao-quing. We also thank the following organisations for library access: British Museum of Natural History, Tring; the Musée Nationale d'Histoire Naturelle, Paris; Station Biologique de la Tour du Valat; the Balfour and Newton Libraries of Cambridge University, the International Council for Bird Preservation (now BirdLife International); Edward Grey Institute for Ornithology; Swansea University; Leiden Museum; and the Raffles Museum Collection.

Chapter 5. We thank W. Tarboton for his help with data on many southern African heron species, also G. Jarry for comments and suggestions concerning herons and wetlands in west Africa, and P. Leonard and U. G. Sorensen for their comments concerning the status of *B. stellaris capensis* in the Bangweulu swamps, Zambia. The author gives special thanks also to H. Hafner for his continued encouragement and assistance, as well as for his invaluable contributions to this chapter.

Chapter 6. We thank many individuals for assistance such as providing personal observations, allowing access to their unpublished data, locating references and commenting on the manuscript. The author especially thanks D. Baker-Gabb, G. S. Baxter, H. Blackburn, R. Chatto, A. Corrick, C. Gaskin, the late B. D. Heather, P. J. Higgins, R. P. Jaensch, W. Johnson, D. G. Geering, K. Gorringe-Smith, M. Hutchison, A. Morris, C. Myers, M. O'Brien, C. O'Donnell, H. Phillips, Project Egret Watch (The

Shortland Wetlands Centre) and Project Egret Watch volunteer observers in Australia and New Zealand, J. Reside, E. Scott, R. Sonnenburg, J. Southeron, G. Winning, and K. Yeadon.

Chapter 7. We thank R. Bayer, G. Castro, M. Dunn, A. M. Lyles, F. MacDonald, K. Shepard for providing information. B. Radke and R. Paul offered unpublished information. We thank R. M. Erwin, B. Fleury, A. M. Lyles, D. McCrimmon, T. Sherry, and J. Spendelow for reviewing the chapter manuscript.

Chapter 8. We thank G. Basili, J. Beltrán, A. H. Beltzer, D. Brooks, J. C. Chebez, R. Clay, M. R. de la Peña, J. L. X. do Nacimiento, R. Franke-Ante, J. C. Gambarotta, A. G. Gantz, S. Hilty, L. Jammes, M. Lentino, L. G. Naranjo, I. Novo, B. L. Reinert, J. V. Remsen, P. Scherer-Neto, C. Sharpe, F. Straube, D. Martins-Teixeira, V. H. Tejera, A. Tovar-Narvaez, D. Ribeiro-Vianna, J. van Vessem, C. Vispo, C. Yamashita, and L. A. Zamudio. The author especially thanks D. Brooks, R. Clay, M. de la Peña, A. M. Lyles, D. Martins-Teixeira, T. Narosky, and F. Olmos for providing unpublished information and authoritative comments on heron status, geographical ranges, and/or environmental problems. The Audubon Society of Venezuela, Econatura, Inparques, The Phelps Ornithological Collection, and Provita kindly allowed the author use of their institutional libraries. His assistants K. Liss, H. Rojas and C. Tineo were immensely helpful throughout the preparation of the manuscript and the map. H. Hafner, J. A. Kushlan, and A. M. Lyles reviewed and made key comments on an earlier version of this chapter. This paper was partially funded by Consejo de Desarrollo Cientifico y Humanistico of U.C.V. The author thanks very especially J. A. Kushlan and H. Hafner for supporting in many ways his participation in this worldwide effort on heron conservation. Finally, the author wishes to dedicate this paper to the memory of Professor J. Pacheco, who first guided him through wading bird ecology.

Chapter 9. We thank the many colleagues who have shared their notes, ideas and enthusiasm for heron conservation with us. The author is particularly grateful for stimulating discussions to the other authors of this book, and to the late F. Bourlière, P. Dugan, J. Dusi, M. Fasola, L. Hoffmann, M. Moser, X. Ruiz, N. Sadoul, A. Johnson, J. A. Valverde and J. Wallace. Their special knowledge of ecological requirements of colonial waterbirds has been a great contribution to this chapter.

Chapter 10. We thank T. Custer, R. M. Erwin, A. Lyles, M. Murdock, C. Perennou, and O. Pineau for their comments and suggestions on an earlier draft of the chapter and wish to take this opportunity to recognise the role and contribution of the Colonial Waterbird Society (now Waterbird Society) in the increase in our knowledge of heron biology in the past twenty years. The society through its meetings and journal has provided the principal venue for discussion, information sharing, and research needs identification for the herons of the world.

Chapter 11. We thank R. M. Erwin, M. Fasola, R. Lansdown, M. Maddock, W. Mullié, T. Mundkur, X. Ruiz, D. Turner, J. van der Kamp and J. Wallace for their help with data and comments. The author wishes to thank particularly H. Hafner and J. Kushlan for their continued encouragement and assistance and to express his gratitude to L. Hoffmann for providing all the necessary facilities to prepare this chapter.

Chapter 12. We thank L. J. Blus, M. A. Mora, H. M Ohlendorf, and M. G. Spalding for comments on earlier drafts of the manuscript of this chapter and R. A. Fuhrmann, L. Garrett and W. Manning for library assistance.

Chapter 13. We thank H. Hafner and the Station Biologique Tour du Valat for translation and J. Kushlan for valuable comments and improvements on the manuscript of this chapter.

Chapter 14. We thank D. Bruning, W. Conway, A. Dobson, S. Elbin, C. King, F. Koontz and C. Sheppard and the editors for helpful discussions and comments. Support for this project, and particularly for participation in the workshops, was provided by the Wildlife Conservation Society and by a grant from the American Ornithologists' Union.

Chapter 15. We thank J. Bickham, C. Henny, D. Hoffman, J. A. Kushlan, and J. Ogden for helping formulate some of these ideas on water bird biomonitoring. R. King helped with the preparation of the manuscript and K. Boone with the figures. We thank R. Butler, H. Hafner, C. Henny, J. Kushlan, and K. Parsons for comments on an earlier draft of the chapter.

Chapter 16. We thank T. Custer, R. M. Erwin, L. Marion, G. Morales, F. Sheldon, and M. Steinkamp for comments on an earlier draft of the chapter.

Chapter 17. We thank the many heron biologists and enthusiasts around the world, too numerous to be cited individually, whose combined insight and knowledge underlie the recommendations of this chapter. To write this synthesis of needed conservation action would have been impossible without their participation. Over the past fifteen years these members and correspondents of the Heron Specialist Group shared their observations, notes, publications, and ideas with the authors and editors of this book. Their invaluable collaboration has substantially increased our knowledge on the status, the biology and the conservation needs of herons. We are most grateful for their dedication and concern for the conservation of herons and their habitats. We hope that this book will help them in their future activities on behalf of herons and their habitats.

Bibliography

AWB (1991). Asian Wetlands Bureau, Kuala Lumpur, Malaysia. Unpublished count data on the Swinhoe's Egret.

Abdulali, H. (1964). The birds of the Andaman and Nicobar islands. *Journal of the Bombay Natural History Society* **61**: 483–571.

Abdulali, H. (1967). A catalogue of the birds in the collection of the Bombay Natural History Society. *Journal of the Bombay Natural History Society* **64**: 139–190.

Adam, M., Billington, C. & Collins, M. (1990). Tropical forests of Asia and the Pacific Rim. IUCN/WCMC Publication (Map), Gland, Switzerland.

Adams, W.M. (1985). River control in West Africa. pp 177–228 in (A.T. Grove, ed.) The Niger and its neighbours. A.A. Balkema, Rotterdam, Netherlands.

Aebischer, N.J. (1995). Philopatry and colony fidelity of shags *Phalacrocorax aristotelis* on the east coast of Britain. *Ibis* **137**: 11–18.

Aladin, N., Eliseyev, D. & Williams, W. (1993). Case study on the Aral Sea. pp 33–37 in (M. Moser and J. Van Vessem, eds.) Wetlands and waterfowl conservation in south and west Asia, IWRB Special Publication 25/AWB Publication 85. Slimbridge, United Kingdom and Kuala Lumpur, Malaysia.

Albanis, T.A., Hela, D., Papakostas, G. & Goutner, V. (1996). Concentration and bioaccumulation of organochlorine pesticide residues in herons and their prey in wetlands of Thermaikos Gulf, Macedonia, Greece. *Science of the Total Environment* **182**: 11–19.

Albers, P.H. (1991). Oil spills and the environment: a review of chemical fate and biological effects of petroleum. pp 1–11 in (J. White, ed.) The effects of oil on wildlife. Sheridan Press, Hanover, Pennsylvania, USA.

Albrecht, G. & Maddock, M. (1985). Avifauna of the Shortland wetlands. *Wetlands Australia* **5**: 53–68.

Alderman, T. (1965). It's a nuisance. *Imperial Oil Review* **49(3)**: 6–10.

Alexander, G.R. (1977). Food of vertebrate predators on trout waters in North Central Lower Michigan. *Michigan Academy* **10**: 181–195.

Ali, S. & Ripley, S.D. (1968). Handbook of the birds of India and Pakistan, Vol. 1. Oxford University Press, London.

Ali, S. & Vijayan, V.S. (1986). Keoladeo National Park Ecological Study. Summary report 1980–85. Bombay Natural History Society, Bombay, India.

Allen, R.R. (1938). Black-crowned Night Heron colonies on Long Island. *Proceedings Linnaean Society New York* **49**: 43–51.

Allport, A.M. & Caroll, D. (1989). Little Bittern breeding in South Yorkshire. *British Birds* **82**: 442–446.

Alonzo-Pasicolan, S. (1992). The bird catchers of Dalton Pass. *Oriental Bird Club Bulletin* **15**: 33–36.

Amadon, D. (1951). Notes on the Chinese Egret *Egretta eulophotes* (Swinhoe). *Philadelphia Journal of Science* **80(1)**: 53–54.

American Ornithologists' Union (1983). Checklist of North American birds. Allen Press, Lawrence, Kansas.

American Ornithologists' Union. (1998). Checklist of North American Birds. Allen Press, Lawrence, Kansas.

Andelt, W.F. & Hopper, S.N. (1996). Effectiveness of alarm-distress calls for frightening herons from a fish rearing facility. *Progressive Fish-Culturist* **58**: 258–262.

Anderson, D.W. & Hickey, J.J. (1972). Eggshell changes in certain North American birds. pp 514–540 in K.H. Voous (ed.) Proceedings of the 15th International Ornithological Congress. The Hague, Netherlands.

Anderson, J.T., Tacha, T.C., Muehl, G.T. & Lobpries, D. (1996). Wetland use by waterbirds that winter in coastal Texas. *National Biological Service Information and Technology Report* 8, Washington, DC.

Andrew, P. (1992). The birds of Indonesia: a checklist (Peter's sequence). Indonesian Ornithological Society, Jakarta, Indonesia.

Andrews, T. (1993). The first record of the Chinese Egret on Java. *Kukila* **6(2)**: 133.

Andrle, R. & Carroll, J. (1988). The atlas of breeding birds in New York State. Cornell University Press, Ithaca, New York.

Angle, T.G. (1992). La scomparsa degli ambienti naturali. pp 11–17 in Habitat, guida alla gestione degli ambienti naturali. Booklet WWF (World Wide Fund for Nature) and CFS (Corpo Forestale del Stato), Rome, Italy.

Anonymous. (1984a). Le Héron cendré et la pêche. *Les cahiers de la pêche* **42**. Office Fédéral de la protection de l'environnement, Berne, Switzerland.

Anonymous. (1984b). The Simpson Estate heronry. *Newsletter for Birdwatchers* **24(5–6)**: 8–9.

Anonymous. (1991). Status of world aquaculture 1990. *Aquaculture Magazine Buyers' Guide* 6,8,10,14,18.

Anonymous. (1992). Florida aquaculture sales total $54 million in 1991. *Aquaculture Magazine* **18(5)**: 55–61.

Anonymous. (1994). Aquaculture continentale: une vague montante. *Bull. Intérieur du Ministère de l'Agriculture* **1417** (Feb.): 16–27.

Anonymous. (1994a). From the field. *Oriental Bird Club Bulletin* **19**: 65–67.

Anonymous. (1994b). Regional reports from Egypt and North Africa. *People & the Planet* **3**: 10–11.

Anonymous. (1998). Little Egret *Egretta garzetta*, Ireland first breeding record. *British Birds* **91**: 242.

Antas, P.T.Z., Silva, F., Alves, M.S. & Lara-Resende, S.M. (1986). Brazil. pp 60–104 in (D. Scott and M. Carbonell, compilers) A directory of neotropical wetlands. IUCN and IWRB, Slimbridge, UK.

Arendt, W.J. (1988). Range expansion of the Cattle Egret (*Bubulcus ibis*) in the Greater Caribbean basin. *Colonial Waterbirds* **11**: 252–262.

Arendt, W.J. & Arendt, A.I. (1988). Aspects of the breeding biology of the Cattle Egret (*Bubulcus ibis*) in Montserrat, West Indies, and its impact on nest vegetation. *Colonial Waterbirds* **11**: 72–84.

Armonía. 1995. Lista de las aves de Bolivia. Asociación Armonía, Santa Cruz de La Sierra, Bolivia.

Arthington, H.A. & Hegerl, E.J. (1988). The distribution, conservation status and management problems of Queensland's athalassic and tidal wetlands. pp 59–101 in (J. A. McComb and P. S. Lake, eds.) The conservation of Australian wetlands. Surrey Beatty and Sons, New South Wales.

Ashkenazi, S. (1983). Biological and ecological aspects of populations of *Nycticorax nycticorax* and *Egretta garzetta* breeding in the Huleh reserve and their influence on fish farms in the Huleh Valley. Ph.D. Thesis: Tel Aviv University, Israel. (In Hebrew with English summary.)

Ashkenazi, S. (1985). Coexistence of herons and fisheries. *South African Journal of Science* **81**: 694.

Ashkenazi, S. & Yom-Tov, Y. (1993). Herons and fish farming in the Huleh Valley, Israel. A matter of conflict or mutual benefit? pp 28 in Colonial Waterbird Society Meeting Abstracts. 6–10 October 1993, Arles, France.

Ashkenazi, S. & Yom-Tov, Y. (1996). Herons and fish farming in the Huleh Valley, Israel: conflict or mutual benefit? *Colonial Waterbirds* (Special Publication) **19**: 143–151.

Austin, O.L., Jr. (1948). The birds of Korea. *Bulletin of the Museum of Comparative Zoology* **1**. Cambridge, Massachusetts, USA.

Austin, O.L., Jr. & Kuroda, N. (1953). The birds of Japan. *Bulletin of the Museum of Comparative Zoology*, Cambridge, Massachusetts, USA.

Awachie, B.J.E. (1976). On fishing and fisheries management in large tropical African rivers with particular reference to Nigeria. pp. 37–45 in (R. Welcomme, ed.) Fisheries management in large rivers, FAO Technical Report No. 194, Rome, Italy.

Backiel, T. & Le Cren, F.D. (1967). Some density relationships for fish population parameters. pp 261–293 in (S.D. Gerking, ed.). The biological basis of freshwater fish production. Blackwell, Oxford.

Baha El Din, S.M. (1993). Notes on recent changes in the status of breeding herons in the Egyptian Nile Valley and Delta. *Ornithological Society of the Middle East Bulletin* **29**: 12–15.

Baha el Din, S.M. & Salama, W. (1991). The catching of birds in North Sinaï, autumn 1990. ICBP Study Report No. 45.

Baillie, J. & Groombridge, B. (eds.). (1996). 1996 IUCN Red list of threatened animals. IUCN, Gland, Switzerland, and Cambridge, UK.

Baker, E.C.S. (1932). Nidification of the birds of the Indian Empire. Taylor & Francis, London.

Baker, S.J. (1986). Irresponsible introductions and reintroductions of animals into Europe with particular reference to Britain. *International Zoo Yearbook* **24/25**: 200–205.

Balança, G. (1987). Etude des stratégies alimentaires de l'Aigrette garzette, *Egretta garzetta*, sur la côte atlantique du Maroc. *Le Gerfaut* **77**: 443–462.

Baluja, G., Murado, M.A. & Hernandez, L.M. (1977). Organochlorine pesticides and PCBs distribution in tissues of Purple Heron and Spoon Duck from the Biological Reserve of Doñana (Spain). *Bulletin of Environmental Contamination and Toxicology* **17**: 603–612.

Bancroft, G.T. (1989). Status and conservation of wading birds in the Everglades. *American Birds* **43**: 1258–1265.

Bancroft, G.T., Jewell, S.D. & Strong, A.M. (1990). Foraging and nesting ecology of herons in the lower Everglades relative to water conditions. Final report. South Florida Water Management District. West Palm Beach, Florida.

Bancroft, G.T., Ogden, J.C. & Patty, B.W. (1988). Wading bird colony formation and turnover relative to rainfall in the Corkscrew Swamp area of Florida during 1982 through 1985. *Wilson Bulletin* **100**: 50–59.

Bankovics, A. (1997). Purple Heron. pp 52–53 in (E.J.M. Hagemeijer and M.J. Blair, eds.) The European bird common census atlas of European breeding birds. Their distribution and abundance. Poyser, London.

Bannerman, D. (1930). The birds of tropical west Africa. Vol. I. Crown Agents, London.

Baral, H.S. (1993). New heronries at Koshi Tappu. *Nepal Bird Watching Club Newsletter* **2(4)**: 1–2.

Bartolomé, J., Fernandez-Cruz, M. & Campos, F. (1996). Band recoveries of Spanish Little Egrets, *Egretta garzetta*. *Colonial Waterbirds* **19**: 220–225.

Basili, G. & Temple, S.A. (1995). A perilous migration. *Natural History* **104**: 40–47.

Bauer, K.M. & Glutz von Blotzheim, U.N. (1966). Handbuch der Vögel Mitteleuropas, Vol. I Akad. Verlag, Frankfurt am Main, Germany.

Baxter, G.S. (1992). The ecology and conservation of egrets. Unpublished Ph.D. thesis, Graduate School of the Environment, Macquarie University, New South Wales, Australia.

Baxter, G.S. (1994). The influence of synchronous breeding, natal tree position and rainfall on egret nesting success. *Colonial Waterbirds* **17**: 120–129.

Baxter, G.S. (1996). Provision of supplementary nest material to colonial egrets. *Emu* **96**: 145–150.

Baxter, G.S. & Fairweather, P.G. (1994). Phosphorus and nitrogen in wetlands with and without egret colonies. *Australian Journal of Ecology* **19**: 404–416.

Beaver, D.L., Osborn, R.G. & Custer, T.W. (1980). Nest site and colony characteristics of wading birds in selected Atlantic coast colonies. *Wilson Bulletin* **92**: 200–220.

Beck, B. (1995). Reintroduction, zoos, conservation, and animal welfare. pp 155–163 in (B.G. Norton, M. Hutchins, E.F. Stevens & T.L. Maple, eds.) Ethics on the ark. Smithsonian Institution Press, Washington DC.

Beehler, B.M., Pratt, T.K. & D Zimmerman, D.A. (1986). Birds of New Guinea. Princeton University Press, Princeton, NJ.

Behlert, R. (1977). Phonoakustische Methode zur Vergrämung von Graureihern *Ardea cinerea* in Fischzuchtanlagen. *Zeitschrift für Jagdwissenschaft* **23**: 144–152.

Beilharz, M.I. (1989). Conservation value assessment of wetlands: discussion paper. Wetlands Unit, National Parks and Wildlife Service, Department of Conservation, Forest and Lands, Victoria, Australia.

Bekhuis, J.F. (1990). Hoe long nog broedende Woudaapjes *Ixobrychus minutus* in Nederland? *Limosa* **63**: 47–50.

Belhadj, G. (1996). Contribution à la cartographie des ornithocénoses en Algérie: Atlas des oiseaux nicheurs du Parc Naturel d'El Kala. Thèse Magister INA (Institut National Agronomique), Algeria.

Bellward, G.D., Norstrom, R.J., Whitehead, P.E., et al. (1990). Comparison of polychlorinated dibenzodioxin levels with hepatic mixed-function oxidase induction in Great Blue Herons. *Journal of Toxicology and Environmental Health* **30**: 33–52.

Bennett, D.C., Bowes, V.A., Hughes, M.R. & Hart, L.E. (1992). Suspected sodium toxicity in hand-reared Great Blue Heron (*Ardea herodias*) chicks. *Avian Diseases* **36**: 743–748.

Benson, C.W. (1960). The birds of the Comoro Islands. *Ibis* **103**: 5–106.

Benson, C.W., Colebrook-Robjent, J.F.R. & Williams, A. (1976). Contribution à l'ornithologie de Madagascar. *L'Oiseau et Revue Française d'Ornithologie* **46**: 103–134.

Bernard, A. (1994). Les zones humides, rapport d'évaluation. Comité interministériel de l'évaluation des politiques publiques, Premier Ministre-Commissariat Général du Plan. La Documentation Française, Paris.

Bernis, F. (1961). Cuatro notas sobre Garzas. *Ardeola* **7**: 204–217.

Berthet, G. (1941–45). Note sur la nidification de l'Aigrette garzette *Egretta garzetta* en Dombes. *Alauda* **13**: 7–10.

Beveridge, M.C.M. (1989). Literature review—Problems caused by birds at inland waters and freshwater fish farms. pp 34–73 in (C.M. Bungenberg de Jong, J. From, L. Marion, and K. Molnar, eds.). Report of the EIFAC working party on prevention and control of bird predation in aquaculture and fisheries operations. EIFAC Technical Paper 51, Rome, Italy.

Beyer, W.N., Spalding, M. & Morrison, D. (1997). Mercury concentrations in feathers of wading birds from Florida. *Ambio* **26**: 97–100.

Bibby, C.J. (1981). Wintering Bitterns in Britain. *British Birds* **74**: 1–10.

Bibby, C.J., Burgess, N.D. & Hill, D.A. (1992). Bird census techniques. Academic Press, London.

Biber-Klemm, S. (1991). International legal instruments for the protection of migratory birds: an overview for the West Palearctic–African flyways. pp 315–344 in (T. Salathé, ed.) Conserving migratory birds. ICBP Technical Publication No.12. ICBP, Cambridge, UK.

Bickham, J.W. (1990). Flow cytometry as a technique to monitor the effects of environmental genotoxins on wildlife populations. pp 97–108 in (S.S. Sandu, W.R. Lower, F.J. de Serres, W.A. Suk and R.R. Tice, eds.) In situ evaluations of biological hazards of environmental pollutants. Plenum Press, New York.

Bildstein, K.L. (1993). White Ibis: Wetland wanderers. Smithsonian Institution Press, Washington, DC.

Bildstein, K.L. (1997). Wading-bird science: a guide for the twenty-first century. *Colonial Waterbirds* **20**: 138–140.

Bildstein, K.L., Bancroft, G.T., Dugan, P.J., et al. (1991). Approaches to the conservation of coastal wetlands in the Western Hemisphere. *Wilson Bulletin* **103**: 218–254.

Billard, R. (1980). La pisciculture en France. INRA Publication. Paris.

Birkin, E.J. (1990). An overview report on the wetlands of the Central Gippsland region. Central Gippsland Region: Wetlands Planning Project, Victoria, Australia.

Björk, S. (1994). Treatment of overgrown shallow lakes—macrophyte control: Lake Hornborga, Sweden. pp 154–168 in (M. Eiseltová, ed.). Restoration of lake ecosystems—a holistic approach. IWRB Publ. No. 32. Slimbridge, UK.

Blake, E.R. (1977). Manual of neotropical birds. Vol. 1. Chicago University Press, Chicago.

Blaker, D. (1969a). Behaviour of the Cattle Egret *Ardeola ibis. Ostrich* **40**: 75–129.

Blaker, D. (1969b). The behaviour of *Egretta garzetta* and *Egretta intermedia. Ostrich* **40**: 150–155.

Blaker, D. (1971). Range expansion of the Cattle Egret. *Ostrich* Supplement **9**: 27–30.

Blakers, M.S., Davies, J.J.F. & Reilly, P.N. (1984). The atlas of Australian Birds. Melbourne University Press, Melbourne.

Blanco, D. & Canevari, P. (1992). Censo neotropical de aves acuáticas 1991. Programa de Ambientes Acuáticos Neotropicales, Buenos Aires, Argentina.

Blok, A.A. & Ross, M. (1977). Grey Heron censuses for 1970–1976. *Het Vogeljaar* **25**: 205–223.

Blondel, J. (1965). Le Héron cendré (*Ardea cinerea* L.) nicheur en Camargue. *L'Oiseau et Revue Française d'Ornithologie* **35**: 59–60.

Blondel, J. & Aronson, J. (1995). Biodiversity and ecosystem function in the Mediterranean: non-human and human determinants. In (G. Davis and D. Richardson, eds.). Biodiversity and ecosystem function in Mediterranean-type ecosystems. Springer Verlag, Heidelberg, Germany.

Blus, L.J., Henny, C.J., Anderson, A. & Fitzner, R.E. (1985). Reproduction, mortality, and heavy metal concentrations in Great Blue Herons from three colonies in Washington and Idaho. *Colonial Waterbirds* **8**: 110–116.

Blus, L.J., Henny, C.J., Hoffman, D.J. & Grove, R.A. (1991). Lead toxicosis in Tundra Swans near a mining and smelting complex in northern Idaho. *Archives of Environmental Contamination and Toxicology* **21**: 549–555.

Blus, L.J., Henny, C.J. & Kaiser, T.E. (1980). Pollution ecology of breeding Great Blue Herons in the Columbia Basin, Oregon and Washington. *Murrelet* **61**: 63–71.

Blus, L.J., Rattner, B.A., Melancon, M.J. & Henny, C.J. (1997). Reproduction of Black-crowned Night Herons related to predation and contaminants in Oregon and Washington, USA. *Colonial Waterbirds* **20**: 185–197.

Böck, F. von. (1975). Der Bestand des Graureiher *Ardea cinerea* in Österreich. *Egretta* **18**: 54–64.

Boehm, E.F. (1953). Water birds of the Mount Mary Plains, South Australia. *Emu* **53**: 291–295.

Boere, G.C. & Lenten, B. (1997). The African–Eurasian Waterbird Agreement: a technical agreement under the Bonn Convention. pp 47–56 in (J. Van Vessem, ed.) Determining priorities for waterbird and wetland conservation. Wetlands International, Kuala Lumpur, Malaysia.

Bolger, P.F. & Wall, L.E. (1959). Egrets in Tasmania. *Emu* **59**: 184–188.

Bonaccorsi, G. & Faggio, G. (1997). Hivernage de la Grande Aigrette *Egretta alba* en Corse. *Alauda* **65**: 105–106.

Borgstrom, G. (1978). The contribution of freshwater fish to human food. In (S. Gerking, ed.). Ecology of freshwater fish production. Blackwell, Oxford, UK.

Bouche, S., Marion, L. & Lefeuvre, J.Cl. (1991). Les zones humides: un patrimoine à sauvegarder. World Wildlife Fund, Paris, France.

Boumphrey, R.S., Harrad, S.J., Jones, K.C. & Osborn, D. (1993). Polychlorinated biphenyl congener patterns in tissues from a selection of British Birds. *Archives of Environmental Contamination and Toxicology* **25**: 346–352.

Bowen, B.S., Koford, R.R. & Vehrencamp, S.L. (1989). Dispersal in the communally breeding Grooved-billed Ani (*Crotophaga sulcirostris*). *Condor* **91**: 52–64.

Bowmaker, A.P. (1963). Cormorant predation on two Central African lakes. *Ostrich* **34**: 3–26.

Boyd, H. & Pirot, J.Y. (1989). Flyway reserve networks for waterbirds. International Waterfowl and Wetlands Research Bureau Special Publication No. 9, Slimbridge, UK.

Braakhekke, W.G. & Marchand, M. (1987). Wetlands in the community wealth. European Environmental Bureau, Brussels, Belgium.

Braaksma, S. (1968). De verspreiding van het Woudaapje (*Ixobrychus minutus*) als broedvegel. *Limosa* **41**: 41–61.

Brazil, M.A. (1992). The birds of Shuangtaizihekou National Nature Reserve, Liaoning Province, China. *Forktail* **7**: 91–124.

Bredin, D. (1983). Contribution à l'étude écologique d'*Ardeola ibis* (L.): Héron gardeboeufs de Camargue. Unpublished thesis, University of Toulouse, France.

Bredin, D. (1984). Régime alimentaire du Héron gardeboeufs à la limite de son expansion géographique récente. *Revue d'Ecologie (Terre Vie)* **39**: 431–445.

Bregulla, H.L. (1992). Birds of Vanuatu. Anthony Nelson, Shropshire, UK.

Bridges, W. (1974). Gathering of animals. Harper & Row, New York.

Bridgewater, P. (1991). Wetland conservation challenges in Oceania. pp 53–60 in (R. Donohue and B. Phillips, eds.) Educating and managing for wetlands conservation. Proceedings of the Wetlands Conservation and Management Workshop. Australian National Parks and Wildlife Service, Canberra.

Bridgman, H.A. & Maddock, M. (1994). Meteorological conditions and Cattle Egret migration: An update. *Notornis* **41**: 189–204.

Bridgman, H.A., Maddock, M. & Geering, D.J. (1997). Cattle Egret migration, satellite telemetry and weather in south east Australia. *Corella* **21**: 69–76.

Bridgman, H.A., Maddock, M. & Geering, D. (1998). Assessing relationships between Cattle Egret migrations and meteorology in the south west Pacific: A review. *International Journal of Biometeorology* **41**: 143–154.

Briggs, S.V., Hodgson, P.H. & Erwin, P. (1995). Changes in population of waterbirds on wetlands following water storage. *Wetlands Australia* **13**: 36–48.

Britton, A.R.C. (1993). Feeding behaviour of Little Egret at Mai Po, Hong Kong. *Hong Kong Bird Report* 1990: 176–184.

Britton, R.H. (1982). Managing the prey fauna. pp 92–98 in (D. Scott, ed.) Manual of active wetland and waterfowl management. IWRB, Slimbridge, UK.

Britton, R.H. & Crivelli, A.J. (1993). Wetlands of southern Europe and North Africa: Mediterranean wetlands. pp 129–194 in (D. F. Wigham et al., eds.). Wetlands of the world I. Kluwer Academic Publishers, The Netherlands.

Broadbent, K. (1910). Birds of Cardwell and Herbert River Districts (N.Q.). *Emu* **10**: 233–245.

Brockelman, W. (1988). Khao Yai: Treks to Sai Yai. *Bangkok Bird Club Bulletin* **5(8)**: 9.

Brooke, R.K. (1984). South African red data book. South African National Scientific Programmes Report No. 97.

Brooker, M.G. (1992). Waterbirds of the Macquarie Marshes. CSIRO Division of Wildlife and Ecology, Canberra, Australia.

Brooks, D.J., Evans, M.I., Martins, R.P. & Porter, R.F. (1987). The status of birds in north Yemen and the records of the OSME expedition in autumn 1985. *Sandgrouse* **9**: 4–66.

Brosselin, M. (1974). Statut 1974 des hérons arboricoles en France. Société Nationale de Protection de la Nature, Paris.

Brosset, A. (1971). Premières observations sur la reproduction de six oiseaux africains. *Alauda* **39**: 112–126.

Brosset, A. (1990). L'évolution récente de l'avifaune du nord-est marocain: pertes et gains depuis 35 ans. *Revue Ecologique (Terre Vie)* **45**: 237–245.

Brosset, A. & Erard, C. (1986). Les Oiseaux des Régions Forestières du Nord-Est du Gabon. Vol 1. Société Nationale de Protection de la Nature, Paris.

Brouwer, K., Smits, S. & Melissen, A. (1995). The 1994 EEP TAG Survey, Part 2. EEP Executive Office, Amsterdam.

Brown, B. (1980). Possible early record of Cattle Egrets in New Zealand. *Notornis* **24**: 285–286.

Brown, L.H., Urban, E.K. & Newmann, K. (1982). The birds of Africa, vol. 1. Academic Press, London.

Broyer, J., Waragnat, P., Constant, G. & Caron, P. (1998). Habitat du Héron pourpré *Ardea purpurea* sur les étangs de pisciculture en France. *Alauda* **66**: 221–228.

Buckley, F.G. & Buckley, P.A. (1980). Habitat selection and marine birds. pp 69–112 in (J. Burger, B.L. Olla and H.E. Winn, eds.) Behaviour of marine animals, vol. 4: Marine birds. Plenum, New York.

Bunck, C.M., Spann, J.W., Pattee, O.H. & Fleming, W.J. (1985). Changes in eggshell thickness during incubation: Implications for evaluating the impact of organochlorine contaminants on productivity. *Bulletin of Environmental Contamination and Toxicology* **35**: 173–182.

Bundy, G. & Warr, E. (1980). A checklist of the birds of the Arabian Gulf States. *Sandgrouse* **1**: 4–49.

Bungenberg de Jong, C.M., From, J., Marion, L. & Molnar, K. (1989). Report of the EIFAC working party on prevention and control of bird predation in aquaculture and fisheries operations. EIFAC Technical Paper 51, Rome.

Burger, J. (1981a). A model for the evolution of mixed-species colonies of Ciconiiformes. *Quarterly Review of Biology* **56**: 143–167.

Burger, J. (1981b). The effects of human activity on birds at a coastal bay. *Biological Conservation* **21**: 231–241.

Burger, J. (1993). Metals in avian feathers: bioindicators of environmental pollution. *Reviews of Environmental Toxicology* **5**: 203–311.

Burger, J. & Gochfeld, M. (1993). Heavy metal and selenium levels in feathers of young egrets and herons from Hong Kong and Szechuan, China. *Archives of Environmental Contamination and Toxicology* **25**: 322–327.

Burger, J. & Gochfeld, M. (1995). Biomonitoring of heavy metals in the Pacific Basin using avian feathers. *Environmental Toxicology and Chemistry* **14**: 1233–1239.

Burger, J. & Hahn, C.D. (1977). Crow predation on Black-crowned Night Heron eggs. *Wilson Bulletin* **89**: 350–351.

Burger, J., Cooper, K., Saliva, J., Gochfeld, D., Lipsky, D. & Gochfeld, M. (1992a). Mercury bioaccumulation in organisms from three Puerto Rican estuaries. *Environmental Monitoring and Assessment* **22**: 181–197.

Burger, J., Parsons, K., Benson, T., Shukla, T., Rothstein, D. & Gochfeld, M. (1992b). Heavy metal and selenium levels in young Cattle Egrets from nesting colonies in the northeastern United States, Puerto Rico, and Egypt. *Archives of Environmental Contamination and Toxicology* **23**: 435–439.

Burton, J.F. (1956). Report on the national census of the heronries, 1954. *Bird Study* **3**: 42–73 (additions and corrections in *Bird Study* **4**: 50–52).

Burton, J.F. (1995). Birds and climate change. Christopher Helm, London, UK.

Butler, P.J. (1992). Parrots, pressures, people, and pride. pp 25–46 in (S.R. Beissinger and

N.F.R. Snyder, eds.) New world parrots in crisis: Solutions from conservation biology. Smithsonian Institution Press, Washington, DC.

Butler, R.W. (1991). Habitat selection and time of breeding in the Great Blue Heron (*Ardea herodias*). PhD thesis, University of British Columbia, Canada.

Butler, R.W. (1992). Great Blue Heron. In (A. Poole, P. Stettenheim and F. Gill, eds.) The birds of North America, No. 25. Academy of Natural Science, Philadelphia, PA, and American Ornithologists' Union, Washington DC.

Butler, R.W. (1993). Time of breeding in relation to food availability of female Great Blue Herons (*Ardea herodias*). *Auk* **110**: 693–701.

Butler, R.W. (1994). Population regulation in Ciconiiform wading birds. *Colonial Waterbirds* **17**: 189–199.

Butler, R.W. (1995). The patient predator: foraging and population ecology of the Great Blue Heron *Ardea herodias* in British Columbia. Canadian Wildlife Service Occasional Paper Number 86, Ottawa.

Butler, R.W. (1997). The Great Blue Heron. University of British Columbia Press, Vancouver.

Butler, R.W. & Campbell, R.W. (1987). The birds of the Fraser River Delta: populations, ecology and international significance. Canadian Wildlife Service Occasional Paper Number 65, Ottawa.

Butler, R.W., Morrison, R.I.G. & Delgado, F. (1992). The distribution of fish-eating, wading and raptorial birds in the Gulf of Panama, October 1991. Canadian Wildlife Service Program Note No. 198, Ottawa.

Butler, R.W., Morrison, R.I.G., Delgado, F.S., Ross, R.K. & Smith, G.E.J. (1997). Habitat associations of coastal birds in Panama. *Colonial Waterbirds* **20**: 518–524.

Butler, R.W., Morrison, R.I.G., Delgado, F.S. & Ross, R.K. (1998). The distribution and abundance of coastal seabirds, wading birds and birds of prey on the coast of Panama. pp 69–89 in (R.I.G. Morrison, R.W. Butler, F.S. Delgado, and R.K. Ross, eds.) Atlas of Nearctic shorebirds and other waterbirds on the coast of Panama. Canadian Wildlife Service Special Publication, Ottawa.

Buxton, R. (1991). New Zealand wetlands. Department of Conservation and the former Environmental Council, Wellington, New Zealand.

Byrd, G.V., Trapp, J.L. & Gibson, D.D. (1978). New information on Asiatic birds in the Aleutian Islands, Alaska. *Condor* **80**: 309–315.

Byrd, M.A. (1978). Dispersal and movements of six North American ciconiiforms. pp 161–185 in (A. Sprunt IV, J.C. Ogden, and S. Winckler, eds.), Wading Birds. National Audubon Society Special Report 7, New York.

Cadbury, C.J. & Fitzherberg-Brockholes (née Meyer), J. (1983). Grey Herons at trout farms in England and Wales. pp 166–171 in (P.R. Evans, H. Hafner, and P. L'Hermite, eds.) Shorebirds and large waterbirds conservation. Commission of the European Community, Brussels, Belgium.

Cairns, J. (1954). The Yellow Bittern. *Malayasian Nature Journal* **9(1)**: 28–31.

Caldwell, H.R. & Caldwell, J.C. (1931). South China Birds. Vanderbourgh, Shanghai.

Call, D.J., Shave, H.J., Binger, H.C., Bergeland, M.E., Ammann, B.D. & Worman, J.J. (1976). DDE poisoning in the wild Great Blue Heron. *Bulletin of Environmental Contamination and Toxicology* **16**: 310–313.

Cameron McNamara (1987). Impact assessment statement Pine Waters Pty. Ltd, unpublished report. Brisbane, Queensland, Australia.

Campbell, B. & Lack, E. (eds.). (1985). A dictionary of birds. T. & A.D. Poyser Ltd, London.

Campbell, R.W., Dawe, N.K., McTaggart-Cowan, I., Cooper, J.M., Kaiser, G.W. & McNall, M.C.E. (1990). The birds of British Columbia, Vol. 1. Royal British Columbia Museum, Victoria.

Campredon, P. (1987). La reproduction des oiseaux d'eau sur le Parc National du Banc d'Arguin (Mauritanie) en 1984–85. *Alauda* **55**: 187–210.

Candeias, D., Rufino R. & Araujo, A. (1987). Ardéidés nicheurs au Portugal. pp 1–6, in (H. Hafner, P J. Dugan and V. Boy, eds.) Herons and wetlands in the Mediterranean , development of indices for quality assessment and management of Mediterranean wetland ecosystems. Final report to the Third Environment Research Programme of the Commission of the European Communities.

Carnaby, J.C. (1933). The birds of Lake Grace District, W.A. *Emu* **33**: 103–109.

Carpenter, J.W. & Spann, J.W. (1979). Diet-related die-off of captive Black-crowned Night Herons. *American Association of Zoo Veterinarians Annual Proceedings*: 51–55.

Carrol, A.L.K. (1970). The White-faced Heron in New Zealand. *Notornis* **17**: 3–24.

Carson, R. (1962). Silent spring. Houghton Mifflin, Boston.

Carss, D.N. (1988). The effects of piscivorous birds on fish farms on the west coast of Scotland. Unpublished PhD thesis, University of Edinburgh.

Carss, D.N. (1993). Grey Heron, *Ardea cinerea* L., predation at cage fish farms in Argyll, western Scotland. *Aquaculture and Fisheries Management* **24**: 29–45.

Carss, D.N. & Marquiss, M. (1992). Avian predation at farmed and natural fisheries. pp 179–196 in (M.C. Lucas, I. Diack, and L. Laird, eds.) Interactions between fisheries and the environment. Proceedings of the Institute of Fisheries Management. 22nd annual study course, 10–12 Sept. 1991, University of Aberdeen, UK.

Carter, M. (1994). Birds of the Cocos–Keeling Islands. *Wingspan* **15**: 14–18.

Casado, S., Florin, M., Molla, S. & Montes, C. (1992). Current status of Spanish wetlands. pp 56–58 in (C.M. Finlayson, G.E. Hollis and T.J. Davis, eds.) Managing Mediterranean wetlands and their birds. IWRB Special Publication 20, Slimbridge, UK.

Casini, L. & Boldreghini, P. (1994). Gli aironi. *Laguna* **14–15**: 34–39.

Castro, G., Ortiz, E.G. & Bertochi, L. (1990). Importancia biológica y conservación de la Laguna El Paraíso, Lima. *Boletín de Lima* **71**: 47–55.

Catuneanu, I.I. (1958). Coloniile de cuibarit din Delta Dunarii si necesitatea crearii unor rezervatii ornitologice. *Ocrotirea Naturii* **3**: 79–115.

Cavé, A.J. (1983). Purple Heron survival and drought in tropical West Africa. *Ardea* **71**: 217–224.

Celmins, A. (1992). List of Latvian birds species. Gandrs Ltd, Riga, Latvia.

Cezilly, F. (1992). Turbidity as an ecological solution to reduce the impact of fish-eating colonial waterbirds on fish farms. *Colonial Waterbirds* **15**: 249–252.

Cezilly, F. (1997). Demographic studies of wading birds: an overview. *Colonial Waterbirds* **20**: 121–128.

Chalmers, M.L. (1986). An annotated checklist of the birds of Hong Kong. Hong Kong Birdwatching Society, Hong Kong.

Chapin, J.P. (1932). The birds of the Belgian Congo. Bulletin of the American Museum of Natural History. Vol. 65, Part I. New York.

Chen, P.H. & Yen, C.W. (1977). A comprehensive survey of Taiwan's heronries. Tourism Bureau, Taipei, Taiwan.

Cheney, M.A., Hacker, C.S. & Schroder, G.D. (1981). Bioaccumulation of lead and cadmium in the Louisiana Heron (*Hydranassa tricolor*) and the Cattle Egret (*Bubulcus ibis*). *Ecotoxicology and Environmental Safety* **5**: 211–224.

Cheng, T.H. (1987). A synopsis of the avifauna of China. Science Press, Beijing and Paul Parey Scientific Publishers, Hamburg and Berlin.

Cherfas, J. (1984). Zoo 2000: A Look Beyond the Bars. British Broadcasting Corporation, London.

Choremi, J. & Spinthakis, E. (1992). Birds and habitat conservation on Chios, Greece. *Avocetta* **16**: 77–80.

Chung, W.Y. (1992). Distribution of heronries in the mid-western and southern lowlands of Taiwan. *Bulletin of the National Museum of Natural Science* **3**: 247–257.

Cintra, R. & Yamashita, C. (1990). Habitats, abundancia e ocorrencia das especies de aves do Pantanal de Poconé, Mato Grosso, Brasil. *Papeis Avulsos de Zoología* **37**: 1–21.

Clancey, P.A. (ed.). (1980). SAOS checklist of southern African birds. South African Ornithological Society, Pretoria.

Claridge, G. & O'Callaghan, B. (eds.). (1997). Community involvement in wetland management: lessons from the field. Wetlands International, Kuala Lumpur, Malaysia.

Clements, F.A. (1992). Recent records of birds from Bhutan. *Forktail* **7**: 57–73.

Coates, B.J., Bishop, K.D. & Gardner, D. (1997). A guide to the birds of Wallacea, Sulawesi, the Moluccas, and the Lesser Sunda Islands, Indonesia. Dove Publications. Alderley, Queensland, Australia.

Collar, N.J. & Andrew, P. (1988). Birds to watch: the ICBP world checklist of threatened birds. International Council for Bird Preservation. Technical Publication 8. Cambridge, UK.

Collar, N.J. & Stuart, S.N. (1985). Threatened birds of Africa and related islands. The ICBP/IUCN red data book. International Council for Bird Preservation and International Union For the Conservation of Nature. Cambridge, UK.

Collar, N.J., Crosby, M.J. & Strattersfield, A.J. (1994). Birds to watch 2. The world list of threatened birds. Birdlife Conservation Series 4. Birdlife International, Cambridge, UK.

Collar, N.J., Gonzaga, L.P., Krabbe, N., Madrono Nieto, A., Naranjo, L.G., Parker, T.A. & Wedge, D.C. (1992). Threatened birds of the Americas: the ICBP/IUCN Red Data Book. International Council for Bird Preservation, Cambridge, UK.

Combridge, P. & Parr, C. (1992). Influx of Little Egrets in Britain and Ireland in 1989. *British Birds* **85(1)**: 16–21.

Conniff, R. (1991). Why catfish farmers want to throttle the crow of the sea. *Smithsonian Journal*, July 1991: 44–55.

Connors, P.G., Anderlini, V.C., Risebrough, R.W., Gilbertson, M. & Hays, H. (1975). Investigations of heavy metals in Common Tern populations. *Canadian Field-Naturalist* **89**: 157–162.

Contreras, J.R. (1993). On some species of birds from the extreme southwest of the Province of Formosa, Argentina. *Notulas faunísticas* **47**: 1–8.

Conway, W.G. (1986). The practical difficulties and financial implications of endangered species breeding programmes. *International Zoo Yearbook* **24/25**: 210–219.

Cook, D.C. (1978). Foraging behavior and food of Grey Herons *Ardea cinerea* on the Ythan Estuary. *Bird Study* **25**: 17–22.

Cooke, A.S., Bell, A. & Prestt, I. (1976). Egg shell characteristics and incidence of shell breakage for Grey Herons *Ardea cinerea* exposed to environmental pollutants. *Environmental Pollution* **11**: 59–84.

Cornish, A.S. (1996). Habitat utilisation by feeding Little Egrets from a Tsim Bei Tsui egretry. *Hong Kong Bird Report* 1995: 238–244.

Cosson, R.P. (1989). Relationships between heavy metal and metallothionein-like protein levels in the liver and kidney of two birds: the Greater Flamingo and the Little Egret. *Comparative Biochemistry and Physiology* **94C**: 243–248.

Cosson, R.P., Amiard, J. & Amiard-Triquet, C. (1988). Trace elements in Little Egrets and Flamingos of Camargue, France. *Ecotoxicology and Environmental Safety* **15**: 107–116.

Costa, L.T., Farinha, J.C., Hecker, N. & Tomàs Vives, P. (1996). Mediterranean wetland inventory: a reference manual. Vol. 1. Medwet, IUCN, Wetlands International, Lisbon, Portugal.

Coverdale, M.A.C., Hancock, J. & Pearson, D.J. (1983). Unusual December–January breeding at the Garsen Heronry, Kenya. *Scopus* **7**: 49–50.

Cracraft, J. (1985). Historical biogeography and patterns of differentiation within the South American avifauna: Areas of endemism. pp 49–84 in (P.A. Buckley, M.S. Foster, E.S. Morton, R.S. Ridgely and F.G. Buckley, eds.) Neotropical ornithology. Ornithological Monographs No. 36. American Ornithologists' Union, Lawrence, Kansas.

Cramp, S. & Simmons, K.E.L. (1977). The birds of Western Palearctic. Handbook of the Birds of Europe, the Middle East and North Africa, Vol. 1. Oxford University Press, Oxford, UK.

Craufurd, R.O. (1966). Notes on the ecology of the Cattle Egret *Ardeola ibis* at Rokupr, Sierra Leone. *Ibis* **108**: 411–418.

Crawford, D.N. (1972). Birds of Darwin area, with some records from other parts of Northern Territory. *Emu* **72**: 131–135.

Creutz, G. (1961). Zur Ernährung des Graureihers (*Ardea cinerea*) und zu seiner Abwehr von Fischteichen. I.N.R.A. Paris. *Annales Epiphyties* **13**: 209–221.

Creutz, G. (1964). Ernährungsweise, Nahrungsauswahl und Abwehr des Graureihers (*Ardea cinerea*). Zoologische Abhandlungen Museum Tierkunde Dresden **237**: 29–64.

Creutz, G. (1981). Der Graureiher. Die Neue Brehm Bücherei, A. Ziemsen Verlag, Wittenberg Lutherstardt, Germany.

Creutz, G. & Schlegel, R. (1961). Das Brutvorkommen des Graureihers in der DDR. *Falke* **92**: 51–58.

Crivelli, A. (1981). Les peuplements de poissons de la Camargue. *Rev. Ecol. (Terre et Vie)* **35**: 617–671.

Crivelli, A. & Hafner, H. (1991). Rapport de mission en U.R.S.S. 15–28 juin 1991. Document polycopié, Tour du Valat, Arles, France.

Crivelli, A.J., Jerrentrup H. & Hallmann, B. (1988). Preliminary results of a complete census of breeding colonial wading birds in Greece, spring 1985–1986. *Hellenic Ornithological Society Newsletter* **4**: 31–32.

Crivelli, A., Grillas, P., Jerrentrup, H. & Nazirides, T. (1995). Effects on fisheries and waterbirds of raising water levels at Kerkini Reservoir, a Ramsar site in northern Greece. *Environmental Management* **19**: 431–443.

Crome, F.J.H. (1988). To drain or not to drain?—Intermittent swamp drainage and waterbird breeding. *Emu* **88**: 243–248.

Curry, P.J. & Sayer, J.A. (1979). The inundation zone of the Niger as an environment for palearctic migrants. *Ibis* **121**: 20–40.

Curry-Lindahl, K. (1981). Bird migration in Africa. Academic Press, London.

Custer, T.W. & Custer, C.M. (1995). Transfer and accumulation of organochlorines from Black-crowned Night-Heron eggs to chicks. *Journal of Environmental Toxicology and Chemistry* **14**: 533–536.

Custer, T.W. & Mulhern, B.L. (1983). Heavy metal residues in prefledging Black-crowned Night-Herons from three Atlantic coast colonies. *Bulletin of Environmental Contamination and Toxicology* **30**: 178–185.

Custer, T.W. & Ohlendorf, H.M. (1989). Brain cholinesterase activity of nestling Great Egrets, Snowy Egrets and Black-crowned Night-Herons. *Journal of Wildlife Disease* **25**: 359–363.

Custer, T.W. & Osborn, R.G. (1978). Feeding habitat used in colonially breeding herons, egrets, and ibises in North Carolina. *Auk* **95**: 733–743.

Custer, T.W. & Peterson, D.W., Jr, (1991). Growth rates of Great Egret, Snowy Egret, and Black-Crowned Night-Heron chicks. *Colonial Waterbirds* **14**: 46–50.

Custer, T.W., Osborn, R.G. & Stout, W. (1980). Distribution, species abundance, and nesting site use of Atlantic coast colonies of herons and their allies. *Auk* **97**: 591–600.

Custer, T.W., Hensler, G.L. & Kaiser, T.E. (1983a). Clutch size, reproductive success, and organo-chlorine contaminants in Atlantic coast Black-crowned Night-Herons. *Auk* **100**: 699–710.

Custer, T.W., Bunck, C.M. & Kaiser, T.E. (1983b). Organochlorine residues in Atlantic coast Black-crowned Night-Heron eggs, 1979. *Colonial Waterbirds* **6**: 160–167.

Custer, T.W., Pendleton, G. & Ohlendorf, H.M. (1990). Within- and among-clutch variation of organochlorine residues in eggs of Black-crowned Night-Herons. *Environmental Monitoring and Assessment* **15**: 83–89.

Custer, T.W., Rattner, B.A., Ohlendorf, H.M. & Melancon, M. (1991). Herons and egrets as proposed indicators of estuarine contamination in the United States. pp 2474–2479 in B.D. Bell (convener), R.V. Cossee, J.E.C. Flux, B.D. Heather, R.A. Hitchmough, C.J.R. Robertson, and M.J. Wiliams (eds.) Proceedings of the 20th International Ornithological Congress. Christchurch, New Zealand.

Custer, T.W., Bickham, J.W., Lewis, T., Rudas, L.A., Custer, C.M. & Melancon, M.J. (1994). Flow cytometry for monitoring contaminant exposure in Black-crowned Night-Herons. *Archives of Environmental Contamination and Toxicology* **27**: 176–179.

Custer, T.W., Hines, R.K., Stewart, P.M., Melancon, M.J., Henshel, D.S. & Sparks, D.W. (1998). Organochlorines, mercury and selenium in great blue heron eggs from Indiana Dunes National Lakeshore, Indiana. *Journal of Great Lakes Research* **24**: 3–11.

Custer, T.W., Hines, R.H., Melancon, M.J., Hoffman, D.J., Bickham, J.W., Martin, J.W. & Henshel, D. (1997). Contaminant concentrations and biomarker response in Great Blue Heron eggs from 10 colonies on the upper Mississippi River, USA. *Environmental Toxicology and Chemistry* **16**: 260–271.

Dahl, T.E. & Johnson, C.E. (1991). Wetland status and trends in the conterminous United States mid-1970s to mid-1980s. US Department of Interior, Fish and Wildlife Service, Washington DC.

David, P.G. (1994). Wading bird nesting at Lake Okeechobee, Florida: a historical perspective. *Colonial Waterbirds* **17**: 69–77.

Davidson, I. (1997). The Western Hemisphere Shorebird Reserve Network (WHSRN): a major programme of Wetlands International—the Americas. pp 3–22 in (J. van Vessem, ed.) Determining priorities for waterbird and wetland conservation. Wetlands International, Kuala Lumpur, Malaysia.

Davidson, I. & Gauthier, M. (1993). Wetland conservation in Central America. Report No. 93-3, North American Wetlands Conservation Council (Canada). Ottawa.

Davis, W.E. Jr. (1993). Black-crowned Night-Heron. In (A. Poole and F. Gill eds.). The birds of North America No. 74. Academy of Natural Science, Philadelphia, and American Ornithologists' Union, Washington, DC.

Davis, W.E. Jr. & Kushlan, J.A. (1994). Green Heron. In (A. Poole, and F. Gill, eds.). The birds of North America, No. 129. Academy of Natural Science, Philadelphia, and American Ornithologists' Union, Washington, DC.

Davis, W.E. & Parsons, K.C. 1991. Effects of investigator disturbance on the survival of Snowy Egret nestlings. *Journal of Field Ornithology* **62**: 432–435.

Dawson, E.W. (1949). Grey Heron (*Ardea cinerea*), in Classified Summarised Notes. N.Z. *Bird Notes* **3**: 88–106.

Dawson, E.W. (1951). Grey Heron (*Ardea cinerea*) in Summarised Classified Notes. *Notornis* **4**: 38–47.

Dawson, E.W. (1974). Sight records of Grey Heron (*Ardea cinerea*) in New Zealand: An elucidation. *Notornis* **21**: 124–128.

Day, J.C.U. (1981). Status of Bitterns in Europe since 1976. *British Birds* **74(1)**: 10–16.

Day, J.C.U. & Wilson, J. (1978). Breeding Bitterns in Britain. *British Birds* **71(7)**: 285–300.

Deignan, H.G. (1945). The birds of northern Thailand. *Smithsonian Institution Bulletin* **186**: 1–616.

Deignan, H.G. (1963). Checklist of the birds of Thailand. Smithsonian Institution, *National Museum* **226**: 1–263.

de Jong, B.H.J., Spaans, A.L. & Held, M. (1986). Suriname. pp 241–255 in (D.A. Scott and M. Carbonell, compilers) A directory of neotropical wetlands. IUCN and IWRB, Slimbridge, UK.

de Kinkelin, P., Michel, L.M. & Ghittino, P. (1985). Précis de pathologie des poissons. Office International des Epizooties, INRA, Paris.

Delestrade, A., McCleery, R.H. & Perrins, C.M. (1996). Natal dispersal in a heterogeneous environment: the case of the Great Tit in Wytham. *Acta Oecologica* **17**: 519–529.

del Hoyo, J., Elliott, A. & Sargatal, J. (eds.). (1992). Handbook of the birds of the world, Vol. 1. Lynx Editions, Barcelona, Spain.

Dell, J. (1985). Irruption of White-necked Heron in south-western Australia in 1975. *West Australian Naturalist* **16**: 28–30.

Dementiev, G.P. & Gladkov, N.A. (1951). The birds of the Soviet Union, Vol. 2. Academy of Sciences USSR, Moscow.

de Naurois, R. (1966). Le Héron pourpré de l'Archipel du Cap Vert. *Ardea purpurea bournei* spp. nov. *L'Oiseau & Revue Française d'Ornithologie* **36**: 89–94.

de Naurois, R. (1969). Peuplement et cycles de reproduction des oiseaux de la côte occidentale d'Afrique (de Cap Barbas, Sahara Espagnol à la République de Guinée). *Mémoires du Muséum National d' Histoire Naturelle* **56**: 1–293.

den Boer, T. (1992). De roerdomp: wintermaatregelen en bescherming. Actie Rapport 5, Vogelbescherming, Nederland.

den Held, J.J. (1981). Population changes in the Purple Heron in relation to drought in wintering area. *Ardea* **69**: 185–191.

Denny, P. (1991). Africa. pp 115–148, in Wetlands. (M. Finlayson and M. Moser, eds) Facts on File Ltd., Oxford, UK and New York.

Department of Water Resources and National Parks and Wildlife Service (1996). Water management plan for the Macquarie Marshes 1996. Water Resources Commission New South Wales, Australia.

de Schauensee, R.M. & Phelps, W.H., Jr. (1979). A guide to the birds of Venezuela. Princeton University Press, Princeton, NJ.

DesGranges, J.L. (1981). Observations sur l'alimentation du Grand Héron *Ardea herodias* au Québec, Canada. *Alauda* **49**: 25–34.

Desk Diary (1998). Environment flows well. *Habitat Australia* **26(3)**: 7.

Devillers, P., Roggeman, W., Tricot, J., Del Marmol, P.J., Kerwijn, C., Jacob, J.P. & Anselin, A. (eds.) (1988). Atlas des oiseaux nicheurs de Belgique. Institut Royal des Sciences Naturelles de Belgique, Brussels, Belgium.

d'Hamonville, L. (1898). Atlas de poche des Oiseaux de France, Belgique et Suisse utiles ou nuisibles. Librairie des Sciences Naturelles Paul Klincksiec, Paris.

Diamond, A.W. & Filion, F.L. (eds) (1987). The value of birds. International Council for Bird Preservation Tech. Publ. No. 6. Slimbridge, UK.

Diamond, A.W. & Presst, I. (1987). Bittern: threatened by loss of its reedbed habitat. In (Diamond A.W., Schreiber, R.J., Attenborough, D., Presst, I., eds) Save the Birds, Cambridge, pp 348–349.

Dias, P.C. (1991). Les Ardéidés nicheurs au Portugal: distribution, biologie et conservation. *Alauda* **59**: 23–26.

Dick, G., Dvorak, M., Grüll, A., Kohler, B. & Rauer, G. (1993). RAMSAR-Bericht 3. Neusiedler See–Seewinkel.

Dickerman, R.W., Parkes, K.C. & Bell, J. (1982). Notes on the plumages of the Boat-billed Heron. *The Living Bird* **19**: 115–120.

Dickinson, E.C., Kennedy, R.S. & Parkes, K.C. (1991). The birds of the Philippines. BOU Check-list No.12. British Ornithologists' Union, Hertfordshire, UK.

Dieter, M.P., Perry, M.C. & Mulhern, B. (1976). Lead and PCBs in Canvasback ducks: Relationship between enzyme levels and residues in blood. *Archives of Environmental Contamination and Toxicology* **5**: 1–13.

di Giacomo, A.G. (1988). Nidificación del Chiflón (*Syrigma sibilatrix*) en Salto, Buenos Aires, Argentina. *El Hornero* **13**: 1–7.

di Giacomo, A.G. (1997). Hallazgo de un nido de *Botaurus pinnatus* en Argentina. *El Hornero* **14**: 262–263.

Dimalexis, A., Pyrovetsi, M. & Sgardelis, S. (1997). Foraging ecology of the Grey Heron (*Ardea cinerea*), Great Egret (*Ardea alba*) and Little Egret (*Egretta garzetta*) in response to habitat at 2 Greek wetlands. *Colonial Waterbirds* **20**: 261–272.

Dodd, M.G. & Murphy, T.M. (1995). Accuracy and precision of techniques for counting Great Blue Heron nests. *Journal of Wildlife Management* **59**: 667–673.

Dodd, M.G. & Murphy, T.M. (1996). The status and distribution of wading birds in South Carolina, 1988–1996. Volume 1. South Carolina Department of Natural Resources, USA.

Dodman, T. & Taylor, V. (1995). African waterfowl census 1995. IWRB, Slimbridge, UK.

Dodman, T. & Taylor, V. (1996). African waterfowl census 1996. Wetlands International, Wageningen, Netherlands.

Dodman, T., de Vaan, C., Hubert, E. & Nivet, C. (1997). African waterfowl census 1997. Wetlands International, Wageningen, Netherlands.

do Nascimiento, J.L.X. (1990). Reproduçao de *Agamia agami* na usina hidrelétrica Balbina, Amazonas, Brasil. *Ararajuba* **1**: 79–83.

Dowsett, R.J. (1981). Breeding and other observations on the Slaty Egret *Egretta vinaceigula*. *Bulletin of the British Ornithological Club* **101**: 323–327.

Dowsett, R.J. & de Vos, A. (1964). *Wildfowl Trust Annual Report* **16**: 67–73.

Dowsett, R. J. & Dowsett-Lemaire, F. (1993). A contribution to the distribution and taxonomy of Afrotropical and Malagasy birds. *Tauraco Research Report* **5**: 325.

Draffan, R.D.W., Garnett, S.T. & Malone, G.J. (1983). Birds of the Torres Strait: An annotated list and bibliographical analysis. *Emu* **83**: 207–234.

Drapeau, P.R., McNeil, R. & Burton, J. (1984). Influences du dérangement humain et de l'activité du Cormoran à aigrettes, *Phalacrocorax auritus*, sur la reproduction du Grand Heron *Ardea herodias*, aux îles de la Madeleine. *Canadian Field Naturalist* **98**: 219–222.

Draulans, D. (1987a). The effect of prey density on foraging behaviour and success of adult and first-year grey herons (*Ardea cinerea*). *Journal Animal Ecology* **56**: 479–493.

Draulans, D. (1987b). The effectiveness of attempts to reduce predation by fish-eating birds; a review. *Biological Conservation* **41**: 219–232.

Draulans, D. (1988). Effects of fish-eating birds on freshwater fish stocks: an evaluation. *Biological Conservation* **44**: 251–263.

Draulans, D. & van Vessem, J. (1985a). De kwestie reigerschade. *Argus* **10**: 7–9.

Draulans, D. & van Vessem, J. (1985b). The effect of disturbance on nocturnal abundance and behaviour of Grey herons (*Ardea cinerea*) at a fish farm in winter. *Journal Applied Ecology* **54**: 771–780.

Draulans, D. & van Vessem, J. (1985c). Age-related differences in the use of time and space by radio-tagged grey herons (*Ardea cinerea*) in winter. *Journal Animal Ecology* **54**: 771–780.

Draulans, D. & van Vessem, J. (1987). Factors affecting abundance, distribution and behaviour of Grey Herons (*Ardea cinerea*) at a fish-farm. *Le Gerfaut* **77**: 43–61.

Draulans, D., van Vessem, J. & Symons, F. (1986). Multivariate analysis of factors affecting foraging success of Grey herons (*Ardea cinerea*) at a fish-farm in winter. *Annales Société Royale Zoologie Belgique* **116**: 211–226.

Duc, Le D. (1992). Results of field survey on waterbird colonies in the Mekong Delta. Waterbird and Wetland Working Group (WWWG), University of Hanoi, Vietnam.

Duffy, D.C., Atkins, N. & Scheinder, D.C. (1981). Do shorebirds compete on their wintering grounds? *Auk* **98**: 215–229.

Dugan, P. (1983). The conservation of Herons during migration and in the wintering areas: a review of present understanding and requirements for future research. pp 141–153, in (P.R. Evans, H. Hafner and P. L'Hermite, eds.) Shorebirds and large waterbirds conservation. Commission of the European Communities, Brussels, Belgium.

Dugan, P. (1993). Wetlands in danger. A world conservation atlas. Mitchell Beazley and IUCN, London.

Dugan, P., Hafner, H. & Boy, V. (1986). Habitat switches and foraging success in the Little Egret (*Egretta garzetta*). pp 1868–1877 in (H. Quellet, ed.) Acta XIX International Ornithological Congress, Volume II. Ottawa.

Duhautois, L. (1984). Inventaire des colonies de Hérons pourprés en France; évaluation des effectifs reproducteurs du Butor étoilé et du Blongios nain en France. Saison de nidification 1983. Société Nationale de Protection de la Nature, Paris.

Duhautois, L. & Marion, L. (1982). Protection des Hérons: des résultats? *Courrier Nature* **78**: 23–32.

Duhautois, L., Charmoy, M-C., Charmoy, F., Reyjal, D. & Trotignon, J. (1974). Seconde prospection post-estivale au Banc d'Arguin (Mauritanie). *Alauda* **42**: 313–327.

Dupuy, A. & Verschuren, J. (1978). Note sur les oiseaux de la région du Parc National du delta du Saloum (Sénégal). *Le Gerfaut* **68**: 321–345.

Dusi, J.C. & Dusi, R.T. (1968). Ecological factors contributing to nesting failure in a heron colony. *Wilson Bulletin* **80**: 458–466.

Dusi, J.L. & Dusi, R.D. (1987) A thirty-four year summary of the status of heron colony sites in the coastal plain of Alabama, USA. *Colonial Waterbirds* **10**: 27–37.

Dusi, J.L. (1979). Heron colony effects on man. *Proceedings Colonial Waterbird Group* **3**: 143–144.

Dustman, E.H., Stickel, L.F. & Elder, J.B. (1972). Mercury in Wild Animals, Lake St. Clair. pp 46–52. in (R. Hartung and B.D. Dinman, eds.) Environmental mercury contamination. Ann Arbor Science Publishers, Ann Arbor, MI, USA.

Dybbro, T. (1970). Fiskehejrens (*Ardea cinerea*) udbredelse i Danmark 1968. *Dansk Ornithologisk Forenings Tidsskrift* **64**: 45–69.

EBBC Atlas of European Birds—see Hagemeijer & Blair 1997.

Edgar, A.T. (1978). The Reef Heron (*Egretta sacra*) in New Zealand. *Notornis* **25**: 25–28.

Eiseltová, M. (ed.). (1994). Restoration of lake ecosystems—a holistic approach. IWRB Publication 32, Slimbridge, UK.

Eisler, R. (1985a). Cadmium hazards to fish, wildlife, and invertebrates: a synoptic review. United States Fish and Wildlife Service Biological Report 85(1.2), Washington, DC.

Eisler, R. (1985b). Selenium hazards to fish, wildlife, and invertebrates: a synoptic review. United States Fish and Wildlife Service Biological Report 85(1.5), Washington, DC.

Eisler, R. (1986). Polychlorinated biphenyl hazards to fish, wildlife, and invertebrates: a synoptic review. United States Fish and Wildlife Service Biological Report 85(1.7), Washington, DC.

Eisler, R. (1987). Mercury hazards to fish, wildlife, and invertebrates: a synoptic review. United States Fish and Wildlife Service Biological Report 85(1.10), Washington, DC.

Eisler, R. (1988). Lead hazards to fish, wildlife, and invertebrates: a synoptic review. United States Fish and Wildlife Service Biological Report 85(1.14), Washington, DC.

El Agbani, M.A. & Dakki, M. (1992). Recensement hivernal d'oiseaux d'eau au Maroc: janvier 1992. *Compte Rendu Institut Scientifique de Rabat* **15**: 1–32.

Elkins, N. (1983). Weather and bird behaviour. T & AD Poyser, London.

Elliott, J.E., Butler, R.W., Norstrom, R.J. & Whitehead, P.E. (1989). Environmental contaminants and reproductive success of Great Blue Herons (*Ardea herodias*) in British Columbia, 1986–87. *Environmental Pollution* **59**: 91–114.

Ellis, W.S. (1990). A Soviet sea lies dying. *National Geographic* **177**: 73–92.

Erard, C., Guillou, J.J. & Mayaud, N. (1986). Le Héron Blanc du Banc d'Arguin *Ardea monicae*. Ses affinités morphologiques. Son histoire. *Alauda* **54**: 161–169.

Erwin, R.M. (1979). Coastal waterbird colonies: Cape Elizabeth, Maine to Virginia. U.S. Fish and Wildlife Service FWS/OBS-79/10, USA.

Erwin, R.M. (1980). Breeding habitat use by colonially nesting waterbirds in two mid-Atlantic U.S. regions under different regimes of human disturbance. *Biological Conservation* **18**: 39–51.

Erwin, R.M. (1983). Feeding habitats of nesting wading birds: spatial use and social influences. *Auk* **100**: 960–970.

Erwin, R.M. (1985a). Foraging decisions, patch use, and seasonality in egrets (Aves: Ciconiiformes). *Ecology* **66**: 837–844.

Erwin, R.M. (1985b). Monitoring colonial waterbird populations in the northeast: historical and future perspectives. Transaction of the 1984 North East Fish and Wildlife Conference, pp 96–108.

Erwin, R.M. (1989a). Predator–prey interactions, resource depression and patch revisitation. *Behavioural Processes* **18**: 1–16.

Erwin, R.M. (1989b). Responses to human intruders by birds nesting in colonies: experimental results and management guidelines. *Colonial Waterbirds* **12**: 104–108.

Erwin, R.M. & Spendelow, J.A. (1991). Colonial wading birds. pp 19.1–19.14 in (S. Funderburk, S. Jordan, J. Mihursky, and D. Riley, eds.) Habitat requirements for Chesapeake Bay living resources. Chesapeake Research Consortium, Inc., Solomons, MD, USA.

Erwin, R.M., Frederick, P.C. & Trapp, J.L. (1993). Monitoring of colonial waterbirds in the United States: needs and priorities. pp 18–22 in (M. Moser, R.C. Prentice, and J. van Vessem, eds.) Waterfowl and wetland conservation in the 1990s, a global perspective. International Waterfowl and Wetland Research Bureau Special Publication No. 26. Slimbridge, UK.

Erwin, R.M., Hatfield, J.S. & Link, W.A. (1991). Social foraging and feeding environment of the Black-crowned Night Heron in an industrialized estuary. *Bird Behaviour* **9**: 94–102.

Erwin, R.M, Geisser, P.H., Shaffer, M.L. & McCrimmon, D.A. Jr. (1985). Colonial waterbird monitoring: a strategy for regional and national evaluation. pp 342–357 in (W. McComb, ed.) Proceedings of a workshop on management of nongame species and ecological communities, University of Kentucky Agricultural Experiment Station, Lexington, KY, USA.

Erwin, R.M., Haig, J.G., Stotts, D.B. & Hatfield, J.S. (1996a). Reproductive success, growth and survival of Black-crowned Night-Heron (*Nycticorax nycticorax*) and Snowy Egret (*Egretta thula*) chicks in coastal Virginia. *Auk* **113**: 119–130.

Erwin, M.E., Haig, J.G., Stotts, D.B. & Hatfield, J.S. (1996b). Dispersal and habitat use by post-fledging juvenile Snowy Egrets and Black-crowned Night Herons, 1996. *Wilson Bulletin* **108**: 342–356.

Erwin, R.M., Spendelow, J.A., Geisler, P.H. & Williams, B.K. (1987). Relationships between nesting populations of wading birds and habitat features along the Atlantic Coast. pp 56–68 in (W.R. Whitman and W.H. Meredith, eds.) Waterfowl and wetlands symposium: Proceedings of a symposium on waterfowl and wetland management in the coastal zone of the Atlantic Flyway. Delaware Department of Natural Resources and Environmental Control. Dover, Delaware, USA.

Eskildsen, U.K. & Vestergaard Jorgensen, P.E. (1973). On the possible transfer of trout pathogenic viruses by gulls. *Rivista Italiana Piscicoltura Ittiopatologia* **8**: 104–105.

European Commission. (1992a). European Community Environmental Legislation. Volume 4—Nature. Office for Official Publications of the European Communities, Luxembourg.

EBD. (1994). European Bird Data Base. BirdLife International, Cambridge, UK. National Bird Population Data collected in collaboration with the European Ornithological Atlas project.

European Commission. (1992b). European Community Environmental Legislation. Volume 7—Water. Office for Official Publications of the European Communities, Luxembourg.

Faber, R.A. & Hickey, J.J. (1973). Eggshell thinning, chlorinated hydrocarbons, and mercury in inland aquatic bird eggs, 1969 and 1970. *Pesticides Monitoring Journal* **7**: 27–36.

Faber, R.A., Risebrough, R.W. & Pratt, H.M. (1972). Organochlorines and mercury in Common Egrets and Great Blue Herons. *Environmental Pollution* **3**: 111–122.

Falla, R.A., Gibson, R.B. & Turbot, E.G. (1975). The new guide to the birds of New Zealand and outlying Islands. Collins, Auckland.

Falzone, C.K. (1989). Breeding Goliath Heron, *Ardea goliath*, at the Dallas Zoo. *AAZPA Regional Proceedings*: 741–745.

Fang, Z. (1993). Preliminary report on some trace of White-eared Night Heron. Unpubl. Report to the Oriental Bird Club, RSPB, Sandy, UK.

Fang, Z. (1996). White-eared Night Heron in Guangxi. Conservation fund in action. *Oriental Bird Bulletin* **23**: 8–9.

Farinha, J.C. (1997). Cattle Egret. pp 54–55 in (E.J.M. Hagemeijer and M.J. Blair, eds.) The European bird common census atlas of European breeding birds. Their distribution and abundance. Poyser, London.

Farinha, J.C. & Leitão, C. (1996). The size of heron colonies in Portugal in relation to foraging habitat. *Colonial Waterbirds* (Special Publication) **19**: 108–114.

Fasola, M. (1983). Herons and Egret colonies in Italy. pp 114–122 in (P.R. Evans, H. Hafner and P. L'Hermite, eds.). Shorebirds and large waterbirds conservation. Proceedings of two workshops held at Durham, UK (1983). Commission of the European Communities, Brussels, Belgium.

Fasola, M. (1986). Resource use of foraging herons in agricultural and non-agricultural habitats in Italy. *Colonial Waterbirds* **9**: 139–148.

Fasola, M. (1994). Opportunistic use of foraging resources by heron communities in Southern Europe. *Ecography* **17**: 113–123.

Fasola, M. & Alieri, R. (1992). Conservation of heronry (Ardeidae) sites in north Italian agricultural landscapes. *Biological Conservation* **62**: 219–228.

Fasola, M. & Barbieri, F. (1978). Factors affecting the distribution of heronries in Northern Italy. *Ibis* **120**: 337–340.

Fasola, M. & Ghidini, M. (1983). Use of feeding habitat by breeding Night Heron and Little Egret. *Avocetta* **7**: 29–36.

Fasola, M. & Hafner, H. (1997a). Species account on the Night-Heron *Nycticorax nycticorax* for BWP Update. A quarterly journal updating Birds of Western Palearctic. Vol. 1, No. 3: 157–165.

Fasola, M. & Hafner, H. (1997b). Little Egret. pp 46–47 in (E.J.M. Hagemeijer and M.J. Blair, eds.) The European bird common census atlas of European breeding birds. Their distribution and abundance. Poyser, London.

Fasola, M. & Hudec, K. (1997). Night-Heron. pp 44–45 in (E.J.M. Hagemeijer and M.J. Blair, eds.) The European bird common census atlas of European breeding birds. Their distribution and abundance. Poyser, London.

Fasola, M. & Ruiz, X. (1996). The value of rice fields as substitutes for natural wetlands for waterbirds in the Mediterranean region. *Colonial Waterbirds* (Special Publication) **19**: 108–114.

Fasola, M., Alieri, R. & Zandonella, D. (1992). Strategia per la conservazione delle colonie di Ardeinae e modello per la gestione di specifiche riserve naturali. *Ricerche Biologia Selvaggina* **90**: 1–50.

Fasola, M., Canova, L. & Saino, N. (1996). Rice fields support a large portion of herons breeding in the Mediterranean Region. *Colonial Waterbirds* (Special Publication) **19**: 129–134.

Fasola, M., Movalli, P.A. & Gandini, C. (1998). Heavy metal, organochlorine pesticide, and PCB residues in eggs and feathers of herons breeding in Northern Italy. *Archives of Environmental Contamination and Toxicology* **34**: 87–93.

Fasola, M., Barbieri, F., Prigioni, C. & Bogliani, G. (1981). Le garzaie in Italia. *Avocetta* **7**: 29–36.

Fasola, M., Hafner, H., Prosper, J., van der Kooij, H. & Schogolev, I. In press. Population changes in European herons: relationships with African climate. Ostrich.

Fasola, M., Vecchio, I., Caccialanza, G., Gandini, C. & Kitsos, M. (1987). Trends of organochlorine residues in eggs of birds from Italy, 1977 to 1985. *Environmental Pollution* **48**: 25–36.

Fernandez Alcazar, G. & Fernandez Cruz, M. (1991). Situacion actual de las garzas coloniales en España. *Quercus* **60**: 8–16.

Fernandez Cruz, M. (1975). Revision de las actuales colonias de Ardeidas de España. *Ardeola* **21**: 65–126.

Fernandez Cruz, M. & Camacho, M. (1987). 1986 Spanish National Census of Heronries. Appendices 6.5, pp 1–15 in (H. Hafner, P.J. Dugan and V. Boy, eds.) Herons and wetlands in the Mediterranean: development of indices for quality assessment and management of Mediterranean wetland ecosystems. Final report to the Third Environment Research Programme of the Commission of the European Communities.

Fernandez Cruz, M. & Farinha, J.C. (1992). Primer Censo de Ardeidas invernantes en la Peninsula Iberica y Baleares (1991–92). *Airo* **3**: 41–54.

Fernandez Cruz, M., Fernandez Alcazar, G., Campos, F. & Dias, P. (1992). Colonies of Ardeids in Spain and Portugal. pp 76–78 in (C.M. Finlayson, G.E. Hollis and T.J. Davis, eds.). Managing Mediterranean wetlands and their birds. Proceedings Symposium Grado, Italy 1991. IWRB Special Publication 20, Slimbridge, UK.

Feunteun, E. & Marion, L. (1989). Ichthyological community and predation by Grey Herons in littoral dammed up marshes. pp 255–256 in (J.C. Lefeuvre, ed.) Proceedings of the Third International Wetland Conference, September 1988. Université de Rennes, Rennes, France.

Feunteun, E. & Marion, L. (1994). Assessment of Grey heron predation on fish communities: the case of the largest European colony. *Hydrobiologia* **279–280**: 327–344.

ffrench, R. (1980). A guide to the birds of Trinidad and Tobago. Harrowood Books, Pennsylvania.

Figueroa, D. & Seijas, A.E. (1986). Venezuela. pp 278–301 in (D.A. Scott and M. Carbonell, compilers) A directory of neotropical wetlands. IUCN and IWRB, Slimbridge, UK.

Fimreite, N. (1971). Effects of dietary methylmercury on Ring-necked Pheasants. Canadian Wildlife Service Occasional Papers No. 9.

Fimreite, N. (1974). Mercury contamination of aquatic birds in northwestern Ontario. *Journal of Wildlife Management* **38**: 120–131.

Finch, B.W. & Howell, L.A. (1982). Observations June–August 1982. *Papua New Guinea Bird Society Newsletter* **193/194**: 37.

Findholt, S.L. (1984). Organochlorine residues, eggshell thickness and reproductive success of Snowy Egrets nesting in Idaho. *Condor* **86**: 163–169.

Findholt, S.J. & Berner, K.L. (1988). Current status and distribution of the ciconiiforms nesting in Wyoming. *Great Basin Naturalist* **48**: 290–297.

Findholt, S.L. & Trost, C.H. (1985). Organochlorine pollutants, eggshell thickness, and reproductive success of Black-crowned Night-Herons in Idaho, 1979. *Colonial Waterbirds* **8**: 32–41.

Finkenstaedt, C. & Heckenroth, H. (1974). Eine künstliche Koloniegründung beim Graureiher (*Ardea cinerea*). *Vogelwelt* **95**: 227–231.

Finlayson C.M. & Larsson, T. (eds.). (1991). Wetland Management and Restoration. Proceedings of Workshop, Sweden 1990. Swedish Environmental Protection Agency Report No. 3992.

Finlayson, C.M., Bailey, B.J., Freeland, W.J. & Fleming, M.R. (1988). Wetlands of the Northern Territory. pp 103–126 in (J.A. McComb and P.S. Lake, eds.) The conservation of Australian wetlands. Surrey Beatty and Sons, New South Wales, Australia.

Finlayson, M. & Moser, M. (1991). Wetlands. Facts on File, Oxford, UK and New York.

Finlayson, M., Hollis, T. & Davis, T. (eds.). (1992). Managing Mediterranean wetlands and their birds. Proceedings of Symposium, Grado, Italy, 1991. IWRB Spec. Publ. No. 20, Slimbridge, UK.

Fischbacher, M. (1984). Standortwahl des Graureihers *Ardea cinerea* an kleineren Fliessgewässern. *Der Ornithologische Beobachter* **81**: 133–147.

Fitzner, R.E., Blus, L.J., Henny, C.J. & Carlile, D.W. (1988). Organochlorine residues in Great Blue Herons from the northwestern United States. *Colonial Waterbirds* **11**: 293–300.

Fitzner, R.E., Gray, R.H. & Hinds, W.J. (1995). Heavy metal concentrations in Great Blue Heron castings in Washington State: A technique for monitoring regional and global trends in environmental contamination. *Bulletin of Environmental Contamination and Toxicology* **55**: 398–403.

Fjeldsa, J. & Krabbe, N. (1990). Birds of the High Andes. Zoological Museum of the University of Copenhagen and Apollo Books, Svendborg, Denmark.

Fleming, W.J., Pullin, B.P. & Swineford, D.M. (1984). Population trends and environmental contaminants in herons in the Tennessee Valley, 1980–81. *Colonial Waterbirds* **7**: 63–73.

Fleury, B.E. (1993). Population trends in Louisiana Herons, Egrets and Ibises from 1949 to 1989, in (J.V. Huner, ed.) Management of fish eating birds on fish farms: a symposium. University of Southwestern Louisiana, College Applied Life Sciences, Lafayette, Louisiana, USA.

Fleury, B.E. (1996). Population trends of colonial wading birds in the southern United States: the response of Louisiana populations to crayfish aquaculture. PhD Dissertation, Tulane University, New Orleans.

Fleury, B.E. & Sherry, T.W. (1995). Long-term population trends of colonial wading birds in the southern United States: impact of crawfish aquaculture on Louisiana populations. *Auk* **112**: 613–632.

Flick, W.A. (1983). Observations on loons as predators on brook trout and as possible transmitters of infectious pancreatic necrosis (IPN). *North American Journal Fish Management* **3**: 95–96.

Flores, E. (1986). Bolivia. pp 39–59 in (D. A. Scott and M. Carbonell, compilers) A directory of neotropical wetlands. IUCN and IWRB, Slimbridge, UK.

Folsom, W.B. & Sanborn, E.A. (1992). World salmon culture 1991–92. *Aquaculture Magazine* **18(6)**: 55–65.

Ford, J. (1965). First occurrence of the Little Egret in south-western Australia. *Emu* **65**: 208.

Ford, J.R. (1969). First Australian record of the Chinese Little Bittern. *Emu* **69**: 233–235.

Forés, E. & Comín, F. (1992). Ricefields, a limnological perspective. *Limnetica* **8**: 101–109.

Fortbush, E.H. (1921). The utility of birds. *Massachusetts Department Agriculture Bulletin* **9**: 1–83.

Fossi, C., Fucardi, S., Leonzio, C. & Renzoni, A. (1984). Trace elements and chlorinated hydrocarbons in birds' eggs from the Delta of the Danube. *Environmental Conservation* **11**: 345–350.

Fox, G.A. (1976). Eggshell quality: its ecological and physiological significance in a DDE-contaminated Common Tern population. *Wilson Bulletin* **88**: 459–477.

Fox, G.A. & Weseloh, D.V. (1987). Colonial waterbirds as bio-indicators of environmental contamination in the Great Lakes. pp 209–216 in (A.W. Diamond and F.L. Filion, eds.) The value of birds. International Council for Bird Preservation Technical Publication No. **6**: 209–216.

Franchimont, J. (1986). Causes de mortalité aux stades des oeufs et des poussins chez les Ardéidés. *Aves* **23**: 34–44.

Franson, J.C. & Custer, T.W. (1994). Prevalence of eustrongyloidosis in wading birds from colonies in California, Texas, and Rhode Island. *Colonial Waterbirds* **17**: 168–172.

Frazier, S. (1996). An overview of the world's Ramsar sites. Wetlands International Publication 39, Oxford, UK.

Frazier, S. (compiler). (1996). Directory of wetlands of international importance; an update. Ramsar Convention Bureau, Gland, Switzerland.

Frederick, P.C. (1997). Tricolored Heron (*Egretta tricolor*). In (A. Poole and F. Gill, eds.) *The birds of North America*, No. 306. Academy of Natural Science, Philadelphia and American Ornithologists' Union, Washington, DC.

Frederick, P.C. & Collopy, M.W. (1988). Reproductive ecology of wading birds in relation to water conditions in the Florida Everglades. Florida Cooperative Fish and Wildlife Research Unit, School of Forest Research and Conservation, University of Florida Tech. Rept. No. 30.

Frederick, P.C. & Collopy, M.W. (1989a). Nesting success of five ciconiiform species in relation to water conditions in the Florida Everglades. *Auk* **106**: 625–634.

Frederick, P.C. & Collopy, M.W. (1989b). The role of predation in determining reproductive success of colonially-nesting wading birds (Ciconiiformes) in the Florida Everglades. *Condor* **91**: 860–867.

Frederick, P.C. & Collopy, M.W. (1989c). Research disturbance in colonies of wading birds: effects of frequency of visits and egg-marking on reproductive parameters. *Colonial Waterbirds* **12**: 152–157.

Frederick, P.C. & McGehee, S.M. (1994). Wading bird use of wastewater treatment wetlands in central Florida, USA. *Colonial Waterbirds* **17**: 50–59.

Frederick, P.C., Bildstein, K.L., Fleury, B. & Ogden, J.C. (1996). Conservation of large, nomadic populations of White Ibises (*Eudocimus albus*) in the United States. *Conservation Biology* **10**: 203–216.

Frederick, P.C., Bjork, R., Bancroft, G.T. & Powell, G.V.N. (1992). Reproductive success of three species of herons relative to habitat in southern Florida. *Colonial Waterbirds* **15**: 192–201.

Frederick, P.C., Towles, T., Sawicki, B.J. & Bancroft, G.T. (1996). Comparison of aerial and ground techniques for discovery and census of wading bird (Ciconiiformes) nesting colonies. *Condor* **98**: 837–841.

Frederiksen, M. (1992). Ynglebestanden af Fiskehejre *Ardea cinerea* i Danmark 1991. *Dansk Ornithologisk Tidsskrift* **86**: 129–136.

Friend, M. (1985). Interpretation of criteria commonly used to determine lead poisoning problem areas. United States Fish and Wildlife Service, Fish and Wildlife Leaflet 2.

Frohring, P.C., Voorhees, D.P. & Kushlan, J.A. (1988). History of wading bird populations in the Florida Everglades: A lesson in the use of historical information. *Colonial Waterbirds* **11**: 328–335.

From, J. (1989). Review of replies of questionnaire on predation in trout culture. pp 7–22 in (C.M. Bungenberg de Jong, J. From, L. Marion, and K. Molnar, eds.) Report of the EIFAC working party on prevention and control of bird predation in aquaculture and fisheries operations. EIFAC Technical Paper 51, Rome, Italy.

Fry, C.H., Hosken, J.H. & Skinner, D. (1986). Further observations on the breeding of Slaty Egrets *Egretta vinaceigula* and Rufous-bellied Herons *Ardeola rufiventris*. *Ostrich* **57**: 61–64.

Fujioka, M. (1985). Sibling competition and siblicide in asynchronously-hatched broods of the Cattle Egret *Bubulcus ibis*. *Animal Behaviour* **33**: 1228–1242.

Fullagar, P. & Davey, C. (1983). Herons, egrets, ibises and spoonbills: Order Ciconiiformes. pp 39–41 in (C. Haigh, ed.) Parks and Wildlife: Wetlands. National Parks and Wildlife Service Sydney, Australia.

Gabriëls, J. (1985). Atlas van de broedvogels in Limburg. BNVR, Brussels, Belgium.

Galet, L. (1931). Notes sur la nidification en Camargue de l'Aigrette garzette, du Bihoreau et du Crabier, *Egretta g. garzetta* (L.), *Nycticorax n. nycticorax* (L.) et *Ardeola r. ralloides* (Scop.). *L'Oiseau* **1**: 54–57.

Garnett, S. (1992). Threatened and extinct birds of Australia. RAOU Report 82. Birds Australia, Melbourne, Australia.

Garnett, S.T. & Bredl, R. (1985). Birds in the vicinity of Edward River Settlement Part 1. Sunbird **15**: 6–23, 25–40.

Gast, S.E. & King, B. (1985). Notes on Philippine birds, 7. Recent records of the Chinese Egret *Egretta eulophotes* from Luzon, Mindoro and Palawan, Philippines. *Bulletin of the British Ornithological Club* **105(4)**: 139–141.

Gauthreaux, S.A. Jr. (1982). The ecology and evolution of avian migration systems. *Avian Biology* **6**: 93–168.

Gee, G.N., Moffat, L.I. & Wilder, G.D. (1948). A tentative list of Chinese birds. Western Art Gallery, Shanghai, China.

Geering, D.J. (1993). The effect of drought-breaking rain on the re-establishment of egret colonies in north coastal New South Wales. *Corella* **17**: 47–51.

Geering, D.J., Maddock, M., Cam, G., Ireland, C., Halse, S.A. & Pearson, G.B. (1998). Movement patterns of Great, Intermediate and Little egrets from Australian breeding colonies. *Corella* **22**: 37–46.

Geiger, C. (1983). Recherches sur les difficultés liées au héron cendré. Les cahiers de la pêche 41. Office Fédéral de la protection de l'environnement, Berne, Switzerland.

Geiger, C. (1984a). Bestand und Verbreitung des Graureihers *Ardea cinerea*, in der Schweiz. *Der Ornithologische Beobachter* **81**: 85–97.

Geiger, C. (1984b). Graureiher *Ardea cinerea* und Fischbestand in Fliessgewässern. *Der Ornithologische Beobachter* **81**: 111–131.

Geldenhuys, J.N. (1984). Status of the Fish Eagle and Goliath Heron in the Orange Free State, South Africa. *Proceedings of the Fifth Pan African Ornithological Congress* **5**: 577–587.

Génard, M., Massé, J., Rigaud, C., Barreau, J.J., Coutant, P., Febvre, S. & Mais, G. (1988). Approche expérimentale de l'impact des oiseaux piscivores en pisciculture extensive littorale. Rapport Gerea-Cemagref-Sretie, Bordeaux, France.

Géroudet, P. (1978). Grands Echassiers, Gallinacés et Râles d'Europe. Delachaux et Niestlé, Neuchâtel, Switzerland.

Gibbs, J.P. (1991). Spatial relationships between nesting colonies and foraging areas of Great Blue Herons. *Auk* **108**: 764–779.

Gibbs, J.P. & Kinkel, L. (1997). Determinants of the size and location of Great Blue Heron colonies. *Colonial Waterbirds* **20**: 1–7.

Gibbs, J.P., Reid, F.A. and Melvin, S. (1992a). Least Bittern. In (A. Poole, P. Stettenheim and F. Gill, eds.) The birds of North America, No. 17. Academy of Natural Science, Philadelphia and American Ornithologists' Union, Washington, DC.

Gibbs, J.P., Melvin, S. & Reid, F.A. (1992b). American Bittern. In (A. Poole, P. Stettenheim and F. Gill, eds.) The birds of North America, No. 18. Academy of Natural Science, Philadelphia and American Ornithologists' Union, Washington, DC.

Gibbs, J.R., Woodward, S., Hunter, M.L. & Hutchinson, A.E. (1987). Determinants of Great Blue Heron colony distribution in coastal Maine. *Auk* **104**: 38–47.

Gibson, A. (1981). Great-billed Heron at Yamba. *Australian Birds* **16**: 32–33.

Gibson-Hill, C.A. (1949). The birds of the Cocos–Keeling Islands (Indian Ocean). *Ibis* **91**: 221–243.

Giesen, W. (1997). Wetlands, biodiversity, and development. Wetlands International, Kuala Lumpur, Malaysia.

Gilbertson, M., Morris, R.D. & Hunter, R.A. (1976). Abnormal chicks and PCB residue levels in eggs of colonial birds of the lower Great Lakes (1971–73). *Auk* **93**: 434–442.

Gilbertson, M., Kubiak, T., Ludwig, J. & Fox, G. (1991). Great lakes embryo mortality, edema, and deformities syndrome, (GLEMEDS) in colonial fish-eating birds: similarity to chick-edema disease. *Journal of Toxicology and Environmental Health* **33**: 455–520.

Giles, J. (1983). Foreword. pp 3–4 in (C. Haigh, ed.) Parks and Wildlife: Wetlands. National Parks and Wildlife Service, Sydney, Australia.

Gill, R., Jr. & Mewaldt, L.R. (1979). Dispersal and migratory patterns of San Francisco Bay produced by herons, egrets, and terns. *North American Bird Bander* **4**: 4–13.

Gilligan, B. (1984). A wetland habitat assessment scheme. *Wetlands Australia* **4**: 49–51.

Gilligan, B.G. (1979). Seaham Swamp Nature Reserve: Water usage and wetland management. Unpubl. Thesis, University of Newcastle, New South Wales, Australia.

Gjiknuri, L. & Peja, N. (1992). Albanian lagoons: their importance and economic development. pp 130–133 in (C.M. Finlayson, G.E. Hollis and T.J. Davis, eds.). Managing Mediterranean wetlands and their birds. IWRB Special Publication 20, Slimbridge, UK.

Goddard, M.T. (1955). Notes on the breeding of the Cattle Egret in north-eastern New South Wales. *Emu* **55**: 275–277.

Godfrey, W.E. (1986). The birds of Canada. National Museum, Ottawa, Canada.

Goering, D.K. & Cherry, R. (1971). Nestling mortality in a Texas heronry. *Wilson Bulletin* **83**: 303–305.

Gonzalez-Martin, M., Ruiz, X. & Llorente, G.A. (1992). Breeding parameters, feeding habits and nestling growth in a recovering population of Purple Herons from the Ebro delta, Spain. *Miscellania Zoologica* (Journal of the Zoology Museum, Barcelona) **16**: 147–160.

Gonzalez-Martin, M. (1994). Reproducion de la garza imperia (*Ardea purpurea*) en el delta del Ebro, Ph.D. Dissertation. University of Barcelona, Spain.

González-Solis, J., Bernadi, X. & Ruiz, X. (1996). Seasonal variation of waterbird prey in the Ebro Delta Rice Fields. *Colonial Waterbirds* **19** (Special Publication): 135–142.

Goodman, S.M. & Meininger, P.L. (eds.). (1989). The birds of Egypt. Oxford University Press, Oxford, UK and New York.

Goodrick, G.N. (1970). A survey of wetlands of coastal NSW. Technical Memorandum No. 5, CSIRO Division of Wildlife Research, Canberra, Australia.

Gore, M.E.J. (1968). A checklist of the birds of Sabah, Borneo. *Ibis* **110**: 165–196.

Gore, M.E.J. & Won, P-O. (1971). The birds of Korea. Royal Asiatic Society, Seoul, Korea.

Gosper, D.G. (1981). Birds of the Hunter and Richmond Rivers, New South Wales. *Corella* **5**: 1–18.

Gosselink, J.G. & Maltby, E. (1990). Wetland losses and gains. In (M. Williams, ed.). Wetlands: A threatened landscape. Blackwell, Oxford, UK.

Gould, J. (1865). Handbook of birds of Australia. Methuen & Co. Ltd, London, UK.

Goutner, V., Jerrentrup, H., Kazantzidis, S. & Nazirides, T. (1991). Occurrence of the Cattle Egret, *Bubulcus ibis*, in Greece. *Rivista Italiana di Ornithologia*, Milano **61**: 107–112.

Government of Canada, (1991). The federal policy on wetland conservation. Canadian Wildlife Service, Ottawa, Canada.

Gowthorpe, P., Lamarche, B., Binaux, R., Gucye, A., Lehlou, S.M., Sall, M.A. and Sakho, A.C. (1996). Les oiseaux nicheurs et les principaux limicoles paléarctiques du Parc National du Banc d'Arguin (Mauritanie). *Alauda* **64**: 81–126.

Gray, J.S. (1980). Why do ecological monitoring? *Marine Pollution Bulletin* **11**: 62–65.

Green, R. (1992). The ornithological importance of the Danube Delta and lakes Razim-Sinoe. pp 61–70, in IUCN Environmental Status Report Vol. 4. Conservation Status of the Danube Delta. Page Brothers. Norwich, UK.

Green R.H. (1977). Birds of Tasmania. Publ. by Author, Launceston, Australia.

Gregory, S.N. (1990). The foraging ecology and feeding behaviour of the Grey heron (*Ardea cinerea*) in the Camargue, S. France. Unpublished Ph.D. thesis, University of Durham, UK.

Grimmet, R.F.A. & Jones, T.A. (1989). Important Bird Areas in Europe. International Council for Bird Preservation Technical Publication 9, Cambridge, UK.

Groombridge, B. (ed.). (1993). 1994 IUCN red list of threatened animals. IUCN, Gland, Switzerland.

Grue, C.E., Fleming, W.J., Busby, D.G. & Hill, E.F. (1983). Assessing hazards of organophosphate pesticides to wildlife. *Transactions of the North American Wildlife and Natural Resources Conference, 1983*. **48**: 200–220.

Grüll, A. (1988). Zur Bedeutung des Südlichen Neusiedlerseebeckens für den Vogelschutz. Biologische Station, Neusiedlersee.

Grummt, W. (1964). Some notes on the breeding of the African Cattle Egret. *Avicultural Magazine* **70**: 222–223.

Grussu, M. (1994). Popolazioni di Ardeidae e Treskiornithidae coloniali in Sardegna. *Gli Uccelli d'Italia* **19**: 3–24.

Grussu, M. (1997). Evoluzione della populazione nidificante di Airone guardabuoi *Bubulcus ibis* in Sardegna: 1993–1996. *Avocetta* **21**: 32.

Gulland, J.A. (1971). Ecological aspects of fishery research. *Advances in Ecological Research* **7**: 115–176.

Gurusami, V. (1988). Simpson Estate, Sembian, Madras-11. Unpublished ms., 2 pp.

Gympie Times (1987). Council to ask questions about Kybong egret habitat. August 11, p. 2.

Hachisuka, M. (1926). A review of the genus *Gorsachius*. *Ibis* **12**: 585–592.

Hachisuka, M. & Udagawa, T. (1951). Contributions to the ornithology of Formosa, part 2. *Quarterly Journal of the Taiwan Museum* **4(1–2)**: 1–180.

Hafner, H. (1970a). A propos d'une population de Hérons Garde-boeufs en Camargue. *Alauda* **38**: 249–254.

Hafner, H. (1970b). La reproduction des Ardéidés en Camargue en 1968 et 1969. *Terre et Vie* **24**: 570–579.

Hafner, H. (1975). Compte rendu ornithologique camarguais pour les années 1972 et 1973. *Terre et Vie* **29**: 100–112.

Hafner H. (1977). Contribution à l'étude écologique de quatre espèces de hérons (*Egretta g. garzetta* L., *Ardeola r. ralloides* Scop., *Ardeola i. ibis* L., *Nycticorax n. nycticorax* L.). Unpublished thesis, Université Paul Sabatier de Toulouse, France.

Hafner, H. (1978). Le succès de reproduction de quatre espèces d'Ardéidés (*Egretta g. garzetta* L., *Ardeola r. ralloides* Scop., *Ardeola i. ibis* L., *Nycticorax n. nycticorax* L.) en Camargue. *Terre et Vie* **32**: 279–289.

Hafner, H. (1982). Creation of a breeding site for tree-nesting herons in the Camargue, France. pp 216–220 in (D. Scott, ed.) Manual of active wetland and waterfowl management. IWRB, Slimbridge, UK.

Hafner, H. (1997a). Ecology of wading birds. *Colonial Waterbirds* **20**: 115–120.

Hafner, H. (1997b). Squacco Heron. pp 39, in (E.J.M. Hagemeijer and M.J. Blair, eds.) The European bird common census atlas of European breeding birds. Their distribution and abundance. Poyser, London, UK.

Hafner, H. & Britton, R. (1983). Changes of foraging sites by nesting Little Egrets *Egretta garzetta* L. in relation to food supply. *Colonial Waterbirds* **6**: 24–30.

Hafner, H. & Didner, E. (1997). Species account on the Squacco Heron *Ardeola ralloides* for *BWP Update*. A quarterly journal updating Birds of Western Palearctic. Vol **1**(3): 166–174.

Hafner, H. & Fasola, M. (1992). The relationship between feeding habitat and colonially nesting Ardeidae. pp 194–201, in (C.M. Finlayson, G.E. Hollis and T.J. Davis, eds.). Managing Mediterranean wetlands and their birds. IWRB Special Publication 20, Slimbridge, UK.

Hafner, H. & Fasola, M. (1997). Long term monitoring and conservation of herons in France and Italy. *Colonial Waterbirds*: 298–305.

Hafner, H. & Moser, M. (1980). Les hérons et la pisciculture en Camargue. Numéro Spécial du *Bulletin mensuel de l'Office National de la Chasse*: 255–260.

Hafner, H., Boy, V. & Gory, G. (1982). Feeding methods, flock size and feeding success in the Little Egret *Egretta garzetta* and the Squacco heron *Ardeola ralloides* in the Camargue, southern France. *Ardea* **70**: 45–54.

Hafner, H., Dugan, P.J. & Boy, V. (1986). Use of artificial and natural wetlands as feeding sites by Little Egrets *Egretta garzetta* L. in the Camargue, Southern France. *Colonial Waterbirds* **9**: 149–154.

Hafner, H., Dugan, P.J. & Boy, V. (1987). Herons and wetlands in the Mediterranean: development of indices for quality assessment and management of Mediterranean wetland ecosystems. Final report to the Third Environment Research Program of the Commission of the European Communities.

Hafner, H., Dugan, P. & Kushlan, J.A. (1986). The ICBP/IWRB Herons Specialist Group: Origin, Present and Future. *Colonial Waterbirds* **9**: 126–127.

Hafner, H., Pineau, O. & Kayser, Y. (1992). The effects of winter climate on the size of the Cattle Egret (*Bubulcus ibis* L.) population in the Camargue. *Revue d'Ecologie (Terre Vie)* **47**: 403–410.

Hafner, H., Pineau, O. & Kayser, Y. (1994). Ecological determinants of annual fluctuations in numbers of breeding Little Egrets *Egretta garzetta* in the Camargue, S. France. *Revue d'Ecologie (Terre Vie)* **49**: 53–62.

Hafner, H., Pineau, O., Kayser, Y. & Bennetts, R. (1999). A re-analysis of the influence of reproduction on the following year's breeding population of Little Egrets in the Camargue, S. France. *Revue d' Ecologie (Terre Vie)*, **54**: 187–188.

Hafner, H., Dugan, P.J., Kersten, M., Pineau, O. & Wallace, J.P. (1993). Flock feeding and food intake in Little Egrets *Egretta garzetta* and their effects on food provisioning and reproductive success. *Ibis* **135**: 25–32.

Hafner, H., Kayser, Y., Boy, V., Fasola, M., Julliard, A-C., Pradel, R. & Cezilly, F. (1998). Local survival, natal dispersal, and recruitment in Little Egrets *Egretta garzetta*. *Journal of Avian Biology* **29**: 216–227.

Hafner, H., Pineau, O., Kayser, Y., Gueye, A., Sall, M.A. & Lamarche, B. (1998). Monitoring of colonial waterbird colonies in the Banc d'Arguin, Islamic Republic of Mauritania. Poster Abstract. 2nd International Conference on Wetlands and Development. Dakar, Senegal.

Hagemeijer, E.J.M. & Blair, M.J. (eds). (1997). The EBCC atlas of European breeding birds: Their distribution and abundance. T.& A.D. Poyser, London, UK.

Hallam, T.G., Trawick, T.L. & Wolff, W.F. (1996). Modeling effects of chemicals on a population: Application to a wading bird nesting colony. *Ecological Modelling* **92**: 155–178.

Halse, S.A., Pearson, G.B., Jaensch, R.P., Kulmoi, P., Gregory, P., Kay, W.R. & Storey, A.W. (1996). Waterbird surveys of the Middle Fly Floodplain, Papua New Guinea. *Wildlife Research* **23**: 557–569.

Hammer, D.A. (1989). Constructed wetlands for wastewater treatment: municipal, industrial, and agricultural. Lewis Publishers, Chelsea, Michigan, USA.

Hancock, J. & Kushlan, J. (1984). The Herons Handbook. Croom Helm, London and Harper & Row, New York.

Hands, H.M., Drobney, R.D. & Ryan, M.R. (1989). Status of the American Bittern in the northcentral United States. US Fish Wildlife Service, Twin Cities, Minnesota.

Hanebrink, E. & Byrd, W. (1989). Predatory birds in relation to aquaculture farming. *Aquaculture Magazine* **15**: 47–51.

Harper, M.J. (1990). Waterbird dynamics at Bool Lagoon, South Australia. *Australian Wildlife Research* **17**: 113–22.

Harrison, C. (1982). An atlas of the birds of the Western Palaearctic. Collins, London.

Hart, L.E., Cheng, K.M., Whitehead, P.E. et al. (1991). Dioxin contamination and growth and development in Great Blue Heron embryos. *Journal of Toxicology and Environmental Health* **32**: 331–344.

Harvey, W.G. (1990). Birds in Bangladesh. University Press Ltd, Dhaka.

Haverschmidt, F. & Mees, G.F. (1994). Birds of Suriname. Vaco, N.V., Uitgeversmaatschappij, Paramaribo, Suriname.

Hayes, F.E. (1996). Seasonal and geographical variation in resident waterbird populations along the Paraguay River. *El Hornero* **14**: 14–26.

Hazavoet, C.J. (1992). A review of the Santiago Purple Heron *Ardea purpurea bournei*, with a report of a new colony. *Bird Conservation International* **2**: 15–23.

Heather, B.D. (1978). The Cattle Egret in New Zealand in 1977. *Notornis* **25**: 215–234.

Heather, B.D. (1982). The Cattle Egret in New Zealand 1978–80. *Notornis* **29**: 241–268.

Heather, B.D. (1986). Cattle Egret numbers in New Zealand in 1984. *Notornis* **33**: 185–189.

Heinz, G.H. (1979). Methylmercury: reproductive and behavioral effects on three generations of Mallard ducks. *Journal of Wildlife Management* **43**: 394–401.

Heinz, G.H., Erdman, T.C., Haseltine, S.D. & Stafford, C. (1985). Contaminant levels in colonial waterbirds from Green Bay and Lake Michigan, 1975–80. *Environmental Monitoring and Assessment* **5**: 223–236.

Henny, C.J. (1972). An analysis of the population dynamics of selected avian species with special reference to changes during the modern pesticide era. United States Department of the Interior, Wildlife Research Report 1. Washington, DC.

Henny, C.J. & Blus, L.J. (1986). Radiotelemetry locates wintering grounds of DDE-contaminated Black-crowned Night-Herons. *Wildlife Society Bulletin* **14**: 236–241.

Henny, C. J., Blus, L.J. & Hulse, C.S. (1985). Trends and effects of organochlorine residues in Oregon and Nevada wading birds, 1979–83. *Colonial Waterbirds* **8**: 117–128.

Henny, C. J., Blus, L.J., Krynitsky, A.J. & Bunck, C.M. (1984). Current impact of DDE on Black-crowned Night-Herons in the intermountain west. *Journal of Wildlife Management* **48**: 1–13.

Henshel, D.S., Cheng, K.M., Norstrom, R., Whitehead, P. & Steeves, J.D. (1992). Morphometric and histological changes in brains of Great Blue Heron hatchlings exposed to PCDDs: preliminary analysis. pp 262–277, in (W.G. Landis, J.S. Hughes, and M.A. Lewis, eds.) Environmental toxicology and risk assessment. American Society for Testing and Materials, Philadelphia, PA.

Hepher, B. (1967). Some biological aspects of warm water fish-pond management. In (Gerking, ed.). The biological basis of freshwater fish production. Blackwell, Oxford, UK.

Hepher, B. & Pruginin, Y. (1981). Commercial fish farming with special reference to fish culture in Israel. John Wiley and Sons, New York.

Hermes, N., Evans, O. & Evans, B. 1986. Norfolk Islands birds: A review 1985. *Notornis* **33**: 141–149.

Hernandez, L.M., Rico, M.C., Gonzalez, M.J., Montero, M.C. & Fernandez, M.A. (1987). Residues of organochlorine chemicals and concentrations of heavy metals in Ciconiiformes eggs in relation to diet and habitat. *Journal of Environmental Science and Health* **22**: 245–258.

Hertzman T. & Larsson, T. (1991). Lake Hornborga—A case study. pp 154–160, in (C.M. Finlayson and T. Larsson, eds.) Wetland management and restoration. Proceedings of Workshop, Sweden 1990. Swedish Environmental Protection Agency Report 3992. Solna, Sweden.

Hewitt, E. R. (1936). Fish-eating birds have no place in trout waters. *Progressive Fish-Culturist* **16**: 11–12.

Hewitt, J.M. (1960). The Cattle Egret in Australia. *Emu* **60**: 99–102.

Hewitt, J.M. (1961). The Cattle Egret near Sydney. *Emu* **61**: 137.

Hickey, J.J. & Anderson, D.W. (1968). Chlorinated hydrocarbons and eggshell changes in raptorial and fish-eating birds. *Science* **162**: 271–273.

Hill, E.F. & Hoffman, D.J. (1984). Avian models for toxicity testing. *Journal of the American College of Toxicology* **3**: 357–376.

Hilty, S.L. (1992). Birding the Venezuelan Llanos. *American Birds* **46**: 360–369.

Hilty, S.L. & Brown, W.L. (1986). A guide to the birds of Colombia. Princeton University Press, Princeton, USA.

Hindwood, K.A. (1993). The Green-backed Heron. *Emu* **33**: 27–43.

Hines, C.G.H. (1992). Observations on the Slaty Egret *Egretta vinaceigula* in northern Namibia. *Ostrich* **63**: 118–122.

Hinrichsen, D. (1994). Coasts under pressure. *People and the Planet* **3**: 6–9.

Hobbs J.M. (1961). Birds of south-west New South Wales. *Emu* **61**: 21–55.

Hoffman, D.J. (1990). Embryotoxicity and teratogenicity of environmental contaminants to bird eggs. *Reviews of Environmental Contamination and Toxicology* **115**: 39–89.

Hoffman, D.J., Smith, G.J. & Rattner, B.A. (1993). Biomarkers of contaminant exposure in Common Terns and Black-crowned Night-Herons in the Great Lakes. *Environmental Toxicology and Chemistry* **12**: 1095–1103.

Hoffman, D.J., Rattner, B.A., Bunck, C.M., Krynitsky, A., Ohlendorf, H.M. & Lowe, R.W. (1986). Association between PCBs and lower embryonic weight in Black-crowned Night Herons in San Francisco Bay. *Journal of Toxicology and Environmental Health* **19**: 383–391.

Hoffmann, L. (1958). An ecological sketch of the Camargue. *British Birds* **51**: 321–349.

Hoffmann, L., Hafner, H. and Salathé, T. (1996). The contribution of colonial waterbird research to wetland conservation in the Mediterranean region. *Colonial Waterbirds* **19** (special publication 1): 12–30.

Hoffman, R.D. & Curnow, R.D. (1979). Mercury in herons, egrets, and their foods. *Journal of Wildlife Management* **43**: 85–93.

Hofstetter, J., Chmetz, I., Baumann, R. & de Crousaz, G. (1949). Une colonie romande de Hérons pourprés sur des arbres. *Nos Oiseaux* **20**: 81–85.

Hollis, G.E. (1986). The Modelling and Management of the Internationally Important Wetland at Garaet El Ichkeul, Tunisia. IWRB Special Publication No. 4, Slimbridge, UK.

Hollis, G.E. (1992). The causes of wetland loss and degradation in the Mediterranean. pp 83–90, in (C.M. Finlayson, G. E. Hollis and T. J. Davis, eds.) Managing Mediterranean wetlands and their birds. IWRB Special Publication 20, Slimbridge, UK.

Hollis, G.E. & Jones, T.A. (1991). Europe and the Mediterranean Basin. pp 27–56, in (M. Finlayson and M. Moser, eds.) Wetlands. Facts on File, Oxford.

Hollis, G.E., Heurteaux, P. & Mercer, F. (1989). The implications of groundwater extraction for the long-term future of the Doñana National Park, Spain. Report to Worldwide Fund for Nature. Department of Geography, University College London.

Holst, O. & Persson, O. (1988). Hägerns *Ardea cinerea* häckningsförekomst i Skäne 1986. *Anser* **27**: 263–266.

Holstein, C. (1927). Fiskehejren. Gad's Forlag, Kobenhavn.

Hölzinger, J. (1987). Rohrdommel—*Botaurus stellaris*. pp 787–790, in (J. Hölzinger, ed.) Vögel Baden-Würtembergs, Karlsruhe.

Honda, K., Min, B.Y. & Tatsukawa, R. (1985). Heavy metal distribution in organs and tissues of the Eastern Great White Egret *Egretta alba modesta*. *Bulletin of Environmental Contamination and Toxicology* **35**: 781–789.

Honda, K., Min, B.Y. & Tatsukawa, R. (1986). Distribution of heavy metals and their age-related changes in the Eastern Great White Egret, *Egretta alba modesta,* in Korea. *Archives of Environmental Contamination and Toxicology* **15**: 185–197.

Hontelez, L.C.M.P., van den Dungen, H.M. & Baars, A.J. (1992). Lead and cadmium in birds in the Netherlands: a preliminary survey. *Archives of Environmental Contamination and Toxicology* **23**: 453–456.

Hothem, R.L., Roster, D.L., King, K.A., Keldsen, T.J., Marois, K.C. & Wainwright, S.E. (1995). Spatial and temporal trends of contaminants in eggs of wading birds from San Francisco Bay, California. *Environmental Toxicology and Chemistry* **8**: 1319–1331.

Houwen, P. (1968). Eigers en Aalsholvers op de Blankaart. *De Belgische Natuur. en Vogelreservaten Bulletin 1968*: 98–102.

Howes, J.R. (1987). Rapid assessment of coastal wetlands in the Philippines. AWB, Kuala Lumpur, Malaysia.

Howes, J.R. and NPWO. (1987). Evaluation of Sarawak wetlands and their importance for waterbirds. Report **3**: Pulau Bruit. Interwader Publication No. 10, Kuala Lumpur, Malaysia.

Hoy, M. D., Jones, J.W. & Bivings, A.E. (1989). Economic impact and control of wading birds at Arkansas minnow ponds. *Proceedings Eastern Wildlife Damage Control Conference* **4**: 105–108.

Hubbard, J.P. (1976). Status of the night heron (*Nycticorax*) of the Philippines and vicinity. *Nemouria* **19**: 1–10.

Hubbell, G. (1962). Breeding the capped heron *Pilherodius pileatus*. *International Zoo Yearbook* **4**: 94.

Huggett, R.J., Klmerle, R.A., Mehrle, P.M. Jr. & Bergmann, H.L. (eds). (1992). Biomarkers: Biochemical, Physiological, and Histological Markers of Anthropogenic Stress. SETAC Special Publication Series. Lewis Publishers, Chelsea, Michigan.

Hulse, M., Mahoney, J.S., Schroder, G.D., Hacker, C.S. & Pier, S.M. (1980). Environmentally acquired lead, cadmium, and manganese in the Cattle Egret, *Bubulcus ibis*, and the Laughing Gull, *Larus atricilla*. *Archives of Environmental Contamination and Toxicology* **9**: 65–78.

Hume, A.O. & Davison, W. (1878). A revised list of the birds of Tenasserim. *Stray Feathers* **6**.

Huner, J.V. (1990). Wading bird and crawfish, a new problem? *Crawfish Tales*, Louisiana Crawfish Farmer's Association. First quarter 1990.

Huner, J.V. (1993a). Management of fish eating birds on fish farms: a symposium. University of Southwestern Louisiana, College Applied Life Sciences, Lafayette, Louisiana.

Huner, J.V. (1993b). The crawfish pond: Louisiana's autumn oasis for waterfowl. *The Aquaculture News*, Dec. 1993: 7.

Huner, J.V. (1995). How crawfish impoundments sustain wetland vertebrates in the South. National Agricultural Ecosystem Management Conference, New Orleans: 32–40.

Husain, M.M. & Kaphalia, B.S. (1990). Bioconcentration of cadmium, manganese and lead in some common species of wild birds from Lucknow City. *Journal of Environmental Biology* **11**: 193–201.

Hustings, F. & van Dijk, K. (eds.). (1994). Bird census in the Kizilirmak delta, Turkey, in spring 1992. WIWO-report 45, Zeist.

ICLARM (1995). Background to press release: From hunting to farming fish. Report of the Consultative Group on International Agricultural Research, International Center for Living Aquatic Resources Management, Washington DC.

Ikeda, S. (1952). Investigations on the relation of wild birds to the industry in Japan. *Inst. Wildl. Service of Japan, Ornithology and Mammalogy Report* **13**: 1–114.

Im, B.H. & Hafner, H. (1984). Impact des oiseaux piscivores et plus particulièrement du Grand Cormoran (*Phalacrocorax carbo sinensis*) sur les exploitations piscicoles en Camargue. Rapport final (contrat No. ENV-491-F (Ss)) à la Communautée Economique Européenne: 84 pp.

Inoue, Y. (1985). The process of asynchronous hatching and sibling competition in the Little Egret *Egretta garzetta*. *Colonial Waterbirds* **8**: 1–12.

Inskipp, C. (1989). Nepal's forest birds: Their status and conservation. International Council for Bird Preservation Monograph 4, Cambridge, UK.

Inskipp, C. & Inskipp, T. (1991). A guide to the birds of Nepal, 2nd edn. Christopher Helm, London.

Inskipp, C. & Inskipp, T. (1993a). Birds recorded during a visit to Bhutan in Autumn 1991. *Forktail* **8**: 97–112.

Inskipp, C. & Inskipp, T. (1993b). Birds recorded during a visit to Bhutan in spring 1993. *Forktail* **9**: 121–142.

Irwin, M.P.S. (1981). The birds of Zimbabwe. Quest Publishing, Harare, Zimbabwe.

Ishizaki, C. & Urich, J. (1985). Mercury contamination of food: a Venezuelan case study. *Interciencia* **10**: 173–178.

IUCN. (1996). 1996 IUCN red list of threatened animals. IUCN, Gland, Switzerland and Cambridge, UK.

IUDZG/CBSG (IUCN/SSC). (1993). The world zoo conservation strategy; the role of the zoos and aquaria of the world in global conservation. Chicago Zoological Society, Brookfield, Illinois.

Jackson, W.R. & Olsen, M. (1988). A study of the Cattle Egret in the Horowhenua. *Notornis* **35**: 83–85.

Jaensch, R.J. & Vervest, R.M. (1989). Breeding Colonies of the Great Egret in Western Australia. RAOU Report 33, Melbourne, Australia.

Jaensch, R.P. (1988). Little Bitterns breeding in northern Australia. *Australian Bird Watcher* **12**: 217–221.

James, C., Nathai-Gyan, N. & Hislop, H. (1986). Trinidad and Tobago. pp 256–265, in (D.A. Scott and M. Carbonell, compilers) A directory of neotropical wetlands. IUCN and IWRB, Slimbridge, UK.

Janz, D.M. & Bellward, G.D. (1997). Effects of acute 2,3,7,8-tetrachlorodibenzo-p-dioxin exposure on plasma thyroid and sex steroid hormone concentrations and estrogen receptor levels in adult Great Blue Herons. *Environmental Toxicology and Chemistry* **16**: 985–989.

Jenni, D.A. (1969). A study of the ecology of four species of herons during the breeding season at Lake Alice, Alachua County, Florida. *Ecological Monographs* **39**: 243–270.

Jepson, P. (1987). Recent reports. *Oriental Bird Club Bull.* **6**: 36–40.

Jones, T. (compiler) (1993). Directory of wetlands of international importance. Ramsar Convention Bureau, Gland, Switzerland.

Joséfik, M. (1969–70). Studies on the Squacco Heron, *Ardeola ralloides*. *Acta Ornithologica Warzawa* **11**: 103–262; **12**: 57–102, 394–504.

Kale, H.W., II. (1978). Birds, in (P.C.H. Pritchard, ed.) Rare and endangered biota of Florida. University Presses of Florida, Gainesville, Florida.

Kasparek, M. (1985). Die Sultanssümpfe. Naturgeschichte eines Vogelparadieses in Anatolien. Heidelberg, Germany.

Katti, M., Singh, P., Manjrekar, N., Sharma, D. & Mukherjee, S. (1992). An ornithological survey in eastern Arunachal Pradesh. *Forktail* **7**: 75–89.

Kayser, Y. (1994). Premier cas d'hivernage du Héron crabier *Ardeola ralloides* en Camargue. *Faune de Provence* **15**: 80.

Kayser, Y., Hafner, H. & Massez, G. (1998). Dénombrement des mâles chanteurs de Butors étoilés *Botaurus stellaris* en Camargue en 1996. *Alauda* **66**: 97–102.

Kayser, Y., Pineau, O. & Hafner, H. (1992). Evolution des effectifs de quelques oiseaux peu communs hivernant en Camargue. *Faune de Provence* **13**: 25–26.

Kayser, Y., Pineau, O,. Hafner, H. & Walmsley, J. (1994a). La nidification de la Grande Aigrette *Egretta alba* en Camargue. *Ornithos* **2**: 81–82.

Kayser, Y., Walmsley, J., Pineau, O. & Hafner, H. (1994b). Evolution récente des effectifs de Hérons cendrés (*Ardea cinerea*) et de Hérons pourprés (*Ardea purpurea*) nicheurs sur le littoral français. *Nos Oiseaux* **42**: 341–355.

Keith, K. & Hines, M.P. (1958). New and rare species of birds at Macquarie Island during 1956 and 1957. *CSIRO Wildlife Research* **3**: 50–53.

Keller, C.E., Spendelow, J.A. & Greer, R.D. (1984). Atlas of wading bird and seabird nesting colonies in coastal Louisiana, Mississippi, and Alabama: 1983. US Fish and Wildlife Service FWS/OBS-84/13, Washington, DC.

Kenyon, M. (1993). Tabasco: hot stuff from the Bayou. *Gourmet* **53(10)**: 122–197.

Kersten, M., Britton, R.H., Dugan, P.J. & Hafner, H. (1991). Flock feeding and food intake in Little Egrets: the effects of prey distribution and behavior. *Journal of Animal Ecology* **60**: 241–252.

King, K.A., Flickinger, E.L. & Hildebrand, H.H. (1978). Shell thinning and pesticide residues in Texas aquatic bird eggs, 1970. *Pesticides Monitoring Journal* **12**: 16–21.

Kingsford, R.T. & Thomas, R.F. (1995). The Macquarie Marshes in arid Australia and its waterbirds: A 50 year history of decline. *Environmental Management* **19**: 867–878.

Kirkpatrick, J.B. & Tyler, P.A. (1988). Tasmanian wetlands and their conservation. pp 1–16, in (A.J. McComb and P.S. Lake, eds.) The conservation of Australian wetlands. Surrey Beatty and Sons, New South Wales, Australia.

Klug, S. & Boswall, J. (1970). Observations from a waterbird colony, Lake Tana, Ethiopia. *Bulletin of the British Ornithological Club* **190**: 97–105.

Knief, W., Ulenaers, P. & van Vessem, J. (1997). Grey Heron. pp 50–51, in (E.J.M. Hagemeijer and M.J. Blair, eds.) The European bird common census atlas of European breeding birds. Their distribution and abundance. Poyser, London.

Knights, P. (1991). New South Wales wetlands: current conservation issues, policies and programs. pp 14–16, in (R. Donohue and B. Phillips, eds.) Educating and managing for wetlands conservation. Proceedings of the Wetlands Conservation and Management Workshop. Australian National Parks and Wildlife Service, Canberra.

Koeman, J.H., Bothof, T., De Vries, R., Van Velzen-Blad, H. & Vos, J.G. (1972). The impact of persistent pollutants on piscivorous and molluscivorous birds. *TNO-niews*, **27**: 561–569.

Konermann, A.D., Wing, L.D. & Richard, J.J. (1978). Great Blue Heron nesting success in two Iowa reservoir ecosystems. pp 117–129, in (A. Sprunt IV, J.C. Ogden, and S. Winckler, eds.) Wading birds. National Audubon Society Research Report Number 7, New York.

Koontz, F. (1995). Wild animal acquisition ethics for zoo biologists. pp 127–145, in (B.G. Norton, M. Hutchins, E. F. Stevens and T. L. Maple, eds.) Ethics on the ark. Smithsonian Institution Press, Washington DC.

Koskimies, P. & Tyler, G. (1997). *Botaurus stellaris,* Bittern. pp 40–41, in (E.J.M. Hagemeijer and M.J. Blair, eds.) The European bird common census atlas of European breeding birds. Their distribution and abundance. Poyser, London.

Kramer, A. (1984). Zum Einfluss des Graureihers *Ardea cinerea* auf den Fischbestand von Forellenbächen. *Der Ornithologische Beobachter* **81**: 149–158.

Krämer, H. (1962). Das Vorkommen des Fischreihers (*Ardea cinerea*) in der BundesRepublik Deutschland. *Journal für Ornithologie* **103**: 401–417.

Krebs, J.R. (1974). Colonial nesting and social feeding as strategies for exploiting food resources in the Great Blue Heron (*Ardea herodias*). *Behaviour* **51**: 99–134.

Krebs, J.R. (1978). Colonial nesting in birds, with special reference to the Ciconiiformes. pp 299–314, in (A. Sprunt, J.C. Ogden and S. Winckler, eds.) Wading birds. National Audubon Society. Research Report No. 7. New York.

Krivenko, V.G. (1991). [Climatic variability and waterfowl populations]. Moscow [in Russian, available in library of Wetlands International, Wageningen, The Netherlands].

Krüger, C. (1946). Kolonier af Fiskehejre *Ardea c. cinerea* i Danmark. *Dansk ornithologisk Tidsskrift* **40**: 216–245.

Kubiak, T.J., Harris, H.J., Smith, L.M. et al. (1989). Microcontaminants and reproductive impairment of the Foster's Tern on Green Bay, Lake Michigan—1983. *Archives of Environmental Contamination and Toxicology* **18**: 706–727.

Kuhk, R. (1955). Beringungs-Ergebnisse beim Silberreiher. *Der Ornithologische Beobachter* **52(1)**: 2–5.

Kushlan, J.A. (1976). Wading bird predation in a seasonally fluctuating pond. *Auk* **93**: 464–476.

Kushlan, J.A. (1977). Significance of plumage color in the formation of feeding aggregations of ciconiiforms. *Ibis* **119**: 361–364.

Kushlan, J.A. (1978a). Feeding ecology of wading birds. pp 249–296, in (A. Sprunt, J.C. Ogden and S. Winckler, eds.) Wading birds. National Audubon Society. Research Report No. 7. New York.

Kushlan, J.A. (1978b). Nonrigorous foraging by robbing egrets. *Ecology* **59**: 649–653.

Kushlan, J.A. (1979a). Design and management of continental wildlife preserves: lessons from the Everglades. *Biological Conservation* **15**: 281–290.

Kushlan, J.A. (1979b). Effects of helicopter censuses on wading bird colonies. *Journal of Wildlife Management* **43**: 756–760.

Kushlan, J.A. (1981). Resource use strategies in wading birds. *Wilson Bulletin* **93**: 145–163.

Kushlan, J.A. (1986). Responses of wading birds to seasonally fluctuating water levels: strategies and their limits. *Colonial Waterbirds* **9**: 155–162.

Kushlan, J.A. (1989a). Avian use of fluctuating wetlands. pp 593–604, in (R.R. Sharitz and J.W. Gibbons, eds.) Freshwater wetlands and wildlife, DOE Symposium Series 61, Oak Ridge, Tennessee, USA.

Kushlan, J.A. (1989b). Wetlands and wildlife, the Everglades perspective. pp 773–796, in (R.R. Sharitz and J.W. Gibbons, eds.) Freshwater wetlands and wildlife, DOE Symposium Series 61, Oak Ridge, Tennessee, USA.

Kushlan, J.A. (1991). The Everglades. pp 121–142, in (R.J. Livingston, ed.) The rivers of Florida. Springer-Verlag, New York.

Kushlan, J.A. (1992). Population biology and conservation of colonial wading birds. *Colonial Waterbirds* **15**: 1–7.

Kushlan, J.A. (1993a). Freshwater wetlands. pp 74–127, in (M.S. Dennison and J.F. Berry) Wetlands: guide to science, technology, and law. Noyes Publications, Park Ridge, New Jersey.

Kushlan, J.A. (1993b). Colonial waterbirds as bioindicators of environmental change. *Colonial Waterbirds* **16**: 223–251.

Kushlan, J.A. (1995). Water regimes and principles for management of wetland systems. pp 27–35, in (J.A. Kusler, D.E. Willard, and H.C. Hull, Jr., eds.) Wetlands and watershed management. Association of State Wetland Managers, Berne, New York.

Kushlan, J.A. (1997). The conservation of wading birds. *Colonial Waterbirds* **20**: 129–137.

Kushlan, J.A. & Frohring, P.C. (1986). The history of the southern Florida Wood Stork population. *Wilson Bulletin* **93**: 368–386.

Kushlan, J.A. & White, D.A. (1977). Nesting wading bird populations in southern Florida. *Florida Scientist* **40**: 65–72.

Kushlan, J.A., Morales, G. & Frohring, P.C. (1985). Foraging niche relations of wading birds in tropical wet savannas. pp 663–682, in (P.A. Buckley, M.S. Foster, E.S. Morton, R.S. Ridgely and F.G. Buckley, eds.) Neotropical ornithology. Ornithological Monographs No. 36. American Ornithologists' Union, Lawrence, Kansas.

Kushlan, J.A., Hancock, J.A., Pinowski, J. & Pinowska, B. (1982). Behavior of Whistling and Capped Herons in the seasonal savannas of Venezuela and Argentina. *Condor* **84**: 255–260.

Kusler, J.A. & Riexinger, P. (eds.). (1986). Proceedings of the National Wetland Assessment Symposium. Association of State Wetland Managers, Chester, Vermont, USA.

Kusler, J.A., Quammen, M.L. & Brooks, G. (eds.). (1988). Proceedings of the National Wetland Symposium: Mitigation of impacts and losses. Association of State Wetland Managers, Berne, New York.

Kusler, J.A., Willard, D.E. & Hull, H.C. Jr. (eds.) (1995). Wetlands and watershed management. Association of State Wetland Managers, Berne, New York.

La Touche, J.D.D. (1913). Untitled. *Ibis* ser. **10**: 282.

La Touche, J.D.D. (1917). Untitled *Ibis* ser. **10**: 562.

La Touche, J.D.D. (1934). A handbook of the birds of eastern China. Vol 2, pp 401–496. Taylor & Francis, London, UK.

Lack, D. (1966). Population studies of birds. Clarendon Press. Oxford.

Lack, P.C. (1986). Ecological correlates of migrants and residents in a tropical African savanna. *Ardea* **74**: 111–119.

Lagler, K.F. (1939). The control of fish predators at hatcheries and rearing stations. *Journal of Wildlife Management* **3**: 169–179.

Lane, J.A.K. & McComb, A.J. (1988). Western Australian wetlands. pp 127–146, in (A.J McComb and P.S. Lake, eds.) The conservation of Australian wetlands. Surrey Beatty and Sons, Chipping Norton, New South Wales, Australia.

Lange, M. (1995). Texas coastal waterbird colonies: 1973–1990 census summary, atlas, and trends. U.S. Fish and Wildlife Service and Texas Parks and Wildlife Department, Arlington TX, USA.

Langley, C.H. (1983). Biology of the Little Bittern in the SW Cape. *Ostrich* **54**: 83–94.

Langrand, O. (1990). Guide to the birds of Madagascar. Yale University Press, New Haven.

Lansdown, R.V. (1987a). Interwader species status report No. 1. Sumatran Heron *Ardea sumatrana*. Interwader, Kuala Lumpur, Malaysia.

Lansdown, R.V. (1987b). Extensions of the known breeding range of the Yellow Bittern *Ixobrychus sinensis*. *Forktail* **4**: 61–63.

Lansdown, R.V. (1988). Some displays, calls and associated morphology of the Cinnamon Bittern *Ixobrychus cinnamomeus*. *Colonial Waterbirds* **11**: 308–310.

Lansdown, R.V. (1990). Little-known oriental birds: The Chinese Egret. *Oriental Bird Club Bulletin* **11**: 27–30.

Lansdown, R.V. (1991). Environmental impact assessment in Asia: A review of the legal and practical status of environmental impact assessment in twenty-two Asian countries. Unpubl. MSc. Thesis, University of Wales, Aberystwyth, UK.

Lansdown, R.V. (1992). The status and conservation of the Sumatran Heron *Ardea sumatrana*. *Heron Conservation Newsletter* **5**: 11–12.

Lansdown, R.V. (1993). Embracing impact assessment in the east. *Environment Risk*, February: 26–28.

Lansdown, R.V. & Rajanathan, R. (1993). Some aspects of the ecology of *Ixobrychus* bitterns nesting in Malaysian ricefields. *Colonial Waterbirds* **16**: 98–101.

Laporte, P. (1982). Organochlorine residues and eggshell measurements of Great Blue Heron eggs from Quebec. *Colonial Waterbirds* **5**: 95–103.

Leach, G.J. (1994). Effects of dam size on waterbirds at farm dams in south-east Queensland. *Corella* **18**: 77–82.

Lean, G. & Hinrichsen, D. (1994). WWF atlas of the environment. 2nd edn. HarperPerennial, London.

Learmonth, N.F. (1953). Bird movements in the Portland district, Victoria in 1951. *Emu* **53**: 86–88.

Lebret, T. (1947). Een kleine broedkolonie van de kwak in Nederland in 1946 en 1947. *Ardea* **35**: 149–156.

Lebreton, J.D., Pradel, R. & Clobert, J. (1993). The statistical analysis of survival in animal populations. *Trends Ecology and Evolution* **8**: 91–95.

Lebreton, P. (1977). Les oiseaux nicheurs rhônalpins. CORA/Ministère de la Culture et de l'Environnement, Paris.

Le Houérou, H.N. (1990). Global change: vegetation, ecosystems and land use in the southern Mediterranean Basin: old approaches to new problems. *Agriculture, Ecosystems and Environment* **33**, 99–109.

Le Houérou H.N. (1991). La Méditerrannée en l'an 2000. *La Météorologie* **36**: 4–37.

Le Louarn, H. (1988). Impact du Héron cendré sur différents systèmes de production. INRA, Rennes, France.

Lee, K.S. (1999). White-eared Night Heron *Gorsachius magnificus* on sale in a Nanning market. *Oriental Bird Club Bulletin* **28**, pp 13.

Lendon, A. (1951). Unidentified egret. *Emu* **51**: 120.

Leslie, D. (1996). Barmah–Millewa Forest water allocation. *Inland Rivers Network News* **1(2)**: 4.

Leven, M.R. & Carey, G.J. (1993). Report on the birds 1992: Systematic list. *Hong Kong Bird Report* 1992: 14–74.

Lever, C. (1987). Naturalized birds of the world. Longman Scientific & Technical. Harlow, UK.

Lillelecht, V. & Leibak, E. (1993). Eesti lindude süstematiline nimestik, staatus ja arvUnited Kingdomus. *Hirundo* **1(12)**: 3–42.

Lingren, E. (1971). Records of new and uncommon species for the island of New Guinea. *Emu* **71**: 134–136.

Lippens, L. & Wille, H. (1969). Le Héron bihoreau, *Nycticorax n. nycticorax* (Linné 1758) en Belgique et en Europe Occidentale. *Le Gerfaut* **59**: 123–156.

Lippens, L. & Wille, H. (1972). Atlas des oiseaux de Belgique et d'Europe occidentale. Tielt.

Littauer, G. (1990a). Avian predators: frightening techniques for reducing bird damage at aquaculture facilities. U.S. Department of Agriculture, Southern Regional Aquaculture Center Publication 401.

Littauer, G. (1990b). Control of bird predation at aquaculture facilities. Strategies and cost estimates. U.S. Department of Agriculture, Southern Regional Aquaculture Center Publication No. 402.

Litvinenko, N.M. & Shibaev, Yu. V. (1999). The Chinese Egret *Egretta eulophotes* – a new breeding species for avifauna of Russia. *Russian Journal of Ornithology*. Express-issue **70**: 7–9.

Livingston, R.J. (1993). Estuarine wetlands. pp 128–152, in (M.S. Dennison and J.F. Berry, eds.) Wetlands: guide to science, technology, and law. Noyes Publications. Park Ridge, New Jersey.

Llamas, M.R. (1988). Conflicts between wetlands conservation and groundwater exploitation. Two case histories in Spain. *Environment, Geology and Water Science* **11**: 241–251.

Lock, L. & Cook, K. (1998). The Little Egret in Britain: a successful colonist. *British Birds* **91(7)**: 273–280.

Locke, L.M., Ohlendorf, H.M., Shillinger, R.B. & Jareed, T. (1974). Salmonellosis in a captive heron colony. *Journal of Wildlife Diseases* **10**: 143–145.

Long, A.J., Poole, C.M., Eldridge, M.I., Won, P.O. & Lee, K.S. (1988). A survey of coastal wetlands and shorebirds in South Korea, spring 1988. Asian Wetland Bureau, Kuala Lumpur, Malaysia.

Lopez-Ornat, A. & Ramo, C. (1992). Colonial waterbird populations in the Sian Ka'an Biosphere Reserve (Quintana Roo, Mexico). *Wilson Bulletin* **104**: 501–515.

Lothian, J.A. & Williams, W.D. (1988). Wetland conservation in South Australia. pp 147–166, in (A.J. McComb and P.S. Lake, eds.) The conservation of Australian wetlands. Surrey Beatty and Sons, New South Wales, Australia.

Lowe, F.A. (1954). The Heron. Collins, London.

Lowen, J.C., Clay, R.P., Mazar Barnett, J. et al. (1997). New and noteworthy observations on the Paraguayan avifauna. *Bulletin of the British Ornithological Club* **117**: 275–293.

Ludke, J.L., Hill, E.F. & Dieter, M.P. (1975). Cholinesterase (ChE) responses and related mortality among birds fed ChE inhibitors. *Archives of Environmental Contamination and Toxicology* **3**: 1–21.

Lukac, S. (1990). Great White Egret *Egretta alba* nests at Becej fish pond. *Ciconia* **2**: 73 (in Serbo–Croat).

Lussana Grasselli, E. (1982). Le zone umide in Italia, ieri e oggi (1861–1961). pp 17–61, in (Atti Conv ed.) Le zone umide dalla bonifica integrale alla utilizzazione per la collettività. Venezia, 25–27 Marzo 1982. FIDC, Rome, Italy.

Lyles, A.M. (ed.). (1994a). Regional collection plan of the AZA Heron, Ibis and Hammerhead Advisory Group. Wildlife Conservation Society, New York.

Lyles, A.M. (ed.). (1994b). Husbandry notebook of AZA's Heron, Ibis and Hammerhead Advisory Group. Wildlife Conservation Society, New York.

Lyster, S. (1985). International Wildlife Law: an analysis of international treaties concerned with the conservation of wildlife. Grotius Publications Limited, Cambridge, UK.

Maccarone, A.D. & Parsons, K.C. (1994). Factors affecting the use of a freshwater and an estuarine foraging site by egrets and ibises during the breeding season in New York City. *Colonial Waterbirds* **17**: 60–68.

Mace, G.M. & Lande, R. (1991). Assessing extinction threats: toward a reevaluation of IUCN threatened species categories. *Conservation Biology* **5**: 148–157.

Mace, G. & Stuart, S. (1994). Draft ICUN red list categories. Version 2.2. *Species* **22**: 13–24.

Mace, G.M., Collar, N., Cooke, J. et al. (1992). The development of the new criteria for listing species on the IUCN Red List. *Species* **19**: 16–22.

Mackrill, E. (1987). Winter breeding of Night Heron in Europe. *Dutch Birding* **9**: 124.

Macdonald, M.A. (1978). The Yellow-billed Egret in West Africa (*Aves Ardeidae*). Revue de Zoologie et Botanique Africaines **92**: 191–200.

Macquarie Marshes Advisory and Audit Committee (1997). Draft Macquarie Marshes 1996 water management plan 1996/97, operation and performance report. Department of Land and Water Conservation, Dubbo, Australia.

Maddock, M. (1990). Cattle Egret: South to Tasmania and New Zealand for the winter. *Notornis* **37**: 1–23.

Maddock, M. (1991a). Observations on the biology of the White-faced Heron *Ardea novaehollandiae*. *Corella* **15**: 29–85.

Maddock, M. (1991b). Education, research and passive recreation: An integrated programme at the Wetlands Centre, Shortland. *International Journal of Science Education* **13(5)**: 561–568.

Maddock, M. (1992). Project Egret Watch: Ornithological research and community education. *Hunter Natural History* **50**: 29–54.

Maddock, M. & Baxter, G.S. (1991). Breeding success of egrets related to rainfall: a six year Australian study. *Colonial Waterbirds* **14**: 133–139.

Maddock, M. & Bridgman, H. (1992). Cattle Egret migration and meteorological conditions. *Notornis* **39**: 73–86.

Maddock, M. & Geering, D.J. (1993). Cattle Egret migration in south-eastern Australia and New Zealand: An update. *Notornis* **40**: 109–122.

Maddock, M. & Geering, D. (1994). Range expansion and migration of the Cattle Egret within Australia and New Zealand: Implications for the spread of the species. *Ostrich* **65**: 191–293.

Maddock, M.N. (1983). Hunter Valley birds raise conservation issues. *Wetlands, Australia* **3**: 71–80.

Magnin, G. (1991). Hunting and persecution of migratory birds in the Mediterranean region. In (T. Salathé, ed.). Conserving migratory birds, ICBP Technical Publications No. 12.

Magrath, M.J.L. (1992). Waterbirds of the Lower Lachlan and Murrumbidgee Valley Wetlands in 1990/91. New South Wales Department of Water Resources, Australia.

Maher, M.T. (1991). Waterbirds back O'Bourke: An inland perspective of the conservation of Australian waterbirds. Unpublished Ph.D. thesis, University of New England, New South Wales, Australia.

Maher, P.N. (1990). Bird Survey of the Lachlan/Murrumbidgee Confluence Wetlands. New South Wales, National Parks and Wildlife Service, Sydney, Australia.

Majic, J. & Mikuska, J. (1970). Heron nesting in the Kopucevski reservation and immediate environs over the period from 1954 to 1970. *Larus* **24**: 65–77.

Mann, C.F. (1976). The Birds of Teso District, Uganda. *Journal of the East African Natural History Society* **156**: 1–16.

Mann, C.F. (1987). A checklist of the birds of Brunei Darussalam. *Brunei Museum Journal* **6**: 170–212.

Mann, C.F. (1989). More notable bird observation from Brunei, Borneo. *Forktail* **5**: 17–22.

Marble, A.D. (1992). A guide to wetland functional design. Lewis Publishers, Boca Raton, Florida.

Marchant, J. (1997). Decrease in heron population but more heronries censused in 1995–96. *British Trust for Ornithology News* **210/211**: 7.

Marchant, S. (1988). Nesting behaviour of the Pacific Heron. *Australian Birds* **21**: 61–65.

Marchant, S. & Higgins, P.J. (1990). Handbook of Australian, New Zealand and Antarctic Birds. Oxford University Press, Melbourne, Australia.

Marin, A.M. (1989). Notes on the breeding of Chestnut-bellied Herons (*Agamia agami*) in Costa Rica. *Condor* **91**: 215–217.

Marion, L. (1976). Contributions à l'écologie des populations de Hérons cendrés, *Ardea cinerea*, en Bretagne. DEA, Université de Rennes, France.

Marion, L. (1979). Stratégie d'utilisation du milieu des colonies de Hérons cendrés, *Ardea cinerea*, en Bretagne. Thèse de troisième cycle, Université de Rennes, France.

Marion, L. (1981). Dynamique d'une population de Hérons cendrés *Ardea cinerea*: exemple de la plus grande colonie d'Europe, le Lac de Grand-Lieu. *L'Oiseau & Revue Française d'Ornithologie* **50**: 219–261.

Marion, L. (1983a). Etat de nos connaissances sur les relations oiseaux piscivores et populations piscicoles naturelles et artificielles, et propositions de recherches prioritaires pour la période 1984–88. Rapport final du Groupe de travail sur les hérons et autres oiseaux piscivores, Secrétariat d'Etat à l'Environnement, Paris.

Marion, L. (1983b). Le Blongios nain. pp 101, in (F. de Beaufort, ed.), Livre rouge des espèces menacées en France. Museum National d'Histoire Naturelle, Paris.

Marion, L. (1984). Mise en évidence par biotélémétrie de territoires alimentaires individuels chez un oiseau colonial, le Héron cendré (*Ardea cinerea*). Mécanisme de répartition et de régulation des effectifs de colonies de hérons. *L'Oiseau & Revue Française d'Ornithologie* **54**: 1–78.

Marion, L. (1987a). Effets de la vague de froid de janvier 1985 sur les populations françaises d'ardéidés (Héron cendré, Aigrette garzette et Héron garde-boeufs). Ministère Environnement, Société Nationale Protection Nature, Université de Rennes, France.

Marion, L. (1987b). Bird predation in open waters. pp 46–57, in (Ir. C. M Bungenberg de Jong, J. From, L. Marion and K. Molnar, eds.) Report of the European Inland Fisheries Advisory Commission Working Party on prevention and control of bird predation in aquaculture and fisheries operations. Food and Agriculture Organization of the United Nations, Rome, Italy.

Marion, L. (1988). Evolution des stratégies démographiques, alimentaires et d'utilisation de l'espace chez le héron cendré en France: importance des contraintes énergétiques et humaines. Thèse d'état, Université de Rennes, France.

Marion, L. (1989a). Review of replies of questionnaire on predation in open waters. pp 23–33, in (C.M. Bungenberg de Jong, J. From, L. Marion, and K. Molnar, eds.) Report of the EIFAC working party on prevention and control of bird predation in aquaculture and fisheries operations. EIFAC Technical Paper 51, Rome, Italy.

Marion, L. (1989b). Territorial feeding and colonial breeding are not necessarily mutually exclusive spatial occupation systems: the case of the Grey Heron (*Ardea cinerea*). *Journal Animal Ecology* **58**: 693–710.

Marion, L. (1990a). Les oiseaux piscivores et les activités piscicoles. Impact et protection. Ministère de l'Environnement et Ministère de l'Agriculture et de la Forêt, Paris.

Marion, L. (1990b). Activités piscicoles et oiseaux piscivores: quels moyens de protection? *L'Oiseau Magazine* **19**: 22–28.

Marion, L. (1991a). Héron cendré *Ardea cinerea*. pp 80–81, in (D.Yeatman-Berthelot and G. Jarry, eds.), Atlas des oiseaux de France en hiver. Société Ornithologique de France, Paris.

Marion, L. (1991b). Inventaire national des héronnières de France 1989: Héron cendré, Héron bihoreau, Héron garde-boeuf, Héron crabier, Aigrette garzette. Ministère Environnement, Museum National d'Histoire Naturelle, Société Nationale Protection Nature, Université de Rennes, France.

Marion, L. (1994a). Le Blongios nain. pp 26–27, in (D. Yeatman-Berthelot and G. Jarry, eds.) Atlas des oiseaux nicheurs de France. Société Ornithologique de France, Paris.

Marion, L. (1994b). Little Bittern. pp 90–91, in (G.M. Tucker and M.F. Heath, eds.). Birds in Europe: their conservation status. BirdLife Conservation Series No. 3. BirdLife International, Cambridge, UK.

Marion, L. (1997a). Les populations de Hérons cendrés en Europe et leur impact sur l'activité piscicole. pp 101–132, in (Ph. Clergeau, ed.) Oiseaux à risques en ville et en campagne. INRA Editions, Paris.

Marion, L. (1997b). Evolution des effectifs nicheurs et de la répartition des hérons coloniaux en France entre 1974 et 1994. *Alauda* **65**: 86–88.

Marion, L. (1997c). *Ixobrychus minutus* Little Bittern. pp 42–43, in (E.J.M. Hagemeijer and M.J. Blair, eds.) The European bird common census atlas of European breeding birds. Their distribution and abundance. Poyser, London.

Marion, L. (1997d). Inventaire national des héronnières de France 1994. Héron cendré, Héron pourpré, Héron bihoreau, Héron garde-bœufs, Héron crabier, Aigrette garzette. Editions du Museum National d' Histoire Naturelle, Paris.

Marion, L. (1997e). Le Grand cormoran en Europe : Dynamique et impacts. pp 133–178, in (P. Clergeau, ed.) Oiseaux à risques en ville et en campagne. INRA Editions, Paris.

Marion, L. (1999). Les réalisations du Programme Life. *Courrier Nature Special Grand-Lieu* **177**: 46.

Marion, L. & Marion, P. (1975). Contribution à l'étude écologique du Lac de Grand-Lieu. *Bulletin Société Sciences Naturelles de l'Ouest de la France* (supplément) 1–611.

Marion, L. & Marion, P. (1982a). Le Héron crabier a-t-il niché en 1981 au lac de Grand-Lieu? Statut de l'espèce en France au XXème siècle. *L'Oiseau & Revue Française d'Ornithologie* **52**: 335–346.

Marion, L. & Marion, P. (1982b). Le Héron garde-boeufs *(Bubulcus ibis)* niche dans l'ouest de la France. Statut de l'espèce en France. *Alauda* **50**: 161–175.

Marion, L. & Marion, P. (1987a). Conséquences de la protection du Héron cendré sur sa dynamique de population et sur ses stratégies d'occupation de l'espace en France. *Revue d'Ecologie (Terre et Vie)*, suppl. **4**: 261–270.

Marion, L. & Marion, P. (1987b). Impact de la prédation exercée par le Héron cendré sur une pisciculture. *Revue d'Ecologie (Terre Vie)*, suppl. **4**: 115–116.

Marion, L. & Marion, P. (1994). Premières nidifications réussies de la Grande Aigrette *Egretta alba* en France, au Lac de Grand-Lieu. *Alauda* **62**: 149–150.

Marion, L. & Reeber, S. (1997). Impact du retard d'exondation sur l'avifaune du Lac de Grand-Lieu. Université de Rennes, France.

Marion, L., Brugière, D. & Grisser, P. (1993). Invasion de Hérons garde-boeufs *Bubulcus ibis* nicheurs en France en 1992. *Alauda* **61**: 129–136.

Marion, L., Marion, P. & Clergeau, P. (1989). Causes and consequences of accelerated eutrophic evolution of the lake of Grand-Lieu, France. *Proceedings of the Third International Conference on Wetlands*, Rennes 1988: 219–220.

Marquiss, M. (1983). Eggshell thinning and the breakage and non-hatching of eggs at Grey heron colonies. Annual report Institute for Terrestrial Ecology for 1982, pp 70–74.

Marquiss, M. (1989). Grey Heron *Ardea cinerea* breeding in Scotland: numbers, distributions and census techniques. *Bird Study* **36**: 181–191.

Marquiss, M. & Carss, D.N. (1994). Fish-eating Birds. Assessing their impact on freshwater fisheries. R&D Report 15, National Rivers Authority, Bristol, UK.

Marquiss, M. & Carss, D.N. (1997). Fish-eating birds and fisheries. *British Trust for Ornithology News* **210–211**: 6–7.

Marquiss, M. & Reynolds, C. (1986). How many herons ? *BTO News* **143**: 12.

Martin, M. (1982). Impact of predators on fish farming. *Aquaculture Magazine* Jan.–Feb.: 36–37, Mar.–Apr.: 44–45, May–June: 46–48.

Martin, R.P. & Lester, G.D. (1991). Atlas and census of wading birds and seabird colonies in Louisiana 1990. Louisiana Department of Wildlife and Fisheries, Special Publication No. 3. Lafayette, Louisiana, USA.

Martinez, A. & Martinez, I. (1983). Nuevas colonias de Garzas en el Delta del Ebro. *Ardeola* **30**: 105–108.

Martinez-Abrain, A. (1991). Avetorillo commun *Ixobrychus minutus*, pp 70–71, in (V. Urios, J.V. Escobar, R. Pardo, R.P Gutierrez and J.A. Gomez, eds.). Atlas de las aves nidificantes de la comunidad Valenciana. Generalitat Valenciana, Conselleria d'agricultura y pesca.

Mather, J.R. (1974). Climatology. Fundamentals and applications. McGraw Hill, New York.

Mathews, G.M. & Iredale, T. (1913). A reference list of the birds of New Zealand. *Ibis* **10(1)**: 402–452.

May, J.B. (1929). Recoveries of Black-crowned Night Herons banded in Massachusetts. *Bulletin of the North Eastern Bird-Banding Assoc.* **5**: 7–16.

McAllister, P.C. & Owens, W.J. (1992). Recovery of infectious pancreatic necrosis virus from the faeces of wild piscivorous birds. *Aquaculture* **106**: 227–232.

McAtee, W.L. & Piper, S.E. (1937). Excluding birds from reservoirs and fishponds. Leaflet 120, U.S. Department of Agriculture.

McBee, K. & Bickham, J.W. (1988). Petrochemical-related DNA damage in wild rodents detected by flow cytometry. *Bulletin of Environmental Contamination and Toxicology* **40**: 343–349.

McComb, A.J. & Lake, P.S. (eds.). (1988). The conservation of Australian wetlands. Surrey Beatty and Sons, New South Wales, Australia.

McCrimmon, D.A. (1978). Nest-site characteristics among five species of herons on the North Carolina coast. *Auk* **95**: 267–280.

McCrimmon, D.A. (1982). Populations of Great Blue Heron *(Ardea herodias)* in New York State from 1964 to 1981. *Colonial Waterbirds* **5**: 87–94.

McCrimmon, D.A. (1987). The collection, management, and exchange of information on colonially nesting birds. pp 187–196, in (A. Sprunt, IV, J.C. Ogden, and S. Winckler eds.) Wading Birds. National Audubon Society Special Report 7, New York.

McCrimmon, D.A. & Parnell, J.F. (1983). The breeding distributions of five colonial waterbirds species in coastal North Carolina. *Colonial Waterbirds* **6**: 168–177.

McCrimmon, D.A., Jr., Fryska, S.T., Ogden, J.C. & Butcher, G.S. (1997). Nonlinear population dynamics of six species of Florida Ciconiiformes assessed by Christmas Bird Counts. *Ecological Applications* **7**: 581–592.

McCulloch, M.N., Tucker, G.M. & Baillie, S.R. (1992). The hunting of migratory birds in Europe: a ringing recovery analysis. *Ibis* **134** suppl.1: 55–65.

McEwen, L.C., Stafford, C.J. & Hensler, G.L. (1984). Organochlorine residues in eggs of Black-crowned Night Herons from Colorado and Wyoming. *Environmental Toxicology and Chemistry* **3**: 367–376.

McIlhenny, E.A. (1934). Bird city. The Christopher Publishing House, Boston.

McKean, J.L. & Hindwood, K.A. (1965). Additional notes on the birds of Lord Howe Island. *Emu* **64**: 79–97.

McKenzie, H.R. & McKenzie, H.M. (1961). Blue Heron at Lake Taupo. *Notornis* **9**: 200.

McKilligan, N.G. (1997). A long term study of factors influencing the breeding success of the Cattle Egret in Australia. *Colonial Waterbirds* **20**: 419–428.

McKilligan, N.G., Reimer, D.S., Seton, D.H.C., Davidson, D. & Willows, J.T. (1993). Survival and seasonal movements of the Cattle Egret in eastern Australia. *Emu* **93**: 19–87.

McNeil, R., Limoges, B. & Rodríguez, J.R. (1990). Corocoro colorado (*Eudocimus ruber*) y otras aves acuáticas coloniales de las lagunas, ciénagas y salinas de la costa centro-oriental de Venezuela. pp 28–45, in (P.C. Frederick, L.G. Morales, A.L. Spaans, and C.S. Luthin, eds.). The Scarlet Ibis (*Eudocimus ruber*): Status, conservation and recent research. International Waterfowl and Wetlands Research Bureau, Slimbridge, UK.

Medway, Lord & Wells, D.R. (1976). The birds of the Malay Peninsula. Vol. 5. Witherby, London and Penerbit University, Malaysia.

Mees, G.F. (1977). Additional records from Formosa (Taiwan). *Zoologische Medelingen* **51**: 243–264.

Mees, G.F. (1982). Birds from the lowlands of southern New Guinea (Merauke and Koembe). *Zoologische Verhandelingen* **191**: 15–18.

Meininger, P.L. & Atta, G.A.M. (eds.). (1994). Ornithological Studies in Egyptian Wetlands 1989/90. Fore-report 94–01, WIWO-report 40, Vlissingen/Zeist.

Meininger, P.L., Sorensen, U.G. & Atta, G.A.M. (1986). Breeding birds of the lakes in the Nile delta, Egypt. *Sandgrouse* **7**: 1–20.

Meininger, P.L., Wolf, P.A., Hadoud, D. & Essghaier, M. (1994). Ornithological survey of the coast of Libya, July 1993. WIWO-report 46, Zeist.

Melancon, M.J. (1996). Development of cytochromes P450 in avian species as a biomarker for environmental contaminant exposure and effect. Procedures and baseline values. pp 95–108 in (D.A. Bengston and D.S. Henshel, eds). Environmental toxicology and risk assessment: biomarker and risk assessment. Vol 5 ASTM STP 1306. American Society for Testing and Materials, Philadelphia, PA, USA.

Mendelssohn, H. (1975). Preliminary report on the influence of pollutants in East Mediterranean sea fish on fish-eating birds. Proceedings of the Sixth Scientific Conference of the Israel Ecological Society, Tel Aviv, Israel.

Merriam–Webster, Inc, (1961). Webster's seventh new collegiate dictionary. Springfield, Massachusetts.

Meyer, J. (1980). Herons at fish farms. pp 58–63, in Proceedings of the Institute of Fisheries Management 11th Annual Study course, 23–25 September 1980, University of Sussex, UK.

Meyer, J. (1981). Room for bird and fish: RSPB's survey of heron damage. *Fish Farmer* **4**: 26.

Michel, C. (1983). Le rôle des oiseaux piscivores en pathologie piscicole. pp 77–83, in (L. Marion, ed.) Etat de nos connaissances sur les relations oiseaux piscivores et populations piscicoles naturelles et artificielles, et propositions de recherches prioritaires pour la période 1984–88. Rapport final du Groupe de travail sur les hérons et autres oiseaux piscivores. Secrétariat d'Etat à l'Environnement, Paris.

Mikhalevich, I., Serebryakov, V. & Grishchenko, V. (1994). Atlas of breeding herons in Ukraine. *Bird Census News* **7/1**: 32–37.

Mikuska, J. (1982). The importance of Kopacki Rit. In IWRB Symposium "Population Ecology of Geese", Debrecen, Hungary. *Aquila* **89**: 205–207.

Mikuska, T. (1992). The population of nesting herons in Croatia. pp 68–69, in (C.M. Finlayson, G.E. Hollis and T.J. Davis, eds.) Managing Mediterranean wetlands and their birds. Proceedings of symposium., Grado, Italy, 1991. IWRB Spec. Publ. No. 20, Slimbridge, UK.

Mikuska, T., Kushlan, J.A. & Hartley, S. (1998). Key areas for wintering North American Herons. *Colonial Waterbirds* **21**: 125–134.

Millener, P.J. (1981). The Quaternary avifauna of the North Island, New Zealand. Unpublished PhD thesis, University of Auckland: 529–530, Auckland, New Zealand.

Miller, K.E. & Smallwood, J.A. (1997). Natal dispersal and philopatry of Southeastern American Kestrels in Florida. *Wilson Bulletin* **109**: 226–232.

Mills, D.H. (1967). Predation on fish by other animals. pp 377–397, in (S. Gerking, ed.) The biological basis of freshwater fish production. Blackwell, Oxford, UK.

Mills, D.H. (1980). Heron—public enemy number 1. *Fish Farmer* **3**: 16.

Milon, P., Petter, J.J. and Randrianasolo, G. (1973). Faune de Madagascar Vol 35: Oiseaux. ORSTOM, Tananarive, and CRNS, Paris, France.

Milstein, P. le S., Prestt, I. & Bell, A.A. (1970). The breeding cycle of the Grey Heron. *Ardea* **58**: 243–254.

Ministère de l'Environnement, (1993). Plan national d'actions prioritaires de conservation des zones humides les plus importantes de Bulgarie. Editions "Bulvest 2000", Ministère de l'Environnement, Bulgarie.

Ministry of the Environment, (1992). Nature Management in Denmark. The Ministry of the Environment, The National Forest and Nature Agency, Copenhagen, Denmark.

Mitchell, C.A., White, D.A. & Kaiser, T.E. (1981). Reproductive success of Great Blue herons at Nueces Bay, Corpus Christi, Texas. *Bulletin of the Texas Ornithological Society* **14**: 18–21.

Mitchell, D. & Roberts, J. (1983). Wetland management: Philosophies and principles. pp 62–66, in (C. Haigh, ed.) Parks and wildlife: wetlands. National Parks and Wildlife Service, Sydney, Australia.

Mitsch, W.J. (1994). Global wetlands, Old World and New. Elsevier, Amsterdam.

Mock, D.W. (1986). Siblicide, parent–offspring conflict, and unequal parents investment by egrets and herons. *Behavioral Ecology and Sociobiology* **20**: 247–256.

Mock, D.W. & Parker, G.A. (1986). Advantages and disadvantages of egret and heron brood reduction. *Evolution* **40**: 459–470.

Mock, D.W., Lamey, T.C. & Ploger, B.J. (1987). Proximate and ultimate roles of food amounts in regulating egret sibling aggression. *Ecology* **68**: 1760–1772.

Moenke, R. & Bick, A. (1990). Records of the Cattle Egret *Bubulcus ibis* L. in the Antarctic. *Mitt. Zool. Mus. Berl.* **66** (suppl.): 69–79.

Moerbeek, D.J. (1984). Afweer van aalscholvers op de viswekerij Nederland anderzoek 1983. Utrecht, Straatbosbeheer.

Moerbeek, D.J., Van Dobben, W.H., Osieck, E.R., Boere, G.C. & Bungenberg de Jong, C.M. (1987). Cormorant damage prevention at a fish farm in the Netherlands. *Biological Conservation* **39**: 23–38.

Moller, N.W. & Olesen, N.S. (1980). Bestander af ynglende Fiskehejre *Ardea cinerea* i Danmark 1978. *Dansk Ornithologisk Tidsskrift* **74**: 105–112.

Moller, N.W. & Olesen, N.S. (1983). Fiskehejren (*Ardea cinerea*) of fiskehejrejagten I Danmark 1976–77. *Danske Viltundersogeisen* **36**: 1–23.

Monet, C. & Varney, A. (1998). Notes on the breeding of the Striated Heron *Butorides striatus* in Tahiti, French Polynesia. *Emu* **98**: 132–135.

Monet, C., Thibault, J.C. & Varney, A. (1993). Stability and changes during the twentieth century in breeding landbirds of Tahiti (Polynesia). *Bird Conservation International* **3**: 261–280.

Moon, G.J.H. (1967). Refocus on New Zealand birds. Reed Wellington, Wellington, New Zealand.

Moore, D.R. (1984). A migrating flock of Grey Heron. *British Birds* **77**: 21.

Mora, M.L. (1991). Organochlorines and breeding success in Cattle Egrets from the Mexicali Valley, Baja California, Mexico. *Colonial Waterbirds* **14**: 127–132.

Mora, M.L. (1996). Congener-specific polychlorinated biphenyl patterns in eggs of aquatic birds from the Lower Laguna Madre. *Environmental Toxicology and Chemistry* **15**: 1003–1010.

Mora, M.L. & Anderson, D.W. (1995). Selenium, boron, and heavy metals in birds from the Mexicali Valley, Baja California, Mexico. *Bulletin of Environmental Contamination and Toxicology* **54**: 198–206.

Morales, G., Pinowski, J., Pacheco, J., Madriz, M. & Gomez, F. (1981). Densidades poblacionales, flujo de energía y hábitos alimentarios de las aves ictiófagas de los Módulos de Apure, Venezuela. *Acta Biologica Venezuelica* **11**: 1–45.

Moreau, R.E. (1967). Water-birds over the Sahara. *Ibis* **109**: 232–259.

Moreau, R.E. (1972). The Palearctic-African bird migration systems. Academic Press, London.

Morel, G.J. & Morel, M.Y. (1989). Une heronnière mixte sur le Lac de Guer (Sénégal) avec référence spéciale à *Ixobrychus m. minutus* et *Platalea leucorodia*. *L'Oiseau & Revue Française d'Ornithologie* **59**: 290–295.

Morris, A. (1979). The spread of the Cattle Egret in New South Wales. *Australian Birds* **13**: 72–74.

Morris, A.K. (1975). The birds of Gosford, Wyong and Newcastle (County Cumberland). *Australian Birds* **9**: 37–76.

Morris, A.K. (1990). Colonial nesting of Striated Herons at Tuggerah, New South Wales. *Corella* **14**: 27–28.

Morris, P. & Hawkins, F. (1998). Birds of Madagascar. A photographic guide. Pica Press. East Sussex, UK.

Morrison, M. (1986). Bird populations as indicators of environmental change. *Current Ornithology* **3**: 429–451.

Morrison, R.I.G. & Ross, R.K. (1989). Atlas of Nearctic shorebirds on the coast of South America. Vols. 1 and 2. Canadian Wildlife Service, Ottawa.

Morrison, R.I.G., Butler, R.W., Delgado, F.S. & Ross, R.K. (1998). Atlas of Nearctic shorebirds and other waterbirds on the coast of Panama. Canadian Wildlife Service Special Publication, Ottawa.

Morrisson, K. (1975). War on birds. *Defenders of Wildlife* **50**: 17–19.

Morton, S.R., Brennan, K.G. & Armstrong, M.D. (1993). Distribution and abundance of herons, egrets, ibises and spoonbills in the Alligator Rivers region, Northern Territory. *Wildlife Research* **20**: 23–44.

Moser, M.E. (1983). Purple Heron colonies in the Camargue. pp. 104–113, in (P. R. Evans, H. Hafner and P. L'Hermite, eds.) Shorebirds and large waterbird conservation. Commission of the European Communities, Brussels, Belgium.

Moser, M.E. (1984). Resource partitioning in colonial herons, with particular reference to the Grey Heron *Ardea cinerea* L. and the Purple Heron *Ardea purpurea* L., in the Camargue, S. France. PhD Thesis, University of Durham, UK.

Moshiri, G.A. (1993). Constructed wetlands for water quality improvement. Lewis Publishers. Boca Raton, Florida.

Mott, D.F. (1978). Control of wading bird predation at fish rearing facilities. pp 131–132, in (A. Sprunt, IV, J.C. Ogden, S. Winckler, eds.) Wading birds. Audubon Society Research Report 7, New York.

Mountfort, G. (1988). Rare birds of the world. Collins/ICBP, London.

Müller, R. (1984). Magenuntersuchungen am Graureiher *Ardea cinerea*. *Der Ornithologische Beobachter* **81**: 159–163.

Mullié, W.C., Brouwer, J., Codjo, S.F. & Decae, R. (1998). Small isolated wetlands in the central Sahel: a resource shared between people and waterbirds. Abstract. Abstract Booklet p. 65, 2nd International conference on Wetlands and Development, Dakar, Senegal.

Mullié, W.C., Massi, A., Focardi, S. & Renzoni, A. (1992). Residue levels of organochlorines and mercury in Cattle Egret, *Bubulcus ibis*, eggs from the Faigom Oasis, Egypt. *Bulletin of Environmental Contaminants and Toxicology* **48**: 739–746.

Mullié, W.C., Verwey, P.J., Berends, A.G., Evert, J.W., Sène, F. & Koeman, J.H. (1991). The impact of pesticides on Palearctic migratory birds in the Western Sahel. In (T. Salathé, ed.) Conserving Migratory Birds, ICBP Technical Publications No. 12.

Mundkur, T. (1991). Nesting and feeding ecology of aquatic birds in Saurashtra and Gulf of Kachchh. Unpub. Ph.D. Thesis, Saurashtra University, Rajkot, India.

Mundkur, T. (1992). First sighting of a colour banded Chinese egret in Singapore. *Singapore Avifauna* **6(4)**: 26.

Mundkur, T. & Matsui, K. (1997). The Asia–Pacific Migratory Waterbird Conservation Strategy: 1996–2000—an international cooperative framework for the conservation of a common resource. pp 57–66, in (J. van Vessem, ed.) Determining priorities for waterbird and wetland conservation. Wetlands International, Kuala Lumpur, Malaysia.

Mundkur, T., Carr, P., Sun Hean & Chhim Somean, (1995). Surveys for Large Waterbirds in Cambodia, March–April 1994. IUCN Species Survival Commission. Gland, Switzerland, and Cambridge, UK.

Munteanu, D. (1998). The Status of Birds in Romania. Romanian Ornithological Society, Cluj–Napoca, Romania.

Munteanu, D. & Ranner, A. (1997). Great White Egret. pp 48–49, in (E.J.M. Hagemeijer and M.J. Blair, eds.) The European Bird Common Census Atlas of European Breeding Birds. Their distribution and abundance. Poyser, London.

Munteanu, D. & Toniuc, N. (1992). The present and future state of the Danube delta. pp 43–46, in (C.M. Finlayson, G.E. Hollis and T.J. Davis, eds.). Managing Mediterranean Wetlands and their birds. IWRB Special Publication No. 20, Slimbridge, UK.

Murphy, W.L. (1992). Notes on the occurrence of the Little Egret (*Egretta garzetta*) in the Americas, with references to other palearctic vagrants. *Colonial Waterbirds* **15**: 113–123.

Murphy, W.L. & Nanan, W. (1987). First confirmed record of the Western Reef Heron, *Egretta gularis*. New record for South America. *American Birds* **41**: 392–394.

Musi, F., Perco, F. & Utmar, P. (1992). Loss, restoration and management of wetlands in Friuli–Venezia Giulia, north eastern Italy. pp 253–257, in (M. Finlayson, G.E. Hollis and T. Davis, eds) Managing Mediterranean wetlands and their birds. IWRB Special Publication 20. Slimbridge, UK.

Mwenya, A.N. (1973). Ornithological notes from southeast of Lake Bangweulu. *Puku* **7**: 151–161.

Myers, J.P. (1981). A test of three hypotheses for latitudinal segregation of the sexes in wintering birds. *Canadian Journal of Zoology* **59**: 1527–1534.

Myers, J.P. (1993). Facts, inferences, and shameless speculations. *American Birds* **47**: 199–201.

Myers, J.P., Morrison, R.I.G., Antas, P.T.Z. et al. (1987). The Western Hemisphere Shorebird Reserve Network. *Wader Study Group Bulletin* **49**: 122–124.

Myers, N. (1993). Gaia: an atlas of planet management. Anchor Books, New York.

Nabhitabhata, J. & Somrang, V. (1986). Threats to migratory birds along the Inner Gulf Coast of Thailand. *Tigerpaper* **13(4)**: 22–23.

Naggiar, M. (1974). Man versus birds. *Florida Wildlife* **27**: 2–5.

Naik, R.M. & Parasharya, B.M. (1987). Impact of the food availability, nesting habitat destruction and regional cultural variation of human settlements on the nesting distribution of a coastal bird, *Egretta gularis. Journal of the Bombay Natural History Society* **84**: 350–360.

Nameer, P.O. (1993). Conserving the Kole Wetlands. A potential Ramsar site from Southern India. pp 105–110, in (A. Verghese, S. Sridhar and A.K. Chakravarthy, eds.) Bird conservation strategies for the nineties and beyond. Ornithological Society of India, Bangalore.

Naranjo, L.G. (1986). Colombia. pp 132–159, in (D.A. Scott and M. Carbonell, compilers) A directory of neotropical wetlands. IUCN and IWRB, Slimbridge, UK.

Narosky, T. & Yzurieta, D. (1987). Guía para la identificación de las aves de Argentina y Uruguay. Asociación Ornitológica del Plata, Buenos Aires, Argentina.

Narusue, M. (1992). Changes in the distribution and extent of breeding colonies of egrets in Saitama Prefecture. *Strix* **11**: 189–209. (In Japanese, English summary.)

Narusue, M. & Uchida, H. (1993). The effect of structural changes of paddy fields on foraging egrets. *Strix* **12**: 121–130. (In Japanese, English summary.)

Nassar, J.R., Zwank, P.J., Hayden, D.C. & Huner, J.V. (1991). Multiple-use impoundments for attracting waterfowl and producing crawfish. U.S. Department Interior, Fish and Wildlife Service, National Wetlands Research Center, Slidell, Louisiana.

National Wetland Working Group (1988). Wetlands of Canada. Ecological Class. Series No. 24, Supply and Service-Canada, Ottawa.

Nazirides, T., Jerrentrup, H. & Crivelli, A.J. (1992). Wintering herons in Greece (1964–1990). pp 73–75, in (C.M. Finlayson, G.E. Hollis and T.J. Davis, eds.) Managing Mediterranean wetlands and their birds. IWRB Special Publication No. 20, Slimbridge, UK.

Nettleship, D.N. & Duffy, D.C. (eds). (1995). The Double-crested Cormorant: biology, conservation and management. *Colonial Waterbirds* **18** (Special Issue 1).

New South Wales National Parks and Wildlife Act 1974. Schedule 12, (Gazettal Date 18 December 1992). NSW National Parks and Wildlife Service, Hurstville, New South Wales, Australia.

Newton, I., Wyllie, I. & Asher, A. (1993). Long-term trends in organochlorine and mercury residues in predatory birds in Britain. *Environmental Pollution* **79**: 143–151.

Newton, I., Wyllie, I. & Asher, A. (1994). Pollutants in Great Britain. *British Birds* **87**: 22–25.

Nichols, J.D. (1991). Extensive monitoring programmes viewed as long-term population studies: the case of North American waterfowl. *Ibis* **133** (supplement I): 89–98.

Nichols, J.D. (1992). Capture–recapture methods. *BioScience* **42**: 94–102.

Nicholson, E.M. (1929). Report of the British birds census of heronries (1928). *British Birds* **22**: 269–232, 333–372.

Nikolaus, G. (1992). Palearctic Cattle Egret *Bubulcus ibis* wintering in tropical Africa; the first ringing recovery. *Scopus* **15**: 135–136.

Nilsson, G. (1981). The bird business: A study of the commercial cage bird trade, 2nd edn. Animal Welfare Institute. Washington, DC.

Nilsson, S.G. & Nilsson I.N., (1976). Numbers, food consumption, and fish predation by birds in Lake Möckeln, southern Sweden. *Ornis Scandinavica* **7**: 61–70.

Nims, R.A. (1987). Accumulation of mercury, cadmium, and selenium in eggs and young of Great Blue Herons. Masters thesis, Ohio State University, Columbus, Ohio.

Nisbet, I.C.T. (1980). Effects of toxic pollutants on productivity in colonial waterbirds. *Transactions of the Linnaean Society of New York* **9**: 103–113.

Nores, M. (1986). Argentina. pp. 1–38, in (D.A. Scott and M. Carbonell, compilers) A directory of neotropical wetlands. IUCN and IWRB, Slimbridge, UK.

Norman, D.M., Breault, A.M. & Moul, I.E. (1989). Bald Eagle incursions and predation at Great Blue Heron Colonies. *Colonial Waterbirds* **12**: 215–217.

Norman, F.I. & Corrick, A.H. (1988). Wetlands in Victoria: A brief review. In (A.J. McComb and P.S. Lake, eds.) The conservation of Australian wetlands. Surrey Beatty and Sons, New South Wales, Australia.

North, M.E.W. (1963). Breeding of the Black-headed Heron at Nairobi, Kenya. *Journal of the East Africa Natural History Society* **106**: 33–63.

North, P.M. (1979). Relating Grey Heron survival rates to winter weather conditions. *Bird Study* **26**: 23–28.

North, P.M. & Morgan, B.J.T. (1979). Modeling heron survival during winter using weather data. *Biometrics* **35**: 667–681.

Norton, S.P.W. (1922). Bird notes from Boree. *Emu* **22**: 39–44.

Nosek, J.A. & Faber, R.A. (1984). Polychlorinated biphenyls and organochlorine insecticides in Great Blue Heron and Great Egret eggs from the upper Mississippi River. pp 241–259, in (J.G. Wiener, R.V. Anderson, and D.R. McConville, eds.) Contaminants in the Upper Mississippi River. Proceedings of the 15th Annual Meeting of the Mississippi River Consortium. Butterworth Publishers, Stonehaven, MA, USA.

O'Brien, R.D. (1967). Insecticides: action and metabolism. Academic Press, New York and London.

Ogden, J.C. (1978). Recent population trends of colonial wading birds on the Atlantic and Gulf coastal plains. pp 135–153, in (A Sprunt, IV, J.C. Ogden, and S. Winckler, eds.) Wading birds Research Report Number 7, National Audubon Society, New York.

Ogden, J.C. (1994). A comparison of wading bird nesting colony dynamics (1931–1946 and 1974–1989) as an indication of ecosystem conditions in the southern Everglades. pp 22/1–22/38, in (S.M. Davis and J.C. Ogden, eds.) Everglades: The ecosystem and its restoration. St. Lucie Press. Delray Beach, Florida.

Ogden, J.C., McCrimmon, D.A., Jr., Bancroft, G.T. & Patty, B. (1987). Breeding populations of the Wood Stork in the southeastern United States. *Condor* **89**: 752–759.

Ogilvie-Grant, W.R. 1899. On new birds from the interior of Hainan. *Ibis* **7**.

Ohlendorf, H.M. (1989). Bioaccumulation and effects of selenium in wildlife. pp 133–177, in (L.W. Jacobs, ed.) Selenium in agriculture and the environment. Soil Science Society of America and American Society of Agronomy. SSSA Special Publication 23, Madison, Wisconsin.

Ohlendorf, H.M. (1993). Marine birds and trace elements in the temperate North Pacific. pp 232–240, in (K. Vermeer, K.T. Briggs, K.H. Morgan, and D. Siegal-Causey, eds.) The status, ecology, and conservation of marine birds of the North Pacific. Special Publication, Canadian Wildlife Service, Ottawa.

Ohlendorf, H.M. & Marois, K.C. (1990). Organochlorines and selenium in Califonia night-heron and egret eggs. *Environmental Monitoring and Assessment* **15**: 91–104.

Ohlendorf, H.M., Klaas, E.E. & Kaiser, T.E. (1974). Environmental pollution in relation to estuarine birds. pp 53–81, in (M.A.Q. Khan and J.P. Bederka, eds.) Survival in toxic environments. Academic Press, New York.

Ohlendorf, H.M., Klaas, E.E. & Kaiser, T.E. (1978a). Environmental pollutants and eggshell thinning in the Black-crowned Night-Heron. pp 63–82, in (A. Sprunt IV, J.C. Ogden, and S. Winckler, eds.) Wading birds. National Audubon Society Research Report Number 7, New York.

Ohlendorf, H.M., Risebrough, R.W. & Vermeer, K. (1978b). Exposure of marine birds to environmental pollutants. United States Fish and Wildlife Service, Wildlife Research Report 9, Washington, DC.

Ohlendorf, H.M., Klaas, E.E. & Kaiser, T.E. (1979a). Environmental pollutants and eggshell thickness: Anhingas and wading birds in the eastern United States. United States Fish and Wildlife Service Special Scientific Report—Wildlife 216, Washington, DC.

Ohlendorf, H.M., Elder, J.B., Stendell, R.C., Hensler, G.L. & Johnson, R.W. (1979b). Organochlorine residues in young herons from the upper Mississippi River—1976. *Pesticides Monitoring Journal* **13**: 115–119.

Ohlendorf, H.M., Swineford, D.M. & Locke, L.N. (1981). Organochlorine residues and mortality of herons. *Pesticides Monitoring Journal* **14**: 125–135.

Ohlendorf, H.M., Custer, T.W., Lowe, R.W., Rigney, M. & Cromartie, E. (1988). Organochlorines and mercury in eggs of coastal terns and herons in California, USA. *Colonial Waterbirds* **11**: 85–94.

Olesen, N.J. & Vestergaard Jorgensen, P.E. (1982). Can and do herons serve as vectors for Egtved virus? *Bulletin European Association Fish Pathology* **3**: 48.

Olmos, F. (1988). A new record of the Streaked Bittern from northeastern Brazil. *Wilson Bulletin* **100**: 510–511.

Oren, D.C. & de Albuquerque, H.G. (1991). Priority areas for new avian collections in Brazilian Amazonia. *Goeldiana Zoology* No. 6.

Ortiz, F. (1986). Ecuador. pp 160–181, in (D.A. Scott and M. Carbonell, compilers) A directory of neotropical wetlands. IUCN and IWRB, Slimbridge, UK.

Osborn, R.G. & Custer, T.W. (1978). Herons and their allies: atlas of Atlantic coast colonies: 1975 and 1976. US Fish and Wildlife Service FWS/OBS—77/08.

Osborne, P.L. (1989). Papua-New Guinea, Introduction. pp 1111–1119, in (D.A. Scott, ed.) A directory of Asian wetlands. International Union for Conservation of Nature, Gland, Switzerland.

Osieck, E.R. (1982). Afweer van aalscholvers op de viswekerij Lelystad; onderzoek 1982. Utrecht, Straatbosbeheer.

Owen, K.L. & Sell, M.G. (1985). The birds of Waimea Inlet. *Notornis* **32**: 271–309.

Padovani, C.R., Forsber, B.R. & Pimentel, T.P. (1995). Contaminação mercurial em peixes do Rio Madeira: Resultados e recomendações para consumo humano. *Acta Amazonica* **25**: 127–136.

Pakenham, R.H.W. (1979). The birds of Zanzibar and Pemba. BOU check-list No. 2. British Ornithologists' Union, London, UK.

Paleologou, E. & Salathé, T. (1993). European Community Instruments for Wetland Conservation: an Overview of the European Community Legal and Financial Instruments Available for Wetland Conservation. Report XI/061/94. Commission of the European Communities, DG XI.B.2. Brussels, Belgium.

Palmer, R.S. (ed) (1962). Handbook of North American birds. Vol 1. Yale University Press. London.

Paran, Y. & Shulter, P. (1981). The diurnal mass migration of the Little Bittern. *Sandgrouse* **1**: 93–94.

Parasharya, B.M. & Naik, R.M. (1988). Breeding biology of the Indian Reef Heron. *Journal of the Bombay Natural History Society* **85**: 251–262.

Parish, D. & Howes, J.R. (1990). Waterbird hunting and management in S.E. Asia. IWRB Special Publication No **2**: 128–131.

Parker, S.A., Eckert, H.J., Ragless, G.B., Cox, J.B. & Reid, N.H.C. (1979). An annotated checklist of the birds of South Australia. Part **1**: Emus and spoonbills. South Australian Ornithological Association, Adelaide.

Parker, T.A. III, Parker, S.A. & Plenge, M.A. (1982). An annotated checklist of Peruvian birds. Buteo Books, Vermillion, USA.

Parkes, K. (1998). First record of the Great Blue Heron in Brazil. *Colonial Waterbirds* **21**: 89–90.

Parkes, K.C. (1974). Buller's New Zealand specimen of Grey Heron. *Notornis* **21**: 121–123.

Parkhurst, J.A., Brooks, R.P. & Arnold, D.E. (1987). A survey of wildlife depredation and control techniques at fish rearing facilities. *Wildlife Society Bulletin* **15**: 386–394.

Parnell, J.F., Ainley, D.G., Blokpoel, H., Cain, B., Custer, T.W., Dusi, J.L., Kress, S., Kushlan, J.A., Southern, W.E., Stenzel, L.E., & Thompson, B.C. (1988). Colonial Waterbird Management in North America. *Colonial Waterbirds* **11**: 129–169.

Parnell. J.F., Golder, G.W., Shield, M.A., Quay, T.L., & Henson, T.M. (1997). Changes in nesting populations of colonial waterbirds in coastal North Carolina, 1900–1995. *Colonial Waterbirds* **20**: 458–469.

Parr, J.W.K., Eames, J., Sun Hean, Chamnan Hong, Som Han, Vi La Pich, & Kim Hout Seng. (1996). Biological and Socio-economic aspects of waterbird exploitation and natural resource utilization at Prek Toal, Tonle Sap Lake, Cambodia. IUCN Species Survival Commission, IUCN, Bangkok, Thailand.

Parsons, K.C. (1994). The Arthur Kill oil spills: biological effects to birds. pp 215–237, in (J. Burger, ed.) Before and after an oil spill: The Arthur Kill. Rutgers University Press, New Brunswick, NJ, USA.

Parsons, K.C. & Burger, J. (1982). Human disturbance and nestling behavior in Black-crowned Night Herons. *Condor* **84**: 184–187.

Paspaleva, M., Kiss, M. & Talpeanu, M. (1985). Les oiseaux coloniaux dans le Delta du Danube. *Travaux du Museum d'Histoire Naturelle Grigore Antipa (République Socialiste de Roumanie)* **27**: 289–304.

Patrekeev, M.V. (1993). Most important areas for waterfowl in Azerbaijan, Eastern Transcaucasus (excluding Kizil Agach Bays or Kirov Bays). pp 78–79, in (M. Moser and J. Van Vessem, eds.) Wetlands and waterfowl conservation in south and west Asia. IWRB Special Publication 25/AWB Publication 85, Slimbridge, UK and Kuala Lumpur, Malaysia.

Patterson, I. J. (1965). Timing and spacing of broods in the Black Headed Gull *Larus ridibundus. Ibis* **107**: 433–459.

Paul, R.T. (1991). Status report, *Egretta rufescens* (Gmelin), Reddish Egret. Unpublished Report, US Fish and Wildlife Service, Albuquerque, New Mexico.

Paz, U. (1986). Plants and Animals of the Land of Israel, an illustrated Encyclopedia. Volume 6, Birds. Ministry of Defence and the Society for Protection of Nature. (In Hebrew, translation of text on herons by Ashkenazi, pers. comm.).

Paz, U. (1987). The birds of Israel. The Stephen Greene Press. Lexington, MA, USA.

Peakall, D.B. (1975). Physiological effects of chlorinated hydrocarbons on avian species. pp 343–360, in (R. Hague and V.H. Freed, eds.) Environmental dynamics of pesticides. Plenum Press, New York.

Peakall, D.B. (1976). Organochlorine residue levels in herons and raptors in the Transvaal. *Ostrich* **47**: 139–141.

Pei, X-M., Wang, L. & Wang, K. (1994). An investigation on herons at Lushun Kou area. In Waterbird Specialist Group of the Chinese Ornithological Association. Waterbird research in China. East China Normal University Press, Beijing.

Penny, M. (1974). The birds of Seychelles. Collins, London.

Penot, J. (1963). Rapport ornithologique (Camargue) pour 1960 et 1961. *Terre et Vie* **17**: 280–288.

Percy, W. (1951). Three studies in bird character. *Country-Life*. London.

Perennou, C. (1986). Haro sur le Héron. Etude de deux causes de mortalité en pisciculture, en particulier de la prédation par le Héron cendré. *Aqua Revue* **4**: 29–30.

Perennou, C. (1990). Peuplements d'oiseaux d'eau en milieu anthropisé: un exemple. Les plaines de la Côte de Coromandel (Inde du Sud-est). Unpublished Ph.D. thesis, Université Lyon-I, Lyon, France.

Perennou, C. (1991). African waterfowl census. IWRB. Slimbridge, UK.

Perennou, C. (1992). African waterfowl census. IWRB. Slimbridge, UK.

Perennou, C., Mundkur, T., Scott, D.A., Follestad, A. & Kvenild, L. (1994). The Asian waterfowl census 1987–91: Distribution and status of Asian waterfowl. AWB Publication No. 86. IWRB Special Publication No. 24. AWB, Kuala Lumpur, Malaysia and IWRB, Slimbridge, UK.

Peris, S.J. & Alabarce, E. (1991). La avifauna postreproductora de los pastizales de altura (Tafí del Valle, sierra del Aconquija, Tucumán). *Acta Zoológica Lilloana* **40**: 125–133.

Perry, A.S., Sidis, I. & Zemach, A. (1990). Organochlorine insecticide residues in birds and bird eggs in the coastal plain of Israel. *Bulletin of Environmental Contamination and Toxicology* **45**: 523–530.

Peter, J.M. (1995). The Eastern Reef Egret in Victoria and Tasmania: Past and present. *Australian Bird Watcher* **16**: 120–125.

Peterjohn, B.G. & Sauer, J.R. (1993). North American breeding birds survey annual summary, 1990–91. *Bird Populations* **1**: 1–15.

Peters, F. & Neukirch, M. (1986). Transmission of some fish pathogenic viruses by the heron (*Ardea cinerea*). *Journal Fish Diseases* **9**: 539–544.

Peterson, R.T. & Fisher, J. (1955). Wild America. The Riverside Press, Cambridge, MA, USA.

Pineau, O. (1992). Key wetlands for the conservation of Little Egrets breeding in the Camargue. pp 210–214, in (C.M. Finlayson, G.E. Hollis, and T.J. Davis, eds.) Managing Mediterranean wetlands and their birds. IWRB Special Publication No. 20, Slimbridge, UK.

Pineau, O., Hafner, H. & Kayser, Y. (1992). Influence of capture and wing-tagging on the Little Egret (*Egretta garzetta*) during the breeding season. *Revue d'Ecologie (Terre Vie)* **47**: 199–204.

Pinkington, C. (ed.). (1981). 99% heron-proof. *Salmonid* **5**: 16–17.

Pinowski, J., Morales, L.G., Pacheco, J., Dobrowolski, K.A. & Pinowska, B. (1980). Estimation of the food consumption of fish-eating birds in the seasonally-flooded savannas (Llanos) of Alto Apure, Venezuela. *Bulletin Académie Polonaise des Sciences* (sér. sci. biol. cl.2) **28**: 163–170.

Plenge, M.A., Parker, T.A. III, Hughes, R.A. & O'Neill, J.P. (1989). Additional notes on the distribution of birds in West-Central Peru. *Le Gerfaut* **79**: 55–68.

Pollock, K.H. & Kendall, W.L. (1987). Visibility bias in aerial surveys: a review of estimation procedures. *Journal of Wildlife Management* **51**: 502–510.

Pons L.J. (1992). Reed exploitation. pp 37–40, in IUCN Environmental Status Reports **4**: Conservation Status of the Danube Delta. Page Brothers. Norwich, UK.

Poole, C.M., Park, J.Y. and Moores, N. (1999). The identification of Chinese Egret and Pacific Reef Egret. *Oriental Bird Club Bulletin* **30**: 39–41.

Poorter, E. (1981). De Zilverreigers van de Oostvaardersplassen. *De Lepelaar*, **66**: 23–24.

Portnoy, J.W. (1977). Nesting colonies of seabirds and wading birds—coastal Louisiana, Mississippi, and Alabama. US Fish and Wildlife Service FWS/OBS-77/07. Washington DC.

Pough, R.H. (1941). The fish-eating bird problem at the fish hatcheries of the north-east. *Transactions North American Wildlife Conference* **5**: 203–206.

Pouteau, C., Franchimont, J. & Sayad, A. (1992). Chronique ornithologique du G.O.MA.C. pour 1991. *Porphyrio* **4**: 39–117.

Powell, G.V.N. (1983). Food availability and reproduction by Great White Herons, *Ardea herodias*: A food addition study. *Colonial Waterbirds* **6**: 139–147.

Powell, G.V.N. & Powell, A.H. (1986). Reproduction by Great White Herons *Ardea herodius* in Florida Bay as an indicator of habitat quality. *Biological Conservation* **36**: 101–113.

Powell, G.V.N., Bjork, R.D., Ogden, J.C., Paul, R.T., Powell, A.H. & Robertson, W.B. Jr. (1989). Population trends in some Florida Bay wading birds. *Wilson Bulletin* **101**: 436–457.

Pratt, E. (1979). The growth of a Cattle Egret colony. *Notornis* **26**: 353–356.

Prentice, C. (1993). Degradation of the Mesopotamian marshes, Iraq. *IWRB News* **10**: 10–11.

Prentice, R.C. & Jaensch, R.P. (1997). Development policies, plans and wetlands. Proceedings of workshop 1 of the International Conference on Wetlands and Development. Wetlands International, Kuala Lumpur, Malaysia.

Pressey, R.L. (1981). A survey of the wetlands on the lower Hunter floodplain, New South Wales. National Parks and Wildlife Service, Sydney, New South Wales, Australia.

Pressey, R.L. (1985). Some problems with wetland evaluation. *Wetlands Australia* **5**: 42–51.

Pressey, R.L. (1986). Wetlands of the River Murray. Australia: River Murray Commission Environmental Report 86/1.

Pressey, R.L. & Harris, J.H. (1988). Wetlands of New South Wales. pp 35–37, in (A.J. McComb and P.S. Lake, eds.) The conservation of Australian wetlands. Surrey Beatty and Sons, New South Wales, Australia.

Prestt, I. (1970a). The heron *Ardea cinerea* and pollution. *Ibis* **112**: 147–148.

Prestt, I. (1970b). Organochlorine Pollution of Rivers and the Heron (*Ardea cinerea* L.). *Proceedings of the Technical Meeting of the International Union for Conservation of Nature and Natural Resources*, **11**: 95–102.

Prévost, J. & Mougin, J.L. (1970). Guide des oiseaux et mammifères des Terres Australes et Antarctiques Francais, guides natur., Deachaux et Niestlé, Neuchâtel, Switzerland.

Price, I.M. (1977). Environmental contaminants in relation to Canadian wildlife. *Transactions of the North American Wildlife and Natural Resources Conference* **42**: 382–396.

Price, I.M. & Nickum, J.G. (1993). Aquaculture and birds: the context for controversy. pp 6–18, in (J.V. Huner, ed.) Management of fish eating birds on fish farms: a symposium, Dec, 1993, University of Southwestern Louisiana, Lafayette, Louisiana, USA.

Procam-Inderena. (1986). Colombia: fauna en peligro. Procam-Inderena, Bogotá, Colombia.

Pullin, B.R. (1987). Restoring great egrets to the Tennessee Valley. Proceedings of Southeastern Nongame and Endangered Species Symposium, Athens, Georgia, USA.

Pycraft, W.P. (1934). Economic ornithology. Royal Society for the Protection of Birds. London, UK.

Quinney, T.E. (1983). Comparison of Great Blue Heron, *Ardea herodias*, reproduction at Boot Island and other Nova Scotia colonies. *Canadian Field Naturalist* **97**: 275–278.

Quinney, T.E. & Smith, P.C. (1980). Comparative foraging behavior and efficiency of adult and juvenile Great Blue Herons. *Canadian Journal Zoology* **58**: 1168–1173.

Rabarisoa, R.G.M. (1993). Recensement des oiseaux d'eau dans les lacs Antsalova. *Newsletter of Working Group on Birds in the Madagascar Region*. Vol 3 (I).

Raffaele, H.A. (1983). A guide to the birds of Puerto Rico and the Virgin Islands. Fondo Educativo Interamaericano, San Juan, Puerto Rico.

Raffaele, H.A., Wiley, J., Garrido, O., Keith, A. & Raffaele, J. (1998). A guide to the birds of the West Indies. Princeton University Press, Princeton, New Jersey.

Ralls, K. & Ballou, J. (1986). Captive breeding programs for populations with a small number of founders. *Trends in Ecology and Evolution* **1**: 19–22.

Ramadan-Jaradi, G. (1988). Notes on some breeding birds of the United Arab Emirates. *Sandgrouse* **10**: 81–84.

Ramesh, A., Tanabe, S., Kannan, K., Subramanian, A.N., Kumaran, P.L. & Tatsukawa, R. (1992). Characteristic trends of persistent organochlorine contamination in wildlife from a tropical agricultural watershed, South India. *Archives of Environmental Contamination and Toxicology* **23**: 26–36.

Ramo, C. & Busto, B. (1982). Notes on the breeding of the Chestnut-bellied Heron (*Agamia agami*) in Venezuela. *Auk* **99**: 784.

Ramo, C. & Busto, B. (1993). Resource use by herons in a Yucatan wetland during the breeding season. *Wilson Bulletin* **105**: 573–586.

Ramsamujh, B. (1990). Status and conservation of the Scarlet Ibis in Guyana. pp 95–99, in (P.C. Frederick, L.G. Morales, A.L. Spaans and C.S. Luthin, eds.). The Scarlet Ibis (*Eudocimus ruber*): Status, conservation and recent research. International Waterfowl and Wetlands Research Bureau, Slimbridge, UK.

Ramsar Convention. (1996a). Recommendation 6.17.4. Resolutions and recommendations. Gland, Switzerland.

Ramsar Convention. (1996b). Recommendation 6.13. Resolutions and recommendations. Gland, Switzerland.

Ramsar Convention Bureau. (1998). List of wetlands of international importance designated by contracting parties. Unpubl. Switzerland.

Ramsay, E.P. (1878). *Proceedings of Linnaean Society: N.S.W.* **2**: 177–212. Sydney, Australia.

Ramsay, E.P. (1888). Tabular list of all the Australian birds at present known to the author over the continent of Australia and adjacent islands. The Author, Sydney, Australia.

Rand, A.L. & Rabor, D.S. (1960). Birds from the Philippine Islands: Siquijor, Mt. Malindang, Bohol and Samar. *Fieldiana Zoologica* **35**: 221–441.

Randall, R. (1975). Deathtraps for birds. *Defenders Wildlife* **50**: 35–38.

Randall, R. (1988). The Ardeidae at the Xaxaba reed-bed. *Babbler* **15**: 31–32.

Randall, R. (1990). Herons and egrets roosting at the Xaxaba reed-bed. *Babbler* **19**: 14–15.

Randall, R. & Herremans, M. (1994). Breeding of the Slaty Egret *Egretta vinaceigula* along the Boro River in the central Okavango Delta (Botswana). *Ostrich* **65**: 39–43.

Ranftl, H., & Zur Mühlen, P. (1976). Graureiher *Ardea cinerea* und Fischereivorläufige Versuchsergebnisse. *Berichte Deutschen Sektion Internationales Rates Vogelschutz* **16**: 69–74.

Ransom, K. & Beveridge, M. (1983). Raiders from the skies. *Fish Farmer* **6**: 22–23.

Ratcliffe, D.A. (1967). Decrease in eggshell weight in certain birds of prey. *Nature* **215**: 208–210.

Ratnam, L., Abdul, J., Gombek, F. & Hawa, S. (1989). Aspects of the demography and reproduction of the Night Heron at Sungai Burung. pp 144–149, in (D. Parish and R.C. Prentice, eds.) Wetland and waterfowl conservation in Asia. Asian Wetland Bureau, Kuala Lumpur, Malaysia.

Rattner, B.A., Hoffman, D.J. & Marn, C.M. (1989). Use of mixed-function oxygenases to monitor contaminant exposure in wildlife. *Environmental Toxicology and Chemistry* **8**: 1093–1102.

Rattner, B.A., Hatfield, J.S., Melancon, M.J., Custer, T.W. & Tillitt, D.E. (1994). Relation among cytochrome P450, AH-active PCB congeners and dioxin-equivalents in pipping Black-crowned Night-Heron embryos. *Environmental Toxicology and Chemistry* **13**: 1805–1812.

Rattner, B.A., Melancon, M.J., Custer, T.W. & Hothem, R.L. (1996). Cytochrome P450 and contaminant burdens in nestling black-crowned night-herons and their interrelation with sibling embryos. *Environmental Toxicology and Chemistry* **15**: 715–721.

Rattner, B.A., Melancon, M.J., Rice, C.P., Riley, W. Jr., Eiseman, J. & Hines, R.K. (1997). Cytochrome P450 and organochlorine contaminants in Black-crowned Night Herons from the Chesapeake Bay Region, USA. *Environmental Toxicology and Chemistry* **16**: 2315–2322.

Rattner, B.A., Melancon, M.J., Custer, T.W. et al. (1993). Biomonitoring environmental contamination with pipping Black-crowned Night-Heron embryos: Induction of Cytochrome P450. *Environmental Toxicology and Chemistry* **12**: 1719–1732.

Recher, H.F. & Recher, J.A. (1969). Comparative foraging efficiency of adult and immature Little Blue Herons (*Egretta caerulea*). *Animal Behavior* **17**: 320–322.

Recher, H.F. & Recher, J.A. (1980). Why are there different kinds of herons? *Transactions of the Linnaean Society of New York* **9**: 135–158.

Recher, H.F., Holmes, R.T., Davis, W.E. Jr. & Morton, S. (1983). Foraging behaviour of Australian herons. *Colonial Waterbirds* **6**: 1–10.

Recovery Roundup. (1985a). Eastern Reef Egret. *Corella* **9(1)**: 33.

Recovery Roundup. (1985b). Rufous Night Heron. *Corella* **9(1)**: 33.

Recovery Roundup. (1985c). Rufous Night Heron. *Corella* **9(2)**: 67.

Recovery Roundup. (1986). Rufous Night Heron. *Corella* **10(2)**: 67.

Recovery Roundup. (1989). Rufous Night Heron. *Corella* **13(1)**: 27.

Recovery Roundup. (1991). Eastern Reef Egret. *Corella* **15(5)**: 152.

Reichholf, J. (1982). Erste Auswirkungen der neuen Schusszeit auf Graureiher *Ardea cinerea*. *Anzeiger der Ornithologischen Gesellschaft Bayern* **21**: 97–100.

Remsen, J.V. Jr. (1986). Aves de una localidad en la sabana húmeda del norte de Bolivia. *Ecología en Bolivia* **8**: 21–35.

Reynolds, C.M. (1979). The heronries census 1972–1977: population changes and a review. *Bird Study* **26**: 7–12.

Rhoades, D.D. & Duke, G.E. (1975). Gastric function in a captive American Bittern. *Auk* **92**: 786–792.

Riddell, W.H. (1944). The Buff-backed Heron, *Ardeola ibis ibis* (Linnaeus). *Ibis* **86**: 503–511.

Ridgely, R.S. & Gwynne, J.A. (1989). A guide to the birds of Panama (Second Edition), Princeton, New Jersey, U.S.A.

Ridgely, R.S. & Gwynne, J.A. (1993). Guía de las aves de Panamá. Asociación Nacional para la Conservación de la Naturaleza. Ciudad de Panamá, Panamá.

Riggert, T.L. (1974). Man and nature: Conservation of wetland areas. A.C.W.W. Triennial Conference, Perth, Western Australia.

Riggert, T.E., Lindgren, E. & Slater, P. (1965). Breeding of White-necked Heron in the southwest. *West Australian Naturalist* **10**: 20.

Risberg, L. (1990). Sveridges faglar. *Var Fagelvärld*, supplement 14, Stockholm, Sweden.

Risebrough, R.W. (1986). Pesticides and bird populations. *Current Ornithology* **3**: 397–427.

Risebrough, R.W. (1991). Indicator species, birds, toxic contaminants, and global change. pp 2480–2486, in (B.D. Bell (convener), R.V. Cossee, J.E.C. Flux, B.D. Heather, R.A. Hitchmough, C.J.R. Robertson, and M.J. Wiliams (eds.) Proceedings of the 20th International Ornithological Congress. Christchurch, New Zealand.

Risley, C. & Blokpoel, H. (1984). Evaluation of effectiveness of bird-scaring operations at a sanitary landfill site near CFB Trenton, Ontario, Canada. pp 265–274, in Proceedings Wildlife hazards to aircraft conference and training workshop. Federal Aviation Administration, Charleston, South Carolina, USA.

Robbins, C.S., Bystrak, D. & Geissler, P.H. (1986). The breeding birds survey: its first fifteen years, 1965–1979. US Fish and Wildlife Service Research Publication 157. Washington, DC.

Robbins, M.B., Capparella, A.P., Ridgely, R.S. & Cardiff, S.W. (1991). Avifauna of the Río Manití and Quebrada Vainilla, Peru. *Proceedings of the Academy of Natural Sciences of Philadelphia* **143**: 145–159.

Roberts, T.J. (1991). The birds of Pakistan. Vol. 1. Oxford University Press, Oxford.

Robson, C.R. (1989). Recent reports. *Oriental Bird Club Bull.* 9 June 1989: 38–44.

Robson, C.R. (1992). Recent reports. *Oriental Bird Club Bull.* 10 November 1989: 41–44.

Robson, C.R., Eames, J.C., Wolstencroft, J.A., Nguyen Chu and Truong Van La (1989). Recent records of birds from Viet Nam. *Forktail* **5**: 71–97.

Rodgers, J.A. Jr. (1997). Pesticide and heavy metal levels of waterbirds in the Everglades agricultural area of south Florida. *Florida Field Naturalist* **25**: 33–41.

Rodgers, J.A. & Smith, H.T. (1995). Set-back distances to protect nesting bird colonies from human disturbance in Florida. *Conservation Biology* **9**: 89–99.

Rodgers, J.A., Linda, S.B. & Nesbitt, S.A. (1995). Comparing aerial estimates with ground counts of nests in Wood Stork colonies. *Journal of Wildlife Management* **59**: 656–666.

Root, T. (1988). Atlas of wintering North American birds, an analysis of Christmas Bird Count data. University of Chicago Press, Chicago.

Rooth, J. & Jonkers, D.A. (1972). *TNO—News* **27**: 551–555.

Rose, P.M. & Scott, D.A. (1994). Waterfowl population estimates. International Waterfowl and Wetlands Research Bureau, IWRB Publication 29. Slimbridge, UK.

Rose P.M. & Scott, D.A. (1997). Waterfowl population estimates. Wetlands International Publication 44. Slimbridge, UK.

Ross, G. & Armstrong, J.B. (1993). Foraging characteristics of wading birds on commercial catfish ponds. pp 36–38, in (J.V. Huner, ed.) Management of fish eating birds on fish farms: a symposium. University of Southwestern Louisiana, Lafayette, Louisiana, USA.

Ross, P.G. (1995). Wading birds consume large amount of catfish. *Catfish Journal*, June 1995: 14.

Round, P.D. (1988). Resident forest birds in Thailand: Their status and conservation. ICBP Monograph No. 2, BirdLife International, Cambridge, UK.

Roux, F. (1973). Censuses of Anatidae in the central Delta of the Niger and the Senegal Delta; January 1972. *Wildfowl* **24**: 63–80.

Roux, F. & Jarry, G. (1984). Numbers, composition and distribution of populations of Anatidae in West Africa. *Wildfowl* **35**: 48–60.

Rüger, A., Prentice, C. & Owen, M. (1986). Results of the IWRB International Waterfowl Census 1967–1983. International Waterfowl Research Bureau, Slimbridge, UK: IWRB Spec. Publ. No. 6.

Ruiz, X. (1985). An analysis of the diet of cattle egret in the Ebro Delta, Spain. *Ardea* **73**: 49–60.

Ruiz, X., Llorente, G.A. & Nadal, J. (1982). Incidence des composantes organochlorés sur la viabilite de l'oeuf du *Bubulcus ibis* dans le Delta de l'Ebre. Proceedings VIth ICSEM/IOC/UNEP Workshop on pollution of the Mediterranean, Cannes: 807–811.

Runde, D.E., Gore, J.A., Hovis, J.A., Robson, M.S. & Southall, P.D. (1991). Florida atlas of breeding sites for herons and their allies, update 1986–1989. Florida Game and Fresh Water Fish Commission, Technical Report 10, Tallahassee, Florida, USA.

Rutschke, E. (1982). Der Brutbestand des Graureihers in DDR. *Falke* **8**: 377–386.

Rutschke, E. (1985). Zur Entwicklung des Brutbestandes des Graureihers in der DDR. *Falke* **32**: 378–388.

Ryder, R.A. (1978). Breeding distribution, movements, and mortality of Snowy Egret in North America. In Wading Birds, Research Report 7, National Audubon Society, New York.

Ryder, R. A. (1979). Status, distribution, and movements of ciconiiforms in Colorado. *Proceedings of the Colonial Waterbird Group* **3**: 49–57.

Rydzewski, W. (1956). The nomadic movements and migrations of the European Common Heron. *Ardea* **44**: 71–188.

Safe, S. (1987). Determination of 2,3,7,8-TCDD toxic equivalent factors (TEFs): Support for the use of the *in vitro* AHH induction assay. *Chemosphere* **16**: 791–802.

Salim, R.V. & Jensen, R.A.C. (1992). Heron colonies in the Sultanate of Oman. *Heron Conservation Newsletter* **5**: 5.

Salmon, T.P. & Conte, F.S. (1981). Control of bird damage at aquaculture facilities. U.S. Fish Wildlife Service (475), Washington, DC.

Salvan, J. (1972). Statut, recensement, reproduction des Oiseaux dulcaquicoles aux environs de Tananarive. *L'Oiseau & Revue Française d'Ornithologie* **42**: 35–51.

Sanderson, J.T., Janz, D.M., Bellward, G.D. & Giesy, J.P. (1997). Effects of embryonic and adult exposure to 2,3,7,8-tetrachlorodibenzo-p-dioxin on hepatic microsomal testosterone hydroxylase activities in Great Blue Herons (*Ardea herodias*). *Environmental Toxicology and Chemistry* **16**: 1304–1310.

Santharam, V. (1987). The Pond Heron *Ardeola grayii*; its local movements. *Newsletter for Birdwatchers* **27(9–10)**: 4–5.

Santharam, V. (1988). Further notes on the local movements of the Pond Heron *Ardeola grayii*. *Newsletter for Birdwatchers* **28(1–2)**: 8–9.

Santos, G.M. (1995). Impactos da Hidrelétrica Samuel sobre as comunidades de peixes do Rio Jamari (Rondonia, Brasil). *Acta Amazonica* **25**: 235–280.

Sarasa, C.G., Bartolome, J., Fernandez-Cruz, M. & Farinha, J.C. (1993). Segundo censo de Ardeidas invernantes en la Peninsula Ibérica y Baleares (1992–93). *Airo* **4**: 41–50.

Scanlon, P.F., Helfrich, L.A. & Stultz, R.E. (1978). Extent and severity of avian predation at federal hatcheries in the U.S. *Proceedings of the Annual Conference of Fish and Wildlife Agencies* **32**: 407–473.

Scheuhammer, A.M. (1987). The chronic toxicity of aluminum, cadmium, mercury, and lead in birds: a review. *Environmental Pollution* **46**: 263–295.

Schiemenz, F. (1936). Fischadler, Fischreiher, Eisvögel und Fischotter in Niedersachsen und die Fischerei, insbesondere die Teichwirtschaft. *Zoologische Fischerei* **34**: 257–288.

Schlatter, R.P. & Espinosa, L.A. (1986). Chile. pp. 105–131, in (D.A. Scott and M. Carbonell, compilers) A directory of neotropical wetlands. IUCN and IWRB, Slimbridge, UK.

Schmidt, von, E. (1977). Auffallende Zunahme des Silberreihers (*Casmerodius albus*) in Ungarn im Jahre 1976. *Egretta* **20**: 68–70.

Schogolev, I.V. (1992). The Dnestr delta, Black Sea: Ornithological importance, conservation problems and management proposals. *Avocetta* **16**: 108–111.

Schulenberg, T.S., Allen, S.E., Stotz, D.F. & Wiedenfeld, D.A. (1984). Distributional records from the Cordillera Yanachaga, Central Peru. *Le Gerfaut* **74**: 57–70.

Schulz, M. (1989). Importance of wetlands of Kakadu National Park to waterbirds. Australian National Parks and Wildlife Service Report, Canberra.

Scientific Advisory Committee (1997). Final submitted recommendation on a nomination for listing: Little Bittern *Ixobrychus minutus* (Scientific Advisory Committee for Flora and Fauna Guarantee nomination no. 439). Department of Natural Resources and Environment, Melbourne, Australia.

Scott, D.A. (1980). A preliminary inventory of wetlands of international importance for waterfowl in West Europe and Northwest Africa. IWRB Special publication, Slimbridge, UK.

Scott, D.A. (1989). A directory of Asian wetlands. IUCN, Gland, Switzerland.

Scott, D.A. (1993a). A Directory of Wetlands in Oceania. International Waterfowl Research Bureau and Asian Wetlands Bureau, Kuala Lumpur, Malaysia.

Scott, D.A. (1993b). Wetlands of West Asia: a regional overview. pp 9–22, in (M. Moser and J. Van Vessem, eds.) Wetlands and waterfowl conservation in south and west Asia, IWRB Special Publication 25/AWB Publication 85, Slimbridge, UK, and Kuala Lumpur, Malaysia.

Scott, D.A. & Carbonell, M. (compilers). (1986). A directory of neotropical wetlands. IUCN and IWRB, Slimbridge, UK.

Scott, D.A. & Carp, E. (1982). A midwinter survey of wetlands in Mesopotamia, Iraq: 1979. *Sandgrouse* **4**: 60–76.

Scott, D.A. & Poole, C.M. (1989). A status overview of Asian wetlands. AWB Publication No 53, Asian Wetland Bureau, Kuala Lumpur, Malaysia.

Scott, D.A. & Rose, P.M. (1989). Asian waterfowl census 1989: Mid-winter waterfowl counts in Southern and Eastern Asia January 1989. IWRB, Slimbridge, UK.

Scott, D.A., Howes, J.R & Duc, L.D. (1989). Recommendations for management of Xuan Thuy Reserve, Red River Delta, Viet Nam. Publ. No. 44 Asian Wetland Bureau, Kuala Lumpur, Malaysia.

Sedgwick, E.H. (1953). Dispersal movement of White-necked Heron (*Notophoyx pacifica*) *Notornis* **5**: 122.

Serebryakov, V.V. & Grishchenko, V.N. (1989). [Number of colonial species of Ardea in the Ukraine in 1986] Ufa: Bashkiz (in Russian).

Servat, J. (1991). Rapport du groupe d'experts chargé d'étudier les missions et l'organisation du Parc naturel régional du Marais Poitevin. Ministère de l'Environnement, Paris.

Serventy, D.L. (1947). The birds of the Swan River District, Western Australia. *Emu* **47**: 241–286.

Serventy, D.L. (1953). The southern invasion of northern birds during 1952. *West Australian Naturalist* **3**: 177–196.

Serventy, D.L. & Whittel, H.M. (1962). Birds of Western Australia. Brokenshaw, Perth, Australia.

Seton, D.H.C. (1973). Observations on breeding of the Great-billed heron in northern Queensland. *Emu* **73**: 9–11.

Shaw, S.P. & Ferdine, C.G. (1956). Wetlands of the United States, their extent, and their value for waterfowl and other wildlife. U.S. Department of Interior, Fish and Wildlife Service, Circular 39, Washington DC.

Sheldon, F.H. & Marin, M.A. (1984). The sympatry of Night Herons in Borneo. *Bulletin of the British Ornithological Club* **105(2)**: 76–78.

Sheldon, F.H. & Slikas, B. (1997). Advances in ciconiiform systematics, 1976–1996. *Colonial Waterbirds* **20**: 106–114.

Shy, E. (1990–1996). Summaries of Mid-Winter Waterfowl census 1989–1995. Nature reserves Authority Bulletin, Israel (in Hebrew).

Shy, E. (1995). Return of waterfowl to the new Hula flooded area. Research Project reports of Hula Restoration Project 1994, MIGAL, Kiryat-Shmona, pp 84–108.

Sibley, C.G. & Monroe, B.L. Jr. (1990). Distribution and taxonomy of the birds of the world. Yale University Press, New Haven and London.

Sick, H. (1984). Ornitologia Brasileira, una Introduçao. Vol 1. Editora Universidade de Brasilia, Brasilia.

Siegel-Causey, D. & Kharitonov, S.P. (1990). The evolution of coloniality. *Current Ornithology* **7**: 285–330.

Siegfried, W.R. (1966). The status of the Cattle Egret in South Africa with notes on the neighbouring territories. *Ostrich* **37**: 157–169.

Siegfried, W.R. (1970). Mortality and dispersal of ringed Cattle Egrets. *Ostrich* **41**: 122–135.

Siegfried, W.R. (1971). Communal roosting of the Cattle egret. *Transvaal Royal Society South Africa* **39**: 419–443.

Siegfried, W.R. (1972). Food requirements and growth of Cattle Egrets in South Africa. *The Living Bird* **11**: 193–206.

Siegfried, W.R. (1988). Habitat and modern range expansion of the Cattle Egret. pp 315–324, in (A. Sprunt, J.C. Ogden, and S. Winckler, eds.) Wading birds. National Audubon Research Report 6, New York.

Silvius, M.J., Verheught, W.J.M. & Iskander, J. (1986). Coastal wetlands inventory of south-east Sumatra. Report of the Sumatran Waterbird Survey Oct.–Dec, 1984. ICBP, Cambridge, UK.

Skinner, J., Wallace, J.P., Altenburg, W. & Bouba, F. (1987). The status of heron colonies in the Inner Niger Delta, Mali. *Malimbus* **9**: 65–82.

Smith, G.J., Spann, J.W. & Hill, E.F. (1986). Cholinesterase activity in Black-crowned Night-Herons exposed to fenthion-treated water. *Archives of Environmental Contamination and Toxicology* **15**: 83–86.

Smith, G.J., Heinz, G.H., Hoffman, D.J., Spann, J.W. & Krynitsky, A.J. (1988). Reproduction in Black-crowned Night-Herons fed selenium. *Lake and Reservoir Management* **4**: 175–180.

Smith, J.P. (1995). Foraging flights and habitat use of nesting wading birds (Ciconiiformes) at Lake Okeechobee, Florida. *Colonial Waterbirds* **18**: 139–158.

Smith, P.W. & Smith, S.A. (1990). Gray Herons on Barabados. *American Birds* **44**: 1096.

Smithers, R.H.N., Irwin, M.P.S. & Paterson, M.L. (1956). A check list of the birds of Southern Rhodesia. Rhodesian Ornithological Society, Cambridge University Press, Cambridge, UK.

Smythies, B.E. (1986). The birds of Burma (3rd edn). Oliver & Boyd, Edinburgh, UK.

Sonobe, K. & Izawa, N. (1987). Endangered bird species in the Korean peninsula. Museum of Korean Nature, Korean University in Tokyo and Wild Bird Society of Japan, Tokyo.

Sonstegard, R.A. & McDermott, L.A. (1972). Epidemiological model for passive transfer of IPNV by homeotherms. *Nature* **237**: 104–105.

Southworth, A.D. (1989). Conserving southeastern coastal wetlands. pp 223–257, in (W.J. Chandler, ed.) Audubon wildlife report—1989/1990. Academic Press, New York.

Spaans, A.L. (1974a). Some bird records from Bonaire. *Ardea* **62**: 36–238.

Spaans, A.L. (1974b). Pesticide effects on fishes and birds in rice fields of Surinam, South America. *Environmental Pollution* **7**: 217–236.

Spaans, A.L. (1990). Problems in assessing trends in breeding populations of Scarlet Ibises and other ciconiiform birds. pp 1–6, in (P.C. Frederick, L.G. Morales, A.L. Spaans, and C.S. Luthin, eds.) The Scarlet Ibis (*Eudocimus ruber*): Status, conservation and recent research. IWRB, Slimbridge, UK.

Spahn, S.A. (1997). Colonial wading birds as bioindicators of food chain contamination by heavy metals and organohalogens: Relationships among tissue concentrations, growth rates and reproduction. Ph.D. dissertation, Tulane University, New Orleans, Louisiana.

Spalding, M.G. (1990). Antemortem diagnosis of eustrongylidosis in wading birds (Ciconiiformes). *Colonial Waterbirds* **13**: 75–77.

Spalding, M.G., Bjork, R.D., Powell, G.V.N. & Sundlof, S.F. (1994a). Mercury and cause of death in Great White Herons. *Journal of Wildlife Management* **58**: 735–739.

Spalding, M.G., Smith, J.P. & Forrester, D.J. (1994b). Natural and experimental infections of *Eustrongylides ignotus*: effect on growth and survival of nestling wading birds. *Auk* **111**: 328–336.

Spanier, E. (1980). The use of distress calls to repel night herons (*Nycticorax nycticorax*) from fishponds. *Journal Applied Ecology* **17**: 287–294.

Speich, S.M., Calambokidas, J., Shea, D.W., Peard, J., Witter, M. & Fry, D.M. (1992). Eggshell thinning and organochlorine contaminants in western Washington waterbirds. *Colonial Waterbirds* **15**: 103–112.

Spellerberg, I. (1991). Monitoring ecological change. Cambridge University Press, Cambridge, UK.

Spendelow, J.A. & Patton, S.R. (1988). National atlas of coastal waterbird colonies in the contiguous United States: 1976–82. US Fish Wildlife Service Biological Report 88(5). Washington, DC.

Speth, J. (1979). Conservation and management of coastal wetlands in California. *Studies in Avian Biology* **2**: 151–155.

Spillett, J.J. (1968). A report on wildlife surveys in South and West India, November–December 1966. *Journal Bombay Natural History Society* **65**: 296–325, 633–663.

Stafford, J. (1971). The Heron population of England and Wales (1928–1970). *Bird Study* **18**: 218–221.

Stanley, D.J. (1988). Subsidence in the northeastern Nile Delta: rapid rates, possible causes, and consequences. *Science* **240**: 497–500.

Stanley-Price, M.R. (1994). Report of Reintroduction Specialist Group. *Species* **21–22**: 126–127.

Staub, F. (1976). Birds of the Mascarenes and Saint Brandon. Organisation Normale des Entreprises Ltee, Port Louis, Mauritius.

Staude, J. (1966). Elektrozaun zur Abwehr von Fischreihern *Ardea cinerea* von Fischteichen. *Emberiza* **1**: 93–94.

Stendell, R.C., Ohlendorf, H.M., Klass, E.E. & Elder, J.B. (1976). Mercury in eggs of aquatic birds, Lake St. Clair—1973. *Pesticides Monitoring Journal* **10**: 7–9.

Stevenson, A.C., Skinner, J., Hollis, G.H. & Smart, M. (1988). The El Kala National Park and environs, Algeria: an ecological evaluation. *Environmental Conservation* **15**: 335–348.

Stickel, W.H., Stickel, L.F. & Spann, J.W. (1969). Tissue residues of dieldrin in relation to mortality in birds and mammals. pp 174–204, in (M.W. Miller and G.G. Berg, eds.) Chemical fallout; Current research on persistent pesticides. Charles C. Thomas, Springfield, Illinois, USA.

Stickley, A.R. (1990). Avian predators on southern aquaculture. Southern Regional Aquaculture Center Publication No. 400.

Stickley, A.R. & Andrews, K.J. (1989). Survey of Mississippi catfish farmers on means, effort, and costs to repel fish-eating birds from ponds. *Proceedings Eastern Wildlife Damage Control Conference* **4**: 106–107.

Stock, E.C. & Venables, I.F. (1988). Conservation and wildlife values of Cattle Egret rookery, Doboy Swamp. Institute of Applied Environmental Research, Griffith University, Queensland, Australia.

Stock, E.C. & Venables, I.F. (1989). Environmental management criteria for Cattle Egret rookery, Doboy Swamp. Institute of Applied Environmental Research, Griffith University, Queensland, Australia.

Stokes, T., Merton, D., Hicks, J. & Tranter, J. (1987). Additional records of birds from Christmas Island, Indian Ocean. *Australian Bird Watcher* **12**: 1–7.

Storey, A.W., Vervest, R.M., Pearson, G.B. & Halse, S.A. (1993). Wetlands of the Swan Coastal Plain, Volume 7: Waterbird usage on the Swan Coastal Plain. Perth, Department of Conservation and Land Management Wildlife Research Centre, Royal Australasian Ornithologists Union Western Australia.

Stotz, D.F, Fitzpatrick, J.W., Parker, T.A. III & Moskovits, D.K. (1996). Neotropical birds, ecology and conservation. University of Chicago Press, Chicago.

Strahler, A.N. (1973). Physical geography. John Wiley, New York.

Streeter, R., Butler, D., Koneff, M. & Schmidt, P. (1997). The North American Waterfowl Management Plan—expanding the commitment. pp 74–78, in (J. van Vessem, ed.) Determining priorities for waterbird and wetland conservation. Wetlands International, Kuala Lumpur, Malaysia.

Stronach, B.W.H. (1968). The Chagana heronry in western Tanzania. *Ibis* **110**: 345–348.

Styan, F.W. (1902). On the occurrence of *Nycticorax magnifica* in the Anwhei Province of China. *Ibis* **8(2)**.

Subramanya, S. (1990). Studies on the birds of ricefields with special reference to certain pest species. Unpublished Ph.D. thesis, University of Agricultural Sciences, Bangalore, India.

Subramanya, S. (1994). Catalogue of Indian heronries. Unpublished report, 11 pp.

Subramanya, S. (1996). Catalogue of Indian heronries: Preliminary report. Unpublished report to the Oriental Bird Club, Sandy, UK.

Suchantke, A. (1960). Herbstlicher Reiherzug und der Camargue-Küste. *Die Vogelwelt* **81**: 33–46.

Sueur, F. (1993). Premier cas de nidification du Héron garde-boeufs *Bubulcus ibis* dans le Marquenterre (Somme). *Alauda* **61**: 195–197.

Sultana, J. (1991). Malta Ornithological Society: a bird protection society in a hostile environment. In (T. Salathé, ed.) Conserving migratory birds. ICBP Technical Publications No. 12.

Sundlof, S., Spalding, M.G., Wentworth, J.D. & Steible, C.K. (1994). Mercury in livers of wading birds (Ciconiiformes) in southern Florida. *Archives of Environmental Contamination and Toxicology* **27**: 299–305.

Suter, W. (1991). Der Einfluss fischfressender Vogelarten auf Süsswasserfisch-Bestände—eine Übersicht. *Journal für Ornithologie* **132**: 29–45.

Svensson, S. (1976). Hägerns *Ardea cinerea* utbredning och antal i Sverige 1972. *Var Vagelvarld* **35**: 26–35.

Swennen, C. & Spaans, A.L. (1985). Habitat use of feeding migratory and local ciconiiform, anseriform and charadriiform birds in coastal wetlands of Surinam. *Le Gerfaut* **75**: 225–251.

Swinhoe, R. 1863. The ornithology of Formosa or Taiwan. *Ibis* ser 1, **5**: 418.

Tapiador, D.D., Henderson, H.F., Delmeudo, M.N. & Tsutsui, H. (1977). Freshwater fisheries and aquaculture in China. F.A.O. Technical Paper 168.

Taraschewski, H. & Paperna, I. (1982). Trematode infections in Pirenella-conica in 3 sites of a mangrove lagoon in Sinai, Egypt. *Zeitschrift fur Parasitenkunde* **67**: 165–174.

Tarboton, W.R. (1967). Rufous Heron *Ardeola rufiventris* breeding in the Transvaal. *Ostrich* **38**: 207.

Tarboton, W.R. (1977). The status of communal herons, ibis and cormorants on the Witwatersrand. *South African Journal of Wildlife Research* **7**: 19–25.

Tate, J. Jr. (1986). The blue list for 1986. *American Birds* **40**: 227–236.

Taylor, J.R. & Edwin, M.D. (1971). Predation on an inland heronry in eastern Texas. *Wilson Bulletin* **83**: 172–177.

Taylor, R.L. & Lott, M. (1978). Transmission of salmonid whirling disease by birds fed trout infected with *Myxosoma cerebralis*. *Journal Protozoology* **25**: 105–106.

Taylor, V. (1993). African waterfowl census 1993. IWRB, Slimbridge, UK.

Taylor, V. & Rose, P.M. (1994). African waterfowl census 1994. IWRB, Slimbridge, UK.

TCWC. (1982). An atlas and census of Texas waterbird colonies 1973–1980. Caesar Kleberg Wildlife Research Insititute, Texas A&I University, Kingsville, TX.

Teixeira, D.M., Otoch, R., Luigi, G., Raposo, M.A. & de Almeida, A.C.C. (1993). Notes on some birds of northeastern Brazil. *Bulletin of the British Ornithological Club* **113**: 48–52.

Telfair, R.C. II (1983). Cattle Egret (*Bubulcus ibis*): a Texas focus and world view. Kleberg Studies in Natural Resources, Texas Agricultural Research Station, Texas A&M University, College Station, TX.

Telfair, R.C. II. (1993). Cattle Egret population trends and dynamics in Texas (1954–1990). Texas Parks and Wildlife Dept., Federal Aid Project Report W-125-R.

Telfair, R.C. II (1994). Cattle Egret. In: (A. Poole and F. Gill eds.) The birds of North America, No. 113. Academy of Natural Science, Philadelphia and American Ornithologists' Union, Washington, DC.

Temple, S. & Wiens, J. (1989). Bird populations and environmental changes: can birds be bio-indicators? *American Birds* **43**: 260–270.

Terborgh, J. (1989). Where have all the birds gone? Princeton University Press, Princeton, NJ.

Terborgh, J.W., Fitzpatrick, J.W. & Emmons, L. (1984). Annotated checklist of bird and mammal species of Cocha Cashu Biological Station, Manu National Park, Peru. *Fieldiana: Zoology*, New Series, No. 21.

Thevenot, M., Beaubrun, P., Baouab, R.E. & Bergier, P. (1982). Compte rendu d'ornithologie Marocaine, année 1981. *Document de l'Institut Scientifique de Rabat* **7**: 1–120.

Thevenot, M., Bergier, P. & Beaubrun, P.C. (1981). Compte rendu d'ornithologie Marocaine, année 1980. *Document de l'Institut Scientifique de Rabat*, **6**: 1–93.

Thewlis, R.M., Duckworth, J.W., Anderson, G.Q.A. et al. (1995). Ornithological records from Laos, 1992–1993. *Forktail* **11**: 47–100.

Thomas, F., Kayser, Y. & Hafner, H. (1999). Nestling size rank in Little Egret (*Egretta garzetta*) influences subsequent breeding success of offspring. *Behavioral Ecology and Sociobiology* **45**: 466–470.

Thompson, D.H. (1977). Declines in populations of colonial waterbirds nesting within the floodplain of the upper Mississippi river. *Proceedings Colonial Waterbird Group* **1**: 26–37.

Thompson, P.M., Harvey, W.C., Johnson, D.L. et al. (1993). Recent notable bird records from Bangladesh. *Forktail* **9**: 13–15.

Thomson P. & Jacobsen, P. (1979). The birds of Tunisia. Jelling Bogtrykkeri APS, Denmark.

Tillitt, D.E., Giesy, J.P. & Ankley, G.T. (1990). Characterization of the H4IIE rat hepatoma cell bioassay as a tool for assessing toxic potency of planar halogenated hydrocarbons in environmental samples. *Environmental Science and Technology* **25**: 87–92.

Tinarelli, R., Rissoli, M. & Boldreghini, P. (1993). Strategies to reduce conflicts between fish-farmers and herons: the use of distress and alarm calls. Colonial Waterbird Society Meeting, Arles 6–10 October 1993, p 5.

Tiner, R.W., Jr, (1984). Wetlands of the United States: current status and recent trends. USFWS, National Wetlands Inventory, Washington, DC.

Tostain, O., Dujardin, J.L., Erard, C. & Thiollay, J.M. (1992). Oiseaux de Guyane. Société d'Etudes Ornithologiques, Brunoy, France.

Traylor, M.A. (1963). Checklist of Angolan birds. Publicacoes Culturais No. 61. Museu do Dundo. Lisbon, Portugal.

Tremblay, J. & Ellison, L.N. (1979). Effects of human disturbance on breeding of Black-crowned Night herons. *Auk* **96**: 364–369.

Tremblay, J. & Ellison, J.N. (1980). Breeding success of the Black-crowned Night Heron in the St. Lawrence Estuary. *Canadian Journal of Zoology* **58**: 1259–1263.

Trent, L., Pullan, E.J. & Proctor, R. (1976). Abundance of macrocrustaceans in a natural marsh and a marsh altered by dredging, bulkheading and filling. *Fishing Bulletin*, **74**: 195–200.

Tucker, G.M. & Heath, M.F. (1994). Birds in Europe: Their conservation status. BirdLife Conservation Series No. 3. BirdLife International, Cambridge, UK.

Tudge, C. (1992). Last Animals at the Zoo. Island Press, Washington, DC.

Turbott, E.G., Braithwaite, D.H. & Wilkin, F.W. (1963). Cattle Egret: A new bird for New Zealand. *Notornis* **10**: 316.

Turner, E.L. (1924). Broadland birds. Tavistock. Country Life, UK.

Turrian, F. & Schmid, T. (1984). Migration d'Ardéidés au delta du Kizilirmak, Turquie du Nord. *Nos Oiseaux* **37**: 289–292.

Tyler, G. (1994). Bittern. pp 88–89, in (G.M. Tucker and M.F. Heath) Birds in Europe: Their Conservation Status. BirdLife Conservation Series No. 3. BirdLife International, Cambridge, UK.

Tyler, S.J. & Ormerod, S.J. (1993). The ecology of river birds in Nepal. *Forktail* **9**: 59–88.

Ueckermann, E., Spittler, H. & Graumann, F. (1981). Technische Massnahmen zur Abwehr des Graureihers (*Ardea cinerea*) von Fischteichen und Fischzuchtanlagen. *Zeitschrift für Jagdwissenschaft* **27**: 271–282.

United States Fish and Wildlife Service, (1985). Endangered and threatened wildlife and plants; removal of the Brown Pelican in the southeastern United States from the list of endangered and threatened wildlife. *Federal Register* **50**: 4938–4945.

Urfi, A.J. (1993a). Heronries in the Delhi region of India. *Oriental Bird Club Bulletin* **17**: 19–21.

Urfi, A.J. (1993b). Breeding patterns of Painted Storks (*Mycteria leucocephala* Pennant) at Delhi Zoo, India. *Colonial Waterbirds* **16**: 95–97.

Usbeck, S. & James, R. (1992). A directory of important wetlands in Australia. Landscape Conservation Unit, Australian Nature Conservation Agency. Canberra.

Utschick, H. (1980). Die Schadwirkung des Graureihers *Ardea cinerea* in Salmonidenbächen in Abhängigkeit von Fischdichte und Bachqualität. *Anzeiger der Ornithologischen Gesellschaft Bayern* **19**: 107–110.

Utschick, H. (1983a). Abwehrstrategie und Abwehrmassnahmen gegen den Graureiher (*Ardea cinerea*) an Fischgewässern. *Garmische Vogelkundliche Berichte* **12**: 18–58.

Utschick, H. (1983b). Die Brutbestandesentwicklung des Graureihers (*Ardea cinerea*) in Bayern. *Journal für Ornithologie* 124: 233–250.

Utschick, H. (1984a). Ökologische Untersuchungen zur Rolle des Graureihers *Ardea cinerea* in der Sportfischerei. *Verhandlungen der Ornithologischen Gesellschaft Bayern* **24**: 87–110.

Utschick, H. (1984b). Untersuchungen zur Rolle des Graureihers *Ardea cinerea* in der Teichwirtschaft. *Verhandlungen der Ornithologischen Gesellschaft Bayern* **24**: 111–124.

Utschick, H. & Weber, E. (1980). Fischdichte in Salmonidengewässern des Erdinger Mooses, Obb., und Nutzung durch den Graureiher. *Garmische Vogelkundliche Berichte* **7**: 28–38.

Uttley, J. (1987). Survey of Sulawesi Selatan to assess the status of wetlands and to identify key sites for migratory birds. Interwader, Kuala Lumpur, Malaysia.

Valverde, J.A. (1955). Essai sur l'Aigrette garzette (*Egretta g. garzetta*) en France. *Alauda* **23**: 147–171; 254–279.

Valverde, J.A. (1955–56). Aves de Marruecos Espanol en julio. *Ardeola* **2**: 87–114; *Ardeola* **3**: 213–240.

Valverde, J.A. (1956). Essai sur l'Aigrette garzette en France (*Egretta garzetta*). *Alauda* **24**: 1–36.

van den Berg, M., Blank, F., Heeremans, C., Wagenaar, H. & Olie, K. (1987). Presence of polychlorinated dibenzo-*p*-dioxins and polychlorinated dibenzofurans in fish-eating birds and fish from the Netherlands. *Archives of Environmental Contamination and Toxicology* **16**: 149–158.

van de Hare, T.M., van der Sant, S., Verkuil, Y. & van der Winder, J. (eds). (1994). Waterbirds in the Sivash, Ukraine, spring 1992. WIWO-report 36. Zeist, The Netherlands.

van der Kooij, H. (1991). Nesthabitat van de Purperreiger *Ardea purpurea* in Nederland. *Limosa* **64**: 103–112.

van der Kooij, H. (1992). Het broedseizoen 1991 van de Purperreiger in Nederland. *Het Vogeljaar* **40(3)**: 119–121.

van der Molen, E.J., Blok, A.A. & De Graaf, G.J. (1982). Winter starvation and mercury intoxication in Grey Herons (*Ardea cinerea*) in the Netherlands. *Ardea* **70**: 173–184.

van der Ven, J. (1964). De Blauwe Reiger in 1963 en 1964 in Nederland. *Limosa* **37**: 308–309.

van Dobben, W.H. (1952). The food of the cormorant in the Netherlands. *Ardea* **40**: 1–63.

van Gessel, F. & Kendall, T. (1972). A checklist of the birds of Kooragang Island. *Hunter Natural History* **4**: 194–215.

van Sanden, P. (1989). Kwak. In: Vogels in Vlaanderen: voorkomen en verspreiding, p. 59. Vlaamse avifauna commissie, I.M.P., Bornem.

van Vessem, J. (1982). Aspects écologiques de la protection des piscicultures contre les Hérons cendrés. *L'Homme & L'Oiseau* **20**: 270–285.

van Vessem, J. (1988). Broedbestand en broedkolonies van de Blauwe Reiger (*Ardea cinerea*) in België von 1982 tot en met 1986. *De Gierfalk* **78**: 69–97.

van Vessem, J. (1997). Determining priorities for waterbird and wetland conservation. Wetlands International, Kuala Lumpur, Malaysia.

van Vessem, J. & Rose, P.M. (1993). Monitoring of waterbirds in the breeding season: The International Waterfowl Census. pp 13–17, in (M. Moser, R.C. Prentice, and J. van Vessem, eds.) Waterfowl and wetland conservation in the 1990s—a global perspective. IWRB Special Publication No. 26, Slimbridge, UK.

van Vessem, J., Draulans, D. & de Bont, A.F. (1982). De status de Blauwe Reiger (*Ardea cinerea*) als broedvogel in België van 1966 tot 1981. *De Giervalk* **72**: 327–335.

van Vessem, J., Draulans, D. & de Bont, A.F. (1984). Movements of radio-tagged Grey Herons *Ardea cinerea* during the breeding season in a large pond area. *Ibis* **126**: 576–587.

van Vessem, J., Draulans, D. & de Bont, A.F. (1985). The effect of killing and removal on the abundance of grey herons at fish farms. pp 337–343, in Proceedings of Seventeenth Congress International of the Union Game Biologists. Brussels, Belgium.

Verhaegen, J.P. (1981). Nidifications du héron bihoreau, *Nycticorax nycticorax*, à Harchies-Hensies. *Le Gerfaut* **71**: 109–111.

Verheyen, R.F. (1966). Het voorkommen van de Blauwe Reiger, *Ardea cinerea* in België. *De Giervalk* **56**: 374–403.

Vermeer, K. & Reynolds, L.M. (1970). Organochlorine residues in aquatic birds in the Canadian prairie provinces. *Canadian Field-Naturalist* **84**: 117–130.

Vermeer, K. & Risebrough, R.W. (1972). Additional information on egg shell thickness in relation to DDE concentrations in Great Blue Heron eggs. *Canadian Field-Naturalist* **86**: 384–385.

Vermeer, K., Armstrong, F.A.J. & Hatch, D.R.M. (1973). Mercury in aquatic birds at Clay Lake, Western Ontario. *Journal of Wildlife Management* **37**: 58–61.

Vermeulen, J.W.C. & Spaans, A.L. (1987). Feeding ecology of Javan Pond Heron *Ardeola speciosa* and Cattle Egret *Bubulcus ibis* in north Sulawesi, Indonesia, with additional notes on the occurrence of Ardeids. Research Institute for Nature Management, Arnhem, Netherlands.

Vernon, C. (1976). Heronries in Rhodesia in 1973–74. *Honeyguide* **86**: 25–29.

Verschuren, J. & Dupuy, A. (1987). Note sur les oiseaux des parcs nationaux littoraux du Sénégal. *Le Gerfaut* **77**: 405–442.

Voisin, C. (1975). Importance des populations de Hérons arboricoles, *Egretta garzetta, Nycticorax nycticorax, Ardeola ralloides* et *Ardeola ibis* dans le Delta du Rhône. Données historiques et situation actuelle. *L'Oiseau & Revue Française d'Ornithologie* **45**: 7–25.

Voisin, C. (1985). Migration et stabilité des populations chez l'Aigrette garzette *Egretta garzetta*. *L'Oiseau et la Revue Française d'Ornithologie* **55**: 291–311.

Voisin, C. (1991). The herons of Europe. T & A D Poyser, London, UK.

Voisin, C. (1996). The migration routes of Purple Herons (*Ardea purpurea*) ringed in France. *Die Vogelwarte* **38**: 155–168.

Voous, K.H. & van Marle, J.G. (1988). The birds of Sumatra: An annotated checklist. BOU Checklist No. 10. BOU, Tring, UK.

Vorobiev, K.A. (1954). Birds of the Ussuri area. Acadamy of Science USSR, Moscow.

Vos, D.K., Ryder, D.A. & Grau, W.D. (1985). Response of breeding Great Blue Herons to human disturbance in north central Colorado. *Colonial Waterbirds* **8**: 13–22.

Voslamber, B. (1992). Zilverreigers *Egretta* sp. in de Oostvaardersplassen in 1991. *Limosa* **65(3)**: 89–92.

Waddington, C.H. (1957). The strategy of the genes. Allen and Unwin, London.

Wallace, J.P. (1990). Cold weather mortality in Little Egret *Egretta garzetta* in the Camargue and its implication for their winter distribution. Unpublished M.Sc. Thesis, University College of Wales, Aberystwyth, UK.

Walmsley, J.G. (1975). The development of a breeding population of Grey Herons (*Ardea cinerea*) in the Camargue. *La Terre et la Vie* **29**: 89–99.

Walter, H. (1985). Vegetation of the Earth and ecological systems of the geo-biosphere. Springer-Verlag, Heidelberg, Germany.

Walters, M. (1976). Some observations of the eggs of the Great White-bellied Heron *Ardea insignis*. *Journal of the Bombay Natural History Society* **73**: 213–214.

Waterbird Specialist Group of the Chinese Ornithological Association. (1994). Waterbird research in China. East China Normal University Press, Beijing.

Watson, I. (1955). Some species seen at the Laverton Saltworks, Victoria, 1950–53, with notes on seasonal changes. *Emu* **55**: 224–248.

Watson, J. (1980). Distribution and nesting of the Yellow Bittern in Seychelles. *Ostrich* **51**: 120–122.

Weibüll, V. (1912). Hejren (*Ardea cinerea*) i Danmark nu og tidligere. *Dansk Ornithologisk Forenings Tidsskrift* **40**: 216–245.

Weise, J.H., Davidson, W.R. & Nettles, V.F. (1977). Large-scale mortality of nesting ardeids caused by nematode infection. *Journal of Wildlife Diseases* **13**: 376–382.

Wells, D.R. (1984). Bird report 1978–79. *Malayan Nature Journal* **38(2)**: 113–150.

Wells, D.R. (1990a). Malayan bird report: 1984–1985. *Malayan Nature* **43(3)**: 148–171.

Wells, D.R. (1990b). Malayan bird report: 1986–1987. *Malayan Nature* **43(3)**: 172–210.

Wen, Z-z. & Sun, R-y. (1994a). Breeding ecology of herons at Xinyang. In Waterbird Specialist Group of the Chinese Ornithological Association. Waterbird research in China. East China Normal University Press, Beijing.

Wen, Z-z. & Sun, R-y. (1994b). Biology of Chinese pond heron (*Ardeola bacchus*) during the breeding season. In Waterbird Specialist Group of the Chinese Ornithological Association. Waterbird research in China. East China Normal University Press, Beijing.

Werschkul, D.F., McMahon, E. & Leitschuh, M. (1976). Some effects of human activities on the Great Blue Heron in Oregon. *Wilson Bulletin* **88**: 660–662.

Werschkul, D.F., McMahon, E. & Leitschuh, M. (1977). Observations on the reproductive ecology of the Great Blue Heron in western Oregon. *Murrelet* **58**: 7–12.

Weseloh, D.V., Ewins, P.J., Neuman, J. & Ludwig, J.P. (1995). Double-crested Cormorants of the Great Lakes: population changes, mortality, recruitment rates and diet. *Colonial Waterbird* **18** (Special Issue 1): 48–59.

White, C.M.N. & Bruce, M.D. (1986). The birds of Wallacea (Sulawesi, the Moluccas and Lesser Sunda Islands, Indonesia): An annotated checklist. BOU Checklist 7. British Ornithologists' Union, London.

White, D.H., Fleming, W.J. & Ensor, K.L. (1988). Pesticide contamination and hatching success of waterbirds in Mississippi. *Journal of Wildlife Management* **52**: 724–729.

White, D.H. & Krynitsky, A.J. (1986). Wildlife in some areas of New Mexico and Texas accumulate elevated DDE residues, 1983. *Archives of Environmental Contamination and Toxicology* **15**: 149–157.

Whitten, A.J., Damanik, S.J., Anwar, J. & Hisyam, N. (1987). The ecology of Sumatra. Gadjah Mada University Press, Yogyakarta, Indonesia.

Whitten, A.J., Mustafa, M. & Henderson, G. (1988). The ecology of Sulawesi. Gadjah Mada University Press, Yogyakarta, Indonesia.

Wiese, R.J., Willis, K. & Hutchins, M. (1994). Is genetic and demographic management conservation? *Zoo Biology* **13**: 297–299.

Wild Bird Society of Japan. (1978). The breeding bird survey 1978. Wild Bird Society of Japan, Tokyo.

Willard, D.E., Foster, M.S., Barrowclough, G.F. et al. (1991). The birds of Cerro La Neblina, Territorio Federal Amazonas, Venezuela. *Fieldiana: Zoology*, New Series, No. 65.

Wille, L.L. & Wille, H. (1969). Le heron bihoreau, *Nycticorax n. nycticorax*, (Linné 1758) en Belgique et en Europe Occidentale. *Le Gerfaut* **59**: 154–156.

Williams, B., Akers, J.W., Via, J.W. & Beck, R.A. (1990). Longitudinal surveys of the beach nesting and colonial waterbirds of the Virginia barrier islands. 1975–1987. *Virginia Journal of Science* **41**: 381–388.

Williams, T. (1992). Killer fish farms. *Audubon*, March/April 1992: 14–22.

Willis, E.O. & Oniki, Y. (1990). Levantamento preliminar das aves de inverno em dez áreas De sudoeste de Mato Grosso, Brasil. *Ararajuba* **1**: 19–38.

Willis, K. & Wiese, R.J. (1993). Effect of new founders on retention of gene diversity in captive populations: a formalization of the nucleus population concept. *Zoo Biology* **12**: 535–548.

Willumsen, B. (1989). Birds and wild fish as potential vectors of *Yersinia ruckeri*. *Journal Fish Disease* **12**: 275–277.

Wilson, A.M. & Moser, M.E. (1994). Conservation of Black Sea wetlands: a review and preliminary action plan. IWRB Special Publication 33, Slimbridge, UK.

Wilson, E.O. (1975). Sociobiology: The new synthesis. Belknap Press, Harvard, USA.

Wilson, M.H. & Ryan, D.A. (1997). Conservation of Mexican wetlands: role of the North American Wetlands Conservation Act. *Wildlife Society Bulletin* **25**: 57–64.

Wingate, D.B. (1973). A checklist and guide to the birds of Bermuda. David B. Wingate, Bermuda.

Wingate, D.B. (1982). Successful reintroduction of the Yellow-crowned Night-Heron as a nesting resident on Bermuda. *Colonial Waterbirds* **5**: 104–115.

Winkler, H., Berthold, P. & Leisler, B. (1994). Monitoring of bird populations in the Lake Neusiedl area. pp 29–36, in (G. Abrecht, G. Dick and C. Prentice, eds.) Monitoring of Ecological Change in Wetlands of Middle Europe. Proceedings International Workshop, Linz, Austria, IWRB Publication No. 30, Slimbridge, UK.

Winning, G. (1990). A scheme for assessment of the nature conservation for wetlands. *Wetlands Australia* **9**: 20–27.

Winning, G. (1991). Some problems in determining the boundaries of SEPP 14 wetlands. *Wetlands Australia* **11**: 10–21.

Winterbottom, J.M. (1942). The birds of Barotseland. (A contribution to the ornithology of Barotseland). *Ibis* **84**: 337–384.

Wittenberger, J.F. & Hunt, G.L. (1985). The adaptive significance of coloniality in birds. *Avian Biology* **8**: 1–78.

Wong, F.K.O. (1991). Habitat utilisation by Little Egrets breeding at Mai Po Egretry. The Hong Kong bird report 1990. *Report Hong Kong Bird Working Society* 1991: 185–190.

Woodall, P.F. (1986). The Cattle Egret *Ardeola ibis* in south-east Queensland. *Australian Wildlife Research* **13**: 575–582.

World Resources Institute. (1992). World Resources 1992–93. Oxford University Press, New York.

World Resources Institute. (1994). World Resources 1994–95. Oxford University Press, New York.

Yamashita, C. & Valle, M.P. (1990a). Ocorrencia de duas aves raras no Brasil Central: *Mergus octosetaceus* e *Tigrisoma fasciatum fasciatum*. *Ararajuba* **1**: 107–109.

Yamashita, C. & Valle, M.P. (1990b). Sobre ninhais de aves do Pantanal do municipio de Poconé, Mato Grosso, Brasil. *Vida Silvestre Neotropical* **2**: 59–63.

Yealand, J.J. (1964). The breeding of the African Cattle Egret. *Avicultural Magazine* **70**: 21–22.

Yeates, G.K. (1950). Flamingo city. Country Life Ltd, London; Charles Scribner's Sons, New York.

Yeatman-Berthelot, D. & Jarry, G. (eds.) 1994. Nouvel atlas des oiseaux nicheurs de France. Société Ornithologique France, Paris.

Yen, C. W. (1992). Distribution of heronries in the mid-western and southern lowlands of Taiwan. *Bulletin of the National Museum of Natural Sciences* **3**: 247–257.

Young, H.G. (1985). Night herons in captivity. *International Zoo News* **32**: 9–14.

Young, L. (1992). Conservation of wildlife in the Deep Bay area: With particular reference to heron species. In (J. Boxall, ed.) Polmet Conference: Pollution in the Metropolitan Environment. Hong Kong Institute of Engineers, Hong Kong.

Young, L. (1993). The ecology of Hong Kong Ardeidae (Aves) with special reference to the Chinese Pond Heron at the Mai Po Marshes Nature Reserve, Hong Kong. Ph.D. thesis, University of Hong Kong.

Young, L. (1998). The importance to ardeids of the Deep Bay fish ponds, Hong Kong. *Biological Conservation*, **84**: 293–300.

Young, L. & Cha, M.W. (1995). The history and status of the egretries in Hong Kong, with notes on those in the Pearl River Delta, Guangdong Province, China. *Hong Kong Bird Report*, 1995: 196–215.

Zinkl, J.G., Jessup, D.A., Bischoff, A.I., Lew, T.E. & Wheeldon, E.B. (1981). Fenthion poisoning of wading birds. *Journal of Wildlife Disease* **17**: 117–119.

Zhou, F. (1996). Conservation Fund in Action: White-eared Night-Heron in Guangxi. *Oriental Bird Club Bulletin* **23**: 8–9.

Zonneveld, I.S. (1983). Principles of bio-indication. *Environmental Monitoring and Assessment* **3**: 207–217.

Index

Abaya, Lake (Ethiopia) 100, 101
Abijatta, Lake (Ethiopia) 100, 101
Acacia drepanolobium woodland 118
Acacia nilotica woodland 208
Acacia seyal woodland 118
acoustic scaring 288–9
action plan for conservation 343–4
adaptability, inherent 377
Aden, Gulf
    Green-backed Heron 114
    Little Egret 112
Adjutant, Lesser 93
Adriatic coastal wetlands 24
Adriatic Sea (Italy) 2, 3
    Squacco Heron population 18
aerial surveys 334
Africa 99, 100, 101
    aquaculture 174, 270
    climate 104
    conservation status 350
    data 105
    drought 30, 31, 40, 367
        hypothesis 30, 31
    environmental conditions 104
    feeding habitats 120
    habitats 104
    status of herons 102–3, 105–17
    wetland management 117–20
African–Eurasian Waterfowl Agreement 233
Agamia agami (Agami Heron) xiv, 151, 360
Aggel Lake (Azerbaijan/Iran) 57, 64
Agreement on the Conservation of African–
        Eurasian Migratory Waterbirds (AEWA) 250
agricultural land 223–4
    pasture 24, 223, 339
agriculture
    Africa 119
    Central America 167
    change 69
    degradation 247

    subsidies and wetlands destruction 23
    see also pesticides; rice fields
Agua Santa Marshes (Peru) 178, 179, 197
Akagera National Park (Tanzania) 101
Alabama (USA) 158
Alaska (USA) 156
    Great Blue Heron 156
Albania 51
    Great White Egret population 40, 41
    Little Egret population 41
    Squacco Heron population 18, 45
Albert, Lake (Australia) 124, 125
Albert National Park (Uganda) 100, 101
Albufera de Valencia (Spain) 2, 3
Aldabra 99, 100
    Cattle Egret 113
    Green-backed Heron 115
    Grey Heron 106, 361
    Little Egret 112
alder 208
aldrin 253
Alexandrina, Lake (Australia) 124, 125
algal blooms 142
Algeria 2, 3, 54
    habitat loss 52
    Little Bittern 50, 368
    Mediterranean wetlands 35, 37, 38, 42, 43, 47, 50
Aliakmon Delta (Greece) 2, 3
Alice Springs (Australia) 132
Alnus (alder) 208
Amazon basin 194
    Agami Heron 188
    Black-crowned Night Heron 189
    Capped Heron 183
    Great Blue Heron 184
    Little Blue Heron 186
    pollution 195
    Rufescent Tiger Heron 191
    Yellow-crowned Night Heron 189
    Zigzag Heron 192

Amazon forest 181, 182
Amazon River (Brazil) 178, 179
Amboromalandy, Lake (Madagascar) 110
delta-aminolevulinic acid dehydratase (ALAD)
    320, 328
Amvrakikos Gulf (Greece) 2, 3
analytical tools 337
Andaman Islands 64, 359
Andes range 181
Andros Island (Bahamas) 152, 153
angling see fishing
Angola 100, 101
    Dwarf Bittern 116
    Eurasian Bittern 117, 362
    wetland management 119
Anlo-Keta Lagoon complex (Ghana) 100, 101
Antananarivo (Madagascar) 109, 110, 112, 114
    Malagasy Pond Heron 114
Antsalova wetlands (Madagascar) 100, 101, 106,
    107, 115
Anzali Marsh (Iran) 57
Ao Pattani (Thailand) 74, 75, 95
aquaculture 174, 225, 232–3, 269
    artificial habitats 341–2
    fish density 284
    fish loss causes 278–9
    habitat degradation 247–8
    industry 269–70
    North America 174
    piscivorous species 272–4
    predation
        beneficial 282
        rates 277–81
    production system diversity 274–8
    site attractiveness to birds 276
    South America 196
    wetland areas 287
        destruction 333
    see also catfish; crawfish/crayfish; fish
        farms/farming; shrimp farming; trout
aquariums 293
Arabian Peninsula 62, 64, 65, 66
Araguaia River (Brazil) 178, 179
Aral Sea 59, 246
Arauca Fauna and Flora Sanctuary (Venezuela)
    178, 179
Arazati Marshes (Uraguay) 178, 179
Archipelago de Sabana (Cuba) 152, 153
Ardea cinerea (Grey Heron) xiii, 1
Ardea cinerea altirostris (Grey Heron) 363
Ardea cinerea firasa (Grey Heron) 99, 106, 363
Ardea cinerea jouyi (Grey Heron) 78
Ardea cinerea monicae (Grey Heron) 105, 106, 203,
    205, 363
Ardea cocoi (Cocoi Heron) xiii
Ardea goliath (Goliath Heron) xiii, 366
Ardea gularis 282
Ardea herodias (Great Blue Heron) 151
Ardea herodias cognata (Great Blue Heron) 184, 198
Ardea herodias fannini (Great Blue Heron) 157, 240
Ardea herodias herodias (Great Blue Heron) 184
Ardea herodias occidentalis (Great Blue Heron) 151,
    157, 364
Ardea humbloti (Malagasy Heron) xiii, 357–8

Ardea imperialis (Imperial Heron) xiii, 254–5
Ardea insignis see Ardea imperialis (Imperial Heron)
Ardea melanocephala (Black-headed Heron) xiii
Ardea pacifica (White-necked Heron) xiii, 123
Ardea purpurea (Purple Heron) xiii, 1
Ardea purpurea bournei (Purple Heron) 107, 362
Ardea purpurea madagascariensis (Purple Heron) 99,
    107, 364
Ardea purpurea manilensis (Purple Heron) 62
Ardea purpurea purpurea (Purple Heron) 367
Ardea rufiventris (Rufous-bellied Heron) xiii, 99
Ardea sumatrana (Sumatran Heron) xiii, 358–9
Ardeinae, colonial nesting 201
Ardeola grayii (Indian Pond Heron) xiii
Ardeola grayii phillipsi (Indian Pond Heron) 364
Ardeola idae (Malagasy Pond Heron) xiii, 114, 359
Ardeola ralloides (Squacco Heron) xiii, 1, 114
Ardeola ralloides ralloides (Squacco Heron) 368
Ardeola rufiventris (Rufous-bellied Heron) xiii, 360
Ardeola speciosa (Javan Pond Heron) xiii
Ardeola speciosa continentalis (Javan Pond Heron)
    85, 91
Ardeola speciosa speciosa (Javan Pond Heron) 85, 91
Argentina 178, 179
    Black-crowned Night Heron 189
    Boat-billed Heron 190
    Cattle Egret 187
    climate 181
    Cocoi Heron 185
    Fasciated Tiger Heron 190
    Great White Egret 185
    Green-backed Heron 187
    Least Bittern 193
    Little Blue Heron 186
    Rufescent Tiger Heron 191
    Snowy Egret 187
    South American Bittern 193
    Streaked Bittern 192
    Whistling Heron 183
Argyle, Lake (Australia) 124, 125
Arizona (USA) 169
    Black-crowned Night Heron 163
Aru Island, Black Bittern 140
Aruba (South America) 178, 179
    Great Blue Heron 184
    Reddish Egret 185
ash tree 208
Asia
    aquaculture 270
    conservation status 350
    see also East and South-east Asia; South and
        West Asia
Asia–Pacific Migratory Waterfowl Conservation
    Strategy 234, 250
Asian Waterfowl Census 60–1, 71
association
    Cattle Egret and grazing animals 220–1, 223, 224
    colonial nesting and social feeding 202
    terrestrial herons and damp/shallow flooded
        grassland 223
Assumption Island 115
Astrakhan Reserve (Russia) 14
Aswan High Dam (Egypt) 246
Atlantic flyway 167–8

Atlantic Ocean coastline 5
Atrato River (Colombia) 178, 179, 197, 370
Aude River (France) 2, 3
Audubon Society 214
    Christmas Bird Counts (CBC) 323, 324
Australia 123, 124, 125
    catchment management 146
    colony threats 146–7
    conservation
        in reserves 144–5
        status 350–1
    environmental conditions 125, 128–9
    pollution 146
    public involvement 147–8
    Purple Heron 81, 205
    status of herons 126–7, 130–40
    Sumatran Heron 79, 359
    urbanisation 147
    wetlands
        assessment 145–6
        management 140–4
Austria 2, 3
    Black-crowned Night Heron 20
    Great White Egret population 11, 12, 41
    Grey Heron population 9
    Little Bittern population 20
    Little Egret population 12
    protection 28
    Purple Heron population 10, 11
Avery Island (Louisiana; USA) 203, 303
aviculturists, reputation of herons 297–8
awareness campaigns see community involve-
        ment; Shortland (Australia), ecotourism
Awassa, Lake (Ethiopia) 100, 101
Axios (Greece) 2, 3, 43, 53
Azerbaijan 56, 57, 64
    Cattle Egret 64
Azov Sea (Russia) 2, 3, 5

bacterial infection 282
Bagmati River (Nepal) 64
Bahamas 152, 153
    conservation 169
    Great White Egret 157
    Little Blue Heron 159
    Reddish Egret 158
    Snowy Egret 160
    Tricoloured Heron 158
    wetlands 155
    Yellow-crowned Night Heron 162
Bahia de Jiguey (Cuba) 152, 153
Bahia de los Perros (Cuba) 152, 153
Bahia Magdalena (Mexico) 152, 153
Bahrain 66
Baltic Sea 5
Baltimore Harbour (Maryland; USA) 261
Baluchistan (Pakistan) 68
Bananal Island (Brazil) 178, 179
Banc D'Arguin (Mauritania) 100, 101, 106, 112,
        120, 362
Bandar Abas marshes (Iran) 57
banding see ringing
Bangladesh 56, 57
    Eastern Reef Heron 64

    Goliath Heron 62
    Imperial Heron 61
    Indian Pond Heron 65
Bangweulu Swamps (Zambia) 100, 101, 109, 114,
        117, 363
Banyuasin Musi River Delta (Indonesia) 74, 75
Barbados 161
Barberspan Nature Reserve (South Africa) 101
Barents Sea 5
Barito Basin swamps (Indonesia) 74, 75
Barmah State Forest (Australia) 124, 125, 143
Barr al Hikman (Oman) 57, 64
Barwon River (Australia) 143
Bassin du Ndiael (Senegal) 100, 101
Baures River (Bolivia) 178, 179
Beilharz's `breeding site for colonial water birds'
        145
Belarus
    Black-crowned Night Heron 19
    Eurasian Bittern population 21
    Little Bittern population 20
Belgium 3
    Black-crowned Night Heron 19, 20
    Eurasian Bittern population 23
    Grey Heron population 6, 7, 9
    Little Bittern population 20–1
    protection 28
    Purple Heron population 11
Belize 152, 153
Bemamba, Lake (Madagascar) 100, 101, 109
    Black Heron 110
Benbach River (New Guinea) 129, 131
Beni Biological Station (Bolivia) 178, 179
Beni Department lakes (Bolivia) 178, 179
Benin, wetland management 119
Bermuda 162
    conservation 167
    Yellow-crowned Night Heron translocation 304
Bern Convention 23
Betsiboka River (Madagascar) 100, 101
Beung Boraphet (Thailand) 74, 75
Bharatpur (India) 56, 57, 63, 64, 70
    artificial nesting site 207–8
Bhavnagar (India) 70
Bhutan 61, 65
Bicavan National Park (Angola) 100, 101
Bigi Pan (Guianas Coast) 178, 179
Bilbeis (Egypt) 46
bill deformities 321
biodiversity preservation 231
bioindicators see indicators
biomonitoring programmes 311–12
Biosphere reserve, Danube delta (Romania) 51
BirdLife International 35, 343
    European threatened species 350
Birds Directive (EU) 23
Bismarck Island (Oceania) 140
Bittern, American xiv, 151, 155, 166
    conservation status 370
    protection 171, 172, 175
    sedentary 239
Bittern, Australian xiv, 129, 140, 145
    captive conservation priority 308
    conservation status 355

Bittern, Black xiv, 67, 90–1, 140, 201
  habitat 222
Bittern, Black-backed 352
Bittern, Cinnamon xiv, 67, 90, 201
  habitat 222, 232
Bittern, Dwarf xiv, 99, 116, 118, 201
Bittern, Eurasian xiv, 1, 4
  Africa 99, 117
  conservation status 350, 363, 370–1
  East and South-east Asia 91
  habitat 24, 26, 27
    loss 22
  latitude tolerance 28
  Mediterranean region 35, 49–50
  migration 22
  population decline 21–2
  population fluctuation 30–1
  South and West Asia 67
  species account for Europe 21–3
  winter mortality 22–3
Bittern, Least xiv, 151, 155
  Americas 164–5, 171, 172, 174, 175
  nesting 201
  South America 192–3, 197
Bittern, Little xiv, 1, 4, 89, 239
  Africa 99, 116, 118
  Australia and Oceania 139
  conservation status 350, 366, 368–70
  East and South-east Asia 89
  habitat 24, 26, 27
  Malagasy 116
  Mediterranean region 35, 48–9, 50
  migration 21, 26, 49, 116, 241, 369
  population fluctuation 30
  South and West Asia 66
  species account for Europe 20–1
Bittern, New Zealand Little 139
Bittern, Schrenck's xiv, 90, 298
  conservation status 361
  migration 240
Bittern, South American xiv, 165, 193, 239
Bittern, Streaked xiv, 182, 192, 197–8
  nesting 205
Bittern, Yellow xiv, 67, 89–90
  Africa 116
  Australia and Oceania 139
  habitat 222
bitterns
  habitat preference 221
  nesting habitat 203
  rice fields 224
Black Sea 5
  Black-crowned Night Heron 46
  conservation action 51
  Eurasian Bittern 49
  Great White Egret 40, 367–8
  Grey Heron 36, 37
  habitat degradation 51
  Little Egret population 41
  Squacco Heron population 18, 45
Blanca Lagoon (Argentina) 178, 179
Blanco River (Ecuador) 178, 179
Blesbokspruit Bird Sanctuary (South Africa) 101
blood sampling 320

Blue Lagoon National Park (Zambia) 100, 101
Boambee (Australia) 147, 148
Boccoo Reef (Tobago) 163
body mass estimate 326
body tissues, contaminants 173–4
Bogotá River (Colombia) 197
Bolivia 178, 179
  Fasciated Tiger Heron 190, 198
  Rufescent Tiger Heron 190
  Streaked Bittern 192
Bon Accord swamp (Tobago) 163
Bonaire (South America) 178, 179
  Great Blue Heron 184
  Reddish Egret 185
Bool Lagoon (South Australia) 124, 125, 141
Booligal Wetlands (Australia) 124, 125, 146
booming, Eurasian Bittern 363
Bopitiya (Sri Lanka) 56, 57
Borneo
  Black-crowned Night Heron 86
  Grey Heron 78
  Nankeen Night Heron 86
  Purple Heron 81
  Swinhoe's Egret 84
Boro River (Botswana) 109
Botaurus lentiginosus (American Bittern) xiv, 361
Botaurus pinnatus (South American Bittern) xiv, 165
Botaurus pinnatus pinnatus (South American Bittern) 193
Botaurus poiciloptilus (Australian Bittern) xiv, 355
Botaurus stellaris (Eurasian Bittern) xiv, 1
Botaurus stellaris capensis (Eurasian Bittern) 99, 117, 362
Botaurus stellaris stellaris (Eurasian Bittern) 117, 370
Botswana 100, 101
  Slaty Egret 109, 356
  wetland management 120
Bou Redim (Tunisia) 46
Bougainville (Oceania) 129
  Yellow Bittern 139
Bracken Ridge (Australia) 147
Brahmaputra flood plain (India/Bangladesh) 56, 57
Braila (Romania) 2, 3
Brazil 178, 179
  Agami Heron 188
  Boat-billed Heron 190
  climate 181
  Fasciated Tiger Heron 190
  Great Blue Heron 184
  Grey Heron 183
  Least Bittern 193
  Little Blue Heron 186
  Rufescent Tiger Heron 191
  South American Bittern 193
  Streaked Bittern 192
  Tricoloured Heron 186
  wetlands 182
  Whistling Heron 183
  Yellow-crowned Night Heron 162, 189
breeding
  conservation 298–303
  sites 26

breeding population monitoring 322–3
`breeding site for colonial water birds' value 145
breeding success
    captive populations 299
    climate 146
Brenne Ponds (France) 2, 3
Briere (France) 2, 3
British Columbia (Canada)
    Bald Eagle predation 170
    Black-crowned Night Heron 163
    dioxins 262
    Great Blue Heron 156
    Green-backed Heron 161
    habitat protection 170
British Isles 1
    see also Ireland; Northern Ireland; United
        Kingdom
British Trust for Ornithology (BTO) 9
Brittany (France) 206
Brouage (France) 2, 3
Bubalis bubalis (water buffalo) 146
Bubulcus ibis (Cattle Egret) xiii, 1, 350
Bubulcus ibis coromandus (Cattle Egret) 64, 113, 137
Bubulcus ibis ibis (Cattle Egret) 187
Bubulcus ibis seychellarum (Cattle Egret) 100, 113
Buenaventura Bay (Colombia) 178, 179
buffer zones 211–12
Bufo marinus (cane toad) 146
Buguey Wetlands Luzon (Philippines) 74, 75
Bulgaria 3
    Great White Egret population 12
    Purple Heron population 10
    Squacco Heron population 18, 45
bullrush 205
bumblefoot 300
Bundaberg (Australia) 128
Burkina Faso 100, 101
    Grey Heron 105
Burundi 100, 101
    Black-crowned Night Heron 115
    Malagasy Pond Heron 114
    wetland management 119
Butorides striatus (Green-backed Heron) xiv, 33, 350
Butorides striatus actophilus (Green-backed Heron)
    85
Butorides striatus albidulus (Green-backed Heron)
    365
Butorides striatus albolimbatus (Green-backed
    Heron) 65, 365
Butorides striatus amurensis (Green-backed Heron)
    85, 86
Butorides striatus atricapillus (Green-backed Heron)
    33, 99, 114
Butorides striatus brevipes (Green-backed Heron)
    65, 114
Butorides striatus carcinophilus (Green-backed
    Heron) 85
Butorides striatus chloriceps (Green-backed Heron)
    65
Butorides striatus crawfordi (Green-backed Heron)
    100, 115
Butorides striatus degens (Green-backed Heron)
    100, 115, 363
Butorides striatus didi (Green-backed Heron) 365

Butorides striatus idenburgi (Green-backed Heron)
    85
Butorides striatus javanicus (Green-backed Heron)
    85, 86, 115
Butorides striatus moluccarum (Green-backed
    Heron) 85
Butorides striatus papuensis (Green-backed Heron)
    85
Butorides striatus patruelis (Green-backed Heron)
    136
Butorides striatus rhizophorae (Green-backed
    Heron) 100, 115
Butorides striatus rutenbergi (Green-backed Heron)
    99, 115
Butorides striatus spodiogaster (Green-backed
    Heron) 85–6
Butorides striatus steini (Green-backed Heron) 86
Butorides striatus striatus (Green-backed Heron)
    187
Butorides striatus sundevalli (Green-backed Heron)
    187, 198
Butorides striatus viriscens (Green-backed Heron)
    187
Butorides sundevalli see *Butorides striatus sundevalli*
    (Green-backed Heron)
Butorides virescens see *Butorides striatus viriscens*
    (Green-backed Heron)

Cabo Orange Marsh (Guianas Coast) 178, 179,
    188, 192
cadmium 264–5, 317
    in feathers 315
California, Gulf of (USA) 158
California (USA)
    American Bittern 166
    Black-crowned Night Heron 163
    Cattle Egret 161
    Great White Egret 157, 158
    Green-backed Heron 161
    habitat protection 170
Camargue (France) 2, 3, 53
    Black-crowned Night Heron population 19, 47
    Cattle Egret population 16, 17, 18, 44
    critical wetlands 24, 29
    diet changes 243
    habitat modification 206
    human disturbance 210
    Little Bittern 48
    Little Egret 13, 14, 15, 42–3, 202, 203
        habitat 230
        migration 240–1
        sensitivity analysis 238
    Purple Heron nesting 11, 205–6
    Squacco Heron population 18, 45, 46
    tree-nesting herons artificial colony 208–10
    water levels 27
Cambodia 365
    egg and chick harvesting 212
    trapping 248
Cameroon 100, 101, 110
    Black-crowned Night Heron 115
    Eurasian Bittern 117
    Squacco Heron 113
    White-crested Tiger Heron 116

Camia National Park (Angola/Zambia) 100, 101
Campeche (Mexico) 169
Canada 152, 153
    Cattle Egret 161
    Great Blue Heron 156
    wetlands 155
        protection 170
Cañada de Los Tres Arboles Marshes (Argentina)
        178, 179
canals 60
Candaba Swamo Luzon (Philippines) 74, 75
Cape Verde Islands
    Grey Heron 105
    Intermediate Egret 110
    Purple Heron 107, 362
Caprivi (Namibia) 109, 356
captive populations 293
    breeding success 299
    censuses 295
    changing status 293–4
    chicks 302
    cleaning 301
    conservation priorities 307–9
    data sources 294–5
    diet 300, 302
    feeding areas 301
    founders 305–6
    handling 300
    health problems 300
    history 295–6
    housing 300–1
    husbandry techniques 299–302
    imprinting 302
    international trade 296
    management 298–9, 305–6
    numbers 296
    observation 304–5
    organised conservation programmes 296–8
    propogation 301–2
        events 299
    sex determination 300
    survival 299
    wild heron contact 306–7
capture–mark–recapture methodology 239
capture–recapture studies 338
    models 335
Carass Island (Falkland Islands) 178, 179
carbamate insecticides 262, 328
    poisoning 321
Caribbean
    Cattle Egret 161
    Great Blue Heron 364
    habitat protection 171
    Reddish Egret 186
    Snowy Egret 160
    Yellow-crowned Night Heron 162, 189, 198
Carlos Anwandter Sanctuary (Chile) 178, 179
carp 270, 276, 278
Carpentaria, Gulf (Australia) 124, 125
    Sumatran Heron 130
Cartagena Bay (Colombia) 178, 179
Caspian lowlands (Iran) 1, 59, 64, 65
Caspian Sea 5
    water levels 19, 30

Cassiporé Marsh (Guianas Coast) 178, 179, 188, 192
Casuarina equisetifolia (Australian pine) 93
Cat Tien (Vietnam) 74, 75
Catalogue of Indian Heronries 60–1, 71
cataloguing 215
catchment management, Australia 146
catfish 269
    losses 280
    predation 280, 284
Caucasus, Squacco Heron population 18
Cayman Islands 158
Ceará (Brazil) 186
censuses 329
    accuracy 322
    captive populations 295
    European data 6
    monitoring infrastructure 334
    population status 332
    techniques 6, 214
    wetlands 323–4
    see also numbers of herons; population size
Central African Republic
    Black-crowned Night Heron 115
    Eurasian Bittern 117
    wetland management 119
Central America 151
    American Bittern 166
    Bare-throated Tiger Heron 164
    Boat-billed Heron 164
    Caribbean coast 155
    Cattle Egret 161
    coastal wetlands 168
    colony site protection 173–4
    conservation 167
    environmental conditions 153, 155
    Fasciated Tiger Heron 360
    Great Blue Heron 156
    Great White Egret 157
    Green-backed Heron 161
    habitat conservation 170–1
    habitat protection 169, 170, 171
    habitat quality 171
    heron fauna 151
    international conservation 172
    Least Bittern 164, 165
    Little Blue Heron 159
    South American Bittern 193
    status of herons 154, 155–166
    Tricoloured Heron 158, 159
    wetland loss 170
    Yellow-crowned Night Heron 162
Central American Biological Corridor Project 172
Central Niger Delta (Mali) 115
Central Valley (USA) 152, 153
cestodes 282
Chaco National Park (Argentina) 178, 179
Chad 100, 101
    Black-crowned Night Heron 115
Chad, Lake (West Africa) 100, 101, 119
Chagos Islands 365
Chashma Barrage Reservoir (Pakistan) 56, 57
Cheju-do (South Korea) 85
Chesapeake Bay (USA) 152, 153, 168
    Great Blue Heron 156

chicks
    brooding 302
    captive populations 302
    contaminant accumulation 314, 328
    hand rearing 302
    harvesting 95, 210, 212–14
    mortality and environmental conditions 315
    predation avoidance 202
Chile 178, 179
    Black-crowned Night Heron 189
    Boat-billed Heron 190
    Cattle Egret 187
    Cocoi Heron 185
    Streaked Bittern 192, 197–8
    Whistling Heron 183
Chilka Lake (India) 56, 57, 59, 61
    Great White Egret 62
    Indian Pond Heron 65
    Intermediate Egret 63
    Little Egret 64
Chilwa Lake (Malawi) 100, 101, 120
China 74, 75
    aquaculture 270
    Black Bittern 90
    Eurasian Bittern 91
    Great White Egret 81
    Grey Heron 78
    habitat loss 93
    Japanese Night Heron 87
    Little Bittern 89
    Malayan Night Heron 88
    Swinhoe's Egret 82, 84, 355
    White-eared Night Heron 86–7
    Yellow Bittern 89
China Kau Kong (China) 74, 75
Chitrangudi Tank (India) 56, 57
chlor-alkali plants 195
chlorophenos 262
cholinesterase
    activity 262, 317
    indicator 317, 328
Christmas Bird Counts (CBC) 323, 324
Christmas Island 125, 128
    Yellow Bittern 139
Churute mangroves (Ecuador) 178, 179
Chuwei Mangrove Swamp (Taiwan) 75
Ciconiiformes 253, 377
Circus aeruginosus (Marsh Harrier) 202
cities
    Africa 106
    South America 185, 187, 189
    South and West Asia 65–6, 70
    see also urbanisation
Clairmarais (France) 7
Clarence Valley (Australia) 140
    White-necked Heron 130
climate
    Africa 104
    breeding success 146
    change 29
    East and South-east Asia 73
    Europe 3, 5
    Mediterranean region 34
    New Guinea 129

New Zealand 129
    South America 181
    South and West Asia 59
clutch size 324, 329
    DDE 324–5
    sedentary species 239
coastal lagoons 34, 120, 222
    Africa 119
    South America 181
Cobourg Peninsula (Australia) 124, 125
Cochlearius cochlearius (Boat-billed Heron) xiv
Cochlearius cochlearius cochlearius (Boat-billed
        Heron) 190
Cocos–Keeling Islands 125, 128
    Nankeen Night Heron 138
Colombia 178, 179
    Agami Heron 188
    Bare-throated Tiger Heron 164, 190, 366
    Boat-billed Heron 190
    Capped Heron 183
    Cattle Egret 187
    Great Blue Heron 184
    Great White Egret 185
    Green-backed Heron 187, 188
    Least Bittern 193
    Little Blue Heron 186
    Reddish Egret 185
    Snowy Egret 160
    South American Bittern 193
    Streaked Bittern 192
    Tricoloured Heron 186
    Whistling Heron 183
    Yellow-crowned Night Heron 162, 189
coloniality, conservation implications 202–3
colonisation, post-fledging dispersal 243
colony
    census techniques 214
    size 53–4
colony sites
    abandonment 173–4, 210–11
    artificial 207–8
    buffer zones 211–12
    East and South-east Asia 92–3
    protection in Americas 173–4
    security zone 204, 205
    use monitoring 327–8
Colorado River (USA)
    Great Blue Heron 156
    Great White Egret 157
    Snowy Egret 160
Colorado (USA) 162, 256
Comachio (Italy) 2, 3
Combermere Bay (Myanmar) 74, 75
commensalism 220
Common Agricultural Policy (EU) 247
community
    beliefs about water usage 148
    rural 120–1
community involvement 148, 149, 378
    wetland conservation 231
community level indicators 327–8
Comores 99, 100
    Cattle Egret 113
    Great White Egret 109

Comores – *contd*
  Green-backed Heron 115
  Grey Heron 106, 363
  Malagasy Heron 357
competition 244–5
congenital anomalies 253, 320–1
Congo Basin (Democratic Republic of Congo) 100, 101
Congo, Democratic Republic of 100, 101
  Black-crowned Night Heron 115
  Eurasian Bittern 117
  Malagasy Pond Heron 114
  Purple Heron 107
  Rufous-bellied Heron 114
  Squacco Heron 113
  wetland management 119
  White-backed Night Heron 115
  White-crested Tiger Heron 116
conservation
  action 343–4
  coordination 378
  habitats 338
  local involvement 148, 149, 231, 378
  plans 29, 228
  populations 337
  scale 342
  status 344–9
    species of the world 346–9
  taxon 351–70
contaminants 342
  accumulation in chicks 314, 328
  concentrations 314–17
  environmental 251
  monitoring 342
  see also pollution
contamination 266–7
  Great Lakes 328
Convention on Biological Diversity 199
Convention on the Conservation of European
    Wildlife and Natural Habitats 23
Convention on International Trade in Endangered
    Species (CITES) 97
Convention on Wetlands of International
    Importance especially as Waterfowl
    Habitat *see* Ramsar Convention
Coongie Lakes (Australia) 124, 125, 143
Cooper Creek (Australia) 124, 125, 143
Coorong (Australia) 124, 125
Coppername River Mouth (Guianas Coast) 178, 179
Coppernamebank (Guianas Coast) 178, 179
coral reefs 129, 339
Corixa (lesser water boatman) 282–3
Coromandel Coast (India) 56, 57, 69
corridor, wildlife 173
Cosmoledo, Little Egret 112
cost–benefit analysis of fish farm protection 290–1
Costa Rica 152, 153
  Agami Heron 162
  border area protection 172
  Fasciated Tiger Heron 164, 190
  Green-backed Heron 161
  Reddish Egret 158
  South American Bittern 165

Cote d'Ivoire
  Black-crowned Night Heron 115
  Grey Heron 106
  wetland management 119
Council of Europe 23
counting 332–3
  bias in techniques 334
  see also censuses; numbers of herons
crawfish/crayfish 232
  farms in Louisiana 271, 273
  predation 285
Criteria for Critically Endangered, Endangered
    and Vulnerable Species (IUCN 1966) 344,
    372–5
critical areas, inaccessibility 334
Crna Mlaka (Croatia) 2, 3
Croatia 2, 3
  Black-crowned Night Heron 19, 48
  Great White Egret population 11, 40–1
  Little Egret population 41
  Purple Heron population 10, 38
  Squacco Heron population 18, 45
Cruces River (Chile) 178, 179
Cuba 152, 153
  Great Blue Heron 156
  Little Blue Heron 159, 160
  Reddish Egret 158
  wetlands 155
  wintering area 168
Cubato mangroves (Brazil) 178, 179
Cucunuba lagoon (South America) 197
Cunene River (Namibia) 116
Cuyabeno Lagoons (Ecuador) 179
cyprinids 269
cytochrome P450 317–19
cytogenetic damage 319–20
Czech Republic
  Black-crowned Night Heron 19
  Great White Egret population 11, 12
  Little Bittern population 20
  Little Egret population 13

Da Ming Shan Nature Reserve (China) 353
dams 141, 142–3
  siltation 246
  South America 195–6
Danau Bankau (Indonesia) 74, 75
Danube delta (Romania) 2, 3, 12, 16
  Biosphere reserve 51
  Black-crowned Night Heron 48
  Cattle Egret population 43
  critical wetlands 24, 27
  Eurasian Bittern 49
  Great White Egret population 40
  Grey Heron 37
    shooting 28
  Little Egret population 41, 43
  pesticides 258
  Purple Heron population 38, 40
  reed bed degradation 50–1
  Squacco Heron population 18, 45
  World Heritage site 51
Darling–Murray river system (Australia) *see*
    Murray–Darling basin (Australia)

Darwin area floodplain (Australia) 125
Dasht-E Moghan (Iran) 57
data management 335
Dawhat Sawqirah (Oman) 57, 64
DDE 258–60
    Black-crowned Night Heron 254–8
    clutch size 324–5
    eggshell thickness 253, 254, 317, 328
DDT 251, 252, 258–9, 313
    Cattle Egret decline 322
    eggshell thickness 254
    poisoning 252, 253
    reproductive success 253
De Hoop Vlei Nature Reserve (South Africa) 100,
        101
de la Virgen Swamp (Colombia) 178, 179
De Mond Nature Reserve (South Africa) 100, 101
deforestation
    Central America 167
    East and South-east Asia 91, 92
    Madagascar 118–19
    mangroves 248
    South and West Asia 70
deformities 253, 320–1
degradation see habitat degradation
Delaware Bay (USA) 152, 153, 168
Delcommune, Lake (Congo) 100, 101
Delhi Zoo (India) 63
Delta du Saloum (Senegal) 100, 101
deltas
    coastline erosion 246
    marshy 5
Denmark 3
    Grey Heron population 7, 9
    Nature Management Act 27
    reed bed management 26
Densu Delta (Ghana) 100, 101
desert, Middle East 59
development see agriculture; urbanisation
Dez Dam (Iran) 57
Dharmasagar Reservoir (India) 65
Dhofar Khawrs (Oman) 57
dibenzofurans, congenital anomalies 321
Diego Suarez (Madagascar) 114
dieldrin 251, 252, 253
    eggshell thickness 253, 254
    poisoning 321
diet
    captive populations 300
    Cattle Egret 17–18
    changes 243–4
    seasonality 327
    young birds 327
dioxin equivalents 318
dioxins 261–2
    congenital anomalies 321
Dipterocarp forest 81
Directive on the Conservation of Natural Habitats
        of Wild Fauna and Flora (92/43/EEC) 23
Directive on the Conservation of Wild Birds
        (79/409/EEC) 23
disease transmission 280, 281–2
dispersal 242–3
    Black-crowned Night Heron 115

Cocoi Heron 185
    Eastern Reef Heron 135
    Great Blue Heron 156
    Great White Egret 41, 108–9
    Indian Pond Heron 65
    Intermediate Egret 110
    Little Egret 229
    Snowy Egret 160
    Swinhoe's Egret 83
distribution xiii–xiv, 336–7
    changes 336
        as indicators 322–4
    migration 336–7
disturbance 210–12, 248–9
ditches 223
diversion from fish farms 287–8
diversity
    aquaculture production systems 274–8
    Europe 2, 28
    habitats 5
Djibouti, wetland management 119
Djoudj National Park (Senegal) 100, 101
DNA 319–20
Dnepr River (Ukraine) 2, 3, 12
    Grey Heron 37
    Little Egret 41
Dnestr Delta (Ukraine) 2, 3, 51
    Black-crowned Night Heron 48
    Eurasian Bittern 49
    Great White Egret population 40
    Grey Heron population 37
    hydrology changes 246
    Purple Heron population 38
    Squacco Heron population 18
Doboy Swamp (Australia) 147
Dobrogea (Romania) 2, 3
Doce River Estuary (Brazil) 178, 179
Dombes, Ponds (France) 2, 3, 13
    Squacco Heron population 18
    water levels 27
Dominican Republic 152, 153
    wintering area 168
Dongting Lakes (China) 74, 75
drainage
    East and South-east Asia 93, 94
    Euphrates and Tigris floodplain 246
    Iran 67
    Iraq 62, 66, 68
    mangrove damage 170
    Mediterranean region 34
    South America 196, 197
    wetlands
        conversion 226
        degradation 247
Drigh lake (Pakistan) 56, 57, 66
drought 229
    Africa 30, 31, 40, 367
    Australia 128
    diet of young 327
    migration 240
    South and West Asia 70
dry–wet cycles 146, 228–9
Dulce River Marshes (Argentina) 178, 179
dumps 223

Duqm (Oman) 57
Dutch Wetlands (Netherlands) 2, 3
dytiscus beetles 278

Eagle, Bald 170–1
East Alligator River (Australia) 146
East and South-east Asia 73
    colony sites 92–3
    conservation priorities 97–8
    data 77–8
    environmental conditions 73, 75, 77
    habitat loss 93–4
    habitat types 73, 75
    heron fauna 73, 76
    hunting 95
    monitoring 95–6
    pesticides 94–5
    planning policy/legislation 96–7
    research 95–6
    status of herons 76, 77–91
    trapping 248–9
    water pollution 94–5
Eber/Aksehir complex (Turkey) 2, 3
Ebro Delta (Spain) 2, 3, 16, 53, 211
    chick exploitation 213
    diet changes 243
    Little Egrets 241
    Purple Heron 38, 39
    rice fields 224
ecological requirements
    feeding 216
    nesting 203–4, 209
ecological studies 206
economics of conservation 332
ecosystem conditions 214
ecosystem level indicators 328
ecotourism 121, 196–7, 215
    see also tourism
Ecuador 178, 179
    Agami Heron 188
    Great Blue Heron 184
    Little Blue Heron 186
    Tricoloured Heron 186
    Zigzag Heron 192
Ecury le Grand (France) 7
education programmes, zoos 305
Edward, Lake (Africa) 107
Edward River (Australia) 132
eggs
    collection 71, 95, 212
    contaminants 172
    harvesting 95, 210, 212–14
    mercury levels 264
    pesticide content 170
    removal in captive breeding 306
eggshell
    quality 317
    thinning 253, 254–6
eggshell thickness
    DDE 254, 317
    indicator 317, 328
    organochlorine insecticides 258–60
Egret, Black see Heron, Black
Egret, Cattle xiii, 1, 4, 24, 172

abundance 167
Africa 100, 112–13, 117, 228
Americas 161
artificial colony 208
Australia and Oceania 123, 125, 128, 136–8, 147
cholinesterase activity 317
colonies 203
conservation status 351
DDT 322
decline 170
diet 17–18
distributional changes 322
disturbance 211
East and South-east Asia 85
egg collection 212
free-ranging in zoos 306
habitat 24, 220, 221, 223, 224
    availability 227–8
hand-rearing 302
lead levels 264
Malagasy 112–13
Mediterranean area 33, 35, 43–4, 50, 52, 53
migration 64, 113, 137
    behaviour change 245
monitoring 323
nests 204
Nile Delta 322
North America 155
organochorine insecticides 259
population fluctuation 30
predator avoidance 202
releases 303
South America 182, 187, 194
South and West Asia 55, 64–5, 68, 71
species account for Europe 15–18
translocation 303
winter temperatures 34, 44
wintering populations 323
Egret, Great
    cholinesterase activity 317
    dieldrin mortality 252
    mercury 263
    organochlorine insecticides 258
    wintering populations 323
Egret, Great White 1, 4
    Africa 99, 108–9, 117, 118
    Americas 157–8
    Australia 123, 131–2, 141, 144, 146–7
    conservation status 362, 367
    contaminant accumulation 314, 315
    East and South-east Asia 81
    feeding
        area 207
        sites 230
    fish predation 278
    genetic characterisation 337
    habitat 24, 222, 223, 224
    hacking 304
    lead levels 264
    Malagasy 108–9
    Mediterranean area 35, 40–1, 50
    mercury 263, 315
    migration 12, 41
    nest construction 203

New Zealand 129
North America 155
Oceania 123, 131–2
piscivory 273
plume trade 214
population fluctuation 30
protection 28
South America 182, 185
South and West Asia 62–3, 68, 70
species account for Europe 11–12
trace elements in feathers 314–15
water levels 27
wintering habit 12, 241, 244
Egret, Intermediate xiii, 63, 70, 71
Africa 99, 110–11, 117
Australia and Oceania 123, 132–4, 141, 142, 144, 146–7
habitat 222, 224
migration 240
wetland management 146
Egret, Little 1, 4
Africa 99–100, 111–12, 117, 118
Americas 160–1
artificial colony 208
Australia and Oceania 134–5, 141
blood sampling 320
capture–recapture models 335
chick harvesting 212, 213
diet change 243–4
disturbance 211
feeding 202, 230
area 207
genetic characterisation 337
habitat 24, 220, 222, 223, 224
flexibility 229
lead levels 264
Malagasy 112
Mediterranean area 33, 35, 41–3, 50, 52, 53
migration 12, 14–15, 43, 111, 240–1
behaviour change 245
nesting 203
New Zealand 129
organochlorine insecticides 260
PCBs 261
plume trade 214
population fluctuation 14, 30
predator avoidance 202
protection 28
range
expansion in Europe 12–13
restricted 167
salinity tolerance 25
sensitivity analysis 238
South America 177, 187
South and West Asia 55, 63–4, 68, 70, 71
species account for Europe 12–15
winter mortality 242
winter temperatures 34
wintering movements 14–15
wintering sites 244
Egret, Reddish xiii, 151, 155, 158
bill deformities 321
conservation 166, 168, 169, 172, 174, 175
status 357

habitat 222
South America 177, 185–6
Egret, Slaty xiii, 99, 109
captive conservation priority 308
conservation status 350, 356–7
Egret, Snowy xii, 155, 160, 170
cholinesterase activity 317
disturbance 211
feeding area 207
fish predation 278
growth rate of young 325, 326
habitat 222, 223, 230
lead levels 264
movements 240
nesting success 325
organochorine insecticides 259
PCBs 261
plume trade 214, 303
South America 182, 186–7
translocation 303
wetland conditions 327
wintering populations 323
Egret, Swinhoe's 81–4, 162
captive 298
conservation priority 307–8
conservation status 355–6
habitat 222
migration 240
Egretta alba (Great White Egret) xiii, 1
Egretta alba alba (Great White Egret) 62, 108, 367
Egretta alba maoriana (Great White Egret) 131–2, 362
Egretta alba melanorhynchos (Great White Egret) 99
Egretta alba modesta (Great White Egret) 62
Egretta ardesiaca (Black Heron) xiii, 110, 359
Egretta caerulea (Little Blue Heron) xiii
Egretta dimorpha see Egretta garzetta dimorpha (Little Egret)
Egretta eulophotes (Swinhoe's Egret) xiii, 81, 355–6
Egretta garzetta (Little Egret) xiii, 1, 242
Egretta garzetta dimorpha (Little Egret) 100, 112
Egretta garzetta garzetta (Little Egret) 111, 161
Egretta garzetta gularis (Western Reef Heron) 33, 111, 112, 117, 161, 187
Egretta garzetta immaculata (Little Egret) 134
Egretta garzetta nigripes (Little Egret) 81
Egretta garzetta schistacea (Little Egret) 112
Egretta gularis see Egretta garzetta gularis (Western Reef Heron)
Egretta intermedia (Intermediate Egret) xiii, 63
Egretta intermedia brachyrhyncha (Intermediate Egret) 99
Egretta intermedia plumifera (Intermediate Egret) 81
Egretta novaehollandiae (White-faced Heron) xiii
Egretta picata (Pied Heron) xiii, 123
Egretta rufescens (Reddish Egret) xiii, 357
Egretta rufescens dickeyi (Reddish Egret) 158
Egretta rufescens rufescens (Reddish Egret) 185
Egretta thula (Snowy Egret) xiii
Egretta tricolor (Tricolored Heron) xiii
Egretta tricolor ruficollis (Tricolored Heron) 186
Egretta tricolor tricolor (Tricolored Heron) 186

Egretta vinaceigula (Slaty Egret) xiii, 356–7
Egypt 2, 3
  Black-crowned Night Heron 48
  Grey Heron 37
  habitat loss 52
  Little Bittern 48, 49
  Mediterranean 35, 37, 38, 41, 42, 43, 46
Eichornia crassipes (water hyacinth) 144
El Hair Watercourse Reserve (Saudi Arabia) 57
El Paraíso (Peru) 178, 179, 197
El Peral Lagoon (Chile) 178, 179
El Pilon Creek (Argentina) 198
El Sonso lagoon (South America) 197
El-Kala wetland complex (Algeria) 2, 3, 34, 35
  Eurasian Bittern 50, 367
  Grey Heron 37
  Little Bittern 48
  Little Egret 42
  Purple Heron 38
Elementaita, Lake (Kenya) 100, 101
embryos, abnormal 321
embryotoxic effects 313
endrin poisoning 252
energy requirements 228
  of fish-eating birds 284
environmental change
  estuarine wetlands 325
  tracking 312–13
environmental conditions
  Africa 104
  Australia 125, 128–9
  Central America 153, 155
  East and South-east Asia 73, 75, 77
  Europe 3, 5
  Malagasy 104
  Mediterranean region 34–5
  nestling mortality 315
  North America 153, 155
  Oceania 125, 128–9
  South America 181–2
  South and West Asia 57, 59–60
  West Indies 153, 155
Environmental Impact Assessments (EIAs) 97
environmentally sensitive management of rice
    fields 53
epidemiology 281–2
Equatorial Trough 104
Eritrea
  Eurasian Bittern 117
  Purple Heron 107
  wetland management 119
EROD activity 318
Esteros del Iber (Argentina) 178, 179
estuarine wetlands 5, 222
  environmental change 325
Ethiopia 100, 101
  Black-crowned Night Heron 115
  Eurasian Bittern 117
  Grey Heron 105, 106
  Little Egret 112
  Purple Heron 107
  Squacco Heron 113
  wetland management 119
Etosha National Park (Namibia) 100, 101, 119

Eturia Lagoons (Argentina) 178, 179
Eucalyptus trees 205
Eudocimus albus (White Ibis) 327
Eudocimus ruber (Scarlet Ibis) 196
Euphrates River (Iran) 67
  floodplain 246
Europe 1
  census data 6
  conservation
    plans 29
    status 350
  critical wetland areas 24
  environmental conditions 3, 5
  habitat management 25–8
  heron fauna 1–3
  important heron areas 2
  international conservation policy 23–4
  landscape alteration 29
  population monitoring 31
  species diversity 28
  wetland conservation 24–5
European Bird Database (1994) 5
  Mediterranean region 35–6
European Union 23
eutrophication 26, 195, 280
Evros Delta (Greece) 2, 3
extinctions 226–7, 352
Eyasi, Lake (Tanzania) 100, 101

faeces of birds 281–2
Falkland Islands 177, 178, 179, 198
  Black-crowned Night Heron 189, 198
  Cattle Egret 187
  Cocoi Heron 185
feathers
  trace elements 314–15, 317, 328
  see also plume trade
feeding
  areas 206–7
    captive populations 301
  behaviour 280
  ecology 216
  effectiveness 284–5
  opportunist 243
  sites 229
    reed beds 26
  social 202
feeding habitat 339–40
  Africa 120
  choice 229–30
  conservation 219
  limitations 227
  North America 155
  requirements 53–4
feral populations 144, 309
Figueroa Marshes (Argentina) 178, 179
Fiji, Green-backed Heron 136
Finniss River (Australia) 146
first-hatched birds 242
fish
  behaviour 285
  consumption 283–4
  density 284
  disease transmission 281–2

invertebrate predators 278, 282–3
migration 195
nematode infections 326
parasites 282
population and water level 27
predation rate 278, 280
predatory 280
proportion in diet 272
secondary infections 282
selection of parasitised by heron 282
stock loss 283–4
fish farms/farming 28, 29, 31, 52, 173, 232–3
    East and South-east Asia 93
    fish-eating bird conflict 270–2
    habitat degradation 247
    habitat value 225
    Madagascar 119
    mangrove clearance 167
    operational measures 287–8
    protective measures 289–91
    site design 286–7
    see also aquaculture; catfish; crawfish/crayfish;
        shrimp farming; trout
fish ponds 225
    design 287
    East and South-east Asia 94
    extensive 276
    intensive 278–9
    production 275
    South America 187
fishermen 213
fishing
    Africa 119
    amateur 276
    commercial 118, 120, 276
fledging success 324–5
    Black-crowned Night Heron 254–5
flooding 229
    feeding habitats 244
    seasonal 246
floodplains
    Africa 119, 120
    South and West Asia 59
Flora and Fauna Guarantee Act (1997; Australia)
        131, 134, 135, 139, 140, 355
Florida Bay (USA) 152, 153, 158
Florida (USA)
    abundance of herons 166
    American Bittern 166
    Black-crowned Night Heron 164
    Cattle Egret 161
    Everglades 152, 153, 171, 233, 278
        drought 327
        hydrology 322
        indicators of deterioration 313
    Great Blue Heron 157, 168, 364
    Great White Egret 157, 158
    Green-backed Heron 161
    Little Blue Heron 159, 160
    mercury 263
    nesting population 168
    population changes 226–7
    Reddish Egret 158
    Snowy Egret 160

Tricoloured Heron 158, 159
    wetland degradation 203
flow cytometry 319, 328
flush distances 211–12
Fly River floodplain (New Guinea) 124, 125, 144
    see also Middle Fly floodplain
fly-ash
    combustion 262
    disposal 265
flyway
    management 233–4
    see also Atlantic flyway; Mississippi River
        (USA), flyway; Pacific flyway
food
    availability 340
    consumption 284
    regurgitation 202
food patch profitability 202
foraging patch 228
forest 338
    conservation 221
    East and South-east Asia 93
    habitats 338
    streamside 220–1
    swamp 119, 129, 145
    see also deforestation
forest fires, Central America 168
forestry
    social 69, 71
    see also deforestation; logging
former USSR, Grey Heron population 10
founders
    captive populations 305–6
    collecting 306
France 2, 3, 5
    Black-crowned Night Heron population 19, 47,
        48
    Cattle Egret population 15–16, 17, 18, 43, 44
    critical wetlands 24
    Great White Egret 12
        population 41
    Grey Heron
        history 7–8
        population 6, 7–9, 37
    Little Bittern population 20, 48
    Little Egret population 12, 13–14, 41, 42
    Mediterranean 34, 35, 37
    protection 28
    Purple Heron population 38, 40
    Squacco Heron population 18, 46
    tourism 51
    water levels 27
    wetland area 25
Fraser's Hill (Malaysia) 90
Fraxinus (ash) 208
French Antilles, wetlands 155
French Guiana 178, 179
    Snowy Egret 160, 187
frog, Australian green 132
fry, fish 278
fuel wood 248
fungal infection 282
Funza marsh (Colombia) 178, 179, 197
Fuquene Lagoons (Colombia) 107, 178, 179

Gabon 100, 101
    Eurasian Bittern 117
    White-crested Tiger Heron 116
Galápagos Islands 177, 198
    Black-crowned Night Heron 189
    Great Blue Heron 156, 184, 198
    Green-backed Heron 187, 198
    saline lagoons 178, 179
    Yellow-crowned Night Heron 162, 189, 198
Galibi (Guianas Coast) 178, 179
Galilee, Sea of (Israel) 47
Gambia
    Black-crowned Night Heron 115
    Eurasian Bittern 117
    Little Egret 111, 112
    Purple Heron 107
    Squacco Heron 113
    wetland management 119
Ganges flood plain (India/Bangladesh) 56, 57, 245
Garonne River floodplain (France) 2, 3
Garzón Lagoon (Uraguay) 178, 179
genetic characterisation 337
genetic damage, indicator 319–20
Georgia, Straight of (Canada) 152, 153
Georgia (USA), American Bittern 166
Germany
    Black-crowned Night Heron 19, 20
    Eurasian Bittern population 23
    Grey Heron population 6, 7, 9
    Little Bittern population 20
    Little Egret population 12
    protection 28
    Purple Heron population 10, 11
Ghana 100, 101
    Black-crowned Night Heron 115
    Eurasian Bittern 117
    Grey Heron 105, 106
    Little Egret 111, 112
    Purple Heron 107
    wetland management 119
Gippsland Lakes (Australia) 124, 125
Gironde estuary (France) 24
Goajiran Peninsula (Colombia) 185
Goksu Delta (Turkey) 2, 3
gold mining 195
Golfo de Ana Maria (Cuba) 152, 153
Golfo de Batabano (Cuba) 152, 153
Golfo de Fonseca 152, 153
Golfo de Guacanayabo (Cuba) 152, 153
Golfo do Montijo (Panama) 152, 153
Gomishan Marsh (Iran) 56, 57, 61
    Great White Egret 62
    Little Egret 64
Gorsachius goisagi (Japanese Night Heron) xiv, 357
Gorsachius magnificus (White-eared Night Heron) xiv, 352–4
Gorsachius melanolophus (Malayan Night Heron) xiv
Gorsachius melanolophus kutteri (Malayan Night Heron) 366
Gorsachius melanolophus melanolophus (Malayan Night Heron) 366
Gorsachius melanolophus minor (Malayan Night Heron) 366
Gorsachius melanolophus rufolineata (Malayan Night Heron) 88, 365
Gosford (Australia) 128
Grado declaration on Mediterranean wetlands 51
Grafton (Australia) 130, 137
Grand-Lieu, Lake (France) 2, 3, 7–8
    Cattle Egret breeding 16
    critical wetlands 24
    Little Egret breeding 13
    Squacco Heron breeding 18
    water levels 27
Great Barrier Reef (Australia) 128, 138
Great Britain see United Kingdom
Great Cumbung Swamp (Australia) 124, 125
Great Lake (Cambodia) 95
Great Lakes (Canada) 320–1
    contamination 328
Great Rann of Kachchh (India) 57
Great Salt Lake (USA) 157
Great Vedaranyam Swamp (India) 59
Greater Antilles
    Cattle Egret 161
    Great Blue Heron 157
    Great White Egret 158
    Least Bittern 164, 165
    Snowy Egret 160
    Tricoloured Heron 158, 159
    Yellow-crowned Night Heron 162
Greater Sundas
    Cinnamon bittern 90
    Grey Heron 363
Greece 2, 3, 34, 53
    Black-crowned Night Heron 48
    Cattle Egret population 16, 43
    Great White Egret population 40, 41
    hunting 248
    pesticides 258
    protection 28
    Purple Heron population 10
    Squacco Heron population 18, 45
    tourism 51
    wetland loss 51
    wintering sites 244
Green Bay (Wisconsin; USA) 258, 260–1
'green' policies 25
Greenland, Grey Heron 156
groundwater extraction 246
growth parameters 325–6
growth rate 325–6
Guadalquivir Delta (Spain) 2, 3
    Black-crowned Night Heron 48
    critical wetlands 24, 29
    Purple Heron 38, 39
Guadeloupe, Little Egret 160
Guadiana River (Spain) 2, 3
    Cattle Egret population 17, 44
    critical wetlands 24, 29
Guajaro Swamp (Colombia) 178, 179
Guam 139
    Cattle Egret 137
Guangdong Province (China) 353
Guangxi (China) 352–3
Guatemala 152, 153
    South American Bittern 165

Yellow-crowned Night Heron 162
Guayaquil, Gulf of (Ecuador) 178, 179
Guerande (France) 2, 3
Gueumbeul Wildlife Reserve (Senegal) 100, 101
Guianas
    Capped Heron 183
    Green-backed Heron 187
    Grey Heron 183
    Least Bittern 193
    South American Bittern 193
    Streaked Bittern 192
Guindy National Park (India) 66
Guinea 100, 101
    Black-crowned Night Heron 115
    Grey Heron 105
    Little Egret 111, 112
    Squacco Heron 113
    wetland management 119
    White-crested Tiger Heron 115
Guinea-Bissau 100, 101, 110
    Little Bittern 116
    Little Egret 111, 112
    wetland management 119
Gujarat (India) 70
gull, herring 317
Gunbower State Forest (Australia) 124, 125, 128, 138
Guyana, Streaked Bittern 198
Gwydir system (Australia) 142–3
Gyobyu Reservoir (Myanmar) 74, 75

H4IIE rat hepatoma cell bioassay 319
habitat
    Africa 104
    artificial 223–5, 341–2
        management 231–3
        predation 278
    availability 227–8
    coastal mudflats 59
    conservation 338
        North America 171–2
    diversity 5
    dry 223
    human activity impact 379
    Malagasy 104
    management 228
        in Europe 25–8
        regional 340
    marine 222
    migratory 237–9
    modification in Camargue 206
    nesting 339
    papyrus swamp 119
    pastureland 223
        damp 24, 339
    quality in Americas 172
    selection 340
    South America 194–5
    types in East and South-east Asia 73, 75
    use as indicator 327–8
    see also coastal lagoons; feeding habitat; forest;
        mangrove swamps; marshes; reed beds;
        salt marshes; tree-nesting herons; upland
        habitat conservation; wetlands; wintering

    areas/sites
habitat degradation 247–8
    artificial colony sites 207
    East and South-east Asia 91, 92, 93
    Israel 52
    South America 195, 197
habitat loss
    East and South-east Asia 93–4
    Mediterranean area 50–1, 54
    New South Wales 140–1
    New Zealand 141
    Swan Coastal Plain (Australia) 140
    wetlands 245–6
Habitats Directive 23
habituation, fish farm protective measures 291
hacking 303–4
Hacks Lagoon (Australia) 124, 125
Hadejia (Nigeria) 100, 101
Hadero Lake (India) 56, 57
Hagoi, Lake (Mariana Islands) 139
Hail Haor Wildlife Sanctuary (Bangladesh) 56, 57, 62
Hainan (China) 86, 87
Haliaeetus leucocephalus (Bald Eagle) 169–70
Hammar Marshes (Iraq) 66
Hamoun-l Helmand (Iran) 57
Hamun-i-Pusak (Afghanistan) 62
hand rearing 302
handling of captive populations 300
Hara Protected Region (Iran) 57
Harrier, Marsh 202
harvest of eggs and chicks 95, 210, 212–14
hatching, asynchronous 242
hatching success 324–5
    Black-crowned Night Heron 254–6
Haur Chubaisah (Iraq) 66
Hawk's Nest Ponds (Falkland Islands) 178, 179
head injuries 300
heavy metals 263–5
heron
    species and distribution xiii–xiv
    see also Night Heron; Pond Heron; Reef Heron;
        Tiger Heron
Heron, Agami xiv, 151, 155, 162, 166, 174, 175
    conservation status 360
    habitat 220–1, 223
    South America 182, 188, 193
Heron, Black xiii, 110, 117, 118
    conservation status 359
    habitat 222
Heron, Black-headed xiii, 57, 99
    Africa 106, 117, 118
    cities 106
    habitat 223
    migration 240
Heron, Boat-billed xiv, 155, 164, 182, 189–90
    captive conservation priority 308
    habitat 222
    hand rearing 302
    sex determination 300
Heron, Capped xiii, 151, 156, 182, 183, 184
    habitat 223
    sedentary 239
Heron, Cocoi xiii, 151, 157, 185

Heron Conservation Action Plan 371
Heron, Goliath xiii
  Africa 107, 118
  conservation status 364
  East and South-east Asia 80
  habitat 222
  hand rearing 302
  South and West Asia 57, 62, 71
Heron, Great Blue xiii, 151, 155, 156–7
  abundance 166
  colony site destruction 173–4
  congenital anomalies 321
  conservation 166, 168, 171, 172, 175
    status 364–5
  contaminant accumulation 318
  cytochrome P450 activity 319
  decline 170
  dieldrin mortality 252
  diet change 243
  dioxins 261–2
  disturbance 211
  feeding area 206
  fish predation 278
  habitat 222, 225, 229
  lead levels 264
  mercury 263
  movements 240
  nesting 201
    success 325
  organochlorine insecticides 258
  PCBs 261
  piscivory 273
  predation 284
  South America 177, 184
  white morph 168, 172, 174, 175
Heron, Green-backed xiv, 33, 65, 85–6, 171
  abundance 166
  Africa 99, 100, 114–15
  Americas 161–2
  Australia and Oceania 123, 136
  conservation status 363, 365
  genetic characterisation 337
  habitat 222, 223, 232
  North America 156
  organochlorine insecticides 258–9
  South America 182, 187–8
  wintering populations 323
Heron, Grey xiii, 1, 4, 24
  abundance 28
  Africa 99, 105–6, 117, 118
  Americas 156
  Australia and Oceania 125
  Black Sea 36
  conservation status 361–2, 363
  diet change 243
  East and South-east Asia 78–9
  eggshell thinning 253–4
  feeding area 206, 207
  food requirements 284
  free-ranging in zoos 306
  habitat 24, 224, 225
  latitude tolerance 28
  lead levels 264
  Malagasy 105

Mediterranean region 35, 36–7, 50, 52
  mercury 264
  migration 8–9, 37, 241
    behaviour change 245
  mixed colonies 7
  monitoring 322, 323
  nesting 201, 203, 204
  organocholorine insecticides 253–4
  persecution 27, 28, 31, 213–14
  pioneering species 29
  piscivory 272–3
  population fluctuations 10
  population stability 29
  predation rate 277
  protection 7, 28, 31
  salinity tolerance 25
  sedentary 239, 240
  South America 177, 183
  South and West Asia 55, 61, 68, 70
  species account for Europe 6–10
  translocation 303
  wintering sites 244
Heron, Imperial
  captive conservation priority 307
  conservation status 350, 354–5
  East and South-east Asia 79
  South and West Asia 55, 59, 61, 70, 71
Heron, Little Blue xiii, 155, 159–60
  cadmium in feathers 315
  fish predation 278
  nesting success 325
  South America 182, 186
  wetland conditions 327
  wintering populations 323
Heron, Malagasy xiii, 107, 298
  captive conservation priority 307
  conservation status 359
Heron, Pied xiii, 123, 132, 144
  habitat 223
Heron, Purple xiii, 1, 4
  Africa 99, 107–8, 118
  breeding range 11
  colonies 203
  conservation status 350, 362, 364, 367
  disturbance 211
  East and South-east Asia 81
  environmental conditions 315
  feeding area 207
  habitat 24, 26, 27, 221
  hunting 249
  Malagasy 99, 107
  Mediterranean region 35, 37–40, 50, 52, 203
  migration 11, 26, 107, 240, 241
  nesting 201, 203
    requirements 205–6
    sites 37
  organochlorine insecticides 259–60
  persecution 52
  pesticide contamination 81
  South and West Asia 62, 68
  species account for Europe 10–11
  water levels 27
  wintering conditions 11, 367
Heron, Rufous-bellied xiii, 114, 240, 360

Heron Specialist Group 332, 337, 343, 371
    IUCN criteria 344
    threat categories 344, 345
Heron, Squacco 1, 4
    Africa 113–14, 117, 118
    conservation status 350, 368
    diet change 243, 244
    feeding area 207
    habitat 24, 26, 221, 224
    Malagasy 113–14
    Mediterranean region 35, 45–8
    migration 26, 240, 241, 242, 244, 245, 368
    organochlorine insecticides 260
    persecution 52
    population fluctuation 18, 19, 25, 30
    protection 28
    ringing 338
    South and West Asia 57, 65, 68
    species account for Europe 18–19
    wintering sites 341
Heron, Sumatran xiii, 358–9
    Australia and Oceania 130–1, 144
    East and South-east Asia 79–81
    South and West Asia 57, 61–2, 71
Heron, Tricolored xiii, 155, 158–59
    fish predation 278
    habitat 222
    lead levels 264
    nesting success 325
    South America 177, 186
    wetland conditions 327
    wintering populations 323
Heron, Whistling xiii, 182, 183
    habitat 222, 223
Heron, White-faced xiii, 123, 128, 129, 134, 141, 145
    habitat 223
    migration 240
Heron, White-necked xiii, 123
    Australia 130, 141
    habitat 222
Heron, Zigzag xiv, 182, 191–2, 193
    conservation status 351, 361
    habitat 222, 223
    nesting 205
    sedentary 239
Herons Handbook 343
Heuningnes Estuary (South Africa) 100, 101
Hidkal Reservoir (India) 57
Hidrovia Project, Paraná–Paraguay river 196
Hispaniola (Dominican Republic)
    Little Blue Heron 159, 160
    north coast 153
    wetlands 155
Honduras 152, 153
    Little Blue Heron 159, 160
    Rufescent Tiger Heron 190
Honduras, Gulf of 153
Hong Kong 77, 78
    Cattle Egret 85
    chick harvesting 213
    colony sites 92, 93
    feeding area 207
    fish ponds 225, 233
    Grey Heron 78

habitat loss 94
hunting 95
Japanese Night Heron 87
research 96
Schrenck's Bittern 90
site protection 96
Swinhoe's Egret 81, 82, 83, 84
wetland loss 226
Hong Kong Mai Po (China) 74, 75
Hornborga, Lake (Sweden), restoration project 27
housing, captive populations 300–1
Huizache–Caimanero lagoon (Mexico) 170
Huleh (Israel) 2, 3
    Black-crowned Night Heron 47
    Cattle Egret 44
    habitat degradation 52
    Little Bittern 49
    Purple Heron 38, 40
humans
    activities and habitat threats 379
    culture 332
    density 26
    disturbance 210
    migration 198
    population 169
Humboldt Bay (California) 158
Hungary 2, 3, 5
    Black-crowned Night Heron 19
    Great White Egret population 11
    Little Egret population 14
    protection 28
    Squacco Heron population 18
Hunter Valley (Australia) 141
    Cattle Egret 137
    Great White Egret 131
    Little Egret 134
    White-faced Heron 134
    White-necked Heron 130
Hunter's Bay (Myanmar) 74, 75
hunting 27–8
    Africa 119
    Americas 173
    Central America 167
    disturbance 248
    East and South-east Asia 95, 96
    Malagasy 107
    Malta 248
    mortality 8
    regulation 249
    South America 196, 197, 249
    South and West Asia 71
    see also plume trade; shooting
husbandry
    research 302–3
    techniques 299–302
hydroelectric power 195, 246
hydrological cycles 153
hydrology 230
    changes 246
    Florida Everglades 322
    manipulation 226, 227

Ibis
    Glossy 25

Ibis – *contd*
  Scarlet 194, 196
  White 327
Ichkeul, Lake (Tunisia) 34, 35
  Grey Heron 37
Ichkeul (Tunisia) 2, 3
Idaho (USA) 256, 257
  Black-crowned Night Heron 164
identification 299–300
Iguazú River (Argentina) 178, 179
Ile Alcatraz (Guinea) 100, 101
Ile Tristao (Guinea) 100, 101
Illinois (USA) 361
Imperial Valley (USA) 152, 153
Important Heron Conservation Areas 337, 340
imprinting, captive populations 302
India 56, 57, 59
  agricultural change 69
  catalogue of known heronries 60–1, 71
  Cattle Egret 64
  Grey Heron 61
  Imperial Heron 61
  Indian Pond Heron 65
  Malayan Night Heron 66
  protection of colonies 212
  Yellow Bittern 89
Indiana (USA) 361
indicators 311–13
  cholinesterase 317
  community level 327–8
  contaminant concentrations 314–17
  diet of young 327
  distributional changes 322–4
  ecosystem level 328
  eggshell thickness 317, 328
  Florida Everglades 313
  genetic damage 319–20
  growth rate of young 325–6
  habitat use 327–8
  metallothionein induction 321
  mortality 321–2, 329
  organism level 313–21
  parasite loads 326–7
  population level 321–7
  reproductive performance 324–6
  selection 328–9
  suborganism level 313–21
  wetland habitat quality 96
Indonesia 66, 74, 75, 124, 125
  Agami Heron 360
  Grey Heron 78
  Malayan Night Heron 88
  Nankeen Night Heron 86
  New Guinea Tiger Heron 360
  Pied Heron 132
  Purple Heron 81
  Sumatran Heron 79, 358–9
  Swinhoe's Egret 84
  trapping 248
Indus Basin (India/Pakistan) 56, 57, 59
industrial development
  disturbance 210
  habitat degradation 247
infections 281–2

  secondary 282
infectious pancreatic necrosis (IPN) 281–2
information needs 331
infrastructure for population counting 334
injuries
  captive birds 300
  to fish 282
Inle Lake (Myanmar) 74, 75
Inner Niger Delta (Mali) 100, 101
  available area 245
  Black Heron 110
  Cattle Egret 113
  egg and chick harvesting 212
  Great White Egret 108
  Intermediate Egret 110
  Little Egret 111, 112
  management 117
  Palearctic migrants 117
  Squacco Heron 113, 242
insecticides *see* pesticides
international cooperation 171–2, 175
International Council for Bird Preservation *see*
      BirdLife International
International Species Information System (ISIS)
      295, 296
international trade 296
International Union for Conservation and Natural
      Resources *see* IUCN (International Union
      for Conservation and Natural Resources)
International Waterfowl Research Bureau *see*
      Wetlands International
International Wildfowl Census 324
International Zoo Yearbook's Breeding Bird
      Census (IZY-BBC) 295
Iowa (USA) 162
Iracoubo marshes (Guianas Coast) 178, 179
Iran 56, 57
  Cattle Egret 65
  Eurasian Bittern 67
  Goliath Heron 62
  Grey Heron 61
  Little Bittern 66
  Purple Heron 62
  Squacco Heron 18
Iraq 56, 57, 59
  Black-crowned Night Heron 66
  drainage of marshes 62, 66, 68
  Goliath Heron 62
  Purple Heron 62, 68
  Squacco Heron 65, 68
Ireland
  Eurasian Bittern population 21
  Grey Heron 239, 240
  Little Egret population 12, 13
  protection 28
iron, feather concentrations 314
Irrawaddy Delta (Myanmar) 74, 75
irrigation 52, 53
  canals 60
  dams 246
  reservoirs 69, 223
Isla de Salamance National Park (Colombia) 178,
      179
islands, oceanic 129

Israel 2, 3
    Black-crowned Night Heron population 48
    Cattle Egret 44
    Eurasian Bittern 50
    Great White Egret 41
    Grey Heron 37
    habitat degradation 52
    hunting 248
    Little Bittern 48–9
    Little Egret population 42, 43
    Mediterranean 35, 37
    pesticides 258
    Purple Heron population 38, 40, 248
    Squacco Heron 46
Italy 2, 3
    Black-crowned Night Heron population 19, 47,
        48, 52–3
    Cattle Egret population 16, 17, 43
    conservation activity 51
    critical wetlands 24
    Great White Egret population 41
    Grey Heron population 7, 10, 37
    Little Bittern population 48
    Little Egret population 12, 14, 41, 42
    Mediterranean 34, 36, 37, 52–3
    PCBs 261
    protection 28
    Purple Heron population 38–9, 80
    Squacco Heron population 18, 45, 46
    tourism 51
    wetland area 25
    see also rice fields, Italy
Ite Lagoon (Peru) 178, 179
IUCN (International Union for Conservation and
        Natural Resources) 343
    criteria 344, 372–5
    Red List of Threatened Animals 307
    threat categories 344, 345
    Wetlands Programme 220
Ivory Coast 100, 101
Ixobrychus cinnamomeus (Cinnamon Bittern) xiv,
        67, 90
Ixobrychus eurhythmus (Schrenck's Bittern) xiv, 361
Ixobrychus exilis (Least Bittern) xiv
Ixobrychus exilis bogotensis (Least Bittern) 193, 197
Ixobrychus exilis erythromelas (Least Bittern) 193
Ixobrychus exilis peruvianus (Least Bittern) 193, 197
Ixobrychus flavicollis (Black Bittern) xiv
Ixobrychus involucris (Streaked Bittern) xiv, 182
Ixobrychus minutus (Little Bittern) xiv, 1
Ixobrychus minutus minutus (Little Bittern) 116,
        368–9
Ixobrychus minutus novaezelandiae see Ixobrychus
        novaezelandiae (New Zealand Little Bittern)
Ixobrychus minutus payesii (Little Bittern) 99, 116,
        239
Ixobrychus minutus podiceps (Little Bittern) 99, 116,
        366
Ixobrychus novaezelandiae (Black-backed Bittern)
        352
Ixobrychus novaezelandiae (New Zealand Little
        Bittern) 139
Ixobrychus sinensis (Yellow Bittern) xiv
Ixobrychus sturmii (Dwarf Bittern) xiv

Izeh Lake (Iran) 57
Izuik Lake (Turkey) 2, 3

Jalisco lagoon (Mexico) 170
Jamaica 152, 153
    Little Blue Heron 160
    wetlands 155
    wintering area 168
Jamari River (Brazil) 196
Japan 74, 75
    aquaculture 270
    conservation work 98
    Great White Egret 81
    Grey Heron 78
    habitat loss 94
    Japanese Night Heron 357
    Malayan Night Heron 88
    rice cultivation 224
    Schrenck's Bittern 90
    Swinhoe's Egret 83, 84, 355
    Yellow Bittern 89
Japura River lakes (Brazil) 178, 179
Jatira–Tacarigue Dam (Venzuela) 178, 179
Java 95
    Black-crowned Night Heron 86
    Cinnamon bittern 90
Jersey Wildlife Preservation Trust 358
Jhaukhali (India/Bangladesh) 56, 57
Jhelum River (India) 70
Jipe, Lake (Kenya/Tanzania) 100, 101
Jonak Char (India/Bangladesh) 56, 57
Jonglei Canal project (Sudan) 119
Jordan 110
José Ignacio Lagoon (Uraguay) 178, 179
Juan Manuel de Aquas Blancas and Aguas Negras
        (Venezuela) 178, 179
Juparana Lakes (Brazil) 178, 179

Kabylie (Algeria) 43
Kachchh, Gulf of (India) 57, 70, 71
Kafue River (Zambia) 100, 101, 107, 109, 356
Kagera wetlands (Tanzania/Rwanda) 100, 101,
        114, 118
Kakadu National Park (Australia) 124, 125, 133,
        144, 145
Kaladan Estuary (Myanmar) 74, 75
Kalimantan, Javan Pond Heron 85
Kaliveli Lake (India) 56, 57, 59
Kangean Archipelago (Indonesia) 74, 75
Kansas (USA) 163
Kapuatai Peat Dome (New Zealand) 124, 125, 145
Karachi Zoo (Pakistan) 64
Karkinitsk (Ukraine) 2, 3
Karnataka (India) 56, 57, 64
Kaw Marshes (Guianas Coast) 178, 179, 193
Kawadighi Haor (India/Bangladesh) 56, 57
Kaziranga National Park (India) 67
Kenya 100, 101
    Black-crowned Night Heron 115
    Grey Heron 105, 106
    Little Egret 112
    Malagasy Pond Heron 114
    Purple Heron 107
    Rufous-bellied Heron 114

Kenya – contd
  tourism 121
  wetland management 119
Keoladeo Ghana National Park (India) 56, 57
Kerala backwaters (India) 59
Kerang Wetlands (Australia) 124, 125
Kerkini reservoir (Greece) 2, 3
  water levels 27
Khambat, Gulf of (India) 57
Khor Kohaly (Iran) 57
Khor Tiab (Iran) 57
Khuzestan marshes (Iran) 59
Kilgwyn swamp (Tobago) 164
killing herons 271, 289
  permits 271
  see also hunting; persecution; poisoning;
    shooting; trapping
Kinabatangan River (Borneo) 81
Kis-Balaton, Lake (Hungary) 2, 3
Kizil-Agach Bay (Iran) 57
Kizilirmak wetland complex (Turkey) 2, 3, 38, 48,
  49
Kneiss Islands (Tunisia) 2, 3, 42
Kole Wetlands (India) 56, 57, 65
Komadugu Gana (Nigeria) 100, 101
Konkoure (Guinea) 100, 101
Kopacki Rit (Croatia) 2, 3
Korea
  Grey Heron 78
  Swinhoe's Egret 81
Koshi Tappu Wildlife Reserve (Nepal) 56, 57, 65
Kosi Bay (Mozambique/South Africa) 100, 101
Kununurra, Lake (Australia) 124, 125
Kura Delta (Iran) 56, 57
Kurbaga Lake (Turkey) 2, 3
Kushiro Marsh (Japan) 74, 75
Kwadighi Haor (Bangladesh) 62
Kwan-Po (North Korea) 74, 75
Kybong (Australia) 147
Kyoga swamp (Africa) 107

La Florida marsh (Colombia) 178, 179, 197
La Herrera Lagoons (Colombia) 178, 179, 197
La Mare aux Hippopotames (Burkina Faso) 100,
  101
La Mare d'Oursi (Burkina Faso) 100, 101
Lac Debo (Mali) 100, 101
Lac Fitri (Chad) 100, 101
Lac Kinkony wetlands (Madagascar) 100, 101
Lac Lagoon (Aruba) 178, 179
Lachlan wetland (Australia) 128, 133, 142–3
Laco Horo (Mali) 100, 101
Lago Atitlan (Guatemala) 153
Lago Chapala (Mexico) 152, 153
Lagoa de Cufada (Guinea) 100, 101
lagoons see coastal lagoons
Laguna de Terminos (Mexico) 169
Laguna di Marano (Italy) 2, 3
Laguna Largo (USA) 158
Laguna Madre (Mexico) 152, 153, 169
Laguna Negra Marshes (Uraguay) 178, 179
Laguna Palo Verde (Costa Rica) 153
Laguna Tamiahua (Mexico) 169
Lanau Mindanao, Lake (Philippines) 74, 75

land reclamation 247
landfill, Oceania 144
Langano, Lake (Ethiopia) 100, 101
Langebaan National Park (South Africa) 100, 101
Laos
  Malayan Night Heron 88, 365
  trapping 248
Larus argentatus (Herring gull) 317
Latvia
  Great White Egret population 11
  Little Bittern population 20
Launillas Lagoon (Peru) 178, 179
law enforcement, South America 195
lead 264
  ALAD blood levels 320, 328
  feather concentrations 314, 317
Lebyazhyi Islands (Crimea) 41
legs, broken 300
Leptoptilis javanicus (Lesser Adjutant) 93
Leslie Matrix model 238
Lesotho 100, 101
Lesser Antilles
  Great Blue Heron 157
  Great White Egret 158
  Least Bittern 164, 165
  Little Egret 187
  Reddish Egret 158
  Snowy Egret 160
  wintering area 168
Liao Marshes (China) 74, 75
Liberia 100, 101
  wetland management 119
  White-crested Tiger Heron 115
Libya 42
Ligula intestinalis (cestode) 282
Limpopo River 110
  valley 116
Lindu, Lake (Indonesia) 74, 75
Linhares Marsh (Brazil) 178, 179
literature 331–2
Litoria aurea (Australian green frog) 132
liver enzyme induction 317–19, 328
livestock industry, Africa 109
Llanos (Venezuela) 178, 179
  available area 245
Lochinvar National Park (Zambia) 100, 101
logging
  New Guinea 144
  see also deforestation
Loire estuary (France) 24
longevity 299
Lonja River (Croatia) 2, 3
Lord Howe Island (Australia) 128
  Cattle Egret 137
  Little Bittern 139
Lorenz proposed park (New Guinea) 125
Los Katios National Park (Colombia) 178, 179
Los Morteros (Argentina) 178, 179
Los Patos Lagoon (Brazil) 178, 179
Los Tumbes mangroves (Ecuador) 178, 179
Lotus (floating macrophyte) 24
Loudias (Greece) 2, 3
Louisiana (USA)
  abundance of herons 167

American Bittern 166
Black-crowned Night Heron 164
Cattle Egret 161
colonies 203
crawfish farms 271, 273
Great Blue Heron 157
Great White Egret 157, 158
Green-backed Heron 161
habitats 169
  protection 169
Least Bittern 165
Little Blue Heron 160
population changes 226–7
Reddish Egret 158
Snowy Egret 160
swamps 152, 153
Tricoloured Heron 158, 159
Loukkos marshes (Morocco) 2, 3, 50
Lowbidgee Floodplain (Australia) 124, 125
Lower Gwydir Wetlands (Australia) 124, 125
Lower Laguna Madre (Texas; USA) 261
Lower Sind (Pakistan) 67
Loyalty Islands (Oceania) 140, 355
Luangwa Valley wetlands (Zambia) 101, 106
Ludasko Lake (Croatia) 2, 3
Lukanga Swamp (Zambia) 100, 101
Lushun Kou (China) 82
Luxembourg
  Eurasian Bittern population 21
  protection 28
Lymnaea snails 282

Macleay floodplain (Australia) 141
Macquarie Island (Antarctic Territory) 128
Macquarie Marshes (Australia) 124, 125, 142, 143,
    144
  Intermediate Egret 132, 133–4
  management 146
  Nankeen Night Heron 138
macrophytes 24
Madagascar 99
  Black Heron 110, 359
  Black-crowned Night Heron 115
  Cattle Egret 113
  Great White Egret 109
  Green-backed Heron 115
  Grey Heron 106, 363
  Little Bittern 116, 366
  Little Egret 112
  Malagasy Heron 357
  Malagasy Pond Heron 114, 359
  Purple Heron 107, 364
  Squacco Heron 113–14
  wetland management 118–19, 120
Madeira River (Brazil) 178, 179
Magadi, Lake (Kenya/Tanzania) 100, 101
Magdalena River basin, pollution 195
Mahaweli Ganga (Sri Lanka) 56, 57, 64, 65
Mahmoud-Chala Lake (Azerbaijan/Iran) 56, 57,
    64
Mai Po and Inner Deep Bay (Hong Kong) 94, 216
Maine (USA) 158
  Great Blue Heron 206
  Little Blue Heron 160

Snowy Egret 160
Makgadakgadi Pan (Botswana) 100, 101
Malagarasi/Moyowosi wetlands (Tanzania) 100,
    101
  Goliath Heron 107
Malagasy 99, 100, 101
  data 105
  environmental conditions 104
  habitats 104
  hunting 107
  Little Egret 112
  rice fields 107
  status of herons 102–3, 105–17
  see also Madagascar
Malawi 100, 101
  Malagasy Pond Heron 114
  wetland management 120
  see also Inner Niger Delta (Mali)
Malawi, Lake 100, 101, 120
Malaysia 66, 74, 75
  Black Bittern 90
  Black-crowned Night Heron 86
  Cinnamon bittern 90
  colony sites 92
  Grey Heron 78
  Intermediate Egret 81
  Javan Pond Heron 85
  Malayan Night Heron 88–9, 365
  Sumatran Heron 79
  Swinhoe's Egret 83, 84
  Yellow Bittern 89
Maldives 65, 364, 365
Mali 100, 101
  Black-crowned Night Heron 115
  Cattle Egret 113
  Eurasian Bittern 117
  Grey Heron 105, 106
  Little Egret 112
  Purple Heron 107
  wetland management 117
Malta
  hunting 248
  shooting 52
Mamoré River (Bolivia) 178, 179, 192
management
  artificial habitats 231–3
  environmentally sensitive of rice fields 53
  habitat 25–8, 228, 340
  regional 233–4
  see also wetlands, management
Managua, Lake (Nicaragua) 152, 153, 155
mandibles, broken 300
mangrove swamps 59, 70, 81, 222
  Africa 119, 120
  aquaculture conversion 175
  Australia 144, 145, 147
  Central America 167
  deforestation 248
  destruction 189, 333
  East and South-east Asia 91, 92, 93
  habitat protection 169
  New Zealand 129
  Oceania 129, 144
  Panama 169

mangrove swamps – *contd*
  South America 181, 194, 196
    loss 189
Mangueira Lagoon (Uraguay/Brazil) 178, 179
Manik Gudilo (Russia) 2, 3
Manitoba (Canada) 163
Mannar, Gulf of (India) 59
Manu National Park (Peru) 178, 179, 188, 192
Manus (Oceania) 129
Manyara, Lake (Tanzania) 100, 101
Manyas, Lake (Turkey) 2, 3
Manzala, Lake (Egypt) 46
Mar Chiquita Lake Delta (Argentina) 178, 179
Marais Poitevin National Regional Park (France)
  23
Mariana Islands (Oceania) 125, 145
  Cattle Egret 137
  Great White Egret 131
  Nankeen Night Heron 138
  Yellow Bittern 139
marine habitat 222
Marismas Nacionales (Mexico) 152, 153
marking schemes 378
marking, visible 337
Maroantsetra (Madagascar) 114
marshes 339
  creation 27
  drainage 26
  freshwater 11
  see also reed beds; salt marshes; wetlands
Martinique 160
  Little Egret 160
Mary River (Australia) 124, 125
Masirah Island (Oman) 57, 64
Massachusetts (USA) 162
Matang Forest Reserve (Malaysia) 33
Matian Haor (India/Bangladesh) 56, 57
Mato Grosso (Brazil) 190, 191, 193
Mauritania 100, 101, 113
  Black-crowned Night Heron 115
  Eurasian Bittern 117
  Squacco Heron 113
  wetland management 119
Mauritius 99
  Cattle Egret 113
  Green-backed Heron 115
Mearim River estuary (Brazil) 178, 179
meat use 248
Medio Mundo Lagoon (Peru) 197
Mediterranean area 1, 33
  colonies 203
  environmental conditions 34–5
  feeding areas 52–3
  habitat destruction 50–1, 54
  hunting 248
  important heron areas 2
  Little Egret population 12
  protection 50
  status of herons 35–6, 50
  tourism 51–2
  wetland destruction 34–5, 51
Mediterranean Sea 5
Mediterranean Wetlands Forum 51
Mejia Lagoon (Peru) 178, 179

Mekhada marshes (Tunisia) 46
Mekong Delta (Vietnam) 74, 75
melaleuca swamp forests 129, 145
mercury 263–4
  feather concentrations 314, 315
Merin Lagoon (Uraguay/Brazil) 178, 179
Mesopotamian marshes (Iraq) 56, 57, 59, 62
  Black-crowned Night Heron 66
  Squacco Heron 65
Meta River (Colombia) 192
metallothionein induction 321
metapopulation analysis, source–sink concept 336
Mexico 152, 153, 169
  Agami Heron 162
  American Bittern 166
  Bare-throated Tiger Heron 164
  Black-crowned Night Heron 164
  Boat-billed Heron 164
  Cattle Egret 161
  conservation 167
  Great White Egret 158
  Green-backed Heron 161
  habitat protection 169, 171
  heron fauna 151
  Least Bittern 164, 165
  Little Blue Heron 159, 160
  nesting habitats 169
  pollution 173
  Reddish Egret 158
  Rufescent Tiger Heron 164
  Snowy Egret 160
  South American Bittern 165
  threatened species 174
  wetlands 155
    loss 170
  Yellow-crowned Night Heron 162
Mexico, Gulf of
  development 174
  Great Blue Heron 157
  Little Blue Heron 160
  Reddish Egret 158
  Snowy Egret 160
  Tricolored Heron 158
  wintering area 168
Michigan (USA) 162
microchip transponders 299
Micronesia 139
Microtus socialis (Social Vole) 52
Middle East, desert 59
Middle Fly floodplain (Papua New Guinea) 138
Middle Fly region survey 132, 133, 134
migration
  African drought hypothesis 30, 31
  Americas 155
  Asian–Pacific routes 55
  Atlantic flyway 167–8
  Black-crowned Night Heron 20, 26, 115, 164
  Black-headed Heron 106
  Cattle Egret 64, 113, 137
  Cinnamon Bittern 90
  competition 237
  diet changes 243
  dispersal 242–3
  distribution 336–7

Eurasian Bittern 22
European species 28
European–African routes 55
fish 195
flyway management 233–4
Great White Egret 12, 41
Grey Heron 8–9, 37
hazards 237
human 198
Indian Pond Heron 65
international cooperation in conservation 171–2
Little Bittern 21, 26, 49, 116, 367
Little Egret 12, 14–15, 43, 111, 240–1, 245
Malagasy Pond Heron 114
Malayan Night Heron 88
Mississippi flyway 168–69
movements 240–1
Nankeen Night Heron 138
overshooting 243
Pacific flyway 169–70
Purple Heron 11, 26, 107
Schrenck's Bittern 90
Squacco Heron 26, 240, 241, 242, 244, 245, 368
status of herons 242
Swinhoe's Egret 83
trans-Sahara 26
weather systems 241
wintering sites 336
migratory bird treaties 172
migratory habitats 237–9
migratory species 239–40
partial/strict 240
migratory status 239–40
changes 245
Millewa Forest (Australia) 124, 125
Mimosa pigra weed invasion 144, 146
mining, South America 195
Mirim Lagoon (Uraguay/Brazil) 178, 179
Mississippi River (USA) 152, 153, 168
Cattle Egret 161
flyway 168–69
Great White Egret 158
habitat protection 169
Little Blue Heron 160
Mita Rapa wetland (Tahiti) 136
Mkri Prespa, Lake (Greece) 2, 3
Mogawng Chaung (Myanmar) 74, 75
Mohingyi Lake (Myanmar) 74, 75
Moissac floodplain (France) 2, 3
Moldova 3
molluscs 270
Mong Pai Lake Proposed Wildlife Sanctuary
    (Myanmar) 74, 75
Mongolia 89
Eurasian Bittern 91
Grey Heron 78
monitoring programmes 322–3, 335–6
numbers 214–15
Montenegro 2, 3
Morocco 2, 3
Black-crowned Night Heron population 47, 48
Eurasian Bittern 50
habitat loss 52
Little Bittern 48

Mediterranean 35, 37, 38, 42, 43, 46
Morowali (Indonesia) 74, 75
Morrocoy National Park (Venezuela) 178, 179
mortality as indicator 321–2, 329
Mosquito Coast (Nicaragua) 152, 153
Moulouya River (Spain) 2, 3
movements 240–2
seasonal 238
see also dispersal; migration
Mozambique 100, 101, 114, 115
Muara Cimanuk (Indonesia) 74, 75
mudflats, coastal 59
Muni Lagoon (Ghana) 100, 101
Murray River (Australia)
Cattle Egret 137
Great White Egret 131
Murray–Darling basin (Australia) 124, 125, 128,
    138, 139
Australian Bittern 140
management 142–3
Murrumbidgee wetlands (Australia) 128, 133, 142,
    143
Murwillumbah (Australia) 147
Muthurajawela (Sri Lanka) 56, 57
Mwea rice scheme (Kenya) 114
Mweru Wantipa wetlands (Zambia) 101
Myanmar 74, 75
Black Bittern 90
Eurasian Bittern 91
Imperial Heron 79
Indian Pond Heron 85
Purple Heron 81
Mycteria americana (Wood Stork) 308, 313
Mycteria cinerea (Milky Stork) 93

Naivasha, Lake (Kenya) 100, 101
Nakdong Estuary (South Korea) 74, 75
Nakuru, Lake (Kenya) 100, 101
Nam Hoi County (China) 74, 75
Namibia 100, 101
Dwarf Bittern 116
Slaty Egret 109, 356
wetland management 119
Napo River (Ecuador) 178, 179
Narasambhudhi Tank (India) 56, 57, 64
Nariva Swamp (Trinidad) 168, 178, 179
Narragansett Bay (Rhode Island, USA) 314
Narran Lakes (Australia) 124, 125, 143
Nasser, Lake (Egypt) 40
Natron, Lake (Kenya/Tanzania) 100, 101
Nature Management Act (Denmark) 27
Nayarit coast (Mexico) 152, 153, 155, 169
Nebraska (USA) 162
Nellapattu (India) 70
nematodes, fish infections 326
Nepal 56, 57, 67
nest construction 203–4
nest sites
artificial 207–10
conservation 201
South and West Asia 70–1
nesting
assemblages 202–3
captive 301

nesting – *contd*
  colonial 201
  ground 83, 203
  habitats 339
    requirements 203–4
  materials 203, 204
  sites 202
  solitary 201, 204–5
  success 324–5, 329
  time 324
nestlings *see* chicks
Netherlands 2, 3
  Black-crowned Night Heron population 19, 20
  Cattle Egret population 15–16, 16
  critical wetlands 29
  Great White Egret population 11, 12
  Grey Heron population 6, 7, 9, 24
  Little Bittern population 20, 22, 23
  Little Egret population 12
  mercury 263
  protection 28
  Purple Heron population 10, 11, 40
  wetlands restoration 27
Netherlands Antilles 177
Neusiedl, Lake (Austria) 2, 3, 12
  Great White Egret 41
  water levels 27
Nevada (USA) 256, 257
New Britain (Oceania) 129, 139
New Caledonia (Oceania) 140, 355
  Nankeen Night Heron 138
New England (USA) 257, 261
New Guinea 123, 124, 125
  Black Bittern 140
  Cattle Egret 137
  climate 129
  Great White Egret 131
  Intermediate Egret 132, 133
  Little Bittern 139
  Little Egret 134
  New Guinea Tiger Heron 139
  Sumatran Heron 130–1
  wetland management 144
  White-necked Heron 130
  see also Papua New Guinea
New Ireland (Oceania) 129
New South Wales (Australia) 147
  Australian Bittern 140
  Black Bittern 140
  Cattle Egret 136, 137
  coast 125
  colony destruction 146–7
  Great White Egret 131, 144
  Green-backed Heron 136
  habitat loss 140–1
  Intermediate Egret 132, 133
  Little Bittern 139
  Little Egret 134, 135
  Nankeen Night Heron 138
  wetland protection 141
  White-faced Heron 134
  White-necked Heron 130
New Zealand 124, 125, 129
  Australian Bittern 140, 355

Cattle Egret 137
climate 129
database for wetlands 141
Eastern Reef Heron 135
Great White Egret 131, 361
habitat loss 141
Little Bittern 139
Little Egret 134, 135
public involvement 148
wetland management 145
Wetland Policy 141
White-necked Heron 130
Newfoundland (Canada) 160
Nicaragua 152, 153
  border area protection 172
  Green-backed Heron 161
  South American Bittern 165
Nicaragua, Lake (Nicaragua) 152, 153, 155
Nicobar Islands (Sumatra) 57, 61, 62, 64
  Malayan Night Heron 88
Nicoya, Gulf of (Costa Rica) 152, 153
Niger 100, 101
  Black-crowned Night Heron 115
  Grey Heron 106
  see also Central Niger Delta (Mali); Inner Niger
      Delta (Mali)
Niger River Delta (Nigeria) 100, 101
Nigeria 100, 101
  Black-crowned Night Heron 115
  Eurasian Bittern 117
  Grey Heron 105, 106
  Little Egret 111, 112
  Squacco Heron 113
night heron
  contaminant accumulation 314
  habitat 222
  South America 182
Night Heron, Black-crowned 1, 4, 14
  Africa 115, 117, 118
  Americas 151, 155, 163–4, 171, 172
  antiChE compounds 262, 317
  artificial colony 208
  Australia and Oceania 125
  chick harvesting 212, 213
  city populations 65–6
  congenital anomalies 321
  conservation status 350, 368
  contaminant accumulation 314, 318
  cytochrome P450 activity 319
  cytogenetic damage 319–20
  diet of young 327
  disturbance 211
  East and South-east Asia 86
  eggshell thickness 317
  Europe species account 19–20
  feral 20
  fish predation 278
  free-ranging in zoos 306
  genetic characterisation 337
  growth rate of young 325, 326
  habitat 24, 27, 224, 225
  hand-rearing 302
  lead levels 264
  Malagasy 115

Mediterranean region 33, 35, 46–8, 52–3
mercury 264
migration 20, 26, 115, 164, 240, 241
migratory status change 245
nesting success 325
organochlorine insecticides 254–8
PCBs 255, 256, 260, 314, 316
petroleum genetic damage 265–6
piscivory 273
population fluctuations 19–20, 30
predator avoidance 202
releases 20
South America 189, 198
South and West Asia 65–6, 68, 70
wintering populations 323
Night Heron, Japanese xiv, 87, 298
    captive conservation priority 308
    conservation status 357
Night Heron, Malayan xiv, 298
    Australia and Oceania 125
    conservation status 365
    East and South-east Asia 87–9
    South and West Asia 55, 59, 66, 70, 71
Night Heron, Mauritius 352
Night Heron, Nankeen xiv, 80, 86
    Australia and Oceania 123, 138, 141, 146–7
    free-ranging in zoos 306
Night Heron, Rodrigues 352
Night Heron, Rufous see Night Heron, Nankeen
Night Heron, White-backed xiv, 99
    Africa 115
Night Heron, White-eared xiv, 86, 308
    conservation status 350, 352–4
Night Heron, Yellow-crowned xiv, 155, 162–3,
    167
    conservation status 366
    free-ranging in zoos 306
    habitat 222, 223
    nesting success 325
    reintroduction 303, 304
    South America 182, 189, 198
Nile delta (Egypt) 2, 3, 34, 40, 41, 246
    Cattle Egret 43, 44, 259, 322
    degradation 34–5
    Eurasian Bittern 50
    Little Bittern 48, 49, 368
    meat use 248
    Squacco Heron 46, 53
Nile River (Egypt) 33, 43
    Goliath Heron 107
Nile Sudd (Sudan) 100, 101, 107, 245
Ninhal do Barreiro (Brazil) 178, 179
Norfolk Island (Australia) 128
    Cattle Egret 137
    White-necked Heron 130
North Africa 52
    conservation status 350
North America 151
    American Bittern 166
    aquaculture 174, 270
    Black-crowned Night Heron 163–4
    colony site protection 173–4
    conservation 167
        status 351

environmental conditions 153, 155
feeding habitats 155
fish predation 280
Green-backed Heron 161
habitat
    conservation 170–1
    protection 169
    quality 171
heron fauna 151
hunting 173
Least Bittern 164, 165
salt marshes 155
status of herons 154, 155–66
wetlands 155
Yellow-crowned Night Heron 162
North American Free Trade Agreement 172
North American Waterfowl Management Plan
    (NAWMP) 172, 233, 250
North Borneo, Yellow Bittern 89
North Carolina (USA) 166
North Island coastal plain (New Zealand) 124,
    125
North Korea 74, 75
    Great White Egret 81
    Swinhoe's Egret 82–3, 84, 355
North Sea 5
North Yongjong Mudflats (South Korea) 74, 75
Northern Ireland, protection 28
Northern Territory (Australia) 144, 145, 146
    Cattle Egret 136
    Green-backed Heron 123, 136
    Intermediate Egret 133
    Nankeen Night Heron 138
Norway, Grey Heron 25
Notonecta (water boatman) 282–3
numbers of herons
    counting 332–3, 334
    Europe 2, 4
    monitoring 214–15
nutrient supplements 300
Nycticorax caledonicus (Nankeen Night Heron)
    xiv
Nycticorax leuconotus (White-backed Night Heron)
    xiv
Nycticorax mauritianus (Mauritius Night Heron)
    352
Nycticorax megacephalus (Rodrigues Night Heron)
    352
Nycticorax nycticorax (Black-crowned Night
    Heron) xiv, 1
Nycticorax nycticorax cyanocephalus (Black-crowned
    Night Heron) 189
Nycticorax nycticorax falklandicus (Black-crowned
    Night Heron) 189, 198
Nycticorax nycticorax hoactli (Black-crowned Night
    Heron) 189
Nycticorax nycticorax nycticorax (Black-crowned
    Night Heron) 368
Nycticorax violaceus (Yellow-crowned Night
    Heron) xiv
Nycticorax violaceus bancrofti (Yellow-crowned
    Night Heron) 162, 189
Nycticorax violaceus calignis (Yellow-crowned
    Night Heron) 189, 198, 366

Nycticorax violaceus cayennensis (Yellow-crowned Night Heron) 189, 198
Nycticorax violaceus pauper (Yellow-crowned Night Heron) 189, 198
Nyl floodplains (Botswana/South Africa) 113, 114, 115, 118
    Purple Heron 107
Nymphea (floating macrophyte) 24

Oceania 123
    environmental conditions 125, 128–9
    siltation 144
    status of herons 126–7, 130–40
    wetland management 144
Ogoovei River (Gabon) 100, 101
Ohio (USA) 370
    Yellow-crowned Night Heron 162
oil spills
    diet of young 327
    nesting success 325
oiling, external 265, 266
Ok Tedi mines (New Guinea) 144
Okarito River (New Zealand) 129, 132, 147
Okavango Delta (Botswana) 100, 101, 114, 120
    Great White Egret 108
    Intermediate Egret 110
    Purple Heron 107
    Slaty Egret 109
Okefenokee Swamp (USA) 152, 153, 166, 168
Oklahoma (USA) 162
Oloiden, Lake (Kenya) 100, 101
Oman 56, 57, 64
Omo Delta (Ethiopia/Kenya) 100, 101
Ontario (Canada) 163
    Yellow-crowned Night Heron 162
Ontario, Lake (Canada) 261
open waters, production 275
opportunist feeders 243
Orange River Mouth (South Africa) 100, 101
Ord River (Australia) 124, 125
    dam scheme 139
Oregon (USA) 256, 257
    Black-crowned Night Heron 164
organochlorine insecticides 52, 251–60
organophosphorus insecticides 262, 328
    poisoning 321
Oriental Bird Club 95
Orinoco basin 181
    Boat-billed Heron 190
    Capped Heron 183
    Fasciated Tiger Heron 164, 190
    flooded savannas 182
    pollution 195
    Yellow-crowned Night Heron 189
Orinoco Delta (Venezuela) 178, 179
    Zigzag Heron 192
Oristano (Sardinia) 2, 3
Oshakati pan (Namibia) 119
Ouarzazat (Morocco) 37, 43
Ousteri Tank (India) 56, 57
Owabi Wildlife Sanctuary (Ghana) 100, 101
oxygen depletion 278
Oyapock River (Guianas Coast) 178, 179
Ozero Sivash (Ukraine) 2, 3

Pacaya-Samiria National Reserve Lagoons (Peru) 178, 179
Pacific flyway 170–1
paddybird *see* Pond Heron, Indian
Paifang Island (Chia) 82
Pakistan 56, 57
    Cattle Egret 64
Palau (Oceania) 139
    Nankeen Night Heron 138
Palo Verde (Costa Rica) 169
Panama 152, 153, 157, 167
    Agami Heron 188
    American Bittern 166
    Boat-billed Heron 190
    Capped Heron 156
    Cocoi Heron 185
    Fasciated Tiger Heron 164, 190
    Great Blue Heron 184
    Green-backed Heron 187
    Least Bittern 193
    mangroves 169
    Reddish Egret 185
Panama, Bay of 169
Pantanal (Brazil/Paraguay) 178, 179, 196
    available area 245
    flooded savanna 182
Panto del Hondo (Spain) 2, 3
Papua New Guinea 89, 125
    Great White Egret 131
    Intermediate Egret 132
    Little Egret 135
    Nankeen Night Heron 138
    New Guinea Tiger Heron 360
    Pied Heron 132
    Sumatran Heron 79, 131
    wetland management 144, 145
    see also New Guinea
papyrus swamp 119
Paracas National Reserve (Peru) 178, 179
Paraguay 178, 179
    climate 181
    Least Bittern 193
    South American Bittern 193
Paraguay River basin 195
Paraña River marshes (Argentina) 178, 179
Paraná–Paraguay river 181, 182, 196
parasites
    loads as indicator 326–7
    transmission 282
Parc National du Djoudj (Senegal) 108, 111, 113, 115, 118
Parc National du `W' (Burkina Faso/Niger) 100, 101
Paroo River system (Australia) 124, 125, 128–9, 143
pastureland 223
    damp 24, 339
Pasua Haor (Bangladesh) 56, 57, 62
patch dynamics 228–30, 231
Pattani Bay (Thailand) 74, 75, 95
Paul de Boquilobo (Portugal) 2, 3
PCBs 255, 256, 260–1, 317, 318
    accumulation in chicks 314, 316
    congenital anomalies 321

Great Lakes contamination 328
PCDD contamination 317, 318
PCDF contamination 317, 318
Pearl River Estuary (Hong Kong) 95
Pecos River (New Mexico) 256
Pekelmeer Lagoon (Aruba) 178, 179
Pennsylvania (USA) 162
permits to kill 271
persecution 27, 29, 52, 213–14
  by fish farmers 247, 271
Persian Gulf 62
Peru 178, 179
  Agami Heron 188
  Black-crowned Night Heron 189
  Cattle Egret 187
  Cocoi Heron 185
  Fasciated Tiger Heron 190
  Least Bittern 193, 197
  Little Blue Heron 186
  Streaked Bittern 192
  Tricoloured Heron 186
  Zigzag Heron 192
pesticides 52, 71, 81
  East and South-east Asia 94–5
  rice fields 71, 232
  South America 195
  see also carbamate insecticides; contaminants;
    eggs; eggshell; eggshell thickness;
    organochlorine insecticides;
    organophosphorus insecticides; pollution
Petit Loango (Gabon) 100, 101
petroleum 265–6
  extraction 145
  genetic damage 265–6
Philippines 66, 74, 75
  Black-crowned Night Heron 86
  Environmental Impact Assessments (EIAs) 97
  Eurasian Bittern 91
  Grey Heron 78
  Intermediate Egret 81
  Japanese Night Heron 87
  Javan Pond Heron 85
  Malayan Night Heron 88, 365
  Nankeen Night Heron 86
  Purple Heron 81
  Schrenk's Bittern 361
  Swinhoe's Egret 81, 83, 84
  trapping 248
Phragmites reed beds 37, 49, 50, 203
Pichavaram Mangrove (India) 56, 57, 66
Pilcomayo River (Argentina) 178, 179
Pilherodius pileatus (Capped Heron) xiii
pine, Australian 93
pinioning 301
Pinus (pine) 211
piscivorous species 272–4
piscivory 243, 271, 274, 280
planar halogenated hydrocarbons (PHHs) 317,
    318–19, 328
planning policy/legislation, East and South-east
    Asia 96–7
plant community
  structure 339
  vegetation 230

Plata River basin 195
Platalea leucorodia (European Spoonbill) 25
Playa Chica Lagoons (Peru) 178, 179, 197
Plegadis falcinellus (Glossy Ibis) 25
plumage, conspicuous 202
plume trade 29, 214
  hunting 160, 173, 187
    Snowy Egret 214, 303
  South America 196
Po River (Italy) 2, 3, 39, 41, 48
  critical wetlands 24, 29
poaching, Central America 167
Point Behague (Guianas Coast) 178, 179
Point Calamere Bird Sanctuary (India) 56, 57
poisoning 271
  DDT 252, 253
  endrin 252
  organophosphate insecticides 321
Poitevin (France) 2, 3
Poland 2, 3
  Black-crowned Night Heron 19
  Eurasian Bittern population 21
  Little Bittern population 20
  protection 28
pollution 266–7
  Australia 146, 147
  contaminants 172–3
  East and South-east Asia 94–5
  Nile delta 35
  Oceania 144
  South America 195, 197
  South and West Asia 71
  water 26
  see also carbamate insecticides; contaminants;
    contamination; dioxins; organochlorine
    insecticides; organophosphorus
    insecticides; pesticides; trace elements
polychlorinated biphenyls *see* PCBs
polychlorinated dibenzo-*p*-dioxins *see* PCDD
polycholorinated dibenzofurans *see* PCDF
Polynesia 145
  Green-backed Heron 136
pond culture *see* aquaculture; fish farms/farming;
    fish ponds; shrimp ponds
pond heron
  habitat preference 222
  organochlorine insecticides 259
Pond Heron, Chinese xiii, 57, 85
  chick harvesting 213
  feeding area 207
Pond Heron, Indian xiii, 239
  conservation status 364
  East and South-east Asia 85
  South and West Asia 55, 65, 70, 71
Pond Heron, Javan xiii, 85, 91, 239
Pond Heron, Malagasy xiii, 99, 114
  captive conservation priority 309
  conservation status 359
poplar 208
population
  changes 333
  conservation 337
  counting 332–3, 334
  density-dependent regulation factors 8

population – *contd*
  estimates 334
  increase in Africa 119
  indices 334
  stability 29–30
  status 332–6
  techniques 334
  trend data evaluation 335–6
population biology 337
Population, Community and/or Ecosystem (PCE)
      indicators 311
population size
  Europe 3
  maximum/minimum 5–6
  monitoring 329
  see also censuses; counting; numbers of herons
Populus (poplar) 208
Porgera mines (New Guinea) 144
Port Moresby (New Guinea) 139
Porto Lago lagoon (Greece) 2, 3, 48
Portugal 2, 3
  Black-crowned Night Heron 47
  Cattle Egret population 15, 16, 24, 43
  Great White Egret 12, 41
  Little Bittern population 20–1
  Little Egret population 41
  Mediterranean 35
  protection 28
  Purple Heron population 10, 40
  Squacco Heron population 45
post-fledging dispersal 243
Posthodiphostomum cuticola (trematode) 282
prairie pothole region (USA/Canada) 155
predation
  avoidance 202
  rates 277–81
  scientific understanding 283–6
  separation from other fish-eating birds 285
prey
  availability 228–9, 340
  base 221
  fluctuations 228–30
  refugia 221
  small mammals 243
  wetlands 221, 226
propogation in captive populations 299, 301–2
protection 27–8, 31
  East and South-east Asia 96
  measures for fish farms 289–91
  Mediterranean area 50
  migratory behaviour change 245
  population recovery 270
Puerto Rico 152, 153
  Little Blue Heron 159, 160
  Little Egret 160
  mangrove swamps 248
Puerto Rico Mudflats (Northern Marianas) 139
Puget Sound (USA) 152, 153
Pulau Betet (Indonesia) 74, 75
Pulau Bukom (Malaysia) 79
Pulau Dua (Indonesia) 74, 75
Pulau Kimaam (New Guinea) 125
Pulau Rambut (Indonesia) 74, 75
Pulicat Lake (India) 56, 57, 59

Purus River (Brazil) 178, 179
Puthupalli Alam (India) 56, 57, 64

Quebec (Canada) 163
Queen Elizabeth National Park (Uganda) 100, 101
Queensland (Australia) 143, 144, 147
  Australian Bittern 140, 355
  Cattle Egret 136, 137
  coast 125, 136
  Little Bittern 139

radiotelemetry 325, 337
Ragay Gulf Luzon (Philippines) 74, 75
Raine Island (Great Barrier Reef, Australia) 138
rainfall, nesting season 146
rainy season
  migration 240
  tropical 245
Rajang Delta Sarawak (Malaysia) 33
Ramsar Bureau 220
Ramsar Convention 25, 120, 250
  adoption in the Americas 170, 172
  European wetlands 23
  South America 195, 199
  water allocation in river systems 142, 146
Ramsar criteria 333, 337
Ramsar Sites
  Africa 120
  Americas 169, 172
  Atlantic Flyway 168
  Australia 128, 142, 143, 144, 145, 355
  Hong Kong 94
  New Zealand 145
  Palo Verde (Costa Rica) 169
  Papua New Guinea 145
  Rio Lagartos 169
  West Indies 169
Ranganathittu (India) 70
range expansion 243
Rap-do (North Korea) 82–3
Rawa Biru (New Guinea) 125
recreational facilities 210
  reed bed areas 26
Red River Estuary (Vietnam) 74, 75
Red Sea
  coast 33
  Green-backed Heron 114
  Little Egret 112
reed beds 26, 203
  artificial nesting sites 208
  cutting in South America 197
  degradation 11, 50–1
  habitat preference 221–2
  harvesting 11, 26
  Phragmites 37, 49, 50, 203
reed mace 205
Reef Heron, Eastern 57, 64, 85
  Australia 123, 135
  habitat 222
  Oceania 123, 125, 129, 135
Reef Heron, Western 33, 64, 70, 117
  South America 187
  West Indies 161
reef systems 144

reforestation 93
    New York 168
    Ontario 168
refuges, zoos 306
regional management 233–4
regurgitation of food 202
reintroduction feasibility 303–4
releases, native 307
reproductive performance indicators 324–6
reproductive strategies 242
reproductive success
    index 329
    pesticides 253
research 331
    integrated multidisciplinary 215–16
reserve networks 172
reservoirs 60, 69, 223, 233
Réunion 99
    Cattle Egret 113
Rhine flood plain, marsh creation 27
Ria Sado (Portugal) 2, 3
rice fields 14, 20, 53, 224–5
    Africa 109
    artificial sites 234
        nesting 208
    Cattle Egret 64
    cultivation changes 232
    double cropping 232
    East and South-east Asia 81, 85, 89–90, 94
    fish production 276
    flooding regimes 232
    Italy 24, 36, 48, 52–3, 208, 323, 327
    Little Egret 63–4
    Madagascar 119
    Malagasy 107
    management 29, 53, 231–2
    pesticides 71, 232
    South America 187, 193, 195, 196
    South and West Asia 60, 69
    Spain 39, 53
    wetland loss 248
    Yellow Bittern 67
rice varieties 232
Richmond River Valley (Australia)
    Great White Egret 131
    Little Egret 134
Rift Valley wetlands (East Africa) 100, 101
ringing 299–300, 337
Rio de Janeiro (Brazil) 189, 192
Rio Kapatchez (Guinea) 100, 101
Rio Lagartos (Mexico) 152, 153, 169
Rio Negro (Argentina), Green-backed Heron 187
Rio Pongo (Guinea) 100, 101
Rio San Juan (Nicaragua) 152, 153
Riverland (Australia) 124, 125
rivers 24
    banks 339
    streamside forests 220–1
    water allocation in systems 141–2
Riyadh wetlands (Saudi Arabia) 57
RNA 319
Rodrigues 99
    Green-backed Heron 115
Romania 2, 3

Black-crowned Night Heron 19, 20
Cattle Egret population 16, 43
critical wetlands 24
Eurasian Bittern population 21
Great White Egret population 11, 40
Little Bittern population 20
protection 28
Purple Heron population 10
Squacco Heron population 18, 45
Royal Society for the Protection of Birds (RSPB)
    214
Ruby Lake (Nevada) 256
Rudbary (Iran) 57
Rukwa Valley wetlands (Tanzania) 100, 101
rural community 120–1
Russia 1, 2, 3, 5
    Black-crowned Night Heron population 19
    Cattle Egret population 16
    critical wetlands 24
    Eurasian Bittern 21, 91, 370
    Great White Egret population 11, 12
    Grey Heron population 6, 10
    Little Bittern population 20
    Little Egret population 12, 14
    Purple Heron population 10
    South and West Asia 56, 57
    Squacco Heron population 18–19
Rwanda 100, 101
    Black-crowned Night Heron 115
    Grey Heron 105, 106
    Malagasy Pond Heron 114
    wetland management 119
Ryongol (North Korea) 74, 75

Sabana de Bogotá (Colombia) 193
Saginaw Bay (Michigan; USA) 260
Sahara crossing 30
St. Clair, Lake (USA) 263, 264
St. Lucia system (Mozambique/South Africa) 100,
    101
St. Lucia (West Indies) 160
St. Martin (West Indies) 160
Saipan (Northern Marianas) 139
Sakumo Lagoon (Ghana) 100, 101
Saladillo River (Argentina) 178, 179
S'Albufera de Mallorca (Spain) 2, 3
salinity tolerance 25
Salix (willow) 208
    forest 24
salmon 270, 276
salmonids 276
Saloum Delta (Senegal) 112
salt marshes 119, 222
    North America 155
salt production, Central America 168
Salto Grande Dam (Paraguay) 178, 179
Salton Sea (USA) 152, 153, 161, 173
    pesticide contamination 256
saltwater intrusion, wetlands 327
Salvinia molesta weed invasion 144, 146
Salwab, Gulf of (Saudi Arabia) 57
Samoa 145
San Agustin Swamp (Colombia) 178, 179
    Reddish Egret 185

San Betino (Spain) 2, 3
San Felipe Lagoon (Peru) 197
San Francisco Bay (USA) 152, 153, 258, 261
San Francisco (USA) 160, 261
San Joaquin River (USA) 166
San Juan Saline Lagoon (Colombia) 178, 179
    Reddish Egret 185
San Marcos Bay (Brazil) 178, 179
San Miguel Marshes (Uruguay/Brazil) 178, 179
Sanambin NHA (Thailand) 74, 75
Santa Elena Penisula (Ecuador) 178, 179
Santa Lucia River (Uruguay) 178, 179
Santa Mart Great Swamp (Colombia) 178, 179
Santa Teresa Marshes (Uraguay) 178, 179
Santos mangroves (Brazil) 178, 179
Sao Tome 112
Sarabar Braji (Turkey) 2, 3
Sardinia, Cattle Egret population 17, 43, 44
Sarrhakhs Fishpool (Iran) 57
Saskatchewan (Canada) 163
satellite telemetry 337
Saudi Arabia 56, 57
    artificial wetlands 69–70
    Grey Heron 61
    Little Bittern 66
Sava River (Croatia) 2, 3
Savanna de Bogotá (Colombia) 197
savannas 182, 223
Scandinavia 5
scaring programmes 288–9
Scirpus lacustris (bullrush) 205
Seaham (Australia) 147, 148
seasonal cycles 146, 228–9
seasonal movements 238
Sebkha Kelbia (Tunisia) 2, 3
Second Island (China) 82
security zone for colonies 204, 205
sedentary species 239, 240
Seistan basin marshes (Iran/Afghanistan) 59
selenium 265
semi-desert 59
Senegal 100, 101
    Black Heron 110
    Black-crowned Night Heron 115
    Cattle Egret 113
    Eurasian Bittern 117
    Grey Heron 105, 106
    Little Bittern 116
    Little Egret 111, 112, 241
    Purple Heron 107
    river damming 246
    Squacco Heron 113
    tourism 121
    wetland management 119
    White-crested Tiger Heron 115
sensitivity analysis 238
Sepik Ramu (Papua New Guinea) 124, 125
Seri (Mali) 100, 101
Serra de Capivara (Brazil) 183
Sette Cama (Gabon) 100, 101
Seudre (France) 2, 3
sewage
    ponds 223
    treatment 195
sex determination 300
Seychelles 99, 100
    Cattle Egret 113
    Eurasian Bittern 117
    Green-backed Heron 115, 363
    Yellow Bittern 116
Sfax-Gabes (Tunisia) 2, 3
Shadegan Marshes (Iran) 57
Shajing Town (China) 353
Shala, Lake (Ethiopia) 100, 101
Shiekhon Lake (Iran) 57
Shijui (China) 74, 75
Shijun-Ho (North Korea) 74, 75
Shin Do (South Korea) 83
Shin Islet (South Korea) 74, 75, 83
Sholavandan (India) 65
shooting 95, 289
    Grey Heron 28
    illegal 271
    permits 271
    see also hunting
Shortland (Australia) 144, 147, 148
    ecotourism 215
    Intermediate Egret 132, 133
shrimp farming 169, 247
    Central America 167
shrimp ponds, South America 187, 196
Shuangtaizi Marshes (China) 74, 75
Sibaya, Lake (Mozambique/South Africa) 100, 101
Siberia 78
    Eurasian Bittern 91
    Great White Egret 81
Sierra Leone 100, 101
    Black-crowned Night Heron 115
    Grey Heron 105
    Squacco Heron 113
    wetland management 119
    White-crested Tiger Heron 115
Silent Valley National Park (India) 66
siltation
    dams 246
    inland forest conversion 167
    Oceania 144
    South America 195, 197
    see also soil erosion
Simpson Estate (India) 56, 57, 66, 70
Sinaloa coast (Mexico) 152, 153
Sine-Saloum delta (Senegal) 114
Singapore
    habitat loss 93
    Malayan Night Heron 88
    Purple Heron 81, 205
    Sumatran Heron 79, 80, 81
    Yellow Bittern 89
Sinnamary marshes (Guianas Coast) 178, 179
sister chromatid exchange 319
site fidelity 240–1
Sites of Special Scientific Interest (SSSIs) 96
Sivash, Lake (Ukraine) 37, 49
Skutari Lake (Montenegro) 2, 3
slaughter *see* killing of herons
Slovakia
    Black-crowned Night Heron 19
    Little Bittern population 20

Little Egret population 14
Purple Heron population 10
Slovenia 20
small mammals as prey 243
socio-economics 332
Sogam-do (North Korea) 74, 75, 83
soil erosion
Madagascar 118–19
Oceania 144
see also siltation
Solimoes River (Brazil) 178, 179
Solomon Islands
Black Bittern 140
Great White Egret 131
Green-backed Heron 136
Nankeen Night Heron 138
Somalia
Squacco Heron 113
wetland management 119
Sonchonrap-to (North Korea) 74, 75
Songor Lagoon (Ghana) 100, 101
Sonora (Mexico) 152, 153
source–sink concept of metapopulation analysis
336
South Africa 100, 101
Cattle Egret 112, 113
Dwarf Bittern 116
Eurasian Bittern 117, 362–3
Goliath Heron 107
Great White Egret 109
Grey Heron 106
Intermediate Egret 110
Little Bittern 116
Little Egret 111, 113
wetland management 119–20
South America 177
aquaculture 175, 270
Boat-billed Heron 164
Cattle Egret 161
climate 181
coastal lagoons 181
conservation 194–5
status 351
data 182–3
endemic genera 177
environmental conditions 181–2
Fasciated Tiger Heron 164, 360
fauna 177
Great White Egret 158
Grey Heron 156
habitat degradation 195
high altitude freshwaters 182
hunting 196, 197, 249
Least Bittern 164, 165
Little Blue Heron 159, 160
managed wetlands 195–6
mangrove swamps 181
pollution 195
Rufescent Tiger Heron 164
Snowy Egret 160
status of herons 180, 183–94
threatened species 197–8
tidal mudflats 181
Tricolored Heron 159

wintering area 168
Yellow-crowned Night Heron 162
Zigzag Heron 361
South Australia 145
Australian Bittern 140
Little Bittern 139
South Caspian lowlands (Azerbaijan/Iran) 57
South Island coastal plain (New Zealand) 124, 125
South Kanghwa (South Korea) 74, 75
South Korea 74, 75
Great White Egret 81
Swinhoe's Egret 83, 84, 355
South Shetland Islands 187
South and West Asia 55
cities 70
climate 59
coastal wetlands 59
data sources 60–1
deforestation 70
environmental conditions 57, 59–60
floodplans 59
habitats 57, 59
heron areas 56, 57
hunting 71
nest-site protection 70–1
pollution 71
species 55, 57
status of herons 58, 60–7
tropical forest 59
wetland conservation 68–70
South-western Drainage Division of Western
Australia 128, 129
Southern Central Plains (Thailand) 74, 75
Spaans Lagoon (Aruba, South America) 178, 179
Spain 2, 3
Black-crowned Night Heron 19, 47, 48, 53
Cattle Egret 15, 16, 24, 43, 203
climate 5
colonies 203
critical wetlands 24
egg collection 212
Great White Egret 12, 41
Grey Heron population 7, 9
groundwater extraction 246
Little Bittern population 20, 48, 53
Little Egret 12, 14, 41, 42, 43, 53, 161
Mediterranean 34, 35, 53
protection 28
Purple Heron population 10, 37–8, 39, 40, 53
Squacco Heron population 18, 45, 46, 53
wetlands
loss 51
rice fields 224, 225
Special Protection Areas (SPAs) 23
Spoonbill, European 25
Sri Lanka 56, 57, 59
Cattle Egret 64
Malayan Night Heron 66
Srinagar City (Kashmir) 65
Srinagar Public Gardens (India) 70
Stagno di Cagliari (Sardinia) 2, 3
Sterna hirundo (Common Tern) 317
stock loss of fish 283–4
stomach contents 284

Stork, Milky 93
Stork, Wood 194, 308, 313, 324
Strug River (Croatia) 2, 3
subspecies categorisation 344
Sudan 100, 101
    Black-crowned Night Heron 115
    Eurasian Bittern 117
    Grey Heron 105, 106
    Purple Heron 107
    Squacco Heron 113
    wetland management 119
Sudd (Sudan) 100, 101, 107
    available area 245
Suesca lagoon (South America) 197
Suez Canal area (Egypt) 259
Sulawesi 132
    Purple Heron 81
    Schrenck's Bittern 90
Sultan Marshes (Turkey) 2, 3, 48
Sumatra 89
    Cinnamon bittern 90
    Grey Heron 363
    Javan Pond Heron 85
    Malayan Night Heron 365
Sundarbans (India/Bangladesh) 56, 57, 59, 61
Sungei Burung Mangroves (Malaysia) 33
Suriname 178, 179
    Boat-billed Heron 190
    Cattle Egret 187
    Little Egret 187
    Streaked Bittern 192
sustainable use, wetlands 231
swamp forest 129, 145
    Africa 119
Swan Coastal Plain (Australia) 128, 129, 141
    habitat loss 140
Swaziland 100, 101
Sweden
    Eurasian Bittern population 21, 23
    Grey Heron population 6, 7, 9
    protection 28
Switzerland
    Grey Heron population 6, 9
    Little Egret population 12
    protection 28
sympatry 378
Syrigma sibilatrix (Whistling Heron) xiii
Syrigma sibilatrix fostersmithi (Whistling Heron) 183
Syrigma sibilatrix sibilatrix (Whistling Heron) 183

Tabasco lagoons (Mexico) 152, 153, 155, 169
    Great White Egret 158
    Snowy Egret 160
Tacarigua Lagoon (Venzuela) 178, 179
Taegam-do (North Korea) 83
Tahiti, Green-backed Heron 136
Taim Marshes (Uraguay/Brazil) 178, 179
Taiwan 74, 75
    colony sites 92–3
    Grey Heron 78
    Japanese Night Heron 87
    Swinhoe's Egret 82, 83, 84
    Yellow Bittern 89

Taiwan Tungshih (Ton-Shou) Mangroves (Taiwan) 74, 75
Tajo River (Spain) 2, 3, 24, 29, 44
Taman Negara (Malaysia) 89
Tambopata Wildlife Reserve (Peru) 178, 179, 192
Tamil Nadu (India) 57, 208
Tampico lagoons (Mexico) 152, 153
Tana Delta wetlands (Kenya) 100, 101, 107, 118
    Black-crowned Night Heron 115
    Cattle Egret 113
    Great White Egret 108
    Intermediate Egret 110
    Squacco Heron 113
Tana, Lake (Ethiopia) 100, 101
    Intermediate Egret 110
Tanganyika, Lake (East Africa) 101
Tanjung Sedari (Indonesia) 74, 75
Tanzania 100, 101
    Black-crowned Night Heron 115
    Great White Egret 108
    Grey Heron 105, 106
    Malagasy Pond Heron 114
    tourism 121
    wetland management 119
Tapajos River (Brazil) 178, 179
Tarat Bay (Saudi Arabia) 57
Tasmania 125, 128
    Australian Bittern 140, 355
    Cattle Egret 137
    Eastern Reef Heron 135
    Little Egret 135
    White-necked Heron 130
Tatu Estuary (Taiwan) 74, 75
taxa, extinct 352
taxon conservation 351–71
taxonomy 344
TCDD 262
    contamination 321
    equivalents 317, 318, 319
Tegam-do (North Korea) 74, 75
telemetry 337
    see also radiotelemetry; satellite telemetry
Tempasuk Plain Sabah (Malaysia) 33
temperature, environmental 240
teratogenic effects 313
Tern, Common 317
territorial behaviour 283
    Grey Heron 10
territorial species, fish farms 287
territoriality 223
Texas (USA) 152, 153, 169
    American Bittern 166
    Black-crowned Night Heron 164
    Cattle Egret 161
    Great White Egret 157, 158
    Little Blue Heron 160
    nesting habitats 169
    Reddish Egret 158
    Tricoloured Heron 158, 159
    Yellow-crowned Night Heron 162
Tha Ton Marsh (Thailand) 74, 75
Thailand 74, 75
    Black Bittern 91
    Eurasian Bittern 91

habitat loss 93
Javan Pond Heron 85
Malayan Night Heron 88, 365
Sumatran Heron 79, 359
Swinhoe's Egret 83, 84
trapping 248
Thika oxidation ponds (Kenya) 114
Third Chala lake 56, 57
threat categories (IUCN) 344, 345
tidal cycles 153, 229
tidal mudflats 222
South America 181
Tierra del Fuego
Black-crowned Night Heron 189
Cattle Egret 187
tiger heron
captive conservation priority 309
nesting 205
North America 155, 166, 174
sedentary species 239
Tiger Heron, Bare-throated xiv, 151, 164, 175, 190, 197
conservation status 366
Tiger Heron, Fasciated xiv, 164, 175, 182, 190, 193, 198
conservation status 360
habitat 222, 223
Tiger Heron, New Guinea xiv, 89, 125, 129, 138–9, 144
clutch size 239
conservation status 360
Tiger Heron, Rufescent xiv, 155, 164, 239
clutch size 239
South America 182, 190–1
Tiger Heron, White-crested xiv, 99, 115–16
clutch size 239
Tigrionis leucolophus (White-crested Tiger Heron) xiv
Tigris River (Iran) 67
floodplain 246
Tigrisoma fasciatum (Fasciated Tiger Heron) xiv, 360
Tigrisoma fasciatum fasciatum (Fasciated Tiger Heron) 190
Tigrisoma fasciatum pallescens (Fasciated Tiger Heron) 190, 198
Tigrisoma fasciatum salmoni (Fasciated Tiger Heron) 190, 198
Tigrisoma lineatum (Rufescent Tiger Heron) xiv
Tigrisoma lineatum lineatum (Rufescent Tiger Heron) 190
Tigrisoma lineatum marmoratum (Rufescent Tiger Heron) 191
Tigrisoma mexicanum (Bare-throated Tiger Heron) xiv, 151
Tigrisoma mexicanum mexicanum (Bare-throated Tiger Heron) 366
tilapia 276
Tilyar Lake (India) 63
Titicaca, Lake (Peru/Bolivia) 178, 179, 189
Tiznit (Morocco) 43
toad, cane 146
Tobago 160, 163, 177
Great Blue Heron 184

Yellow-crowned Night Heron 189, 198
Tocantins River (Brazil) 178, 179
toes, cracked 300
Togo
Grey Heron 105
wetland management 119
Tolibin, Lake (Australia) 124, 125
Tonda Wildlife Management Area (New Guinea) 125, 129, 131, 145
Tonga, Green-backed Heron 136
Tonga, Lake (Tunisia) 46
Tongaland (Mozambique/South Africa) 100, 101
Toronto (Australia) 147
Torres Strait 128
Torres Strait Islands 132
Tota, Lake (Colombia) 178, 179, 197
Totumo Swamp (Colombia) 178, 179
Toulouse floodplain (France) 2, 3
tourism 25
Africa 109, 120–1
Australia 145
Central America 167
disturbance 210, 248
East and South-east Asia 91
Galápagos 198
mass 51–2, 249
Oceania 144
South America 196
West Indies 163
wetland protection 249
see also ecotourism
trace elements 263–5
feathers 314–15, 317, 328
Tramandi Lagoons (Brazil) 178, 179, 193
translocation of herons 303
Transvaal (South Africa) 258, 363
trapping 95, 248–9, 289
tree-nesting herons, artificial colony 208–10
trematodes 282
trend analysis 335–6
Trinidad 160, 177, 178, 179
ecotourism 197
Great Blue Heron 184
Grey Heron 183
Least Bittern 193
Little Egret 187
South American Bittern 193
Streaked Bittern 192
Tricolored Heron 186
wintering area 168
Trobriand Islands (Oceania) 129
tropical forest 59
trout 269–70
culture 274, 275, 276
losses 280
Tshangalele, Lake (Congo) 100, 101
Tulear (Madagascar) 114
Tumi Chucua Lake (Bolivia) 192
Tunisia 2, 3
Mediterranean 35, 37, 41, 42, 43, 46
water shortage 52
Turkana, Lake (Ethiopia/Kenya) 100, 101
Turkey 2, 3, 54
Cattle Egret population 16

Turkey – *contd*
  Eurasian Bittern 49
  Great White Egret population 11, 12, 40, 41
  Grey Heron 37
  Little Bittern population 20, 48
  Little Egret population 12, 41
  Mediterranean 34, 35, 37, 53
  Purple Heron population 38
  Squacco Heron population 18, 45
Turkmenistan 62, 64, 67
Typha (reed mace) 205

Uelle river system (Congo) 115
Uganda 100, 101
  Black-crowned Night Heron 115
  Dwarf Bittern 116
  Malagasy Pond Heron 114
  Purple Heron 107
  Rufous-bellied Heron 114
  wetland management 119
Ujong Kulon National Park (Sumatra) 89
Ukraine 2, 3
  Eurasian Bittern population 21, 49
  Great White Egret population 11, 12, 40
  Grey Heron population 6, 37
  Little Bittern population 20
  Purple Heron population 10, 38
  Squacco Heron population 18
Ulla-Ulla National Biological Reserve (Bolivia)
      178, 179, 189
Umayo (Peru) 178, 179, 189
Unare, Gulf of (Venezuela) 178, 179
United Arab Emirates 63, 65, 66
United Kingdom 3, 5
  Eurasian Bittern population 21, 22, 23
  Grey Heron population 6, 7, 9, 239, 240
  Little Egret population 12, 13
  PCBs 261
  protection 28
United States of America 152, 153
  wetland protection 170
upland habitat conservation 220–1, 231
Upo Marshes (South Korea) 74, 75
Upper Irrawaddy (Myanmar) 74, 75
Urabá, Gulf of (Colombia) 178, 179, 190, 197, 366
Uraguay
  Boat-billed Heron 190
  South American Bittern 193
  wetlands 182
urbanisation 248
  Africa 119
  Australia 144, 147
  colony sites 173
  disturbance 210
  habitat degradation 247
  see also cities
Uru-Uru Lake (Bolivia) 178, 179, 189
Uruguay 178, 179
Usumacinta Delta (Mexico) 169

Valencia (Spain) 53
Vanuatu, Green-backed Heron 136
Vasej Ab-Bandans (Iran) 56, 57
Vedanthangal Bird Sanctuary (India) 56, 57

Vedaranyam Great Salt Swamp (India) 56, 57
Vedathangal (India) 70
vegetation 230
  plant community structure 339
Vendre marshes (France) 2, 3
Venetian Lagoons (Italy) 2, 3, 39
  critical wetlands 24, 29
Venezuela 178, 179
  Agami Heron 188
  Boat-billed Heron 190
  Fasciated Tiger Heron 164, 190
  Great Blue Heron 184
  Green-backed Heron 187
  Least Bittern 193
  Little Blue Heron 186
  Reddish Egret 185
  Snowy Egret 160, 187
  South American Bittern 193
  Streaked Bittern 192
  Tricoloured Heron 186
  Whistling Heron 183
  Yellow-crowned Night Heron 162, 189
  Zigzag Heron 192
Verlorenvlei (South Africa) 100, 101
Victoria (Australia) 134, 143, 144
  Australian Bittern 140, 355
  Eastern Reef Heron 135
  Green-backed Heron 136
  Little Bittern 139
  Little Egret 135
  Nankeen Night Heron 138
Victoria, Lake (East Africa) 100, 101
Victoria River (Australia) 124, 125
Vietnam 74, 75
  colony sites 92
  habitat loss 93
  Javan Pond Heron 85
  Malayan Night Heron 88, 365
  Purple Heron 81
  survey 78, 79
  Swinhoe's Egret 84
Villa marshes (Peru) 197
viral haemorrhagic septicaemia (VHS) 281
viral infections 281–2
Virgin Islands
  Great Blue Heron 156
  Yellow-crowned Night Heron 162
Vistonis, Lake (Greece) 2, 3
vitamin supplements 300
Vole, Social 52
Volga Delta (Russia) 2, 3, 5, 10, 56, 57
  Cattle Egret population 16, 17, 19
  critical wetland area 24, 25, 29
  hydrological changes 246
  Little Egret population 14
Volongo (Spain) 2, 3

Wadi Hanifah (Saudi Arabia) 57
Wag naar Zee (Guianas Coast) 178, 179
Wageningen Swamps (Guianas Coast) 178, 179
Waitangiroto Nature Reserve (New Zealand) 124,
      125
Waituna Lagoon (New Zealand) 124, 125, 145
Walado Debo (Mali) 100, 101, 113

Washington State (USA) 256, 257
  Bald Eagle predation 170
  Great Blue Heron 157
  Green-backed Heron 161
Wasur (New Guinea) 124, 125
water
  commmunity beliefs about usage 148
  deep 339
  depth for foraging 155
  management sites 223
  open 275
  resources in Africa 118
  storage 69
  supply 52
  see also pollution
water boatman 282–3
water buffalo, feral 144, 146
water level 25
  management 26–7, 141, 234
  predation rates 278
  Purple Heron nesting 11
water quality 26
  fish loss 280
  Oceania 144
  prey availability 228
  South America 195
watershed management 234
Way Kambas (Indonesia) 74, 75
weather systems, migration 241
Wembere swamps (Tanzania) 100, 101
  Black-crowned Night Heron 115
  Cattle Egret 113
  Goliath Heron 107
  Little Egret 111
  management 117–18
  Squacco Heron 113
West Indies 151
  American Bittern 166
  Black-crowned Night Heron 164
  colony site protection 173–4
  environmental conditions 153, 155
  Green-backed Heron 161
  Grey Heron 156
  habitat quality 171
  heron fauna 151
  Least Bittern 164, 165
  Little Blue Heron 159
  Snowy Egret 160
  status of herons 154, 155–66
  Tricoloured Heron 158
  Yellow-crowned Night Heron 163
West New Britain (Oceania) 139
Western Australia
  Black Bittern 140
  Cattle Egret 136
  Great White Egret 144
  Green-backed Heron 123, 136
  Little Egret 135
Western Hemisphere Shorebird Reserve Network
    233
wet–dry seasonal cycles 229
Wetland Conservation Act (USA) 172
wetlands
  alteration 226–7

aquaculture expansion 287
artificial 54, 59–60, 69–70, 94, 246
    Australia 141
assessment in Australia 145–6
Canada 155
censuses 323–4
coastal 5, 24
condition indicators 327
conservation 219–20
    in Europe 24–5
conversion 226–7
degradation 54
destruction 333
    in Mediterranean region 34–5, 51
East and South-east Asia 92, 93, 94, 98
estuarine 5, 222, 325
habitat 340
    loss 245–6
    preferences 221–2
inventories 231
loss 226–7, 245–6, 248, 332
managed in South America 195–6
management
    in Africa 117–20
    in Australia 140–4
    in Madagascar 118–19
    plans 27
    strategies 230–1
monitoring programmes 322–3
North America 155
pressures 245–6
prey 226
protection for other species 51
restoration 27, 340
South America 194–6
South and West Asia 68–70
species dependence 378–9
subsidies for destruction 23
transformation
    sudden 246
    in twentieth century 25
tropical rains 245
types 221
see also coastal lagoons; mangrove swamps;
      marshes; mudflats; reed beds; rice fields;
      salt marshes; swamp forest
Wetlands International 95, 220, 323, 343
Whangamarino (New Zealand) 124, 125, 145
Wia-wia (Guianas Coast) 178, 179
Wild Bird Society of Japan (WBSJ) 87
Wilderness Lakes (South Africa) 100, 101
willow 208
Wingha (Gabon) 100, 101
Winghe (Gabon) 100, 101
winter, survival 242
wintering areas/sites 340–1
  Americas 172–3
  bird size 244
  counting 332–3
  habitats 237–9
  migration 336
  outside Europe 26
wintering populations 323–4
Wisconsin (USA) 162

Witwatersrand (Transvaal, South Africa) 110, 113
World Heritage site, Danube delta (Romania) 51
World Wide Fund for Nature 95, 358
wounding of fish 282
Wyoming (USA) 256

Xi Jiang (Pearl River) Delta (China) 74, 75
Xingu River (Brazil) 178, 179

Yancheng Marshes (China) 74, 75
Yap (Micronesia) 139
Yellow River Delta (China) 74, 75
Yellow Sea 355
Yemen, Goliath Heron 62
Yob-do (North Korea) 83
Yugoslavia 40

Zaire *see* Congo, Democratic Republic of
Zalew Wislany (Poland, Russia) 2, 3
Zambesi River (Namibia/Zambia) 109, 110, 115, 356
Zambia 100, 101
  Black Heron 110
  Eurasian Bittern 117, 362
  Great White Egret 108
  Intermediate Egret 110, 111
  Little Egret 111
  Malagasy Pond Heron 114
  Slaty Egret 109, 356
  wetland management 120
  White-backed Night Heron 115
Zapata Swamp (Cuba) 153, 155, 169

Zapatosa Swamp (Colombia) 178, 179, 193
Zapecos River (Bolivia) 178, 179
Zebrilus undulatus (Zigzag Heron) xiv, 361
Zhalong Marshes and Nature Reserve (China) 74, 75
Zimbabwe 118
  Black-headed Heron 106
  Cattle Egret 113
  Dwarf Bittern 116
  Great White Egret 108
  Grey Heron 106
  Intermediate Egret 110
  Little Egret 111
  Malagasy Pond Heron 114
  tourism 121
  wetland management 120
zinc 321
Ziway, Lake (Ethiopia) 100, 101
Zonerodius heliosylus (New Guinea Tiger Heron) xiv, 360
zoos 293
  conservation breeding feasibility 298–303
  education programmes 305
  escapes 303
  free-flying herons 306
  husbandry research 302–3
  in situ conservation 305
  intensive techniques 304–5
  numbers of herons 295
  organised conservation programmes 296–8
  refuges 306
  release 303
  species kept 295–6, 298